THE COLLECTED
ESSAYS, JOURNALISM
AND LETTERS OF
GEORGE ORWELL

Volume IV

In Front of Your Nose
1945–1950

More detailed lay-out.

The ship. The other passengers. C's inadequacy — 1 chap.

More about the ship, crunch up Mr McG. C's antih... to "get on."

The younger passenger — 1 chap.

His memories — the bungalow at N'zeile. — 1 (2?) chap.

First meetings with B.J. The Mission — 1 chap.

Return — the Planters — his reaction to the Mission. — 1 chap.

Incidents of the ship. The other ship (Spanish). C's line — 1 chap.

The incident in the picture — 1 chap.

C's brightness period — 1 chap.

The ship — 1 chap.

The opportunist — 1 chap

Finale — 1 chap.

11 chaps?

A synopsis of the long short story, called "A Smoking Room Story",
in the note-book Orwell kept in 1949

George Orwell with his adopted son Richard, November 1946

THE COLLECTED
ESSAYS, JOURNALISM
AND LETTERS OF

GEORGE
ORWELL

Volume IV

In Front of Your Nose

1945–1950

Edited by
SONIA ORWELL AND IAN ANGUS

LONDON · SECKER & WARBURG

First published in England 1968 by
Martin Secker & Warburg Limited
14 Carlisle Street, London W1

SBN: 436 35015 7

Printed in Great Britain by
The Camelot Press Ltd., London and Southampton

Contents

viii   *Contents*

Acknowledgements

The editors wish to express their grateful thanks to the following institutions and libraries, their trustees, curators and staffs for their co-operation and valuable help and for making copies of Orwell material available: Sir Frank Francis, Director and Principal Librarian of the British Museum (for: II: 37; III: 105; IV: 8); Dr John D. Gordan, Curator of the Henry W. and Albert A. Berg Collection of the New York Public Library, Astor, Lenox and Tilden Foundations (for: I: 18, 22, 23, 31, 33, 36, 38, 48, 50–2, 54, 58, 60, 61, 73, 75, 76, 86, 92, 98, 108, 112, 116, 121, 124, 128, 133, 139, 140, 141, 146, 154: III: 53, 97, 106; IV: 29, 59, 92, 95, 100, 106, 107, 110, 115, 121, 126, 136, 137, 142, 144, 159, 164, 165); Dr Warren Roberts, Director of the Humanities Research Center, University of Texas (for: I: 65, 66, 79, 102, 122, 123, 161; II: 4, 6, 10, 50; III: 52); S. C. Sutton, Librarian and Keeper of India Office Records (for: I: 115); Robert L. Collison, Librarian of the BBC Library (for: II: 38, 39, 52); Dr G. Chandler, Librarian of Liverpool City Library (for: I: 94); Wilbur Smith, Head of the Department of Special Collections, Library of the University of California, Los Angeles (for: I: 84); Anne Abley, Librarian of St Antony's College, Oxford (for: IV: 31, 32); and J.W. Scott, Librarian of University College London, for the material in the George Orwell Archive.

We are also deeply indebted to all those recipients of letters from Orwell, or their executors, who have been kind enough to make available the correspondence published in these volumes.

We would like to thank the following publications for permission to reproduce material first published in their pages: *Commentary*; *Encounter*; the *Evening Standard*; *Forward*; *Life*; the *Listener*; the *London Magazine*; the *Manchester Evening News*; the *New Leader* (NY); the *New Statesman and Nation*; the *New Yorker*; *New York Times Book Review*; the *Observer*; *Partisan Review*; *Peace News*; the *Socialist Leader*; *Time and Tide*; *The Times*; *Tribune*; and *Wiadomości*.

We would like to thank the following for allowing us to use material whose copyright they own: the executors of the late Frank Richards for his "Reply to George Orwell" in *Horizon*; H.W. Wilson & Co. for Orwell's entry in *Twentieth Century Authors*; George Allen & Unwin Ltd for "The Rediscovery of Europe" in *Talking to India*; Professor George Woodcock and D.S. Savage for their contributions to the controversy "Pacifism and the War" in *Partisan Review*; Dr Alex Comfort for his contribution to the same controversy and for his "Letter to an American Visitor" in *Tribune*; William Collins Sons & Co. Ltd for *The English People*; the executors of the late James Agate for his contribution to the controversy in the *Manchester Evening News*; the executors of Gerard Manley Hopkins and the Oxford University Press for "Felix Randal"; Elek Books Ltd for the Introduction to Jack London's *Love of Life*; Eyre and Spottiswoode Ltd for the Introduction to Leonard Merrick's *The Position of Peggy Harper*; and the executors of the late Konni Zilliacus for his letter to *Tribune*.

We would like to thank the following for their co-operation and invaluable help: Mrs Evelyn Anderson, the Hon. David Astor, Frank D. Barber, Dennis Collings, Dr Alex Comfort, Jack Common, Lettice Cooper, Stafford Cottman, Humphrey Dakin, Mrs John Deiner, Mrs William Dunn, Mrs T.S. Eliot, Dr McDonald Emslie, Faber & Faber Ltd, Mr and Mrs Francis Fierz, Roy Fuller, T.R. Fyvel, Livia Gollancz, Victor Gollancz Ltd, Mrs Arthur Goodman, A.S.F. Gow, James Hanley, Rayner Heppenstall, Inez Holden, Mrs Humphry House, Mrs Lydia Jackson, Frank Jellinek, Dr Shirley E. Jones, Jon Kimche, Denys King-Farlow, Arthur Koestler, Mrs Georges Kopp, James Laughlin, F.A. Lea, John Lehmann, John McNair, Michael Meyer, Henry Miller, Raymond Mortimer, Mrs Middleton Murry, Mrs Rosalind Obermeyer, Laurence O'Shaughnessy, *Partisan Review*, Professor R.S. Peters, Ruth Pitter, Joyce Pritchard, Philip Rahv, Sir Herbert Read, Vernon Richards, the Rev. Herbert Rogers, the Hon. Sir Steven Runciman, Brenda Salkeld, John Sceats, Roger Senhouse, Stephen Spender, Professor Gleb Struve, Julian Symons, F.J. Warburg and Professor George Woodcock. We would also like to thank: Angus Calder (for allowing us to consult his unpublished thesis on the Common Wealth Party); Howard Fink (for allowing us to consult his unpublished *Chronology of Orwell's Loci and Activities*); and I.R. Willison (whose *George Orwell: Some Materials for a Bibliography*, School

of Librarianship, London University, 1953, was indispensable).
Finally, this edition would not have been possible but for the patient and understanding editorial help of Aubrey Davis and the support and help of the Library staff of University College London, particularly that of J.W. Scott, the Librarian, Margaret Skerl, Karen Bishop, Mrs Michael Kraushaar and Mrs Gordon Leitch.

A Note on the Editing

The contents are arranged in order of publication except where the time lag between writing and appearance in print is unusually large, when we have chosen the date of writing. There are one or two rare exceptions to this rule, generally made for the sake of illustrating the development in Orwell's thought, but a note at the end of each article or review states when, and in which publication, it appeared first. If it was not published or the date of writing has determined its position the date of writing is given. Where there is no mention of a periodical at the end of an article, it has never been published before. "Why I Write", written in 1946, has been placed at the beginning of Volume I, as it seems a suitable introduction to the whole collection. Where the article was reprinted in the major collections of his writing, this has been indicated and the following abbreviations used for the various books: CE, *Collected Essays*; CrE, *Critical Essays*; DD, *Dickens, Dali and Others*; EYE, *England Your England*; ITW, *Inside the Whale*; OR, *The Orwell Reader*; SE, *Shooting an Elephant*; SJ, *Such, Such Were the Joys*.

Any title in square brackets at the head of an article or review has been supplied by us. All the others are either Orwell's own or those of the editors of the publication in question. He certainly wrote his own titles for his *Tribune* pieces; some of the others read as if he had written them but with most it is hard to tell and there is no way of finally checking.

Only when the article has never been printed before have we had the manuscript to work from and none of these were revised by Orwell as they would have been had he published them. With everything else we have had to use the text as it appeared in print. As anyone who has ever done any journalism or book reviewing knows, this means the text which appears here may well be slightly, if not very, different from the text Orwell originally wrote. Editors cut, printers make errors which are not thought of as very important in journalism, and it is only when the writer wants to reprint his pieces in book form that he bothers to restore the cuts, correct the errors and generally prepare them to survive in more lasting form: the reader therefore should bear in mind that they might well be very different if Orwell himself had revised them for re-publication. Both to these previously printed essays and journalism and to the hitherto unpublished articles and diaries we have given a uniform style in spelling, quotation marks and punctuation.

The letters were written, nearly always in haste, with scant attention to style and hardly any to punctuation; but throughout them we have corrected spelling mistakes, regularised the punctuation and have put book and periodical titles in italics. In a few cases postscripts of an unimportant nature have been omitted without indication. Otherwise cuts in both the letters and the journalism have been indicated by three dots, with a fourth dot to indicate a period. The same method was used by Orwell for indicating omissions when abridging excerpts he was quoting in reviews and essays, but as we have not made cuts in any of these excerpts there should be no confusion between our cuts and Orwell's own.

Orwell's "As I Please" column often consisted of two or more sections each devoted to a specific topic. Whenever one of the self-contained sections has been entirely omitted, this has not been indicated, but any cut made within a section is indicated by the usual three or four dots.

George Orwell never legally changed his name from Eric Blair and all the friends he made when young knew him and addressed him as Eric Blair. Later on new friends and acquaintances knew him and addressed him as George Orwell. In his letters he signs himself by the name his correspondent used. His earlier articles were signed E.A. Blair or Eric Blair and we have indicated these. From the moment this name is dropped in his published writing it is entirely signed George Orwell. Where a footnote deals with a period or a situation in which he would have looked upon himself primarily as Eric Blair we have referred to him by this name.

As this is an Anglo-American edition, many of the footnotes have been provided for the benefit of American readers and contain information we know to be familiar to English readers. We have put in the minimum of footnotes. This is largely because of the great difficulty of annotating the history of the period during which he wrote. It is still too recent for standard histories of it to exist and the events and people he discussed are often still the subjects of fierce polemic making it difficult to give an "objective" footnote. We have only footnoted the text in some detail where he talks about people or events in his personal life or where there is a reference to some topic about which the reader could find nothing in any existing book of reference. The numbers in the cross-references in the footnotes refer to items, not pages.

The Editors

1945

1. Revenge Is Sour

Whenever I read phrases like "war guilt trials", "punishment of war criminals", and so forth, there comes back into my mind the memory of something I saw in a prisoner-of-war camp in South Germany, earlier this year.

Another correspondent and myself were being shown round the camp by a little Viennese Jew who had been enlisted in the branch of the American army which deals with the interrogation of prisoners. He was an alert, fair-haired, rather good-looking youth of about twenty-five, and politically so much more knowledgeable than the average American officer that it was a pleasure to be with him. The camp was on an airfield, and, after we had been round the cages, our guide led us to a hangar where various prisoners who were in a different category from the others were being "screened".

Up at one end of the hangar about a dozen men were lying in a row on the concrete floor. These, it was explained, were SS officers who had been segregated from the other prisoners. Among them was a man in dingy civilian clothes who was lying with his arm across his face and apparently asleep. He had strangely and horribly deformed feet. The two of them were quite symmetrical, but they were clubbed out into an extraordinary globular shape which made them more like a horse's hoof than anything human. As we approached the group the little Jew seemed to be working himself up into a state of excitement.

"That's the real swine!" he said, and suddenly he lashed out with his heavy army boot and caught the prostrate man a fearful kick right on the bulge of one of his deformed feet.

"Get up, you swine!" he shouted as the man started out of sleep, and then repeated something of the kind in German. The prisoner scrambled to his feet and stood clumsily to attention. With the same air of working himself up into a fury—indeed he was almost dancing up and down as he spoke—the Jew told us the prisoner's history. He

was a "real" Nazi: his party number indicated that he had been a
member since the very early days, and he had held a post corresponding to a General in the political branch of the SS. It could be taken as
quite certain that he had had charge of concentration camps and had
presided over tortures and hangings. In short, he represented everything that we had been fighting against during the past five years.

Meanwhile, I was studying his appearance. Quite apart from the
scrubby, unfed, unshaven look that a newly captured man generally
has, he was a disgusting specimen. But he did not look brutal or in
any way frightening: merely neurotic and, in a low way, intellectual.
His pale, shifty eyes were deformed by powerful spectacles. He could
have been an unfrocked clergyman, an actor ruined by drink, or a
spiritualist medium. I have seen very similar people in London common lodging houses, and also in the Reading Room of the British
Museum. Quite obviously he was mentally unbalanced—indeed, only
doubtfully sane, though at this moment sufficiently in his right mind
to be frightened of getting another kick. And yet everything that the
Jew was telling me of his history could have been true, and probably
was true! So the Nazi torturer of one's imagination, the monstrous
figure against whom one had struggled for so many years, dwindled
to this pitiful wretch, whose obvious need was not for punishment,
but for some kind of psychological treatment.

Later, there were further humiliations. Another SS officer, a large,
brawny man, was ordered to strip to the waist and show the blood-
group number tattooed on his under-arm; another was forced to
explain to us how he had lied about being a member of the SS and
attempted to pass himself off as an ordinary soldier of the Wehr-
macht. I wondered whether the Jew was getting any real kick out of
this new-found power that he was exercising. I concluded that he
wasn't really enjoying it, and that he was merely—like a man in a
brothel, or a boy smoking his first cigar, or a tourist traipsing round
a picture gallery—*telling* himself that he was enjoying it, and behaving as he had planned to behave in the days when he was helpless.

It is absurd to blame any German or Austrian Jew for getting his
own back on the Nazis. Heaven knows what scores this particular
man may have had to wipe out; very likely his whole family had been
murdered; and, after all, even a wanton kick to a prisoner is a very
tiny thing compared with the outrages committed by the Hitler
régime. But what this scene, and much else that I saw in Germany,
brought home to me was that the whole idea of revenge and punish-

ment is a childish day-dream. Properly speaking, there is no such thing as revenge. Revenge is an act which you want to commit when you are powerless and because you are powerless: as soon as the sense of impotence is removed, the desire evaporates also.

Who would not have jumped for joy, in 1940, at the thought of seeing SS officers kicked and humiliated? But when the thing becomes possible, it is merely pathetic and disgusting. It is said that when Mussolini's corpse was exhibited in public, an old woman drew a revolver and fired five shots into it, exclaiming, "Those are for my five sons!" It is the kind of story that the newspapers make up, but it might be true. I wonder how much satisfaction she got out of those five shots, which, doubtless, she had dreamed years earlier of firing. The condition of her being able to get near enough to Mussolini to shoot at him was that he should be a corpse.

In so far as the big public in this country is responsible for the monstrous peace settlement now being forced on Germany, it is because of a failure to see in advance that punishing an enemy brings no satisfaction. We acquiesced in crimes like the expulsion of all Germans from East Prussia—crimes which in some cases we could not prevent but might at least have protested against—because the Germans had angered and frightened us, and therefore we were certain that when they were down we should feel no pity for them. We persist in these policies, or let others persist in them on our behalf, because of a vague feeling that, having set out to punish Germany, we ought to go ahead and do it. Actually there is little acute hatred of Germany left in this country, and even less, I should expect to find, in the army of occupation. Only the minority of sadists, who must have their "atrocities" from one source or another, take a keen interest in the hunting-down of war criminals and quis-lings. If you ask the average man what crime Goering, Ribbentrop and the rest are to be charged with at their trial, he cannot tell you. Somehow the punishment of these monsters ceases to seem attractive when it becomes possible: indeed, once under lock and key, they almost cease to be monsters.

Unfortunately, there is often need of some concrete incident before one can discover the real state of one's feelings. Here is another memory from Germany. A few hours after Stuttgart was captured by the French army, a Belgian journalist and myself entered the town, which was still in some disorder. The Belgian had been broadcasting throughout the war for the European Service of the BBC, and, like

nearly all Frenchmen or Belgians, he had a very much tougher
attitude towards "the Boche" than an Englishman or an American
would have. All the main bridges into the town had been blown up,
and we had to enter by a small footbridge which the Germans had
evidently made efforts to defend. A dead German soldier was lying
supine at the foot of the steps. His face was a waxy yellow. On his
breast someone had laid a bunch of the lilac which was blossoming
everywhere.

The Belgian averted his face as we went past. When we were well
over the bridge he confided to me that this was the first time he had
seen a dead man. I suppose he was thirty-five years old, and for four
years he had been doing war propaganda over the radio. For several
days after this, his attitude was quite different from what it had been
earlier. He looked with disgust at the bomb-wrecked town and the
humiliations the Germans were undergoing, and even on one
occasion intervened to prevent a particularly bad bit of looting.
When he left, he gave the residue of the coffee we had brought with
us to the Germans on whom we were billeted. A week earlier he
would probably have been scandalised at the idea of giving coffee to
a "Boche". But his feelings, he told me, had undergone a change at
the sight of "ce pauvre mort" beside the bridge: it had suddenly
brought home to him the meaning of war. And yet, if we had happened to enter the town by another route, he might have been spared
the experience of seeing even one corpse out of the—perhaps—
twenty million that the war has produced.

Tribune, 9 November 1945.

2. You and the Atom Bomb

Considering how likely we all are to be blown to pieces by it within
the next five years, the atomic bomb has not roused so much discussion as might have been expected. The newspapers have published
numerous diagrams, not very helpful to the average man, of protons
and neutrons doing their stuff, and there has been much reiteration
of the useless statement that the bomb "ought to be put under
international control". But curiously little has been said, at any
rate in print, about the question that is of most urgent interest to

all of us, namely: "How difficult are these things to manufacture?"

Such information as we—that is, the big public—possess on this subject has come to us in a rather indirect way, apropos of President Truman's decision not to hand over certain secrets to the USSR. Some months ago, when the bomb was still only a rumour, there was a widespread belief that splitting the atom was merely a problem for the physicists, and that when they had solved it a new and devastating weapon would be within reach of almost everybody. (At any moment, so the rumour went, some lonely lunatic in a laboratory might blow civilisation to smithereens, as easily as touching off a firework.)

Had that been true, the whole trend of history would have been abruptly altered. The distinction between great states and small states would have been wiped out, and the power of the State over the individual would have been greatly weakened. However, it appears from President Truman's remarks, and various comments that have been made on them, that the bomb is fantastically expensive and that its manufacture demands an enormous industrial effort, such as only three or four countries in the world are capable of making. This point is of cardinal importance, because it may mean that the discovery of the atomic bomb, so far from reversing history, will simply intensify the trends which have been apparent for a dozen years past.

It is a commonplace that the history of civilisation is largely the history of weapons. In particular, the connection between the discovery of gunpowder and the overthrow of feudalism by the bourgeoisie has been pointed out over and over again. And though I have no doubt exceptions can be brought forward, I think the following rule would be found generally true: that ages in which the dominant weapon is expensive or difficult to make will tend to be ages of despotism, whereas when the dominant weapon is cheap and simple, the common people have a chance. Thus, for example, tanks, battleships and bombing planes are inherently tyrannical weapons, while rifles, muskets, long-bows and hand-grenades are inherently democratic weapons. A complex weapon makes the strong stronger, while a simple weapon—so long as there is no answer to it—gives claws to the weak.

The great age of democracy and of national self-determination was the age of the musket and the rifle. After the invention of the flintlock, and before the invention of the percussion cap, the musket was a fairly efficient weapon, and at the same time so simple that it could be produced almost anywhere. Its combination of qualities made possible the success of the American and French revolutions, and made a popular insurrection a more serious business than it could be in our own day. After the musket came the breech-loading rifle. This was a comparatively complex thing, but it could still be produced in scores of countries, and it was cheap, easily smuggled and economical of ammunition. Even the most backward nation could always get hold of rifles from one source or another, so that Boers, Bulgars, Abyssinians, Moroccans—even Tibetans—could put up a fight for their independence, sometimes with success. But thereafter every development in military technique has favoured the State as against the individual, and the industrialised country as against the backward one. There are fewer and fewer foci of power. Already, in 1939, there were only five states capable of waging war on the grand scale, and now there are only three—ultimately, perhaps, only two. This trend has been obvious for years, and was pointed out by a few observers even before 1914. The one thing that might reverse it is the discovery of a weapon—or, to put it more broadly, of a method of fighting—not dependent on huge concentrations of industrial plant.

From various symptoms one can infer that the Russians do not yet possess the secret of making the atomic bomb; on the other hand, the consensus of opinion seems to be that they will possess it within a few years. So we have before us the prospect of two or three monstrous super-states, each possessed of a weapon by which millions of people can be wiped out in a few seconds, dividing the world between them. It has been rather hastily assumed that this means bigger and bloodier wars, and perhaps an actual end to the machine civilisation. But suppose—and really this is the likeliest development—that the surviving great nations make a tacit agreement never to use the atomic bomb against one another? Suppose they only use it, or the threat of it, against people who are unable to retaliate? In that case we are back where we were before, the only difference being that power is concentrated in still fewer hands and that the outlook for subject peoples and oppressed classes is still more hopeless.

When James Burnham wrote *The Managerial Revolution* it seemed probable to many Americans that the Germans would win the European end of the war, and it was therefore natural to assume that Germany and not Russia would dominate the Eurasian land mass, while Japan would remain master of East Asia. This was a miscalculation, but it does not affect the main argument. For Burnham's geographical picture of the new world has turned out to be correct. More and more obviously the surface of the earth is being parcelled off into three great empires, each self-contained and cut off from contact with the outer world, and each ruled, under one disguise or another, by a self-elected oligarchy. The haggling as to where the frontiers are to be drawn is still going on, and will continue for some years, and the third of the three super-states—East Asia, dominated by China—is still potential rather than actual. But the general drift is unmistakable, and every scientific discovery of recent years has accelerated it.

We were once told that the aeroplane had "abolished frontiers"; actually it is only since the aeroplane became a serious weapon that frontiers have become definitely impassable. The radio was once expected to promote international understanding and co-operation; it has turned out to be a means of insulating one nation from another. The atomic bomb may complete the process by robbing the exploited classes and peoples of all power to revolt, and at the same time putting the possessors of the bomb on a basis of military equality. Unable to conquer one another, they are likely to continue ruling the world between them, and it is difficult to see how the balance can be upset except by slow and unpredictable demographic changes.

For forty or fifty years past, Mr H.G. Wells and others have been warning us that man is in danger of destroying himself with his own weapons, leaving the ants or some other gregarious species to take over. Anyone who has seen the ruined cities of Germany will find this notion at least thinkable. Nevertheless, looking at the world as a whole, the drift for many decades has been not towards anarchy but towards the reimposition of slavery. We may be heading not for general breakdown but for an epoch as horribly stable as the slave empires of antiquity. James Burnham's theory has been much discussed, but few people have yet considered its ideological implications—that is, the kind of world-view, the kind of beliefs, and the social structure that would probably prevail in a state which was at once *unconquerable* and in a permanent state of "cold war" with its neighbours.

Had the atomic bomb turned out to be something as cheap and easily manufactured as a bicycle or an alarm clock, it might well have plunged us back into barbarism, but it might, on the other hand, have meant the end of national sovereignty and of the highly-centralised police state. If, as seems to be the case, it is a rare and costly object as difficult to produce as a battleship, it is likelier to put an end to large-scale wars at the cost of prolonging indefinitely a "peace that is no peace".

Tribune, 19 October 1945

3. What Is Science?

In last week's *Tribune*, there was an interesting letter from Mr J. Stewart Cook, in which he suggested that the best way of avoiding the danger of a "scientific hierarchy" would be to see to it that every member of the general public was, as far as possible, scientifically educated. At the same time, scientists should be brought out of their isolation and encouraged to take a greater part in politics and administration.

As a general statement, I think most of us would agree with this, but I notice that, as usual, Mr Cook does not define science, and merely implies in passing that it means certain exact sciences whose experiments can be made under laboratory conditions. Thus, adult education tends "to neglect scientific studies in favour of literary, economic and social subjects", economics and sociology not being regarded as branches of science, apparently. This point is of great importance. For the word science is at present used in at least two meanings, and the whole question of scientific education is obscured by the current tendency to dodge from one meaning to the other.

Science is generally taken as meaning either (a) the exact sciences, such as chemistry, physics, etc, or (b) a method of thought which obtains verifiable results by reasoning logically from observed fact.

If you ask any scientist, or indeed almost any educated person, "What is science?" you are likely to get an answer approximating to (b). In everyday life, however, both in speaking and in writing, when people say "science" they mean (a). Science means something that happens in a laboratory: the very word calls up a picture of graphs, test-tubes, balances, Bunsen burners, microscopes. A biologist, an astronomer, perhaps a psychologist or a mathematician, is described as a "man of science": no one would think of applying this term to a statesman, a poet, a journalist or even a philosopher. And those who tell us that the young must be scientifically educated mean, almost invariably, that they should be taught more about radioactivity, or the stars, or the physiology of their own bodies, rather than that they should be taught to think more exactly.

This confusion of meaning, which is partly deliberate, has in it a great danger. Implied in the demand for more scientific education is the claim that if one has been scientifically trained one's approach to *all* subjects will be more intelligent than if one had had no such training. A scientist's political opinions, it is assumed, his opinions on sociological questions, on morals, on philosophy, perhaps even on the arts, will be more valuable than those of a layman. The world, in other words, would be a better place if the scientists were in control of it. But a "scientist", as we have just seen, means in practice a specialist in one of the exact sciences. It follows that a chemist or a physicist, as such, is politically more intelligent than a poet or a lawyer, as such. And, in fact, there are already millions of people who do believe this.

But is it really true that a "scientist", in this narrower sense, is any likelier than other people to approach non-scientific problems in an objective way? There is not much reason for thinking so. Take one simple test—the ability to withstand nationalism. It is often loosely said that "Science is international", but in practice the scientific workers of all countries line up behind their own governments with fewer scruples than are felt by the writers and the artists. The German scientific community, as a whole, made no resistance to Hitler. Hitler may have ruined the long-term prospects of German science, but there were still plenty of gifted men to do the necessary research on such things as synthetic oil, jet planes, rocket projectiles and the atomic bomb. Without them the German war machine could never have been built up.

On the other hand, what happened to German literature when the Nazis came to power? I believe no exhaustive lists have been published, but I imagine that the number of German scientists—Jews apart—who voluntarily exiled themselves or were persecuted by the régime was much smaller than the number of writers and journalists. More sinister than this, a number of German scientists swallowed the monstrosity of "racial science". You can find some of the statements to which they set their names in Professor Brady's *The Spirit and Structure of German Fascism*.

But, in slightly different forms, it is the same picture everywhere. In England, a large proportion of our leading scientists accept the structure of capitalist society, as can be seen from the comparative freedom with which they are given knighthoods, baronetcies and even peerages. Since Tennyson, no English writer worth reading— one might, perhaps, make an exception of Sir Max Beerbohm—has been given a title. And those English scientists who do not simply accept the *status quo* are frequently Communists, which means that, however intellectually scrupulous they may be in their own line of work, they are ready to be uncritical and even dishonest on certain subjects. The fact is that a mere training in one or more of the exact sciences, even combined with very high gifts, is no guarantee of a humane or sceptical outlook. The physicists of half a dozen great nations, all feverishly and secretly working away at the atomic bomb, are a demonstration of this.

But does all this mean that the general public should *not* be more scientifically educated? On the contrary! All it means is that scientific education for the masses will do little good, and probably a lot of harm, if it simply boils down to more physics, more chemistry, more biology, etc to the detriment of literature and history. Its probable effect on the average human being would be to narrow the range of his thoughts and make him more than ever contemptuous of such knowledge as he did not possess: and his political reactions would probably be somewhat less intelligent than those of an illiterate peasant who retained a few historical memories and a fairly sound aesthetic sense.

Clearly, scientific education ought to mean the implanting of a rational, sceptical, experimental habit of mind. It ought to mean acquiring a *method*—a method that can be used on any problem that one meets—and not simply piling up a lot of facts. Put it in those words, and the apologist of scientific education will usually agree. Press him further, ask him to particularise, and somehow it always turns out that scientific education means more attention to the exact sciences, in other words—more *facts*. The idea that science means a way of looking at the world, and not simply a body of knowledge, is in practice strongly resisted. I think sheer professional jealousy is part of the reason for this. For if science is simply a method or an attitude, so that anyone whose thought-processes are sufficiently rational can in some sense be described as a scientist—what then becomes of the enormous prestige now enjoyed by the chemist, the physicist, etc and his claim to be somehow wiser than the rest of us?

A hundred years ago, Charles Kingsley described science as

"making nasty smells in a laboratory". A year or two ago a young industrial chemist informed me, smugly, that he "could not see what was the use of poetry". So the pendulum swings to and fro, but it does not seem to me that one attitude is any better than the other. At the moment, science is on the up-grade, and so we hear, quite rightly, the claim that the masses should be scientifically educated: we do not hear, as we ought, the counter-claim that the scientists themselves would benefit by a little education. Just before writing this, I saw in an American magazine the statement that a number of British and American physicists refused from the start to do research on the atomic bomb, well knowing what use would be made of it. Here you have a group of sane men in the middle of a world of lunatics. And though no names were published, I think it would be a safe guess that all of them were people with some kind of general cultural background, some acquaintance with history or literature or the arts—in short, people whose interests were not, in the current sense of the word, purely scientific.

Tribune, 26 October 1945

4. Review

Drums under the Windows by Sean O'Casey

W.B. Yeats said once that a dog does not praise its fleas, but this is somewhat contradicted by the special status enjoyed in this country by Irish nationalist writers. Considering what the history of Anglo-Irish relations has been, it is not surprising that there should be Irishmen whose life-work is abusing England: what does call for remark is that they should be able to look to the English public for support and in some cases should even, like Mr O'Casey himself, prefer to live in the country which is the object of their hatred.

This is the third volume of Mr O'Casey's autobiography, and it seems to cover roughly the period 1910 to 1916. In so far as one can dig it out from masses of pretentious writing, the subject-matter is valuable and interesting. Mr O'Casey, younger son of a poverty-stricken Protestant family, worked for years as a navvy, and was at the same time deeply involved in the nationalist movement and the various cultural movements that were mixed up with it. Several of his brothers and sisters died in circumstances of gaunt poverty which would excuse a good deal of bitterness against the English occupation. He was the associate of Larkin, Connolly, the Countess Markievicz, and other leading political figures, and he had a front-seat view of the Easter Rebellion in 1916. But the cloudy manner in which the book is written makes it difficult to pin down facts or chronology. It is all in the third person ("Sean did this" and "Sean did that"), which gives an unbearable effect of narcissism, and large portions of it are written in a simplified imitation of the style of *Finnegans Wake*, a sort of Basic Joyce, which is sometimes effective in a humorous aside, but is hopeless for narrative purposes.

However, Mr O'Casey's outstanding characteristic is the romantic nationalism which he manages to combine with Communism. This book contains literally no reference to England which is not hostile or contemptuous. On the other hand, there is hardly a page which does not contain some such passage as this:

> Cathleen ni Houlihan, in her bare feet, is singing, for her pride that had almost gone is come back again. In tattered gown, and hair uncombed, she sings, shaking the ashes from her hair, and smoothing out the bigger creases in her dress; she is

> Singing of men that in battle array,
> Ready in heart and ready in hand,
> March with banner and bugle and fife
> To the death, for their native land.

Or again:

> Cathleen, the daughter of Houlihan, walks firm now, a flush on her haughty cheek. She hears the murmur in the people's hearts. Her lovers are gathering round her, for things are changed, changed utterly: "A terrible beauty is born".

If one substitutes "Britannia" for "Cathleen ni Houlihan" in these and similar passages (Cathleen ni Houlihan, incidentally, makes her appearance several times in every chapter), they can be seen at a glance for the bombast that they are. But why is it that the worst extremes of jingoism and racialism have to be tolerated when they come from an Irishman? Why is a statement like "My country right or wrong" reprehensible if applied to England and worthy of respect if applied to Ireland (or for that matter to India)? For there is no doubt that some such convention exists and that "enlightened" opinion in England can swallow even the most blatant nationalism so long as it is not British nationalism. Poems like "Rule, Britannia!" or "Ye Mariners of England" would be taken seriously if one inserted at the right places the name of some foreign country, as one can see by the respect accorded to various French and Russian war poets today.

So far as Ireland goes, the basic reason is probably England's bad conscience. It is difficult to object to Irish nationalism without seeming to condone centuries of English tyranny and exploitation. In particular, the incident with which Mr O'Casey's book ends, the summary execution of some twenty or thirty rebels who ought to have been treated as prisoners of war, was a crime and a mistake. Therefore anything that is said about it has to pass unchallenged, and Yeats's poem on the subject, which makes a sort of theme song for Mr O'Casey's book, has to be accepted uncriticised as a great poem. Actually it is not one of Yeats's better poems. But how can an Englishman, conscious that his country was in the wrong on that and many other occasions, say anything of the kind? So literary judgement is perverted by political sympathy, and Mr O'Casey and others like him are able to remain almost immune from criticism. It seems time to revise our attitude, for there is no real reason why Cromwell's massacres should cause us to mistake a bad or indifferent book for a good one.

Observer, 28 October 1945

5. Catastrophic Gradualism

There is a theory which has not yet been accurately formulated or given a name, but which is very widely accepted and is brought forward whenever it is necessary to justify some action which conflicts with the sense of decency of the average human being. It might be called, until some better name is found, the Theory of Catastrophic Gradualism. According to this theory, nothing is ever achieved without bloodshed, lies, tyranny and injustice, but on the other hand no considerable change for the better is to be expected as the result of even the greatest upheaval. History necessarily proceeds by calamities, but each succeeding age will be as bad, or nearly as bad, as the last. One must not protest against purges, deportations, secret police forces and so forth, because these are the price that has to be paid for progress: but on the other hand "human nature" will always see to it that progress is slow or even imperceptible. If you object to dictatorship you are a reactionary, but if you expect dictatorship to produce good results you are a sentimentalist.

At present this theory is most often used to justify the Stalin régime in the USSR, but it obviously could be—and, given appropriate circumstances, would be—used to justify other forms of totalitarianism. It has gained ground as a result of the failure of the Russian Revolution—failure, that is, in the sense that the Revolution has not fulfilled the hopes that it aroused twenty-five years ago. In the name of Socialism the Russian régime has committed almost every crime that can be imagined, but at the same time its evolution is *away* from Socialism, unless one redefines that word in terms that no Socialist of 1917 would have accepted. To those who admit these facts, only two courses are open. One is simply to repudiate the whole theory of totalitarianism, which few English intellectuals have the courage to do: the other is to fall back on Catastrophic Gradualism. The formula usually employed is "You can't make an omelette without breaking eggs." And if one replies, "Yes, but where is the omelette?", the answer is likely to be: "Oh well, you can't expect everything to happen all in a moment."

Naturally this argument is pushed backward into history, the design being to show that every advance was achieved at the cost of atrocious crimes, and could not have been achieved otherwise. The instance generally used is the overthrow of feudalism by the bourgeoisie, which is supposed to foreshadow the overthrow of capitalism by Socialism in our own age. Capitalism, it is argued, was once a progressive force, and therefore its crimes were justified, or at least were unimportant. Thus, in a recent number of the *New Statesman*, Mr Kingsley Martin, reproaching Arthur Koestler for not possessing a true "historical perspective", compared Stalin with Henry VIII. Stalin, he admitted, had done terrible things, but on balance he had served the cause of "progress", and a few million "liquidations" must not be allowed to obscure this fact. Similarly, Henry VIII's character left much to be desired, but after all he had made possible the rise of capitalism, and therefore on balance could be regarded as a friend of humanity.

Now, Henry VIII has not a very close resemblance to Stalin;

Cromwell would provide a better analogy; but, granting Henry VIII the importance given to him by Mr Martin, where does this argument lead? Henry VIII made possible the rise of capitalism, which led to the horrors of the Industrial Revolution and thence to a cycle of enormous wars, the next of which may well destroy civilisation altogether. So, telescoping the process, we can put it like this: "Everything is to be forgiven Henry VIII, because it was ultimately he who enabled us to blow ourselves to pieces with atomic bombs." You are led into similar absurdities if you make Stalin responsible for our present condition and the future which appears to lie before us, and at the same time insist that his policies must be supported. The motives of those English intellectuals who support the Russian dictatorship are, I think, different from what they publicly admit, but it is logical to condone tyranny and massacre if one assumes that progress is inevitable. If each epoch is as a matter of course better than the last, then any crime or any folly that pushes the historical process forward can be justified. Between, roughly, 1750 and 1930 one could be forgiven for imagining that progress of a solid, measurable kind was taking place. Latterly, this has become more and more difficult, whence the theory of Catastrophic Gradualism. Crime follows crime, one ruling class replaces another, the Tower of Babel rises and falls, but one mustn't resist the process—indeed, one must be ready to applaud any piece of scoundrelism that comes off— because in some mystical way, in the sight of God, or perhaps in the sight of Marx, this is Progress. The alternative would be to stop and consider (a) to what extent is history predetermined? and (b) what is meant by progress? At this point one has to call in the Yogi to correct the Commissar.

In his much-discussed essay, Koestler is generally assumed to have come down heavily on the side of the Yogi. Actually, if one assumes the Yogi and the Commissar to be at opposite points of the scale, Koestler is somewhat nearer to the Commissar's end. He believes in action, in violence where necessary, in government, and consequently in the shifts and compromises that are inseparable from government. He supported the war, and the Popular Front before it. Since the appearance of Fascism he has struggled against it to the best of his ability, and for many years he was a member of the Communist Party. The long chapter in his book in which he criticises the USSR is even vitiated by a lingering loyalty to his old Party and by a resulting tendency to make all bad developments date from the rise of

Stalin: whereas one ought, I believe, to admit that all the seeds of
evil were there from the start and that things would not have been
substantially different if Lenin or Trotsky had remained in control.
No one is less likely than Koestler to claim that we can put everything
right by watching our navels in California. Nor is he claiming, as
religious thinkers usually do, that a "change of heart" must come
before any genuine political improvement. To quote his own words:

> Neither the saint nor the revolutionary can save us; only the
> synthesis of the two. Whether we are capable of achieving it I do
> not know. But if the answer is in the negative, there seems to be
> no reasonable hope of preventing the destruction of European
> civilisation, either by total war's successor Absolute War, or by
> Byzantine conquest—within the next few decades.

That is to say, the "change of heart" must happen, but it is not
really happening unless at each step it issues in action. On the other
hand, no change in the structure of society can by itself effect a real
improvement. Socialism used to be defined as "common ownership
of the means of production", but it is now seen that if common
ownership means no more than centralised control, it merely paves
the way for a new form of oligarchy. Centralised control is a necessary pre-condition of Socialism, but it no more produces Socialism
than my typewriter would of itself produce this article I am writing.
Throughout history, one revolution after another—although usually
producing a temporary relief, such as a sick man gets by turning
over in bed—has simply led to a change of masters, because no
serious effort has been made to eliminate the power instinct: or if
such an effort has been made, it has been made only by the saint, the
Yogi, the man who saves his own soul at the expense of ignoring the
community. In the minds of active revolutionaries, at any rate the
ones who "got there", the longing for a just society has always been
fatally mixed up with the intention to secure power for themselves.

Koestler says that we must learn once again the technique of contemplation, which "remains the only source of guidance in ethical
dilemmas where the rule-of-thumb criteria of social utility fail". By
"contemplation" he means "the will not to will", the conquest of the
desire for power. The practical men have led us to the edge of the
abyss, and the intellectuals in whom acceptance of power politics has
killed first the moral sense, and then the sense of reality, are urging us
to march rapidly forward without changing direction. Koestler

maintains that history is not at all moments predetermined, but that there are turning-points at which humanity is free to choose the better or the worse road. One such turning-point (which had not appeared when he wrote the book), is the atomic bomb. Either we renounce it, or it destroys us. But renouncing it is both a moral effort and a political effort. Koestler calls for "a new fraternity in a new spiritual climate, whose leaders are tied by a vow of poverty to share the life of the masses, and debarred by the laws of the fraternity from attaining unchecked power". He adds: "If this seems Utopian, then Socialism is a Utopia." It may not even be a Utopia—its very name may in a couple of generations have ceased to be a memory—unless we can escape from the folly of "realism". But that will not happen without a change in the individual heart. To that extent, though no further, the Yogi is right as against the Commissar.

C[ommon] W[ealth] Review, November 1945; *Politics*, September 1946

6. Good Bad Books

Not long ago a publisher commissioned me to write an introduction for a reprint of a novel by Leonard Merrick. This publishing house, it appears, is going to reissue a long series of minor and partly-forgotten novels of the twentieth century. It is a valuable service in these bookless days, and I rather envy the person whose job it will be to scout round the threepenny boxes, hunting down copies of his boyhood favourites.

A type of book which we hardly seem to produce in these days, but which flowered with great richness in the late nineteenth and early twentieth centuries, is what Chesterton called the "good bad book": that is, the kind of book that has no literary pretensions but which remains readable when more serious productions have perished. Obviously outstanding books in this line are *Raffles* and the Sherlock Holmes stories, which have kept their place when innumerable "problem novels", "human documents" and "terrible indictments" of this or that have fallen into deserved oblivion. (Who has worn better, Conan Doyle or Meredith?) Almost in the same class as these I put R. Austin Freeman's earlier stories—"The Singing Bone", "The Eye of Osiris" and others—Ernest Bramah's *Max Carrados*, and, dropping the standard a bit, Guy Boothby's Tibetan thriller, *Dr Nikola*, a sort of schoolboy version of Huc's *Travels in Tartary*, which would probably make a real visit to Central Asia seem a dismal anticlimax.

But apart from thrillers, there were the minor humorous writers of the period. For example, Pett Ridge—but I admit his full-length books no longer seem readable—E. Nesbit (*The Treasure Seekers*), George Birmingham, who was good so long as he kept off politics, the pornographic Binstead ("Pitcher" of the *Pink 'Un*), and, if American books can be included, Booth Tarkington's Penrod stories. A cut above most of these was Barry Pain. Some of Pain's humorous writings are, I suppose, still in print, but to anyone who comes across it I recommend what must now be a very rare book— *The Octave of Claudius*, a brilliant exercise in the macabre. Somewhat later in time there was Peter Blundell, who wrote in the W.W. Jacobs vein about Far Eastern seaport towns, and who seems to be rather unaccountably forgotten, in spite of having been praised in print by H.G. Wells.

However, all the books I have been speaking of are frankly "escape" literature. They form pleasant patches in one's memory, quiet corners where the mind can browse at odd moments, but they hardly pretend to have anything to do with real life. There is another kind of good bad book which is more seriously intended, and which tells us, I think, something about the nature of the novel and the reasons for its present decadence. During the last fifty years there has been a whole series of writers—some of them are still writing— whom it is quite impossible to call "good" by any strictly literary standard, but who are natural novelists and who seem to attain sincerity partly because they are not inhibited by good taste. In this class I put Leonard Merrick himself, W.L. George, J.D. Beresford, Ernest Raymond, May Sinclair, and—at a lower level than the others but still essentially similar—A.S.M. Hutchinson.

Most of these have been prolific writers, and their output has naturally varied in quality. I am thinking in each case of one or two outstanding books: for example, Merrick's *Cynthia*, J.D. Beresford's *A Candidate for Truth*, W.L. George's *Caliban*, May Sinclair's *The Combined Maze* and Ernest Raymond's *We, the Accused*. In each of these books the author has been able to identify himself with his imagined characters, to feel with them and invite sympathy on their behalf, with a kind of abandonment that cleverer people would find it difficult to achieve. They bring out the fact that intellectual refinement can be a disadvantage to a story-teller, as it would be to a music-hall comedian.

Take, for example, Ernest Raymond's *We, the Accused*—a peculiarly sordid and convincing murder story, probably based on the Crippen case. I think it gains a great deal from the fact that the author only partly grasps the pathetic vulgarity of the people he is writing about, and therefore does not despise them. Perhaps it even —like Theodore Dreiser's *An American Tragedy*—gains something from the clumsy long-winded manner in which it is written; detail is piled on detail, with almost no attempt at selection, and in the process an effect of terrible, grinding cruelty is slowly built up. So also with *A Candidate for Truth*. Here there is not the same clumsiness, but there is the same ability to take seriously the problems of commonplace people. So also with *Cynthia* and at any rate the earlier part of *Caliban*. The greater part of what W.L. George wrote was shoddy rubbish, but in this particular book, based on the career of Northcliffe, he achieved some memorable and truthful pictures of lower-middle-class London life. Parts of this book are probably autobiographical, and one of the advantages of good bad writers is their lack of shame in writing autobiography. Exhibitionism and self-pity are the bane of the novelist, and yet if he is too frightened of them his creative gift may suffer.

The existence of good bad literature—the fact that one can be amused or excited or even moved by a book that one's intellect simply refuses to take seriously—is a reminder that art is not the same thing as cerebration. I imagine that by any test that could be devised, Carlyle would be found to be a more intelligent man than Trollope. Yet Trollope has remained readable and Carlyle has not: with all his cleverness he had not even the wit to write in plain straightforward English. In novelists, almost as much as in poets, the connection between intelligence and creative power is hard to establish. A good novelist may be a prodigy of self-discipline like Flaubert, or he may be an intellectual sprawl like Dickens. Enough talent to set up dozens of ordinary writers has been poured into Wyndham Lewis's so-called novels, such as *Tarr* or *Snooty Baronet*. Yet it would be a very heavy labour to read one of these books right through. Some indefinable quality, a sort of literary vitamin, which exists even in a book like *If Winter Comes*, is absent from them.

Perhaps the supreme example of the "good bad" book is *Uncle*

Tom's Cabin. It is an unintentionally ludicrous book, full of preposterous melodramatic incidents; it is also deeply moving and essentially true; it is hard to say which quality outweighs the other. But
Uncle Tom's Cabin, after all, is trying to be serious and to deal with
the real world. How about the frankly escapist writers, the purveyors
of thrills and "light" humour? How about *Sherlock Holmes, Vice
Versa, Dracula, Helen's Babies* or *King Solomon's Mines*? All of
these are definitely absurd books, books which one is more inclined
to laugh *at* than *with*, and which were hardly taken seriously even by
their authors; yet they have survived, and will probably continue to
do so. All one can say is that, while civilisation remains such that one
needs distraction from time to time, "light" literature has its appointed place; also that there is such a thing as sheer skill, or native
grace, which may have more survival value than erudition or intellectual power. There are music-hall songs which are better poems
than three-quarters of the stuff that gets into the anthologies:

> Come where the booze is cheaper,
> Come where the pots hold more,
> Come where the boss is a bit of a sport,
> Come to the pub next door!

Or again:

> Two lovely black eyes—
> Oh, what a surprise!
> Only for calling another man wrong,
> Two lovely black eyes!

I would far rather have written either of those than, say, "The Blessed
Damozel" or "Love in the Valley". And by the same token I would
back *Uncle Tom's Cabin* to outlive the complete works of Virginia
Woolf or George Moore, though I know of no strictly literary test
which would show where the superiority lies.

Tribune, 2 November 1945; SE

7. Introduction to *Love of Life and Other Stories* by Jack London

In her little book, *Memories of Lenin*, Nadezhda Krupskaya relates that when Lenin was in his last illness she used to read aloud to him in the evenings:

> Two days before his death I read to him in the evening a tale by Jack London, "Love of Life"—it is still lying on the table in his room. It was a very fine story. In a wilderness of ice, where no human being had set foot, a sick man, dying of hunger, is making for the harbour of a big river. His strength is giving out, he cannot walk but keeps slipping, and beside him there slides a wolf— also dying of hunger. There is a fight between them: the man wins. Half dead, half demented, he reaches his goal. That tale greatly pleased Ilyich (Lenin). Next day he asked me to read him more Jack London.

However, Krupskaya goes on, the next tale turned out to be "saturated with bourgeois morals," and "Ilyich smiled and dismissed it with a wave of his hand." These two pieces by Jack London were the last things that she read to him.

The story, "Love of Life", is even grimmer than Krupskaya suggests in her short summary of it, for it actually ends with the man eating the wolf, or at any rate biting into its throat hard enough to draw blood. That is the sort of theme towards which Jack London was irresistibly drawn, and this episode of Lenin's death bed readings is of itself not a bad criticism of London's work. He was a writer who excelled in describing cruelty, whose main theme, indeed, was the cruelty of Nature, or at any rate of contemporary life; he was also an extremely variable writer, much of whose work was produced hurriedly and at low pressure; and he had in him a strain of feeling which Krupskaya is probably right in calling "bourgeois"—at any rate, a strain which did not accord with his democratic and Socialist convictions.

During the last twenty years Jack London's short stories have been rather unaccountably forgotten—how thoroughly forgotten, one could gauge by the completeness with which they were out of print. So far as the big public went, he was remembered by various animal books, particularly *White Fang* and *The Call of the Wild*—

books which appealed to the Anglo-Saxon sentimentality about animals—and after 1933 his reputation took an upward bound because of *The Iron Heel*, which had been written in 1907, and is in some sense a prophecy of Fascism. *The Iron Heel* is not a good book, and on the whole its predictions have not been borne out. Its dates and its geography are ridiculous, and London makes the mistake, which was usual at that time, of assuming that revolution would break out first in the highly industrialised countries. But on several points London was right where nearly all other prophets were wrong, and he was right because of just that strain in his nature that made him a good short-story writer and a doubtfully reliable Socialist.

London imagines a proletarian revolution breaking out in the United States and being crushed, or partially crushed, by a counter-offensive of the capitalist class; and, following on this, a long period during which society is ruled over by a small group of tyrants known as the Oligarchs, who are served by a kind of SS known as the Mercenaries. An underground struggle against dictatorship was the kind of thing that London could imagine, and he foresaw certain of the details with surprising accuracy; he foresaw, for instance, that peculiar horror of totalitarian society, the way in which suspected enemies of the régime *simply disappear*. But the book is chiefly notable for maintaining that capitalist society would not perish of its "contradictions", but that the possessing class would be able to form itself into a vast corporation and even evolve a sort of perverted Socialism, sacrificing many of its privileges in order to preserve its superior status. The passages in which London analyses the mentality of the Oligarchs are of great interest:

They, as a class (writes the imaginary author of the book), believed that they alone maintained civilisation. It was their belief that, if they ever weakened, the great beast would engulf them and everything of beauty and joy and wonder and good in its cavernous and slime-dripping maw. Without them, anarchy would reign and humanity would drop backward into the primitive night out of which it had so painfully emerged. . . . In short, they alone, by their unremitting toil and self-sacrifice, stood between weak humanity and the all-devouring beast: and they believed it, firmly believed it.

I cannot lay too great stress upon this high ethical righteousness of the whole Oligarch class. This has been the strength of the Iron Heel, and too many of the comrades have been slow or loath to realise it. Many of them have ascribed the strength of the Iron Heel to its system of reward and punishment. This is a mistake. Heaven and hell may be the prime factors of zeal in the religion of a fanatic; but for the great majority of the religious, heaven and hell are incidental to right and wrong. Love of the right, desire for the right, unhappiness with anything less than the right—in short, right conduct, is the prime factor of religion. And so with the Oligarchy. . . . The great driving force of the Oligarchs is the belief that they are doing right.

From these and similar passages it can be seen that London's understanding of the nature of a ruling class—that is, the characteristics which a ruling class must have if it is to survive—went very deep. According to the conventional left-wing view, the "capitalist" is simply a cynical scoundrel, without honour or courage, and intent only on filling his own pockets. London knew that that view is false. But why, one might justly ask, should this hurried, sensational, in some ways childish writer have understood that particular thing so much better than the majority of his fellow Socialists?

The answer is surely that London could foresee Fascism because he had a Fascist streak in himself: or at any rate a marked strain of brutality and an almost unconquerable preference for the strong man as against the weak man. He knew instinctively that the American businessmen would fight when their possessions were menaced, because in their place he would have fought himself. He was an adventurer and a man of action as few writers have ever been. Born into dire poverty, he had already escaped from it at sixteen, thanks to his commanding character and powerful physique: his early years were spent among oyster pirates, gold prospectors, tramps and prize-fighters, and he was ready to admire toughness wherever he found it. On the other hand he never forgot the sordid miseries of his childhood, and he never faltered in his loyalty to the exploited classes. Much of his time was spent in working and lecturing for the Socialist movement, and when he was already a successful and famous man he could explore the worst depths of poverty in the London slums, passing himself off as an American sailor, and compile a book (*The People of the Abyss*) which still has sociological value. His outlook was democratic in the sense that he hated exploitation and hereditary privilege, and that he felt most at home in the company of people who worked with their hands: but his instinct lay towards acceptance of a "natural aristocracy" of strength, beauty and talent. Intellectually he knew, as one can see from various remarks in *The Iron Heel*, that Socialism ought to mean the meek inheriting the earth, but that was not what his temperament demanded. In much of his work one strain in his character simply kills the other off: he is at his best where they interact, as they do in certain of his short stories.

Jack London's great theme is the cruelty of Nature. Life is a savage struggle, and victory has nothing to do with justice. In the best of his short stories there is a startling lack of comment, a suspension of judgement, arising out of the fact that he both delights in the struggle and perceives its cruelty. Perhaps the best thing he ever wrote is "Just Meat". Two burglars have got away with a big haul of jewellery: each is intent on swindling the other out of his share, and they poison one another simultaneously with strychnine, the story ending with the two men dead on the floor. There is almost no comment, and certainly no "moral". As Jack London sees it, it is simply a fragment of life, the kind of thing that happens in the present-day world: nevertheless it is doubtful whether such a plot would occur to any writer who was not fascinated by cruelty. Or take a story like "The *Francis Spaight*". The starving crew of a waterlogged ship have decided to resort to cannibalism, and have just nerved themselves to begin when another ship heaves in sight. It is characteristic of Jack London that the second ship should appear after and not before the cabin boy's throat has been cut. A still more typical story is "A Piece of Steak". London's love of boxing and admiration for sheer physical strength, his perception of the meanness and cruelty of a competitive society, and at the same time his instinctive tendency to accept *vae victis* as a law of Nature, are all expressed here. An old prize-fighter is fighting his last battle: his opponent is a beginner, young and full of vigour, but without experience. The old man nearly wins, but in the end his ring-craft is no match for the youthful resilience of the other. Even when he has him at his mercy he is unable to strike the blow that would finish him, because he has been underfed for weeks before the fight and his muscles cannot make the necessary effort. He is left bitterly reflecting that if only he had had a good piece of steak on the day of the fight he would have won.

The old man's thoughts all run upon the theme: "Youth will be served". First you are young and strong, and you knock out older men and make money which you squander: then your strength wanes and in turn you are knocked out by younger men, and then you sink into poverty. This does in fact tell the story of the average boxer's life, and it would be a gross exaggeration to say that Jack London *approves* of the way in which men are used up like gladiators by a society which cannot even bother to feed them. The detail of the piece of steak—not strictly necessary, since the main point of the story is that the younger man is bound to win by virtue of his youth —rubs in the economic implication. And yet there is something in London that takes a kind of pleasure in the whole cruel process. It is not so much an approval of the harshness of Nature, as a mystical belief that Nature *is* like that. Nature is "red in tooth and claw". Perhaps fierceness is bad, but fierceness is the price of survival. The young slay the old, the strong slay the weak, by an inexorable law. Man fights against the elements or against his fellow man, and there is nothing except his own toughness to help him through. London would have said that he was merely describing life as it is actually lived, and in his best stories he does so: still, the constant recurrence of the same theme—struggle, toughness, survival—shows which way his inclinations pointed.

London had been deeply influenced by the theory of the Survival of the Fittest. His book, *Before Adam*—an inaccurate but very readable story of prehistory, in which ape-man and early and late Palaeolithic men are all shown as existing simultaneously—is an attempt to popularise Darwin. Although Darwin's main thesis has not been shaken, there has been, during the past twenty or thirty years, a change in the interpretation put upon it by the average thinking man. In the late nineteenth century Darwinism was used as a justification for *laissez-faire* capitalism, for power politics and for the exploiting of subject peoples. Life was a free-for-all in which the fact of survival was proof of fitness to survive: this was a comforting thought for successful businessmen, and it also led naturally, though not very logically, to the notion of "superior" and "inferior" races. In our day we are less willing to apply biology to politics, partly because we have watched the Nazis do just that thing, with great thoroughness and with horrible results. But when London was writing, a crude version of Darwinism was widespread and must have been difficult to escape. He himself was even capable at times of succumbing to racial mysticism. He toyed for a while with a race theory similar to that of the Nazis, and throughout his work the cult of the "nordic" is fairly well marked. It ties up on the one hand with his admiration for prize-fighters, and on the other with his anthropomorphic view of animals: for there seems to be good reason for thinking that an exaggerated love of animals generally goes with a rather brutal attitude towards human beings. London was a Socialist with the instincts of a buc- caneer and the education of a nineteenth-century materialist. In general the background of his stories is not industrial, nor even civilised. Most of them take place—and much of his own life was lived—on ranches or South Sea islands, in ships, in prison or in the wastes of the Arctic: places where a man is either alone and depen- dent on his own strength and cunning, or where life is naturally patriarchal.

Nevertheless, London did write from time to time about con- temporary industrial society, and on the whole he was at his best when he did so. Apart from his short stories, there are *The People of the Abyss*, *The Road* (a brilliant little book describing London's youthful experiences as a tramp), and certain passages in *The Valley of the Moon*, which have the tumultuous history of American trade unionism as their background. Although the tug of his impulses was away from civilisation, London had read deeply in the literature of the Socialist movement, and his early life had taught him all he needed to know about urban poverty. He himself was working in a factory at the age of eleven, and without that experience behind him he could hardly have written such a story as "The Apostate". In this story, as in all his best work, London does not comment, but he does unquestionably aim at rousing pity and indignation. It is generally when he writes of more primitive scenes that his moral attitude becomes equivocal. Take, for instance, a story like "Make Westing". With whom do London's sympathies lie—with Captain Cullen or with George Dorety? One has the impression that if he were forced to make a choice he would side with the Captain, who commits two murders but does succeed in getting his ship round Cape Horn. On the other hand, in a story like "The Chinago", although it is told in the usual pitiless style, the "moral" is plain enough for anyone who wants to find it. London's better angel is his Socialist convictions, which come into play when he deals with such subjects as coloured exploitation, child labour or the treatment of criminals, but are hardly involved when he is writing about explorers or animals. It is probably for this reason that a high proportion of his better writings deal with urban life. In stories like "The Apostate", "Just Meat", "A Piece of Steak" and "Semper Idem", however cruel and sordid they may seem, something is keeping him on the rails and checking his natural urge towards the glorification of brutality. That "something" is his knowledge, theoretical as well as practical, of what industrial capitalism means in terms of human suffering.

Jack London is a very uneven writer. In his short and restless life he poured forth an immense quantity of work, setting himself to produce 1,000 words every day and generally achieving it. Even his best stories have the curious quality of being well told and yet not well written: they are told with admirable economy, with just the right incidents in just the right place, but the texture of the writing is poor, the phrases are worn and obvious, and the dialogue is erratic. His reputation has had its ups and downs, and for a long period he seems to have been much more admired in France and Germany than in the English-speaking countries. Even before the triumph of Hitler, which brought *The Iron Heel* out of its obscurity, he had a certain renown as a left-wing and "proletarian" writer—rather the same kind of renown as attaches to Robert Tressell, W.B. Traven or Upton Sinclair. He has also been attacked by Marxist writers for his "Fascist tendencies". These tendencies unquestionably existed in him, so much so that if one imagines him as living on into our own day, instead of dying in 1915, it is very hard to be sure where his political allegiance would have lain. One can imagine him in the Communist Party, one can imagine him falling a victim to Nazi racial theory, and one can imagine him the quixotic champion of some Trotskyist or Anarchist sect. But, as I have tried to make clear, if he had been a politically reliable person he would probably have left behind nothing of interest. Meanwhile his reputation rests mainly on *The Iron Heel,* and the excellence of his short stories has been almost forgotten. A dozen of the best of them are collected in this volume, and a few more are worth rescuing from the museum shelves and the second-hand boxes. It is to be hoped, too, that new editions of *The Road, The Jacket, Before Adam* and *The Valley of the Moon* will appear when paper becomes more plentiful. Much of Jack London's work is scamped and unconvincing, but he produced at least six volumes which deserve to stay in print, and that is not a bad achievement from a life of only forty-one years.

Written [November 1945]; published by Paul Elek, November 1946

8. Letter[1] to the Duchess of Atholl

27B Canonbury Square
Islington
London N1
15 November 1945

Dear Duchess of Atholl,[2]

I have only just received your letter dated November 13th.

I am afraid I cannot speak for the League for European Freedom. I could easily get out of it by saying that the date is impossible or—what is quite true—that I know nothing about Jugoslavia, but I prefer to tell you plainly that I am not in agreement with the League's ultimate objectives as I understand them. I went to the first public meeting, or one of the first, and wrote something about it in *Tribune* which you may have seen.[3] Certainly what is said on your platforms is more truthful than the lying propaganda to be found in most of the press, but I cannot associate myself with an essentially Conservative body which claims to defend democracy in Europe but has nothing to say about British imperialism. It seems to me that one can only denounce the crimes now being committed in Poland, Jugoslavia, etc if one is equally insistent on ending Britain's unwanted rule in India. I belong to the Left and must work inside it, much as I hate Russian totalitarianism and its poisonous influence in this country.

Yours truly
[Geo. Orwell]

9. Review

The Prussian Officer and Other Stories by D.H. Lawrence

Reviews ought not to consist of personal reminiscences, but perhaps it is worth recording how I first became acquainted with D.H.

[1] From a carbon copy.

[2] The Duchess of Atholl (1874–1960), a Unionist MP 1923–38, became in 1924 one of the first two women to be a Minister in a British Government. She was known as "The Red Duchess" for her very strong anti-Franco feelings during the Spanish civil war. Throughout her life she campaigned for various "causes".

[3] See III, 91.

Lawrence's work, because it happened that I read him before I had
heard of him, and the qualities which then impressed me were
probably the essential ones.

In 1919 I went into my schoolmaster's study for some purpose,
and, not finding him there, picked up a magazine with a blue cover
which was on the table. I was then sixteen and wallowing in Georgian
poetry. My idea of a good poem would have been Rupert Brooke's
"Grantchester". As soon as I opened the magazine I was completely
overwhelmed by a poem which describes a woman standing in the
kitchen and watching her husband approaching across the fields.
On the way he takes a rabbit out of a snare and kills it. Then he
comes in, throws the dead rabbit on the table, and, his hands still
stinking of rabbit's fur, takes the woman in his arms. In a sense she
hates him, but she is utterly swallowed up in him. More than the
sexual encounter, the "beauty of Nature" which Lawrence deeply
felt, but which he was also able to turn on and off like a tap, impressed me; especially the lines (referring to a flower):

> Then her bright breast she will uncover
> And yield her honeydrop to her lover.

But I failed to notice the name of the author, or even of the magazine,
which must have been the *English Review*.

Four or five years later, still not having heard of Lawrence, I got
hold of the volume of short stories now reprinted as a Penguin. Both
"The Prussian Officer" and "The Thorn in the Flesh" impressed me
deeply. What struck me was not so much Lawrence's horror and
hatred of military discipline, as his understanding of its nature.
Something told me that he had never been a soldier, and yet he
could project himself into the atmosphere of an army, and the
German army at that. He had built all this up, I reflected, from
watching a few German soldiers walking about in some garrison
town. From another story, "The White Stocking" (also in this collection, though I think I read it later), I deduced the moral that women
behave better if they get a sock on the jaw occasionally.

Clearly there is more in Lawrence than this, but I think these first
impacts left me with a broadly true picture of him. He was in essence
a lyric poet, and an undisciplined enthusiasm for "Nature", i.e. the
surface of the earth, was one of his principal qualities, though it has
been much less noticed than his preoccupation with sex. And on top
of this he had the power of understanding, or seeming to understand,

people totally different from himself, such as farmers, gamekeepers, clergymen and soldiers—one might add coal miners, for though Lawrence himself had worked in the pit at the age of thirteen, clearly he was not a typical miner. His stories are a kind of lyric poem, produced by just looking at some alien, inscrutable human being and suddenly experiencing an intense imaginative vision of his inner life.

How true these visions were is debatable. Like some Russian writers of the nineteenth century, Lawrence often seems to by-pass the novelist's problem by making all his characters equally sensitive. All the people in his stories, even those to whom he is hostile, seem to experience the same kind of emotions, everyone can make contact with everyone else, and class barriers, in the form in which we know them, are almost obliterated. Yet he does often seem to have an extraordinary power of knowing imaginatively something that he could not have known by observation. Somewhere in one of his books he remarks that when you shoot at a wild animal, the action is not the same as shooting at a target. You do not look along the sights: you aim by an instinctive movement of the whole body, and it is as though your will were driving the bullet forward. This is quite true, and yet I do not suppose Lawrence had ever shot at a wild animal. Or consider the death scene at the end of "England my England" (which is not in the present collection, unfortunately). Lawrence had never been in circumstances remotely similar to those he was describing. He had merely had a private vision of the feelings of a soldier under fire. Perhaps it is true to experience, perhaps not; but at least it is emotionally true, and therefore convincing.

With few exceptions Lawrence's full-length novels are, it is generally admitted, difficult to get through. In the short stories his faults do not matter so much, because a short story can be purely lyrical, whereas a novel has to take account of probability and has to be cold-bloodedly constructed. In *The Prussian Officer* there is an extraordinarily good, longish story called "Daughters of the Vicar". An Anglican clergyman of the ordinary middle-class type is marooned in a mining village where he and his family are half-starved on a tiny stipend, and where he has no function, the mining folk having no need of him and no sympathy with him. It is the typical impoverished middle-class family in which the children grow up with a false consciousness of social superiority dragging upon them like a ball and fetter. The usual problem arises: how are the daughters to get married? The elder daughter gets the chance to marry a comparatively well-to-do clergyman. He happens to be a dwarf, suffering from some internal disease, and an utterly inhuman creature, more like a precocious and disagreeable child than a man. By the standards of most of the family she has done the right thing: she has married a gentleman. The younger daughter, whose vitality is not to be defeated by snobbishness, throws family prestige overboard and marries a healthy young coal miner.

It will be seen that this story has a close resemblance to *Lady Chatterley's Lover*. But in my opinion it is much better and more convincing than the novel, because the single imaginative impulse is strong enough to sustain it. Probably Lawrence had watched, somewhere or other, the underfed, downtrodden, organ-playing daughter of a clergyman wearing out her youth, and had a sudden vision of her escaping into the warmer world of the working class, where husbands are plentiful. It is a fit subject for a short story, but when drawn out to novel length it raises difficulties to which Lawrence was unequal. In another story in this book, "The Shades of Spring", there is a gamekeeper who is presented as a wild natural creature, the opposite of the over-conscious intellectual. Such figures appear again and again in Lawrence's books, and I think it is true to say that they are more convincing in the short stories, where we do not have to know too much about them, than in the novels (for example, *Lady Chatterley's Lover* or *The Woman Who Rode Away*), where, in order to be set into action, they have to be credited with complex thoughts which destroy their status as unspoiled animals. Another story, "Odour of Chrysanthemums", deals with the death of a miner in a pit accident. He is a drunkard and up to the moment of his death his wife has wanted nothing so much as to be rid of him. Only when she is washing his dead body does she perceive, as though for the first time, how beautiful he is. That is the kind of thing Lawrence could do, and in the first paragraph of the story there is a wonderful example of his power of visual description. But one could not make a full-length novel out of such an episode, nor, without other more prosaic ingredients, out of a series of such episodes. . . .

Tribune, 16 November 1945

34

10. Through a Glass, Rosily

The recent article by *Tribune's* Vienna correspondent[1] provoked a spate of angry letters which, besides calling him a fool and a liar and making other charges of what one might call a routine nature, also carried the very serious implication that he ought to have kept silent even if he knew that he was speaking the truth. He himself made a brief answer in *Tribune*, but the question involved is so important that it is worth discussing it at greater length.

Whenever A and B are in opposition to one another, anyone who attacks or criticises A is accused of aiding and abetting B. And it is often true, objectively and on a short-term analysis, that he *is* making things easier for B. Therefore, say the supporters of A, shut up and don't criticise: or at least criticise "constructively", which in practice always means favourably. And from this it is only a short step to arguing that the suppression and distortion of known facts is the highest duty of a journalist.

Now, if one divides the world into A and B and assumes that A represents progress and B reaction, it is just arguable that no fact detrimental to A ought ever to be revealed. But before making this claim one ought to realise where it leads. What do we mean by reaction? I suppose it would be agreed that Nazi Germany represented reaction in its worst form or one of its worst. Well, the people in this country who gave most ammunition to the Nazi propagandists during the war are exactly the ones who tell us that it is "objectively" pro-Fascist to criticise the USSR. I am not referring to the Communists during their anti-war phase: I am referring to the Left as a whole. By and large, the Nazi radio got more material from the British left-wing press than from that of the Right. And it could hardly be otherwise, for it is chiefly in the left-wing press that serious criticism of British institutions is to be found. Every revelation about slums or social inequality, every attack on the leaders of the Tory Party, every denunciation of British imperialism, was a gift for Goebbels. And not necessarily a worthless gift, for German propaganda about "British plutocracy" had considerable effect in neutral countries, especially in the earlier part of the war.

[1] When *Tribune's* Vienna correspondent had reported the appalling conditions in the city and, quite truthfully, described the monstrous behaviour of some of the Russian occupying troops, several readers protested against what they called "this slander" on the Red army.

Here are two examples of the kind of source from which the Axis propagandists were liable to take their material. The Japanese, in one of their English-speaking magazines in China, serialised Briffault's *Decline and Fall of the British Empire*. Briffault, if not actually a Communist, was vehemently pro-Soviet, and the book incidentally contained some cracks at the Japanese themselves; but from the Japanese point of view this didn't matter, since the main tendency of the book was anti-British. About the same time the German radio broadcast shortened versions of books which they considered damaging to British prestige. Among others they broadcast E.M. Forster's *A Passage to India*. And so far as I know they didn't even have to resort to dishonest quotation. Just because the book was essentially truthful, it could be made to serve the purposes of Fascist propaganda. According to Blake,

> A truth that's told with bad intent
> Beats all the lies you can invent,

and anyone who has seen his own statements coming back at him on the Axis radio will feel the force of this. Indeed, anyone who has ever written in defence of unpopular causes or been the witness of events which are likely to cause controversy, knows the fearful temptation to distort or suppress the facts, simply because any honest statement will contain revelations which can be made use of by unscrupulous opponents. But what one has to consider are the long-term effects. In the long run, can the cause of progress be served by lies, or can it not? The readers who attacked *Tribune's* Vienna correspondent so violently accused him of untruthfulness, but they also seemed to imply that the facts he brought forward ought not to be published even if true. 100,000 rape cases in Vienna are not a good advertisement for the Soviet régime: therefore, even if they have happened, don't mention them. Anglo-Russian relations are more likely to prosper if inconvenient facts are kept dark.

The trouble is that if you lie to people, their reaction is all the more violent when the truth leaks out, as it is apt to do in the end. Here is an example of untruthful propaganda coming home to roost. Many English people of goodwill draw from the left-wing press an unduly favourable picture of the Indian Congress Party. They not only believe it to be in the right (as it is), but are also apt to imagine that it is a sort of left-wing organisation with democratic and internationalist aims. Such people, if they are suddenly confronted with

an actual, flesh-and-blood Indian Nationalist, are liable to recoil into
the attitudes of a Blimp. I have seen this happen a number of times.
And it is the same with pro-Soviet propaganda. Those who have
swallowed it whole are always in danger of a sudden revulsion in
which they may reject the whole idea of Socialism. In this and other
ways I should say that the net effect of Communist and near-Com-
munist propaganda has been simply to retard the cause of Socialism,
though it may have temporarily aided Russian foreign policy.

There are always the most excellent, high-minded reasons for
concealing the truth, and these reasons are brought forward in almost
the same words by supporters of the most diverse causes. I have had
writings of my own kept out of print because it was feared that the
Russians would not like them, and I have had others kept out of
print because they attacked British imperialism and might be quoted
by anti-British Americans. We are told *now* that any frank criticism
of the Stalin régime will "increase Russian suspicions", but it is only
seven years since we were being told (in some cases by the same newspapers) that frank criticism of the Nazi régime would increase Hitler's
suspicions. As late as 1941, some of the Catholic papers declared that
the presence of Labour Ministers in the British Government increased
Franco's suspicions and made him incline more towards the Axis.
Looking back, it is possible to see that if only the British and American peoples had grasped in 1933 or thereabouts what Hitler stood for,
war might have been averted. Similarly, the first step towards decent
Anglo-Russian relations is the dropping of illusions. In principle
most people would agree to this: but the dropping of illusions means
the publication of facts, and facts are apt to be unpleasant.

The whole argument that one mustn't speak plainly because it
"plays into the hands of" this or that sinister influence is dishonest,
in the sense that people only use it when it suits them. As I have
pointed out, those who are most concerned about playing into the
hands of the Tories were least concerned about playing into the
hands of the Nazis. The Catholics who said "Don't offend Franco
because it helps Hitler" had been more or less consciously helping
Hitler for years beforehand. Beneath this argument there always lies
the intention to do propaganda for some single sectional interest, and
to browbeat critics into silence by telling them that they are "objectively" reactionary. It is a tempting manoeuvre, and I have used it
myself more than once, but it is dishonest. I think one is less likely to
use it if one remembers that the advantages of a lie are always short-

lived. So often it seems a positive duty to suppress or colour the facts! And yet genuine progress can only happen through increasing enlightenment, which means the continuous destruction of myths.

Meanwhile there is a curious backhanded tribute to the values of liberalism in the fact that the opponents of free speech write letters to *Tribune* at all. "Don't criticise," such people are in effect saying: "don't reveal inconvenient facts. Don't play into the hands of the enemy!" Yet they themselves are attacking *Tribune*'s policy with all the violence at their command. Does it not occur to them that if the principles they advocate were put into practice, their letters would never get printed?

Tribune, 23 November 1945

11. Freedom of the Park

A few weeks ago, five people who were selling papers outside Hyde Park were arrested by the police for obstruction. When taken before the magistrates they were all found guilty, four of them being bound over for six months and the other sentenced to forty shillings' fine or a month's imprisonment. He preferred to serve his term, so I suppose he is still in jail at this moment.

The papers these people were selling were *Peace News*, *Forward* and *Freedom*, besides other kindred literature. *Peace News* is the organ of the Peace Pledge Union, *Freedom* (till recently called *War Commentary*) is that of the Anarchists: as for *Forward*, its politics defy definition, but at any rate it is violently Left. The magistrate, in passing sentence, stated that he was not influenced by the nature of the literature that was being sold: he was concerned merely with the fact of obstruction, and that this offence had technically been committed.

This raises several important points. To begin with, how does the law stand on the subject? As far as I can discover, selling newspapers in the street *is* technically obstruction, at any rate if you fail to move on when the police tell you to. So it would be legally possible for any policeman who felt like it to arrest any newsboy for selling the *Evening News*. Obviously this doesn't happen, so that the enforcement of the law depends on the discretion of the police.

And what makes the police decide to arrest one man rather than another? However it may have been with the magistrate, I find it hard to believe that in this case the police were not influenced by political considerations. It is a bit too much of a coincidence that they should have picked on people selling just those papers. If they had also arrested someone who was selling *Truth*, or the *Tablet*, or the *Spectator*, or even the *Church Times*, their impartiality would be easier to believe in.

The British police are not like a continental *gendarmerie* or Gestapo, but I do not think one maligns them in saying that, in the past, they have been unfriendly to left-wing activities. They have generally shown a tendency to side with those whom they regarded as the defenders of private property. There were some scandalous cases at the time of the Mosley disturbances. At the only big Mosley meeting I ever attended, the police collaborated with the Blackshirts in "keeping order", in a way in which they certainly would not have collaborated with Socialists or Communists. Till quite recently "red" and "illegal" were almost synonymous, and it was always the seller of, say, the *Daily Worker*, never the seller of, say, the *Daily Telegraph*, who was moved on and generally harassed. Apparently it can be the same, at any rate at moments, under a Labour Government.

A thing I would like to know—it is a thing we hear very little about—is what changes are made in the administrative personnel when there has been a change of government. Does the police officer who has a vague notion that "Socialism" means something against the law carry on just the same when the government itself is Socialist? It is a sound principle that the official should have no party affiliations, should serve successive governments faithfully and should not be victimised for his political opinions. Still, no government can afford to leave its enemies in key positions, and when Labour is in undisputed power for the first time—and therefore when it is taking over an administration formed by Conservatives—it clearly must make sufficient changes to prevent sabotage. The official, even when friendly to the government in power, is all too conscious that he is a permanency and can frustrate the short-lived Ministers whom he is supposed to serve.

When a Labour Government takes over, I wonder what happens to Scotland Yard Special Branch? To Military Intelligence? To the Consular Service? To the various colonial administrations—and so on and so forth? We are not told, but such symptoms as there are do not suggest that any very extensive reshuffling is going on. We are still represented abroad by the same ambassadors, and BBC censorship seems to have the same subtly reactionary colour that it always had. The BBC claims, of course, to be both independent and non-political. I was told once that its "line", if any, was to represent the left-wing of the government in power. But that was in the days of the Churchill Government. If it represents the left wing of the present Government, I have not noticed the fact.

However, the main point of this episode is that the sellers of newspapers and pamphlets should be interfered with at all. Which particular minority is singled out—whether Pacifists, Communists, Anarchists, Jehovah's Witnesses or the Legion of Christian Reformers who recently declared Hitler to be Jesus Christ—is a secondary matter. It is of symptomatic importance that these people should have been arrested at that particular spot. You are not allowed to sell literature inside Hyde Park, but for many years past it has been usual for the paper-sellers to station themselves just outside the gates and distribute literature connected with the open-air meetings a hundred yards away. Every kind of publication has been sold there without interference.

As for the meetings inside the Park, they are one of the minor wonders of the world. At different times I have listened there to Indian Nationalists, Temperance reformers, Communists, Trotskyists, the SPGB,[1] the Catholic Evidence Society, Freethinkers, vegetarians, Mormons, the Salvation Army, the Church Army, and a large variety of plain lunatics, all taking their turn at the rostrum in an orderly way and receiving a fairly good-humoured hearing from the crowd. Granted that Hyde Park is a special area, a sort of Alsatia where outlawed opinions are permitted to walk—still, there are very few countries in the world where you can see a similar spectacle. I have known continental Europeans, long before Hitler seized power, come away from Hyde Park astonished and even perturbed by the things they had heard Indian or Irish Nationalists saying about the British Empire.

The degree of freedom of the press existing in this country is often overrated. Technically there is great freedom, but the fact that most of the press is owned by a few people operates in much the same way

[1] Socialist Party of Great Britain, a Marxist organisation with no connection with the Labour Party.

as a state censorship. On the other hand, freedom of speech is real. On the platform, or in certain recognised open-air spaces like Hyde Park, you can say almost anything; and, what is perhaps more significant, no one is frightened to utter his true opinions in pubs, on the tops of buses, and so forth.

The point is that the relative freedom which we enjoy depends on public opinion. The law is no protection. Governments make laws, but whether they are carried out, and how the police behave, depends on the general temper of the country. If large numbers of people are interested in freedom of speech, there will be freedom of speech, even if the law forbids it; if public opinion is sluggish, inconvenient minorities will be persecuted, even if laws exist to protect them. The decline in the desire for intellectual liberty has not been so sharp as I would have predicted six years ago, when the war was starting, but still there has been a decline. The notion that certain opinions cannot safely be allowed a hearing is growing. It is given currency by intellectuals who confuse the issue by not distinguishing between democratic opposition and open rebellion, and it is reflected in our growing indifference to tyranny and injustice abroad. And even those who declare themselves to be in favour of freedom of opinion generally drop their claim when it is their own adversaries who are being persecuted.

I am not suggesting that the arrest of five people for selling harmless newspapers is a major calamity. When you see what is happening in the world today, it hardly seems worth squealing about such a tiny incident. All the same, it is not a good symptom that such things should happen when the war is well over, and I should feel happier if this, and the long series of similar episodes that have preceded it, were capable of raising a genuine popular clamour, and not merely a mild flutter in sections of the minority press.

Tribune, 7 December 1945

12. The Sporting Spirit

Now that the brief visit of the Dynamo football team[1] has come to an end, it is possible to say publicly what many thinking people were

---

[1] The Moscow Dynamos, a Russian football team, toured Britain in the autumn of 1945 playing against leading British clubs.

saying privately before the Dynamos ever arrived. That is, that sport is an unfailing cause of ill-will, and that if such a visit as this had any effect at all on Anglo-Soviet relations, it could only be to make them slightly worse than before.

Even the newspapers have been unable to conceal the fact that at least two of the four matches played led to much bad feeling. At the Arsenal match, I am told by someone who was there, a British and a Russian player came to blows and the crowd booed the referee. The Glasgow match, someone else informs me, was simply a free-for-all from the start. And then there was the controversy, typical of our nationalistic age, about the composition of the Arsenal team. Was it really an all-England team, as claimed by the Russians, or merely a league team, as claimed by the British? And did the Dynamos end their tour abruptly in order to avoid playing an all-England team? As usual, everyone answers these questions according to his political predilections. Not quite everyone, however. I noted with interest, as an instance of the vicious passions that football provokes, that the sporting correspondent of the russophile *News Chronicle* took the anti-Russian line and maintained that Arsenal was not an all-England team. No doubt the controversy will continue to echo for years in the footnotes of history books. Meanwhile the result of the Dynamos' tour, in so far as it has had any result, will have been to create fresh animosity on both sides.

And how could it be otherwise? I am always amazed when I hear people saying that sport creates goodwill between the nations, and that if only the common peoples of the world could meet one another at football or cricket, they would have no inclination to meet on the battlefield. Even if one didn't know from concrete examples (the 1936 Olympic Games, for instance) that international sporting contests lead to orgies of hatred, one could deduce it from general principles.

Nearly all the sports practised nowadays are competitive. You play to win, and the game has little meaning unless you do your utmost to win. On the village green, where you pick up sides and no feeling of local patriotism is involved, it is possible to play simply for the fun and exercise: but as soon as the question of prestige arises, as soon as you feel that you and some larger unit will be disgraced if you lose, the most savage combative instincts are aroused. Anyone who has played even in a school football match knows this. At the international level sport is frankly mimic warfare. But the significant thing is not the behaviour of the players but the attitude of the spectators: and, behind the spectators, of the nations who work themselves into furies over these absurd contests, and seriously believe—at any rate for short periods—that running, jumping and kicking a ball are tests of national virtue.

Even a leisurely game like cricket, demanding grace rather than strength, can cause much ill-will, as we saw in the controversy over body-line bowling and over the rough tactics of the Australian team that visited England in 1921. Football, a game in which everyone gets hurt and every nation has its own style of play which seems unfair to foreigners, is far worse. Worst of all is boxing. One of the most horrible sights in the world is a fight between white and coloured boxers before a mixed audience. But a boxing audience is always disgusting, and the behaviour of the women, in particular, is such that the army, I believe, does not allow them to attend its contests. At any rate, two or three years ago, when Home Guards and regular troops were holding a boxing tournament, I was placed on guard at the door of the hall, with orders to keep the women out.

In England, the obsession with sport is bad enough, but even fiercer passions are aroused in young countries where games playing and nationalism are both recent developments. In countries like India or Burma, it is necessary at football matches to have strong cordons of police to keep the crowd from invading the field. In Burma, I have seen the supporters of one side break through the police and disable the goalkeeper of the opposing side at a critical moment. The first big football match that was played in Spain about fifteen years ago led to an uncontrollable riot. As soon as strong feelings of rivalry are aroused, the notion of playing the game according to the rules always vanishes. People want to see one side on top and the other side humiliated, and they forget that victory gained through cheating or through the intervention of the crowd is meaningless. Even when the spectators don't intervene physically they try to influence the game by cheering their own side and "rattling" opposing players with boos and insults. Serious sport has nothing to do with fair play. It is bound up with hatred, jealousy, boastfulness, disregard of all rules and sadistic pleasure in witnessing violence: in other words it is war minus the shooting.

Instead of blah-blahing about the clean, healthy rivalry of the football field and the great part played by the Olympic Games in bringing the nations together, it is more useful to inquire how and why this modern cult of sport arose. Most of the games we now play are of ancient origin, but sport does not seem to have been taken very seriously between Roman times and the nineteenth century. Even in the English public schools the games cult did not start till the later part of the last century. Dr Arnold, generally regarded as the founder of the modern public school, looked on games as simply a waste of time. Then, chiefly in England and the United States, games were built up into a heavily-financed activity, capable of attracting vast crowds and rousing savage passions, and the infection spread from country to country. It is the most violently combative sports, football and boxing, that have spread the widest. There cannot be much doubt that the whole thing is bound up with the rise of nationalism— that is, with the lunatic modern habit of identifying oneself with large power units and seeing everything in terms of competitive prestige. Also, organised games are more likely to flourish in urban communities where the average human being lives a sedentary or at least a confined life, and does not get much opportunity for creative labour. In a rustic community a boy or young man works off a good deal of his surplus energy by walking, swimming, snowballing, climbing trees, riding horses, and by various sports involving cruelty to animals, such as fishing, cock-fighting and ferreting for rats. In a big town one must indulge in group activities if one wants an outlet for one's physical strength or for one's sadistic impulses. Games are taken seriously in London and New York, and they were taken seriously in Rome and Byzantium: in the Middle Ages they were played, and probably played with much physical brutality, but they were not mixed up with politics nor a cause of group hatreds.

If you wanted to add to the vast fund of ill-will existing in the world at this moment, you could hardly do it better than by a series of football matches between Jews and Arabs, Germans and Czechs, Indians and British, Russians and Poles, and Italians and Jugoslavs, each match to be watched by a mixed audience of 100,000 spectators. I do not, of course, suggest that sport is one of the main causes of international rivalry; big-scale sport is itself, I think, merely another effect of the causes that have produced nationalism. Still, you do make things worse by sending forth a team of eleven men, labelled as national champions, to do battle against some rival team, and allowing it to be felt on all sides that whichever nation is defeated will "lose face".

I hope, therefore, that we shan't follow up the visit of the Dynamos by sending a British team to the USSR. If we must do so, then let us

send a second-rate team which is sure to be beaten and cannot be
claimed to represent Britain as a whole. There are quite enough real
causes of trouble already, and we need not add to them by encouraging young men to kick each other on the shins amid the roars of
infuriated spectators.

Tribune, 14 December 1945; SE

13. Nonsense Poetry

In many languages, it is said, there is no nonsense poetry, and there
is not a great deal of it even in English. The bulk of it is in nursery
rhymes and scraps of folk poetry, some of which may not have been
strictly nonsensical at the start, but have become so because their
original application has been forgotten. For example, the rhyme
about Margery Daw:

> See-saw, Margery Daw,
> Dobbin shall have a new master.
> He shall have but a penny a day
> Because he can't go any faster.

Or the other version that I learned in Oxfordshire as a little boy:

> See-saw, Margery Daw,
> Sold her bed and lay upon straw.
> Wasn't she a silly slut
> To sell her bed and lie upon dirt?

It may be that there was once a real person called Margery Daw, and
perhaps there was even a Dobbin who somehow came into the story.
When Shakespeare makes Edgar in *King Lear* quote "Pillicock sat on
Pillicock hill", and similar fragments, he is uttering nonsense, but no
doubt these fragments come from forgotten ballads in which they
once had a meaning. The typical scrap of folk poetry which one
quotes almost unconsciously is not exactly nonsense but a sort of
musical comment on some recurring event, such as "One a penny,
two a penny, Hot-Cross buns", or "Polly, put the kettle on, we'll all
have tea". Some of these seemingly frivolous rhymes actually express
a deeply pessimistic view of life, the churchyard wisdom of the peasant. For instance:

> Solomon Grundy,
> Born on Monday,
> Christened on Tuesday,
> Married on Wednesday,
> Took ill on Thursday,
> Worse on Friday,
> Died on Saturday,
> Buried on Sunday,
> And that was the end of Solomon Grundy.

which is a gloomy story, but remarkably similar to yours or mine.

Until Surrealism made a deliberate raid on the unconscious, poetry that aimed at being nonsense, apart from the meaningless refrains of songs, does not seem to have been common. This gives a special position to Edward Lear, whose nonsense rhymes have just been edited by Mr R.L. Megroz,[1] who was also responsible for the Penguin edition a year or two before the war. Lear was one of the first writers to deal in pure fantasy, with imaginary countries and made-up words, without any satirical purpose. His poems are not all of them equally nonsensical; some of them get their effect by a perversion of logic, but they are all alike in that their underlying feeling is sad and not bitter. They express a kind of amiable lunacy, a natural sympathy with whatever is weak and absurd. Lear could fairly be called the originator of the limerick, though verses in almost the same metrical form are to be found in earlier writers, and what is sometimes considered a weakness in his limericks—that is, the fact that the rhyme is the same in the first and last lines—is part of their charm. The very slight change increases the impression of ineffectuality, which might be spoiled if there were some striking surprise. For example:

> There was a young lady of Portugal
> Whose ideas were excessively nautical;
> She climbed up a tree
> To examine the sea,
> But declared she would never leave Portugal.

It is significant that almost no limericks since Lear's have been both printable and funny enough to seem worth quoting. But he is really seen at his best in certain longer poems, such as "The Owl and the Pussy-Cat" or "The Courtship of the Yonghy-Bonghy-Bò":

[1] *The Lear Omnibus* edited by R.L. Megroz.

On the Coast of Coromandel,
Where the early pumpkins blow,
In the middle of the woods
Lived the Yonghy-Bonghy-Bò.
Two old chairs, and half a candle—
One old jug without a handle—
These were all his worldly goods:
In the middle of the woods,
These were all the worldly goods
Of the Yonghy-Bonghy-Bò,
Of the Yonghy-Bonghy-Bò.

Later there appears a lady with some white Dorking hens, and an inconclusive love affair follows. Mr Megroz thinks, plausibly enough, that this may refer to some incident in Lear's own life. He never married, and it is easy to guess that there was something seriously wrong in his sex life. A psychiatrist could no doubt find all kinds of significance in his drawings and in the recurrence of certain made-up words such as "runcible". His health was bad, and as he was the youngest of twenty-one children in a poor family, he must have known anxiety and hardship in very early life. It is clear that he was unhappy and by nature solitary, in spite of having good friends.

Aldous Huxley, in praising Lear's fantasies as a sort of assertion of freedom, has pointed out that the "They" of the limericks represent common sense, legality and the duller virtues generally. "They" are the realists, the practical men, the sober citizens in bowler hats who are always anxious to stop you doing anything worth doing. For instance:

There was an Old Man of Whitehaven,
Who danced a quadrille with a raven;
But they said, "It's absurd
To encourage this bird!"
So they smashed that Old Man of Whitehaven.

To smash somebody just for dancing a quadrille with a raven is exactly the kind of thing that "They" would do. Herbert Read has also praised Lear, and is inclined to prefer his verse to that of Lewis Carroll, as being purer fantasy. For myself, I must say that I find Lear funniest when he is least arbitrary and when a touch of burlesque or perverted logic makes its appearance. When he gives his fancy free play, as in his imaginary names, or in things like "Three Receipts for Domestic Cookery", he can be silly and tiresome. "The Pobble Who Has No Toes" is haunted by the ghost of logic, and I think it is the element of sense in it that makes it funny. The Pobble, it may be remembered, went fishing in the Bristol Channel:

> And all the Sailors and Admirals cried,
> When they saw him nearing the further side—
> "He has gone to fish, for his Aunt Jobiska's
> Runcible Cat with crimson whiskers!"

The thing that is funny here is the burlesque touch, the Admirals. What is arbitrary—the word "runcible", and the cat's crimson whiskers—is merely rather embarrassing. While the Pobble was in the water some unidentified creatures came and ate his toes off, and when he got home his aunt remarked:

> "It's a fact the whole world knows,
> That Pobbles are happier without their toes,"

which once again is funny because it has a meaning, and one might even say a political significance. For the whole theory of authoritarian governments is summed up in the statement that Pobbles were happier without their toes. So also with the well-known limerick:

> There was an Old Person of Basing,
> Whose presence of mind was amazing;
> He purchased a steed,
> Which he rode at full speed,
> And escaped from the people of Basing.

It is not quite arbitrary. The funniness is in the gentle implied criticism of the people of Basing, who once again are "They", the respectable ones, the right-thinking, art-hating majority.

The writer closest to Lear among his contemporaries was Lewis Carroll, who, however, was less essentially fantastic—and, in my opinion, funnier. Since then, as Mr Megroz points out in his Introduction, Lear's influence has been considerable, but it is hard to believe that it has been altogether good. The silly whimsiness of present-day children's books could perhaps be partly traced back to sense, though it came off in Lear's case, is a doubtful one. Probably the best nonsense poetry is produced gradually and accidentally, by communities rather than by individuals. As a comic draughtsman, on the other hand, Lear's influence must have been beneficial. James Thurber, for instance, must surely owe something to Lear, directly or indirectly.

Tribune, 21 December 1945; SE

14. Review

A Coat of Many Colours: Occasional Essays by Herbert Read

The essays and reviews in this moderate-sized volume cover such subjects as Anarchism, war books, Toulouse-Lautrec, Paul Klee, Eric Gill, Havelock Ellis, prose style, Lawrence of Arabia, Gerard Manley Hopkins, Socialist Realism, George Saintsbury, Verlaine, Stendhal, Wordsworth's *Prelude*, Marlowe's *Faustus*, Chinese painting, Salvador Dali, Kierkegaard, and Henry James. Those I have named make up roughly a quarter of the subjects that Herbert Read discusses, and obviously such a book cannot be exhaustively dealt with in a thousand or fifteen hundred words. I prefer to concentrate mainly on one point—the clash between Read's political beliefs and his aesthetic theory. But the multiplicity of subjects is in itself a point to be noticed. Even if one regards Read simply as a critic of painting the range of his interests and sympathies is very wide, and his open-mindedness has been his strength and weakness as a writer.

Read is an Anarchist, and an Anarchist of an uncompromising kind; he admits that the ideal society cannot be realised at this moment, but he refuses to be satisfied with anything less or to abandon the belief that Man is perfectible. He is also an accepter of the Machine Age and a defender, on aesthetic grounds, of the products of the machine. In some of the essays in this book, notably "Art and Autarky" and the essay on Eric Gill, he seems to hedge a little, but in general he sticks to it that an anarchistic form of society is compatible with a high level of technical development:
him. At any rate, the idea of deliberately setting out to write non-

Anarchism implies a universal decentralisation of authority, and a universal simplification of life. Inhuman entities like the modern city will disappear. But Anarchism does not necessarily imply a reversion to handicraft and outdoor sanitation. There is no contradiction between Anarchism and electric power, Anarchism and air transport, Anarchism and division of labour, Anarchism and industrial efficiency. Since the functional groups will all be working for their mutual benefit, and not for other people's profit or for mutual destruction, the measure of efficiency will be the appetite for fullness of living.

The vague generalisation contained in the last sentence avoids the enormous question: how are freedom and organisation to be reconciled? If one considers the probabilities one is driven to the conclusion that Anarchism implies a low standard of living. It need not imply a hungry or uncomfortable world, but it rules out the kind of air-conditioned, chromium-plated, gadget-ridden existence which is now considered desirable and enlightened. The processes involved in making, say, an aeroplane are so complex as to be only possible in a planned, centralised society, with all the repressive apparatus that that implies. Unless there is some unpredictable change in human nature, liberty and efficiency must pull in opposite directions. Read will not admit this, and he will not fully admit that the machine has frustrated the creative instincts and degraded aesthetic feeling. Indeed, he takes what looks like a perverse pleasure in praising the things that are mechanically and collectively produced as against the achievement of the individual craftsman:

> The new aesthetic must be based on the fundamentally new factor in modern civilisation—large-scale machine production. That method of production involves certain characteristics which contradict the accepted notion of beauty—they are generally indicated by the word *standardisation*. In itself, standardisation is not an aesthetic question. If a thing is beautiful you do not diminish that beauty by reproducing it. . . . Standardised machine products are exact replicas of one another, and if one is beautiful, the rest are beautiful. . . . We may admit that certain forms of personal expression are not suitable for mechanical reproduction as standardised objects, but we claim that the creative will of the artist can and should be adapted to the new conditions. We draw attention to a

certain type of modern art (abstract, non-representational or
constructivist art) which, while still remaining a very personal
expression of the individual artists who produce it, is nevertheless the prototype of machine art. Such works of art could be
reproduced without losing any of their aesthetic qualities.

At first glance this looks reasonable and the objections likely to
be urged against it look sentimental and arty-and-crafty. But just
test it by a few concrete examples. "If a thing is beautiful you do not
diminish that beauty by reproducing it." I suppose that "Whether on
Ida's shady brow" is beautiful. (If you don't care for that particular
poem, substitute some other that you do care for.) Well, would you
like to hear it read aloud five thousand times running? Would it still
be beautiful at the end of such a process? On the contrary, it would
seem the most hideous collection of words that has ever existed. Any
shape, any sound, any colour, any smell becomes odious through too
much repetition, because repetition fatigues the senses to which
beauty must make its appeal. Read often speaks of beauty as though
it were a kind of Platonic Absolute existing somewhere or other in
its own right and in no way dependent on human appreciation. If one
takes this view, one must assume that the value of, say, a picture
resides in the picture itself, and that the method by which it has been
produced is irrelevant. It may be produced by machinery, or, like
certain Surrealist pictures, by accident. But how about books? It is
just thinkable that books may some day be written by machinery,
and it is quite easy to imagine poems being produced partly by
fortuitous means—by some device similar to the kaleidoscope, for
instance. And if they were "good" poems I do not see how Read
could consistently object to such a process. It is a queer position for
an Anarchist to be driven into.

But of course Read is not consistent in his acceptance of the
machine. In this book we find him praising the beauties of modern
car design, and we find him pointing out that the masses in the
industrialised countries have been brought into a state of "mental
sickness" by "deadening labours and devitalised environment". We
find him writing sympathetically of Paul Klee and Ben Nicholson,
but also of Ruskin and Walter de la Mare. We find him saying
"personally, I am against the grandiose in art," and we find him
praising the Pyramids. The fact is, as anyone who has been reviewed
by him knows, that Read is too kind a critic. The range of his sym-

pathies, as I pointed out earlier, is very wide, perhaps too wide. The only thing he acutely dislikes is conservatism, or, to put it more precisely, academicism. He is always on the side of the young against the old. He is in favour of abstract painting and streamlined teapots because the aesthetic conservatives don't like them: and he is in favour of Anarchism because the political Conservatives, including the official Left, don't like that. The contradiction into which this leads him remains unresolved.

It would be difficult to overpraise Read as a populariser and as a champion of unfashionable causes. I suppose no one in our time has done more to encourage young poets and keep the British public informed about artistic developments in Europe, and no one of equal standing has had the guts to speak out against the russomania of the last ten years. But all the same, wide sympathies have their penalty. It is probably a mistake for any kind of artist, even a critic, to endeavour to "keep up" beyond a certain point. This does not mean that one has to accept the normal academic assumption that literature and art came to an end about forty years ago. Clearly the young and the middle-aged ought to try to appreciate one another. But one ought also to recognise that one's aesthetic judgement is only fully valid between fairly well-defined dates. Not to admit this is to throw away the advantage that one derives from being born into one's own particular time. Among people now alive there are two very sharp dividing lines. One is between those who can and those who can't remember the period before 1914; the other is between those who were adult before 1933 and those who were not. Other things being equal, who is likelier to have the truer vision at this moment, a person of twenty or a person of fifty? One can't say, though on some points posterity may decide. Each generation imagines itself to be more intelligent than the one that went before it, and wiser than the one that comes after it. This is an illusion, and one should recognise it as such, but one ought also to stick to one's own world-view, even at the price of seeming old-fashioned: for that world-view springs out of experiences that the younger generation has not had, and to abandon it is to kill one's intellectual roots.

If I apply to Read the simple test, "How much of it sticks?" I find that none of his critical work has left so deep an impression on me as certain passages in his writings about his childhood, and a handful of poems. At this moment I recall particularly a passage describing the making of lead buckshot in a bullet-mould—and the joy of the act,

he said, was not in the usefulness of the bullet but in the beauty of the
silvery new-minted lead—and a poem written early in this war, "The
Contrary Experience". In these and similar writings Read is simply
speaking out of his experience: he is not trying to be open-minded, or
up-to-date, or cosmopolitan, or public-spirited. In politics Read is an
Anarchist, in aesthetic theory he is a Europeaniser, but in his origins
he is a Yorkshireman—that is, a member of a small, rustic, rather
uncouth tribe whose members secretly believe all the other peoples
of the earth to be just a little inferior to themselves. I think his best
work comes from the Yorkshire strain in him. I am not decrying his
critical activities. They have been a civilising influence which it
would be ungrateful not to acknowledge. But in contrast to his autobiographical writings, and to some of his poems and certain passages
in his political pamphlets, his purely critical work has a sort of
diffuseness, a wateriness, which comes from being too open-minded,
too charitable, too civilised, too anxious to keep abreast of modern
thought and remain in touch with all movements simultaneously,
instead of giving expression to the vehement likes and dislikes which
must be present in his mind, just as much as in any other writer's.

Poetry Quarterly, Winter 1945

15. Introduction to *The Position of Peggy Harper* by Leonard Merrick

Leonard Merrick died in 1939, but during the later part of his life he
wrote, or at any rate published, nothing but short stories. Except for
one early and now forgotten book, *Violet Moses*, his full-length
novels all belong to the period between 1900 and 1914. There are
about a dozen of them in all, and their general level is so high that,
though it would be fairly easy to pick out six of them as being better
worth reprinting than the rest, it is not easy to narrow the choice
down to a single volume.

   Merrick has the peculiarity that, though he is by no means a
"highbrow" writer, the background of his stories is almost invariably
one or other of the arts. Among his full-length novels, the only exceptions to this rule are *The Worldlings*, a story of imposture founded on

the Tichborne case, and *One Man's View*, which is a partial exception in so much that the central character is a lawyer. Otherwise the people he habitually writes about are novelists, poets, painters and, most characteristically of all, actors. If there is one thing above all others for which he deserves to be remembered, it is his extraordinarily convincing and glamourless picture of stage life; and this, perhaps, justifies the reprinting of *The Position of Peggy Harper* rather than of, say, *Cynthia* or *The Worldlings*, which are equally good in their different way.

Although nearly all of Merrick's books are about writers or artists, they can be divided fairly sharply into two classes. One class, by which unfortunately he is best known, are his Paris books, mostly collections of short stories, such as *A Chair on the Boulevard*. These stories describe a kind of Bohemianism which Merrick had not experienced from the inside and which only doubtfully exists; the atmosphere they are trying to reproduce is that of *Trilby* or even, at their worst, that of W.J. Locke's *Aristide Pujol*. Where Merrick describes *his own* adventures in Paris, as he obviously does in certain chapters in *Cynthia*, for instance, it is quite a different story. Picturesqueness disappears, and in its place there enters that dreadful thing which he understood so well, poverty against a background of gentility. Merrick's shabby-genteel novels are the ones that matter: the best of them, apart from those that have been mentioned already, are *The Man Who Was Good*, *The Actor Manager*, *The House of Lynch* and *The Quaint Companions*. *Conrad in Quest of His Youth*, one of Merrick's most successful books, deals partly with stage life, but differs from the others in that poverty is not a leading theme in it.

Money is always a fascinating subject, provided that only small sums are involved. Brute starvation is not interesting, and neither are transactions involving thousands of millions of pounds; but an out-of-work actor pawning his watch-chain and wondering whether next week the watch will have to follow it—that is interesting. However, Merrick's books are not simply concerned with the difficulty of making a living. His theme is rather the humiliation which a sensitive and honest person feels when he is forced into contact with people whose standards are commercial. Christopher Tatham, the hero of *Peggy Harper*, writes a melodrama which scores a thunderous success while the comedies into which he has put his real work grow dog-eared on their journey from agent to agent. It is an interesting detail —a reminder that, after all, the status of the literary man *has* risen

during the past thirty or forty years—that the sum Tatham receives
for his five-act melodrama is fifteen pounds! But the fact that he is
underpaid is socially less significant than the fact that he is isolated.
Until it is almost too late, he simply does not have the opportunity of
making contact with people in any way similar to himself. His silly,
snobbish mother, and his prosperous uncle who is "associated with
hops", are somewhat further from understanding his point of view
than the vulgar actor-manager who buys his melodrama. The foolish
engagement into which he enters is the direct result of isolation.
When he first meets Peggy Harper, at the age of twenty-one or thereabouts, he probably does not know—never having had the chance to
find out—that there exist women who are both attractive and intelligent. Until he has made his mark by individual effort, society has no
place for him. The dull commercial world of his family and the
vulgar, down-at-heel world of the touring companies are equally
hostile to him, and it is largely luck that the one or the other does not
swallow him up for good.

Merrick is not consciously, or at any rate not overtly, a "writer
with a purpose". The commercialism and philistinism of the English-
speaking civilisation is something that he inveighs against but
assumes to be unchangeable, like the English climate. And there are
many of the accepted values of his time that he does not even question. In particular, he everywhere takes for granted the superiority of
a "gentleman" to a "bounder" and of a "good accent" to cockney;
and in most of his books there are passages which if they were written
today would be called snobbish. Actually, Merrick is not a snobbish
writer—if he were he would probably write about wealthy or titled
people instead of concentrating on the shabby-genteel—but he is too
honest to disguise his instinctive preferences. He feels strongly that
good manners and delicate sensibilities are important, and that one
of the worst horrors of poverty is having to take orders from ill-bred,
coarse-fibred people. A beautiful little scene in *Peggy Harper* illustrates the kind of servitude that an educated man in a low-class
touring company must be ready to put up with. The word "menace"
has occurred in the script of the play that is being rehearsed, and the
ignoramus of a stage manager insists that it should be pronounced
"manace":

"What's that—what d'ye call it? 'Menace?' Rats! That's extant,
that's altogether extant." He evidently relished his discovery of

"extant", which he seemed to believe was a scholarly synonym
for "out of date". He looked round for Tatham. "Isn't 'menace'
extant, eh?" he enquired.

"Quite," said Tatham.

Peggy Harper, like most of Merrick's books (the outstanding exception is *The Man Who Was Good*), has a "happy ending", but it is
implied all the way through that decency and intelligence are very
serious handicaps. In *Cynthia*, which is a story about a novelist, the
clash between honesty and bread and butter is even more painful.
Cynthia is a book which it would not be altogether absurd to mention
in the same sentence as George Gissing's *New Grub Street*, but its
theme is one that a good many different writers have handled. The
special thing that Merrick could do, and which no one else seems to
have done, is to reproduce the atmosphere of low-class theatrical
life: the smell of greasepaint and fish and chips, the sordid rivalries,
the comfortless Sunday journeys, the lugging of suitcases through the
back streets of unfamiliar towns, the "professional" lodgings
presided over by "Ma", the poky bedrooms with the rickety wash-
hand-stand and the grim white chamber-pot under the bed (does
Merrick ever mention the chamber-pot? Probably not: one just
seems to imagine it), and the trudging up and down the Strand on
worn-out boot-soles, the agents' offices where women in dyed frocks
sit waiting their turn, the forlorn collection of press cuttings, the
manager who bolts in the middle of the tour with all the takings.

Although Merrick was fairly successful, especially towards the end
of his life, as a short-story writer, his full-length novels never "sold"
in this country. About 1918 Messrs Hodder and Stoughton issued a
uniform edition of his works with introductions by H.G. Wells,
G.K. Chesterton, W.D. Howells and other well-known writers who
admired him and felt that he was underrated. The introduction to
Peggy Harper was written by Sir Arthur Pinero. The uniform edition,
however, was no more successful than earlier editions had been—a
fact which is all the more puzzling because throughout his life
Merrick's books sold relatively well in the United States.[1] The
obvious explanation of his unpopularity is that he chose to write
about artists, whereas the big public, as he himself often remarked,
would sooner read about politicians or businessmen; also that his

---

[1] The American uniform edition was issued by Messrs E.P. Dutton, who also
issued a limited edition. [Author's footnote.]

books are what people call "grey", or "gloomy", or "too like real life". It is quite true that the majority of Merrick's books are far from being cheer-up stories. They are lightly written, and for the sake of preserving the comedy form they usually have a "happy ending", but their underlying mood is a bitter one. But it is still not clear why Merrick should have been more popular in America. The American public is presumably no more inclined than the British to take sides with the artist against society: nor did Merrick make any special concessions to American readers, for the subject-matter and the whole atmosphere of most of his books are intensely English.

Possibly, from the American point of view, the Englishness was an exotic attraction, while the kind of poverty and failure that Merrick was describing were not quite the kind that Americans are afraid of. At any rate, Merrick's steady refusal to see silver linings where none existed must have had something to do with his unpopularity. It is perhaps significant that *Conrad in Quest of His Youth*, the hero of which is wealthy, was about the most successful of his books. Now that the fear of poverty is a less urgent emotion, and the demand for sunshine stories less insistent, he seems overdue for revival.

Written [late 1945] for Eyre and Spottiswoode who wanted to publish a reprint of *The Position of Peggy Harper* with this introduction. The book, however, was never published.

1946

16. The Prevention of Literature

About a year ago I attended a meeting of the PEN Club, the occasion being the tercentenary of Milton's *Areopagitica*—a pamphlet, it may be remembered, in defence of freedom of the press. Milton's famous phrase about the sin of "killing" a book was printed on the leaflets, advertising the meeting, which had been circulated beforehand.

There were four speakers on the platform. One of them delivered a speech which did deal with the freedom of the press, but only in relation to India; another said, hesitantly, and in very general terms, that liberty was a good thing; a third delivered an attack on the laws relating to obscenity in literature. The fourth devoted most of his speech to a defence of the Russian purges. Of the speeches from the body of the hall, some reverted to the question of obscenity and the laws that deal with it, others were simply eulogies of Soviet Russia. Moral liberty—the liberty to discuss sex questions frankly in print— seemed to be generally approved, but political liberty was not mentioned. Out of this concourse of several hundred people, perhaps half of whom were directly connected with the writing trade, there was not a single one who could point out that freedom of the press, if it means anything at all, means the freedom to criticise and oppose. Significantly, no speaker quoted from the pamphlet which was ostensibly being commemorated. Nor was there any mention of the various books that have been "killed" in this country and the United States during the war. In its net effect the meeting was a demonstration in favour of censorship.[1]

There was nothing particularly surprising in this. In our age, the idea of intellectual liberty is under attack from two directions. On the

---

[1] It is fair to say that the PEN Club celebrations, which lasted a week or more, did not always stick at quite the same level. I happened to strike a bad day. But an examination of the speeches (printed under the title *Freedom of Expression*) shows that almost nobody in our own day is able to speak out as roundly in favour of intellectual liberty as Milton could do 300 years ago—and this in spite of the fact Milton was writing in a period of civil war. [Author's footnote.]

one side are its theoretical enemies, the apologists of totalitarianism, and on the other its immediate, practical enemies, monopoly and bureaucracy. Any writer or journalist who wants to retain his integrity finds himself thwarted by the general drift of society rather than by active persecution. The sort of things that are working against him are the concentration of the press in the hands of a few rich men, the grip of monopoly on radio and the films, the unwillingness of the public to spend money on books, making it necessary for nearly every writer to earn part of his living by hack work, the encroachment of official bodies like the MOI[1] and the British Council, which help the writer to keep alive but also waste his time and dictate his opinions, and the continuous war atmosphere of the past ten years, whose distorting effects no one has been able to escape. Everything in our age conspires to turn the writer, and every other kind of artist as well, into a minor official, working on themes handed to him from above and never telling what seems to him the whole of the truth. But in struggling against this fate he gets no help from his own side: that is, there is no large body of opinion which will assure him that he is in the right. In the past, at any rate throughout the Protestant centuries, the idea of rebellion and the idea of intellectual integrity were mixed up. A heretic—political, moral, religious, or aesthetic—was one who refused to outrage his own conscience. His outlook was summed up in the words of the Revivalist hymn:

> Dare to be a Daniel,
> Dare to stand alone;
> Dare to have a purpose firm,
> Dare to make it known.

To bring this hymn up to date one would have to add a "Don't" at the beginning of each line. For it is the peculiarity of our age that the rebels against the existing order, at any rate the most numerous and characteristic of them, are also rebelling against the idea of individual integrity. "Daring to stand alone" is ideologically criminal as well as practically dangerous. The independence of the writer and the artist is eaten away by vague economic forces, and at the same time it is undermined by those who should be its defenders. It is with the second process that I am concerned here.

Freedom of thought and of the press are usually attacked by arguments which are not worth bothering about. Anyone who has experi-

[1] Ministry of Information.

ence of lecturing and debating knows them off backwards. Here I am not trying to deal with the familiar claim that freedom is an illusion, or with the claim that there is more freedom in totalitarian countries than in democratic ones, but with the much more tenable and dangerous proposition that freedom is undesirable and that intellectual honesty is a form of antisocial selfishness. Although other aspects of the question are usually in the foreground the controversy over freedom of speech and of the press is at the bottom a controversy over the desirability, or otherwise, of telling lies. What is really at issue is the right to report contemporary events truthfully, or as truthfully as is consistent with the ignorance, bias and self-deception from which every observer necessarily suffers. In saying this I may seem to be saying that straightforward "reportage" is the only branch of literature that matters: but I will try to show later that at every literary level, and probably in every one of the arts, the same issue arises in more or less subtilised forms. Meanwhile, it is necessary to strip away the irrelevancies in which this controversy is usually wrapped up.

The enemies of intellectual liberty always try to present their case as a plea for discipline versus individualism. The issue truth-versus-untruth is as far as possible kept in the background. Although the point of emphasis may vary, the writer who refuses to sell his opinions is always branded as a mere egoist. He is accused, that is, either of wanting to shut himself up in an ivory tower, or of making an exhibitionist display of his own personality, or of resisting the inevitable current of history in an attempt to cling to unjustified privileges. The Catholic and the Communist are alike in assuming that an opponent cannot be both honest and intelligent. Each of them tacitly claims that "the truth" has already been revealed, and that the heretic, if he is not simply a fool, is secretly aware of "the truth" and merely resists it out of selfish motives. In Communist literature the attack on intellectual liberty is usually masked by oratory about "petty-bourgeois individualism", "the illusions of nineteenth-century liberalism", etc, and backed up by words of abuse such as "romantic" and "sentimental", which, since they do not have any agreed meaning, are difficult to answer. In this way the controversy is manoeuvred away from its real issue. One can accept, and most enlightened people would accept, the Communist thesis that pure freedom will only exist in a classless society, and that one is most nearly free when one is working to bring such a society about. But slipped in with this is the quite unfounded claim that the Communist Party is itself aiming at the establishment of the classless society, and that in the USSR this aim is actually on the way to being realised. If the first claim is allowed to entail the second, there is almost no assault on common sense and common decency that cannot be justified. But meanwhile, the real point has been dodged. Freedom of the intellect means the freedom to report what one has seen, heard, and felt, and not to be obliged to fabricate imaginary facts and feelings. The familiar tirades against "escapism", "individualism", "romanticism" and so forth, are merely a forensic device, the aim of which is to make the perversion of history seem respectable.

Fifteen years ago, when one defended the freedom of the intellect, one had to defend it against Conservatives, against Catholics, and to some extent—for they were not of great importance in England— against Fascists. Today one has to defend it against Communists and "fellow-travellers". One ought not to exaggerate the direct influence of the small English Communist Party, but there can be no question about the poisonous effect of the Russian *mythos* on English intellectual life. Because of it, known facts are suppressed and distorted to such an extent as to make it doubtful whether a true history of our times can ever be written. Let me give just one instance out of the hundreds that could be cited. When Germany collapsed, it was found that very large numbers of Soviet Russians—mostly, no doubt, from non-political motives—had changed sides and were fighting for the Germans. Also, a small but not negligible proportion of the Russian prisoners and Displaced Persons refused to go back to the USSR, and some of them, at least, were repatriated against their will. These facts, known to many journalists on the spot, went almost unmentioned in the British press, while at the same time russophile publicists in England continued to justify the purges and deportations of 1936–8 by claiming that the USSR "had no quislings". The fog of lies and misinformation that surrounds such subjects as the Ukraine famine, the Spanish civil war, Russian policy in Poland, and so forth, is not due entirely to conscious dishonesty, but any writer or journalist who is fully sympathetic to the USSR—sympathetic, that is, in the way the Russians themselves would want him to be—does have to acquiesce in deliberate falsification on important issues. I have before me what must be a very rare pamphlet, written by Maxim Litvinov in 1918 and outlining the recent events in the Russian Revolution. It makes no mention of Stalin, but gives high praise to

Trotsky, and also to Zinoviev, Kamenev and others. What could be the attitude of even the most intellectually scrupulous Communist towards such a pamphlet? At best, the obscurantist attitude of saying that it is an undesirable document and better suppressed. And if for some reason it were decided to issue a garbled version of the pamphlet, denigrating Trotsky and inserting references to Stalin, no Communist who remained faithful to his Party could protest. Forgeries almost as gross as this have been committed in recent years. But the significant thing is not that they happen, but that even when they are known about they provoke no reaction from the left-wing intelligentsia as a whole. The argument that to tell the truth would be "inopportune" or would "play into the hands of" somebody or other is felt to be unanswerable, and few people are bothered by the prospect of the lies which they condone getting out of the newspapers and into the history books.

The organised lying practised by totalitarian states is not, as is sometimes claimed, a temporary expedient of the same nature as military deception. It is something integral to totalitarianism, something that would still continue even if concentration camps and secret police forces had ceased to be necessary. Among intelligent Communists there is an underground legend to the effect that although the Russian Government is obliged now to deal in lying propaganda, frame-up trials, and so forth, it is secretly recording the true facts and will publish them at some future time. We can, I believe, be quite certain that this is not the case, because the mentality implied by such an action is that of a liberal historian who believes that the past cannot be altered and that a correct knowledge of history is valuable as a matter of course. From the totalitarian point of view history is something to be created rather than learned. A totalitarian state is in effect a theocracy, and its ruling caste, in order to keep its position, has to be thought of as infallible. But since, in practice, no one is infallible, it is frequently necessary to rearrange past events in order to show that this or that mistake was not made, or that this or that imaginary triumph actually happened. Then, again, every major change in policy demands a corresponding change of doctrine and a revaluation of prominent historical figures. This kind of thing happens everywhere, but is clearly likelier to lead to outright falsification in societies where only one opinion is permissible at any given moment. Totalitarianism demands, in fact, the continuous alteration of the past, and in the long run probably demands a disbelief in the very existence of objective truth. The friends of totalitarianism in this country usually tend to argue that since absolute truth is not attainable, a big lie is no worse than a little lie. It is pointed out that all historical records are biassed and inaccurate, or, on the other hand, that modern physics has proved that what seems to us the real world is an illusion, so that to believe in the evidence of one's senses is simply vulgar philistinism. A totalitarian society which succeeded in perpetuating itself would probably set up a schizophrenic system of thought, in which the laws of common sense held good in everyday life and in certain exact sciences, but could be disregarded by the politician, the historian, and the sociologist. Already there are countless people who would think it scandalous to falsify a scientific text-book, but would see nothing wrong in falsifying an historical fact. It is at the point where literature and politics cross that totalitarianism exerts its greatest pressure on the intellectual. The exact sciences are not, at this date, menaced to anything like the same extent. This partly accounts for the fact that in all countries it is easier for the scientists than for the writers to line up behind their respective governments.

To keep the matter in perspective, let me repeat what I said at the beginning of this essay: that in England the immediate enemies of truthfulness, and hence of freedom of thought, are the press lords, the film magnates, and the bureaucrats, but that on a long view the weakening of the desire for liberty among the intellectuals themselves is the most serious symptom of all. It may seem that all this time I have been talking about the effects of censorship, not on literature as a whole, but merely on one department of political journalism. Granted that Soviet Russia constitutes a sort of forbidden area in the British press, granted that issues like Poland, the Spanish civil war, the Russo-German Pact, and so forth, are debarred from serious discussion, and that if you possess information that conflicts with the prevailing orthodoxy you are expected to distort it or to keep quiet about it—granted all this, why should literature in the wider sense be affected? Is every writer a politician, and is every book necessarily a work of straightforward "reportage"? Even under the tightest dictatorship, cannot the individual writer remain free inside his own mind and distil or disguise his unorthodox ideas in such a way that the authorities will be too stupid to recognise them? And in any case, if the writer himself is in agreement with the prevailing orthodoxy, why should it have a cramping effect on him? Is not literature, or any of the arts, likeliest to flourish in societies in which there are no major conflicts of opinion and no sharp distinction between the artist and his audience? Does one have to assume that every writer is a rebel, or even that a writer as such is an exceptional person?

Whenever one attempts to defend intellectual liberty against the claims of totalitarianism, one meets with these arguments in one form or another. They are based on a complete misunderstanding of what literature is, and how—one should perhaps rather say why—it comes into being. They assume that a writer is either a mere entertainer or else a venal hack who can switch from one line of propaganda to another as easily as an organ-grinder changing tunes. But after all, how is it that books ever come to be written? Above a quite low level, literature is an attempt to influence the viewpoint of one's contemporaries by recording experience. And so far as freedom of expression is concerned, there is not much difference between a mere journalist and the most "unpolitical" imaginative writer. The journalist is unfree, and is conscious of unfreedom, when he is forced to write lies or suppress what seems to him important news: the imaginative writer is unfree when he has to falsify his subjective feelings, which from his point of view are facts. He may distort and caricature reality in order to make his meaning clearer, but he cannot misrepresent the scenery of his own mind: he cannot say with any conviction that he likes what he dislikes, or believes what he disbelieves. If he is forced to do so, the only result is that his creative faculties dry up. Nor can he solve the problem by keeping away from controversial topics. There is no such thing as genuinely non-political literature, and least of all in an age like our own, when fears, hatreds, and loyalties of a directly political kind are near to the surface of everyone's consciousness. Even a single taboo can have an all-round crippling effect upon the mind, because there is always the danger that any thought which is freely followed up may lead to the forbidden thought. It follows that the atmosphere of totalitarianism is deadly to any kind of prose writer, though a poet, at any rate a lyric poet, might possibly find it breathable. And in any totalitarian society that survives for more than a couple of generations, it is probable that prose literature, of the kind that has existed during the past four hundred years, must actually come to an end.

Literature has sometimes flourished under despotic régimes, but, as has often been pointed out, the despotisms of the past were not totalitarian. Their repressive apparatus was always inefficient, their ruling classes were usually either corrupt or apathetic or half-liberal in outlook, and the prevailing religious doctrines usually worked against perfectionism and the notion of human infallibility. Even so it is broadly true that prose literature has reached its highest levels in periods of democracy and free speculation. What is new in totalitarianism is that its doctrines are not only unchallengeable but also unstable. They have to be accepted on pain of damnation, but on the other hand they are always liable to be altered at a moment's notice. Consider, for example, the various attitudes, completely incompatible with one another, which an English Communist or "fellow-traveller" has had to adopt towards the war between Britain and Germany. For years before September 1939 he was expected to be in a continuous stew about "the horrors of Nazism" and to twist everything he wrote into a denunciation of Hitler: after September 1939, for twenty months, he had to believe that Germany was more sinned against that sinning, and the word "Nazi", at least so far as print went, had to drop right out of his vocabulary. Immediately after hearing the 8 o'clock news bulletin on the morning of June 22, 1941, he had to start believing once again that Nazism was the most hideous evil the world had ever seen. Now, it is easy for a politician to make such changes: for a writer the case is somewhat different. If he is to switch his allegiance at exactly the right moment, he must either tell lies about his subjective feelings, or else suppress them altogether. In either case he has destroyed his dynamo. Not only will ideas refuse to come to him, but the very words he uses will seem to stiffen under his touch. Political writing in our time consists almost entirely of prefabricated phrases bolted together like the pieces of a child's Meccano set. It is the unavoidable result of self-censorship. To write in plain, vigorous language one has to think fearlessly, and if one thinks fearlessly one cannot be politically orthodox. It might be otherwise in an "age of faith", when the prevailing orthodoxy has been long established and is not taken too seriously. In that case it would be possible, or might be possible, for large areas of one's mind to remain unaffected by what one officially believed. Even so, it is worth noticing that prose literature almost disappeared during the only age of faith that Europe has ever enjoyed. Throughout the whole of the Middle Ages there was almost no imaginative prose literature and very little in the way of historical writing: and the intellectual leaders of society expressed their most serious thoughts in a dead language which barely altered during a thousand years.

Totalitarianism, however, does not so much promise an age of faith as an age of schizophrenia. A society becomes totalitarian when its structure becomes flagrantly artificial: that is, when its ruling class has lost its function but succeeds in clinging to power by force or fraud. Such a society, no matter how long it persists, can never afford to become either tolerant or intellectually stable. It can never permit either the truthful recording of facts, or the emotional sincerity, that literary creation demands. But to be corrupted by totalitarianism one does not have to live in a totalitarian country. The mere prevalence of certain ideas can spread a kind of poison that makes one subject after another impossible for literary purposes. Wherever there is an enforced orthodoxy—or even two orthodoxies, as often happens— good writing stops. This was well illustrated by the Spanish civil war. To many English intellectuals the war was a deeply moving experience, but not an experience about which they could write sincerely. There were only two things that you were allowed to say, and both of them were palpable lies: as a result, the war produced acres of print but almost nothing worth reading.

It is not certain whether the effects of totalitarianism upon verse need be so deadly as its effects on prose. There is a whole series of converging reasons why it is somewhat easier for a poet than for a prose writer to feel at home in an authoritarian society. To begin with, bureaucrats and other "practical" men usually despise the poet too deeply to be much interested in what he is saying. Secondly, what the poet is saying—that is, what his poem "means" if translated into prose—is relatively unimportant even to himself. The thought contained in a poem is always simple, and is no more the primary purpose of the poem than the anecdote is the primary purpose of a picture. A poem is an arrangement of sounds and associations, as a painting is an arrangement of brush-marks. For short snatches, indeed, as in the refrain of a song, poetry can even dispense with meaning altogether. It is therefore fairly easy for a poet to keep away from dangerous subjects and avoid uttering heresies: and even when he does utter them, they may escape notice. But above all, good verse, unlike good prose, is not necessarily an individual product. Certain kinds of poems, such as ballads, or, on the other hand, very artificial verse forms, can be composed co-operatively by groups of people. Whether the ancient English and Scottish ballads were originally produced by individuals, or by the people at large, is disputed; but at any rate they are non-individual in the sense that they constantly change in passing from mouth to mouth. Even in print no two versions of a ballad are ever quite the same. Many primitive peoples compose verse communally. Someone begins to improvise, probably accompanying himself on a musical instrument, somebody else chips in with a line or a rhyme when the first singer breaks down, and so the process continues until there exists a whole song or ballad which has no identifiable author.

In prose, this kind of intimate collaboration is quite impossible. Serious prose, in any case, has to be composed in solitude, whereas the excitement of being part of a group is actually an aid to certain kinds of versification. Verse—and perhaps good verse of its kind, though it would not be the highest kind—might survive under even the most inquisitorial régime. Even in a society where liberty and individuality had been extinguished, there would still be need either for patriotic songs and heroic ballads celebrating victories, or for elaborate exercises in flattery: and these are the kinds of poem that can be written to order, or composed communally, without necessarily lacking artistic value. Prose is a different matter, since the prose writer cannot narrow the range of his thoughts without killing his inventiveness. But the history of totalitarian societies, or of groups of people who have adopted the totalitarian outlook, suggests that loss of liberty is inimical to all forms of literature. German literature almost disappeared during the Hitler régime, and the case was not much better in Italy. Russian literature, so far as one can judge by translations, has deteriorated markedly since the early days of the Revolution, though some of the verse appears to be better than the prose. Few if any Russian novels that it is possible to take seriously have been translated for about fifteen years. In western Europe and America large sections of the literary intelligentsia have either passed through the Communist Party or been warmly sympathetic to it, but this whole leftward movement has produced extraordinarily few books worth reading. Orthodox Catholicism, again, seems to have a crushing effect upon certain literary forms, especially the novel. During a period of three hundred years, how many people have been at once good novelists and good Catholics? The fact is that certain themes cannot be celebrated in words, and tyranny is one of them. No one ever wrote a good book in praise of the Inquisition. Poetry might survive, in a totalitarian age, and certain arts or half-arts, such as architecture, might even find tyranny beneficial, but the prose writer would have no choice between silence and death. Prose literature as we know it is the product of rationalism, of the Protestant centuries, of the autonomous individual. And the destruction of intellectual liberty cripples the journalist, the sociological writer, the historian, the novelist, the critic and the poet, in that order. In the future it is possible that a new kind of literature, not involving individual feeling or truthful observation, may arise, but no such thing is at present imaginable. It seems much likelier that if the liberal culture that we have lived in since the Renaissance actually comes to an end, the literary art will perish with it.

Of course, print will continue to be used, and it is interesting to speculate what kinds of reading matter would survive in a rigidly totalitarian society. Newspapers will presumably continue until television technique reaches a higher level, but apart from newspapers it is doubtful even now whether the great mass of people in the industrialised countries feel the need for any kind of literature. They are unwilling, at any rate, to spend anywhere near as much on reading matter as they spend on several other recreations. Probably novels and stories will be completely superseded by film and radio productions. Or perhaps some kind of low-grade sensational fiction will survive, produced by a sort of conveyor-belt process that reduces human initiative to the minimum.

It would probably not be beyond human ingenuity to write books by machinery. But a sort of mechanising process can already be seen at work in the film and radio, in publicity and propaganda, and in the lower reaches of journalism. The Disney films, for instance, are produced by what is essentially a factory process, the work being done partly mechanically and partly by teams of artists who have to subordinate their individual style. Radio features are commonly written by tired hacks to whom the subject and the manner of treatment are dictated beforehand: even so, what they write is merely a kind of raw material to be chopped into shape by producers and censors. So also with the innumerable books and pamphlets commissioned by government departments. Even more machine-like is the production of short stories, serials, and poems for the very cheap magazines. Papers such as the *Writer* abound with advertisements of Literary Schools, all of them offering you ready-made plots at a few shillings a time. Some, together with the plot, supply the opening and closing sentences of each chapter. Others furnish you with a sort of algebraical formula by the use of which you can construct your plots for yourself. Others offer packs of cards marked with characters and situations, which have only to be shuffled and dealt in order to produce ingenious stories automatically. It is probably in some such way that the literature of a totalitarian society would be produced, if literature were still felt to be necessary. Imagination—even consciousness, so far as possible—would be eliminated from the process of writing. Books would be planned in their broad lines by bureaucrats, and would pass through so many hands that when finished they would be no more an individual product than a Ford car at the end of the assembly line. It goes without saying that anything so produced would be rubbish; but anything that was not rubbish would endanger the structure of the State. As for the surviving literature of the past, it would have to be suppressed or at least elaborately rewritten.

Meanwhile totalitarianism has not fully triumphed everywhere. Our own society is still, broadly speaking, liberal. To exercise your right of free speech you have to fight against economic pressure and against strong sections of public opinion, but not, as yet, against a secret police force. You can say or print almost anything so long as you are willing to do it in a hole-and-corner way. But what is sinister, as I said at the beginning of this essay, is that the conscious enemies of liberty are those to whom liberty ought to mean most. The big public do not care about the matter one way or the other. They are not in favour of persecuting the heretic, and they will not exert themselves to defend him. They are at once too sane and too stupid to acquire the totalitarian outlook. The direct, conscious attack on intellectual decency comes from the intellectuals themselves.

It is possible that the russophile intelligentsia, if they had not succumbed to that particular myth, would have succumbed to another of much the same kind. But at any rate the Russian myth is there, and the corruption it causes stinks. When one sees highly educated men looking on indifferently at oppression and persecution, one wonders which to despise more, their cynicism or their short-sightedness. Many scientists, for example, are the uncritical admirers of the USSR. They appear to think that the destruction of liberty is of no importance so long as their own line of work is for the moment unaffected. The USSR is a large, rapidly developing country which has acute need of scientific workers and, consequently, treats them generously. Provided that they steer clear of dangerous subjects such as psychology, scientists are privileged persons. Writers, on the other hand, are viciously persecuted. It is true that literary prostitutes like

Ilya Ehrenburg or Alexei Tolstoy are paid huge sums of money, but the only thing which is of any value to the writer as such—his freedom of expression—is taken away from him. Some, at least, of the English scientists who speak so enthusiastically of the opportunities enjoyed by scientists in Russia are capable of understanding this. But their reflection appears to be: "Writers are persecuted in Russia. So what? I am not a writer". They do not see that any attack on intellectual liberty, and on the concept of objective truth, threatens in the long run every department of thought.

For the moment the totalitarian state tolerates the scientist because it needs him. Even in Nazi Germany, scientists, other than Jews, were relatively well treated, and the German scientific community, as a whole, offered no resistance to Hitler. At this stage of history, even the most autocratic ruler is forced to take account of physical reality, partly because of the lingering-on of liberal habits of thought, partly because of the need to prepare for war. So long as physical reality cannot be altogether ignored, so long as two and two have to make four when you are, for example, drawing the blue-print of an aeroplane, the scientist has his function, and can even be allowed a measure of liberty. His awakening will come later, when the totalitarian state is firmly established. Meanwhile, if he wants to safeguard the integrity of science, it is his job to develop some kind of solidarity with his literary colleagues and not regard it as a matter of indifference when writers are silenced or driven to suicide, and newspapers systematically falsified.

But however it may be with the physical sciences, or with music, painting, and architecture, it is—as I have tried to show—certain that literature is doomed if liberty of thought perishes. Not only is it doomed in any country which retains a totalitarian structure; but any writer who adopts the totalitarian outlook, who finds excuses for persecution and the falsification of reality, thereby destroys himself as a writer. There is no way out of this. No tirades against "individualism" and "the ivory tower", no pious platitudes to the effect that "true individuality is only attained through identification with the community", can get over the fact that a bought mind is a spoiled mind. Unless spontaneity enters at some point or another, literary creation is impossible, and language itself becomes ossified. At some time in the future, if the human mind becomes something totally different from what it now is, we may learn to separate literary creation from intellectual honesty. At present we know only that the imagination, like certain wild animals, will not breed in captivity. Any writer or journalist who denies that fact—and nearly all the current praise of the Soviet Union contains or implies such a denial— is, in effect, demanding his own destruction.

Polemic, No. 2, January 1946; SE; OR; CE

17. Review

We by E.I. Zamyatin

Several years after hearing of its existence, I have at last got my hands on a copy of Zamyatin's *We*, which is one of the literary curiosities of this book-burning age. Looking it up in Gleb Struve's *Twenty-Five Years of Soviet Russian Literature*, I find its history to have been this:

Zamyatin, who died in Paris in 1937, was a Russian novelist and critic who published a number of books both before and after the Revolution. *We* was written about 1923, and though it is not about Russia and has no direct connection with contemporary politics—it is a fantasy dealing with the twenty-sixth century AD—it was refused publication on the ground that it was ideologically undesirable. A copy of the manuscript found its way out of the country, and the book has appeared in English, French and Czech translations, but never in Russian. The English translation was published in the United States, and I have never been able to procure a copy: but copies of the French translation (the title is *Nous Autres*) do exist, and I have at last succeeded in borrowing one. So far as I can judge it is not a book of the first order, but it is certainly an unusual one, and it is astonishing that no English publisher has been enterprising enough to reissue it.

The first thing anyone would notice about *We* is the fact—never pointed out, I believe—that Aldous Huxley's *Brave New World* must be partly derived from it. Both books deal with the rebellion of the primitive human spirit against a rationalised, mechanised, painless world, and both stories are supposed to take place about six hundred years hence. The atmosphere of the two books is similar, and it is roughly speaking the same kind of society that is being described, though Huxley's book shows less political awareness and is more influenced by recent biological and psychological theories.

In the twenty-sixth century, in Zamyatin's vision of it, the inhabitants of Utopia have so completely lost their individuality as to be known only by numbers. They live in glass houses (this was written before television was invented), which enables the political police, known as the "Guardians", to supervise them more easily. They all wear identical uniforms, and a human being is commonly referred to either as "a number" or "a unif" (uniform). They live on synthetic food, and their usual recreation is to march in fours while the anthem of the Single State is played through loudspeakers. At stated intervals they are allowed for one hour (known as "the sex hour") to lower the curtains round their glass apartments. There is, of course, no marriage, though sex life does not appear to be completely promiscuous. For purposes of love-making everyone has a sort of ration book of pink tickets, and the partner with whom he spends one of his allotted sex hours signs the counterfoil. The Single State is ruled over by a personage known as The Benefactor, who is annually re-elected by the entire population, the vote being always unanimous. The guiding principle of the State is that happiness and freedom are incompatible. In the Garden of Eden man was happy, but in his folly he demanded freedom and was driven out into the wilderness. Now the Single State has restored his happiness by removing his freedom.

So far the resemblance with *Brave New World* is striking. But though Zamyatin's book is less well put together—it has a rather weak and episodic plot which is too complex to summarise—it has a political point which the other lacks. In Huxley's book the problem of "human nature" is in a sense solved, because it assumes that by pre-natal treatment, drugs and hypnotic suggestion the human organism can be specialised in any way that is desired. A first-rate scientific worker is as easily produced as an Epsilon semi-moron, and in either case the vestiges of primitive instincts, such as maternal feeling or the desire for liberty, are easily dealt with. At the same time no clear reason is given why society should be stratified in the elaborate way that is described. The aim is not economic exploitation, but the desire to bully and dominate does not seem to be a motive either. There is no power hunger, no sadism, no hardness of any kind. Those at the top have no strong motive for staying at the top, and though everyone is happy in a vacuous way, life has become so pointless that it is difficult to believe that such a society could endure.

Zamyatin's book is on the whole more relevant to our own situation. In spite of education and the vigilance of the Guardians, many of the ancient human instincts are still there. The teller of the story, D-503, who, though a gifted engineer, is a poor conventional creature, a sort of Utopian Billy Brown of London Town, is constantly horrified by the atavistic impulses which seize upon him. He falls in love (this is a crime, of course) with a certain I-330 who is a member of an underground resistance movement and succeeds for a while in leading him into rebellion. When the rebellion breaks out it appears that the enemies of The Benefactor are in fact fairly numerous, and these people, apart from plotting the overthrow of the State, even indulge, at the moment when their curtains are down, in such vices as smoking cigarettes and drinking alcohol. D-503 is ultimately saved from the consequences of his own folly. The authorities announce that they have discovered the cause of the recent disorders: it is that some human beings suffer from a disease called imagination. The nerve-centre responsible for imagination has now been located, and the disease can be cured by X-ray treatment. D-503 undergoes the operation, after which it is easy for him to do what he has known all along that he ought to do—that is, betray his confederates to the police. With complete equanimity he watches I-330 tortured by means of compressed air under a glass bell:

> She looked at me, her hands clasping the arms of the chair, until her eyes were completely shut. They took her out, brought her to herself by means of an electric shock, and put her under the bell again. This operation was repeated three times, and not a word issued from her lips.
>
> The others who had been brought along with her showed themselves more honest. Many of them confessed after one application. Tomorrow they will all be sent to the Machine of The Benefactor.

The Machine of The Benefactor is the guillotine. There are many executions in Zamyatin's Utopia. They take place publicly, in the presence of The Benefactor, and are accompanied by triumphal odes recited by the official poets. The guillotine, of course, is not the old crude instrument but a much improved model which literally liquidates its victim, reducing him in an instant to a puff of smoke and a pool of clear water. The execution is, in fact, a human sacrifice, and the scene describing it is given deliberately the colour of the sinister slave civilisations of the ancient world. It is this intuitive grasp of the irrational side of totalitarianism—human sacrifice, cruelty as an end in itself, the worship of a Leader who is credited with divine attributes —that makes Zamyatin's book superior to Huxley's.

It is easy to see why the book was refused publication. The following conversation (I abridge it slightly) between D-503 and I-330 would have been quite enough to set the blue pencils working:

"Do you realise that what you are suggesting is revolution?"

"Of course, it's revolution. Why not?"

"Because there can't *be* a revolution. *Our* revolution was the last and there can never be another. Everybody knows that."

"My dear, you're a mathematician: tell me, which is the last number?"

"What do you mean, the last number?"

"Well, then, the biggest number!"

"But that's absurd. Numbers are infinite. There can't be a last one."

"Then why do you talk about the last revolution?"

There are other similar passages. It may well be, however, that Zamyatin did not intend the Soviet régime to be the special target of his satire. Writing at about the time of Lenin's death, he cannot have had the Stalin dictatorship in mind, and conditions in Russia in 1923 were not such that anyone would revolt against them on the ground that life was becoming too safe and comfortable. What Zamyatin seems to be aiming at is not any particular country but the implied aims of industrial civilisation. I have not read any of his other books, but I learn from Gleb Struve that he had spent several years in England and had written some blistering satires on English life. It is evident from *We* that he had a strong leaning towards primitivism. Imprisoned by the Czarist Government in 1906, and then imprisoned by the Bolsheviks in 1922 in the same corridor of the same prison, he had cause to dislike the political régimes he had lived under, but his book is not simply the expression of a grievance. It is in effect a study of the Machine, the genie that man has thoughtlessly let out of its bottle and cannot put back again. This is a book to look out for when an English version appears.

Tribune, 4 January 1946

18. Letter to Arthur Koestler

27B Canonbury Square
Islington
London N1
10 January 1946

Dear Arthur,

I saw Barbara Ward[1] and Tom Hopkinson[2] today and told them about our project. They were both a little timid, chiefly I think because they realise that an organisation[3] of this type would in practice be anti-Russian, or would be compelled to become anti-Russian, and they are going through an acute phase of anti-Americanism. However they are anxious to hear more and certainly are not hostile to the idea. I said the next step would be to show them copies of the draft manifesto, or whatever it is, when drawn up. I wonder if you have seen Bertrand Russell, and if so, what he said. I have no doubt these two would help to the extent of passing our ideas on to others, but at some stage it might be more useful to contact Hulton[4] personally, which I could do. I haven't found out anything significant about the League for the Rights of Man. No one seems to have much about it in their files. All I can discover is that it is still in existence in France, and that it did exist in Germany up to Hitler, so it must have been an international organisation. There is something about it in Wells's *Crux Ansata* (which I can't get hold of), so it is possible that it drew up the Declaration of the Rights of Man which Wells is always burbling about. But I am certain that some years before the

[1] Barbara Ward, now Lady Jackson (1914–   ), economist and writer on politics. Assistant editor of the *Economist* 1939–57. Known for her interest and concern in all matters relating to individual freedom and civil rights.

[2] Tom Hopkinson (1905–   ), author and well-known journalist of liberal and left-wing views; 1940–50 editor of *Picture Post*.

[3] In late 1945 both Orwell and Koestler felt that the decline in democratic feeling throughout the world called for an *international* organisation, similar to the pre-war League for the Rights of Man. Its aims were to protect the individual, in no matter which country, against arbitrary arrest and imprisonment without trial, deportation from his homeland or restriction of movement within it, the promotion of freedom of speech and of the press and the right of each individual to nominate and vote for the candidate of his choice. Suggested names for the new organisation were: *League for the Defence and Development of Democracy* and *League for the Freedom and Dignity of Man*.

[4] Edward Hulton (1906–   ), Kt, 1957; magazine publisher of liberal views, at this time proprietor of *Picture Post*.

war it had become a Stalinist organisation, as I distinctly remember that it refused to intervene in favour of the Trotskyists in Spain: nor so far as I remember did it do anything about the Moscow trials. But one ought to verify all this.

I hope you are all well. I am very busy as usual. I had lunch with Negrin[1] the other day, but couldn't get much information out of him. I never manage to see him quite alone. But I still feel fairly sure that he is *not* the Russians' man, as he was credited with being during the civil war. However I don't suppose it makes much difference, as I am afraid there is not much chance of Negrin's lot getting back when Franco moves out. I am also having lunch with Beaverbrook next week. If I get a chance to speak to him on equal terms at all I shall ask him about Stalin, whom after all he has seen at close quarters a number of times.

The French publisher who had signed a contract to translate *Animal Farm* has got cold feet and says it is impossible "for political reasons". It's really sad to think of a thing like that happening in France, of all countries in the world. However I dare say one of the others will risk it. Did I tell you I had fixed an American edition?

The book of essays is printing and they say they can't make alterations in the text, but we are going to put in an erratum slip, at any rate about the German-English business.[2]

Please give my love to Mamaine.[3] Richard[4] is very well. Celia[5] came to tea on Tuesday and saw him have his bath.

Yours
George

PS. I don't think I ever thanked you for our stay. I have a sort of inhibition about that, because as a child I was taught to say "Thank you for having me" after a party, and it seemed to me such an awful phrase.

[1] Juan Negrin, the Spanish Prime Minister during the last phase of the civil war, after which he set up a Spanish Government in exile.

[2] The correction in the book of essays, *Critical Essays*, is in Orwell's essay "Arthur Koestler" making it clear that Koestler's early books had been written in German.

[3] Mamaine Koestler, *née* Paget (1916–56), Arthur Koestler's wife.

[4] Richard Blair, Orwell's adopted son, twenty months old at this time.

[5] Celia Kirwan, *née* Paget (1916–), now Mrs Arthur Goodman, the twin sister of Mamaine Koestler.

19. Pleasure Spots

Some months ago I cut out of a shiny magazine some paragraphs written by a female journalist and describing the pleasure resort of the future. She had recently been spending some time at Honolulu, where the rigours of war do not seem to have been very noticeable. However, "a transport pilot . . . told me that with all the inventiveness packed into this war, it was a pity someone hadn't found out how a tired and life-hungry man could relax, rest, play poker, drink, and make love, all at once, and round the clock, and come out of it feeling good and fresh and ready for the job again." This reminded her of an entrepreneur she had met recently who was planning a "pleasure spot which he thinks will catch on tomorrow as dog racing and dance halls did yesterday." The entrepreneur's dream is described in some detail:

His blue-prints pictured a space covering several acres, under a series of sliding roofs—for the British weather is unreliable—and with a central space spread over with an immense dance floor made of translucent plastic which can be illuminated from beneath. Around it are grouped other functional spaces, at different levels. Balcony bars and restaurants commanding high views of the city roofs, and ground-level replicas. A battery of skittle alleys. Two blue lagoons: one, periodically agitated by waves, for strong swimmers, and another, a smooth and summery pool, for playtime bathers. Sunlight lamps over the pools to simulate high summer on days when the roofs don't slide back to disclose a hot sun in a cloudless sky. Rows of bunks on which people wearing sun-glasses and slips can lie and start a tan or deepen an existing one under a sunray lamp.

Music seeping through hundreds of grills connected with a central distributing stage, where dance or symphonic orchestras play or the radio programme can be caught, amplified, and disseminated. Outside, two 1,000-car parks. One, free. The other, an open-air cinema drive-in, cars queueing to move through turnstiles, and the film thrown on a giant screen facing a row of assembled cars. Uniformed male attendants check the cars, provide free aid and water, sell petrol and oil. Girls in white satin slacks take orders for buffet dishes and drinks, and bring them on trays.

Whenever one hears such phrases as "pleasure spot", "pleasure resort", "pleasure city", it is difficult not to remember the often-quoted opening of Coleridge's "Kubla Khan".

> In Xanadu did Kubla Khan
> A stately pleasure-dome decree:
> Where Alph, the sacred river, ran
> Through caverns measureless to man
> > Down to a sunless sea.
> So twice five miles of fertile ground
> With walls and towers were girdled round:
> And there were gardens bright with sinuous rills
> Where blossomed many an incense-bearing tree;
> And here were forests ancient as the hills,
> Enfolding sunny spots of greenery.

But it will be seen that Coleridge has got it all wrong. He strikes a false note straight off with that talk about "sacred" rivers and "measureless" caverns. In the hands of the above-mentioned entrepreneur, Kubla Khan's project would have become something quite different. The caverns, air-conditioned, discreetly lighted and with their original rocky interior buried under layers of tastefully-coloured plastics, would be turned into a series of tea-grottoes in the Moorish, Caucasian or Hawaiian styles. Alph, the sacred river, would be dammed up to make an artificially-warmed bathing pool, while the sunless sea would be illuminated from below with pink electric lights, and one would cruise over it in real Venetian gondolas each equipped with its own radio set. The forests and "spots of greenery" referred to by Coleridge would be cleaned up to make way for glass-covered tennis courts, a bandstand, a roller-skating rink and perhaps a nine-hole golf course. In short, there would be everything that a "life-hungry" man could desire.

I have no doubt that, all over the world, hundreds of pleasure resorts similar to the one described above are now being planned, and perhaps are even being built. It is unlikely that they will be finished—world events will see to that—but they represent faithfully enough the modern civilised man's idea of pleasure. Something of the kind is already partially attained in the more magnificent dance halls, movie palaces, hotels, restaurants and luxury liners. On a pleasure cruise or in a Lyons Corner House one already gets something more than a glimpse of this future paradise. Analysed, its main characteristics are these:

Do—IV

1. One is never alone.
2. One never does anything for oneself.
3. One is never within sight of wild vegetation or natural objects of any kind.
4. Light and temperature are always artificially regulated.
5. One is never out of the sound of music.

The music—and if possible it should be the same music for everybody—is the most important ingredient. Its function is to prevent thought and conversation, and to shut out any natural sound, such as the song of birds or the whistling of the wind, that might otherwise intrude. The radio is already consciously used for this purpose by innumerable people. In very many English homes the radio is literally never turned off, though it is manipulated from time to time so as to make sure that only light music will come out of it. I know people who will keep the radio playing all through a meal and at the same time continue talking just loudly enough for the voices and the music to cancel out. This is done with a definite purpose. The music prevents the conversation from becoming serious or even coherent, while the chatter of voices stops one from listening attentively to the music and thus prevents the onset of that dreaded thing, thought. For

> The lights must never go out.
> The music must always play,
> Lest we should see where we are;
> Lost in a haunted wood,
> Children afraid of the dark
> Who have never been happy or good.

It is difficult not to feel that the unconscious aim in the most typical modern pleasure resorts is a return to the womb. For there, too, one was never alone, one never saw daylight, the temperature was always regulated, one did not have to worry about work or food, and one's thoughts, if any, were drowned by a continuous rhythmic throbbing.

When one looks at Coleridge's very different conception of a "pleasure dome", one sees that it revolves partly round gardens and partly round caverns, rivers, forests and mountains with "deep romantic chasms"—in short, round what is called Nature. But the whole notion of admiring Nature, and feeling a sort of religious awe in the presence of glaciers, deserts or waterfalls, is bound up with the sense of man's littleness and weakness against the power of the universe. The moon is beautiful partly because we cannot reach it, the sea is impressive because one can never be sure of crossing it safely. Even the pleasure one takes in a flower—and this is true even of a botanist who knows all there is to be known about the flower— is dependent partly on the sense of mystery. But meanwhile man's power over Nature is steadily increasing. With the aid of the atomic bomb we could literally move mountains: we could even, so it is said, alter the climate of the earth by melting the polar ice-caps and irrigating the Sahara. Isn't there, therefore, something sentimental and obscurantist in preferring bird-song to swing music and in wanting to leave a few patches of wildness here and there instead of covering the whole surface of the earth with a network of *Autobahnen* flooded by artificial sunlight?

The question only arises because in exploring the physical universe man has made no attempt to explore himself. Much of what goes by the name of pleasure is simply an effort to destroy consciousness. If one started by asking, what is man? what are his needs? how can he best express himself? one would discover that merely having the power to avoid work and live one's life from birth to death in electric light and to the tune of tinned music is not a reason for doing so. Man needs warmth, society, leisure, comfort and security: he also needs solitude, creative work and the sense of wonder. If he recognised this he could use the products of science and industrialism eclectically, applying always the same test: does this make me more human or less human? He would then learn that the highest happiness does *not* lie in relaxing, resting, playing poker, drinking and making love simultaneously. And the instinctive horror which all sensitive people feel at the progressive mechanisation of life would be seen not to be a mere sentimental archaism, but to be fully justified. For man only stays human by preserving large patches of simplicity in his life, while the tendency of many modern inventions—in particular the film, the radio and the aeroplane—is to weaken his consciousness, dull his curiosity, and, in general, drive him nearer to the animals.

Tribune, 11 January 1946

82

20. The Politics of Starvation

A few days ago I received a wad of literature from the "Save Europe Now" Committee, which has been attempting—without much encouragement from the Government or help from the press—to increase the supply of food from this country to Europe. They quote a series of statements from authoritative sources, which I will come back to in a moment, and which go to show that whereas we are reasonably well off and the United States is enjoying an orgy of over-eating, a good part of Europe is lapsing into brute starvation.

In the *Observer* of January 13, however, I have just read a signed article by Air Chief Marshal Sir Philip Joubert, expressing the contrary opinion:

> To one returning from overseas in this seventh winter of war (writes Sir Philip), the appearance of the British people is tragic. They seem morose, lacking in spring; and laughter comes with difficulty. The children look pallid and suety—fat but not fit. They compare very ill with the rosy-cheeked youngsters of Denmark, who have all the meat and fat they need, with plenty of fruit in season.

His main thesis is that we need more meat, fats and eggs—i.e. more of the rationed foods—and less starch. The official figures showing that, in fact, we are healthier than we were before the war convey a false impression: first—this is a quite extraordinary argument—because health and nutrition were admittedly in a bad way before the war, so that the present improvement is nothing to write home about; secondly because the drop in the death-rate merely means a "greater expectation of existence" and one must not "confuse existence with life". Unless we can attain "liveliness, vitality, vigour", for which meat, fat, fruit and cane sugar are required, we cannot make the effort needed for the task of reconstruction. Sir Philip ends his article:

> As for those who would cut our present rations further so as to give more to the Germans, there must be many who would reply to their demands: "I would sooner that my children, brought up in freedom and goodwill towards men, should enjoy full vigour than the Germans, who may be using their strength to make war on the world again in another generation."

It will be seen that he is assuming (a) that any further export of food means a cut in rations here, and (b) that it is only proposed to send food to Germany. And in fact that is the form in which the big public has heard of this project, although those responsible have emphasised from the start that they were only proposing a *voluntary* surrender of certain foodstuffs, by those sections of the population to whom it would do no harm, and were *not* proposing it for the sole benefit of Germany.

Now here are a few facts from the latest bulletin of the "Save Europe Now" Committee. In Budapest, in November, the chemists were closing down for lack of supplies, the hospitals had neither windows, fuel nor anaesthetics, and it was calculated that the town contained 30,000 stray children, some of whom had formed themselves into criminal bands. In December, "independent observers" considered that unless fresh food supplies were brought quickly, a million people would die of starvation in Hungary this winter. In Vienna (November) "the food for hospital surgeons consists of unsweetened coffee, a very thin soup and bread. Less than 500 calories in all", while the Austrian Secretary of State, in December, described the thickly populated areas of eastern Austria as being menaced by "boundless misery, epidemics, crime, physical and moral decline". In Czechoslovakia, in November, the Foreign Minister appealed to Britain and the USA to send fats and meat to save 700,000 "very badly fed children, of whom fifty per cent already have tuberculosis". In Germany, the Saar children are "slowly starving". In the British zone, Field-Marshal Montgomery said that he was "entirely dependent on imports of wheat if he was to maintain the present ration scales for the German people, ranging from 1,200 to 1,500 calories". This was in November. About the same time General Eisenhower, speaking of the French zone, said that "the normal ration of 1,100 calories a day for the average consumer was consistently not met". And so on. Meanwhile it appears that our own average consumption is about 2,800 or 2,900 calories a day, while the most recent figures of deaths from tuberculosis, and of deaths of mothers in childbirth and of children of all ages up to five, are the lowest ever recorded. As for the USA, consumption of butter has just risen largely and meat rationing has come to an end. The Secretary of Agriculture estimates that "the lifting of rationing will make meat available for civilians at the rate of 165 lb annually—the pre-war supply was in the neighbourhood of 125 lb".

Even if the above figures do not convey much impression, who has not seen the photographs of skeleton-like children in Greece and other places—children to whom no one would think of applying Sir Philip Joubert's term, "suety"? Yet there has undoubtedly been considerable resistance to the idea that we should send more food to Europe. The "Save Europe Now" Committee, though they are now pursuing more limited aims, started off with the suggestion that those who felt inclined should sacrifice their points,[1] or some of their points, and that the Government should forward the food so saved to the famine-stricken areas. The scheme was discouraged officially, but it also had a cold reception from many private persons. People who would have been in a position to give it good publicity were frankly frightened of it, and the general public was allowed to imagine that what was proposed was to take food from British housewives in order to give it to German war criminals. Indeed, the whole manner in which this business has been discussed illustrates the curious dishonesty that infects every political issue nowadays.

There are two things that make what one might call the official Left, Labour or Communist, nervous of any scheme which might mean sending extra food to Germany. One is fear of the working-class reaction. The working classes, so it is said, would resent even a voluntary arrangement which meant, in effect, that people in the higher income groups, who buy unrationed foods and eat some of their meals in restaurants, should give up their surplus. The average woman in the fish queue, it is feared, would answer: "If there's really any food to spare, let *us* have it. Or why not give it to the coal miners?" I don't know whether this would really be the reaction, if the issues were fully explained. I suspect that some of the people who argue thus have in mind the sordid consideration that if we are to sacrifice food in sufficient quantities to make any difference, it would mean not merely giving up points but curtailing restaurant feeding. In practice, whatever it may be in intention, our rationing system is thoroughly undemocratic, and an all-round row on the subject of the export of food might draw attention to this fact. That is part of the reason, I think, why this question has not been fully discussed in print.

But another consideration, even less mentionable, also enters.

---

[1] When food was rationed in Britain the basic commodities were allocated on "coupons", but luxuries like tinned fruit or tinned meat were allocated on a system of "points".

Food is a political weapon, or is thought of as a political weapon. The hungriest areas are either in the Russian zone or in the parts of Europe that are divided between the USSR and the western Allies. Many people calculate that if we send more food to, say, Hungary, British or American influence in Hungary will increase: whereas if we let the Hungarians starve and the Russians feed them, they are more likely to look towards the USSR. All those who are strongly russophile are therefore against sending extra food to Europe, while some people are probably in favour of sending food merely because they see it as a way of weakening Russian prestige. No one has been honest enough to avow such motives, but you have only to look through the lists of those who have—and of those who haven't— supported the "Save Europe Now" campaign to see how the land lies.

The folly of all such calculations lies in supposing that you can ever get good results from starvation. Whatever the ultimate political settlement in Europe may be, it can only be worse if it has been preceded by years of hunger, misery, banditry and ignorance. Air Marshal Joubert advises us to feed ourselves rather than feed German children who will be fighting against us a generation hence. This is the "realistic" view. In 1918 the "realistic" ones were also in favour of keeping up the blockade after the Armistice. We did keep up the blockade, and the children we starved then were the young men who were bombing us in 1940. No one, perhaps, could have foreseen just that result, but people of goodwill could and did foresee that the results of wantonly starving Germany, and of making a vindictive peace, would be evil. So also with raising our own rations, as we shall perhaps be doing before long, while famine descends on Europe. But if we do decide to do this, at least let the issues be plainly discussed, and let the photographs of starving children be well publicised in the press, so that the people of this country may realise just what they are doing.

Tribune, 18 January 1946

21. Letter to Geoffrey Gorer [in the United States]

27B Canonbury Square
Islington
London N1
22 January 1946

Dear Geoffrey,[1]

It was too good of you to send all those things. They were greatly appreciated here, especially by Richard, who had a big whack of the plum pudding and seemed none the worse afterwards. I was amused by the "this is an unsolicited gift" on the outside, which I suppose is a formula necessitated by people over here writing cadging letters. I had quite a good Christmas. I went to Wales to stay with Arthur Koestler for a few days while the nurse went away with her own kid. Richard went out to a lot of parties where he was the only child, and except for occasionally dirtying his trousers (I still can't get him house-trained) behaved with great aplomb and sat up to table in an ordinary chair. But of course the travelling just before and just after Xmas was fearful. To leave London you had to queue up 2 hours before the train left, and coming back the train was 4 hours late and landed one in town about half an hour after the undergrounds had stopped. However, fortunately Richard enjoys travelling, and I think when you are carrying a child you have a slightly better chance with porters.

It is foully cold here and the fuel shortage is just at its worst. We only got a ton of coal for the whole winter and it's almost impossible to get logs. Meanwhile the gas pressure is so low that one can hardly get a gas fire to light, and one can only get about $1\frac{1}{2}$ gallons of lamp oil a week. What I do is to light the fires with a little of the coal I have left and keep them damped down all day with blocks of wet peat of which I happen to have a few. It's so much easier in the country where if you're absolutely forced to you can go out and scrounge firewood. Otherwise things aren't bad here. Food is about the same as ever. Yesterday I took Silone[2] and his wife out to dinner. They were

---

[1] Geoffrey Gorer (1905–), social anthropologist, whose books include *Africa Dances*, *The Revolutionary Ideas of the Marquis de Sade*, *The American People* and *Exploring English Character*. In the early 'thirties he had written Orwell a fan letter about *Burmese Days*, they had met and remained friends until Orwell's death.

[2] Ignazio Silone, Italian writer and novelist.

only here for a few days and were still in a state of being astonished at the food, all the English in Rome having told them we were starving over here. I am always ashamed when people come to England for the first time like that, and say to them "Don't think England is like this in peace time," but the Ss said that for cleanness and state of repair London was a dream compared with Rome. They said that in Rome you could get anything if you had enough money, but an overcoat, for instance, cost the equivalent of £120.

Didn't you tell me you met Dennis Collings[1] in Malaya? He was an anthropologist, and I think latterly was curator of the museum in Singapore. I used to know him very well. He got home recently and I heard from him the other day. He had been captured in Java and appeared not to have had absolutely too bad a time, having been a camp interpreter.

I forget if I'd started doing weekly articles for the *Evening Standard* before you left. In spite of—by my standards—enormous fees it doesn't do me much good financially, because one extra article a week just turns the scale and makes it necessary for me to have a secretary. However, even with the extra article she takes a certain amount of drudgery off me, and I am using her to arrange and catalogue my collection of pamphlets.[2] I find that up to date I have about 1200, but of course they keep on accumulating. I have definitely arranged I am going to stop doing the *Evening Standard* stuff and most other journalism in May, and take six months off to write another novel. If the Jura place[3] can be put in order this year I shall go there, otherwise I shall take a furnished house somewhere in the country, preferably by the sea, but anyway somewhere where I can't be telephoned to. My book of reprints ought to be out soon and the American title is *Dickens, Dali and Others*. Scribners are doing that one, and Harcourt Brace (I think that is the name) are doing *Animal Farm*. I don't fancy that one will sell in the USA, though of course it *might* sell heavily, as with most books in America it seems you either

[1] Dennis Collings (1905–), a friend of Orwell's since 1921 when they had both lived in Southwold. An anthropologist, he had become assistant curator of the Raffles Museum, Singapore, when he joined the Colonial Service in 1934.

[2] From 1935 on Orwell had made a habit of collecting pamphlets representing minority points of view. This collection of pamphlets is now in the British Museum.

[3] Orwell had rented a house, which had been empty for several years, on the island of Jura in the Inner Hebrides.

sell 100,000 copies or nothing. I have arranged a lot of translations of *AF*, but the French publishers who signed the first contract have already got cold feet and say it's impossible at present "for political reasons". I think it's sad to think of a thing like that happening, in France of all countries.

I must knock off now as this is Susan's[1] day off and I have to go out and do the shopping. Richard has been trying to help me with the typing of this letter. He is now 20 months old and weighs about 32 lbs. He still doesn't talk but is very alert in other ways and extremely active, in fact you can't keep him still for a moment. Three times in the last month he got all the radiants out of the gas fire and smashed them to bits, which is a nuisance because they're very difficult to buy. I think he could talk if he wanted to, but he hardly needs to as he can usually get what he wants by making an inarticulate noise and point-ing—at least he does not exactly point but throws both arms out in the general direction of the thing he wants.

Let me hear how you are getting on and how things are in the USA. I hear they hate us more than ever now.

Yours
George

22. Review

The Reilly Plan by Lawrence Wolfe

The much-discussed Reilly Plan for rehousing is in itself merely an effort to get rid of the waste, noise, drudgery and loneliness which are usual in any ordinary town or built-up area, without altogether sacrificing cultural continuity or the desire of the average human being to have "a home of your own". This book, written by an enthusiastic supporter of the Plan, develops its social and psycho-logical implications. Sir Charles Reilly, who confesses that he did not originally foresee the far-reaching consequences deduced by his disciple—indeed he has slightly the air of a man who has mounted a hobby-horse which turns out to be a unicorn—contributes an Intro-duction.

In the Reilly Plan, the majority of the houses are not built along

[1] Susan Watson, whom Orwell employed as housekeeper and nurse for his adopted son Richard.

roads but round greens. A Reilly "unit" consists of about 250 houses grouped round five or six greens: most of the greens are roughly oval in shape, and the number of houses surrounding them will vary from 30 to 60. Each unit has its own Community Centre, nursery school, shopping centre, restaurant and meals service, and is self-contained to the extent that no main traffic roads run through it. The houses run round the greens in long blocks: behind each house there is a small garden, but the front door gives straight on the green. They are warmed by "area heating", there is continuous hot water, and rubbish removal is done by suction. Some of the houses or flats have kitchens, some not. If you prefer to live in a kitchenless house, you can have all your meals delivered from the meals centre in thermos containers which are left on the doorstep like the milk, the dirty dishes being afterwards removed by the same agency. A town can be built up of as many Reilly "units" as there is need and space for. Of course, any large town will have its central shopping and administrative area, but the main idea of the plan is to split the town up into self-contained communities, practically villages, of about 1,000 people each.

Supposing that it could actually be put into operation—and, according to Mr Wolfe, this method of rehousing is cheaper and quicker than the normal methods—the advantages of the plan are obvious. The proper provision of day nurseries near at hand, the "area heating", the ability to get cheap meals at the Community Centre whenever you wanted them, the absence of noise and of anxiety about traffic (with towns so planned, there would be no danger of small children straying on to the motor roads), would take an immense load of unnecessary work off the housewife. Living round a green would almost certainly promote sociability, and it is an important detail that each of the Community Centres would only be serving about 1,000 people, all of whom might be expected to know one another by sight. The green spaces, the easily accessible playing fields, the absence of smoke, and the ever-running hot water would make for health and cleanliness, and the children would grow up in the constant society of others of the same age instead of being alternately nagged and coddled at home. Mr Wolfe is probably within his rights in claiming that in such communities there would be less drudgery, less disease, less ignorance, earlier marriages, a higher birthrate, less crime and fewer neuroses than we have at present. And yet—!

Mr Wolfe uses the Reilly Plan as the occasion for an almost non-stop attack on what he calls "isolationism": meaning not only the chaos and aimlessness of life in great cities, but the whole English tradition of having a home of your own and keeping yourself *to* yourself. He is probably right in saying that this has increased in recent years, and certainly right in saying that house-ownership, stimulated by the building societies (just before the war no less than four million people in Britain owned or were buying their houses), encourages it. Life in little family units, with few communal facilities, naturally increases the drudgery of household work, and the average woman is middle-aged at thirty, thanks to the labour of preparing six or seven meals a day in an inconvenient kitchen and looking after, say, two children. Mr Wolfe proceeds to build up a picture of Britain which would suggest that it is the most overworked, poverty-stricken, crime and disease-ridden country under the sun. What he does not say is that most of the social change of the present century has been in the direction which he advocates.

Life in Britain may be more "isolationist" than it was, but it is also very much more comfortable and less laborious. As against thirty years ago, people are larger and heavier, live longer, work shorter hours, eat more, spend more on amusements, and have household facilities which their parents would have found unimaginable. By most of the standards which Mr Wolfe is applying, the mass of the people were far better off in 1939 than they had been in 1909, and though the war has diminished national "real" income, it has also tended to produce greater equality. These facts are known to anyone whose memories go far back enough, but they can be checked by figures. A book to study side by side with Mr Wolfe's is *The Condition of the British People, 1911- 45*, by Mark Abrams, recently published by Gollancz. This shows unmistakably the physical improvement that has taken place. It also shows, so far as one can draw an inference from its figures, that we have not grown any happier or any more conscious of a reason for living. The slump in the birthrate, which Mr Wolfe rightly deplores, has coincided with the rise in material standards. The recent Mass Observation book, *Britain and her Birthrate*, seems to show that the two phenomena are directly connected.

Evidently what is needed to change the existing trend is the growth of a sense of purpose, and it is not certain that this will happen merely because people are removed from their old-fashioned, isolated homes

and resettled in labour-saving colonies where they will lose much of
their privacy. Naturally Mr Wolfe claims that he has no wish to break
up the family, but various of the innovations that he favours would
tend to have that effect. He is remarkably enthusiastic about the
kitchenless house and "the abolition of the muddlesome, costly and
wasteful apparatus of the kitchen". The family that dispenses with its
kitchen, he says, "has a more attractive and comfortable home".
The food is delivered in a thermos container "shaped like a medium
suitcase" which "will keep the contents hot for several hours, even in
cold weather, and even if left on the doorstep". When you feel hungry
just open the door, and there the stuff is. It is not stated whether you
can choose what meals you will have, but presumably you cannot.
You are, of course, using other people's crockery all the time, but it
doesn't matter because it is sterilised in between whiles.

It is perhaps hardly necessary to dwell on the objections to this
kind of thing. What is more to the point is that nearly everyone,
including the overworked housewives whom Mr Wolfe pities, would
recoil from such a prospect. Comparatively few people, as a Gallup
poll has just shown, even want their houses centrally heated. Further-
more, for the moment the main preoccupation is to get houses built
and not sacrifice any that are still habitable.

Yet, sooner or later the replanning of whole areas will be possible,
and then it will be necessary to decide once and for all whether the
old style of house, and the old manner of arranging houses, is to
survive. The question has not been properly thrashed out, and people
have to fall back on instincts which may be partly perverted. They
want to live near their work, but they want to live in houses and not
in flats. They want day nurseries and welfare clinics, but they also
want privacy. They want to save work, but they want to cook their
own meals and not eat meals chosen by other people and delivered in
thermos containers. A deep instinct warns them not to destroy the
family, which in the modern world is the sole refuge from the State,
but all the while the forces of the machine age are slowly destroying
the family. So they look on while our culture perishes, and yet irra-
tionally cling to such fragments of it as the whitened doorstep and
the open fireplace.

Even in the Reilly Plan a chunk of the old culture, in the form of a
church, survives in each unit: and to judge from the sketches in this
book, the churches are to be in the Gothic style. A question not asked
by Mr Wolfe, and seldom asked by anybody, is why we are on earth

at all, and, leading out of this, what kind of lives we want to live. Yet till we have an answer to this question we shall never solve our housing problem and are merely making it rather more likely that the atom bombs will solve it for us.

Tribune, 25 January 1946

23. Books v. Cigarettes

A couple of years ago a friend of mine, a newspaper editor, was fire-watching with some factory workers. They fell to talking about his newspaper, which most of them read and approved of, but when he asked them what they thought of the literary section, the answer he got was: "You don't suppose we read that stuff, do you? Why, half the time you're talking about books that cost twelve and sixpence! Chaps like us couldn't spend twelve and sixpence on a book." These, he said, were men who thought nothing of spending several pounds on a day trip to Blackpool.

This idea that the buying, or even the reading, of books is an expensive hobby and beyond the reach of the average person is so widespread that it deserves some detailed examination. Exactly what reading costs, reckoned in terms of pence per hour, is difficult to estimate, but I have made a start by inventorying my own books and adding up their total price. After allowing for various other expenses, I can make a fairly good guess at my expenditure over the last fifteen years.

The books that I have counted and priced are the ones I have here, in my flat. I have about an equal number stored in another place, so that I shall double the final figure in order to arrive at the complete amount. I have not counted oddments such as proof copies, defaced volumes, cheap paper-covered editions, pamphlets, or magazines, unless bound up into book form. Nor have I counted the kind of junky books—old school text-books and so forth—that accumulate in the bottoms of cupboards. I have counted only those books which I have acquired voluntarily, or else would have acquired voluntarily, and which I intend to keep. In this category I find that I have 442 books, acquired in the following ways:

Bought (mostly second-hand)	251
Given to me or bought with book tokens	33
Review copies and complimentary copies	143
Borrowed and not returned	10
Temporarily on loan	5
Total	442

Now as to the method of pricing. Those books that I have bought I have listed at their full price, as closely as I can determine it. I have also listed at their full price the books that have been given to me, and those that I have temporarily borrowed, or borrowed and kept. This is because book-giving, book-borrowing and book-stealing more or less even out. I possess books that do not strictly speaking belong to me, but many other people also have books of mine: so that the books I have not paid for can be taken as balancing others which I have paid for but no longer possess. On the other hand I have listed the review and complimentary copies at half-price. That is about what I would have paid for them second-hand, and they are mostly books that I would only have bought second-hand, if at all. For the prices I have sometimes had to rely on guesswork, but my figures will not be far out. The costs were as follows:

	£	s.	d.
Bought	36	9	0
Gifts	10	10	0
Review copies, etc	25	11	9
Borrowed and not returned	4	16	9
On loan	3	10	0
Shelves	2	0	0
Total	82	17	6

Adding the other batch of books that I have elsewhere, it seems that I possess altogether nearly 900 books, at a cost of £165 15s. This is the accumulation of about fifteen years—actually more, since some of these books date from my childhood: but call it fifteen years. This works out at £11 1s. a year, but there are other charges that must be added in order to estimate my full reading expenses. The biggest will be for newspapers and periodicals, and for this I think £8 a year would be a reasonable figure. Eight pounds a year covers the cost of two daily papers, one evening paper, two Sunday papers, one weekly review and one or two monthly magazines. This brings the figure up to £19 1s, but to arrive at the grand total one has to make a guess. Obviously one often spends money on books without afterwards having anything to show for it. There are library subscriptions, and there are also the books, chiefly Penguins and other cheap editions, which one buys and then loses or throws away. However, on the basis of my other figures, it looks as though £6 a year would be quite enough to add for expenditure of this kind. So my total reading expenses over the past fifteen years have been in the neighbourhood of £25 a year.

Twenty-five pounds a year sounds quite a lot until you begin to measure it against other kinds of expenditure. It is nearly 9s 9d a week, and at present 9s 9d is the equivalent of about 83 cigarettes (Players): even before the war it would have bought you less than 200 cigarettes. With prices as they now are, I am spending far more on tobacco than I do on books. I smoke six ounces a week, at half-a-crown an ounce, making nearly £40 a year. Even before the war when the same tobacco cost 8d an ounce, I was spending over £10 a year on it: and if I also averaged a pint of beer a day, at sixpence, these two items together will have cost me close on £20 a year. This was probably not much above the national average. In 1938 the people of this country spent nearly £10 per head per annum on alcohol and tobacco: however, 20 per cent of the population were children under fifteen and another 40 per cent were women, so that the average smoker and drinker must have been spending much more than £10. In 1944, the annual expenditure per head on these items was no less than £23. Allow for the women and children as before, and £40 is a reasonable individual figure. Forty pounds a year would just about pay for a packet of Woodbines every day and half a pint of mild six days a week—not a magnificent allowance. Of course, all prices are now inflated, including the price of books: still, it looks as though the cost of reading, even if you buy books instead of borrowing them and take in a fairly large number of periodicals, does not amount to more than the combined cost of smoking and drinking.

It is difficult to establish any relationship between the price of books and the value one gets out of them. "Books" includes novels, poetry, text-books, works of reference, sociological treatises and much else, and length and price do not correspond to one another, especially if one habitually buys books second-hand. You may spend ten shillings on a poem of 500 lines, and you may spend sixpence on a dictionary which you consult at odd moments over a period of twenty

years. There are books that one reads over and over again, books
that become part of the furniture of one's mind and alter one's whole
attitude to life, books that one dips into but never reads through,
books that one reads at a single sitting and forgets a week later: and
the cost, in terms of money, may be the same in each case. But if one
regards reading simply as a recreation, like going to the pictures, then
it is possible to make a rough estimate of what it costs. If you read
nothing but novels and "light" literature, and bought every book
that you read, you would be spending—allowing eight shillings as the
price of a book, and four hours as the time spent in reading it—two
shillings an hour. This is about what it costs to sit in one of the more
expensive seats in the cinema. If you concentrated on more serious
books, and still bought everything that you read, your expenses
would be about the same. The books would cost more but they would
take longer to read. In either case you would still possess the books
after you had read them, and they would be saleable at about a third
of their purchase price. If you bought only second-hand books, your
reading expenses would, of course, be much less: perhaps sixpence an
hour would be a fair estimate. And on the other hand if you don't
buy books, but merely borrow them from the lending library, reading
costs you round about a halfpenny an hour: if you borrow them
from the public library, it costs you next door to nothing.

I have said enough to show that reading is one of the cheaper
recreations: after listening to the radio probably *the* cheapest. Meanwhile, what is the actual amount that the British public spends on
books? I cannot discover any figures, though no doubt they exist.
But I do know that before the war this country was publishing annually about 15,000 books, which included reprints and school books.
If as many as 10,000 copies of each book were sold—and even allowing for the school books, this is probably a high estimate—the average person was only buying, directly or indirectly, about three books
a year. These three books taken together might cost £1, or probably
less.

These figures are guesswork, and I should be interested if someone
would correct them for me. But if my estimate is anywhere near
right, it is not a proud record for a country which is nearly 100 per
cent literate and where the ordinary man spends more on cigarettes
than an Indian peasant has for his whole livelihood. And if our book
consumption remains as low as it has been, at least let us admit that
it is because reading is a less exciting pastime than going to the dogs,

the pictures or the pub, and not because books, whether bought or
borrowed, are too expensive.

Tribune, 8 February 1946; SE

24. Review

The Democrat at the Supper Table by Colm Brogan

Narcissism is a normal motive of novelists, including some of the
best novelists. To act with firmness and daring in moments of danger,
to right injustices, to be a dominating personality, to exercise fascination on the opposite sex and to horsewhip one's private enemies—
these things are more easily achieved on paper than in real life, and
it is an unusual novel that does not contain somewhere or other a
portrait of the author, thinly disguised as hero, saint, or martyr. This
is particularly noticeable in conversational novels, to which class
Mr Brogan's book belongs. Without actually imitating Chesterton,
Mr Brogan has obviously been influenced by him, and his central
character has a Father Brown-like capacity for getting the better of
an argument, and also for surrounding himself with fools and
scoundrels whose function is to lead up to his wisecracks.

The action—or rather the series of discussions of which the book
consists—takes place in a private hotel. The "I" of the story describes
himself as a Democrat, and also appears to be a Catholic: sharing
the supper table with him are a Jewish Communist, a schoolmaster
of advanced views, an Indian Nationalist, a businessman, a poet, and
the proprietress of the hotel. The three first-named are frankly
stooges. The businessman, on the other hand, is allowed to show
occasional gleams of common sense, while the poet is an enigmatic
character inclined at times to take sides with the narrator, and the
proprietress is the typical Chestertonian female, a being devoid of
logic but possessing a wisdom which goes beyond that of the mere
male. As the arguments turn chiefly upon the questions of free enterprise versus state control and the extension of the school-leaving age,
the experienced reader can foresee in advance a good deal of what
each of the debaters will say.

Nevertheless, when one compares this book with its predecessors

of ten or twenty years ago, one cannot help being struck by the
retreat that conservatism—using this word in a wide sense—has
already had to make. Mr Brogan is defending capitalism, and he
expends considerable ingenuity in showing that Britain would have
a better chance of recapturing her share of the world markets with a
"free" economy than with nationalised industries. He does not, like
Chesterton, pretend that it would be possible to step back into the
Middle Ages and that great blocks of the people are yearning to do
so. He even defends mass production and is ready to accept the
principle of social insurance, though he is opposed to making it
compulsory. He opposes a unitary educational system and the raising
of the school-leaving age, but on the other hand he wants to spend
more money on the infant schools, and he does not say, as similar
thinkers would have said a little while ago, that parents should have
the right to decide whether their children are to be educated or not.
In effect the book is a rearguard action—a defence of the past, but
inspired by a consciousness that there is not very much left to defend.

However, the conversations follow the usual pattern. The Communist is a bad-blooded creature who drags references to Soviet
Russia into almost every sentence. The schoolmaster is a windbag.
The Indian is a mass of vague uplift and imaginary grievances, and
even the businessman, hard-headed in his own line, is taken in by
the Dean of Canterbury's sermons. As for the narrator, he is a para-
gon of wit, learning, intellectuality, broad-mindedness, and common
sense, and if he finally fails to convert the others to his point of view
it is because their minds have already been rotted by the follies of
modern education.

The trouble with all books of this kind is a sort of querulousness
that arises from not really having a practical programme to offer.
Mr Brogan is probably aware that there will be no return to *laissez-
faire* capitalism, just as Chesterton must have been aware at moments
that there would be no return to peasant proprietorship. Probably,
too, he is aware that it is not much use telling people that compulsory
education, compulsory social insurance, control of investments, and
direction of labour add up to slavery, since, even if it is true, the great
mass of the people would far rather have slavery than the alternative.

The world is going in a certain direction that he does not like, but
he is unable to think of any other direction in which it could actually
be induced to go. So he takes the essentially defensive line of pointing
out the absurdities and monstrosities of "advanced" thought—

which, after all, is not very difficult. But it is not by these methods that anyone who is not in agreement with him already will be brought to think twice about Communism, feminism, atheism, pacifism, or any of the other -isms that Mr Brogan dislikes.

Observer, 10 February 1946

Critical Essays was published in London by Secker & Warburg on 14 February 1946 and in New York with the title **Dickens, Dali and Others** *by Reynal & Hitchcock on 29 April the same year.*

25. Decline of the English Murder

It is Sunday afternoon, preferably before the war. The wife is already asleep in the armchair, and the children have been sent out for a nice long walk. You put your feet up on the sofa, settle your spectacles on your nose, and open the *News of the World*. Roast beef and York-shire, or roast pork and apple sauce, followed up by suet pudding and driven home, as it were, by a cup of mahogany-brown tea, have put you in just the right mood. Your pipe is drawing sweetly, the sofa cushions are soft underneath you, the fire is well alight, the air is warm and stagnant. In these blissful circumstances, what is it that you want to read about?

Naturally, about a murder. But what kind of murder? If one examines the murders which have given the greatest amount of pleasure to the British public, the murders whose story is known in its general outline to almost everyone and which have been made into novels and rehashed over and over again by the Sunday papers, one finds a fairly strong family resemblance running through the greater number of them. Our great period in murder, our Elizabethan period, so to speak, seems to have been between roughly 1850 and 1925, and the murderers whose reputation has stood the test of time are the following: Dr Palmer of Rugeley, Jack the Ripper, Neill Cream, Mrs Maybrick, Dr Crippen, Seddon, Joseph Smith, Armstrong, and Bywaters and Thompson. In addition, in 1919 or thereabouts, there was another very celebrated case which fits into the general pattern but which I had better not mention by name, because the accused man was acquitted.

Of the above-mentioned nine cases, at least four have had success-ful novels based on them, one has been made into a popular melo-drama, and the amount of literature surrounding them, in the form of newspaper write-ups, criminological treatises and reminiscences by lawyers and police officers, would make a considerable library. It is difficult to believe that any recent English crime will be remembered so long and so intimately, and not only because the violence of external events has made murder seem unimportant, but because the prevalent type of crime seems to be changing. The principle *cause célèbre* of the war years was the so-called Cleft Chin Murder, which has now been written up in a popular booklet;[1] the verbatim account of the trial was published some time last year by Messrs Jarrolds with an introduction by Mr Bechhofer-Roberts. Before returning to this pitiful and sordid case, which is only interesting from a sociological and perhaps a legal point of view, let me try to define what it is that the readers of Sunday papers mean when they say fretfully that "you never seem to get a good murder nowadays".

In considering the nine murders I named above, one can start by excluding the Jack the Ripper case, which is in a class by itself. Of the other eight, six were poisoning cases, and eight of the ten criminals belonged to the middle class. In one way or another, sex was a powerful motive in all but two cases, and in at least four cases respectability—the desire to gain a secure position in life, or not to forfeit one's social position by some scandal such as a divorce—was one of the main reasons for committing murder. In more than half the cases, the object was to get hold of a certain known sum of money such as a legacy or an insurance policy, but the amount involved was nearly always small. In most of the cases the crime only came to light slowly, as the result of careful investigation which started off with the suspicions of neighbours or relatives; and in nearly every case there was some dramatic coincidence, in which the finger of Providence could be clearly seen, or one of those episodes that no novelist would dare to make up, such as Crippen's flight across the Atlantic with his mistress dressed as a boy, or Joseph Smith playing "Nearer, my God, to Thee" on the harmonium while one of his wives was drowning in the next room. The background of all these crimes, except Neill Cream's, was essentially domestic; of twelve victims, seven were either wife or husband of the murderer.

With all this in mind one can construct what would be, from a

[1] *The Cleft Chin Murder* by R. Alwyn Raymond.

News of the World reader's point of view, the "perfect" murder. The murderer should be a little man of the professional class—a dentist or a solicitor, say—living an intensely respectable life somewhere in the suburbs, and preferably in a semi-detached house, which will allow the neighbours to hear suspicious sounds through the wall. He should be either chairman of the local Conservative Party branch, or a leading Nonconformist and strong Temperance advocate. He should go astray through cherishing a guilty passion for his secretary or the wife of a rival professional man, and should only bring himself to the point of murder after long and terrible wrestles with his conscience. Having decided on murder, he should plan it all with the utmost cunning, and only slip up over some tiny, unforeseeable detail. The means chosen should, of course, be poison. In the last analysis he should commit murder because this seems to him less disgraceful, and less damaging to his career, than being detected in adultery. With this kind of background, a crime can have dramatic and even tragic qualities which make it memorable and excite pity for both victim and murderer. Most of the crimes mentioned above have a touch of this atmosphere, and in three cases, including the one I referred to but did not name, the story approximates to the one I have outlined.

Now compare the Cleft Chin Murder. There is no depth of feeling in it. It was almost chance that the two people concerned committed that particular murder, and it was only by good luck that they did not commit several others. The background was not domesticity, but the anonymous life of the dance halls and the false values of the American film. The two culprits were an eighteen-year-old ex-waitress named Elizabeth Jones, and an American army deserter, posing as an officer, named Karl Hulten. They were only together for six days, and it seems doubtful whether, until they were arrested, they even learned one another's true names. They met casually in a teashop, and that night went out for a ride in a stolen army truck. Jones described herself as a strip-tease artist, which was not strictly true (she had given one unsuccessful performance in this line), and declared that she wanted to do something dangerous, "like being a gun-moll". Hulten described himself as a big-time Chicago gangster, which was also untrue. They met a girl bicycling along the road, and to show how tough he was Hulten ran over her with his truck, after which the pair robbed her of the few shillings that were on her. On another occasion they knocked out a girl to whom they had offered a lift, took her coat and handbag and threw her into a river. Finally, in the most wanton way, they murdered a taxi-driver who happened to have £8 in his pocket. Soon afterwards they parted. Hulten was caught because he had foolishly kept the dead man's car, and Jones made spontaneous confessions to the police. In court each prisoner incriminated the other. In between crimes, both of them seem to have behaved with the utmost callousness: they spent the dead taxi-driver's £8 at the dog races.

Judging from her letters, the girl's case has a certain amount of psychological interest, but this murder probably captured the headlines because it provided distraction amid the doodlebugs and the anxieties of the Battle of France. Jones and Hulten committed their murder to the tune of V1,[1] and were convicted to the tune of V2.[2] There was also considerable excitement because—as has become usual in England—the man was sentenced to death and the girl to imprisonment. According to Mr Raymond, the reprieving of Jones caused widespread indignation and streams of telegrams to the Home Secretary: in her native town, "She should hang" was chalked on the walls beside pictures of a figure dangling from a gallows. Considering that only ten women have been hanged in Britain in this century, and that the practice has gone out largely because of popular feeling against it, it is difficult not to feel that this clamour to hang an eighteen-year-old girl was due partly to the brutalising effects of war. Indeed, the whole meaningless story, with its atmosphere of dance-halls, movie palaces, cheap perfume, false names and stolen cars, belongs essentially to a war period.

Perhaps it is significant that the most talked-of English murder of recent years should have been committed by an American and an English girl who had become partly americanised. But it is difficult to believe that this case will be so long remembered as the old domestic poisoning dramas, product of a stable society where the all-prevailing hypocrisy did at least ensure that crimes as serious as murder should have strong emotions behind them.

Tribune, 15 February, 1946; SE; OR

[1] The V1, an unmanned aircraft developed by the Germans and used by them to bomb London from June 1944: they were nicknamed "doodlebugs" by the Londoners.
[2] The V2, a rocket bomb used by the Germans on London from September 1944.

26. Letter to the Reverend Herbert Rogers

27B, Canonbury Square
Islington, London N1
18 February 1946

Dear Mr Rogers,[1]

I only received your letter of the 10th about three days ago. I cannot answer it in detail, but will take up two main points.

First, as to Brogan's derivation from Chesterton. I assumed that the kind of person I was writing for would know more or less what Chesterton stood for, i.e. for a return to a peasant society with a wide distribution of private property. Even in Chesterton's lifetime, it was perfectly obvious that this was a hopeless programme in the sense that no large number of people effectively wanted it, and after Chesterton's death the movement which he had tried to found disintegrated. In Brogan's case you have once again a defence of private property, but on a slightly more realistic level. Brogan is now arguing in favour of laissez-faire capitalism and against planning, social insurance and State interference generally. This is not strictly Chesterton's position, but it is as near as one could get to Chesterton's position now without being simply laughed down. Chesterton's line was "no Government interference of any kind". He even, for instance, was against State protection for children neglected by their parents, on the ground that the children's welfare was the parents' concern. Brogan knew that this attitude would be hopeless nowadays, so his line is "as little interference as possible". He is therefore not openly against social insurance or extension of the school leaving age, but is against making them compulsory. This attitude sounds Liberal, but when a real choice has to be made, the people who take it always end up by siding with Fascism as being a little nearer to their views than Socialism. Chesterton, you will remember, ended up as an admirer of Mussolini.

Secondly, as to the whole of this kind of writing being essentially defensive and negative. The *Observer* cut out of my review a sentence or two in which I pointed out that ever since W.H. Mallock's *New Republic* there has been a continuous stream of what one might call

[1] The Reverend Herbert Rogers, Chaplain to St Mungo's School, Ayrshire, Colm Brogan's brother-in-law, who had written to Orwell complaining that the review of *The Democrat at the Supper Table* gave an inadequate idea of the book.

"clever Conservative" books, opposing the current trend without being able to offer any viable programme in its place. If you look back twenty years, you will find people like Ronald Knox,[1] Cyril Alington,[2] Chesterton himself and his many followers, talking as though such things as Socialism, Industrialism, the theory of evolution, psycho-therapy, universal compulsory education, radio, aeroplanes and what not could be simply laughed out of existence. At any given moment it is always very easy to be funny about the "advanced" ideas of the moment. But the fact is that the world is going in a certain direction which is broadly discernible and one has to recognise this as the starting-point for any serious thought. I don't myself feel at all certain that this civilisation will survive, but if it does survive I think it is quite obvious that it will not revert again towards economic chaos and individualism. Whether we like it or not, the trend is towards centralism and planning and it is more useful to try to humanise the collectivist society that is certainly coming than to pretend, like Brogan, that we could revert to a past phase. It is arguable that the nineteenth-century economic system was more satisfactory than the present one, but the point is that no significant number of people wish to revert to it. I think that Brogan realises this and that the consciousness of not having an answer makes him take refuge in the very easy game of poking fun at parlour Communists, the Brains Trust etc. I applied the term Narcissistic both to this book and to Chesterton's because the kind of book which consists of conversations where the person whom the author agrees with has the best of it is quite obviously a way of revenging the conversational defeats which one suffers in real life. I can hardly think of an instance in Brogan's book, and I certainly cannot think of one in any of Chesterton's, where it is not the Catholic who makes the wise and witty retort. But have you noticed in real life that Catholics as such are better conversationalists than other people?

Yours sincerely,
Geo. Orwell

---

[1] Monsignor Ronald Arbuthnot Knox (1888–1957), classical and Biblical scholar, Catholic apologist, prolific writer and wit. He became a Catholic convert and priest in 1917, after having been a clergyman of the Church of England.

[2] The Very Reverend Cyril Alington (1872–1955). Scholar, writer, headmaster of several schools and, from 1916 to 1933, of Eton.

27. Letter to Dorothy Plowman

27B Canonbury Square
Islington, London N1
19 February 1946

Dear Dorothy,[1]
I enclose cheque for £150 as a first instalment of repayment of that £300 anonymously lent to me in 1938—it's a terribly long time afterwards to start repaying, but until this year I was really unable to. Just latterly I have started making money. I got your address from Richard Rees.[2] It's a long time since I heard from you, and I do not think I even wrote to you when Max died.[3] One does not know what to say when these things happen. I reviewed Max's book of letters[4] for the *Manchester Evening News*, which you may have seen. My book *Animal Farm* has sold quite well, and the new one, which is merely a book of reprints,[5] also seems to be doing well. It was a terrible shame that Eileen[6] didn't live to see the publication of *Animal Farm*, which she was particularly fond of and even helped in the planning of. I suppose you know I was in France when she died. It was a terribly cruel and stupid thing to happen. No doubt you know I have a little boy named Richard whom we adopted in 1944 when he was 3 weeks old. He was ten months old when Eileen died and is 21 months old now. Her last letter to me was to tell me he was

---

[1] Dorothy Plowman (1887–1967), widow of Max Plowman (1883–1941), journalist and author who worked on the *Adelphi* 1929–41 where he had met Orwell as a young contributor. He encouraged Orwell in his early writing and, with his wife, remained friends with him. In the summer of 1938 when Orwell was advised by his doctors to winter in a warm climate, L.H. Myers (1881–1944), the novelist, gave Dorothy Plowman £300 to enable him to do so. She had never told Orwell the source of the money although he realised she had acted as an intermediary on behalf of someone else.

[2] Sir Richard Rees Bt. (1900–), painter, author and critic whose writings include *George Orwell: Fugitive from the Camp of Victory* and *Simone Weil*. From 1930–36 he edited the *Adelphi* and met Orwell as a young contributor. They remained close friends until Orwell's death. Throughout the years Rees was constant in his devotion, help and encouragement.

[3] See II, 24.

[4] Orwell reviewed *Bridge into the Future: Letters of Max Plowman* in the *Manchester Evening News*, 7 December 1944.

[5] *Critical Essays*.

[6] Eileen Blair, Orwell's wife, had died in March 1945.

beginning to crawl. Now he has grown into a big strong child and is very active and intelligent, although he doesn't talk yet. I have a nurse-housekeeper who looks after him and me, and luckily we are able to get a char as well. He is so full of beans that it is getting difficult to keep him in the flat, and I am looking forward to getting him out of London for the whole summer. I am not quite certain where we are going. I am supposed to be the tenant of a cottage in the Hebrides, but it's possible they won't have it in living order this year, in which case I shall probably take him to the east coast somewhere. I want a place where he can run in and out of the house all day with no fear of traffic. I am anxious to get out of London for my own sake as well, because I am constantly smothered under journalism—at present I am doing 4 articles every week—and I want to write another book which is impossible unless I can get 6 months quiet. I have been in London almost the whole of the war. Eileen was working for 4 or 5 years in government offices, generally for 10 hours a day or more, and it was partly overwork that killed her. I shall probably go back to the country in 1947, but at present it's impossible to get hold of unfurnished houses and so I daren't let go of my flat.

Richard Rees is living in Chelsea and has kept his beard, although demobilised. Rayner Heppenstall[1] has a job in the BBC and seems to be quite liking it. It's funny that you should be at Royston, so near where we used to live.[2] I have got to go down some time to the cottage I still have there, to sort out the furniture and books, but I have been putting it off because last time I was there it was with Eileen and it upsets me to go there. What has become of Piers?[3] I hope all goes well with you both.

Yours,
Eric Blair

---

[1] Rayner Heppenstall (1911–   ), novelist, poet and critic whose works include *The Blaze of Noon* and *Four Absentees*, met Orwell in the spring of 1935 through Sir Richard Rees and had remained friends with him.
[2] At Wallington in Hertfordshire where Orwell rented a cottage from 1936–47.
[3] The Plowmans' son.

28. Review

The Cosmological Eye by Henry Miller

It is a pity that some publisher cannot take his courage in his hands and reissue *Tropic of Cancer*. About a year later he could recoup his losses by publishing a book entitled *What I Saw in Prison*, or words to that effect, and meanwhile a few copies of the forbidden text would have reached the public before the entire edition was burned by the public hangman, or whoever it is that has the job of burning banned books in this country. As it is, *Tropic of Cancer* must be one of the rarest of contemporary books—though it is said that a pirated edition was circulating in America two or three years ago—and even *Black Spring* is not easily procurable. Fragments of Henry Miller's writings are printed all over the place, while the parts that are worth anything remain inaccessible. In criticising him one has to rely on memory, and since the person who reads the criticism may never get a chance to read the books, the whole process is rather like taking a blind man to see a firework display.

The present selection includes the short story—it is perhaps rather a sketch than a story—"Max", the excellent autobiographical sketch "Via Dieppe-Newhaven", three chapters, heavily blue-pencilled, from *Black Spring*, a scenario for a Surrealist film, and a number of critical essays and fragments. The book closes with a biographical note which is probably truthful in its main outlines, and which ends like this:

> I want to be read by less and less people; I have no interest in the life of the masses, nor in the intentions of the existing governments of the world. I hope and believe that the whole civilised world will be wiped out in the next hundred years or so. I believe that man can exist, and in an infinitely better, larger way, without "civilisation".

To compare "Via Newhaven-Dieppe" with, for instance, the fragment from *Hamlet*, the enormous book of letters which Miller wrote in collaboration with Michael Fraenkel, is to get a good idea of what Miller can and cannot do. "Via Newhaven-Dieppe" is a truthful and even moving piece of writing. It records an unsuccessful attempt by Miller to pay a short visit to England in 1935. The immigration officials nosed out the fact that he had very little money in his pockets, and he was promptly clapped into a police-court cell and sent back across the Channel on the following day, the whole thing being done with the maximum of stupidity and offensiveness. The only person who showed a spark of decency in the whole affair was the simple police constable who had to guard Miller through the night. The book in which this sketch occurs was published in 1938, and I remember reading it just after Munich and reflecting that, though the Munich settlement was not a thing to be proud of, this little episode made me feel more ashamed of my country. Not that the British officials at Newhaven behaved much worse than that kind of person behaves everywhere. But somehow the whole thing was saddening. A couple of bureaucrats had got an artist at their mercy, and the mixture of spite, cunning and stupidity with which they handled him made one wonder what is the use of all this talk about democracy, freedom of the press, and whatnot.

"Via Newhaven-Dieppe" is in the same vein as *Tropic of Cancer*. For forty years or more Miller had led an insecure, disreputable kind of life, and he had two outstanding gifts, both of which could perhaps be traced back to a common origin. One was a complete lack of ordinary shame, and the other was an ability to write a bold, florid, rhythmical prose of a kind that had hardly been seen in English for twenty years past. On the other hand he had no power of self-discipline, no sense of responsibility, and perhaps not much imagination, as opposed to fancy. He was therefore best equipped as an autobiographical writer, and liable to dry up when the material drawn from his past life came to an end.

After *Black Spring* it was to be expected that Miller would descend into charlatanism of one kind or another, and in fact a great deal of his later writing is simply a banging on the big drum—noise proceeding from emptiness. Let anyone read the two essays in this book, "The Universe of Death" (a criticism of Proust and Joyce) and "An Open Letter to Surrealists Everywhere". In nearly seventy pages, it is astonishing how little he says, and how impressively he says it. The arresting but in fact almost meaningless phrase "universe of death" strikes a characteristic note. One of Miller's tricks is to be constantly using apocalyptic language, to sprinkle every page with phrases like "cosmological flux", "lunar attraction" and "interstellar spaces" or with sentences like "The orbit over which I am travelling leads me farther and farther away from the dead sun which gave me birth." The second sentence in the essay on Proust and Joyce is:

"Whatever has happened in literature since Dostoievski has happened on the other side of death." What rubbish it is, when you think it out! The key words in this kind of writing are "death", "life", "birth," "sun", "moon", "womb", "cosmic" and "catastrophe", and by free use of them the most banal statement can be made to sound picturesque, while what is outright meaningless can be given an air of mystery and profundity. Even the title of this book, *The Cosmological Eye*, doesn't actually mean anything, but it sounds as though it *ought* to mean something.

When one digs them out from beneath the flamboyant language, Miller's opinions are mostly commonplace, and often reactionary. They boil down to a sort of nihilistic quietism. He disclaims interest in politics—at the beginning of this book he announces that he has "become God" and is "absolutely indifferent to the fate of the world" —but in fact he is constantly making political pronouncements, including flimsy racial generalisations about the "French soul", the "German soul", etc. He is an extreme pacifist and on the other hand has a yearning for violence, provided that it is happening somewhere else, thinks life wonderful but hopes and expects to see everything blown to pieces before long, and talks a good deal about "great men" and "aristocrats of the spirit". He refuses to bother about the difference between Fascism and Communism, because "society is made up of individuals". This has come to be a familiar attitude nowadays, and it would be a respectable one if it were carried to its logical conclusion, which would mean remaining passive in the face of war, revolution, Fascism or anything else. Actually, those who talk in the same vein as Miller always take care to stay inside bourgeois-democratic society, making use of its protection while disclaiming responsibility for it: on the other hand, when a real choice has to be made, the quietist attitude never seems to survive. At bottom, Miller's outlook is that of a simple individualist who recognises no obligations to anyone else—at any rate, no obligations to society as a whole—and does not even feel the need to be consistent in his opinions. Much of his later work is merely a statement of this fact in more resounding words.

As long as Miller was simply an outcast and vagabond, having unpleasant experiences with policemen, landladies, wives, duns, whores, editors and such-like, his irresponsible attitude did no harm —indeed, as a basis for a book like *Tropic of Cancer*, it was the best attitude. The great thing about *Tropic of Cancer* was that it had no moral. But if you are going to utter judgements on God, the universe, war, revolution, Hitler, Marxism and "the Jews", then Miller's particular brand of intellectual honesty is not enough. Either one must genuinely keep out of politics, or one must recognise that politics is the science of the possible. Here and there in Miller's later writing there is a slab of unpretentious autobiography—"Via New-haven-Dieppe" is one example, and there are comparable passages even in the unreadable Hamlet book—and then once again the old magic reappears. Miller's real gift is his power of describing the under side of life, but probably he needs misfortune to prod him into using it. However, it seems that his life in California during the past five or six years has not been all jam, and perhaps one of these days he will stop writing empty sentences about death and the universe and revert to the thing that he is really fitted to do. But he must give up "being God", because the only good book that God ever wrote was the Old Testament.

Meanwhile this selection will give new readers a not too misleading impression of Miller's work. But as it was found possible to print three chapters of *Black Spring*, with asterisks here and there, it was a pity not to do the same with *Tropic of Cancer*, parts of which are not markedly obscene and could easily be made presentable with an occasional row of dots in the right places.

Tribune, 22 February 1946

29. Letter to Leonard Moore

27B Canonbury Square
Islington
London N1
23 February 1946

Dear Mr Moore,[1]
Many thanks for the cuttings from the *Sydney Morning Herald*, which I return herewith. I think they are quite good, but I don't think they are quite the kind of thing that would be worth incorporating in a book if it were ever decided to do an illustrated edition of *Animal*

---

[1] Leonard Moore of Christy & Moore Ltd, Orwell's literary agent until his death.

Farm. I'll talk this over with Warburg[1] again. I suppose the book will
be re-issued some time, and certainly it would be nice to have it
illustrated. There was some vague idea of Low[2] doing it, as according
to Horrabin[3] he (Low) once remarked he would like to do it. But I
don't suppose that will come to anything, and I dare say some time
I'll run across some young artist whose style would be suitable.

I enclose also the Italian contract, duly signed. If later it should
turn out that there is any difficulty about the sterling, i.e. for the
advance, don't press them. It is important that the book should be
translated into Italian, and if they found they could only pay in lire I
could always find ways of spending the money in Italy. In that case I
would re-imburse you for your commission. I am very glad to hear
about the projected Norwegian and Danish translations. The woman
who is doing the Polish one has I believe completed it. It is some
Polish publisher in Glasgow who is issuing it. A Russian woman who
wrote to me is also trying to interest some Russian publishers who
exist in New York. I have told her, as in the Polish case, that I don't
want any money for it, but curiously enough, if they take the book
up, it ought to be possible to dispose of quite a few copies of a Russian translation, because of the hordes of DPs and other nondescript
Russians now at large in Germany and France. The write-up in
Time was very good and ought to help the American edition if the
latter appears fairly soon. I suppose the publishers are alive to this.
You mentioned in your last letter something about giving Harcourt
Brace an option on future books. It's a bit premature as I have no
book in preparation yet, but I should think Harcourt Brace would be
the people to tie up with, as they had the courage to publish *Animal
Farm.* But of course they may be put off the idea if the book flops in
the USA, as it well may. I am not sure whether one can count on the
American public grasping what it is about. You may remember that
the Dial Press had been asking me for some years for a manuscript,
but when I sent the MS of *AF* in 1944 they returned it, saying shortly
that "it was impossible to sell animal stories in the USA". Just
recently they wrote saying that "there had been some mistake" and
that they would like to make another offer for the book. I rather

---

[1] F.J. Warburg, managing director of Secker & Warburg Ltd, publishers of
Homage to Catalonia and *Animal Farm.*
[2] David Low (1891–1965), Kt 1962. Left-wing in sympathy, he was the best-
known British political cartoonist of his generation.
[3] J.F. Horrabin (1884–1962), left-wing journalist and illustrator.

gather they had at first taken it for a bona fide animal story. So I
suppose it might be worth indicating on the dust-jacket of the
American edition what the book is about. However, Harcourt Brace
would be the best judges of that.

I am going to drop all journalism for six months as from the end of
April and get on with another book. I don't suppose I shall finish one
in that time but I shall break the back of it. It is to be a novel,[1] but I
don't care to say more than that about it at present.

Yours sincerely
Eric Blair

30. Review

The Story of Burma by F. Tennyson Jesse

Burmese history is legendary until the eleventh century and remains
hazy until the mid-eighteenth century when the Burmese finally over-
came the original inhabitants of the country, the Talaings. Miss
Tennyson Jesse's book is not intended to be primarily a chronicle of
events, and she rightly skates over the earlier period and concentrates
on the real turning-point in modern Burmese history—the annexa-
tion of Upper Burma in 1885. The mistakes then made, she thinks,
were responsible for the failure of the British to build up a sound and
popular administration, and hence were partly to blame for the
collapse of 1942.

The behaviour of the British in Burma has perhaps not been so
blameless as Miss Tennyson Jesse makes it appear, but it is certain
that if the Burmese had not lost their independence to the British they
would have lost it to some other Power, probably France. Geo-
graphically, Burma is an isolated country, and for centuries the
Burmese had remained exceptionally ignorant of the outside world.
It is curious to reflect that in 1820, or thereabouts, a Burmese army
was sent to invade India, with orders to bring back the Governor-
General in chains, and, if necessary, to march on and capture
London. Once Lower Burma had been annexed, Upper Burma was

[1] *Nineteen Eighty-Four.*

Eo—IV

bound to follow sooner or later, but even so the drunken King
Thibaw and his wife Supayalat made every mistake that it was
possible to make. British and Indian traders were insulted in unbearable ways, while Thibaw's periodical massacres of his own
subjects—he celebrated his accession to the throne by executing his
brothers, to the number of eighty or thereabouts—dismayed even the
British anti-imperialists. When the invasion finally happened,
Thibaw's regular army dispersed without fighting, though bands of
guerrillas kept up the struggle for years afterwards.

The great error, Miss Tennyson Jesse thinks, was to abolish the
monarchy. Thibaw had to be deposed, but another prince should
have been put upon the throne. As it was, the symbol of authority to
which the Burmese had been accustomed for centuries was destroyed,
and indirectly the power of the priesthood, on which the moral life
of the country depended, was greatly weakened. The old order was
broken up, and Burma was burdened with a system of law, administration, and education which was alien to the country and which
never took root. As a result, violent crime flourished, the priesthood
took to politics, the universities turned out an unemployed intelligentsia which became the backbone of the nationalist movement,
and the entire lower ranks of the administration were incurably
corrupt. At the same time Burma remained in many ways very backward, and practically all large-scale trade remained in the hands of
the British, or of Indians and Chinese. Even the armed forces were
recruited mainly from non-Burmese peoples. Naturally, resentment
mounted up, and though the Japanese invaders may not have enjoyed
very much active support, loyalty to the British régime was hardly a
factor in the situation, so far as the Burmese proper were concerned.

Miss Tennyson Jesse's views are shared by other observers sympathetic to Burma, and no doubt they contain part of the truth. She
implies, however, that it would have been better to encourage Burma
to emerge only very slowly from the Middle Ages, and that, above all,
we should have tried to preserve the Buddhist religion in its full
purity. Underlying this is probably the belief that if we had not tact-
lessly forced western institutions on Burma, an anti-British nationalist movement would never have grown up. This seems very questionable. National consciousness, which in the circumstances could
only be anti-British, was bound to develop by one route or another,
and it was the promise to modernise the country rapidly that gave
Japanese propaganda much of its appeal. Miss Tennyson Jesse

seems everywhere to minimise the importance of Asiatic nationalism and colour-consciousness. She puts the number of the Burmese fifth column during the 1942 campaign at 5,000, which must surely be a serious underestimate. This book is a useful popular survey provided that the reader bears in mind that it is written from the angle of what might be called benevolent imperialism and, while genuinely affectionate towards the Burmese, is decidedly over-charitable towards the British.

Observer, 24 February 1946

31. Letter¹ to F. Tennyson Jesse

27B Canonbury Square
Islington, London N1
4 March 1946

Dear Miss Tennyson Jesse,²
You ask what is my knowledge of Burma. It is out of date, but it is quite good of its kind. I was in the Imperial Police in Burma from 1922 to 1927, so that I know from the inside a little about the work of governing a country of that kind. I also know how the Europeans used to behave, and from what I could learn from Burmese and English acquaintances, they had not improved greatly in more recent years. In your book you said nothing about our economic exploitation of the country, the way in which, for instance, we could get oil and other raw materials at a fraction of what they would have cost if Burma were an independent country, and though you did mention it, you soft-pedalled the social misbehaviour of the British and the friction to which it has led over a long period. As to the figures for the Burmese fifth column, I simply can't accept 5,000 as anywhere near the truth, though I can well believe that the number was smaller than was reported at the time. The figure of 5,000 being official doesn't make it any more credible—rather the opposite, as naturally those responsible for the administration would minimise the amount

¹ From a typed copy.
² F. Tennyson Jesse (d. 1958), novelist and journalist, who took great exception to Orwell's review of her book *The Story of Burma* and wrote him two letters saying so.

of opposition. Ever since 1931 sporadic guerilla fighting had been happening in Burma, involving much larger numbers of people than that, and it was admitted during the 1942 campaign that enough Burmese were operating with the Japs to affect the military issue to some extent. I had accounts from one or two people who were in Burma at the time. The whole administration of the country simply folded up in the face of a serious threat, and it had been possible to foresee years beforehand that this would happen. We have treated Burma better than we have treated some countries, but on the whole it is a sordid story and one ought to begin any book about Burma by saying so. Did you ever read my novel about Burma (*Burmese Days*)? I dare say it's unfair in some ways and inaccurate in some details, but much of it is simply reporting of what I have seen.

Yours sincerely,
George Orwell

32. Letter to[1] F. Tennyson Jesse

27B Canonbury Square,
Islington, London N1
14 March 1946

Dear Miss Tennyson Jesse,
I am ill in bed, which is why I haven't answered earlier, and even now I cannot write a proper letter.

I think you have missed my point. It isn't what you did say about the British in Burma, but what you didn't say. No one would infer from your book that the British had done anything worse than be a little stupid and sometimes follow mistaken policies. Nothing about the economic milching of the country via such concerns as the Burma Oil Company, nor about the disgusting social behaviour of the British till very recently. I do know something about this. Apart from my own time there I have family connections with the country over three generations. My grandmother lived forty years in Burma and at the end could not speak a word of Burmese—typical of the ordinary Englishwoman's attitude.

Yours sincerely,
George Orwell

[1] From a typed copy.

33. Letter to the Editor of *Forward*

Sir,[1]

During the Moscow political trials of 1936 and 1937, many references were made to an alleged association between Leon Trotsky and other of the accused on the one hand and the Nazi Government and Gestapo on the other.

Following the Moscow trials a Commission of Enquiry, initiated by the American Committee for the Defence of Leon Trotsky and having the mandate of similar organisations in other countries, was set up.

Meeting in America, it acted under the Chairmanship of Dr John Dewey, eminent liberal publicist and educationist, was served as Secretary by Suzanne La Follette, author and journalist, and as Counsel by John P. Finnerty, famous as counsel for Sacco and Vanzetti and for Tom Mooney.

The remainder of the Commission was composed of well-known public figures—sociologists, educationists, editors, journalists, authors. In the voluminous *Report* subsequently issued by the Commission, the Commissioners describe themselves as ". . . holding widely divergent political and social opinions, and none of them being a political adherent of Leon Trotsky . . ."

The Commission completely exonerated Trotsky of the charges made against him.

In 1936 and 1937, when the trials in Moscow took place, and in 1937 when the Commission of Enquiry was held, it was not, of course, possible for either side to check the allegations of collusion between Trotsky and the Nazis by reference to Nazi sources.

Now, however, the position is different. The whole of the Gestapo records are in the hands of the Allied Powers, and Hess—the only Nazi named in the Moscow indictment—is available at Nuremberg for public questioning.

The opportunity thus presented for an investigation aimed at the establishment of historical truth and bearing upon the political integrity of figures and tendencies of international standing is invaluable.

We therefore suggest the following:

[1] In the margin of the press-cutting of this letter Orwell wrote, "Circulated widely to British press. Published only (I think) in *Forward* and M[anchester] G[uardian]." [It did not appear in the *Manchester Guardian*.]

1. That Hess be interrogated at Nuremberg in regard to his alleged meeting with Trotsky.

2. That an accredited representative of Natalia Sedov-Trotsky (Leon Trotsky's widow) be invited to attend this session of the Nuremberg trial with authority to cross-examine the accused and witnesses.

3. That the Allied experts examining Gestapo records be instructed to state whether there are any documents proving or disproving liaison between the Nazi Party or State and Trotsky or the other old Bolshevik leaders indicted at the Moscow trials and if so, to make them available for publication. Yours, etc,

(Signed)	George Padmore
John Baird	Paul Potts
A.A. Ballard	F.A. Ridley
Frank Horrabin	Henry Sara
C.E.M. Joad	C.A. Smith
Arthur Koestler	Julian Symons
George Orwell	H.G. Wells

25th February, 1946

Forward, 16 March 1946

34. Review

The Martyrdom of Man by Winwood Reade

If one were obliged to write a history of the world, would it be better to record the true facts, so far as one could discover them, or would it be better simply to make the whole thing up? The answer is not so self-evident as it appears. The purpose of anyone who writes the history of any large epoch must necessarily be to impose a pattern on events, or at least to discover a pattern, and for that purpose a sound general theory, or even an instinctive grasp of probability, might be more useful than a mountain of learning. A history constructed imaginatively would never be right about any single event, but it might come nearer to essential truth than a mere compilation of names and dates in which no one statement was demonstrably untrue.

One feels this strongly with that queer, unhonoured masterpiece, Winwood Reade's *The Martyrdom of Man*. Not, of course, that Reade was simply making his history up. In a way, indeed, he was reasserting the value of empirical knowledge as against tradition and authority, since his main aim was to attack current religious beliefs, and his method of doing so was to insist on the known facts, including New Testament texts which orthodox believers prefer to forget about. Again, he was ready to take over large blocks of information from specialists in various fields, and in his preface to the book he indicates some of his sources, stating plainly that "there is scarcely anything in this work which I can claim as my own. I have taken not only facts and ideas, but phrases and even paragraphs, from other writers." And yet his book is essentially a work of imagination and not merely a record of events. He did not, perhaps, start out with a preconceived idea of the pattern of history, but by his reading and his travels he believes that he has found the pattern, and once it is found the details drop into place. The book is a kind of vision, or epic, inspired by the conception of progress. Man is Prometheus: he has stolen the fire and been terribly punished for it, but in the end he will turn the gods out of heaven and the reign of reason will begin.

In spite of its clear and powerful writing, *The Martyrdom of Man* is not a well-arranged book. It is somewhat uncouthly divided into four main parts, headed War, Religion, Liberty and Intellect, which are supposed to summarise the main stages of human development, and the fourth section partly recapitulates what has been said earlier. And of course it is inclined to be lopsided, as any attempt at universal history probably always must be. For a European it is almost impossible not to think of "the world" as meaning the fringes of the Mediterranean and the Atlantic, and neither India nor China enter much into Reade's scheme of things. Neither do England, Russia or South America. The centre of the world, as he sees it, is Egypt and the countries of the Middle East, and he is at his best in dealing with the slave empires of antiquity and the rise of the Semitic religions. Take this typical passage:

> Rome lived upon its principal till ruin stared it in the face.
> Industry is the only true source of wealth, and there was no

industry in Rome. By day the Ostia road was crowded with carts and muleteers, carrying to the great city the silks and spices of the East, the marble of Asia Minor, the timber of the Atlas, the grain of Africa and Egypt; and the carts brought out nothing but loads of dung. That was their return cargo.

In the mingled qualities of this passage—its irony, its air of assured knowledge, its insistence on the importance of economic processes, and alongside with this its retention of picturesqueness—one can see, I think, the reason for Reade's popular appeal. People felt that for once they were getting history from someone who knew all the facts and yet was not a professor—not a hanger-on of the upper classes and the Established Church. Reade has no resemblance to the dry-as-dust "economic historian". The romantic, pageant-like side of history, the swelling sails of the Phoenician galleys, the brass shields of the Roman soldiers, the knights, the castles, the tournaments, and the resounding names—Caesar, Alexander, Hannibal, Nebuchadnezzar, Charlemagne—it is all present in his work, but somehow with a new slant, as though he were saying all the while: "Just look at it like this, and it all falls into place." An outstanding quality of the book is its masterly handling of time. History is made to flow: great epochs are summarised in a paragraph, Egyptians merge into Persians, Persians into Greeks, Greeks into Romans, barbarism fades into feudalism, feudalism into capitalism, in such a way that one seems to see it streaming past like a panorama, with its essential principles laid bare and yet with its colour and much of its detail retained.

In the Introduction to the Thinker's Library edition Mr J.M. Robertson points out that *The Martyrdom of Man* is remarkable

> at once for its continuous impact on two generations of readers and for its steady success in the face of a bitterly or contemptuously hostile literary and newspaper press. Without a word of respectable literary approval, without an advertisement by the publishers, it made its way from the year of publication, and it it has gone on selling for more than sixty years, edition following edition up to the present.

The book is, as it were, unofficial history. Reade was aiming at the emancipated, at people not frightened of the truth, but his book was essentially a popular one, repudiating almost from its first pages the values of bourgeois society. One may guess that its deepest appeal, as well as the reason for the hostility of the press, lay in its humanist interpretation of Christianity. In 1872, when the book was published, it needed courage to take this line, but it still seemed a revolutionary book forty or fifty years later. I well remember its effect on me when I first read it at the age of about seventeen. When I came upon Reade's description of the typical Hebrew prophet, and saw the words "As soon as he received his mission he ceased to wash," I felt profoundly "This man is on my side". Then I went on and read Reade's examination of the character of Jesus. It was a curiously liberating experience. Here was somebody who neither accepted Jesus as the Son of God, nor, as was the fashion at that time, as a Great Moral Teacher, but simply presented him as a fallible human being like any other—a noble character on the whole, but with serious faults, and, in any case, only one of a long line of very similar Jewish fanatics. Not till a century after his death, said Reade, did various pagan legends belonging to Osiris and Apollo become attached to him.

Was this a true explanation? I did not know then, and do not know now. One would have to be a specialist to give an opinion. But at least Reade's account of the life of Jesus *could* be a true one, whereas the version that was thrust upon me by my schoolmasters outraged common sense. Reade was an emancipating writer because he seemed to speak as man to man, to resolve history into an intelligible pattern in which there was no need for miracles. Even if he was wrong, he was grown-up.

Although it is inspired by the concept of progress, and although it has influenced the left-wing movement over two generations, one ought not to regard *The Martyrdom of Man* as a Socialist book. Reade had been much influenced by the Darwinian theory of the struggle for survival, and in some ways his outlook is distinctly reactionary. He explicitly declares his disbelief in Socialism, is convinced of the valuable effects of commercial competition, thinks that imperialism should be encouraged, and seems to regard orientals as natural inferiors. He also toys with the dangerous idea that there are different orders of truth and that a false belief should sometimes not be exploded if it is socially valuable. But he says some very prescient things—he says, for instance, that Communism, if estab-lished, might harden into a caste system, which was a penetrating remark to make in 1871—and he sees clearly that human equality cannot be realised except at a high level of mechanical civilisation.

His objectives are such as most Socialists would accept, although his attitude towards existing society is not. He is a sort of irregular ally of the Socialist movement, fighting chiefly on the religious front. Many thousands of working-class readers must have disagreed with some of his conclusions and yet felt that they had a good friend in this scholar who had turned against the priests, and so could make the past not only intelligible but also alive.

Tribune, 15 March 1946

35. Letter to Arthur Koestler

27B Canonbury Square
Islington
London N1
16 March 1946

Dear Arthur,

I have been very ill all this week (something vaguely called gastritis, which means something wrong with your belly—I suppose if it was your head they call it cephalitis and so on), and have only just got out of bed. While I was still in bed an American called Henson[1] came to see me and tell me about an American organisation along partly the same lines as our own, with which we obviously should be affiliated. I enclose herewith a sheet of their notepaper, on which you can see who is sponsoring it, and also a copy of a memorandum on Anglo-American relations which he left with me. The purpose of the International Rescue and Relief Committee, as I understand it, is to assist victims of totalitarianism, particularly in such matters as giving relief to destitute people, helping political refugees to get out of totalitarian territory, etc. He impressed me that this is very definitely a non-Stalinist organisation, that they know all about the Stalinists' ways and are keeping them out of it, and that the organisation is anti-Stalinist to the extent that the people they assist are largely Trotskyists etc. They appear to have considerable funds at their disposal and are therefore able to help people in a solid way. The

---

[1] Francis A. Henson (d. 1963), an American, one of the International Rescue and Relief Committee's representatives in Europe. In 1949 he was Education Director of the United Automobile Workers.

organisation to which the other enclosed draft refers, the UDA,[1] is, I gather, in some sort of loose tie-up with the IRRC, but I understood him to say that Stalinists or fellow-travellers have not been completely excluded from that one.

He asked me about our organisation, and I told him how far it had got and who was associated with it. He will be very interested to get any particulars about our meeting at Easter.[2] He was going to see various people in the Labour Party before proceeding to Paris. I gather that he will be in Paris for some time and can be written to at the address he has written on the attached (Blvd des Capucines). Obviously these are the sort of people we should keep in close touch with, as it is all more or less up the same street.

I told him that as soon as we had anything definite to go upon we should circularise suitable American intellectuals and publicists, and he gave me two addresses which I did not know. One is Bertram Wolfe,[3] whose pamphlets you have perhaps seen. Another is Bert Jolis, whom you probably don't know but who is very much of our way of thinking. I add the address of Victor Serge[4] from whom I heard recently. I suppose you or somebody is beginning to file suitable addresses. Obviously we should have comprehensive lists of sympathisers in all countries.

Bertram Wolfe
68 Montague Street,
Brooklyn, New York

Bert Jolis
270 West End Avenue
New York City

[1] Union for Democratic Action.

[2] In January 1946 Koestler had approached Bertrand Russell about his and Orwell's idea for an international organisation (see 18). Russell liked the idea and suggested a conference be called with no more than a dozen people, all experts—one on the Far East, one on the Middle East etc—to work out a programme of action. Koestler and Orwell convened such a conference for Easter 1946 but, through various difficulties, it never took place.

[3] Bertram Wolfe (1895–), an American writer and scholar, among whose works are *Diego Rivera, Three Who Made a Revolution* and *Rosa Luxemburg and the Russian Revolution*.

[4] Victor Serge (1890–1947), Russian by parentage, French by adoption, one of the most literate of the early Communists and author of some twenty books. A Left oppositionist in Russia ; Paris correspondent for POUM during the Spanish civil war. In 1941 he settled in Mexico where he died impoverished.

Victor Serge
V. Paderewski
Hermosillo 19
Dep. 5
Mexico D.F.
I won't write any more now because I still feel a bit sick.

Yours
George

36. In Front of Your Nose

Many recent statements in the press have declared that it is almost,
if not quite, impossible for us to mine as much coal as we need for
home and export purposes, because of the impossibility of induc-
ing a sufficient number of miners to remain in the pits. One set of
figures which I saw last week estimated the annual "wastage" of
mine workers at 60,000 and the annual intake of new workers at
10,000. Simultaneously with this—and sometimes in the same column
of the same paper—there have been statements that it would be
undesirable to make use of Poles or Germans because this might lead
to unemployment in the coal industry. The two utterances do not
always come from the same sources, but there must certainly be
many people who are capable of holding these totally contradictory
ideas in their heads at a single moment.

  This is merely one example of a habit of mind which is extremely
widespread, and perhaps always has been. Bernard Shaw, in the
preface to *Androcles and the Lion,* cites as another example the first
chapter of the Gospel of Matthew, which starts off by establishing
the descent of Joseph, father of Jesus, from Abraham. In the first
verse, Jesus is described as "the son of David, the son of Abraham",
and the genealogy is then followed up through fifteen verses: then, in
the next verse but one, it is explained that as a matter of fact Jesus
was *not* descended from Abraham, since he was not the son of
Joseph. This, says Shaw, presents no difficulty to a religious believer,
and he names as a parallel case the rioting in the East End of London
by the partisans of the Tichborne Claimant, who declared that a
British working man was being done out of his rights.

Medically, I believe, this manner of thinking is called schizophrenia: at any rate, it is the power of holding simultaneously two beliefs which cancel out. Closely allied to it is the power of ignoring facts which are obvious and unalterable, and which will have to be faced sooner or later. It is especially in our political thinking that these vices flourish. Let me take a few sample subjects out of the hat. They have no organic connection with each other: they are merely cases, taken almost at random, of plain, unmistakable facts being shirked by people who in another part of their mind are aware of those facts.

Hong Kong. For years before the war everyone with knowledge of Far Eastern conditions knew that our position in Hong Kong was untenable and that we should lose it as soon as a major war started. This knowledge, however, was intolerable, and government after government continued to cling to Hong Kong instead of giving it back to the Chinese. Fresh troops were even pushed into it, with the certainty that they would be uselessly taken prisoner, a few weeks before the Japanese attack began. Then war came, and Hong Kong promptly fell—as everyone had known all along that it would do.

Conscription. For years before the war, nearly all enlightened people were in favour of standing up to Germany: the majority of them were also against having enough armaments to make such a stand effective. I know very well the arguments that are put forward in defence of this attitude; some of them are justified, but in the main they are simply forensic excuses. As late as 1939, the Labour Party voted against conscription, a step which probably played its part in bringing about the Russo-German Pact and certainly had a disastrous effect on morale in France. Then came 1940 and we nearly perished for lack of a large, efficient army, which we could only have had if we had introduced conscription at least three years earlier.

The Birthrate. Twenty or twenty-five years ago, contraception and enlightenment were held to be almost synonymous. To this day, the majority of people argue—the argument is variously expressed, but always boils down to more or less the same thing—that large families are impossible for economic reasons. At the same time, it is widely known that the birthrate is highest among the low-standard nations, and, in our population, highest among the worst-paid groups. It is also argued that a smaller population would mean less unemployment and more comfort for everybody, while on the other hand it is well established that a dwindling and ageing population is faced with calamitous and perhaps insoluble economic problems. Necessarily the figures are uncertain, but it is quite possible that in only seventy years our population will amount to about eleven millions, over half of whom will be Old Age Pensioners. Since, for complex reasons, most people don't want large families, the frightening facts can exist somewhere or other in their consciousness, simultaneously known and not known.

UNO. In order to have any efficacy whatever, a world organisation must be able to override big states as well as small ones. It must have power to inspect and limit armaments, which means that its officials must have access to every square inch of every country. It must also have at its disposal an armed force bigger than any other armed force and responsible only to the organisation itself. The two or three great states that really matter have never even pretended to agree to any of these conditions, and they have so arranged the constitution of UNO that their own actions cannot even be discussed. In other words, UNO's usefulness as an instrument of world peace is nil. This was just as obvious before it began functioning as it is now. Yet only a few months ago millions of well-informed people believed that it was going to be a success.

There is no use in multiplying examples. The point is that we are all capable of believing things which we *know* to be untrue, and then, when we are finally proved wrong, impudently twisting the facts so as to show that we were right. Intellectually, it is possible to carry on this process for an indefinite time: the only check on it is that sooner or later a false belief bumps up against solid reality, usually on a battlefield.

When one looks at the all-prevailing schizophrenia of democratic societies, the lies that have to be told for vote-catching purposes, the silence about major issues, the distortions of the press, it is tempting to believe that in totalitarian countries there is less humbug, more facing of the facts. There, at least, the ruling groups are not dependent on popular favour and can utter the truth crudely and brutally. Goering could say "Guns before butter", while his democratic opposite numbers had to wrap the same sentiment up in hundreds of hypocritical words.

Actually, however, the avoidance of reality is much the same everywhere, and has much the same consequences. The Russian people were taught for years that they were better off than everybody else, and propaganda posters showed Russian families sitting down to abundant meals while the proletariat of other countries starved in the gutter. Meanwhile the workers in the western countries were so much better off than those of the USSR that non-contact between Soviet citizens and outsiders had to be a guiding principle of policy. Then, as a result of the war, millions of ordinary Russians penetrated far into Europe, and when they return home the original avoidance of reality will inevitably be paid for in frictions of various kinds. The Germans and the Japanese lost the war quite largely because their rulers were unable to see facts which were plain to any dispassionate eye.

To see what is in front of one's nose needs a constant struggle. One thing that helps towards it is to keep a diary, or, at any rate, to keep some kind of record of one's opinions about important events. Otherwise, when some particularly absurd belief is exploded by events, one may simply forget that one ever held it. Political predictions are usually wrong, but even when one makes a correct one, to discover *why* one was right can be very illuminating. In general, one is only right when either wish or fear coincides with reality. If one recognises this, one cannot, of course, get rid of one's subjective feelings, but one can to some extent insulate them from one's thinking and make predictions cold-bloodedly, by the book of arithmetic. In private life most people are fairly realistic. When one is making out one's weekly budget, two and two invariably make four. Politics, on the other hand, is a sort of sub-atomic or non-Euclidean world where it is quite easy for the part to be greater than the whole or for two objects to be in the same place simultaneously. Hence the contradictions and absurdities I have chronicled above, all finally traceable to a secret belief that one's political opinions, unlike the weekly budget, will not have to be tested against solid reality.

Tribune, 22 March 1946

37. Letter to Arthur Koestler

27B Canonbury Square
Islington
London N1
31 March 1946

Dear Arthur,

I enclose a letter from the IRRC people, about whom I wrote to you before, and a copy of their bulletin. The part of it about Jennie Lee[1] and Michael Foot[2] is rather vague and I am not sure what it is he wants me to do, but I hope to see Jennie Lee tomorrow and will speak to her about it. Michael is in Teheran, I think.

I am seeing Malory Brown on Wednesday, and will tell him the Easter Conference is off. Has anyone told Michael?

I think my Jura cottage is going to be ready by May and I am arranging to send my furniture up about the end of April and then, if all is well, go up there early in May. If anything falls through I shall go somewhere else, but in any case I shall leave London and do no writing or anything of the kind for two months. I feel desperately tired and jaded. Richard is very well and active but still not talking.

I have at last got hold of a book by that scientist I spoke to you of, John Baker.[3] He is evidently one of the people we should circularise when we have a draft proposal ready. He could probably also be useful in telling us about other scientists who are not totalitarian-minded, which is important because as a body they are much more subject to totalitarian habits of thought than writers, and have more popular prestige. Humphrey[4] got Waddington,[5] who is a borderline

---

[1] Jennie Lee (1904–), MP 1929–31, 1945– , politician on the Left wing of the Labour Party, the wife of Aneurin Bevan. In 1965 she became Joint Parliamentary Under-Secretary of State, Department of Education and Science, Britain's first "Minister for the Arts".

[2] Michael Foot (1913–), politician, writer and journalist, on the extreme Left of the Labour Party. MP for Devonport 1945–55. Since 1960 MP for Ebbw Vale, the constituency held by Aneurin Bevan whose official biography he wrote and whose friend he had been. Assistant editor of *Tribune* 1937–8 and editor 1948–52 and 1955–60. One of the most able debaters in the post war House of Commons.

[3] John Randal Baker (1900–), Reader in Cytology, Oxford University. His books include *The Scientific Life*, 1942, *Science and the Planned State*, 1945, and *Principles of Biological Microtechnique*, 1958.

[4] Hugh (Humphrey) Slater (1906–58), painter, author and ex-Communist.

case, to do an article for *Polemic*, which I think was a good move, as it will appear in the same number as our opening volley against the *Modern Quarterly*.[1] Unfortunately it was a very bad article.

Love to Mamaine. It is beautiful spring weather at last and daffodils out all over the place. Each winter I find it harder and harder to believe that spring will actually come.

Yours
George

38. Politics and the English Language

Most people who bother with the matter at all would admit that the English language is in a bad way, but it is generally assumed that we cannot by conscious action do anything about it. Our civilisation is decadent, and our language—so the argument runs—must inevitably share in the general collapse. It follows that any struggle against the abuse of language is a sentimental archaism, like preferring candles to electric light or hansom cabs to aeroplanes. Underneath this lies the half-conscious belief that language is a natural growth and not an instrument which we shape for our own purposes.

Now, it is clear that the decline of a language must ultimately have political and economic causes: it is not due simply to the bad influence of this or that individual writer. But an effect can become a cause, reinforcing the original cause and producing the same effect in an intensified form, and so on indefinitely. A man may take to drink because he feels himself to be a failure, and then fail all the

---

Went to Spain as a political journalist and fought for the Republicans 1936–8, becoming Chief of Operations in the International Brigade. Edited *Polemic* 1945–7, a magazine of philosophy, psychology and aesthetics, for which Orwell wrote five long essays.

[5] C.H. Waddington (1905–), biologist, greatly interested in politics and the application of science to social ends.

[1] The *Modern Quarterly*, founded 1938, aimed at contributing to a realistic, social revaluation of the arts and sciences, devoting special attention to studies based upon the materialistic interpretation of the universe. It lapsed during the war and was revived in December 1945 with Dr John Lewis as editor. Marxist in outlook, with many eminent scientists as contributors, it attacked, among other things, what it called "persistent attempts to confuse moral issues" e.g. Orwell's "sophistries" in "Notes on Nationalism" in *Polemic*.

more completely because he drinks. It is rather the same thing that is happening to the English language. It becomes ugly and inaccurate because our thoughts are foolish, but the slovenliness of our language makes it easier for us to have foolish thoughts. The point is that the process is reversible. Modern English, especially written English, is full of bad habits which spread by imitation and which can be avoided if one is willing to take the necessary trouble. If one gets rid of these habits one can think more clearly, and to think clearly is a necessary first step towards political regeneration: so that the fight against bad English is not frivolous and is not the exclusive concern of professional writers. I will come back to this presently, and I hope that by that time the meaning of what I have said here will have become clearer. Meanwhile, here are five specimens of the English language as it is now habitually written.

These five passages have not been picked out because they are especially bad—I could have quoted far worse if I had chosen—but because they illustrate various of the mental vices from which we now suffer. They are a little below the average, but are fairly representative samples. I number them so that I can refer back to them when necessary:

1. I am not, indeed, sure whether it is not true to say that the Milton who once seemed not unlike a seventeenth-century Shelley had not become, out of an experience ever more bitter in each year, more alien (sic) to the founder of that Jesuit sect which nothing could induce him to tolerate.

Professor Harold Laski (Essay in *Freedom of Expression*).

2. Above all, we cannot play ducks and drakes with a native battery of idioms which prescribes such egregious collocations of vocables as the Basic *put up with* for *tolerate* or *put at a loss* for *bewilder*.

Professor Lancelot Hogben (*Interglossa*).

3. On the one side we have the free personality: by definition it is not neurotic, for it has neither conflict nor dream. Its desires, such as they are, are transparent, for they are just what institutional approval keeps in the forefront of consciousness; another institutional pattern would alter their number and intensity; there is little in them that is natural, irreducible, or culturally dangerous. But *on the other side*, the social bond itself is nothing

but the mutual reflection of these self-secure integrities. Recall the definition of love. Is not this the very picture of a small academic? Where is there a place in this hall of mirrors for either personality or fraternity?

Essay on psychology in *Politics* (New York).

4. All the "best people" from the gentlemen's clubs, and all the frantic Fascist captains, united in common hatred of Socialism and bestial horror of the rising tide of the mass revolutionary movement, have turned to acts of provocation, to foul incendiarism, to medieval legends of poisoned wells, to legalise their own destruction to proletarian organisations, and rouse the agitated petty-bourgeoisie to chauvinistic fervour on behalf of the fight against the revolutionary way out of the crisis.

Communist pamphlet.

5. If a new spirit *is* to be infused into this old country, there is one thorny and contentious reform which must be tackled, and that is the humanisation and galvanisation of the BBC. Timidity here will bespeak canker and atrophy of the soul. The heart of Britain may be sound and of strong beat, for instance, but the British lion's roar at present is like that of Bottom in Shakespeare's *Midsummer Night's Dream*—as gentle as any sucking dove. A virile new Britain cannot continue indefinitely to be traduced in the eyes, or rather ears, of the world by the effete languors of Langham Place, brazenly masquerading as "standard English". When the Voice of Britain is heard at nine o'clock, better far and infinitely less ludicrous to hear aitches honestly dropped than the present priggish, inflated, inhibited, school-ma'amish arch braying of blameless bashful mewing maidens!

Letter in *Tribune*.

Each of these passages has faults of its own, but, quite apart from avoidable ugliness, two qualities are common to all of them. The first is staleness of imagery: the other is lack of precision. The writer either has a meaning and cannot express it, or he inadvertently says something else, or he is almost indifferent as to whether his words mean anything or not. This mixture of vagueness and sheer incompetence is the most marked characteristic of modern English prose, and especially of any kind of political writing. As soon as certain topics are raised, the concrete melts into the abstract and no one seems able to think of turns of speech that are not hackneyed: prose consists less and less of *words* chosen for the sake of their meaning, and more of *phrases* tacked together like the sections of a pre-fabricated hen-house. I list below, with notes and examples, various of the tricks by means of which the work of prose construction is habitually dodged:

Dying metaphors. A newly invented metaphor assists thought by evoking a visual image, while on the other hand a metaphor which is technically "dead" (e.g. *iron resolution*) has in effect reverted to being an ordinary word and can generally be used without loss of vividness. But in between these two classes there is a huge dump of worn-out metaphors which have lost all evocative power and are merely used because they save people the trouble of inventing phrases for them-selves. Examples are: *Ring the changes on, take up the cudgels for, toe the line, ride roughshod over, stand shoulder to shoulder with, play into the hands of, no axe to grind, grist to the mill, fishing in troubled waters, rift within the lute, on the order of the day, Achilles' heel, swan song, hotbed.* Many of these are used without knowledge of their meaning (what is a "rift", for instance?), and incompatible metaphors are frequently mixed, a sure sign that the writer is not interested in what he is saying. Some metaphors now current have been twisted out of their original meaning without those who use them even being aware of the fact. For example, *toe the line* is sometimes written *tow the line.* Another example is *the hammer and the anvil,* now always used with the implication that the anvil gets the worst of it. In real life it is always the anvil that breaks the hammer, never the other way about: a writer who stopped to think what he was saying would be aware of this, and would avoid perverting the original phrase.

Operators, or *verbal false limbs.* These save the trouble of picking out appropriate verbs and nouns, and at the same time pad each sentence with extra syllables which give it an appearance of symmetry. Characteristic phrases are: *render inoperative, militate against, prove unacceptable, make contact with, be subjected to, give rise to, give grounds for, have the effect of, play a leading part (rôle) in, make itself felt, take effect, exhibit a tendency to, serve the purpose of,* etc etc. The keynote is the elimination of simple verbs. Instead of being a single word, such as *break, stop, spoil, mend, kill,* a verb becomes a *phrase,* made up of a noun or adjective tacked on to some general-purposes verb such as *prove, serve, form, play, render*. In addition, the passive voice is wherever possible used in preference to the active, and noun constructions are used instead of gerunds (*by examination of* instead of *by examining*). The range of verbs is further cut down by means of the *-ise* and *de-* formations, and banal statements are given an appearance of profundity by means of the *not un-* formation. Simple conjunctions and prepositions are replaced by such phrases as *with respect to, having regard to, the fact that, by dint of, in view of, in the interests of, on the hypothesis that*; and the ends of sentences are saved from anticlimax by such resounding commonplaces as *greatly to be desired, cannot be left out of account, a development to be expected in the near future, deserving of serious consideration, brought to a satisfactory conclusion,* and so on and so forth.

Pretentious diction. Words like *phenomenon, element, individual* (as noun), *objective, categorical, effective, virtual, basic, primary, promote, constitute, exhibit, exploit, utilise, eliminate, liquidate,* are used to dress up simple statements and give an air of scientific impartiality to biassed judgements. Adjectives like *epoch-making, epic, historic, unforgettable, triumphant, age-old, inevitable, inexorable, veritable,* are used to dignify the sordid processes of international politics, while writing that aims at glorifying war usually takes on an archaic colour, its characteristic words being: *realm, throne, chariot, mailed fist, trident, sword, shield, buckler, banner, jackboot, clarion.* Foreign words and expressions such as *cul de sac, ancien régime, deus ex machina, mutatis mutandis, status quo, Gleichschaltung, Weltanschauung,* are used to give an air of culture and elegance. Except for the useful abbreviations *i.e., e.g.,* and *etc,* there is no real need for any of the hundreds of foreign phrases now current in English. Bad writers, and especially scientific, political and sociological writers, are nearly always haunted by the notion that Latin or Greek words are grander than Saxon ones, and unnecessary words like *expedite, ameliorate, predict, extraneous, deracinated, clandestine, sub-aqueous* and hundreds of others constantly gain ground from their Anglo-Saxon opposite numbers.[1] The jargon peculiar to Marxist writing

[1] An interesting illustration of this is the way in which the English flower names which were in use till very recently are being ousted by Greek ones, *snapdragon* becoming *antirrhinum, forget-me-not* becoming *myosotis,* etc. It is hard to see any practical reason for this change of fashion: it is probably due to an instinctive

(*hyena, hangman, cannibal, petty bourgeois, these gentry, lacquey, flunkey, mad dog, White Guard*, etc) consists largely of words and phrases translated from Russian, German or French; but the normal way of coining a new word is to use a Latin or Greek root with the appropriate affix and, where necessary, the *-ise* formation. It is often easier to make up words of this kind (*deregionalise, impermissible, extramarital, non-fragmentatory* and so forth) than to think up the English words that will cover one's meaning. The result, in general, is an increase in slovenliness and vagueness.

Meaningless words. In certain kinds of writing, particularly in art criticism and literary criticism, it is normal to come across long passages which are almost completely lacking in meaning.[1] Words like *romantic, plastic, values, human, dead, sentimental, natural, vitality*, as used in art criticism, are strictly meaningless, in the sense that they not only do not point to any discoverable object, but are hardly even expected to do so by the reader. When one critic writes, "The outstanding features of Mr X's work is its living quality", while another writes, "The immediately striking thing about Mr X's work is its peculiar deadness", the reader accepts this as a simple difference of opinion. If words like *black* and *white* were involved, instead of the jargon words *dead* and *living*, he would see at once that language was being used in an improper way. Many political words are similarly abused. The word *Fascism* has now no meaning except in so far as it signifies "something not desirable". The words *democracy, socialism, freedom, patriotic, realistic, justice*, have each of them several different meanings which cannot be reconciled with one another. In the case of a word like *democracy*, not only is there no agreed definition, but the attempt to make one is resisted from all sides. It is almost universally felt that when we call a country democratic we are praising it: consequently the defenders of every kind of régime claim that it is a democracy, and fear that they might have to

---

turning-away from the more homely word and a vague feeling that the Greek word is scientific. [Author's footnote.]

[1] Example: "Comfort's catholicity of perception and image, strangely Whitmanesque in range, almost the exact opposite in aesthetic compulsion, continues to evoke that trembling atmospheric accumulative hinting at a cruel, an inexorably serene timelessness . . . Wrey Gardiner scores by aiming at simple bullseyes with precision. Only they are not so simple, and through this contented sadness runs more than the surface bitter-sweet of resignation." (*Poetry Quarterly.*) [Author's footnote.]

stop using the word if it were tied down to any one meaning. Words of this kind are often used in a consciously dishonest way. That is, the person who uses them has his own private definition, but allows his hearer to think he means something quite different. Statements like *Marshal Pétain was a true patriot, The Soviet press is the freest in the world, The Catholic Church is opposed to persecution,* are almost always made with intent to deceive. Other words used in variable meanings, in most cases more or less dishonestly, are: *class, totalitarian, science, progressive, reactionary, bourgeois, equality.*

Now that I have made this catalogue of swindles and perversions, let me give another example of the kind of writing that they lead to. This time it must of its nature be an imaginary one. I am going to translate a passage of good English into modern English of the worst sort. Here is a well-known verse from *Ecclesiastes*:

> I returned, and saw under the sun, that the race is not to the swift, nor the battle to the strong, neither yet bread to the wise, nor yet riches to men of understanding, nor yet favour to men of skill; but time and chance happeneth to them all.

Here it is in modern English:

> Objective consideration of contemporary phenomena compels the conclusion that success or failure in competitive activities exhibits no tendency to be commensurate with innate capacity, but that a considerable element of the unpredictable must invariably be taken into account.

This is a parody, but not a very gross one. Exhibit 3, above, for instance, contains several patches of the same kind of English. It will be seen that I have not made a full translation. The beginning and ending of the sentence follow the original meaning fairly closely, but in the middle the concrete illustrations—race, battle, bread—dissolve into the vague phrase "success or failure in competitive activities". This had to be so, because no modern writer of the kind I am discussing—no one capable of using phrases like "objective consideration of contemporary phenomena"—would ever tabulate his thoughts in that precise and detailed way. The whole tendency of modern prose is away from concreteness. Now analyse these two sentences a little more closely. The first contains 49 words but only 60 syllables, and all its words are those of everyday life. The second contains 38 words of 90 syllables: 18 of its words are from Latin roots, and one from

Greek. The first sentence contains six vivid images, and only one phrase ("time and chance") that could be called vague. The second contains not a single fresh, arresting phrase, and in spite of its 90 syllables it gives only a shortened version of the meaning contained in the first. Yet without a doubt it is the second kind of sentence that is gaining ground in modern English. I do not want to exaggerate. This kind of writing is not yet universal, and outcrops of simplicity will occur here and there in the worst-written page. Still, if you or I were told to write a few lines on the uncertainty of human fortunes, we should probably come much nearer to my imaginary sentence than to the one from *Ecclesiastes*.

As I have tried to show, modern writing at its worst does not consist in picking out words for the sake of their meaning and inventing images in order to make the meaning clearer. It consists in gumming together long strips of words which have already been set in order by someone else, and making the results presentable by sheer humbug. The attraction of this way of writing is that it is easy. It is easier—even quicker, once you have the habit—to say *In my opinion it is a not unjustifiable assumption that* than to say *I think*. If you use ready-made phrases, you not only don't have to hunt about for words; you also don't have to bother with the rhythms of your sentences, since these phrases are generally so arranged as to be more or less euphonious. When you are composing in a hurry—when you are dictating to a stenographer, for instance, or making a public speech—it is natural to fall into a pretentious, latinised style. Tags like *a consideration which we should do well to bear in mind* or *a conclusion to which all of us would readily assent* will save many a sentence from coming down with a bump. By using stale metaphors, similes and idioms, you save much mental effort, at the cost of leaving your meaning vague, not only for your reader but for yourself. This is the significance of mixed metaphors. The sole aim of a metaphor is to call up a visual image. When these images clash—as in *The Fascist octopus has sung its swan song, the jackboot is thrown into the melting-pot*—it can be taken as certain that the writer is not seeing a mental image of the objects he is naming; in other words he is not really thinking. Look again at the examples I gave at the beginning of this essay. Professor Laski (1) uses five negatives in 53 words. One of these is superfluous, making nonsense of the whole passage, and in addition there is the slip *alien* for akin, making further nonsense, and several avoidable pieces of clumsiness which increase the general

vagueness. Professor Hogben (2) plays ducks and drakes with a
battery which is able to write prescriptions, and, while disapproving
of the everyday phrase *put up with*, is unwilling to look *egregious* up
in the dictionary and see what it means. (3), if one takes an unchari-
able attitude towards it, is simply meaningless: probably one could
work out its intended meaning by reading the whole of the article in
which it occurs. In (4) the writer knows more or less what he wants to
say, but an accumulation of stale phrases chokes him like tea-leaves
blocking a sink. In (5) words and meaning have almost parted
company. People who write in this manner usually have a general
emotional meaning—they dislike one thing and want to express
solidarity with another—but they are not interested in the detail of
what they are saying. A scrupulous writer, in every sentence that he
writes, will ask himself at least four questions, thus: What am I
trying to say? What words will express it? What image or idiom will
make it clearer? Is this image fresh enough to have an effect? And he
will probably ask himself two more: Could I put it more shortly?
Have I said anything that is avoidably ugly? But you are not obliged
to go to all this trouble. You can shirk it by simply throwing your
mind open and letting the ready-made phrases come crowding in.
They will construct your sentences for you—even think your thoughts
for you, to a certain extent—and at need they will perform the important service of partially concealing your meaning even from yourself.
It is at this point that the special connection between politics and the
debasement of language becomes clear.

In our time it is broadly true that political writing is bad writing.
Where it is not true, it will generally be found that the writer is some
kind of rebel, expressing his private opinions, and not a "party line".
Orthodoxy, of whatever colour, seems to demand a lifeless, imitative
style. The political dialects to be found in pamphlets, leading articles,
manifestos, White Papers and the speeches of Under-Secretaries do,
of course, vary from party to party, but they are all alike in that one
almost never finds in them a fresh, vivid, home-made turn of speech.
When one watches some tired hack on the platform mechanically
repeating the familiar phrases—*bestial atrocities, iron heel, blood-
stained tyranny, free peoples of the world, stand shoulder to shoulder*—
one often has a curious feeling that one is not watching a live human
being but some kind of dummy: a feeling which suddenly becomes
stronger at moments when the light catches the speaker's spectacles
and turns them into blank discs which seem to have no eyes behind

them. And this is not altogether fanciful. A speaker who uses that kind of phraseology has gone some distance towards turning himself into a machine. The appropriate noises are coming out of his larynx, but his brain is not involved as it would be if he were choosing his words for himself. If the speech he is making is one that he is accustomed to make over and over again, he may be almost unconscious of what he is saying, as one is when one utters the responses in church. And this reduced state of consciousness, if not indispensable, is at any rate favourable to political conformity.

In our time, political speech and writing are largely the defence of the indefensible. Things like the continuance of British rule in India, the Russian purges and deportations, the dropping of the atom bombs on Japan, can indeed be defended, but only by arguments which are too brutal for most people to face, and which do not square with the professed aims of political parties. Thus political language has to consist largely of euphemism, question-begging and sheer cloudy vagueness. Defenceless villages are bombarded from the air, the inhabitants driven out into the countryside, the cattle machine-gunned, the huts set on fire with incendiary bullets: this is called *pacification*. Millions of peasants are robbed of their farms and sent trudging along the roads with no more than they can carry: this is called *transfer of population* or *rectification of frontiers*. People are imprisoned for years without trial, or shot in the back of the neck or sent to die of scurvy in Arctic lumber camps: this is called *elimination of unreliable elements*. Such phraseology is needed if one wants to name things without calling up mental pictures of them. Consider for instance some comfortable English professor defending Russian totalitarianism. He cannot say outright, "I believe in killing off your opponents when you can get good results by doing so". Probably, therefore, he will say something like this:

> While freely conceding that the Soviet régime exhibits certain features which the humanitarian may be inclined to deplore, we must, I think, agree that a certain curtailment of the right to political opposition is an unavoidable concomitant of transitional periods, and that the rigours which the Russian people have been called upon to undergo have been amply justified in the sphere of concrete achievement.

The inflated style is itself a kind of euphemism. A mass of Latin words falls upon the facts like soft snow, blurring the outlines and covering up all the details. The great enemy of clear language is insincerity. When there is a gap between one's real and one's declared aims, one turns as it were instinctively to long words and exhausted idioms, like a cuttlefish squirting out ink. In our age there is no such thing as "keeping out of politics". All issues are political issues, and politics itself is a mass of lies, evasions, folly, hatred and schizophrenia. When the general atmosphere is bad, language must suffer. I should expect to find—this is a guess which I have not sufficient knowledge to verify—that the German, Russian and Italian languages have all deteriorated in the last ten or fifteen years, as a result of dictatorship.

But if thought corrupts language, language can also corrupt thought. A bad usage can spread by tradition and imitation, even among people who should and do know better. The debased language that I have been discussing is in some ways very convenient. Phrases like *a not unjustifiable assumption, leaves much to be desired, would serve no good purpose, a consideration which we should do well to bear in mind,* are a continuous temptation, a packet of aspirins always at one's elbow. Look back through this essay, and for certain you will find that I have again and again committed the very faults I am protesting against. By this morning's post I have received a pamphlet dealing with conditions in Germany. The author tells me that he "felt impelled" to write it. I open it at random, and here is almost the first sentence that I see: "(The Allies) have an opportunity not only of achieving a radical transformation of Germany's social and political structure in such a way as to avoid a nationalistic reaction in Germany itself, but at the same time of laying the foundations of a co-operative and unified Europe." You see, he "feels impelled" to write—feels, presumably, that he has something new to say—and yet his words, like cavalry horses answering the bugle, group themselves automatically into the familiar dreary pattern. This invasion of one's mind by ready-made phrases (*lay the foundations, achieve a radical transformation*) can only be prevented if one is constantly on guard against them, and every such phrase anaesthetises a portion of one's brain.

I said earlier that the decadence of our language is probably curable. Those who deny this would argue, if they produced an argument at all, that language merely reflects existing social conditions, and that we cannot influence its development by any direct tinkering with words and constructions. So far as the general tone

or spirit of a language goes, this may be true, but it is not true in
detail. Silly words and expressions have often disappeared, not
through any evolutionary process but owing to the conscious action
of a minority. Two recent examples were *explore every avenue* and
leave no stone unturned, which were killed by the jeers of a few
journalists. There is a long list of fly-blown metaphors which could
similarly be got rid of if enough people would interest themselves
in the job; and it should also be possible to laugh the *not un-* formation out of existence,[1] to reduce the amount of Latin and Greek in
the average sentence, to drive out foreign phrases and strayed
scientific words, and, in general, to make pretentiousness unfashionable. But all these are minor points. The defence of the English
language implies more than this, and perhaps it is best to start by
saying what it does *not* imply.

To begin with, it has nothing to do with archaism, with the salvag-
ing of obsolete words and turns of speech, or with the setting-up of a
"standard English" which must never be departed from. On the
contrary, it is especially concerned with the scrapping of every word
or idiom which has outworn its usefulness. It has nothing to do with
correct grammar and syntax, which are of no importance so long as
one makes one's meaning clear, or with the avoidance of Ameri-
canisms, or with having what is called a "good prose style". On the
other hand it is not concerned with fake simplicity and the attempt
to make written English colloquial. Nor does it even imply in every
case preferring the Saxon word to the Latin one, though it does
imply using the fewest and shortest words that will cover one's
meaning. What is above all needed is to let the meaning choose the
word, and not the other way about. In prose, the worst thing one
can do with words is to surrender to them. When you think of a
concrete object, you think wordlessly, and then, if you want to
describe the thing you have been visualising, you probably hunt
about till you find the exact words that seem to fit it. When you think
of something abstract you are more inclined to use words from the
start, and unless you make a conscious effort to prevent it, the existing dialect will come rushing in and do the job for you, at the
expense of blurring or even changing your meaning. Probably it
is better to put off using words as long as possible and get one's

[1] One can cure oneself of the *not un-* formation by memorising this sentence:
A not unblack dog was chasing a not unsmall rabbit across a not ungreen field.
[Author's footnote.]

meaning as clear as one can through pictures or sensations. After-wards one can choose—not simply *accept*—the phrases that will best cover the meaning, and then switch round and decide what impression one's words are likely to make on another person. This last effort of the mind cuts out all stale or mixed images, all prefabricated phrases, needless repetitions, and humbug and vagueness generally. But one can often be in doubt about the effect of a word or a phrase, and one needs rules that one can rely on when instinct fails. I think the following rules will cover most cases:

i. Never use a metaphor, simile or other figure of speech which you are used to seeing in print.

ii. Never use a long word where a short one will do.

iii. If it is possible to cut a word out, always cut it out.

iv. Never use the passive where you can use the active.

v. Never use a foreign phrase, a scientific word or a jargon word if you can think of an everyday English equivalent.

vi. Break any of these rules sooner than say anything outright barbarous.

These rules sound elementary, and so they are, but they demand a deep change of attitude in anyone who has grown used to writing in the style now fashionable. One could keep all of them and still write bad English, but one could not write the kind of stuff that I quoted in those five specimens at the beginning of this article.

I have not here been considering the literary use of language, but merely language as an instrument for expressing and not for concealing or preventing thought. Stuart Chase and others have come near to claiming that all abstract words are meaningless, and have used this as a pretext for advocating a kind of political quietism. Since you don't know what Fascism is, how can you struggle against Fascism? One need not swallow such absurdities as this, but one ought to recognise that the present political chaos is connected with the decay of language, and that one can probably bring about some improvement by starting at the verbal end. If you simplify your English, you are freed from the worst follies of orthodoxy. You cannot speak any of the necessary dialects, and when you make a stupid remark its stupidity will be obvious, even to yourself. Political language—and with variations this is true of all political parties, from Conservatives to Anarchists—is designed to make lies sound truthful and murder respectable, and to give an appearance of solidity to pure wind. One cannot change this all in a moment, but one can at least change one's own habits, and from time to time one can even, if one jeers loudly enough, send some worn-out and useless phrase— some *jackboot, Achilles' heel, hotbed, melting pot, acid test, veritable inferno* or other lump of verbal refuse—into the dustbin where it belongs.

Horizon, April 1946; *Modern British Writing* ed. Denys Val Baker, 1947; SE; OR; CE

39. Letter to Philip Rahv

27B Canonbury Square
Islington
London N1
9 April 1946

Dear Rahv,

Thanks for your letter of April 4th. I note that you want the next London Letter by about May 20th, and I will despatch it early in May. I am going to drop all my journalistic work here and go to Scotland for 6 months as from about the end of April, but I haven't definitely fixed the date of leaving yet. As soon as I do I'll send you my new address, but anyway letters sent to the above would get to me.

Yes, I saw the article in *Time*, which was a bit of good luck. I have no doubt the book[1] will be subject to some boycotting, but so far as this country is concerned I have been surprised by the unfriendly reactions it *didn't* get. It is being translated into 9 languages. The most difficult to arrange was French. One publisher signed a contract and then said it was "impossible" for political reasons, others made similar answers—however, I have fixed it with a publisher who is in Monte Carlo, and thus feels a bit safer. She is a woman, Odile Pathé, and worth keeping in mind for people who have unpopular books to translate, as she seems to have courage, which is not common in France these last few years. I have no doubt what Camus said was quite true. I am told French publishers are now "commanded" by Aragon and others not to publish undesirable books (according to my information, Hemingway's *For Whom the Bell Tolls* was one

[1] *Animal Farm.*

such). The Communists have no actual jurisdiction in the matter, but it would be in their power, e.g. to set fire to a publisher's building with the connivance of the police. I don't know how long this kind of thing will go on. In England a feeling has undoubtedly been growing against the CP. In France a year ago I got the impression that hardly anyone cares a damn any longer about freedom of the press etc. The occupation seemed to me to have had a terrible crushing effect even upon people like Trotskyists: or maybe a sort of intellectual decadence had set in years before the war. The only Frenchman I met at that [time] to whom I felt I could talk freely was a man named Raimbaud, a hunchback, who was one of the editors of the little near-Trotskyist weekly *Libertés*. The queer thing is that with all this moral decay there has over the past decade or so been much more literary *talent* in France than in England, or anywhere else, I should say.

I don't know whether you have seen *Polemic*, the new bi-monthly review. In the third number I have a long article on James Burnham which I shall reprint afterwards as a pamphlet.[1] He won't like it— however, it is what I think.

Yours
Geo. Orwell

40. Some Thoughts on the Common Toad

Before the swallow, before the daffodil, and not much later than the snowdrop, the common toad salutes the coming of spring after his own fashion, which is to emerge from a hole in the ground, where he has lain buried since the previous autumn, and crawl as rapidly as possible towards the nearest suitable patch of water. Something— some kind of shudder in the earth, or perhaps merely a rise of a few degrees in the temperature—has told him that it is time to wake up: though a few toads appear to sleep the clock round and miss out a year from time to time—at any rate, I have more than once dug them up, alive and apparently well, in the middle of the summer.

At this period, after his long fast, the toad has a very spiritual look, like a strict Anglo-Catholic towards the end of Lent. His

---

[1] "Second Thoughts on James Burnham" (reprinted in this volume as "James Burnham and the Managerial Revolution") *Polemic*, May 1946. See 46.

movements are languid but purposeful, his body is shrunken, and by contrast his eyes look abnormally large. This allows one to notice, what one might not at another time, that a toad has about the most beautiful eye of any living creature. It is like gold, or more exactly it is like the golden-coloured semi-precious stone which one some-times sees in signet-rings, and which I think is called a chrysoberyl.

For a few days after getting into the water the toad concentrates on building up his strength by eating small insects. Presently he has swollen to his normal size again, and then he goes through a phase of intense sexiness. All he knows, at least if he is a male toad, is that he wants to get his arms round something, and if you offer him a stick, or even your finger, he will cling to it with surprising strength and take a long time to discover that it is not a female toad. Frequently one comes upon shapeless masses of ten or twenty toads rolling over and over in the water, one clinging to another without distinction of sex. By degrees, however, they sort themselves out into couples, with the male duly sitting on the female's back. You can now distinguish males from females, because the male is smaller, darker and sits on top, with his arms tightly clasped round the female's neck. After a day or two the spawn is laid in long strings which wind themselves in and out of the reeds and soon become invisible. A few more weeks, and the water is alive with masses of tiny tadpoles which rapidly grow larger, sprout hind-legs, then forelegs, then shed their tails: and finally, about the middle of the summer, the new generation of toads, smaller than one's thumb-nail but perfect in every particular, crawl out of the water to begin the game anew.

I mention the spawning of the toads because it is one of the pheno-mena of spring which most deeply appeal to me, and because the toad, unlike the skylark and the primrose, has never had much of a boost from the poets. But I am aware that many people do not like reptiles or amphibians, and I am not suggesting that in order to enjoy the spring you have to take an interest in toads. There are also the crocus, the missel-thrush, the cuckoo, the blackthorn, etc. The point is that the pleasures of spring are available to everybody, and cost nothing. Even in the most sordid street the coming of spring will register itself by some sign or other, if it is only a brighter blue between the chimney pots or the vivid green of an elder sprouting on a blitzed site. Indeed it is remarkable how Nature goes on existing unofficially, as it were, in the very heart of London. I have seen a kestrel flying over the Deptford gasworks, and I have heard a first-rate performance by a blackbird in the Euston Road. There must be some hundreds of thousands, it not millions, of birds living inside the four-mile radius, and if is rather a pleasing thought that none of them pays a halfpenny of rent.

As for spring, not even the narrow and gloomy streets round the Bank of England are quite able to exclude it. It comes seeping in everywhere, like one of those new poison gases which pass through all filters. The spring is commonly referred to as "a miracle", and during the past five or six years this worn-out figure of speech has taken on a new lease of life. After the sort of winters we have had to endure recently, the spring does seem miraculous, because it has become gradually harder and harder to believe that it is actually going to happen. Every February since 1940 I have found myself thinking that this time winter is going to be permanent. But Persephone, like the toads, always rises from the dead at about the same moment. Suddenly, towards the end of March, the miracle happens and the decaying slum in which I live is transfigured. Down in the square the sooty privets have turned bright green, the leaves are thickening on the chestnut trees, the daffodils are out, the wallflowers are budding, the policeman's tunic looks positively a pleasant shade of blue, the fishmonger greets this customers with a smile, and even the sparrows are quite a different colour, having felt the balminess of the air and nerved themselves to take a bath, their first since last September.

Is it wicked to take a pleasure in spring and other seasonal changes? To put it more precisely, is it politically reprehensible, while we are all groaning, or at any rate ought to be groaning, under the shackles of the capitalist system, to point out that life is frequently more worth living because of a blackbird's song, a yellow elm tree in October, or some other natural phenomenon which does not cost money and does not have what the editors of left-wing newspapers call a class angle? There is no doubt that many people think so. I know by experience that a favourable reference to "Nature" in one of my articles is liable to bring me abusive letters, and though the key-word in these letters is usually "sentimental", two ideas seem to be mixed up in them. One is that any pleasure in the actual process of life encourages a sort of political quietism. People, so the thought runs, ought to be discontented, and it is our job to multiply our wants and not simply to increase our enjoyment of the things we have already. The other idea is that this is the age of machines and that to dislike the machine, or even to want to limit its domination, is backward-looking, reactionary and slightly ridiculous. This is often backed up by the statement that a love of Nature is a foible of urbanised people who have no notion what Nature is really like. Those who really have to deal with the soil, so it is argued, do not love the soil, and do not take the faintest interest in birds or flowers, except from a strictly utilitarian point of view. To love the country one must live in the town, merely taking an occasional week-end ramble at the warmer times of year.

This last idea is demonstrably false. Medieval literature, for instance, including the popular ballads, is full of an almost Georgian enthusiasm for Nature, and the art of agricultural peoples such as the Chinese and Japanese centres always round trees, birds, flowers, rivers, mountains. The other idea seems to me to be wrong in a subtler way. Certainly we ought to be discontented, we ought not simply to find out ways of making the best of a bad job, and yet if we kill all pleasure in the actual process of life, what sort of future are we preparing for ourselves? If a man cannot enjoy the return of spring, why should he be happy in a labour-saving Utopia? What will he do with the leisure that the machine will give him? I have always suspected that if our economic and political problems are ever really solved, life will become simpler instead of more complex, and that the sort of pleasure one gets from finding the first primrose will loom larger than the sort of pleasure one gets from eating an ice to the tune of a Wurlitzer. I think that by retaining one's childhood love of such things as trees, fishes, butterflies and—to return to my first instance—toads, one makes a peaceful and decent future a little more probable, and that by preaching the doctrine that nothing is to be admired except steel and concrete, one merely makes it a little surer that human beings will have no outlet for their surplus energy except in hatred and leader worship.

At any rate, spring is here, even in London N.1, and they can't stop you enjoying it. This is a satisfying reflection. How many a time have I stood watching the toads mating, or a pair of hares having a boxing match in the young corn, and thought of all the important persons who would stop me enjoying this if they could. But luckily they can't. So long as you are not actually ill, hungry, frightened or immured in a prison or a holiday camp, spring is still spring. The atom bombs are piling up in the factories, the police are prowling through the cities, the lies are streaming from the loudspeakers, but the earth is still going round the sun, and neither the dictators nor the bureaucrats, deeply as they disapprove of the process, are able to prevent it.

Tribune, 12 April 1946; *New Republic,* 20 May 1946; SE; OR

41. Letter to Arthur Koestler

27B Canonbury Square
Islington
London N1
13 April 1946

Dear Arthur,

I return Stephen King-Hall's[1] memorial, which I read with interest.

I have passed on to David Astor[2] your suggestion that you might do two pieces a month for the *Obs[erver]*. I should think they would jump at that. I suggested to David that someone from the *Obs.* should now write to you.

As to the PEN, I have just had a routine letter from Desmond McCarthy[3] asking me to join it. He actually has the cheek to refer to that dreadful book *Freedom of Expression* which they published last year. I am going to send him a cutting of the review I did of the book at the time.[4] Even if they asked me to become something on

[1] Commander Stephen King-Hall (1893–1966), retired from the navy 1929 after a distinguished naval career. Independent-National MP 1939–44. Started the *K.-H. News Service Letter,* 1936, which became the *National News Letter* from 1941 onwards. Right-wing and outspoken, he was highly regarded as a political commentator for his individual interpretation of events. It is not known what was the subject of King-Hall's confidential circular or memorial to which Orwell refers here.

[2] The Hon. David Astor (1912–), foreign editor of the *Observer* 1946 and editor from 1948. He met Orwell at the beginning of the war and they remained friends until Orwell's death.

[3] Desmond MacCarthy (1877–1952), Kt 1951, man of letters, one of the most enlightened, delightful and generous-hearted of critics. For many years literary editor of the *New Statesman and Nation,* he later contributed weekly to the *Sunday Times.* At this time he was President of the English PEN.

[4] Orwell reviewed *Freedom and Expression* edited by Herman Ould, in *Tribune* 12 October 1945, and his essay "The Prevention of Literature" (see 16), was triggered off by it.

the Executive Committee, I *cannot* do that kind of work. It is just throwing one's time and abilities down the drain. In any case as you know I am going away for the whole summer and cutting loose from all this. Everyone keeps coming at me wanting me to lecture, to write commissioned booklets, to join this and that, etc—you don't know how I pine to get free of it all and have time to think again.

Love to Mamaine.

Yours
George

42. Letter to A.S.F. Gow

27B Canonbury Square
Islington
London N1
13 April 1946

Dear Mr Gow,[1]

It was very nice to hear from you after all this time. I heard almost simultaneously from M.D. Hill,[2] who wrote to me apropos of the *Gem* and *Magnet*,[3] and George Lyttelton, who is now editing a series for Home & Van Thal and wanted me to write something. To my sorrow I had to say no, at any rate for the time being, because I am just on the point of dropping all journalism and other casual work for six months. I may start another book during the period, but I have resolved to stop hackwork for a bit, because I have been writing three articles a week for two years and for two years previous to that had been in the BBC where I wrote enough rubbish (news commentaries and so on) to fill a shelf of books. I have become more and more like a sucked orange and I am going to get out of it and go to Scotland for six months to a place where there is no telephone and not much of a postal service.

[1] A.S.F. Gow (1886–   ), classical scholar, Assistant Master at Eton College 1914–25 and Orwell's classical tutor. A Fellow of Trinity College, Cambridge, he went to live their permanently in 1925.

[2] M.D. Hill and the Hon. George Lyttelton were two masters at Eton in Orwell's time.

[3] "Boys' Weeklies". See I, 163.

A lot has happened to me since I saw you. I am very sorry to say I lost my wife a little over a year ago, very suddenly and unexpectedly although her health had been indifferent for some time. I have a little adopted son who is now nearly 2 and was about 10 months old when his mother, i.e. my wife, died. He was 3 weeks old when we adopted him. He is a splendid child and fortunately very healthy, and is a great pleasure to me. I didn't do much in the war because I was class IV, having a disease called bronchiectasis and also a lesion in one lung which was never diagnosed when I was a boy. But actually my health has been much better the last few years thanks to M and B. The only bit of war I saw apart from blitzes and the Home Guard was being a war correspondent for a little while in Germany about the time of the collapse, which was quite interesting. I was in the Spanish war for a bit and was wounded through the neck, which paralysed one vocal cord, but this doesn't affect my voice. As you gathered I had a difficult time making a living out of writing at the start, though looking back now, and knowing what a racket literary journalism is, I see that I could have managed much better if I had known the ropes. At present the difficulty with all writers I know is that whereas it is quite easy to make a living by journalism or broadcasting, it is practically impossible to live by books. Before the war my wife and I used to live off my books, but then we lived in the country on £5 a week, which you could do then, and we didn't have a child. The last few years life has been so ghastly expensive that I find the only way I can write books is to write long essays for the magazines and then reprint them. However all this hack work I have done in the last few years has had the advantage that it gets me a new public, and when I do publish a book it sells a lot more than mine used to before the war.

You mentioned Freddie Ayer.[1] I didn't know you knew him. He is a great friend of mine. This new magazine, *Polemic*, has only made two appearances so far, but I have great hopes that it will develop into something good. Bertrand Russell is of course the chief star in the constellation. It was a bad job Bobby Longden[2] getting killed.

[1] A.J. Ayer (1910–) philosopher, whose *Language, Truth and Logic*, 1936, was a revolutionary work, being the first extensive presentation of Logical Positivism in English. He was Grote Professor of the Philosophy of Mind and Logic, London University, 1946–9; since 1959 he has been Professor of Logic at Oxford University.

[2] Robert (Bobby) Longden, a contemporary of Orwell and Connolly at Eton, had a brilliant academic career, became Headmaster of Wellington School just before the war and was killed in 1940 by a stray bomb that hit the school.

I believe Wellington became very enlightened while he was there. A boy whom you may know called Michael Meyer,[1] who was in the RAF and is now I think back at Cambridge again, was at Wellington under Bobby and has a great regard for him.

I will certainly come and see you next time I am at Cambridge, but I don't quite know when that will be. I thought of you last time I was there about 2 years ago when I was lecturing to the London School of Economics which was evacuated there. About my name. I have used the name Orwell as a pen-name for a dozen years or more, and most of the people I know call me George, but I have never actually changed my name and some people still call me Blair. It is getting to be such a nuisance that I keep meaning to change it by deed poll, but you have to go to a solicitor etc which puts me off.

Yours
Eric Blair

PS. You couldn't be expected to read all the books your ex-pupils have produced, but I wonder whether you saw my last book but one, *Animal Farm*? If not I'd be happy to send you a copy. It is very short and might amuse you.

43. Letter to Stafford Cottman

27B Canonbury Square
Islington, London N1
25 April 1946
CAN 3751

Dear Staff,[2]

It was very nice to hear from you. I didn't realise you were still in the RAF. Be sure and look me up if you're in London when I'm here (if I am the above telephone number will always get me), but I'm

---

[1] Michael Meyer (1921–), author and translator, had first met Orwell in 1943 and they became friends. At this time he was engaged on postgraduate English studies at Oxford. He went to Upsala in 1948 and has since made numerous translations of Strindberg and Ibsen.

[2] Stafford Cottman (1918–) had been a clerk in local government before he joined the ILP (Independent Labour Party) Contingent in Spain where Orwell met him in 1937. At this time he was a Sergeant in the RAF.

shortly going away for 6 months. I've been doing too much hack journalism for several years past and have decided to drop it for a bit—for two months I mean to do nothing at all, then maybe I shall start another book, but any way, no journalism until next autumn. I have written three articles a week for two years, in addition to all the bilge I had to write for the BBC for two years before that. I have given up the cottage in Hertfordshire and taken another in the island of Jura in the Hebrides, and hope to go up there about May 10th if my furniture has arrived by that time. It's in an extremely un-get-atable place, but it's a nice house and I think I can make it quite comfortable with a little trouble, and then I shall have a nice place to retire to occasionally at almost no rent. My little boy whom I think you have never seen is now nearly 2 and extremely active, which is one of the reasons why I am anxious to get out of London for the summer. He was 10 months old when Eileen died. It was an awful shame—she had been so overworked for years and in wretched health, then things just seemed to be getting better and that happened. The only good thing was that I don't think she expected anything to go wrong with the operation. She died as a result of the anaesthetic almost as soon as they gave it her. I was in France at the time, as neither of us had expected the operation to be very serious. The child I think was just too young to miss her, and he has done very well in health and everything else. I have a good housekeeper who looks after him and me.

The other day I ran into Paddy Donovan[1] in the Edgware Road. He has a job cleaning windows and he said he would ring me up, but he hasn't done so yet. He was wounded in Germany about the time of the crossing of the Rhine. Don't forget to ring me up if you're in town this coming autumn.

Yours
Eric Blair

44. A Good Word for the Vicar of Bray

Some years ago a friend took me to the little Berkshire church of which the celebrated Vicar of Bray was once the incumbent. (Actually it is a few miles from Bray, but perhaps at that time the two

---

[1] John (Paddy) Donovan (1905–), a labourer who had been Orwell's Sergeant in Spain.

livings were one.) In the churchyard there stands a magnificent yew tree which, according to a notice at its foot, was planted by no less a person than the Vicar of Bray himself. And it struck me at the time as curious that such a man should have left such a relic behind him.

The Vicar of Bray, though he was well equipped to be a leader-writer on *The Times,* could hardly be described as an admirable character. Yet, after this lapse of time, all that is left of him is a comic song and a beautiful tree, which has rested the eyes of generation after generation and must surely have outweighed any bad effects which he produced by his political quislingism.

Thibaw, the last King of Burma, was also far from being a good man. He was a drunkard, he had five hundred wives—he seems to have kept them chiefly for show, however—and when he came to the throne his first act was to decapitate seventy or eighty of his brothers. Yet he did posterity a good turn by planting the dusty streets of Mandalay with tamarind trees which cast a pleasant shade until the Japanese incendiary bombs burned them down in 1942.

The poet, James Shirley, seems to have generalised too freely when he said that "Only the actions of the just Smell sweet and blossom in their dust". Sometimes the actions of the unjust make quite a good showing after the appropriate lapse of time. When I saw the Vicar of Bray's yew tree it reminded me of something, and afterwards I got hold of a book of selections from the writings of John Aubrey and reread a pastoral poem which must have been written some time in the first half of the seventeenth century, and which was inspired by a certain Mrs Overall.

Mrs Overall was the wife of a Dean and was extensively unfaithful to him. According to Aubrey she "could scarcely denie any one", and she had "the loveliest Eies that were ever seen, but wondrous wanton". The poem (the "shepherd swaine" seems to have been somebody called Sir John Selby) starts off:

> Downe lay the Shepherd Swaine
> So sober and demure
> Wishing for his wench againe
> So bonny and so pure
> With his head on hillock lowe
> And his arms akimboe
> And all was for the losse of his
> Hye nonny nonny noe. . . .

> Sweet she was, as kind a love
> As ever fetter'd Swaine;
> Never such a daynty one
> Shall man enjoy again.
> Sett a thousand on a rowe
> I forbid that any showe
> Ever the like of her
> Hye nonny nonny noe.

As the poem proceeds through another six verses, the refrain "Hye nonny nonny noe" takes on an unmistakably obscene meaning, but it ends with the exquisite stanza:

> But gone she is the prettiest lasse
> That ever trod on plaine.
> What ever hath betide of her
> Blame not the Shepherd Swaine.
> For why? She was her owne Foe,
> And gave herself the overthrowe
> By being so franke of her
> Hye nonny nonny noe.

Mrs Overall was no more an exemplary character than the Vicar of Bray, though a more attractive one. Yet in the end all that remains of her is a poem which still gives pleasure to many people, though for some reason it never gets into the anthologies. The suffering which she presumably caused, and the misery and futility in which her own life must have ended, have been transformed into a sort of lingering fragrance like the smell of tobacco-plants on a summer evening.

But to come back to trees. The planting of a tree, especially one of the long-living hardwood trees, is a gift which you can make to posterity at almost no cost and with almost no trouble, and if the tree takes root it will far outlive the visible effect of any of your other actions, good or evil. A year or two ago I wrote a few paragraphs in *Tribune* about some sixpenny rambler roses from Woolworth's which I had planted before the war. This brought me an indignant letter from a reader who said that roses are bourgeois, but I still think that my sixpence was better spent than if it had gone on cigarettes or even on one of the excellent Fabian Research Pamphlets.

Recently, I spent a day at the cottage where I used to live, and noted with a pleased surprise—to be exact, it was a feeling of having done good unconsciously—the progress of the things I had planted nearly ten years ago. I think it is worth recording what some of them cost, just to show what you can do with a few shillings if you invest them in something that grows.

First of all there were the two ramblers from Woolworth's, and three polyantha roses, all at sixpence each. Then there were two bush roses which were part of a job lot from a nursery garden. This job lot consisted of six fruit trees, three rose bushes and two gooseberry bushes, all for ten shillings. One of the fruit trees and one of the rose bushes died, but the rest are all flourishing. The sum total is five fruit trees, seven roses and two gooseberry bushes, all for twelve and sixpence. These plants have not entailed much work, and have had nothing spent on them beyond the original amount. They never even received any manure, except what I occasionally collected in a bucket when one of the farm horses happened to have halted outside the gate.

Between them, in nine years, those seven rose bushes will have given what would add up to a hundred or a hundred and fifty months of bloom. The fruit trees, which were mere saplings when I put them in, are now just about getting in their stride. Last week one them, a plum, was a mass of blossom, and the apples looked as if they were going to do fairly well. What had originally been the weakling of the family, a Cox's Orange Pippin—it would hardly have been included in the job lot if it had been a good plant—had grown into a sturdy tree with plenty of fruit spurs on it. I maintain that it was a public-spirited action to plant that Cox, for these trees do not fruit quickly and I did not expect to stay there long. I never had an apple off it myself, but it looks as if someone else will have quite a lot. By their fruits ye shall know them, and the Cox's Orange Pippin is a good fruit to be known by. Yet I did not plant it with the conscious intention of doing anybody a good turn. I just saw the job lot going cheap and stuck the things into the ground without much preparation.

A thing which I regret, and which I will try to remedy some time, is that I have never in my life planted a walnut. Nobody does plant them nowadays—when you see a walnut it is almost invariably an old tree. If you plant a walnut you are planting it for your grand-children, and who cares a damn for his grandchildren? Nor does anybody plant a quince, a mulberry or a medlar. But these are garden trees which you can only be expected to plant if you have a patch of ground of your own. On the other hand, in any hedge or in any piece of waste ground you happen to be walking through, you can do something to remedy the appalling massacre of trees, especially oaks, ashes, elms and beeches, which has happened during the war years.

Even an apple tree is liable to live for about 100 years, so that the Cox I planted in 1936 may still be bearing fruit well into the twenty-first century. An oak or a beech may live for hundreds of years and be a pleasure to thousands or tens of thousands of people before it is finally sawn up into timber. I am not suggesting that one can discharge all one's obligations towards society by means of a private re-afforestation scheme. Still, it might not be a bad idea, every time you commit an antisocial act, to make a note of it in your diary, and then, at the appropriate season, push an acorn into the ground.

And, if even one in twenty of them came to maturity, you might do quite a lot of harm in your lifetime, and still, like the Vicar of Bray, end up as a public benefactor after all.

Tribune, 26 April 1946; SE; OR

45. Editorial to *Polemic*

The December number of the *Modern Quarterly* devotes one paragraph of its editorial to an attack upon *Polemic*, which, it seems, is guilty of "persistent attempts to confuse moral issues, to break down the distinction between right and wrong". It is perhaps of some significance that *Polemic*—and not, shall we say, *Truth*, the *Tablet* or the *Nineteenth Century and After*—is the only periodical that the Communist-controlled *Modern Quarterly* singles out for attack. But before dealing with this point, it is worth casting a glance at the moral code whose champion the *Modern Quarterly* sets out to be.

The above-quoted statement implies that there are two definite entities called "right" and "wrong", which are clearly distinguishable from one another and are of a more or less permanent nature. Without some such assumption, it has no meaning. In the next paragraph of the editorial we find the statement that "the whole basis of ethics needs re-examination"—which implies, of course, that the distinction between right and wrong is *not* obvious and unchallenge-able, and that to break it down, or to define it in a new way, may well be a duty. Later in the same number, in an essay entitled "Belief and Action", we find Professor J.D. Bernal[1] in effect claiming that almost any moral standard can and should be scrapped when political expediency demands it. Needless to say, Professor Bernal does not put it quite so plainly as that, but if his words mean anything, that is what they mean. Here is one of various passages in which his doctrine is set forth. The emphasis is ours:

> A radical change in morality is in any case required by the new social relations which men are already entering into in an organ-ised and planned society. The relative importance of different virtues are bound to be affected. Old virtues may even appear as vices and new virtues instituted (sic). Many of the basic virtues —truthfulness and good fellowship—are, of course, as old as humanity and need no changing, but *those based on excessive concern with individual rectitude need reorienting in the direction of social responsibility.*

Put in plain English, the passage emphasised means that public spirit and common decency pull in opposite directions; while the paragraph as a whole means that we must alter our conception of right and wrong from year to year, and if necessary from minute to minute. And there can be no doubt that Professor Bernal and his fellow thinkers have shown great alacrity in doing this. During the past five or six years right and wrong have changed into one another at dizzying speed, and it is even probably true that actions which were wrong at one moment have afterwards become retrospectively right, and vice versa. Thus, in 1939, the Moscow radio denounced the British naval blockade of Germany as an inhuman measure which struck at women and children, while, in 1945, those who objected to some ten million German peasants being driven out of their homes were denounced by the same radio as pro-Nazis. So that the starvation of German women and children had changed from a bad action into a good one, and probably the earlier starvation had also become good with the passage of time. We may assume that Professor Bernal was in agreement with the Moscow radio on both

[1] Professor J.D. Bernal (1901–   ), physicist and crystallographer, Marxist and author of books on science and sociology including *The Freedom of Necessity*, 1949.

occasions. Similarly, in 1945, the German invasion of Norway was a treacherous attack upon a defenceless neutral while, in 1940, it was a well-justified counter to a previous invasion by the British. One could multiply such examples indefinitely. But it is evident that from Professor Bernal's point of view any virtue can become a vice, and any vice a virtue, according to the political needs of the moment. When he makes a specific exception of "truthfulness", he is presumably actuated by mere prudence. The implication of the whole passage is that telling lies might also be a virtue. But that is not the kind of thing that it pays to put in print.

A little later in the essay we read: "Because collective action in the industrial and political field is the only effective action, it is the only virtuous action." This contains the doctrine that an action—at any rate in political and industrial affairs—is only right when it is successful. It would be unfair to take this as meaning that every action which is successful is right, but the general tone of the essay does not leave much doubt that power and virtue are inextricably mixed up in Professor Bernal's mind. Right action does not lie in obeying your conscience, or a traditional moral code: right action lies in pushing history in the direction in which it is actually going. And what is that direction? Naturally, the direction of the classless society which all decent people desire. But, though that is where we are going, it needs effort to get there. And precisely what kind of effort? Well, of course, close co-operation with the Soviet Union—which, as any Communist would and must interpret it, means subservience to the Soviet Union. Here are some bits from Professor Bernal's peroration:

> The war has been won and the world is about to enter the hard but glorious period of recovery and reconstruction. . . . The great alliance of the United Nations which has been achieved through the bitter needs of the war has now become even more important as a guarantee against future wars which might be far worse than that through which we have passed. To maintain that alliance and to guard it against its open enemies and the more subtle disseminators of mutual suspicion will require constant vigilance and continued efforts to reach ever-closer understanding. . . . To the degree to which we can see things in the same light we can go forward together in fellowship and hope.

What exactly does Professor Bernal mean by "fellowship" and

"ever-closer understanding" between Britain and the USSR? Does he mean, for instance, that independent British observers in large numbers should be allowed to travel freely through Soviet territory and send home uncensored reports? Or that Soviet citizens should be encouraged to read British newspapers, listen to the BBC and view the institutions of this country with a friendly eye? Obviously he doesn't mean that. All he can mean, therefore, is that Russian propaganda in this country should be intensified, and that critics of the Soviet régime (darkly referred to as "subtle disseminators of mutual suspicion") should be silenced. He says much the same thing in several other places in his essay. So that, if we reduce his message to its essentials, we get the following propositions:

Apart from "truthfulness and good fellowship", no quality can be definitely labelled good or bad. Any action which serves the cause of progress is virtuous.

Progress means moving towards a classless and scientifically planned society.

The quickest way to get there is to co-operate with the Soviet Union.

Co-operation with the Soviet Union means not criticising the Stalin régime.

To put it even more shortly: anything is right which furthers the aims of Russian foreign policy. Professor Bernal would probably not admit that this is what he means, but it is in effect what he is saying, though it takes him fifteen pages to do so.

A thing that is especially noticeable in Professor Bernal's article is the English, at once pompous and slovenly, in which it is written. It is not pedantic to draw attention to this, because the connection between totalitarian habits of thought and the corruption of language is an important subject which has not been sufficiently studied. Like all writers of his school, Professor Bernal has a strong tendency to drop into Latin when something unpleasant has to be said. It is worth looking again at the passage italicised in the first of the quotations given above. To say "party loyalty means doing dirt on your own conscience" would be too crude: to say "(virtues) based on excessive concern with individual rectitude need reorienting in the direction of social responsibility" comes to much the same thing, but far less courage is required in saying it. The long, vague words express the intended meaning and at the same time blur the moral squalor of what is being said. A remark that occurs in F. Anstey's *Vice Versa*, "Drastic measures is Latin for a whopping", illustrates well enough the essential principle of this style of writing. But there is another characteristic of writers friendly to totalitarianism which has been less noticed. This is a tendency to play tricks with syntax and produce unbuttoned-up or outright meaningless sentences. It will be seen that one of the sentences quoted from Professor Bernal has had to be given a "sic" to show that there is no misprint, and there are other and more extreme instances. In the *Partisan Review* for the winter of 1944, the American critic Edmund Wilson makes some interesting remarks on this subject, apropos of the film "Mission to Moccow".

"Mission to Moscow" was founded on a book by Joseph E. Davies, who had been United States ambassador in Moscow during the period of the purges. In the book he expressed grave doubts about the justice of the verdicts in the sabotage trials, whereas in the film (in which he figures as a character) he is represented as feeling no doubts whatever. By the time the film was made the USA and the USSR were allies, and part of its object was to "build up" the Russian purges as a fully-justified extermination of traitors. The first version even contained "shots" of Trotsky engaged in secret negotiations with Ribbentrop: these were afterwards cut out, perhaps in deference to the feelings of the Jewish community, or possibly because they were too like the real photographs of Ribbentrop negotiating with Stalin. Davies gave his *imprimatur* to the film, which was in effect a falsification of what he had said. Discussing this, Wilson gives some samples of Davies's prose, for the sake of the light that they probably cast on his mentality. Two extracts will do:

> The peace of Europe, if maintained, is in imminent danger of being a peace imposed by the dictators, under conditions where all of the smaller countries will speedily rush in to get under the shield of the German aegis, and under conditions where, even though there be a concert of power, as I have predicted to you two years ago, with "Hitler leading the band".

Here is Mr Davies on the subject of Eugen Onegin:

> Both the opera and the ballet were based on Pushkin's works, and the music was by the great Tchaikovsky. The opera was "Eugen Onegin", a romantic story of two young men of position whose friendship was broken up over a misunderstanding and lovers' quarrel, which resulted in a duel in which the poet was

killed. It was significant of Pushkin's own end and, oddly
enough, was written by him.

The confusion in this passage is such that it takes several minutes
to sort out the various errors. But here is Professor Bernal:

> Our British democracy, from long practice, does enable us to
> secure without coercion or bloodshed, but clumsily, far too
> slowly and with a heavy bias on ancient privilege.

What word, or phrase, is missing here? We do not know, and probably Professor Bernal does not either, but at any rate the sentence is
meaningless. And curiously enough a rather similar kind of English
turns up in the editorial:

> If science has much to teach us which we still have to learn,
> science must also be aware that it is fiercely assailed today by
> those who fear that man has power at his disposal beyond his
> moral capacity to control it. This is precisely one of those glib
> and pretentious ideas that is in need of ruthless criticism.

One non sequitur, one tautological phrase and two grammatical
errors, all in sixty words. And the writing of the editorial nowhere
rises far above this level. It is not suggested, of course, that the causes
of slovenly or meaningless writing are the same in every case. Sometimes "Freudian errors" are to blame, sometimes sheer mental
incompetence, and sometimes an instinctive feeling that clear
thought is dangerous to orthodoxy. But there does seem to be a
direct connection between acceptance of totalitarian doctrines and
the writing of bad English, and we think it important that this should
be pointed out.

To return to the *Modern Quarterly*'s attack on *Polemic*. We have
shown that Professor Bernal teaches, and the editorial seems to
endorse, the doctrine that nearly anything is right if it is politically
expedient. Why then do they simultaneously charge *Polemic* with
"confusing moral issues", as though "right" and "wrong" were fixed
entities which every decent person knows how to distinguish already?
The reason can only be that they are a little nervous about the reactions of their more tender-minded readers, and think that their real
aims should not be stated too bluntly. So, also, with their claim that
they will give a hearing to all viewpoints, or very many viewpoints:[1]

[1] Professor Bernal was asked to write for the first and second *Polemics*. He is
now invited to contribute to the next. [Author's footnote.] Professor Bernal never
wrote for *Polemic*.

There is (says the editorial) wide scope for differences of opinion within our terms of reference. A certain speculative freedom and adventurousness of presentation is not only allowable but eminently desirable. No one should be deterred by feeling that his views may shock any kind of orthodoxy, left or right, from stating his case. On the other hand, if the holiest canons seem to be unwisely and ignorantly challenged, there is always a remedy—instant and effective reply.

It would be interesting to subject this statement to a few tests. Would the *Modern Quarterly*, for instance, print a full history of the arrest and execution of Ehrlich and Alter, the Polish Socialist leaders? Would it reprint any extract from the Communist Party's "Stop the War" pamphlets of 1940? Would it publish articles by Anton Ciliga or Victor Serge? It would not. The above-quoted statement, therefore, is simply a falsehood, the aim of which is to make an impression of broad-mindedness on inexperienced readers.

The reason for the *Modern Quarterly*'s hostility to *Polemic* is not difficult to guess. *Polemic* is attacked because it upholds certain moral and intellectual values whose survival is dangerous from the totalitarian point of view. These are what is loosely called the liberal values —using the word "liberal" in its old sense of "liberty-loving". Its aim, before all else, is to defend the freedom of thought and speech that has been painfully won during the past four hundred years. It is only natural that Professor Bernal and others like him should regard this as a worse offence than the setting-up of some rival form of totalitarianism. According to Professor Bernal:

The liberal, individualistic, almost atomic philosophy started in the Renaissance and grew to full stature with the French Revolution. It is a philosophy of the "rights of man", of "liberty, equality, and fraternity", of private property, free enterprise, and free trade. We have known it in such a debased form, so unrelated to the pattern of the needs of the times, that only lip-service is paid to it, and honest but ignorant minds have preferred even the bestialities of Fascism to its unreal and useless tenets.

We have to contend here with the usual cloudy language and confusion of ideas, but if the last sentence means anything, it means that Professor Bernal considers Fascism to be slightly preferable to liberalism. Presumably the editors of the *Modern Quarterly* are in agreement with him about this. So we arrive at the old, true, and unpalatable conclusion that a Communist and a Fascist are some-what nearer to one another than either is to a democrat. As to the special accusation levelled against us, of "breaking down the distinction between right and wrong", it arose particularly out of the fact that one of our contributors objected to the disgusting gloating in the British press over the spectacle of dangling corpses. We think we have said enough to show that our real crime, in the eyes of the *Modern Quarterly*, lies in *defending* a conception of right and wrong, and of intellectual decency, which has been responsible for all true progress for centuries past, and without which the very continuance of civilised life is by no means certain.

[Unsigned]

Polemic, No. 3, May 1946

46. James Burnham and the Managerial Revolution[1]

James Burnham's book, *The Managerial Revolution*, made a considerable stir both in the United States and in this country at the time when it was published, and its main thesis has been so much discussed that a detailed exposition of it is hardly necessary. As shortly as I can summarise it, the thesis is this:

Capitalism is disappearing, but Socialism is not replacing it. What is now arising is a new kind of planned, centralised society which will be neither capitalist nor, in any accepted sense of the word, democratic. The rulers of this new society will be the people who effectively control the means of production: that is, business executives, technicians, bureaucrats and soldiers, lumped together by Burnham under the name of "managers". These people will eliminate the old capitalist class, crush the working class, and so organise society that all power and economic privilege remain in their own hands. Private property rights will be abolished, but common ownership will not be established. The new "managerial" societies will not consist of a patchwork of small, independent states, but of great super-states

---

[1] This essay was originally printed in *Polemic* under the title "Second Thoughts on James Burnham", and later reprinted as a pamphlet with the present title.

grouped round the main industrial centres in Europe, Asia, and America. These super-states will fight among themselves for possession of the remaining uncaptured portions of the earth, but will probably be unable to conquer one another completely. Internally, each society will be hierarchical, with an aristocracy of talent at the top and a mass of semi-slaves at the bottom.

In his next published book, *The Machiavellians*, Burnham elaborates and also modifies his original statement. The greater part of the book is an exposition of the theories of Machiavelli and of his modern disciples, Mosca, Michels, and Pareto: with doubtful justification, Burnham adds to these the syndicalist writer, Georges Sorel. What Burnham is mainly concerned to show is that a democratic society has never existed and, so far as we can see, never will exist. Society is of its nature oligarchical, and the power of the oligarchy always rests upon force and fraud. Burnham does not deny that "good" motives may operate in private life, but he maintains that politics consists of the struggle for power, and nothing else. All historical changes finally boil down to the replacement of one ruling class by another. All talk about democracy, liberty, equality, fraternity, all revolutionary movements, all visions of Utopia, or "the classless society", or "the Kingdom of Heaven on earth", are humbug (not necessarily conscious humbug) covering the ambitions of some new class which is elbowing its way into power. The English Puritans, the Jacobins, the Bolsheviks, were in each case simply power seekers using the hopes of the masses in order to win a privileged position for themselves. Power can sometimes be won or maintained without violence, but never without fraud, because it is necessary to make use of the masses, and the masses would not co-operate if they knew that they were simply serving the purposes of a minority. In each great revolutionary struggle the masses are led on by vague dreams of human brotherhood, and then, when the new ruling class is well established in power, they are thrust back into servitude. This is practically the whole of political history, as Burnham sees it.

Where the second book departs from the earlier one is in asserting that the whole process could be somewhat moralised if the facts were faced more honestly. *The Machiavellians* is sub-titled *Defenders of Freedom*. Machiavelli and his followers taught that in politics decency simply does not exist, and, by doing so, Burnham claims, made it possible to conduct political affairs more intelligently and less oppressively. A ruling class which recognised that its real aim was to stay in power would also recognise that it would be more likely to succeed if it served the common good, and might avoid stiffening into a hereditary aristocracy. Burnham lays much stress on Pareto's theory of the "circulation of the élites". If it is to stay in power a ruling class must constantly admit suitable recruits from below, so that the ablest men may always be at the top and a new class of power-hungry malcontents cannot come into being. This is likeliest to happen, Burnham considers, in a society which retains democratic habits—that is, where opposition is permitted and certain bodies such as the press and the trade unions can keep their autonomy. Here Burnham undoubtedly contradicts his earlier opinion. In *The Managerial Revolution*, which was written in 1940, it is taken as a matter of course that "managerial" Germany is in all ways more efficient than a capitalist democracy such as France or Britain. In the second book, written in 1942, Burnham admits that the Germans might have avoided some of their more serious strategic errors if they had permitted freedom of speech. However, the main thesis is not abandoned. Capitalism is doomed, and Socialism is a dream. If we grasp what is at issue we may guide the course of the managerial revolution to some extent, but that revolution *is happening*, whether we like it or not. In both books, but especially the earlier one, there is a note of unmistakable relish over the cruelty and wickedness of the processes that are being discussed. Although he reiterates that he is merely setting forth the facts and not stating his own preferences, it is clear that Burnham is fascinated by the spectacle of power, and that his sympathies were with Germany so long as Germany appeared to be winning the war. A more recent essay, "Lenin's Heir", published in the *Partisan Review* about the beginning of 1945, suggests that this sympathy has since been transferred to the USSR. "Lenin's Heir", which provoked violent controversy in the American left-wing press, has not yet been reprinted in England, and I must return to it later.

It will be seen that Burnham's theory is not, strictly speaking, a new one. Many earlier writers have foreseen the emergence of a new kind of society, neither capitalist nor Socialist, and probably based upon slavery: though most of them have differed from Burnham in not assuming this development to be *inevitable*. A good example is Hilaire Belloc's book, *The Servile State*, published in 1911. *The Servile State* is written in a tiresome style, and the remedy it suggests (a return to small-scale peasant ownership) is for many reasons impossible: still, it does foretell with remarkable insight the kind of things that have been happening from about 1930 onwards. Chesterton, in a less methodical way, predicted the disappearance of democracy and private property, and the rise of a slave society which might be called either capitalist or Communist. Jack London, in *The Iron Heel* (1909), foretold some of the essential features of Fascism, and such books as Wells's *The Sleeper Awakes* (1900), Zamyatin's *We* (1923), and Aldous Huxley's *Brave New World* (1930), all described imaginary worlds in which the special problems of capitalism had been solved without bringing liberty, equality, or true happiness any nearer. More recently, writers like Peter Drucker and F.A. Voigt have argued that Fascism and Communism are substantially the same thing. And indeed, it has always been obvious that a planned and centralised society is liable to develop into an oligarchy or a dictatorship. Orthodox Conservatives were unable to see this, because it comforted them to assume that Socialism "wouldn't work", and that the disappearance of capitalism would mean chaos and anarchy. Orthodox Socialists could not see it, because they wished to think that they themselves would soon be in power, and therefore assumed that when capitalism disappears, Socialism takes its place. As a result they were unable to foresee the rise of Fascism, or to make correct predictions about it after it had appeared. Later, the need to justify the Russian dictatorship and to explain away the obvious resemblances between Communism and Nazism clouded the issue still more. But the notion that industrialism must end in monopoly, and that monopoly must imply tyranny, is not a startling one.

Where Burnham differs from most other thinkers is in trying to plot the course of the "managerial revolution" accurately on a world scale, and in assuming that the drift towards totalitarianism is irresistible and must not be fought against, though it may be guided. According to Burnham, writing in 1940, "managerialism" has reached its fullest development in the USSR, but is almost equally well developed in Germany, and has made its appearance in the United States. He describes the New Deal as "primitive managerialism". But the trend is the same everywhere, or almost everywhere. Always *laissez-faire* capitalism gives way to planning and state interference, the mere *owner* loses power as against the technician and the bureaucrat, but Socialism—that is to say, what used to be called Socialism—shows no sign of emerging:

Some apologists try to excuse Marxism by saying that it has "never had a chance". This is far from the truth. Marxism and the Marxist parties have had dozens of chances. In Russia, a Marxist party took power. Within a short time it abandoned Socialism; if not in words, at any rate in the effect of its actions. In most European nations there were during the last months of the first world war and the years immediately thereafter, social crises which left a wide-open door for the Marxist parties: without exception they proved unable to take and hold power. In a large number of countries—Germany, Denmark, Norway, Sweden, Austria, England, Australia, New Zealand, Spain, France—the reformist Marxist parties have administered the governments, and have uniformly failed to introduce Socialism or make any genuine step towards Socialism. . . . These parties have, in practice, at every historical test—and there have been many—either failed Socialism or abandoned it. This is the fact which neither the bitterest foe nor the most ardent friend of Socialism can erase. This fact does not, as some think, prove anything about the moral quality of the Socialist ideal. But it does constitute unblinkable evidence that, whatever its moral quality, Socialism is not going to come.

Burnham does not, of course, deny that the new "managerial" régimes, like the régimes of Russia and Nazi Germany, may be *called* Socialist. He means merely that they will not *be* Socialist in any sense of the word which would have been accepted by Marx, or Lenin, or Keir Hardie, or William Morris, or indeed, by any representative Socialist prior to about 1930. Socialism, until recently, was supposed to connote political democracy, social equality and internationalism. There is not the smallest sign that any of these things is in a way to being established anywhere, and the one great country in which something described as a proletarian revolution once happened, i.e. the USSR, has moved steadily away from the old concept of a free and equal society aiming at universal human brotherhood. In an almost unbroken progress since the early days of the Revolution, liberty has been chipped away and representative institutions smothered, while inequalities have increased and nationalism and militarism have grown stronger. But at the same time, Burnham insists, there has been no tendency to return to capitalism. What is happening is simply the growth of "managerialism", which, according to Burnham, is in progress everywhere, though the manner in which it comes about may vary from country to country.

Now, as an interpretation of what *is happening*, Burnham's theory is extremely plausible, to put it at the lowest. The events of, at any rate, the last fifteen years in the USSR can be far more easily explained by this theory than by any other. Evidently the USSR is not Socialist, and can only be called Socialist if one gives the word a meaning different from what it would have in any other context. On the other hand, prophecies that the Russian régime would revert to capitalism have always been falsified, and now seem further than ever from being fulfilled. In claiming that the process had gone almost equally far in Nazi Germany, Burnham probably exaggerates, but it seems certain that the drift was away from old-style capitalism and towards a planned economy with an adoptive oligarchy in control. In Russia the capitalists were destroyed first and the workers were crushed later. In Germany the workers were crushed first, but the elimination of the capitalists had at any rate begun, and calculations based on the assumption that Nazism was "simply capitalism" were always contradicted by events. Where Burnham seems to go most astray is in believing "managerialism" to be on the up-grade in the United States, the one great country where free capitalism is still vigorous. But if one considers the world movement as a whole, his conclusions are difficult to resist; and even in the United States the all-prevailing faith in *laissez-faire* may not survive the next great economic crisis. It has been urged against Burnham that he assigns far too much importance to the "managers", in the narrow sense of the word—that is, factory bosses, planners and technicians—and seems to assume that even in Soviet Russia it is these people, and not the Communist Party chiefs, who are the real holders of power. However, this is a secondary error, and it is partially corrected in *The Machiavellians*. The real question is not whether the people who wipe their boots on us during the next fifty years are to be called managers, bureaucrats, or politicians: the question is whether capitalism, now obviously doomed, is to give way to oligarchy or to true democracy.

But curiously enough, when one examines the predictions which Burnham has based on his general theory, one finds that in so far as they are verifiable, they have been falsified. Numbers of people have pointed this out already. However, it is worth following up Burnham's predictions in detail, because they form a sort of pattern which

is related to contemporary events, and which reveals, I believe, a
very important weakness in present-day political thought.

To begin with, writing in 1940, Burnham takes a German victory
more or less for granted. Britain is described as "dissolving", and as
displaying "all the characteristics which have distinguished decadent
cultures in past historical transitions", while the conquest and
integration of Europe which Germany achieved in 1940 is described
as "irreversible". "England," writes Burnham, "no matter with what
non-European allies, cannot conceivably hope to conquer the
European continent." Even if Germany should somehow manage to
lose the war, she could not be dismembered or reduced to the status
of the Weimar Republic, but is bound to remain as the nucleus of a
unified Europe. The future map of the world, with its three great
super-states is, in any case, already settled in its main outlines: and
"the nuclei of these three super-states are, whatever may be their
future names, the previously existing nations, Japan, Germany, and
the United States."

Burnham also commits himself to the opinion that Germany will
not attack the USSR until after Britain has been defeated. In a
condensation of his book published in the *Partisan Review* of May-
June 1941, and presumably written later than the book itself, he says:

> As in the case of Russia, so with Germany, the third part of the
> managerial problem—the contest for dominance with other
> sections of managerial society—remains for the future. First
> had to come the death-blow that assured the toppling of the
> capitalist world order, which meant above all the destruction of
> the foundations of the British Empire (the keystone of the
> capitalist world order) both directly and through the smashing of
> the European political structure, which was a necessary prop
> of the Empire. This is the basic explanation of the Nazi-Soviet
> Pact, which is not intelligible on other grounds. The future
> conflict between Germany and Russia will be a managerial
> conflict proper; prior to the great world-managerial battles, the
> end of the capitalist order must be assured. The belief that
> Nazism is "decadent capitalism" . . . makes it impossible to
> explain reasonably the Nazi-Soviet Pact. From this belief
> followed the always expected war between Germany and
> Russia, not the actual war to the death between Germany and
> the British Empire. The war between Germany and Russia is

one of the managerial wars of the future, not of the anti-capitalist wars of yesterday and today.

However, the attack on Russia will come later, and Russia is certain, or almost certain, to be defeated. "There is every reason to believe . . . that Russia will split apart, with the western half gravitating towards the European base and the eastern towards the Asiatic." This quotation comes from *The Managerial Revolution*. In the above-quoted article, written probably about six months later, it is put more forcibly: "the Russian weaknesses indicate that Russia will not be able to endure, that it will crack apart, and fall towards east and west." And in a supplementary note which was added to the English (Pelican) edition, and which appears to have been written at the end of 1941, Burnham speaks as though the "cracking apart" process were already happening. The war, he says, "is part of the means whereby the western half of Russia is being integrated into the European super-state".

Sorting these various statements out, we have the following prophecies:

1. Germany is bound to win the war.
2. Germany and Japan are bound to survive as great states, and to remain the nuclei of power in their respective areas.
3. Germany will not attack the USSR until after the defeat of Britain.
4. The USSR is bound to be defeated.

However, Burnham has made other predictions besides these. In a short article in the *Partisan Review*, in the summer of 1944, he gives his opinion that the USSR will gang up with Japan in order to prevent the total defeat of the latter, while the American Communists will be set to work to sabotage the eastern end of the war. And finally, in an article in the same magazine in the winter of 1944–5, he claims that Russia, destined so short a while ago to "crack apart", is within sight of conquering the whole of Eurasia. This article, which was the cause of violent controversies among the American intelligentsia, has not been reprinted in England. I must give some account of it here, because its manner of approach and its emotional tone are of a peculiar kind, and by studying them one can get nearer to the real roots of Burnham's theory.

The article is entitled "Lenin's Heir", and it sets out to show that

Stalin is the true and legitimate guardian of the Russian Revolution, which he has not in any sense "betrayed" but has merely carried forward on lines that were implicit in it from the start. In itself, this is an easier opinion to swallow than the usual Trotskyist claim that Stalin is a mere crook who has perverted the Revolution to his own ends, and that things would somehow have been different if Lenin had lived or Trotsky had remained in power. Actually there is no strong reason for thinking that the main lines of development would have been very different. Well before 1923 the seeds of a totalitarian society were quite plainly there. Lenin, indeed, is one of those politicians who win an undeserved reputation by dying prematurely.[1] Had he lived, it is probable that he would either have been thrown out, like Trotsky, or would have kept himself in power by methods as barbarous, or nearly as barbarous, as those of Stalin. The *title* of Burnham's essay, therefore, sets forth a reasonable thesis, and one would expect him to support it by an appeal to the facts.

However, the essay barely touches upon its ostensible subject-matter. It is obvious that anyone genuinely concerned to show that there has been continuity of policy as between Lenin and Stalin would start by outlining Lenin's policy and then explain in what way Stalin's has resembled it. Burnham does not do this. Except for one or two cursory sentences he says nothing about Lenin's policy, and Lenin's name only occurs five times in an essay of twelve pages: in the first seven pages, apart from the title, it does not occur at all. The real aim of the essay is to present Stalin as a towering, super-human figure, indeed a species of demigod, and Bolshevism as an irresistible force which is flowing over the earth and cannot be halted until it reaches the outermost borders of Eurasia. In so far as he makes any attempt to prove his case, Burnham does so by repeating over and over again that Stalin is "a great man"—which is probably true, but is almost completely irrelevant. Moreover, though he does advance some solid arguments for believing in Stalin's genius, it is

[1] It is difficult to think of any politician who has lived to be eighty and still been regarded as a success. What we call a "great" statesman normally means one who dies before his policy has had time to take effect. If Cromwell had lived a few years longer he would probably have fallen from power, in which case we should now regard him as a failure. If Pétain had died in 1930, France would have venerated him as a hero and patriot. Napoleon remarked once that if only a cannon-ball had happened to hit him when he was riding into Moscow, he would have gone down to history as the greatest man who ever lived. [Author's footnote.]

clear that in his mind the idea of "greatness" is inextricably mixed up with the idea of cruelty and dishonesty. There are curious passages in which it seems to be suggested that Stalin is to be admired *because of* the limitless suffering that he has caused:

> Stalin proves himself a "great man", in the grand style. The accounts of the banquets, staged in Moscow for the visiting dignitaries, set the symbolic tone. With their enormous menus of sturgeon, and roasts, and fowl, and sweets; their streams of liquor; the scores of toasts with which they end; the silent, unmoving secret police behind each guest; all against the winter background of the starving multitudes of besieged Leningrad; the dying millions at the front; the jammed concentration camps; the city crowds kept by their minute rations just at the edge of life; there is little trace of dull mediocrity or the hand of Babbitt. We recognise, rather, the tradition of the most spectacular of the Tsars, of the Great Kings of the Medes and Persians, of the Khanate of the Golden Horde, of the banquet we assign to the gods of the Heroic Ages in tribute to the insight that insolence, and indifference, and brutality on such a scale remove beings from the human level. . . . Stalin's political techniques shows a freedom from conventional restrictions that is incompatible with mediocrity: the mediocre man is custom-bound. Often it is the scale of their operations that sets them apart. It is usual, for example, for men active in practical life to engineer an occasional frame-up. But to carry out a frame-up against tens of thousands of persons, important percentages of whole strata of society, including most of one's own comrades, is so far out of the ordinary that the long-run mass conclusion is either that the frame-up must be true—at least "have some truth in it"—or that power so immense must be submitted to— is a "historical necessity", as intellectuals put it. . . . There is nothing unexpected in letting a few individuals starve for reasons of state; but to starve by deliberate decision, several millions, is a type of action attributed ordinarily only to gods.

In these and other similar passages there may be a tinge of irony, but it is difficult not to feel that there is also a sort of fascinated admiration. Towards the end of the essay Burnham compares Stalin with those semi-mythical heroes, like Moses or Asoka, who embody in themselves a whole epoch, and can justly be credited with feats that they did not actually perform. In writing of Soviet foreign policy and its supposed objectives, he touches an even more mystical note:

> Starting from the magnetic core of the Eurasian heartland, the Soviet power, like the reality of the One of Neo-Platonism overflowing in the descending series of the emanative progression, flows outward, west into Europe, south into the Near East, east into China, already lapping the shores of the Atlantic, the Yellow and China Seas, the Mediterranean, and the Persian Gulf. As the undifferentiated One, in its progression, descends through the stages of Mind, Soul, and Matter, and then through its fatal Return back to itself; so does the Soviet power, emanating from the integrally totalitarian centre, proceed outwards by Absorption (the Baltics, Bessarabia, Bukovina, East Poland), Domination (Finland, the Balkans, Mongolia, North China and, tomorrow, Germany), Orienting Influence (Italy, France, Turkey, Iran, Central and south China . . .), until it is dissipated in *MH ON*, the outer material sphere, beyond the Eurasian boundaries, of momentary Appeasement and Infiltration (England, the United States).

I do not think it is fanciful to suggest that the unnecessary capital letters with which this passage is loaded are intended to have a hypnotic effect on the reader. Burnham is trying to build up a picture of terrifying, irresistible power, and to turn a normal political manoeuvre like infiltration into Infiltration adds to the general portentousness. The essay should be read in full. Although it is not the kind of tribute that the average russophile would consider acceptable, and although Burnham himself would probably claim that he is being strictly objective, he is in effect performing an act of homage, and even of self-abasement. Meanwhile, this essay gives us another prophecy to add to the list: i.e. that the USSR will conquer the whole of Eurasia, and probably a great deal more. And one must remember that Burnham's basic theory contains, in itself, a prediction which still has to be tested—that is, that whatever else happens, the "managerial" form of society is bound to prevail.

Burnham's earlier prophecy, of a Germany victory in the war and the integration of Europe round the German nucleus, was falsified, not only in its main outlines, but in some important details. Burnham insists all the way through that "managerialism" is not only more efficient than capitalist democracy or Marxian Socialism, but also more acceptable to the masses. The slogans of democracy and national self-determination, he says, no longer have any mass appeal: "managerialism", on the other hand, can rouse enthusiasm, produce intelligible war aims, establish fifth columns everywhere, and inspire its soldiers with a fanatical morale. The "fanaticism" of the Germans, as against the "apathy" or "indifference" of the British, French, etc, is much emphasised, and Nazism is represented as a revolutionary force sweeping across Europe and spreading its philosophy "by contagion". The Nazi fifth columns "cannot be wiped out", and the democratic nations are quite incapable of projecting any settlement which the German or other European masses would prefer to the New Order. In any case, the democracies can only defeat Germany if they go "still further along the managerial road than Germany has yet gone".

The germ of truth in all this is that the smaller European states, demoralised by the chaos and stagnation of the pre-war years, collapsed rather more quickly than they need have done, and might conceivably have accepted the New Order if the Germans had kept some of their promises. But the actual experience of German rule aroused almost at once such a fury of hatred and vindictiveness as the world has seldom seen. After about the beginning of 1941 there was hardly any need of a positive war aim, since getting rid of the Germans was a sufficient objective. The question of morale, and its relation to national solidarity, is a nebulous one, and the evidence can be so manipulated as to prove almost anything. But if one goes by the proportion of prisoners to other casualties, and the amount of quislingism, the totalitarian states come out of the comparison worse than the democracies. Hundreds of thousands of Russians appear to have gone over to the Germans during the course of the war, while comparable numbers of Germans and Italians had gone over to the Allies before the war started: the corresponding number of American or British renegades would have amounted to a few scores. As an example of the inability of "capitalist ideologies" to enlist support, Burnham cites "the complete failure of voluntary military recruiting in England (as well as the entire British Empire) and in the United States". One would gather from this that the armies of the totalitarian states were manned by volunteers. Actually, no totalitarian state has ever so much as considered voluntary recruitment for any purpose, nor, throughout history, has a large army ever been raised by voluntary means.[1] It is not worth listing the many similar arguments that Burnham puts forward. The point is that he assumes that the Germans must win the propaganda war as well as the military one, and that, at any rate in Europe, this estimate was not borne out by events.

It will be seen that Burnham's predictions have not merely, when they were verifiable, turned out to be wrong, but that they have sometimes contradicted one another in a sensational way. It is this last fact that is significant. Political predictions are usually wrong, because they are usually based on wish-thinking, but they can have symptomatic value, especially when they change abruptly. Often the revealing factor is the date at which they are made. Dating Burnham's various writings as accurately as can be done from internal evidence, and then noting what events they coincided with, we find the following relationships:

In *The Managerial Revolution* Burnham prophesies a German victory, postponement of the Russo-German war until after Britain is defeated, and, subsequently, the defeat of Russia. The book, or much of it, was written in the second half of 1940—i.e. at a time when the Germans had overrun western Europe and were bombing Britain, and the Russians were collaborating with them fairly closely, and in what appeared, at any rate, to be a spirit of appeasement.

In the supplementary note added to the English edition of the book, Burnham appears to assume that the USSR is already beaten and the splitting-up process is about to begin. This was published in the spring of 1942 and presumably written at the end of 1941; i.e. when the Germans were in the suburbs of Moscow.

The prediction that Russia would gang up with Japan against the USA was written early in 1944, soon after the conclusion of a new Russo-Japanese treaty.

The prophecy of Russian world conquest was written in the winter of 1944, when the Russians were advancing rapidly in eastern Europe while the Western Allies were still held up in Italy and northern France.

It will be seen that at each point Burnham is predicting *a con-*

---

[1] Great Britain raised a million volunteers in the earlier part of the 1914–18 war. This must be a world's record, but the pressures applied were such that it is doubtful whether the recruitment ought to be described as voluntary. Even the most "ideological" wars have been fought largely by pressed men. In the English civil war, the Napoleonic wars, the American civil war, the Spanish civil war, etc, both sides resorted to conscription or the press gang. [Author's footnote.]

tinuation of the thing that is happening. Now the tendency to do this
is not simply a bad habit, like inaccuracy or exaggeration, which one
can correct by taking thought. It is a major mental disease, and its
roots lie partly in cowardice and partly in the worship of power,
which is not fully separable from cowardice.

Suppose in 1940 you had taken a Gallup poll, in England, on the
question "Will Germany win the war?" You would have found,
curiously enough, that the group answering "Yes" contained a far
higher percentage of intelligent people—people with IQ of over 120,
shall we say—than the group answering "No". The same would have
held good in the middle of 1942. In this case the figures would not
have been so striking, but if you had made the question "Will the
Germans capture Alexandria?" or "Will the Japanese be able to
hold on to the territories they have captured?", then once again there
would have been a very marked tendency for intelligence to concentrate in the "Yes" group. In every case the less-gifted person
would have been likelier to give a right answer.

If one went simply by these instances, one might assume that high
intelligence and bad military judgement always go together. However, it is not so simple as that. The English intelligentsia, on the
whole, were more defeatist than the mass of the people—and some
of them went on being defeatist at a time when the war was quite
plainly won—partly because they were better able to visualise the
dreary years of warfare that lay ahead. Their morale was worse
because their imaginations were stronger. The quickest way of ending
a war is to lose it, and if one finds the prospect of a long war intolerable, it is natural to disbelieve in the possibility of victory. But there
was more to it than that. There was also the disaffection of large
numbers of intellectuals, which made it difficult for them not to side
with any country hostile to Britain. And deepest of all, there was
admiration—though only in a very few cases conscious admiration—
for the power, energy, and cruelty of the Nazi régime. It would be a
useful though tedious labour to go through the left-wing press and
enumerate all the hostile references to Nazism during the years
1935–45. One would find, I have little doubt, that they reached their
high-water mark in 1937–8 and 1944–5, and dropped off noticeably
in the years 1939–42—that is, during the period when Germany
seemed to be winning. One would find, also, the same people advocating a compromise peace in 1940 and approving the dismemberment
of Germany in 1945. And if one studied the reactions of the English

intelligentsia towards the USSR, there, too, one would find genuinely progressive impulses mixed up with admiration for power and cruelty. It would be grossly unfair to suggest that power worship is the only motive for russophile feeling, but it is one motive, and among intellectuals it is probably the strongest one.

Power worship blurs political judgement because it leads, almost unavoidably, to the belief that present trends will continue. Whoever is winning at the moment will always seem to be invincible. If the Japanese have conquered south Asia, then they will keep south Asia for ever, if the Germans have captured Tobruk, they will infallibly capture Cairo; if the Russians are in Berlin, it will not be long before they are in London: and so on. This habit of mind leads also to the belief that things will happen more quickly, completely, and cata-strophically than they ever do in practice. The rise and fall of empires, the disappearance of cultures and religions, are expected to happen with earthquake suddenness, and processes which have barely started are talked about as though they were already at an end. Burnham's writings are full of apocalyptic visions. Nations, governments, classes and social systems are constantly described as expanding, contracting, decaying, dissolving, toppling, crashing, crumbling, crystallising, and, in general, behaving in an unstable and melo-dramatic way. The slowness of historical change, the fact that any epoch always contains a great deal of the last epoch, is never suffi-ciently allowed for. Such a manner of thinking is bound to lead to mistaken prophecies, because, even when it gauges the direction of events rightly, it will miscalculate their tempo. Within the space of five years Burnham foretold the domination of Russia by Germany and of Germany by Russia. In each case he was obeying the same instinct: the instinct to bow down before the conqueror of the moment, to accept the existing trend as irreversible. With this in mind one can criticise his theory in a broader way.

The mistakes I have pointed out do not disprove Burnham's theory, but they do cast light on his probable reasons for holding it. In this connection one cannot leave out of account the fact that Burnham is an American. Every political theory has a certain regional tinge about it, and every nation, every culture, has its own charac-teristic prejudices and patches of ignorance. There are certain problems that must almost inevitably be seen in a different perspec-tive according to the geographical situation from which one is looking at them. Now, the attitude that Burnham adopts, of classifying

Communism and Fascism as much the same thing, and at the same time accepting both of them—or, at any rate, not assuming that either must be violently struggled against—is essentially an American attitude, and would be almost impossible for an Englishman or any other western European. English writers who consider Communism and Fascism to be *the same thing* invariably hold that both are monstrous evils which must be fought to the death: on the other hand, any Englishman who believes Communism and Fascism to be opposites will feel that he ought to side with one or the other.[1] The reason for this difference of outlook is simple enough and, as usual, is bound up with wish-thinking. If totalitarianism triumphs and the dreams of the geopoliticians come true, Britain will disappear as a world power and the whole of western Europe will be swallowed by some single great state. This is not a prospect that it is easy for an Englishman to contemplate with detachment. Either he does not want Britain to disappear—in which case he will tend to construct theories proving the thing that he wants—or, like a minority of intellectuals, he will decide that his country is finished and transfer his allegiance to some foreign power. An American does not have to make the same choice. Whatever happens, the United States will survive as a great power, and from the American point of view it does not make much difference whether Europe is dominated by Russia or by Germany. Most Americans who think of the matter at all would prefer to see the world divided between two or three monster states which had reached their natural boundaries and could bargain with one another on economic issues without being troubled by ideological differences. Such a world-picture fits in with the American tendency to admire size for its own sake and to feel that success constitutes justification, and it fits in with the all-prevailing anti-British sentiment. In practice, Britain and the United States have twice been forced into alliance against Germany, and will probably, before long, be forced into alliance against Russia: but, subjectively, a majority of Americans would prefer either Russia or Germany to Britain, and, as between Russia and Germany, would prefer whichever seemed stronger at the moment.[2] It is, therefore,

[1] The only exception I am able to think of is Bernard Shaw, who, for some years at any rate, declared Communism and Fascism to be much the same thing, and was in favour of both of them. But Shaw, after all, is not an Englishman, and probably does not feel his fate to be bound up with that of Britain. [Author's footnote.]

[2] As late as the autumn of 1945, a Gallup poll taken among the American

not surprising that Burnham's world-view should often be noticeably close to that of the American imperialists on the one side, or to that of the isolationists on the other. It is a "tough" or "realistic" world-view which fits in with the American form of wish-thinking. The almost open admiration for Nazi methods which Burnham shows in the earlier of his two books, and which would seem shocking to almost any English reader, depends ultimately on the fact that the Atlantic is wider than the Channel.

As I have said earlier, Burnham has probably been more right than wrong about the present and the immediate past. For quite fifty years past the general drift has almost certainly been towards oligarchy. The ever-increasing concentration of industrial and financial power; the diminishing importance of the individual capitalist or shareholder, and the growth of the new "managerial" class of scientists, technicians, and bureaucrats; the weakness of the proletariat against the centralised state; the increasing helplessness of small countries against big ones; the decay of representative institutions and the appearance of one-party régimes based on police terrorism, faked plebiscites, etc: all these things seem to point in the same direction. Burnham sees the trend and assumes that it is irresistible, rather as a rabbit fascinated by a boa constrictor might assume that a boa constrictor is the strongest thing in the world. When one looks a little deeper, one sees that all his ideas rest upon two axioms which are taken for granted in the earlier book and made partly explicit in the second one. They are:

1. Politics is essentially the same in all ages.
2. Political behaviour is different from other kinds of behaviour.

To take the second point first. In *The Machiavellians*, Burnham insists that politics is simply the struggle for power. Every great social movement, every war, every revolution, every political programme, however edifying and Utopian, really has behind it the ambitions of some sectional group which is out to grab power for itself. Power can never be restrained by any ethical or religious code, but only by other power. The nearest possible approach to altruistic

---

troops in Germany showed that 51 per cent "thought Hitler did much good before 1939". This was after five years of anti-Hitler propaganda.

The verdict, as quoted, is not very strongly favourable to Germany, but it is hard to believe that a verdict equally favourable to Britain would be given by anywhere near 51 per cent of the American army. [Author's footnote.]

behaviour is the perception by a ruling group that it will probably
stay in power longer if it behaves decently. But curiously enough,
these generalisations only apply to political behaviour, not to any
other kind of behaviour. In everyday life, as Burnham sees and
admits, one cannot explain every human action by applying the
principle of *cui bono*? Obviously, human beings have impulses which
are not selfish. Man, therefore, is an animal that can act morally
when he acts as an individual, but becomes unmoral when he acts
collectively. But even this generalisation only holds good for the
higher groups. The masses, it seems, have vague aspirations towards
liberty and human brotherhood, which are easily played upon by
power-hungry individuals or minorities. So that history consists of a
series of swindles, in which the masses are first lured into revolt by
the promise of Utopia, and then, when they have done their job,
enslaved over again by new masters.

Political activity, therefore, is a special kind of behaviour, charac-
terised by its complete unscrupulousness, and occurring only among
small groups of the population, especially among dissatisfied groups
whose talents do not get free play under the existing form of society.
The great mass of the people—and this is where (2) ties up with (1)
—will always be unpolitical. In effect, therefore, humanity is divided
into two classes: the self-seeking, hypocritical minority, and the
brainless mob whose destiny is always to be led or driven, as one gets
a pig back to the sty by kicking it on the bottom or by rattling a stick
inside a swill-bucket, according to the needs of the moment. And
this beautiful pattern is to continue for ever. Individuals may pass
from one category to another, whole classes may destroy other
classes and rise to the dominant position, but the division of humanity
into rulers and ruled is unalterable. In their capabilities, as in their
desires and needs, men are not equal. There is an "iron law of
oligarchy", which would operate even if democracy were not
impossible for mechanical reasons.

It is curious that in all his talk about the struggle for power,
Burnham never stops to ask *why* people want power. He seems to
assume that power hunger, although only dominant in comparatively few people, is a natural instinct that does not have to be
explained, like the desire for food. He also assumes that the division
of society into classes serves the same purpose in all ages. This is
practically to ignore the history of hundreds of years. When Burnham's master, Machiavelli, was writing, class divisions were not

only unavoidable, but desirable. So long as methods of production were primitive, the great mass of the people were necessarily tied down to dreary, exhausting manual labour: and a few people had to be set free from such labour, otherwise civilisation could not maintain itself, let alone make any progress. But since the arrival of the machine the whole pattern has altered. The justification for class distinctions, if there is a justification, is no longer the same, because there is no mechanical reason why the average human being should continue to be a drudge. True, drudgery persists; class distinctions are probably re-establishing themselves in a new form, and individual liberty is on the down-grade: but as these developments are now technically avoidable, they must have some psychological cause which Burnham makes no attempt to discover. The question that he ought to ask, and never does ask, is: Why does the lust for naked power become a major human motive exactly *now*, when the dominion of man over man is ceasing to be necessary? As for the claim that "human nature", or "inexorable laws" of this and that, make Socialism impossible, it is simply a projection of the past into the future. In effect, Burnham argues that because a society of free and equal human beings has never existed, it never can exist. By the same argument one could have demonstrated the impossibility of aeroplanes in 1900, or of motor cars in 1850.

The notion that the machine has altered human relationships, and that in consequence Machiavelli is out of date, is a very obvious one. If Burnham fails to deal with it, it can, I think, only be because his own power instinct leads him to brush aside any suggestion that the Machiavellian world of force, fraud, and tyranny may somehow come to an end. It is important to bear in mind what I said above: that Burnham's theory is only a variant—an American variant, and interesting because of its comprehensiveness—of the power worship now so prevalent among intellectuals. A more normal variant, at any rate in England, is Communism. If one examines the people who, having some idea of what the Russian régime is like, are strongly russophile, one finds that, on the whole, they belong to the "managerial" class of which Burnham writes. That is, they are not managers in the narrow sense, but scientists, technicians, teachers, journalists, broadcasters, bureaucrats, professional politicians: in general, middling people who feel themselves cramped by a system that is still partly aristocratic, and are hungry for more power and more prestige. These people look towards the USSR and see in it, or think they see, a system which eliminates the upper class, keeps the working class in its place, and hands unlimited power to people very similar to themselves. It was only *after* the Soviet régime became unmistakably totalitarian that English intellectuals, in large numbers, began to show an interest in it. Burnham, although the English russophile intelligentsia would repudiate him, is really voicing their secret wish: the wish to destroy the old, equalitarian version of Socialism and usher in a hierarchical society where the intellectual can at last get his hands on the whip. Burnham at least has the honesty to say that Socialism isn't coming; the others merely say that Socialism *is* coming, and then give the word "Socialism" a new meaning which makes nonsense of the old one. But his theory, for all its appearance of objectivity, is the rationalisation of a wish. There is no strong reason for thinking that it tells us anything about the future, except perhaps the immediate future. It merely tells us what kind of world the "managerial" class themselves, or at least the more conscious and ambitious members of the class, would like to live in.

Fortunately the "managers" are not so invincible as Burnham believes. It is curious how persistently, in *The Managerial Revolution*, he ignores the advantages, military as well as social, enjoyed by a democratic country. At every point the evidence is squeezed in order to show the strength, vitality, and durability of Hitler's crazy régime. Germany is expanding rapidly, and "rapid territorial expansion has always been a sign, not of decadence . . . but of renewal". Germany makes war successfully, and "the ability to make war well is never a sign of decadence but of its opposite". Germany also "inspires in millions of persons a fanatical loyalty. This, too, never accompanies decadence". Even the cruelty and dishonesty of the Nazi régime are cited in its favour, since "the young, new, rising social order is, as against the old, more likely to resort on a large scale to lies, terror, persecution". Yet, within only five years this young, new, rising social order had smashed itself to pieces and become, in Burnham's usage of the word, decadent. And this had happened quite largely because of the "managerial" (i.e. undemocratic) structure which Burnham admires. The immediate cause of the German defeat was the unheard-of folly of attacking the USSR while Britain was still undefeated and America was manifestly getting ready to fight. Mistakes of this magnitude can only be made, or at any rate they are most likely to be made, in countries where public opinion has no power. So long as the common man can get a hearing, such elementary rules as not fighting all your enemies simultaneously are less likely to be violated.

But, in any case, one should have been able to see from the start that such a movement as Nazism could not produce any good or stable result. Actually, so long as they were winning, Burnham seems to have seen nothing wrong with the methods of the Nazis. Such methods, he says, only appear wicked because they are new:

> There is no historical law that polite manners and "justice" shall conquer. In history there is always the question of *whose* manners and *whose* justice. A rising social class and a new order of society have got to break through the old moral codes just as they must break through the old economic and political institutions. Naturally, from the point of view of the old, they are monsters. If they win, they take care in due time of manners and morals.

This implies that literally anything can become right or wrong if the dominant class of the moment so wills it. It ignores the fact that certain rules of conduct have to be observed if human society is to hold together at all. Burnham, therefore, was unable to see that the crimes and follies of the Nazi régime *must* lead by one route or another to disaster. So also with his new-found admiration for Stalinism. It is too early to say in just what way the Russian régime will destroy itself. If I had to make a prophecy, I should say that a continuation of the Russian policies of the last fifteen years—and internal and external policy, of course, are merely two facets of the same thing—can only lead to a war conducted with atomic bombs, which will make Hitler's invasion look like a tea-party. But at any rate, the Russian régime will either democratise itself, or it will perish. The huge, invincible, everlasting slave empire of which Burnham appears to dream will not be established, or, if established, will not endure, because slavery is no longer a stable basis for human society.

One cannot always make positive prophecies, but there are times when one ought to be able to make negative ones. No one could have been expected to foresee the exact results of the Treaty of Versailles, but millions of thinking people could and did foresee that those results would be bad. Plenty of people, though not so many in this case, can foresee that the results of the settlement now being forced on Europe will also be bad. And to refrain from admiring Hitler or Stalin—that, too, should not require an enormous intellectual effort.

But it is partly a moral effort. That a man of Burnham's gifts should have been able for a while to think of Nazism as something rather admirable, something that could and probably would build up a workable and durable social order, shows what damage is done to the sense of reality by the cultivation of what is now called "realism".

With title "Second Thoughts on James Burnham", *Polemic*, No. 3, May 1946; SE; OR; CE; with title "James Burnham", *University Observer* (Chicago), Summer 1947; printed as a pamphlet with title "James Burnham and the Managerial Revolution" by the Socialist Book Centre, summer 1946

47. Confessions of a Book Reviewer

In a cold but stuffy bed-sitting room littered with cigarette ends and half-empty cups of tea, a man in a moth-eaten dressing-gown sits at a rickety table, trying to find room for his typewriter among the piles of dusty papers that surround it. He cannot throw the papers away because the wastepaper basket is already overflowing, and besides, somewhere among the unanswered letters and unpaid bills it is possible that there is a cheque for two guineas which he is nearly certain he forgot to pay into the bank. There are also letters with addresses which ought to be entered in his address book. He has lost his address book, and the thought of looking for it, or indeed of looking for anything, afflicts him with acute suicidal impulses.

He is a man of 35, but looks 50. He is bald, has varicose veins and wears spectacles, or would wear them if his only pair were not chronically lost. If things are normal with him he will be suffering from malnutrition, but if he has recently had a lucky streak he will be suffering from a hangover. At present it is half-past eleven in the morning, and according to his schedule he should have started work two hours ago; but even if he had made any serious effort to start he would have been frustrated by the almost continuous ringing of the telephone bell, the yells of the baby, the rattle of an electric drill out in the street, and the heavy boots of his creditors clumping up and down the stairs. The most recent interruption was the arrival of the second post, which brought him two circulars and an income-tax demand printed in red.

Needless to say this person is a writer. He might be a poet, a novelist, or a writer of film scripts or radio features, for all literary people are very much alike, but let us say that he is a book reviewer. Half hidden among the pile of papers is a bulky parcel containing five volumes which his editor has sent with a note suggesting that they "ought to go well together". They arrived four days ago, but for 48 hours the reviewer was prevented by moral paralysis from opening the parcel. Yesterday in a resolute moment he ripped the string off it and found the five volumes to be *Palestine at the Cross Roads, Scientific Dairy Farming, A Short History of European Democracy* (this one is 680 pages and weighs four pounds), *Tribal Customs in Portuguese East Africa*, and a novel, *It's Nicer Lying Down*, probably included by mistake. His review—800 words, say— has got to be "in" by midday tomorrow.

Three of these books deal with subjects of which he is so ignorant that he will have to read at least 50 pages if he is to avoid making some howler which will betray him not merely to the author (who of course knows all about the habits of book reviewers), but even to the general reader. By four in the afternoon he will have taken the books out of their wrapping paper but will still be suffering from a nervous inability to open them. The prospect of having to read them, and even the smell of the paper, affects him like the prospect of eating cold ground-rice pudding flavoured with castor oil. And yet curiously enough his copy will get to the office in time. Somehow it always does get there in time. At about nine pm his mind will grow relatively clear, and until the small hours he will sit in a room which grows colder and colder, while the cigarette smoke grows thicker and thicker, skipping expertly through one book after another and laying each down with the final comment, "God, what tripe!" In the morning, blear-eyed, surly and unshaven, he will gaze for an hour or two at a blank sheet of paper until the menacing finger of the clock frightens him into action. Then suddenly he will snap into it. All the stale old phrases—"a book that no one should miss", "something memorable on every page", "of special value are the chapters dealing with, etc etc"—will jump into their places like iron filings obeying the magnet, and the review will end up at exactly the right length and with just about three minutes to go. Meanwhile another wad of ill-assorted, unappetising books will have arrived by post. So it goes on. And yet with what high hopes this downtrodden, nerve-racked creature started his career, only a few years ago.

Do I seem to exaggerate? I ask any regular reviewer—anyone

who reviews, say, a minimum of 100 books a year—whether he can deny in honesty that his habits and character are such as I have described. Every writer, in any case, is rather that kind of person, but the prolonged, indiscriminate reviewing of books is a quite exceptionally thankless, irritating and exhausting job. It not only involves praising trash—though it does involve that, as I will show in a moment—but constantly *inventing* reactions towards books about which one has no spontaneous feelings whatever. The reviewer, jaded though he may be, is professionally interested in books, and out of the thousands that appear annually, there are probably fifty or a hundred that he would enjoy writing about. If he is a top-notcher in his profession he may get hold of ten or twenty of them: more probably he gets hold of two or three. The rest of his work, however conscientious he may be in praising or damning, is in essence humbug. He is pouring his immortal spirit down the drain, half a pint at a time.

The great majority of reviews give an inadequate or misleading account of the book that is dealt with. Since the war publishers have been less able than before to twist the tails of literary editors and evoke a paean of praise for every book that they produce, but on the other hand the standard of reviewing has gone down owing to lack of space and other inconveniences. Seeing the results, people sometimes suggest that the solution lies in getting book reviewing out of the hands of hacks. Books on specialised subjects ought to be dealt with by experts, and on the other hand a good deal of reviewing, especially of novels, might well be done by amateurs. Nearly every book is capable of arousing passionate feeling, if it is only a passionate dislike, in some or other reader, whose ideas about it would surely be worth more than those of a bored professional. But, unfortunately, as every editor knows, that kind of thing is very difficult to organise. In practice the editor always finds himself reverting to his team of hacks—his "regulars", as he calls them.

None of this is remediable so long as it is taken for granted that every book deserves to be reviewed. It is almost impossible to mention books in bulk without grossly overpraising the great majority of them. Until one has some kind of professional relationship with books one does not discover how bad the majority of them are. In much more than nine cases out of ten the only objectively truthful criticism would be "This book is worthless", while the truth about the reviewer's own reaction would probably be "This book does not interest me in any way, and I would not write about it unless I were paid to." But the public will not pay to read that kind of thing. Why should they? They want some kind of guide to the books they are asked to read, and they want some kind of evaluation. But as soon as values are mentioned, standards collapse. For if one says—and nearly every reviewer says this kind of thing at least once a week—that *King Lear* is a good play and *The Four Just Men* is a good thriller, what meaning is there in the word "good"?

The best practice, it has always seemed to me, would be simply to ignore the great majority of books and to give very long reviews— 1,000 words is a bare minimum—to the few that seem to matter. Short notes of a line or two on forthcoming books can be useful, but the usual middle-length review of about 600 words is bound to be worthless even if the reviewer genuinely wants to write it. Normally he doesn't want to write it, and the week-in, week-out production of snippets soon reduces him to the crushed figure in a dressing-gown whom I described at the beginning of this article. However, everyone in this world has someone else whom he can look down on, and I must say, from experience of both trades, that the book reviewer is better off than the film critic, who cannot even do his work at home, but has to attend trade shows at eleven in the morning and, with one or two notable exceptions, is expected to sell his honour for a glass of inferior sherry.

Tribune, 3 May 1946; *New Republic*, 5 August 1946; SE

48. London Letter to *Partisan Review*

[Early May? 1946]
Dear Editors,
It is unfortunate that in order to get this letter off in time I must write it before any definite result has emerged from the negotiations in India, and before the battle over Communist affiliation to the Labour Party is fully joined. The big masses are not alive to the importance of the Indian issue, and until something dramatic happens it will be difficult to judge what their feelings about Indian independence really are. The Communist issue arouses perceptibly

more interest. It is not yet certain whether the Communists will have
another try at affiliation, and, if they do, the move will probably be
defeated by one means or another at the forthcoming Labour Party
Conference. But, owing to the anomalies in the constitution of the
Labour Party, it is just thinkable that they might bring it off, with
disastrous results. The leaders of the Labour Party evidently regard
the danger as serious and have been denouncing the Communists in
no uncertain terms. It is a complicated issue, but I think I can make
it clearer if I first sketch in the general political background.

First of all, as to the standing of the Labour Government with the
nation as a whole. There is no question in my mind that this continues to be good, and all evidence in the form of local elections and
public opinion polls confirms this. At the same time we have as yet
had no solid advantage from the change of the Government, and
people in general are aware of this. For anyone outside the armed
forces, life since the armistice has been physically as unpleasant as it
was during the war, perhaps more so, because the effects of certain
shortages are cumulative. The clothing shortage, for instance,
becomes less and less tolerable as our clothes become more and more
completely worn out, and during last winter the fuel situation was
worse than it had been at any time during the war. Food is as dull
as ever, the queues do not get any shorter, the contrast between the
wealthy person who eats in restaurants and the housewife who has
to make do on her rations is as glaring as it always was, and every
kind of privation seems more irritating because there is no war to
justify it. Black-market activities are said to have increased since the
war stopped. Then, again, the housing situation does not improve,
and is unlikely to do so for a long time to come, and there is already
an appreciable amount of unemployment. On the other hand there
is resentment against long hours and bad working conditions, which
has shown itself in a series of "unofficial" strikes. When you listen
to the conversations in the fish queue you can hardly doubt that the
average working-class person is discontented, feels that the ending
of the war ought to have brought him more comfort and amusement,
and does not see why our loaves should be made smaller or our beer
reduced in order to prevent Europe from starving.

And yet there seems to be extraordinarily little hostile criticism on
strictly political grounds. One cannot get a true idea of the general
reaction from the British press, because the big newspapers are
mostly owned by Tories while part of the minority press is under

Communist influence. I have heard almost endless grumbling because "they" are not providing new houses quickly enough, or because "they" won't let you have enough coal to last through the winter, or because of bad travelling conditions, income tax, slowness of demobilisation, the expensiveness of vegetables, the smallness of the milk ration, and I do not know what else: but what I have not heard any ordinary person say is that the Government has not made any perceptible step towards the introduction of Socialism. Even allowing for the fact that everything takes time, it is astonishing how little change seems to have happened as yet in the structure of society. In a purely economic sense, I suppose, the drift is towards Socialism, or at least towards state ownership. Transport, for example, is being nationalised. The railway shareholders are being bought out at prices they would hardly get in the open market: still, the control of the railways is being taken out of private hands. But in the social set-up there is no symptom by which one could infer that we are not living under a Conservative government. No move has been made against the House of Lords, for example, there has been no talk of disestablishing the Church, there has been very little replacement of Tory ambassadors, service chiefs or other high officials, and if any effort is really being made to democratise education, it has borne no fruit as yet. Allowing for the general impoverishment, the upper classes are still living their accustomed life, and though they certainly dislike the Labour Government, they don't appear to be frightened of it. All this fits in with the British preference for doing things slowly and not stirring up class hatred—still, I think almost any observer would have expected a greater change in the social atmosphere when a Labour Government with a crushing majority had been in power for eight months.

But it is not on these grounds that the average person expresses discontent. In so far as they bother with politics, people still feel that they won a great victory last summer—as indeed they did—and though the deeds of the new Government are perhaps somewhat uninspiring, there is no competing ideology in sight. The Conservative Party is bankrupt of ideas, as even its own publicists admit. All it can do is to yap against "state interference" and "bureaucracy", which the ordinary person may slightly dislike but far prefers to economic insecurity. A good many Tories now believe that their best hope lies in the Communists, who might succeed in splitting the Labour Party nad forcing the right-wing Labour leaders to form another coalition. I don't myself believe that this will happen, but it is a fact that the Communists are at present the main danger to the Government, and might become a real political force if some calamity abroad—for instance, large-scale fighting in India—made the Government's foreign policy acutely unpopular.

The actual number of Communists and "fellow-travellers" is still only a few score thousands, and has no doubt dwindled over the past year. But while they have somewhat lost ground with the general public, they have now succeeded in capturing the leadership of several important unions, and in addition there is the group of "underground" Communist MPs—that is, MPs elected as Labour men but secretly members of the CP or reliably sympathetic to it. The number of these is uncertain, but I should say there are twenty or thirty of them, out of a total of something over 300 Labour MPs. Their tactic, needless to say, is to clamour inside and outside Parliament for a policy of appeasement towards the USSR, and at the same time to try to group the Left elements in the country round them by playing on domestic discontent. At present they have rather isolated themselves by making their aims too obvious, and expressions like "infiltration" and "crypto-Communist" are now being bandied about by people who had hardly heard of such things a year ago. When Bevin had a show-down with the Parliamentary Labour Party on the question of his foreign policy, only six MPs would actually vote against him, though others abstained. Considering that the USSR is and must be implacably hostile to a social democratic government of the British type, it is clear that a combination of open Communists like Arthur Horner at the head of big trade unions, "underground" Communists like Zilliacus in Parliament, and "sympathisers" like Priestley in the popular press, could be very dangerous. But the difficulty for these people is that they cannot lay their main emphasis on domestic grievances. They are tied to the defence of Russian foreign policy, which the ordinary person feels to be simply indefensible. From reading the minority left-wing press you might get the idea that the Labour Party is seething with revolt and that the rank-and-file Labour supporter is full of enthusiasm for the Russian actions in Iran, Rumania, etc, and is also pining to hand over the secrets of the atomic bomb without getting any military information in return. It is certain, however, that this is not so. The public opinion polls taken by the *News Chronicle* showed that Bevin's popularity went sensationally *up* after his battle with Vishinsky, and went up most of all among Labour Party supporters. I doubt even whether there is widespread feeling against Bevin's policies in Greece and Indonesia, in so far as these are still live issues. But as for the USSR, it is hardly denied even by russophiles that the popular enthusiasm of a year or two ago has worn very thin. If there were no other symptoms at all, I could infer this merely from my own postbag. As open apologists of the Stalin régime, the Communists are now playing on a losing wicket. And yet if they could get inside the Labour Party as an organised body, they might be able to do enormous mischief. Even the worst kind of split could hardly result in a Communist-controlled government, but it might bring back the Conservatives—which, I suppose, would be less dangerous from the Russian point of view than the spectacle of a Labour Government making a success of things.

Politically there is not much else happening. There has been some slight activity on the part of the Mosleyites and other Fascist groups, but there is no sign that they have any mass following. The intellectual struggle between Stalinists and anti-Stalinists goes on and on, with frequent sensational defections from one side or the other. Wyndham Lewis, I am credibly informed, has become a Communist or at least a strong sympathiser, and is writing a book in praise of Stalin to balance his previous books in favour of Hitler. All who bother about politics are immersed in the day-to-day struggle over Trieste, Palestine, India, Egypt, the nationalisation of steel, the American loan, rehousing, the Health Service Bill, and I do not know what else, but no thoughtful person whom I know has any hopeful picture of the future. The notion that a war between Russia and America is inevitable within the next few decades, and that Britain, in its unfavourable geographical position, is bound to be blown to pieces by atomic bombs, is accepted with a sort of vague resignation, rather as people accept the statement that sooner or later the sun will cool down and we shall all freeze to death. The general public seems to have forgotten about the atomic bomb, which seldom figures in the news. Everyone is intent on having a good time, so far as our reduced circumstances permit. Football matches are attended by enormous crowds, pubs and picture houses are always packed, and motoring has revived to a surprising extent considering that petrol is still theoretically rationed, the "basic" ration being only five gallons a month. Second-hand cars sell for fantastic prices, and extraordinary objects, some of them twenty or thirty years old, are to be seen puffing along on the roads. The forgery of petrol coupons is said to have reached such a pitch that the authorities may actually give up rationing in despair. With some difficulty you can now buy a vacuum cleaner, but I still haven't seen a refrigerator for sale, and it would be impossible to furnish a house in even the barest way without spending hundreds of pounds and having to make do with a great deal of ugly and ill-made stuff. There is still, for instance, no crockery except the hideous "utility" ware or second-hand sets at impossible prices. The general scarcity makes everyone competitive about small possessions, and when you succeed in buying something like a wrist-watch or a fountain pen you boast of it for weeks afterwards. The snob note is definitely returning to the advertisements, and in spite of the all-round shabbiness one can feel a sort of quiet pressure to make people dress in a more formal manner again. The other day when I was passing St Paul's some kind of ceremony was going on, and I was interested to see top-hats in fairly large numbers, for the first time in six years or more. But they were rather mangy-looking top-hats, and the aspect of the crowd was such that I could not tell whether the function was a wedding or a funeral.

Very little to report on the literary front. The newspapers are still at their reduced size and likely to remain so for some time to come, but there are constant rumours of the starting of two or three new evening papers and of a new weekly political review of the type of the *New Statesman* or *Tribune*. Books are as scarce and easy to sell as ever. Most of the time I can't even buy copies of my own books. Scissors-and-paste anthologies and miscellanies continue to appear in great numbers, and since I wrote to you last a whole lot more literary monthlies and quarterlies have come into being. Most of these are poor little things and unlikely to live long, but the kind of streamlined, high-powered, slickly got-up, semi-intellectual magazine which you are familiar with in the USA is now beginning to appear here also. Two recent examples are *Future* and *Contact*. Hatry, the financial wizard, who went into the book trade after he came out of prison, is said to be behind some of these new ventures. Thoughtful people watch these developments with dismay, but it is clear that you can only get a large circulation for the kind of magazine in which the letter-press exists round the edges of photographs, and which gives the average reader the feeling of being "advanced" without actually forcing him to think. It is also well known that a great part of the

British periodical press is hopelessly antiquated, and that if it does not modernise itself it may be suddenly supplanted by any magazines which the Americans may decide to start over here. The "digest" type of magazine is more and more popular, and even the Central Office of Information (previously the MOI) runs magazines of this type in numerous languages for distribution in Europe. In the BBC what may possibly turn out to be an important change is taking place. After years of struggle it has been decided to set aside one wavelength for intelligent programmes. One of the great troubles of broadcasting in this country has been that no programme is regarded as economic unless it can appeal to millions of people, and that anything in the smallest degree highbrow provokes storms of indignation from ordinary radio-users, who claim that the time they pay for is being wasted on stuff that can only appeal to a small minority. Also, as the BBC is a chartered corporation and, during the war, has been heavily subsidised by the government, it is subject to a great deal of ignorant and hostile criticism in Parliament, of which its directors are terrified. If the highbrow stuff is isolated in a separate wavelength where the average listener who keeps his radio tuned in to the Home Service for twenty-three hours a day need not be bored by it, much of the criticism will drop off and the more intelligent people inside the BBC may get a free hand. As I well know, there are in the BBC, mostly in its lower ranks, many gifted people who realise that the possibilities of radio have not yet been explored and cannot be explored unless one is content with a minority audience. However, although it is claimed that the "C" programmes (i.e. those on the separate wavelength) will be highly experimental and almost completely uncensored, the people ultimately in charge of them are still high-up permanent officials of the BBC, so it may be that no real change is contemplated.

I can't think of any more news. It is a beautiful spring, with everything in bloom very early. The railings round the parks have not been restored, but the statues are returning to their pedestals. London looks as shabby and dirty as ever, but even after an interval of a year the cessation of the black-out is still an acute pleasure.

Partisan Review, Summer 1946

49. Two Letters to the Editor of *Tribune*

[On reading Orwell's "London Letter", the previous item, Konni Zilliacus MP[1] wrote the following letter.]

A friend in the USA has sent me a copy of the *Partisan Review* (Vol XIII, No. 3, Summer, 1946), containing a "London Letter", by Mr George Orwell, in which he expresses his alarm and indignation at the damage that may be done to Mr Bevin's glorious foreign policy by the opposition of what he calls "'underground' Communist MPs —that is, MPs elected as Labour men, but secretly members of the CP or reliably sympathetic to it." Later he writes of "'underground' Communists like Zilliacus in Parliament and 'sympathisers' like Priestley in the press."

It would be a shabby thing even for a Tory to slander Labour Members of Parliament in the American press, for that indirectly traduces Parliament itself. It seems to me a quite despicable thing for Mr Orwell to do, as he is supposed to be a supporter of the Labour Party.

Since he has seen fit publicly to slander the Labour opponents of the Bevin-Churchill foreign policy in general, and myself in particular, I hope you will allow me to expose him by drawing attention to his article and asking him a few questions.

Does Mr Orwell contend that I am secretly a member of the CP, although I have the honour to be a Labour MP? I am not a member of the CP, never have been a member of the CP, and would consider it a disgraceful thing to do, to be secretly a member of any party or organisation, membership of which was not compatible with membership of the Labour Party. I am proud of the fact that I joined the Labour Party when I was demobilised after the first world war nearly 28 years ago, and have stuck to it and worked for it ever since, in good times and bad.

As for my being "reliably sympathetic" to the CP, readers of *Tribune* may remember how bitterly I denounced the CP's going into opposition against the war (also my criticism of the Soviet-German treaty of friendship and non-aggression, when I still think I was right,

[1] Konni Zilliacus (1894–1967), politician, pamphleteer and writer of some seventeen books on political subjects. Left-wing Labour MP 1945–50 and again from 1955 till his death, he was in frequent trouble with the Labour Party because of his extreme pro-Soviet attitudes.

and my strong hostility to the USSR in the Soviet-Finnish war, when
I now believe I was wrong).

Or does Mr Orwell claim that my present views on foreign policy
are inconsistent with the foreign policy on which the Labour Party
won the general election, or with my own election address and
election campaign? Because, if so, he is wrong there too. Consis-
tency is not necessarily a virtue. But it is a fact that I have been
consistent on this issue.

Or finally, is Mr Orwell trying to make out that I am in some way
dishonest in these matters, not speaking and writing on foreign
affairs—which so far as I am concerned are the medium in which I
have lived and moved and had my being for most of my adult life—
to the best of my knowledge and judgement and according to my
conscience, but with some unavowed ulterior motive? For that also
is untrue.

In short, can Mr Orwell suggest any explanation not wholly
discreditable to himself, for having uttered the silly and offensive
falsehood in an American publication that Labour MPs who feel it
their duty to oppose the Bevin-Churchill under-the-counter coalition
in foreign policy, are "secretly members of the CP"?

K. Zilliacus, MP
House of Commons

Tribune, 17 January 1947

[To which Orwell replied:]

If you strip Mr Zilliacus's letter of its abusive words ("disgraceful",
"despicable" etc), the substance of it boils down to this: that he *says*
he is not a "crypto-Communist". But of course he does! What else
could he say? A pickpocket does not go to the races wearing a label
"pickpocket" on his coat lapel, and a propagandist does not describe
himself as a propagandist. The whole effectiveness of Mr Zilliacus
and his associates depends on their *not* being branded as Communists.

I do not think Mr Zilliacus's past record is evidence. He himself
admits that he has changed some of his views, a fact which I noticed
several years ago. Nor do I care whether he has a Communist Party
ticket or any direct connection with the CP. What I believe, and will

go on believing until I see evidence to the contrary, is that he and others like him are pursuing a policy barely distinguishable from that of the CP, that they are in effect the publicity agents of the USSR in this country, and that when Soviet and British interests appear to them to clash, they will support the Soviet interest. I could not prove this in a court of law, any more than I could have proved before the war that the Catholic Church was sympathetic to Fascism. I merely infer it from the speeches, writings and other political acts of Mr Zilliacus and his group, and in particular their persistent efforts to persuade the public of this country that the puppet régimes of eastern Europe are democracies. If Mr Zilliacus is *not* "reliably sympathetic" to the CP, let him show it by his actions. This letter of his, I should say, somewhat supports my thesis. For if what I have suggested is obviously untrue, why does he get so hot and bothered about it? Recently I found myself described by an American paper as a Fascist. I did not write a letter denouncing this as a "slander", because no one whose opinion mattered would pay any attention to it. Why does not Mr Zilliacus feel himself equally able to disregard the suggestion that he himself is a "crypto"?

Mr Zilliacus misrepresents what I said in the *Partisan Review*, making it appear that I am an uncritical supporter of Bevin's foreign policy and that I look on it, and perhaps even have described it, as "glorious". Actually I made only a short mention of foreign policy in the article referred to, and the main point I was making was that if the "cryptos" succeeded in splitting the Labour Party, the beneficiaries would be the Tories. Mr Zilliacus also appears to think that it is "shabby", "despicable" and so forth to make accusations against a British MP in the press of a foreign country. Why? An MP is a public figure on whom the electorate have every right to comment, and I should have been shirking my duty in my "London Letters" to the *Partisan Review* if I had not said exactly what I thought about the leading men of this country. In his present letter Mr Zilliacus alleges a "Bevin-Churchill under-the-counter coalition". Would he hesitate to repeat this accusation in New York, or for that matter in Moscow? And if not, why should I refrain from speaking my mind about the group known as the "cryptos"? Looking back through four years of "London Letters" I find references at least equally hostile to Attlee, Churchill, Beaverbrook, Halifax, etc, but on those occasions I did not see Mr Zilliacus springing to the rescue on the ground that I was "traducing Parliament". Does he imagine that he and the little group who think like him ought to be specially exempted from criticism? Or is he under the impression that he can frighten me into silence? Let him be sure that I shall continue my efforts to counter totalitarian propaganda in this country. On the other hand, if at any time he changes his views and becomes once again a supporter of democracy, I shall probably be one of the first to notice it, and certainly I shall be very ready to acknowledge it.

George Orwell
London N1

Tribune, 17 January 1947

50. Letter to F. J. Warburg

27B Canonbury Square
Islington
London N1
4 May 1946

Dear Fred,
I am sending under separate cover on Monday Trotsky's *Life of Stalin* and Victor Serge's memoirs, which I received yesterday. I have only looked at the latter to the extent of seeing that it is an untidy manuscript, but if it is up to the extracts which were printed in *Politics* it should be a worth-while book. I thought it better to send it straight on because I might not get time to read it. I have been called out of London at rather short notice. I am sorry to say one of my sisters[1] has died unexpectedly, and I have to go up to Nottingham on Monday. However, I'll be back in London before finally leaving about next Friday, and I hope to see you and Roger[2] then.

As to the Trotsky book. I haven't read all of it, but I have read a good deal of it, mostly the bits dealing with Stalin's childhood, with the civil war and with the alleged murder of Lenin. With regard to the reason for its previous withdrawal by Harper's, an editorial note in the *Partisan Review* for March–April 1942 states:

[1] His elder sister, Marjorie Dakin.
[2] Roger Senhouse, a director of Secker & Warburg.

Three books, either critical or definitely hostile to the present régime in Russia, have been withdrawn from publication after having been publicly announced . . . also Trotsky's *Life of Stalin*. The latter book was actually sent out for review, only to be recalled a few days later (on December 12) by a note signed by President Cass Canfield which concludes, "We hope you will co-operate with us in the matter of avoiding any comment whatever regarding the biography and its postponement."

I think it is clear, especially having regard to the date (a week after the USA entered the war) that the reason for withdrawal must have been to avoid offending Russian sentiment and not, as subsequently alleged, because of objections raised by the Trotskyists. If there had been any of the latter I should have heard of them, especially as I have once or twice referred in print to the existence of this suppressed book. And in any case, if Harper's previously withdrew the book because the Trotskyists objected, why are they reissuing it now?

As to the book's intrinsic value. I should think it would be well worth publishing if you could buy sheets for say 1,000 copies and bind them up. To produce it anew would, I suppose, be very expensive and would use up a lot of paper for a rather specialised book. It seems to me that it is quite a bona fide book in the sense of being either Trotsky's own work or, in the uncompleted passages, the kind of thing that he would have said. It was unfinished when he was murdered and was completed by the translator. The earlier parts are almost completely Trotsky, but towards the end there are long passages written almost completely by the translator. Wherever it is not Trotsky this is indicated by square brackets, and one could presumably verify from Trotsky's widow and others near to him that the emendation has been done honestly. I found the earlier parts, referring to Stalin's childhood and early history as a revolutionary, particularly interesting because they demonstrate the difficulty of establishing *any* fact about a public figure who has become a subject for propaganda. I think all this part, and that referring to the civil war, successfully brings out, what can hardly be said too often, that Stalin was a secondary figure until about 1925 and the picture now presented of him as Lenin's right-hand man etc is a fabrication. The passages referring to the inner politics of the party are to me somewhat tedious, but I suppose they can have an interest for specialists. By and large I should say that the book has historical value and,

though of course it is *not* unprejudiced, is grown-up compared with
what is written about similar subjects on the other side. The whole
history of the Russian revolution has to be pieced together from
fragments lying here and there among huge mounds of lies, and the
more unofficial first-hand documents that get into print, the better.
As for the suggestion that Stalin was responsible for Lenin's death,
Trotsky does not claim to be able to prove it but merely puts it
forward as something inherently probable and presents a certain
amount of supporting evidence. It seems to me the sort of inference
that a historian ought to be allowed to draw, even if one does not
agree with it. Stalin, after all, *did* have Trotsky assassinated.

This is not the sort of book that I myself would want to read in
toto for its own sake, but I think it is the sort of book that ought to
be in print. If one were adding an introduction for the English edition,
it might be worth trying to get a little more information about the
circumstances of Trotsky's assassination, which may have been
partly decided on because of the knowledge that he was writing this
very book. There had been an earlier attempt on his life, and one
might be able to infer something from knowing the date of this. . . .

Yours
George

51. Letter to Michael Meyer

Barnhill
Isle of Jura
Argyllshire
23 May 1946

Dear Michael,
Thanks so much for your efforts. No, I haven't a licence[1] (there's no
policeman on this island!) so don't worry abt the black powder. I
made some which is not as good as commercial stuff but will do. If
you *could* get the percussion caps I'd be much obliged. Tell them the
largest size they have, i.e. something abt this size ☐.

I'm just settling in here—up to my eyes getting the house straight,
but it's a lovely house. Richard isn't coming till the end of June,

[1] To carry firearms.

because Susan has to have a minor operation & I couldn't cope with him singlehanded, so I've had to board him out. However the reports are that he is getting on well. Only difficulties at present are (a) that I can't yet get a jeep (hope to get one at the end of the month) & am having to make do with a motor bike which is hell on these roads, & (b) owing to the drought there's no water for baths, though enough to drink. However one doesn't get very dirty here. Come & stay sometime. It's not such an impossible journey (abt 48 hours from London) & there's plenty of room in this house, though of course conditions are rough.

All the best
George

52. Letter to Vernon Richards

Barnhill
Isle of Jura
Argyllshire
6 August 1946

Dear Richards,[1]
I enclose the copy of the Nunn May petition, which I have signed, not without slight misgivings. I think it is right to petition, (a) because the sentence was too long and (b) because the less spy-hunting that is indulged in the better, but I can't help feeling privately that the petition as worded doesn't state the facts quite correctly. It seems pretty clear that Nunn May's[2] motive was simply to hand over a military secret to the USSR and not to the world at large. He did not publish his information, but on the contrary handed it over secretly to an intelligence agent and, according to the evidence at the first

[1] Vernon Richards (Vero Ricchione) (1915–), Soho born, civil engineer, journalist and Anarchist. Editor of *Spain and the World* and its successor, *Revolt*, 1936–9 and frequently editor 1939–49 of *War Commentary*, afterwards *Freedom*, the Anarchist newspaper.

[2] Alan Nunn May (1911–), nuclear physicist; together with Klaus Fuchs, with whom he was employed on top-secret research, he passed information to the USSR, thereby probably considerably assisting the Russians in their development of the atom bomb. Arrested in March 1946, he was sentenced on 1 May 1946 to ten years' imprisonment.

hearing, also made a rendezvous to meet some other agent later in London. I certainly don't think he wanted or expected to be paid, but as the Russians did pay him something they evidently considered that they were simply buying a piece of information, and he must have known what kind of people he was dealing with. I should have thought the strongest point to make was the date. I forget what date it was, but didn't this happen after the war was over?

My best regards to Marie Louise.[1] I expect to be back in London in October. I have had several glorious months doing no work whatever. Richard is very well and beginning to talk a little.

Yours sincerely
Geo. Orwell

53. Letter to Celia Kirwan

Barnhill
Isle of Jura
Argyllshire
17 August 1946

Dearest Celia,[2]

How marvellous of you to get the brandy and send it off on your own initiative. I enclose cheque for £9–15–0. I hope you weren't put to any other expense about it—if so please let me know.

I forgot to say, I think one or two of the titles (of pamphlets and so on) in the Swift essay[3] are incorrect, as I was quoting them from memory, but so long as I see a galley proof it will be easy to put this right.

I am sorry you are pining away in London. It must be lousy being there at this time of year, especially if you have been having such marvellous weather as we have had here for the last week or

---

[1] Marie Louise Richards (1918–1949), daughter of the distinguished Italian Anarchist, Camillo Berneri, who was killed by the Communists in Barcelona in early May 1937; wife of Vernon Richards. She was a continuous contributor to *Spain and the World* and editor, from time to time during the 'forties, of *Freedom*.

[2] At this time Celia Kirwan was editorial assistant on *Polemic*.

[3] "Politics vs. Literature". See 57.

two. I still haven't done any work to speak of, there always seems to be so much to do of other kinds, and the journeys one makes are quite astonishing. Susan's child came up here yesterday, and I was supposed to go to Glasgow to meet her. I set out the day before yesterday morning, but punctured my motor bike on the way and thus missed the boat. I then got a lift first in a lorry, then in a car, and crossed the ferry to the next island in hopes there would be a plane to Glasgow, however the plane was full up, so I took a bus on to Port Ellen, where there would be a boat on Friday morning. Port Ellen was full to the brim owing to a cattle show, all the hotels were full up, so I slept in a cell in the police station along with a lot of other people including a married couple with a perambulator. In the morning I got the boat, picked the child up and brought her back, then we hired a car for the first 20 miles and walked the last five home. This morning I got a lift in a motor boat to where my bike was, mended the puncture and rode home—all this in 3 days. I think we are going to get a motor boat, i.e. a boat with an outboard engine, as it is the best way of travelling here when the weather is decent. At present we have only a little rowing boat which is good for fishing but which you can't go far out to sea in. We go fishing nearly every night, as we are partly dependent on fish for food, and we have also got two lobster pots and catch a certain number of lobsters and crabs. I have now learned how to tie up a lobster's claws, which you have to do if you are going to keep them alive, but it is very dangerous, especially when you have to do it in the dark. We also have to shoot rabbits when the larder gets low, and grow vegetables, though of course I haven't been here long enough to get much return from the ground yet, as it was simply a jungle when I got here. With all this you can imagine that I don't do much work— however I have actually begun my new book and hope to have done four or five chapters by the time I come back in October. I am glad Humphrey[1] has been getting on with his—I wonder how *The Heretics* sold? I saw Norman Collins[2] gave it rather a snooty review in the *Observer*.

Richard now wears real shorts, which another child had grown

[1] Hugh (Humphrey) Slater.

[2] Norman Collins (1907–), writer and journalist, author of *London Belongs To Me* (published in the United States as *Dulcimers Street*) and *Children of the Archbishop*; deputy Chairman of Victor Gollancz, 1934–41, Controller, Light Programme BBC 1946–47, at present Deputy Chairman, Associated Television.

out of, and braces, and I have got him some real farm labourer's
boots. He has to wear boots here when he goes far from the house,
because if he has shoes he is liable to take them off, and there are
snakes here. I think you would like this place. Do come any time if
you want to. But if you do, try and let me know in advance (it means
writing about a week in advance, because we only get letters twice a
week here), so that I can arrange about hiring a car. Also, don't
bring more luggage than, say, a rucksack and a haversack, but on
the other hand do bring a little flour if you can. We are nearly always
short of bread and flour here since the rationing. You don't want
many clothes so long as you have a raincoat and stout boots or
shoes. Remember the boats sail on Mondays, Wednesdays and
Fridays, and you have to leave Glasgow about 8 am. I expect to
be here till about the 10th of October.

With love
George

PS. You might ask Freddie[1] from me, now that he has a chair in
Mental Philosophy, who has the chair in non-mental philosophy.

54. The Cost of Letters

[George Orwell's answers to a questionnaire "The Cost of Letters" in
Horizon, September 1946, in which several writers were asked:

1. How much do you think a writer needs to live on?
2. Do you think a serious writer can earn this sum by his writing, and if
   so, how?
3. If not, what do you think is the most suitable second occupation for
   him?
4. Do you think literature suffers from the diversion of a writer's energy
   into other employments or is enriched by it?
5. Do you think the State or any other institution should do more for
   writers?
6. Are you satisfied with your own solution of the problem and have
   you any specific advice to give to young people who wish to earn
   their living by writing?]

---

[1] A.J. Ayer.

1. At the present purchasing value of money, I think £10 a week after payment of income tax is a minimum for a married man, and perhaps £6 a week for an unmarried man. The *best* income for a writer, I should say—again at the present value of money—is about £1,000 a year. With that he can live in reasonable comfort, free from duns and the necessity to do hack work, without having the feeling that he has definitely moved into the privileged class. I do not think one can with justice expect a writer to do his best on a working-class income. His first necessity, just as indispensable to him as are tools to a carpenter, is a comfortable, well-warmed room where he can be sure of not being interrupted; and, although this does not sound much, if one works out what it means in terms of domestic arrangements, it implies fairly large earnings. A writer's work is done at home, and if he lets it happen he will be subjected to almost constant interruption. To be protected against interruption always costs money, directly or indirectly. Then again, writers need books and periodicals in great numbers, they need space and furniture for filing papers, they spend a great deal on correspondence, they need at any rate part-time secretarial help, and most of them probably benefit by travelling, by living in what they consider sympathetic surroundings, and by eating and drinking the things they like best and by being able to take their friends out to meals or have them to stay. It all costs money. Ideally I would like to see every human being have the same income, provided that it were a fairly high income: but so long as there is to be differentiation, I think the writer's place is in the middle bracket, which means, at present standards, round about £1,000 a year.

2. No. I am told that at most a few hundred people in Great Britain earn their living solely by writing books, and most of those are probably writers of detective stories, etc. In a way it is easier for people like Ethel M. Dell to avoid prostitution than it is for a serious writer.

3. If it can be so arranged as not to take up the whole of his time, I think a writer's second occupation should be something non-literary. I suppose it would be better if it were also something congenial. But I can just imagine, for instance, a bank clerk or an insurance agent going home and doing serious work in his evenings; whereas the effort is too much to make if one has already squandered one's energies on semi-creative work such as teaching, broadcasting or composing propaganda for bodies such as the British Council.

4. Provided one's whole time and energies are not used up, I think it benefits. After all, one must make some sort of contact with the ordinary world. Otherwise, what is one to write about?

5. The only thing the State could usefully do is to divert more of the public money into buying books for the public libraries. If we are to have full Socialism, then clearly the writer must be State-supported, and ought to be placed among the better-paid groups. But so long as we have an economy like the present one, in which there is a great deal of State enterprise but also large areas of private capitalism, then the less truck a writer has with the State, or any other organised body, the better for him and his work. There are invariably strings tied to any kind of organised patronage. On the other hand, the old kind of private patronage, in which the writer is in effect the dependant of some individual rich man, is obviously undesirable. By far the best and least exacting patron is the big public. Unfortunately the British public won't at present spend money on books, although it reads more and more and its average of taste, I should say, has risen greatly in the last twenty years. At present, I believe, the average British citizen spends round about £1 a year on books, whereas he spends getting on for £25 on tobacco and alcohol combined. Via the rates and taxes he could easily be made to spend more without even knowing it—as, during the war years, he spent far more than usual on radio, owing to the subsidising of the BBC by the Treasury. If the Government could be induced simply to earmark larger sums for the purchase of books, without in the process taking over the whole book trade and turning it into a propaganda machine, I think the writer's position would be eased and literature might also benefit.

6. Personally I am satisfied, i.e. in a financial sense, because I have been lucky, at any rate during the last few years. I had to struggle desperately at the beginning, and if I had listened to what people said to me I would never have been a writer. Even until quite recently, whenever I have written anything which I took seriously, there have been strenuous efforts, sometimes by quite influential people, to keep it out of print. To a young writer who is conscious of having something in him, the only advice I can give is not to take advice. Financially, of course, there are tips I could give, but even those are of no use unless one has some kind of talent. If one simply wants to make a living by putting words on paper, then the BBC, the film companies and the like are reasonably helpful. But if one wants

to be primarily a *writer*, then, in our society, one is an animal that is tolerated but not encouraged—something rather like a house sparrow—and one gets on better if one realises one's position from the start.

Horizon, September 1946; *Current British Thought*, No. 1, 1947

55. Letter to George Woodcock

Barnhill
Isle of Jura
Argyllshire
2 September 1946

Dear George,[1]

Thanks ever so for the tea—it came just at the right moment because this week the whole of the nearest village is being brought here in lorries to get in the field of corn in front of our house, and of course tea will have to flow like water while the job is on. We have been helping the crofter who is our only neighbour with his hay and corn, at least when rain hasn't made it impossible to work. Everything is done here in an incredibly primitive way. Even when the field is ploughed with a tractor the corn is still sown broadcast, then scythed and bound up into sheaves by hand. They seem to broadcast corn, i.e. oats, all over Scotland, and I must say they seem to get it almost as even as can be done by a machine. Owing to the wet they don't get the hay in till about the end of September or even later, sometimes as late as November, and they can't leave it in the open but have to store it all in lofts. A lot of the corn doesn't quite ripen and is fed to the cattle in sheaves like hay. The crofters have to work very hard, but in many ways they are better off and more independent than a town labourer, and they would be quite comfortable if they could get a bit of help in the way of machinery, electrical power and roads, and could get the landlords off their backs and get rid of the

---

[1] George Woodcock (1912–), author, Anarchist, editor of *Now* 1940–7, at present Professor of English at the University of British Columbia and, since 1959, editor of *Canadian Literature*. After his controversy with Orwell in "Pacifism and the War" (see II, 34) they corresponded and remained friends until Orwell's death.

deer. These animals are so common on this particular island that they are an absolute curse. They eat up the pastures where there ought to be sheep, and they make fencing immensely more expensive than it need be. The crofters aren't allowed to shoot them, and are constantly having to waste their time dragging carcases of deer down from the hill during the stalking season. Everything is sacrificed to the brutes because they are an easy source of meat and therefore profitable to the people who own them. I suppose sooner or later these islands will be taken in hand, and then they could either be turned into a first-rate area for dairy produce and meat, or else they would support a large population of small peasants living off cattle and fishing. In the 18th century the population here was 10,000—now less than 300.

My love to Inge.[1] I hope to be back in London about October 13th.

Yours
Georg e

56. Letter to George Woodcock

Barnhill
Isle of Jura
Argyllshire
28 September 1946

Dear George,
I was quite stunned on hearing from you about Collet's[2] taking over the SBC.[3] How could it have happened? I thought they were doing quite well. And what happens about their publications, for instance the pamphlets they were issuing from time to time? There was one of mine[4] they published a few months back and, I don't even know how many copies it sold. It is simply calamitous if there isn't one large left-wing bookshop not under CP control. However, I shouldn't say it would be impossible to set up a successful rival, because any CP bookshop must be hampered as a shop by being unable to stock

[1] Later Mrs George Woodcock.
[2] The official Communist bookshop in London.
[3] Socialist Book Centre.
[4] "James Burnham and the Managerial Revolution". See 46.

"the wrong" kind of literature. We must talk it over when I get back. I have no idea what capital you need to set up a well-stocked book-shop but I fancy it is several thousand pounds. It is not inconceivable that one might dig the money out of some well-intentioned person like Hulton,[1] if he saw his way to not making a loss on it. The thing is to have a shop which apart from selling all the left-wing stuff is a good *bookshop*, has a lending library and is managed by someone who knows something about books. Having worked in a bookshop I have got ideas on the subject, which I'll tell you about when I get back.

Of course it's very flattering to have that article in *Politics*.[2] I haven't a copy of *Keep the Aspidistra Flying*. I picked up a copy in a second-hand shop some months back, but I gave it away. There are two or three books which I am ashamed of and have not allowed to be reprinted or translated, and that is one of them. There is an even worse one called *A Clergyman's Daughter*. This was written simply as an exercise and I oughtn't to have published it, but I was desperate for money, ditto when I wrote *Keep the A*. At that time I simply hadn't a book in me, but I was half starved and had to turn out something to bring in £100 or so.

I'm leaving here on the 9th and shall reach London on the 13th. I'll ring you up then. Love to Inge. Richard is blooming.

Yours
George

57. Politics vs. Literature: An Examination of *Gulliver's Travels*

In *Gulliver's Travels* humanity is attacked, or criticised, from at least three different angles, and the implied character of Gulliver himself necessarily changes somewhat in the process. In Part I he is the typical eighteenth-century voyager, bold, practical and unromantic, his homely outlook skilfully impressed on the reader by the biographical details at the beginning, by his age (he is a man of forty,

[1] Edward Hulton.
[2] "George Orwell, Nineteenth Century Liberal" by George Woodcock, *Politics*, December 1946.

with two children, when his adventures start), and by the inventory of the things in his pockets, especially his spectacles, which make several appearances. In Part II he has in general the same character, but at moments when the story demands it he has a tendency to develop into an imbecile who is capable of boasting of "our noble Country, the Mistress of Arts and Arms, the Scourge of France" etc etc, and at the same time of betraying every available scandalous fact about the country which he professes to love. In Part III he is much as he was in Part I, though, as he is consorting chiefly with courtiers and men of learning, one has the impression that he has risen in the social scale. In Part IV he conceives a horror of the human race which is not apparent, or only intermittently apparent, in the earlier books, and changes into a sort of unreligious anchorite whose one desire is to live in some desolate spot where he can devote himself to meditating on the goodness of the Houyhnhnms. However, these inconsistencies are forced upon Swift by the fact that Gulliver is there chiefly to provide a contrast. It is necessary, for instance, that he should appear sensible in Part I and at least intermittently silly in Part II, because in both books the essential manoeuvre is the same, i.e. to make the human being look ridiculous by imagining him as a creature six inches high. Whenever Gulliver is not acting as a stooge there is a sort of continuity in his character, which comes out especially in his resourcefulness and his observation of physical detail. He is much the same kind of person, with the same prose style, when he bears off the warships of Blefuscu, when he rips open the belly of the monstrous rat, and when he sails away upon the ocean in his frail coracle made from the skins of Yahoos. Moreover, it is difficult not to feel that in his shrewder moments Gulliver is simply Swift himself, and there is at least one incident in which Swift seems to be venting his private grievance against contemporary society. It will be remembered that when the Emperor of Lilliput's palace catches fire, Gulliver puts it out by urinating on it. Instead of being congratulated on his presence of mind, he finds that he has committed a capital offence by making water in the precincts of the palace, and

> I was privately assured, that the Empress, conceiving the greatest Abhorrence of what I had done, removed to the most distant Side of the Court, firmly resolved that those buildings should never be repaired for her Use; and, in the Presence of her chief Confidents, could not forbear vowing Revenge.

According to Professor G.M. Trevelyan (*England under Queen Anne*), part of the reason for Swift's failure to get preferment was that the Queen was scandalised by *A Tale of a Tub*—a pamphlet in which Swift probably felt that he had done a great service to the English Crown, since it scarifies the Dissenters and still more the Catholics while leaving the Established Church alone. In any case no one would deny that *Gulliver's Travels* is a rancorous as well as a pessimistic book, and that especially in Parts I and III it often descends into political partisanship of a narrow kind. Pettiness and magnanimity, republicanism and authoritarianism, love of reason and lack of curiosity, are all mixed up in it. The hatred of the human body with which Swift is especially associated is only dominant in Part IV, but somehow this new preoccupation does not come as a surprise. One feels that all these adventures, and all these changes of mood, could have happened to the same person, and the inter-connection between Swift's political loyalties and his ultimate despair is one of the most interesting features of the book.

Politically, Swift was one of those people who are driven into a sort of perverse Toryism by the follies of the progressive party of the moment. Part I of *Gulliver's Travels*, ostensibly a satire on human greatness, can be seen, if one looks a little deeper, to be simply an attack on England, on the dominant Whig Party, and on the war with France, which—however bad the motives of the Allies may have been —did save Europe from being tyrannised over by a single reactionary power. Swift was not a Jacobite nor strictly speaking a Tory, and his declared aim in the war was merely a moderate peace treaty and not the outright defeat of England. Nevertheless there is a tinge of quislingism in his attitude, which comes out in the ending of Part I and slightly interferes with the allegory. When Gulliver flees from Lilliput (England) to Blefuscu (France) the assumption that a human being six inches high is inherently contemptible seems to be dropped. Whereas the people of Lilliput have behaved towards Gulliver with the utmost treachery and meanness, those of Blefuscu behave generously and straightforwardly, and indeed this section of the book ends on a different note from the all-round disillusionment of the earlier chapters. Evidently Swift's animus is, in the first place, against *England*. It is "your Natives" (i.e. Gulliver's fellow country-men) whom the King of Brobdingnag considers to be "the most pernicious Race of little odious Vermin that Nature ever suffered to crawl upon the surface of the Earth", and the long passage at the end, denouncing colonisation and foreign conquest, is plainly aimed at England, although the contrary is elaborately stated. The Dutch, England's allies and target of one of Swift's most famous pamphlets, are also more or less wantonly attacked in Part III. There is even what sounds like a personal note in the passage in which Gulliver records his satisfaction that the various countries he has discovered cannot be made colonies of the British Crown:

> The *Houyhnhnms*, indeed, appear not to be so well prepared for War, a Science to which they are perfect Strangers, and especially against missive Weapons. However, supposing myself to be a Minister of State, I could never give my advice for invading them. . . . Imagine twenty thousand of them breaking into the midst of an *European* army, confounding the Ranks, overturning the Carriages, battering the Warriors' Faces into Mummy, by terrible Yerks from their hinder Hoofs . . .

Considering that Swift does not waste words, that phrase, "battering the warriors' faces into mummy", probably indicates a secret wish to see the invincible armies of the Duke of Marlborough treated in a like manner. There are similar touches elsewhere. Even the country mentioned in Part III, where "the Bulk of the People consist, in a Manner, wholly of Discoverers, Witnesses, Informers, Accusers, Prosecutors, Evidences, Swearers, together with their several subservient and subaltern Instruments, all under the Colours, the Conduct, and Pay of Ministers of State", is called Langdon, which is within one letter of being an anagram of England. (As the early editions of the book contain misprints, it may perhaps have been intended as a complete anagram.) Swift's *physical* repulsion from humanity is certainly real enough, but one has the feeling that his debunking of human grandeur, his diatribes against lords, politicians, court favourites, etc have mainly a local application and spring from the fact that he belonged to the unsuccessful party. He denounces injustice and oppression, but he gives no evidence of liking democracy. In spite of his enormously greater powers, his implied position is very similar to that of the innumerable silly-clever Conservatives of our own day—people like Sir Alan Herbert, Professor G.M. Young, Lord Elton, the Tory Reform Committee or the long line of Catholic apologists from W.H. Mallock onwards: people who specialise in cracking neat jokes at the expense of whatever is "modern" and "progressive", and whose opinions are often all the more extreme because they know that they cannot influence the actual drift of events. After all, such a pamphlet as *An Argument to prove that the Abolishing of Christianity* etc is very like "Timothy Shy" having a bit of clean fun with the Brains Trust, or Father Ronald Knox exposing the errors of Bertrand Russell. And the ease with which Swift has been forgiven—and forgiven, sometimes, by devout believers—for the blasphemies of *A Tale of a Tub* demonstrates clearly enough the feebleness of religious sentiments as compared with political ones.

However, the reactionary cast of Swift's mind does not show itself chiefly in his political affiliations. The important thing is his attitude towards science, and, more broadly, towards intellectual curiosity. The famous Academy of Lagado, described in Part III of *Gulliver's Travels*, is no doubt a justified satire on most of the so-called scientists of Swift's own day. Significantly, the people at work in it are described as "Projectors", that is, people not engaged in disinterested research but merely on the look-out for gadgets which will save labour and bring in money. But there is no sign—indeed, all through the book there are many signs to the contrary—that "pure" science would have struck Swift as a worth-while activity. The more serious kind of scientist has already had a kick in the pants in Part II, when the "Scholars" patronised by the King of Brobdingnag try to account for Gulliver's small stature:

> After much Debate, they concluded unanimously that I was only *Relplum Scalcath*, which is interpreted literally, *Lusus Naturae*; a Determination exactly agreeable to the modern philosophy of *Europe*, whose Professors, disdaining the old Evasion of *occult Causes*, whereby the followers of *Aristotle* endeavoured in vain to disguise their Ignorance, have invented this wonderful Solution of all Difficulties, to the unspeakable Advancement of human Knowledge.

If this stood by itself one might assume that Swift is merely the enemy of *sham* science. In a number of places, however, he goes out of his way to proclaim the uselessness of all learning or speculation not directed towards some practical end:

> The Learning of (the Brobdingnagians) is very defective, consisting only in Morality, History, Poetry, and Mathematics, wherein they must be allowed to excel. But, the last of these is wholly applied to what may be useful in Life, to the Improvement of Agriculture, and all mechanical Arts; so that among us

it would be little esteemed. And as to Ideas, Entities, Abstractions, and Transcendentals, I could never drive the least Conception into their Heads.

The Houyhnhnms, Swift's ideal beings, are backward even in a mechanical sense. They are unacquainted with metals, have never heard of boats, do not, properly speaking, practise agriculture (we are told that the oats which they live upon "grow naturally"), and appear not to have invented wheels.[1] They have no alphabet, and evidently have not much curiosity about the physical world. They do not believe that any inhabited country exists beside their own, and though they understand the motions of the sun and moon, and the nature of eclipses, "this is the utmost Progress of their *Astronomy*". By contrast, the philosophers of the flying island of Laputa are so continuously absorbed in mathematical speculations that before speaking to them one has to attract their attention by flapping them on the ear with a bladder. They have catalogued ten thousand fixed stars, have settled the periods of ninety-three comets, and have discovered, in advance of the astronomers of Europe, that Mars has two moons—all of which information Swift evidently regards as ridiculous, useless and uninteresting. As one might expect, he believes that the scientist's place, if he has a place, is in the laboratory, and that scientific knowledge has no bearing on political matters:

> What I . . . thought altogether unaccountable, was the strong Disposition I observed in them towards News and Politics, perpetually enquiring into Public Affairs, giving their judgements in Matters of State, and passionately disputing every Inch of a Party Opinion. I have, indeed, observed the same Disposition among most of the Mathematicians I have known in *Europe*, though I could never discover the least Analogy between the two Sciences; unless those People suppose, that, because the smallest Circle hath as many Degrees as the largest, therefore the Regulation and Management of the World require no more Abilities, than the Handling and Turning of a Globe.

Is there not something familiar in that phrase "I could never discover

---

[1] Houyhnhnms too old to walk are described as being carried in "sledges" or in "a kind of vehicle, drawn like a sledge". Presumably these had no wheels. [Author's footnote.]

the least analogy between the two sciences"? It has precisely the note of the popular Catholic apologists who profess to be astonished when a scientist utters an opinion on such questions as the existence of God or the immortality of the soul. The scientist, we are told, is an expert only in one restricted field: why should his opinions be of value in any other? The implication is that theology is just as much an exact science as, for instance, chemistry, and that the priest is also an expert whose conclusions on certain subjects must be accepted. Swift in effect makes the same claim for the politician, but he goes one better in that he will not allow the scientist—either the "pure" scientist or the *ad hoc* investigator—to be a useful person in his own line. Even if he had not written Part III of *Gulliver's Travels*, one could infer from the rest of the book that, like Tolstoy and like Blake, he hates the very idea of studying the processes of Nature. The "Reason" which he so admires in the Houyhnhnms does not primarily mean the power of drawing logical inferences from observed facts. Although he never defines it, it appears in most contexts to mean either common sense—i.e. acceptance of the obvious and contempt for quibbles and abstractions—or absence of passion and superstition. In general he assumes that we know all that we need to know already, and merely use our knowledge incorrectly. Medicine, for instance, is a useless science, because if we lived in a more natural way, there would be no diseases. Swift, however, is not a simple-lifer or an admirer of the Noble Savage. He is in favour of civilisation and the arts of civilisation. Not only does he see the value of good manners, good conversation, and even learning of a literary and historical kind, he also sees that agriculture, navigation and architecture need to be studied and could with advantage be improved. But his implied aim is a static, incurious civilisation—the world of his own day, a little cleaner, a little saner, with no radical change and no poking into the unknowable. More than one would expect in anyone so free from accepted fallacies, he reveres the past, especially classical antiquity, and believes that modern man has degenerated sharply during the past hundred years.[1] In the island of sorcerers, where the spirits of the dead can be called up at will:

[1] The physical decadence which Swift claims to have observed may have been a reality at that date. He attributes it to syphilis, which was a new disease in Europe and may have been more virulent than it is now. Distilled liquors, also, were a novelty in the seventeenth century and must have led at first to a great increase in drunkenness. [Author's footnote.]

I desired that the Senate of *Rome* might appear before me in one
large Chamber, and a modern Representative in Counterview,
in another. The first seemed to be an Assembly of Heroes and
Demy-Gods, the other a Knot of Pedlars, Pick-pockets, High-
waymen, and Bullies.

Although Swift uses this section of Part III to attack the truthfulness
of recorded history, his critical spirit deserts him as soon as he is
dealing with Greeks and Romans. He remarks, of course, upon the
corruption of imperial Rome, but he has an almost unreasoning
admiration for some of the leading figures of the ancient world:

I was struck with profound Veneration at the Sight of *Brutus*,
and could easily discover the most consummate Virtue, the
greatest Intrepidity and Firmness of Mind, the truest Love of
his Country, and general Benevolence for mankind, in every
Lineament of his Countenance. . . . I had the Honour to have
much Conversation with *Brutus*, and was told, that his Ancestor
Junius, *Socrates*, *Epaminondas*, *Cato* the younger, *Sir Thomas
More*, and himself, were perpetually together: a *Sextumvirate*,
to which all the Ages of the World cannot add a seventh.

It will be noticed that of these six people only one is a Christian. This
is an important point. If one adds together Swift's pessimism, his
reverence for the past, his incuriosity and his horror of the human
body, one arrives at an attitude common among religious reactionaries—that is, people who defend an unjust order of society by
claiming that this world cannot be substantially improved and only
the "next world" matters. However, Swift shows no sign of having
any religious beliefs, at least in any ordinary sense of the words. He
does not appear to believe seriously in life after death, and his idea
of goodness is bound up with republicanism, love of liberty, courage,
"benevolence" (meaning in effect public spirit), "reason" and other
pagan qualities. This reminds one that there is another strain in
Swift, not quite congruous with his disbelief in progress and his
general hatred of humanity.

To begin with, he has moments when he is "constructive" and even
"advanced". To be occasionally inconsistent is almost a mark of
vitality in Utopia books, and Swift sometimes inserts a word of praise
into a passage that ought to be purely satirical. Thus, his ideas about
the education of the young are fathered on to the Lilliputians, who
have much the same views on this subject as the Houyhnhnms. The

Lilliputians also have various social and legal institutions (for instance, there are old age pensions, and people are rewarded for keeping the law as well as punished for breaking it) which Swift would have liked to see prevailing in his own country. In the middle of this passage Swift remembers his satirical intention and adds, "In relating these and the following Laws, I would only be understood to mean the original Institutions, and not the most scandalous Corruptions into which these people are fallen by the degenerate Nature of Man": but as Lilliput is supposed to represent England, and the laws he is speaking of have never had their parallel in England, it is clear that the impulse to make constructive suggestions has been too much for him. But Swift's greatest contribution to political thought, in the narrower sense of the words, is his attack, especially in Part III, on what would now be called totalitarianism. He has an extraordinarily clear prevision of the spy-haunted "police State", with its endless heresy-hunts and treason trials, all really designed to neutralise popular discontent by changing it into war hysteria. And one must remember that Swift is here inferring the whole from a quite small part, for the feeble governments of his own day did not give him illustrations ready-made. For example, there is the professor at the School of Political Projectors who "shewed me a large Paper of Instructions for discovering Plots and Conspiracies", and who claimed that one can find people's secret thoughts by examining their excrement:

> Because Men are never so serious, thoughtful, and intent, as when they are at Stool, which he found by frequent Experiment: for in such Conjunctures, when he used merely as a Trial to consider what was the best Way of murdering the King, his Ordure would have a Tincture of Green; but quite different when he thought only of raising an Insurrection, or burning the Metropolis.

The professor and his theory are said to have been suggested to Swift by the—from our point of view—not particularly astonishing or disgusting fact that in a recent State Trial some letters found in somebody's privy had been put in evidence. Later in the same chapter we seem to be positively in the middle of the Russian purges:

> In the Kingdom of Tribnia, by the Natives called Langdon . . . the Bulk of the People consist, in a Manner, wholly of Discoverers, Witnesses, Informers, Accusers, Prosecutors,

Evidences, Swearers. . . . It is first agreed, and settled among
them, what suspected Persons shall be accused of a Plot: Then,
effectual Care is taken to secure all their Letters and Papers,
and put the Owners in Chains. These papers are delivered to a
Sett of Artists, very dexterous in finding out the mysterious
Meanings of Words, Syllables, and Letters. . . . Where this
Method fails, they have two others more effectual, which the
Learned among them call *Acrostics* and *Anagrams. First,* they
can decypher all initial Letters into political Meanings: Thus, N
shall signify a Plot, B a Regiment of Horse, L a Fleet at Sea: Or,
Secondly, by transposing the Letters of the Alphabet in any
suspected Paper, they can lay open the deepest Designs of a
discontented Party. So, for Example, if I should say in a Letter
to a Friend, *Our Brother Tom has just got the Piles,* a skilful
Decypherer would discover that the same Letters, which compose that Sentence, may be analysed in the following Words:
Resist—a Plot is brought Home—The Tour.[1] And this is the
anagrammatic Method.

Other professors at the same school invent simplified languages,
write books by machinery, educate their pupils by inscribing the
lessons on a wafer and causing them to swallow it, or propose to
abolish individuality altogether by cutting off part of the brain of
one man and grafting it on to the head of another. There is something
queerly familiar in the atmosphere of these chapters, because, mixed
up with much fooling, there is a perception that one of the aims of
totalitarianism is not merely to make sure that people will think the
right thoughts, but actually to make them *less conscious.* Then,
again, Swift's account of the Leader who is usually to be found
ruling over a tribe of Yahoos, and of the "favourite" who acts first
as a dirty-worker and later as a scapegoat, fits remarkably well into
the pattern of our own times. But are we to infer from all this that
Swift was first and foremost an enemy of tyranny and a champion of
the free intelligence? No: his own views, so far as one can discern
them, are not markedly liberal. No doubt he hates lords, kings,
bishops, generals, ladies of fashion, orders, titles and flummery
generally, but he does not seem to think better of the common
people than of their rulers, or to be in favour of increased social
equality, or to be enthusiastic about representative institutions. The

[1] Tower. [Author's footnote.]

Houyhnhnms are organised upon a sort of caste system which is racial in character, the horses which do the menial work being of different colours from their masters and not interbreeding with them. The educational system which Swift admires in the Lilliputians takes hereditary class distinctions for granted, and the children of the poorest class do not go to school, because "their Business being only to till and cultivate the Earth . . . therefore their Education is of little Consequence to the Public". Nor does he seem to have been strongly in favour of freedom of speech and the press, in spite of the toleration which his own writings enjoyed. The King of Brobdingnag is astonished at the multiplicity of religious and political sects in England, and considers that those who hold "opinions prejudicial to the public" (in the context this seems to mean simply heretical opinions), though they need not be obliged to change them, ought to be obliged to conceal them: for "as it was Tyranny in any Government to require the first, so it was Weakness not to enforce the second". There is a subtler indication of Swift's own attitude in the manner in which Gulliver leaves the land of the Houyhnhnms. Intermittently, at least, Swift was a kind of anarchist, and Part IV of *Gulliver's Travels* is a picture of an anarchistic society, not governed by law in the ordinary sense, but by the dictates of "Reason", which are voluntarily accepted by everyone. The General Assembly of the Houyhnhnms "exhorts" Gulliver's master to get rid of him, and his neighbours put pressure on him to make him comply. Two reasons are given. One is that the presence of this unusual Yahoo may unsettle the rest of the tribe, and the other is that a friendly relationship between a Houyhnhnm and a Yahoo is "not agreeable to Reason or Nature, or a Thing ever heard of before among them". Gulliver's master is somewhat unwilling to obey, but the "exhortation" (a Houyhnhnm, we are told, is never *compelled* to do anything, he is merely "exhorted" or "advised") cannot be disregarded. This illustrates very well the totalitarian tendency which is implicit in the anarchist or pacifist vision of society. In a society in which there is no law, and in theory no compulsion, the only arbiter of behaviour is public opinion. But public opinion, because of the tremendous urge to conformity in gregarious animals, is less tolerant than any system of law. When human beings are governed by "thou shalt not", the individual can practise a certain amount of eccentricity: when they are supposedly governed by "love" or "reason", he is under continuous pressure to make him behave and think in exactly the same

way as everyone else. The Houyhnhnms, we are told, were unanimous
on almost all subjects. The only question they ever *discussed* was how
to deal with the Yahoos. Otherwise there was no room for disagreement among them, because the truth is always either self-evident, or
else it is undiscoverable and unimportant. They had apparently no
word for "opinion" in their language, and in their conversations
there was no "difference of sentiments". They had reached, in fact,
the highest stage of totalitarian organisation, the stage when conformity has become so general that there is no need for a police force.
Swift approves of this kind of thing because among his many gifts
neither curiosity nor good nature was included. Disagreement would
always seem to him sheer perversity. "Reason", among the Houyhnhnms, he says, "is not a Point Problematical, as with us, where men
can argue with Plausibility on both Sides of a Question; but strikes
you with immediate Conviction; as it must needs do, where it is not
mingled, obscured, or discoloured by Passion and Interest." In other
words, we know everything already, so why should dissident opinions
be tolerated? The totalitarian society of the Houyhnhnms, where there
can be no freedom and no development, follows naturally from this.

We are right to think of Swift as a rebel and iconoclast, but except
in certain secondary matters, such as his insistence that women
should receive the same education as men, he cannot be labelled
"left". He is a Tory anarchist, despising authority while disbeliev-
ing in liberty, and preserving the aristocratic outlook while seeing
clearly that the existing aristocracy is degenerate and contemptible.
When Swift utters one of his characteristic diatribes against the
rich and powerful, one must probably, as I said earlier, write off
something for the fact that he himself belonged to the less successful
party, and was personally disappointed. The "outs", for obvious
reasons, are always more radical than the "ins".[1] But the most

[1] At the end of the book, as typical specimens of human folly and viciousness,
Swift names "a Lawyer, a Pickpocket, a Colonel, a Fool, a Lord, a Gamester, a
Politician, a Whore-master, a Physician, an Evidence, a Suborner, an Attorney, a
Traitor, or the like". One sees here the irresponsible violence of the powerless. The
list lumps together those who break the conventional code, and those who keep
it. For instance, if you automatically condemn a colonel, as such, on what grounds
do you condemn a traitor? Or again, if you want to suppress pickpockets, you
must have laws, which means that you must have lawyers. But the whole closing
passage, in which the hatred is so authentic, and the reason given for it so
inadequate, is somehow unconvincing. One has the feeling that personal animosity
is at work. [Author's footnote.]

essential thing in Swift is his inability to believe that life—ordinary life on the solid earth, and not some rationalised, deodorised version of it—could be made worth living. Of course, no honest person claims that happiness is *now* a normal condition among adult human beings; but perhaps it *could* be made normal, and it is upon this question that all serious political controversy really turns. Swift has much in common—more, I believe, than has been noticed—with Tolstoy, another disbeliever in the possibility of happiness. In both men you have the same anarchistic outlook covering an authoritarian cast of mind; in both a similar hostility to science, the same impatience with opponents, the same inability to see the importance of any question not interesting to themselves; and in both cases a sort of horror of the actual process of life, though in Tolstoy's case it was arrived at later and in a different way. The sexual unhappiness of the two men was not of the same kind, but there was this in common, that in both of them a sincere loathing was mixed up with a morbid fascination. Tolstoy was a reformed rake who ended by preaching complete celibacy, while continuing to practise the opposite into extreme old age. Swift was presumably impotent, and had an exaggerated horror of human dung: he also thought about it incessantly, as is evident throughout this works. Such people are not likely to enjoy even the small amount of happiness that falls to most human beings, and, from obvious motives, are not likely to admit that earthly life is capable of much improvement. Their incuriosity, and hence their intolerance, spring from the same root.

Swift's disgust, rancour and pessimism would make sense against the background of a "next world" to which this one is the prelude. As he does not appear to believe seriously in any such thing, it becomes necessary to construct a paradise supposedly existing on the surface of the earth, but something quite different from anything we know, with all that he disapproves of—lies, folly, change, enthusiasm, pleasure, love and dirt—eliminated from it. As his ideal being he chooses the horse, an animal whose excrement is not offensive. The Houyhnhnms are dreary beasts—this is so generally admitted that the point is not worth labouring. Swift's genius can make them credible, but there can have been very few readers in whom they have excited any feeling beyond dislike. And this is not from wounded vanity at seeing animals preferred to men; for, of the two, the Houyhnhnms are much liker to human beings than are the Yahoos, and Gulliver's horror of the Yahoos, together with his recognition that they are the same kind of creature as himself, contains a logical absurdity. This horror comes upon him at his very first sight of them. "I never beheld," he says, "in all my Travels, so disagreeable an Animal, nor one against which I naturally conceived so strong an Antipathy." But in comparison with what are the Yahoos disgusting? Not with the Houyhnhnms, because at this time Gulliver has not seen a Houyhnhnm. It can only be in comparison with himself, i.e. with a human being. Later, however, we are to be told that the Yahoos *are* human beings, and human society becomes insupportable to Gulliver because all men are Yahoos. In that case why did he not conceive his disgust of humanity earlier? In effect we are told that the Yahoos are fantastically different from men, and yet are the same. Swift has overreached himself in his fury, and is shouting at his fellow creatures: "You are filthier than you are!" However, it is impossible to feel much sympathy with the Yahoos, and it is not because they oppress the Yahoos that the Houyhnhnms are unattractive. They are unattractive because the "Reason" by which they are governed is really a desire for death. They are exempt from love, friendship, curiosity, fear, sorrow and—except in their feelings towards the Yahoos, who occupy rather the same place in their community as the Jews in Nazi Germany—anger and hatred. "They have no Fondness for their Colts or Foles, but the Care they take, in educating them, proceeds entirely from the Dictates of *Reason*." They lay store by "Friendship" and "Benevolence", but "these are not confined to particular Objects, but universal to the whole Race". They also value conversation, but in their conversations there are no differences of opinion, and "nothing passed but what was useful, expressed in the fewest and most significant Words". They practise strict birth control, each couple producing two offspring and thereafter abstaining from sexual intercourse. Their marriages are arranged for them by their elders, on eugenic principles, and their language contains no word for "love", in the sexual sense. When somebody dies they carry on exactly as before, without feeling any grief. It will be seen that their aim is to be as like a corpse as is possible while retaining physical life. One or two of their characteristics, it is true, do not seem to be strictly "reasonable" in their own usage of the word. Thus, they place a great value not only on physical hardihood but on athleticism, and they are devoted to poetry. But these exceptions may be less arbitrary than they seem. Swift probably emphasises the physical strength of the Houyhnhnms in order to make clear that they could never be conquered by the hated human race, while a taste for poetry may figure among their qualities because poetry appeared to Swift as the antithesis of science, from his point of view the most useless of all pursuits. In Part III he names "Imagination, Fancy, and Invention" as desirable faculties in which the Laputan mathematicians (in spite of their love of music) were wholly lacking. One must remember that although Swift was an admirable writer of comic verse, the kind of poetry he thought valuable would probably be didactic poetry. The poetry of the Houyhnhnms, he says:

> must be allowed to excel (that of) all other Mortals; wherein the Justness of their Similes, and the Minuteness, as well as exactness, of their Descriptions, are, indeed, inimitable. Their Verses abound very much in both of these; and usually contain either some exalted Notions of Friendship and Benevolence, or the Praises of those who were Victors in Races, and other bodily Exercises.

Alas, not even the genius of Swift was equal to producing a specimen by which we could judge the poetry of the Houyhnhnms. But it sounds as though it were chilly stuff (in heroic couplets, presumably), and not seriously in conflict with the principles of "Reason".

Happiness is notoriously difficult to describe, and pictures of a just and well-ordered society are seldom either attractive or convincing. Most creators of "favourable" Utopias, however, are concerned to show what life could be like if it were lived more fully. Swift advocates a simple refusal of life, justifying this by the claim that "Reason" consists in thwarting your instincts. The Houyhnhnms, creatures without a history, continue for generation after generation to live prudently, maintaining their population at exactly the same level, avoiding all passion, suffering from no diseases, meeting death indifferently, training up their young in the same principles—and all for what? In order that the same process may continue indefinitely. The notions that life here and now is worth living, or that it could be made worth living, or that it must be sacrificed for some future good, are all absent. The dreary world of the Houyhnhnms was about as good a Utopia as Swift could construct, granting that he neither believed in a "next world" nor could get any pleasure out of certain normal activities. But it is not really set up as something desirable in itself, but as the justification for another attack on humanity. The aim, as usual, is to humiliate Man by reminding him that he is weak and ridiculous, and above all that he stinks; and the ultimate motive, probably, is a kind of envy, the envy of the ghost for the living, of the man who knows he cannot be happy for the others who—so he fears —may be a little happier than himself. The political expression of such an outlook must be either reactionary or nihilistic, because the person who holds it will want to prevent society from developing in some direction in which his pessimism may be cheated. One can do this either by blowing everything to pieces, or by averting social change. Swift ultimately blew everything to pieces in the only way that was feasible before the atomic bomb—that is, he went mad— but, as I have tried to show, his political aims were on the whole reactionary ones.

From what I have written it may have seemed that I am *against* Swift, and that my object is to refute him and even to belittle him. In a political and moral sense I am against him, so far as I understand him. Yet curiously enough he is one of the writers I admire with least reserve, and *Gulliver's Travels*, in particular, is a book which it seems impossible for me to grow tired of. I read it first when I was eight— one day short of eight, to be exact, for I stole and furtively read the copy which was to be given me next day on my eighth birthday—and I have certainly not read it less than half a dozen times since. Its fascination seems inexhaustible. If I had to make a list of six books which were to be preserved when all others were destroyed, I would certainly put *Gulliver's Travels* among them. This raises the question: what is the relationship between agreement with a writer's opinions, and enjoyment of his work?

If one is capable of intellectual detachment, one can *perceive* merit in a writer whom one deeply disagrees with, but *enjoyment* is a different matter. Supposing that there is such a thing as good or bad art, then the goodness or badness must reside in the work of art itself—not independently of the observer, indeed, but independently of the mood of the observer. In one sense, therefore, it cannot be true that a poem is good on Monday and bad on Tuesday. But if one judges the poem by the appreciation it arouses, then it can certainly be true, because appreciation, or enjoyment, is a subjective condition which cannot be commanded. For a great deal of his waking life, even the most cultivated person has no aesthetic feelings whatever, and the power to have aesthetic feelings is very easily destroyed. When you are frightened, or hungry, or are suffering from toothache or seasickness, *King Lear* is no better from your point of view than

Peter Pan. You may know in an intellectual sense that it is better, but that is simply a fact which you remember: you will not *feel* the merit of *King Lear* until you are normal again. And aesthetic judgement can be upset just as disastrously—more disastrously, because the cause is less readily recognised—by political or moral disagreement. If a book angers, wounds or alarms you, then you will not enjoy it, whatever its merits may be. If it seems to you a really pernicious book, likely to influence other people in some undesirable way, then you will probably construct an aesthetic theory to show that it *has* no merits. Current literary criticism consists quite largely of this kind of dodging to and fro between two sets of standards. And yet the opposite process can also happen: enjoyment can overwhelm disapproval, even though one clearly recognises that one is enjoying something inimical. Swift, whose world-view is so peculiarly unacceptable, but who is nevertheless an extremely popular writer, is a good instance of this. Why is it that we don't mind being called Yahoos, although firmly convinced that we are *not* Yahoos?

It is not enough to make the usual answer that of course Swift was wrong, in fact he was insane, but he was "a good writer". It is true that the literary quality of a book is to some small extent separable from its subject-matter. Some people have a native gift for using words, as some people have a naturally "good eye" at games. It is largely a question of timing and of instinctively knowing how much emphasis to use. As an example near at hand, look back at the passage I quoted earlier, starting "In the Kingdom of Tribnia, by the Natives called Langdon". It derives much of its force from the final sentence: "And this is the anagrammatic Method". Strictly speaking this sentence is unnecessary, for we have already seen the anagram deciphered, but the mock-solemn repetition, in which one seems to hear Swift's own voice uttering the words, drives home the idiocy of the activities described, like the final tap to a nail. But not all the power and simplicity of Swift's prose, nor the imaginative effort that has been able to make not one but a whole series of impossible worlds more credible than the majority of history books—none of this would enable us to enjoy Swift if his world-view were truly wounding or shocking. Millions of people, in many countries, must have enjoyed *Gulliver's Travels* while more or less seeing its anti-human implications: and even the child who accepts Parts I and II as a simple story gets a sense of absurdity from thinking of human beings six inches high. The explanation must be that Swift's world-view is felt to be *not* altogether false—or it would probably be more accurate to say, not false all the time. Swift is a diseased writer. He remains permanently in a depressed mood which in most people is only intermittent, rather as though someone suffering from jaundice or the after-effects of influenza should have the energy to write books. But we all know that mood, and something in us responds to the expression of it. Take, for instance, one of his most characteristic works, "The Lady's Dressing Room": one might add the kindred poem, "Upon a Beautiful Young Nymph Going to Bed". Which is truer, the viewpoint expressed in these poems, or the viewpoint implied in Blake's phrase, "The naked female human form divine"? No doubt Blake is nearer the truth, and yet who can fail to feel a sort of pleasure in seeing that fraud, feminine delicacy, exploded for once? Swift falsifies his picture of the whole world by refusing to see anything in human life except dirt, folly and wickedness, but the part which he abstracts from the whole does exist, and it is something which we all know about while shrinking from mentioning it. Part of our minds—in any normal person it is the dominant part—believes that man is a noble animal and life is worth living: but there is also a sort of inner self which at least intermittently stands aghast at the horror of existence. In the queerest way, pleasure and disgust are linked together. The human body is beautiful: it is also repulsive and ridiculous, a fact which can be verified at any swimming pool. The sexual organs are objects of desire and also of loathing, so much so that in many languages, if not in all languages, their names are used as words of abuse. Meat is delicious, but a butcher's shop makes one feel sick: and indeed all our food springs ultimately from dung and dead bodies, the two things which of all others seem to us the most horrible. A child, when it is past the infantile stage but still looking at the world with fresh eyes, is moved by horror almost as often as by wonder—horror of snot and spittle, of the dogs' excrement on the pavement, the dying toad full of maggots, the sweaty smell of grown-ups, the hideousness of old men, with their bald heads and bulbous noses. In his endless harping on disease, dirt and deformity, Swift is not actually inventing anything, he is merely leaving something out. Human behaviour, too, especially in politics, is as he describes it, although it contains other more important factors which he refuses to admit. So far as we can see, both horror and pain are necessary to the continuance of life on this planet, and it is therefore open to pessimists like Swift to say: "If horror and pain must always be with us, how can life be significantly improved?" His attitude is in effect the Christian attitude, minus the bribe of a "next world"—which, however, probably has less hold upon the minds of believers than the conviction that this world is a vale of tears and the grave is a place of rest. It is, I am certain, a wrong attitude, and one which could have harmful effects upon behaviour; but something in us responds to it, as it responds to the gloomy words of the burial service and the sweetish smell of corpses in a country church.

It is often argued, at least by people who admit the importance of subject-matter, that a book cannot be "good" if it expresses a palpably false view of life. We are told that in our own age, for instance, any book that has genuine literary merit will also be more or less "progressive" in tendency. This ignores the fact that throughout history a similar struggle between progress and reaction has been raging, and that the best books of any one age have always been written from several different viewpoints, some of them palpably more false than others. In so far as a writer is a propagandist, the most one can ask of him is that he shall genuinely believe in what he is saying, and that it shall not be something blazingly silly. Today, for example, one can imagine a good book being written by a Catholic, a Communist, a Fascist, a Pacifist, an Anarchist, perhaps by an old-style Liberal or an ordinary Conservative: one cannot imagine a good book being written by a spiritualist, a Buchmanite or a member of the Ku Klux Klan. The views that a writer holds must be compatible with sanity, in the medical sense, and with the power of continuous thought: beyond that what we ask of him is talent, which is probably another name for conviction. Swift did not possess ordinary wisdom, but he did possess a terrible intensity of vision, capable of picking out a single hidden truth and then magnifying it and distorting it. The durability of *Gulliver's Travels* goes to show that, if the force of belief is behind it, a world-view which only just passes the test of sanity is sufficient to produce a great work of art.

Polemic, No. 5, September–October 1946; SE; OR; CE

58. How the Poor Die

In the year 1929 I spent several weeks in the Hôpital X, in the fifteenth *arrondissement* of Paris. The clerks put me through the usual

third-degree at the reception desk, and indeed I was kept answering
questions for some twenty minutes before they would let me in. If you
have ever had to fill up forms in a Latin country you will know the
kind of questions I mean. For some days past I had been unequal to
translating Réaumur into Fahrenheit, but I know that my temperature was round about 103, and by the end of the interview I had
some difficulty in standing on my feet. At my back a resigned little
knot of patients, carrying bundles done up in coloured handkerchiefs,
waited their turn to be questioned.

After the questioning came the bath—a compulsory routine for
all newcomers, apparently, just as in prison or the workhouse. My
clothes were taken away from me, and after I had sat shivering for
some minutes in five inches of warm water I was given a linen nightshirt and a short blue flannel dressing-gown—no slippers, they had
none big enough for me, they said—and led out into the open air.
This was a night in February and I was suffering from pneumonia.
The ward we were going to was 200 yards away and it seemed that to
get to it you had to cross the hospital grounds. Someone stumbled in
front of me with a lantern. The gravel path was frosty underfoot,
and the wind whipped the nightshirt round my bare calves. When we
got into the ward I was aware of a strange feeling of familiarity
whose origin I did not succeed in pinning down till later in the night.
It was a long, rather low, ill-lit room, full of murmuring voices and
with three rows of beds surprisingly close together. There was a foul
smell, faecal and yet sweetish. As I lay down I saw on a bed nearly
opposite me a small, round-shouldered, sandy-haired man sitting
half naked while a doctor and a student performed some strange
operation on him. First the doctor produced from his black bag a
dozen small glasses like wine glasses, then the student burned a match
inside each glass to exhaust the air, then the glass was popped on to
the man's back or chest and the vacuum drew up a huge yellow
blister. Only after some moments did I realise what they were doing
to him. It was something called cupping, a treatment which you can
read about in old medical text-books but which till then I had vaguely
thought of as one of those things they do to horses.

The cold air outside had probably lowered my temperature, and
I watched this barbarous remedy with detachment and even a certain
amount of amusement. The next moment, however, the doctor and
the student came across to my bed, hoisted me upright and without a
word began applying the same set of glasses, which had not been

sterilised in any way. A few feeble protests that I uttered got no more response than if I had been an animal. I was very much impressed by the impersonal way in which the two men started on me. I had never been in the public ward of a hospital before, and it was my first experience of doctors who handle you without speaking to you, or, in a human sense, taking any notice of you. They only put on six glasses in my case, but after doing so they scarified the blisters and applied the glasses again. Each glass now drew out about a dessert-spoonful of dark-coloured blood. As I lay down again, humiliated, disgusted and frightened by the thing that had been done to me, I reflected that now at least they would leave me alone. But no, not a bit of it. There was another treatment coming, the mustard poultice, seemingly a matter of routine like the hot bath. Two slatternly nurses had already got the poultice ready, and they lashed it round my chest as tight as a strait jacket while some men who were wandering about the ward in shirt and trousers began to collect round my bed with half-sympathetic grins. I learned later that watching a patient have a mustard poultice was a favourite pastime in the ward. These things are normally applied for a quarter of an hour and certainly they are funny enough if you don't happen to be the person inside. For the first five minutes the pain is severe, but you believe you can bear it. During the second five minutes this belief evaporates, but the poultice is buckled at the back and you can't get it off. This is the period the onlookers most enjoy. During the last five minutes, I noted a sort of numbness supervenes. After the poultice had been removed a waterproof pillow packed with ice was thrust beneath my head and I was left alone. I did not sleep and to the best of my knowledge this was the only night of my life—I mean the only night spent in bed—in which I have not slept at all, not even a minute.

During my first hour in the Hôpital X, I had had a whole series of different and contradictory treatments, but this was misleading, for in general you got very little treatment at all, either good or bad, unless you were ill in some interesting and instructive way. At five in the morning the nurses came round, woke the patients and took their temperatures, but did not wash them. If you were well enough you washed yourself, otherwise you depended on the kindness of some walking patient. It was generally patients, too, who carried the bed-bottles and the grim bed-pan, nicknamed *la casserole*. At eight breakfast arrived, called army-fashion *la soupe*. It was soup, too, a thin vegetable soup with slimy hunks of bread floating about in it. Later in the day the tall, solemn, black-bearded doctor made his rounds, with an *interne* and a troop of students following at his heels, but there were about sixty of us in the ward and it was evident that he had other wards to attend to as well. There were many beds past which he walked day after day, sometimes followed by imploring cries. On the other hand if you had some disease with which the students wanted to familiarise themselves you got plenty of attention of a kind. I myself, with an exceptionally fine specimen of a bronchial rattle, sometimes had as many as a dozen students queueing up to listen to my chest. It was a very queer feeling—queer, I mean, because of their intense interest in learning their job, together with a seeming lack of any perception that the patients were human beings. It is strange to relate, but sometimes as some young student stepped forward to take his turn at manipulating you he would be actually tremulous with excitement, like a boy who has at last got his hands on some expensive piece of machinery. And then ear after ear—ears of young men, of girls, of Negroes—pressed against your back, relays of fingers solemnly but clumsily tapping, and not from any one of them did you get a word of conversation or a look direct in your face. As a non-paying patient, in the uniform nightshirt, you were primarily *a specimen*, a thing I did not resent but could never quite get used to.

After some days I grew well enough to sit up and study the surrounding patients. The stuffy room, with its narrow beds so close together that you could easily touch your neighbour's hand, had every sort of disease in it except, I suppose, acutely infectious cases. My right-hand neighbour was a little red-haired cobbler with one leg shorter than the other, who used to announce the death of any other patient (this happened a number of times, and my neighbour was always the first to hear of it) by whistling to me, exclaiming "*Numéro 43!*" (or whatever it was) and flinging his arms above his head. This man had not much wrong with him, but in most of the other beds within my angle of vision some squalid tragedy or some plain horror was being enacted. In the bed that was foot to foot with mine there lay, until he died (I didn't see him die—they moved him to another bed), a little weazened man who was suffering from I do not know what disease, but something that made his whole body so intensely sensitive that any movement from side to side, sometimes even the weight of the bed-clothes, would make him shout out with pain. His worst suffering was when he urinated, which he did with the greatest difficulty. A nurse would bring him the bed-bottle and then for a long time stand beside his bed, whistling, as grooms are said to do with horses, until at last with an agonised shriek of *"Je pisse!"* he would get started. In the bed next to him the sandy-haired man whom I had seen being cupped used to cough up blood-streaked mucus at all hours. My left-hand neighbour was a tall, flaccid-looking young man who used periodically to have a tube inserted into his back and astonishing quantities of frothy liquid drawn off from some part of his body. In the bed beyond that a veteran of the war of 1870 was dying, a handsome old man with a white imperial, round whose bed, at all hours when visiting was allowed, four elderly female relatives dressed all in black sat exactly like crows, obviously scheming for some pitiful legacy. In the bed opposite me in the further row was an old bald-headed man with drooping moustaches and greatly swollen face and body, who was suffering from some disease that made him urinate almost incessantly. A huge glass receptable stood always beside his bed. One day his wife and daughter came to visit him. At the sight of them the old man's bloated face lit up with a smile of surprising sweetness, and as his daughter, a pretty girl of about twenty, approached the bed I saw that his hand was slowly working its way from under the bed-clothes. I seemed to see in advance the gesture that was coming—the girl kneeling beside the bed, the old man's hand laid on her head in his dying blessing. But no, he merely handed her the bed-bottle, which she promptly took from him and emptied into the receptacle.

About a dozen beds away from me was *numéro 57*—I think that was his number—a cirrhosis of the liver case. Everyone in the ward knew him by sight because he was sometimes the subject of a medical lecture. On two afternoons a week the tall, grave doctor would lecture in the ward to a party of students, and on more than one occasion old *numéro 57* was wheeled on a sort of trolley into the middle of the ward, where the doctor would roll back his nightshirt, dilate with his fingers a huge flabby protuberance on the man's belly —the diseased liver, I suppose—and explain solemnly that this was a disease attributable to alcoholism, commoner in the wine-drinking countries. As usual he neither spoke to his patient nor gave him a smile, a nod or any kind of recognition. While he talked, very grave and upright, he would hold the wasted body beneath his two hands, sometimes giving it a gentle roll to and fro, in just the attitude of a woman handling a rolling-pin. Not that *numéro 57* minded this kind of thing. Obviously he was an old hospital inmate, a regular exhibit at lectures, his liver long since marked down for a bottle in some pathological museum. Utterly uninterested in what was said about him, he would lie with his colourless eyes gazing at nothing, while the doctor showed him off like a piece of antique china. He was a man of about sixty, astonishingly shrunken. His face, pale as vellum, had shrunken away till it seemed no bigger than a doll's.

One morning my cobbler neighbour woke me by plucking at my pillow before the nurses arrived. *"Numéro 57!"*—he flung his arms above his head. There was a light in the ward, enough to see by. I could see old *numéro 57* lying crumpled up on his side, his face sticking out over the side of the bed, and towards me. He had died some time during the night, nobody knew when. When the nurses came they received the news of his death indifferently and went about their work. After a long time, an hour or more, two other nurses marched in abreast like soldiers, with a great clumping of sabots, and knotted the corpse up in the sheets, but it was not removed till some time later. Meanwhile, in the better light, I had had time for a good look at *numéro 57*. Indeed I lay on my side to look at him. Curiously enough he was the first dead European I had seen. I had seen dead men before, but always Asiatics and usually people who had died violent deaths. *Numéro 57*'s eyes were still open, his mouth also open, his small face contorted into an expression of agony. What most impressed me however was the whiteness of his face. It had been pale before, but now it was little darker than the sheets. As I gazed at the tiny, screwed-up face it struck me that this disgusting piece of refuse, waiting to be carted away and dumped on a slab in the dissecting room, was an example of "natural" death, one of the things you pray for in the Litany. There you are, then, I thought, that's what is waiting for you, twenty, thirty, forty years hence: that is how the lucky ones die, the ones who live to be old. One wants to live, of course, indeed one only stays alive by virtue of the fear of death, but I think now, as I thought then, that it's better to die violently and not too old. People talk about the horrors of war, but what weapon has man invented that even approaches in cruelty some of the commoner diseases? "Natural" death, almost by definition, means something slow, smelly and painful. Even at that, it makes a difference if you can achieve it in your own home and not in a public institution. This poor old wretch who had just flickered out like a candle-end was not even important enough to have anyone watching by his deathbed. He was merely a number, then a "subject" for the students' scalpels. And the sordid publicity of dying in such a place! In the Hôpital X the beds were very close together and there were no screens. Fancy, for instance, dying like the little man whose bed was for a while foot to foot with mine, the one who cried out when the bed-clothes touched him! I dare say *Je pisse!* were his last recorded words. Perhaps the dying don't bother about such things— that at least would be the standard answer: nevertheless dying people are often more or less normal in their minds till within a day or so of the end.

In the public wards of a hospital you see horrors that you don't seem to meet with among people who manage to die in their own homes, as though certain diseases only attacked people at the lower income levels. But it is a fact that you would not in any English hospitals see some of the things I saw in the Hôpital X. This business of people just dying like animals, for instance, with nobody standing by, nobody interested, the death not even noticed till the morning— this happened more than once. You certainly would not see that in England, and still less would you see a corpse left exposed to the view of the other patients. I remember that once in a cottage hospital in England a man died while we were at tea, and though there were only six of us in the ward the nurses managed things so adroitly that the man was dead and his body removed without our even hearing about it till tea was over. A thing we perhaps underrate in England is the advantage we enjoy in having large numbers of well-trained and rigidly-disciplined nurses. No doubt English nurses are dumb enough, they may tell fortunes with tea-leaves, wear Union Jack badges and keep photographs of the Queen on their mantelpieces, but at least they don't let you lie unwashed and constipated on an unmade bed, out of sheer laziness. The nurses at the Hôpital X still had a tinge of Mrs Gamp about them, and later, in the military hospitals of Republican Spain, I was to see nurses almost too ignorant to take a temperature. You wouldn't, either, see in England such dirt as existed in the Hôpital X. Later on, when I was well enough to wash myself in the bathroom, I found that there was kept there a huge packing-case into which the scraps of food and dirty dressings from the ward were flung, and the wainscottings were infested by crickets.

When I had got back my clothes and grown strong on my legs I fled from the Hôpital X, before my time was up and without waiting for a medical discharge. It was not the only hospital I have fled

from, but its gloom and bareness, its sickly smell and, above all,
something in its mental atmosphere stand out in my memory as
exceptional. I had been taken there because it was the hospital
belonging to my *arrondissement*, and I did not learn till after I was
in it that it bore a bad reputation. A year or two later the celebrated
swindler, Madame Hanaud, who was ill while on remand, was taken
to the Hôpital X, and after a few days of it she managed to elude her
guards, took a taxi and drove back to the prison, explaining that she
was more comfortable there. I have no doubt that the Hôpital X was
quite untypical of French hospitals even at that date. But the patients,
nearly all of them working men, were surprisingly resigned. Some of
them seemed to find the conditions almost comfortable, for at least
two were destitute malingerers who found this a good way of getting
through the winter. The nurses connived because the malingerers
made themselves useful by doing odd jobs. But the attitude of the
majority was: of course this is a lousy place, but what else do you
expect? It did not seem strange to them that you should be woken
at five and then wait three hours before starting the day on watery
soup, or that people should die with no one at their bedside, or even
that your chance of getting medical attention should depend on
catching the doctor's eye as he went past. According to their traditions
that was what hospitals were like. If you are seriously ill, and if you
are too poor to be treated in your own home, then you must go into
hospital, and once there you must put up with harshness and discomfort, just as you would in the army. But on top of this I was interested
to find a lingering belief in the old stories that have now almost
faded from memory in England—stories, for instance, about doctors
cutting you open out of sheer curiosity or thinking it funny to start
operating before you were properly "under". There were dark tales
about a little operating room said to be situated just beyond the
bathroom. Dreadful screams were said to issue from this room. I saw
nothing to confirm these stories and no doubt they were all nonsense,
though I did see two students kill a sixteen-year-old boy, or nearly
kill him (he appeared to be dying when I left the hospital, but he
may have recovered later) by a mischievous experiment which they
probably could not have tried on a paying patient. Well within living
memory it used to be believed in London that in some of the big
hospitals patients were killed off to get dissection subjects. I didn't
hear this tale repeated at the Hôpital X, but I should think some of
the men there would have found it credible. For it was a hospital in

which not the methods, perhaps, but something of the atmosphere of the nineteenth century had managed to survive, and therein lay its peculiar interest.

During the past fifty years or so there has been a great change in the relationship between doctor and patient. If you look at almost any literature before the later part of the nineteenth century, you find that a hospital is popularly regarded as much the same thing as a prison, and an old-fashioned, dungeon-like prison at that. A hospital is a place of filth, torture and death, a sort of antechamber to the tomb. No one who was not more or less destitute would have thought of going into such a place for treatment. And especially in the early part of the last century, when medical science had grown bolder than before without being any more successful, the whole business of doctoring was looked on with horror and dread by ordinary people. Surgery, in particular, was believed to be no more than a peculiarly gruesome form of sadism, and dissection, possible only with the aid of body-snatchers, was even confused with necromancy. From the nineteenth century you could collect a large horror-literature connected with doctors and hospitals. Think of poor old George III, in his dotage, shrieking for mercy as he sees his surgeons approaching to "bleed him till he faints"! Think of the conversations of Bob Sawyer and Benjamin Allen, which no doubt are hardly parodies, or the field hospitals in *La Débâcle* and *War and Peace*, or that shocking description of an amputation in Melville's *Whitejacket*! Even the names given to doctors in nineteenth-century English fiction, Slasher, Carver, Sawyer, Fillgrave and so on, and the generic nickname "sawbones", are about as grim as they are comic. The anti-surgery tradition is perhaps best expressed in Tennyson's poem, "The Children's Hospital", which is essentially a pre-chloroform document though it seems to have been written as late as 1880. Moreover, the outlook which Tennyson records in this poem had a lot to be said for it. When you consider what an operation without anaesthetics must have been like, what it notoriously *was* like, it is difficult not to suspect the motives of people who would undertake such things. For these bloody horrors which the students so eagerly looked forward to ("A magnificent sight if Slasher does it!") were admittedly more or less useless: the patient who did not die of shock usually died of gangrene, a result which was taken for granted. Even now doctors can be found whose motives are questionable. Anyone who has had much illness, or who has listened to medical students talking, will know what I mean. But anaesthetics were a turning-point, and disinfectants were another. Nowhere in the world, probably, would you now see the kind of scene described by Axel Munthe in *The Story of San Michele*, when the sinister surgeon in top-hat and frock-coat, his starched shirtfront spattered with blood and pus, carves up patient after patient with the same knife and flings the severed limbs into a pile beside the table. Moreover, national health insurance has partly done away with the idea that a working-class patient is a pauper who deserves little consideration. Well into this century it was usual for "free" patients at the big hospitals to have their teeth extracted with no anaesthetic. They didn't pay, so why should they have an anaesthetic—that was the attitude. That too has changed.

And yet every institution will always bear upon it some lingering memory of its past. A barrack-room is still haunted by the ghost of Kipling, and it is difficult to enter a workhouse without being reminded of *Oliver Twist*. Hospitals began as a kind of casual ward for lepers and the like to die in, and they continued as places where medical students learned their art on the bodies of the poor. You can still catch a faint suggestion of their history in their characteristically gloomy architecture. I would be far from complaining about the treatment I have received in any English hospital, but I do know that it is a sound instinct that warns people to keep out of hospitals if possible, and especially out of the public wards. Whatever the legal position may be, it is unquestionable that you have far less control over your own treatment, far less certainty that frivolous experiments will not be tried on you, when it is a case of "accept the discipline or get out". And it is a great thing to die in your own bed, though it is better still to die in your boots. However great the kindness and the efficiency, in every hospital death there will be some cruel, squalid detail, something perhaps too small to be told but leaving terribly painful memories behind, arising out of the haste, the crowding, the impersonality of a place where every day people are dying among strangers.

The dread of hospitals probably still survives among the very poor and in all of us it has only recently disappeared. It is a dark patch not far beneath the surface of our minds. I have said earlier that, when I entered the ward at the Hôpital X, I was conscious of a strange feeling of familiarity. What the scene reminded me of, of course, was the reeking, pain-filled hospitals of the nineteenth century, which I had never seen but of which I had a traditional knowledge. And something, perhaps the black-clad doctor with his frowsy black bag, or perhaps only the sickly smell, played the queer trick of unearthing from my memory that poem of Tennyson's, "The Children's Hospital", which I had not thought of for twenty years. It happened that as a child I had had it read aloud to me by a sick-nurse whose own working life might have stretched back to the time when Tennyson wrote the poem. The horrors and sufferings of the old-style hospitals were a vivid memory to her. We had shuddered over the poem together, and then seemingly I had forgotten it. Even its name would probably have recalled nothing to me. But the first glimpse of the ill-lit, murmurous room, with the beds so close together, suddenly roused the train of thought to which it belonged, and in the night that followed I found myself remembering the whole story and atmosphere of the poem, with many of its lines complete.

Now, [N.S.], No. 6 [November 1946]; SE; OR; CE

59. Letter to Leonard Moore

27B Canonbury Square
Islington
London N1
2 November 1946

Dear Moore,

Many thanks for your letter dated 1st November.

I have read through the *New Yorker's* proposals carefully, and I do not think there is anything to object to. Only two doubtful points arise, i.e. the point referred to by them as (c), reprinting of articles of mine in books issued by the *New Yorker*, and the question of "editing" my reviews. I am not much concerned about reprints of this type of article because they would be strictly book reviews and would not be much more than 1,500 words, if that. I would never reprint in book form anything of less than 2,000 words, so I don't particularly mind if they choose to include things of mine in collections of snippets. When one has anything included in a book of this type, as one does from time to time, one never seems to get more than a few pounds out of it, and I don't see how anything else can be expected, since the royalties obviously have to be split up among the various contributors. I don't think it is worth asking the *New Yorker* to depart from its usual practice in this matter. The question of "editing" might be more difficult. In my experience one can never be sure that one's stuff will get to press unaltered in any daily or weekly periodical. The *Observer*, for instance, habitually cuts my articles without consulting me if there is a last-minute shortage of space. In writing for papers like the *Evening Standard*, I have had things not merely cut but actually altered, and of course even a cut always modifies the sense of an article to some extent. What really matters here is whether or not one is dealing with a civilised and intelligent paper. The *New Yorker* would be bound to make cuts occasionally, and would not as a rule have time to consult me, but I don't fancy they would alter my articles in any way I strongly objected to. So all in all I think we can accept their proposition as it stands. . . .

Yours sincerely
E.A. Blair

60. As I Please

Someone has just sent me a copy of an American fashion magazine which shall be nameless. It consists of 325 large quarto pages, of which no fewer than 15 are given up to articles on world politics, literature, etc. The rest consists entirely of pictures with a little letter-press creeping round their edges: pictures of ball dresses, mink coats, step-ins, panties, brassières, silk stockings, slippers, perfumes, lipsticks, nail varnish—and, of course, of the women, unrelievedly beautiful, who wear them or make use of them. I do not know just how many drawings or photographs of women occur throughout the whole volume, but as there are 45 of them, all beautiful, in the first 50 pages, one can work it out roughly.

One striking thing when one looks at these pictures is the overbred, exhausted, even decadent style of beauty that now seems to be striven after. Nearly all of these women are immensely elongated. A thin-boned, ancient-Egyptian type of face seems to predominate: narrow hips are general, and slender non-prehensile hands like those of a lizard are everywhere. Evidently it is a real physical type, for it occurs as much in the photographs as in the drawings. Another striking thing is the prose style of the advertisements, an extraordinary mixture of sheer lushness with clipped and sometimes very expressive technical jargon. Words like suave-mannered, custom-finished, contour-conforming, mitt-back, innersole, backdip, midriff, swoosh, swash, curvaceous, slenderise and pet-smooth are flung about with evident full expectation that the reader will understand them at a glance. Here are a few sample sentences taken at random:

"A new Shimmer Sheen colour that sets your hands and his head in a whirl." "Bared and beautifully bosomy." "Feathery-light Milliken Fleece to keep her kitten-snug!" "Others see you through a veil of sheer beauty, *and they wonder why!*" "Gentle discipline for curves in lacy lastex pantie-girdle." "An exclamation point of a dress that depends on fluid fabric for much of its drama." "Suddenly your figure lifts . . . lovely in the litheness of a Foundette pantie-girdle." "Lovely to look at, lovelier to wear is this original Lady Duff gown with its shirred cap sleeves and accentuated midriff." "Supple and tissue-light, yet wonderfully curve-holding." "The miracle of figure flattery!" "Moulds your bosom into proud feminine lines." "Isn't it wonderful to know that Corsees wash and wear and whittle you down . . . even though they weigh only four ounces!" "The distilled witchery of one woman who was forever desirable . . . forever beloved . . . Forever Amber." And so on and so on and so on.

A fairly diligent search through the magazine reveals two discreet allusions to grey hair, but if there is anywhere a direct mention of fatness or middle age I have not found it. Birth and death are not mentioned either: nor is work, except that a few recipes for breakfast dishes are given. The male sex enters directly or indirectly into perhaps one advertisement in twenty, and photographs of dogs or kittens appear here and there. In only two pictures, out of about three hundred, is a child represented.

On the front cover there is a coloured photograph of the usual elegant female standing on a chair while a grey-haired, spectacled, crushed-looking man in shirt-sleeves kneels at her feet, doing something to the edge of her skirt. If one looks closely one finds that actually he is about to take a measurement with a yard-measure. But to a casual glance he looks as though he were kissing the hem of the woman's garment—not a bad symbolical picture of American civilisation, or at least of one important side of it.

One interesting example of our unwillingness to face facts and our consequent readiness to make gestures which are known in advance to be useless, is the present campaign to Keep Death off the Roads.

The newspapers have just announced that road deaths for September dropped by nearly 80 as compared with the previous September. This is very well so far as it goes, but the improvement will probably not be kept up—at any rate, it will not be progressive —and meanwhile everyone knows that you *can't* solve the problem while our traffic system remains what it is. Accidents happen because on narrow, inadequate roads, full of blind corners and surrounded by dwelling houses, vehicles and pedestrians are moving in all directions at all speeds from three miles an hour to sixty or seventy. If you really want to keep death off the roads, you would have to replan the whole road system in such a way as to make collisions impossible. Think out what this means (it would involve, for example, pulling down and rebuilding the whole of London), and you can see that it is quite beyond the power of any nation at this moment. Short of that you can only take palliative measures, which ultimately boil down to making people more careful.

But the only palliative measure that would make a real difference is a drastic reduction in speed. Cut down the speed limit to twelve miles an hour in all built-up areas, and you would cut out the vast majority of accidents. But this, everyone will assure you, is "impossible". Why is it impossible? Well, it would be unbearably irksome. It would mean that every road journey took twice or three times as long as it takes at present. Besides, you could never get people to observe such a speed limit. What driver is going to crawl along at twelve miles an hour when he knows that his engine would do fifty? It is not even easy to keep a modern car down to twelve miles an hour and remain in high gear—and so on and so forth, all adding up to the statement that slow travel is of its nature intolerable.

In other words we value speed more highly than we value human life. Then why not say so, instead of every few years having one of these hypocritical campaigns (at present it is "Keep Death off the Roads"—a few years back it was "Learn the Kerb Step"), in the full knowledge that while our roads remain as they are, and present speeds are kept up, the slaughter must continue?

A sidelight on bread rationing. My neighbour in Scotland this summer was a crofter engaged on the enormous labour of reclaiming a farm which has been derelict for several years. He has no helper except a sister, he has only one horse, and he possesses only the most primitive machinery, which does not even include a reaper. Throughout this summer he certainly did not work less than fourteen hours a day, six days a week. When bread rationing started he put in for the extra ration, only to find that, though he could, indeed, get more bread than a sedentary worker, he was not entitled to the full agricultural labourer's ration. The reason? That within the meaning of the act he is not an agricultural labourer! Since he is "on his own" he ranks as a farmer, and it is assumed that he eats less bread than he would do if he were working for wages for somebody else.

Tribune, 8 November 1946

61. As I Please

As the clouds, most of them much larger and dirtier than a man's hand, come blowing up over the political horizon, there is one fact that obtrudes itself over and over again. This is that the Government's troubles, present and future, arise quite largely from its failure to publicise itself properly.

People are not told with sufficient clarity what is happening, and why, and what may be expected to happen in the near future. As a result, every calamity, great or small, takes the mass of the public by surprise, and the Government incurs unpopularity by doing things which any government, of whatever colour, would have to do in the same circumstances.

Take one question which has been much in the news lately but has never been properly thrashed out: the immigration of foreign labour into this country. Recently we have seen a tremendous outcry at the TUC[1] conference against allowing Poles to work in the two places where labour is most urgently needed—in the mines and on the land.

It will not do to write this off as something "got up" by Communist sympathisers, nor on the other hand to justify it by saying that

[1] Trades Union Congress.

the Polish refugees are all Fascists who "strut about" wearing monocles and carrying brief-cases.

The question is, would the attitude of the British trade unions be any friendlier if it were a question, not of alleged Fascists but of the admitted victims of Fascism?

For example, hundreds of thousands of homeless Jews are now trying desperately to get to Palestine. No doubt many of them will ultimately succeed, but others will fail. How about inviting, say, 100,000 Jewish refugees to settle in this country? Or what about the Displaced Persons, numbering nearly a million, who are dotted in camps all over Germany, with no future and no place to go, the United States and the British Dominions having already refused to admit them in significant numbers? Why not solve their problem by offering them British citizenship?

It is easy to imagine what the average Briton's answer would be. Even before the war, with the Nazi persecutions in full swing, there was no popular support for the idea of allowing large numbers of Jewish refugees into this country: nor was there any strong move to admit the hundreds of thousands of Spaniards who had fled from Franco to be penned up behind barbed wire in France.

For that matter, there was very little protest against the internment of the wretched German refugees in 1940. The comments I most often overheard at the time were "What did they want to come here for?" and "They're only after our jobs".

The fact is that there is strong popular feeling in this country against foreign immigration. It arises partly from simple xenophobia, partly from fear of undercutting in wages, but above all from the out-of-date notion that Britain is overpopulated and that more population means more unemployment.

Actually, so far from having more workers than jobs, we have a serious labour shortage which will be accentuated by the continuance of conscription, and which will grow worse, not better, because of the ageing of the population.

Meanwhile our birthrate is still frighteningly low, and several hundred thousand women of marriageable age have no chance of getting husbands. But how widely are these facts known or understood?

In the end it is doubtful whether we can solve our problems without encouraging immigration from Europe. In a tentative way the Government has already tried to do this, only to be met by ignorant hostility, because the public has not been told the relevant facts beforehand. So also with countless other unpopular things that will have to be done from time to time.

But the most necessary step is not to prepare public opinion for particular emergencies, but to raise the general level of political understanding: above all, to drive home the fact, which has never been properly grasped, that British prosperity depends largely on factors outside Britain.

This business of publicising and explaining itself is not easy for a Labour Government, faced by a press which at bottom is mostly hostile. Nevertheless, there are other ways of communicating with the public, and Mr Attlee and his colleagues might well pay more attention to the radio, a medium which very few politicians in this country have ever taken seriously.

There is one question which at first sight looks both petty and disgusting but which I should like to see answered. It is this. In the innumerable hangings of war criminals which have taken place all over Europe during the past few years, which method has been followed—the old method of strangulation, or the modern, comparatively humane method which is supposed to break the victim's neck at one snap?

A hundred years ago or more, people were hanged by simply hauling them up and letting them kick and struggle until they died, which might take a quarter of an hour or so. Later the drop was introduced, theoretically making death instantaneous, though it does not always work very well.

In recent years, however, there seems to have been a tendency to revert to strangulation. I did not see the news film of the hanging of the German war criminals at Kharkov, but the descriptions in the British press appeared to show that the older method was used. So also with various executions in the Balkan countries.

The newspaper accounts of the Nuremberg hangings were ambiguous. There was talk of a drop, but there was also talk of the condemned men taking ten or twenty minutes to die. Perhaps, by a typically Anglo-Saxon piece of compromise, it was decided to use a drop but to make it too short to be effective.

It is not a good symptom that hanging should still be the accepted form of capital punishment in this country. Hanging is a barbarous, inefficient way of killing anybody, and at least one fact about it—

quite widely known, I believe—is so obscene as to be almost unprintable.

Still, until recently we did feel rather uneasy on the subject, and we did have our hangings in private. Indeed, before the war, public execution was a thing of the past in nearly every civilised country. Now it seems to be returning, at least for political crimes, and though we ourselves have not actually reintroduced it as yet, we participate at second hand by watching the news films.

It is queer to look back and think that only a dozen years ago the abolition of the death penalty was one of those things that every enlightened person advocated as a matter of course, like divorce reform or the independence of India. Now, on the other hand, it is a mark of enlightenment not merely to approve of executions but to raise an outcry because there are not more of them.

Therefore it seems to me of some importance to know whether strangulation is now coming to be the normal practice. For if people are being taught to gloat not only over death but over a peculiarly horrible form of torture, it marks another turn on the downward spiral that we have been following ever since 1933.

Quotation wanted.

A character in one of Chekhov's stories, I forget which, remarks: "As Shakespeare says, 'Happy is he who in his youth is young.'" I have never been able to find this line, nor does it sound like Shakespeare. Possibly the translator retranslated it from the Russian instead of looking up the original. Can anybody tell me where it occurs?

Tribune, 15 November 1946

62. As I Please

In current discussions of the Royal Commission that is to enquire into the press, the talk is always of the debasing influence exerted by owners and advertisers. It is not said often enough that a nation gets the newspapers it deserves. Admittedly, this is not the whole of the truth. When the bulk of the press is owned by a handful of people, one has not much choice, and the fact that during the war the newspapers temporarily became more intelligent without losing circulation, suggests that the public taste is not quite so bad as it seems. Still, our newspapers are not all alike; some of them are more intelligent than others, and some are more popular than others. And when you study the relationship between intelligence and popularity, what do you find?

Below I list in two columns our nine leading national daily papers. In the first column these are ranged in order of intelligence, so far as I am able to judge it: in the other they are ranged in order of popularity, as measured by circulation. By intelligence I do not mean agreement with my own opinions. I mean a readiness to present news objectively, to give prominence to the things that really matter, to discuss serious questions even when they are dull, and to advocate policies which are at least coherent and intelligible. As to the circulation, I may have misplaced one or two papers, as I have no recent figures, but my list will not be far out. Here are the two lists:

INTELLIGENCE	POPULARITY
1. *Manchester Guardian.*	1. *Express.*
2. *Times.*	2. *Herald.*
3. *News Chronicle.*	3. *Mirror.*
4. *Telegraph.*	4. *News Chronicle.*
5. *Herald.*	5. *Mail.*
6. *Mail.*	6. *Graphic.*
7. *Mirror.*	7. *Telegraph.*
8. *Express.*	8. *Times.*
9. *Graphic.*	9. *Manchester Guardian.*

It will be seen that the second list is very nearly—not quite, for life is never so neat as that—the first turned upside down. And even if I have not ranged these papers in quite the right order, the general relationship holds good. The paper that has the best reputation for truthfulness, the *Manchester Guardian*, is the one that is not read even by those who admire it. People complain that it is "so dull". On the other hand countless people read the *Daily* —— while saying frankly that they "don't believe a word of it".

In these circumstances it is difficult to foresee a radical change, even if the special kind of pressure exerted by owners and advertisers is removed. What matters is that in England we do possess juridical liberty of the press, which makes it possible to utter one's true opinions fearlessly in papers of comparatively small circulation. It is vitally important to hang on to that. But no Royal Commission can make the big-circulation press much better than it is, however much it manipulates the methods of control. We shall have a serious and truthful popular press when public opinion actively demands it. Till then, if the news is not distorted by businessmen it will be distorted by bureaucrats, who are only one degree better.

Tribune, 22 November 1946

63. Riding Down from Bangor

The reappearance of *Helen's Babies*,[1] in its day one of the most popular books in the world—within the British Empire alone it was pirated by twenty different publishing firms, the author receiving a total profit of £40 from a sale of some hundreds of thousands or millions of copies—will ring a bell in any literate person over thirty-five. Not that the present edition is an altogether satisfactory one. It is a cheap little book with rather unsuitable illustrations, various American dialect words appear to have been cut out of it, and the sequel, *Other People's Children*, which was often bound up with it in earlier editions, is missing. Still, it is pleasant to see *Helen's Babies* in print again. It had become almost a rarity in recent years, and it is one of the best of the little library of American books on which people born at about the turn of the century were brought up.

The books one reads in childhood, and perhaps most of all the bad and good bad books, create in one's mind a sort of false map of the world, a series of fabulous countries into which one can retreat at odd moments throughout the rest of life, and which in some cases can even survive a visit to the real countries which they are supposed to represent. The pampas, the Amazon, the coral islands of the Pacific, Russia, land of birch-tree and samovar, Transylvania with its boyars and vampires, the China of Guy Boothby, the Paris of du Maurier—one could continue the list for a long time. But one other imaginary country that I acquired early in life was called America. If I pause on the word "America", and, deliberately putting aside the existing reality, call up my childhood vision of it, I see two pictures

[1] *Helen's Babies* by John Habberton, first published in 1876.

—composite pictures, of course, from which I am omitting a good deal of the detail.

One is of a boy sitting in a whitewashed stone schoolroom. He wears braces and has patches on his shirt, and if it is summer he is barefooted. In the corner of the school room there is a bucket of drinking water with a dipper. The boy lives in a farm-house, also of stone and also whitewashed, which has a mortgage on it. He aspires to be President, and is expected to keep the woodpile full. Somewhere in the background of the picture, but completely dominating it, is a huge black Bible. The other picture is of a tall, angular man, with a shapeless hat pulled down over his eyes, leaning against a wooden paling and whittling at a stick. His lower jaw moves slowly but ceaselessly. At very long intervals he emits some piece of wisdom such as "A woman is the orneriest critter there is, 'ceptin' a mule", or "When you don't know a thing to do, don't do a thing"; but more often it is a jet of tobacco juice that issues from the gap in his front teeth. Between them those two pictures summed up my earliest impression of America. And of the two, the first—which, I suppose, represented New England, the other representing the South—had the stronger hold upon me.

The books from which these pictures were derived included, of course, books which it is still possible to take seriously, such as *Tom Sawyer* and *Uncle Tom's Cabin*, but the most richly American flavour was to be found in minor works which are now almost forgotten. I wonder, for instance, if anyone still reads *Rebecca of Sunnybrook Farm*, which remained a popular favourite long enough to be filmed with Mary Pickford in the leading part. Or how about the "Katy" books by Susan Coolidge (*What Katy Did at School*, etc), which, although girls' books and therefore "soppy", had the fascination of foreignness? Louisa M. Alcott's *Little Women* and *Good Wives* are, I suppose, still flickeringly in print, and certainly they still have their devotees. As a child I loved both of them, though I was less pleased by the third of the trilogy, *Little Men*. That model school where the worst punishment was to have to whack the schoolmaster, on "this hurts me more than it hurts you" principles, was rather difficult to swallow.

Helen's Babies belonged in much the same world as *Little Women*, and must have been published round about the same date. Then there were Artemus Ward, Bret Harte, and various songs, hymns and ballads, besides poems dealing with the civil war, such as

"Barbara Fritchie" ("'Shoot if you must this old grey head, But spare your country's flag,' she said") and "Little Gifford of Tennessee". There were other books so obscure that it hardly seems worth mentioning them, and magazine stories of which I remember nothing except that the old homestead always seemed to have a mortgage on it. There was also *Beautiful Joe*, the American reply to *Black Beauty*, of which you might just possibly pick up a copy in a sixpenny box. All the books I have mentioned were written well before 1900, but something of the special American flavour lingered on into this century in, for instance, the Buster Brown coloured supplements, and even in Booth Tarkington's "Penrod" stories, which will have been written round about 1910. Perhaps there was even a tinge of it in Ernest Thompson Seton's animal books (*Wild Animals I Have Known*, etc), which have now fallen from favour but which drew tears from the pre-1914 child as surely as *Misunderstood* had done from the children of a generation earlier.

Somewhat later my picture of nineteenth-century America was given greater precision by a song which is still fairly well known and which can be found (I think) in the *Scottish Students' Song Book*. As usual in these bookless days I cannot get hold of a copy, and I must quote fragments from memory. It begins:

> Riding down from Bangor
> On an Eastern train,
> Bronzed with weeks of hunting
> In the woods of Maine—
> Quite extensive whiskers,
> Beard, moustache as well—
> Sat a student fellow,
> Tall and slim and swell.

Presently an aged couple and a "village maiden", described as "beautiful, petite", get into the carriage. Quantities of cinders are flying about, and before long the student fellow gets one in his eye: the village maiden extracts it for him, to the scandal of the aged couple. Soon after this the train shoots into a long tunnel, "black as Egypt's night". When it emerges into the daylight again the maiden is covered with blushes, and the cause of her confusion is revealed when

> There suddenly appeared
> A tiny little ear-ring
> In that horrid student's beard!

I do not know the date of the song, but the primitiveness of the train (no lights in the carriage, and a cinder in one's eye a normal accident) suggests that it belongs well back in the nineteenth century.

What connects this song with books like *Helen's Babies* is first of all a sort of sweet innocence—the climax, the thing you are supposed to be slightly shocked at, is an episode with which any modern piece of naughty-naughty would *start*—and, secondly, a faint vulgarity of language mixed up with a certain cultural pretentiousness. *Helen's Babies* is intended as a humorous, even a farcical book, but it is haunted all the way through by words like "tasteful" and "ladylike", and it is funny chiefly because its tiny disasters happen against a background of conscious gentility. "Handsome, intelligent, composed, tastefully dressed, without a suspicion of the flirt or the languid woman of fashion about her, she awakened to the utmost my every admiring sentiment"—thus is the heroine described, figuring elsewhere as "erect, fresh, neat, composed, bright-eyed, fair-faced, smiling and observant". One gets beautiful glimpses of a now-vanished world in such remarks as: "I believe you arranged the floral decorations at St Zephaniah's Fair last winter, Mr Burton? 'Twas the most tasteful display of the season." But in spite of the occasional use of "'twas" and other archaisms—"parlour" for sitting-room, "chamber" for bedroom, "real" as an adverb, and so forth—the book does not "date" very markedly, and many of its admirers imagine it to have been written round about 1900. Actually it was written in 1875, a fact which one might infer from internal evidence, since the hero, aged twenty-eight, is a veteran of the civil war.

The book is very short and the story is a simple one. A young bachelor is prevailed on by his sister to look after her house and her two sons, aged five and three, while she and her husband go on a fortnight's holiday. The children drive him almost mad by an endless succession of such acts as falling into ponds, swallowing poison, throwing keys down wells, cutting themselves with razors, and the like, but also facilitate his engagement to "a charming girl, whom, for about a year, I had been adoring from afar". These events take place in an outer suburb of New York, in a society which now seems astonishingly sedate, formal, domesticated and, according to current conceptions, un-American. Every action is governed by etiquette. To pass a carriage full of ladies when your hat is crooked is an ordeal; to recognise an acquaintance in church is ill-bred; to become engaged after a ten days' courtship is a severe social lapse. We are accustomed to thinking of American society as more crude, adventurous and, in a cultural sense, democratic than our own, and from writers like Mark Twain, Whitman and Bret Harte, not to mention the cowboy and Red Indian stories of the weekly papers, one draws a picture of a wild anarchic world peopled by eccentrics and desperadoes who have no traditions and no attachment to one place. That aspect of nineteenth-century America did of course exist, but in the more populous eastern States a society similar to Jane Austen's seems to have survived longer than it did in England. And it is hard not to feel that it was a better kind of society than that which arose from the sudden industrialisation of the later part of the century. The people in *Helen's Babies* or *Little Women* may be mildly ridiculous, but they are uncorrupted. They have something that is perhaps best described as integrity, or good morale, founded partly on an unthinking piety. It is a matter of course that everyone attends church on Sunday morning and says grace before meals and prayers at bedtime: to amuse the children one tells them Bible stories, and if they ask for a song it is probably "Glory, glory Hallelujah". Perhaps it is also a sign of spiritual health in the light literature of this period that death is mentioned freely. "Baby Phil", the brother of Budge and Toddie, has died shortly before *Helen's Babies* opens, and there are various tear-jerking references to his "tiny coffin". A modern writer attempting a story of this kind would have kept coffins out of it

English children are still americanised by way of the films, but it would no longer be generally claimed that American books are the best ones for children. Who, without misgivings, would bring up a child on the coloured "comics" in which sinister professors manufacture atomic bombs in underground laboratories while Superman whizzes through the clouds, the machine-gun bullets bouncing off his chest like peas, and platinum blondes are raped, or very nearly, by steel robots and fifty-foot dinosaurs? It is a far cry from Superman to the Bible and the woodpile. The earlier children's books, or books readable by children, had not only innocence but a sort of native gaiety, a buoyant, carefree feeling, which was the product, presumably, of the unheard-of freedom and security which nineteenth-century America enjoyed. That is the connecting link between books so seemingly far apart as *Little Women* and *Life on the Mississippi*. The society described in the one is subdued, bookish and home-loving, while the other tells of a crazy world of bandits, gold mines, duels, drunkenness and gambling hells: but in both one can detect an underlying confidence in the future, a sense of freedom and opportunity.

Nineteenth-century America was a rich, empty country which lay outside the main stream of world events, and in which the twin nightmares that beset nearly every modern man, the nightmare of unemployment and the nightmare of State interference, had hardly come into being. There were social distinctions, more marked than those of today, and there was poverty (in *Little Women*, it will be remembered, the family is at one time so hard up that one of the girls sells her hair to the barber), but there was not, as there is now, an all-prevailing sense of helplessness. There was room for everybody, and if you worked hard you could be certain of a living—could even be certain of growing rich: this was generally believed, and for the greater part of the population it was even broadly true. In other words, the civilisation of nineteenth-century America was capitalist civilisation at its best. Soon after the civil war the inevitable deterioration started. But for some decades, at least, life in America was much better fun than life in Europe—there was more happening, more colour, more variety, more opportunity—and the books and songs of that period had a sort of bloom, a childlike quality. Hence, I think, the popularity of *Helen's Babies* and other "light" literature, which made it normal for the English child of thirty or forty years ago to grow up with a theoretical knowledge of racoons, woodchucks, chipmunks, gophers, hickory trees, water-melons and other unfamiliar fragments of the American scene.

Tribune, 22 November 1946; SE

64. As I Please

Here is an analysis of the front page of my morning newspaper, on an ordinary, uneventful day in November, 1946.

The big headline goes to the UN conference, at which the USSR is putting forward demands for an enquiry into the strength of Anglo-American forces in ex-enemy or allied countries. This is obviously intended to forestall a demand for inspection of forces inside the USSR, and it is plain to see that the resulting discussion will lead to nothing except recriminations and a prestige victory for this side or that, with no advance, and no attempt at any advance, towards genuine international agreement.

The fighting in Greece is growing more serious. The constitutional opposition is swinging more and more towards support of the rebels, while the Government is alleging that the so-called rebels are in fact guerrillas operating from across the frontier.

There is further delay in calling the Indian Constituent Assembly (this column has a footnote: "Blood-bath in India: Page Two"), and Mr Gandhi has starved himself into a condition which is causing anxiety.

The American coal strike is continuing, and is likely to "have disastrous effects on world grain supplies". Owing to other recent strikes, the United States has cancelled delivery of two million tons of steel to Britain, which will further complicate the British housing problem. There is also an unofficial "go slow" movement on the Great Western Railway.

Another bomb has gone off in Jerusalem, with a number of casualties. There is also news of various minor unavoidable calamities, such as a plane crash, the likelihood of floods all over England, and a collision of ships in the Mersey, with the apparent loss of 100 head of cattle, which I suppose would represent one week's meat ration for about 40,000 people.

There is no definitely good news at all on the front page. There are items, such as a rise in British exports during October, which look as if they might be good, but which might turn out to be bad if one had sufficient knowledge to interpret them. There is also a short statement to the effect that the occupying powers in Germany "may" shortly reach a better agreement. But this is hardly more than the expression of a pious wish, unsupported by evidence.

I repeat that this pageful of disasters is merely the record of an average day, when nothing much is happening: and incidentally it occurs in a newspaper which, rather more than most, tries to put a good face on things.

When one considers how things have gone since 1930 or thereabouts, it is not easy to believe in the survival of civilisation. I do not argue from this that the only thing to do is to abjure practical politics, retire to some remote place and concentrate either on individual salvation or on building up self-supporting communities against the day when the atom bombs have done their work. I think one must continue the political struggle, just as a doctor must try to save the life of a patient who is probably going to die. But I do suggest that we shall get nowhere unless we start by recognising that political behaviour is largely non-rational, that the world is suffering from some kind of mental disease which must be diagnosed before it can be cured. The significant point is that nearly all the calamities that happen to us are quite unnecessary. It is commonly assumed that what human beings want is to be comfortable. Well, we now have it in our power to be comfortable, as our ancestors had not. Nature may occasionally hit back with an earthquake or a cyclone, but by and large she is beaten. And yet exactly at the moment when there is, or could be, plenty of everything for everybody, nearly our whole energies have to be taken up in trying to grab territories, markets and raw materials from one another. Exactly at the moment when wealth might be so generally diffused that no government need fear serious opposition, political liberty is declared to be impossible and half the world is ruled by secret police forces. Exactly at the moment when superstition crumbles and a rational attitude towards the universe becomes feasible, the right to think one's own thoughts is denied as never before. The fact is that human beings only started fighting one another in earnest when there was no longer anything to fight about.

It is not easy to find a direct economic explanation of the behaviour of the people who now rule the world. The desire for pure power seems to be much more dominant than the desire for wealth. This has often been pointed out, but curiously enough the desire for power seems to be taken for granted as a natural instinct, equally prevalent in all ages, like the desire for food. Actually it is no more natural, in the sense of being biologically necessary, than drunkenness or gambling. And if it has reached new levels of lunacy in our own age, as I think it has, then the question becomes: What is the special quality in modern life that makes a major human motive out of the impulse to bully others? If we could answer that question —seldom asked, never followed up—there might occasionally be a bit of good news on the front page of your morning paper.

However, it is always possible, in spite of appearances, that the age we live in is *not* worse than the other ages that have preceded it, nor perhaps even greatly different. At least this possibility occurs to me when I think of an Indian proverb which a friend of mine once translated:

> In April was the jackal born,
> In June the rain-fed rivers swelled:
> "Never in all my life," said he,
> "Have I so great a flood beheld."[1]

I suppose the shortage of clocks and watches is nobody's fault, but is it necessary to let their prices rocket as they have done in the last year or two?

Early this year I saw ex-army watches exhibited in a showcase at a little under £4 each. A week or two later I succeeded in buying one of them for £5. Recently their price seems to have risen to £8. A year or two ago, alarm clocks, which at that time could not be bought without a permit, were on sale at 16 shillings each. This was the controlled price, and presumably it did not represent an actual loss to the manufacturer. The other day I saw precisely similar clocks at 45 shillings—a jump of 180 per cent. Is it really conceivable that the cost price has increased correspondingly?

Incidentally, for 45 shillings you can, if you are on the phone, arrange for the telephone operator to call you every morning for nearly 18 months, which is a lot longer than the life of the average alarm clock.

Under the heading, "The Return of the Jews to Palestine", Samuel Butler records in his *Note-Books*:

> A man called on me last week and proposed gravely that I should write a book upon an idea which had occurred to a friend of his, a Jew living in New Bond Street. . . . If only I would help, the return of the Jews to Palestine would be rendered certain and easy. There was no trouble about the poor Jews, he knew how he could get them back at any time; the difficulty lay with the Rothschilds, the Oppenheims and such; with my assistance, however, the thing could be done.
>
> I am afraid I was rude enough to decline to go into the scheme on the ground that I did not care twopence whether the Roths-

[1] In "As I Please", *Tribune* 24 January 1947, Orwell wrote; "A few weeks ago I quoted an Indian proverb in this column, and erroneously said that it had been translated by a friend of mine. Actually the verse I quoted comes from Kipling. This illustrates something I have pointed out elsewhere (see II, 30)—that Kipling is one of those writers whom one quotes unconsciously."

childs and Oppenheims went back to Palestine or not. This was felt to be an obstacle; but then he began to try and make me care, whereupon, of course, I had to get rid of him.

This was written in 1883. And who would have foreseen that only about sixty years later nearly all the Jews in Europe would be trying to get back to Palestine of their own accord, while nearly everybody else would be trying to stop them?

Tribune, 29 November 1946

65. As I Please

With great enjoyment I have just been rereading *Trilby*, George du Maurier's justly popular novel, one of the finest specimens of that "good bad" literature which the English-speaking peoples seem to have lost the secret of producing. *Trilby* is an imitation of Thackeray, a very good imitation and immensely readable—Bernard Shaw, if I remember rightly, considered it to be *better* than Thackeray in many ways—but to me the most interesting thing about it is the different impressions one derives from reading it first before and then after the career of Hitler.

The thing that now hits one in the eye in reading *Trilby* is its antisemitism. I suppose, although few people actually read the book now, its central story is fairly widely known, the name of Svengali having become a by-word, like that of Sherlock Holmes. A Jewish musician—not a composer, but a brilliant pianist and music-teacher—gets into his power an orphaned Irish girl, a painters' model, who has a magnificent voice but happens to be tone-deaf. Having hypnotised her one day to cure an attack of neuralgia, he discovers that when she is in the hypnotic trance she can be taught to sing in tune.

Thereafter, for about two years, the pair of them travel from one European capital to another, the girl singing every night to enormous and ecstatic audiences, and never even knowing, in her waking life, that she is a singer. The end comes when Svengali dies suddenly in the middle of a concert and Trilby breaks down and is booed off the stage. That is the main story, though of course there is much else, including an unhappy love affair and three clean-living English painters who make a foil for Svengali's villainy.

There is no question that the book is antisemitic. Apart from the fact that Svengali's vanity, treacherousness, selfishness, personal uncleanliness and so forth are constantly connected with the fact that he is a Jew, there are the illustrations. Du Maurier, better known for his drawings in *Punch* than for his writings, illustrated his own book, and he made Svengali into a sinister caricature of the traditional type. But what is most interesting is the divergence of the antisemitism of that date—1895, the period of the Dreyfus Case—and that of today.

To begin with, du Maurier evidently holds that there are two kinds of Jew, good ones and bad ones, and that there is a racial difference between them. There enters briefly into the story another Jew, Glorioli, who possesses all the virtues and qualities that Svengali lacks. Glorioli is "one of the Sephardim"—of Spanish extraction, that is—whereas Svengali, who comes from German Poland, is "an oriental Israelite Hebrew Jew". Secondly du Maurier considers that to have a dash of Jewish blood is an advantage. We are told that the hero, Little Billee, may have had some Jewish blood, of which there was a suggestion in his features, and "fortunately for the world, and especially for ourselves, most of us have in our veins at least a minimum of that precious fluid". Clearly, this is not the Nazi form of antisemitism.

And yet the tone of all the references to Svengali is almost unconsciously contemptuous, and the fact that du Maurier chose a Jew to play such a part is significant. Svengali, who cannot sing himself and has to sing, as it were, through Trilby's lungs, represents that well-known type, the clever underling who acts as the brains of some more impressive person.

It is queer how freely du Maurier admits that Svengali is more gifted than the three Englishmen, even than Little Billee, who is represented, unconvincingly, as a brilliant painter. Svengali has "genius", but the others have "character", and "character" is what matters. It is the attitude of the rugger-playing prefect towards the spectacled "swot", and it was probably the normal attitude towards Jews at that time. They were natural inferiors, but of course they were cleverer, more sensitive and more artistic than ourselves, because such qualities are of secondary importance. Nowadays the English are less sure of themselves, less confident that stupidity always wins in the end, and the prevailing form of antisemitism has changed, not altogether for the better.

In last week's *Tribune* Mr Julian Symons remarked—rightly, I think —that Aldous Huxley's later novels are much inferior to his earlier ones. But he might have added that this kind of falling-off is usual in imaginative writers, and that it only goes unnoticed when a writer is, so to speak, carried forward by the momentum of his earlier books. We value H.G. Wells, for example, for *Tono-Bungay*, *Mr Polly*, *The Time Machine*, etc. If he had stopped writing in 1920 his reputation would stand quite as high as it does: if we knew him only by the books he wrote after that date, we should have rather a low opinion of him. A novelist does not, any more than a boxer or a ballet dancer, last for ever. He has an initial impulse which is good for three or four books, perhaps even for a dozen, but which must exhaust itself sooner or later. Obviously one cannot lay down any rigid rule, but in many cases the creative impulse seems to last for about 15 years: in a prose writer these 15 years would probably be between the ages of 30 and 45, or thereabouts. A few writers, it is true, have a much longer lease of life, and can go on developing when they are middle-aged or even old. But these are usually writers (examples: Yeats, Eliot, Hardy, Tolstoy) who make a sudden, almost violent change in their style, or their subject-matter, or both, and who may even tend to repudiate their earlier work.

Many writers, perhaps most, ought simply to stop writing when they reach middle age. Unfortunately our society will not let them stop. Most of them know no other way of earning a living, and writing, with all that goes with it—quarrels, rivalries, flattery, the sense of being a semi-public figure—is habit-forming. In a reasonable world a writer who had said his say would simply take up some other profession. In a competitive society he feels, just as a politician does, that retirement is death. So he continues long after his impulse is spent, and, as a rule, the less conscious he is of imitating himself, the more grossly he does it.

Early this year I met an American publisher who told me that his firm had just had a nine-months lawsuit from which it had emerged partially victorious, though out of pocket. It concerned the printing of a four-letter word which most of us use every day, generally in the present participle.

The United States is usually a few years ahead of Britain in these matters. You could print "b———" in full in American books at a time when it had to appear in English ones as B dash. Recently it has become possible in England to print the word in full in a book, but in periodicals it still has to be B dash. Only five or six years ago it was printed in a well-known monthly magazine, but the last-minute panic was so great that a weary staff had to black the word out by hand.

As to the other word, the four-letter one, it is still unprintable in periodicals in this country, but in books it can be represented by its first letter and a dash. In the United States this point was reached at least a dozen years ago. Last year the publishing firm in question tried the experiment of printing the word in full. The book was suppressed, and after nine months of litigation the suppression was upheld. But in the process an important step forward was made. It was ruled that you may now print the first and last letters of the word with two asterisks in between, clearly indicating that it had four letters. This makes it reasonably sure that within a few years the word will be printable in full.

So does progress continue—and it is genuine progress, in my opinion, for if only our half-dozen "bad" words could be got off the lavatory wall and on to the printed page, they would soon lose their magical quality, and the habit of swearing, degrading to our thoughts and weakening to our language, might become less common.

Tribune, 6 December 1946

66. As I Please

When one reads the reports of UNO conferences, or international negotiations of any kind, it is difficult not to be reminded of *l'Attaque* and similar war games that children used to play, with cardboard pieces representing battleships, aeroplanes and so forth, each of which had a fixed value and could be countered in some recognised way. In fact, one might almost invent a new game called Uno, to be played in enlightened homes where the parents do not want their children to grow up with a militaristic outlook.

The pieces in this game are called the proposal, the *démarche*, the formula, the stumbling-block, the stalemate, the deadlock, the bottle-neck and the vicious circle. The object of the game is to arrive at a formula, and though details vary, the general outline of play is always much the same. First the players assemble, and somebody leads off with the proposal. This is countered by the stumbling-block, without which the game could not develop. The stumbling-block then changes into a bottle-neck, or more often into a deadlock or a vicious circle. A deadlock and a vicious circle occurring simultaneously produce a stalemate, which may last for weeks. Then suddenly someone plays the *démarche*. The *démarche* makes it possible to produce a formula, and once the formula has been found the players can go home, leaving everything as it was at the beginning.

At the moment of writing, the front page of my morning paper has broken out into a pink rash of optimism. It seems that everything is going to be all right after all. The Russians will agree to inspection of armaments, and the Americans will internationalise the atomic bomb. On another page of the same paper are reports of events in Greece which amount to a state of war between the two groups of powers who are being so chummy in New York.

But while the game of deadlocks and bottle-necks goes on, another more serious game is also being played. It is governed by two axioms. One is that there can be no peace without a general surrender of sovereignty: the other is that no country capable of defending its sovereignty ever surrenders it. If one keeps these axioms in mind one can generally see the relevant facts in international affairs through the smoke-screen with which the newspapers surround them. At the moment the main facts are:

1. The Russians, whatever they may say, will not agree to genuine inspection of their territories by foreign observers.

2. The Americans, whatever they may say, will not let slip the technological lead in armaments.

3. No country is now in a condition to fight an all-out major war.

These, although they may be superseded later, are at present the real counters in the real game, and one gets nearer the truth by constantly remembering them than by alternately rejoicing and despairing over the day-to-day humbug of conferences.

Tribune, 13 December 1946

67. As I Please

An advertisement in my Sunday paper sets forth in the form of a picture the four things that are needed for a successful Christmas. At the top of the picture is a roast turkey; below that, a Christmas pudding; below that, a dish of mince pies; and below that, a tin of ——'s Liver Salt.

It is a simple recipe for happiness. First the meal, then the antidote, then another meal. The ancient Romans were the great masters of this technique. However, having just looked up the word *vomitorium* in the Latin dictionary, I find that after all it does *not* mean a place where you went to be sick after dinner. So perhaps this was not a normal feature of every Roman home, as is commonly believed.

Implied in the above-mentioned advertisement is the notion that a good meal means a meal at which you overeat yourself. In principle I agree. I only add in passing that when we gorge ourselves this Christmas, if we do get the chance to gorge ourselves, it is worth giving a thought to the thousand million human beings, or there-abouts, who will be doing no such thing. For in the long run our Christmas dinners would be safer if we could make sure that everyone else had a Christmas dinner as well. But I will come back to that presently.

The only reasonable motive for not overeating at Christmas would be that somebody else needs the food more than you do. A deliberately austere Christmas would be an absurdity. The whole point of Christmas is that it is a debauch—as it was probably long before the birth of Christ was arbitrarily fixed at that date. Children know this very well. From their point of view Christmas is not a day of temperate enjoyment, but of fierce pleasures which they are quite willing to pay for with a certain amount of pain. The awakening at about 4 am to inspect your stocking; the quarrels over toys all through the morning, and the exciting whiffs of mincemeat and sage-and-onions escaping from the kitchen door; the battle with enormous platefuls of turkey, and the pulling of the wishbone; the darkening of the windows and the entry of the flaming plum pudding; the hurry to make sure that everyone has a piece on his plate while the brandy is still alight; the momentary panic when it is rumoured that Baby has swallowed the threepenny bit; the stupor all through the after-noon; the Christmas cake with almond icing an inch thick; the

peevishness next morning and the castor oil on December 27th—
it is an up-and-down business, by no means all pleasant, but well
worth while for the sake of its more dramatic moments.

Teetotallers and vegetarians are always scandalised by this attitude.
As they see it, the only rational objective is to avoid pain and to stay
alive as long as possible. If you refrain from drinking alcohol, or
eating meat, or whatever it is, you may expect to live an extra five
years, while if you overeat or overdrink you will pay for it in acute
physical pain on the following day. Surely it follows that all excesses,
even a once-a-year outbreak such as Christmas, should be avoided
as a matter of course?

Actually it doesn't follow at all. One may decide, with full knowledge of what one is doing, that an occasional good time is
worth the damage it inflicts on one's liver. For health is not the only
thing that matters: friendship, hospitality, and the heightened spirits
and change of outlook that one gets by eating and drinking in good
company are also valuable. I doubt whether, on balance, even outright drunkenness does harm, provided it is infrequent—twice a year,
say. The whole experience, including the repentance afterwards,
makes a sort of break in one's mental routine, comparable to a week-
end in a foreign country, which is probably beneficial.

In all ages men have realised this. There is a wide consensus of
opinion, stretching back to the days before the alphabet, that whereas
habitual soaking is bad, conviviality is good, even if one does sometimes feel sorry for it next morning. How enormous is the literature
of eating and drinking, especially drinking, and how little that is
worth while has been said on the other side! Offhand I can't remember a single poem in praise of water, i.e. water regarded as a drink.
It is hard to imagine what one could say about it. It quenches thirst:
that is the end of the story. As for poems in praise of wine, on the
other hand, even the surviving ones would fill a shelf of books. The
poets started turning them out on the very day when the fermentation
of the grape was first discovered. Whisky, brandy and other distilled
liquors have been less eloquently praised, partly because they came
later in time. But beer has had quite a good press, starting well back
in the Middle Ages, long before anyone had learned to put hops in it.
Curiously enough, I can't remember a poem in praise of stout, not
even draught stout, which is better than the bottled variety, in my
opinion. There is an extremely disgusting description in *Ulysses* of
the stout-vats in Dublin. But there is a sort of back-handed tribute

to stout in the fact that this description, though widely known, has not done much towards putting the Irish off their favourite drink.

The literature of eating is also large, though mostly in prose. But in all the writers who have enjoyed describing food, from Rabelais to Dickens and from Petronius to Mrs Beeton, I cannot remember a single passage which puts dietetic considerations first. Always food is felt to be an end in itself. No one has written memorable prose about vitamins, or the dangers of an excess of proteins, or the importance of masticating everything thirty-two times. All in all, there seems to be a heavy weight of testimony on the side of overeating and over-drinking, provided always that they take place on recognised occasions and not too frequently.

But ought we to overeat and overdrink this Christmas? We ought not to, nor will most of us get the opportunity. I am writing in praise of Christmas, but in praise of Christmas 1947, or perhaps 1948. The world as a whole is not exactly in a condition for festivities this year. Between the Rhine and the Pacific there cannot be very many people who are in need of ——'s Liver Salt. In India there are, and always have been, about 100 million people who only get one square meal a day. In China, conditions are no doubt much the same. In Germany, Austria, Greece and elsewhere, scores of millions of people are existing on a diet which keeps breath in the body but leaves no strength for work. All over the war-wrecked areas from Brussels to Stalingrad, other uncounted millions are living in the cellars of bombed houses, in hide-outs in the forests, or in squalid huts behind barbed wire. It is not so pleasant to read almost simul-taneously that a large proportion of our Christmas turkeys will come from Hungary, and that the Hungarian writers and journalists—presumably not the worst-paid section of the community—are in such desperate straits that they would be glad to receive presents of saccharine and cast-off clothing from English sympathisers. In such circumstances we could hardly have a "proper" Christmas, even if the materials for it existed.

But we will have one sooner or later, in 1947, or 1948, or maybe even in 1949. And when we do, may there be no gloomy voices of vegetarians or teetotallers to lecture us about the things that we are doing to the linings of our stomachs. One celebrates a feast for its own sake, and not for any supposed benefit to the lining of one's stomach. Meanwhile Christmas is here, or nearly. Santa Claus is rounding up his reindeer, the postman staggers from door to door beneath his bulging sack of Christmas cards, the black markets are humming, and Britain has imported over 7,000 crates of mistletoe from France. So I wish everyone an old-fashioned Christmas in 1947, and meanwhile, half a turkey, three tangerines, and a bottle of whisky at not more than double the legal price.

Tribune, 20 December 1946

68. As I Please

Somewhere or other—I think it is in the preface to *Saint Joan*—Bernard Shaw remarks that we are more gullible and superstitious today than we were in the Middle Ages, and as an example of modern credulity he cites the widespread belief that the earth is round. The average man, says Shaw, can advance not a single reason for thinking that the earth is round. He merely swallows this theory because there is something about it that appeals to the twentieth-century mentality.

Now, Shaw is exaggerating, but there is something in what he says, and the question is worth following up, for the sake of the light it throws on modern knowledge. Just why *do* we believe that the earth is round? I am not speaking of the few thousand astronomers, geographers and so forth who could give ocular proof, or have a theoretical knowledge of the proof, but of the ordinary newspaper-reading citizen, such as you or me.

As for the Flat Earth theory, I believe I could refute it. If you stand by the seashore on a clear day, you can see the masts and funnels of invisible ships passing along the horizon. This phenomenon can only be explained by assuming that the earth's surface is curved. But it does not follow that the earth is spherical. Imagine another theory called the Oval Earth theory, which claims that the earth is shaped like an egg. What can I say against it?

Against the Oval Earth man, the first card I can play is the analogy of the sun and moon. The Oval Earth man promptly answers that I don't know, by my own observation, that those bodies are spherical. I only know that they are round, and they may perfectly well be flat discs. I have no answer to that one. Besides, he goes on, what reason have I for thinking that the earth must be the same shape as the sun and moon? I can't answer that one either.

My second card is the earth's shadow: when cast on the moon during eclipses, it appears to be the shadow of a round object. But how do I know, demands the Oval Earth man, that eclipses of the moon are caused by the shadow of the earth? The answer is that I don't know, but have taken this piece of information blindly from newspaper articles and science booklets.

Defeated in the minor exchanges, I now play my queen of trumps: the opinion of the experts. The Astronomer Royal, who ought to know, tells me that the earth is round. The Oval Earth man covers the queen with his king. Have I tested the Astronomer Royal's statement, and would I even know a way of testing it? Here I bring out my ace. Yes, I do know one test. The astronomers can foretell eclipses, and this suggests that their opinions about the solar system are pretty sound. I am therefore justified in accepting their say-so about the shape of the earth.

If the Oval Earth man answers—what I believe is true—that the ancient Egyptians, who thought the sun goes round the earth, could also predict eclipses, then bang goes my ace. I have only one card left: navigation. People can sail ships round the world, and reach the places they aim at, by calculations which assume that the earth is spherical. I believe that finishes the Oval Earth man, though even then he may possibly have some kind of counter.

It will be seen that my reasons for thinking that the earth is round are rather precarious ones. Yet this is an exceptionally elementary piece of information. On most other questions I should have to fall back on the expert much earlier, and would be less able to test his pronouncements. And much the greater part of our knowledge is at this level. It does not rest on reasoning or on experiment, but on authority. And how can it be otherwise, when the range of knowledge is so vast that the expert himself is an ignoramus as soon as he strays away from his own speciality? Most people, if asked to prove that the earth is round, would not even bother to produce the rather weak arguments I have outlined above. They would start off by saying that "everyone knows" the earth to be round, and if pressed further, would become angry. In a way Shaw is right. This *is* a credulous age, and the burden of knowledge which we now have to carry is partly responsible.

Opinions may differ about the verdict in Professor Laski's libel case.[1]

[1] Professor Harold J. Laski, former Chairman of the National Executive of

But even if one feels that the verdict was technically justified, I think it should be remembered that Professor Laski took this action—in effect—on behalf of the Labour Party. It was an incident in the General Election—a reply, felt at the time to be necessary, to the anti-Red propaganda of part of the Conservative press. It will therefore be extremely unfair if he is left to pay the very heavy costs unaided. May I remind everyone again that contributions should be sent to Morgan Phillips, Secretary, Labour Party, Transport House.

The Laski case will presumably lead to further discussions about the composition of juries, particularly Special Juries, but I wish it would have the incidental effect of drawing people's attention once again to the present state of the law of libel.

I believe the libel trade, like some other trades, went through a slack period during the war, but a few years before that the bringing of frivolous libel actions was a major racket and a nightmare to editors, publishers, authors and journalists alike. Some people used to declare that it would be better if the libel laws were abolished altogether, or at any rate greatly relaxed, so that newspapers had as much latitude as they used to have, for instance, in pre-war France. I cannot agree with this. Innocent people have a right to protection against slander. The racket arose not so much because the law is unduly strict as because it is possible to obtain damages for a libel from which one has not suffered any pecuniary loss.

The sufferers are not so much the big newspapers, which have fleets of retained lawyers and can afford to pay damages, as publishers and small periodicals. I do not know the exact provisions of the law, but from interviews with terrified solicitors which I have sometimes had before a book went to press, I gather that it is almost impossible to invent a fictitious character which might not be held to be a portrait of a real person. As a result, a blackmailing libel action is an easy way of picking up money. Publishing houses and periodicals are often insured against libel up to a certain sum, which means that they will pay a smallish claim sooner than fight an action. In one case

---

the Labour Party, had sued the *Newark Advertiser* for libel. He claimed that the account in the *Newark Advertiser* of his speech at Newark on 20 June 1945, in support of the local Labour candidate, was damaging as it implied that he had advocated revolution by violence. The court rejected Laski's claim and ruled for the defendants. On 2 December 1945, Mr Morgan Phillips, Secretary of the Labour Party, opened a fund to help Laski with the very considerable costs of the legal action.

I have even heard of collusion being practised. A arranged to libel B, B threatened an action, and the pair of them split the proceeds.

It seems to me that the way to put this right is to make sure that a libel action cannot be profitable. Except where it can be shown that actual loss has been suffered, let no damages be paid. On the other hand, where a libel is proved, the guilty party should make a retractation in print, which at present does not usually happen. Big newspapers would be much more frightened of that than of paying out £10,000 damages, while, if no money payments were made, the motive for blackmailing actions would have disappeared.

A correspondent has sent me a copy of one of the disgusting American "comics" which I referred to a few weeks ago. The two main stories in it are about a beautiful creature called The Hangman, who has a green face, and, like so many characters in American strips, can fly. On the front page there is a picture of what is either an ape-like lunatic, or an actual ape dressed up as a man, strangling a woman so realistically that her tongue is sticking four inches out of her mouth. Another item is a python looping itself round a man's neck and then hanging him by suspending itself over a balustrade. Another is a man jumping out of a skyscraper window and hitting the pavement with a splash. There is much else of the same kind.

My correspondent asks me whether I think this is the kind of thing that should be put into the hands of children, and also whether we could not find something better on which to spend our dwindling dollars.

Certainly I would keep these things out of children's hands if possible. But I would not be in favour of actually prohibiting their sale. The precedent is too dangerous. But meanwhile, *are* we actually using dollars to pay for this pernicious rubbish? The point is not completely unimportant, and I should like to see it cleared up.

Tribune, 27 December 1946

1947

69. As I Please

Nearly a quarter of a century ago I was travelling on a liner to Burma. Though not a big ship, it was a comfortable and even a luxurious one, and when one was not asleep or playing deck games one usually seemed to be eating. The meals were of that stupendous kind that steamship companies used to vie with one another in producing, and in between times there were snacks such as apples, ices, biscuits and cups of soup, lest anyone should find himself fainting from hunger. Moreover, the bars opened at ten in the morning, and, since we were at sea, alcohol was relatively cheap.

The ships of this line were mostly manned by Indians, but apart from the officers and the stewards they carried four European quartermasters whose job was to take the wheel. One of these quartermasters, though I suppose he was only aged forty or so, was one of those old sailors on whose back you almost expect to see barnacles growing. He was a short, powerful, rather ape-like man, with enormous forearms covered by a mat of golden hair. A blond moustache which might have belonged to Charlemagne completely hid his mouth. I was only twenty years old and very conscious of my parasitic status as a mere passenger, and I looked up to the quarter-masters, especially the fair-haired one, as godlike beings on a par with the officers. It would not have occurred to me to speak to one of them without being spoken to first.

One day, for some reason, I came up from lunch early. The deck was empty except for the fair-haired quartermaster, who was scurry-ing like a rat along the side of the deck-houses, with something partially concealed between his monstrous hands. I had just time to see what it was before he shot past me and vanished into a doorway. It was a pie dish containing a half-eaten baked custard pudding.

At one glance I took in the situation—indeed, the man's air of guilt made it unmistakable. The pudding was a left-over from one of the passengers' tables. It had been illicitly given to him by a steward, and he was carrying it off to the seamen's quarters to devour it at leisure. Across more than twenty years I can still faintly feel the shock of astonishment that I felt at that moment. It took me some-time to see the incident in all its bearings: but do I seem to exaggerate when I say that this sudden revelation of the gap between function and reward—the revelation that a highly-skilled craftsman, who might literally hold all our lives in his hands, was glad to steal scraps of food from our table—taught me more than I could have learned from half a dozen Socialist pamphlets?

A news item to the effect that Jugoslavia is now engaged on a purge of writers and artists led me to look once again at the reports of the recent literary purge in the USSR, when Zoschenko, Akhmatova and others were expelled from the Writers' Union.

In England this kind of thing is not happening to us as yet, so that we can view it with a certain detachment, and, curiously enough, as I look again at the accounts of what happened, I feel somewhat more sorry for the persecutors than for their victims. Chief among the persecutors is Andrei Zhdanov, considered by some to be Stalin's probable successor. Zhdanov, though he has conducted literary purges before, is a full-time politician with—to judge from his speeches—about as much knowledge of literature as I have of aero-dynamics. He does not give the impression of being, according to his own lights, a wicked or dishonest man. He is truly shocked by the defection of certain Soviet writers, which appears to him as an incom-prehensible piece of treachery, like a military mutiny in the middle of a battle. The purpose of literature is to glorify the Soviet Union; surely that must be obvious to everyone? But instead of carrying out their plain duty, these misguided writers keep straying away from the paths of propaganda, producing non-political works, and even in the case of Zoschenko, allowing a satirical note to creep into their writings. It is all very painful and bewildering. It is as though you set a man to work in an excellent, up-to-date, air-conditioned factory, gave him high wages, short hours, good canteens and playing-grounds, a comfortable flat, a nursery-school for his children, all-round social insurance and music while you work—only to find the ungrateful fellow throwing spanners into the machinery on his very first day.

What makes the whole thing somewhat pathetic is the general admission—an honest admission, seeing that Soviet publicists are

not in the habit of decrying their own country—that Russian literature as a whole is not what it ought to be. Since the USSR represents
the highest existing form of civilisation, it is obvious that it ought to
lead the world in literature as in everything else. "Surely", says
Zhdanov, "our new Socialist system, embodying all that is best in
the history of human civilisation and culture, is capable of creating
the most advanced literature, which will leave far behind the best
creations of olden times." *Izvestia* (as quoted by the New York
paper, *Politics*) goes further: "Our culture stands on an immeasur-
ably higher level than bourgeois culture. . . . Is it not clear that our
culture has the right not to act as pupil and imitator but, on the
contrary, to teach others the general human morals?" And yet
somehow the expected thing never happens. Directives are issued,
resolutions are passed unanimously, recalcitrant writers are silenced:
and yet for some reason a vigorous and original literature, unmistakably superior to that of capitalist countries, fails to emerge.

All this has happened before, and more than once. Freedom of
expression has had its ups and downs in the USSR, but the general
tendency has been towards tighter censorship. The thing that
politicians are seemingly unable to understand is that you cannot
produce a vigorous literature by terrorising everyone into conformity.
A writer's inventive faculties will not work unless he is allowed to
say approximately what he feels. You can destroy spontaneity and
produce a literature which is orthodox but feeble, or you can let
people say what they choose and take the risk that some of them will
utter heresies. There is no way out of that dilemma so long as books
have to be written by individuals.

That is why, in a way, I feel sorrier for the persecutors than for
the victims. It is probable that Zoschenko and the others at least
have the satisfaction of understanding what is happening to them:
the politicians who harry them are merely attempting the impossible.
For Zhdanov and his kind to say, "The Soviet Union can exist
without literature" would be reasonable. But that is just what they
can't say. They don't know what literature is, but they know that it is
important, that it has prestige value, and that it is necessary for
propaganda purposes, and they would like to encourage it, if only
they knew how. So they continue with their purges and directives,
like a fish bashing its nose against the wall of an aquarium again
and again, too dim-witted to realise that glass and water are not the
same thing.

From *The Thoughts of the Emperor Marcus Aurelius*:

In the morning when thou risest unwillingly, let this thought be present—I am rising to the work of a human being. Why then am I dissatisfied if I am going to do the things for which I exist and for which I was brought into the world? Or have I been made for this, to lie in the bed-clothes and keep myself warm?— But this is more pleasant—Dost thou exist then to take thy pleasure, and not at all for action or exertion? Dost thou not see the little plants, the little birds, the ants, the spiders, the bees working together to put in order their several parts of the universe? And art thou unwilling to do the work of a human being, and dost thou not make haste to do that which is according to thy nature?

It is a good plan to print this well-known exhortation in large letters and hang it on the wall opposite your bed. And if that fails, as I am told it sometimes does, another good plan is to buy the loudest alarm clock you can get and place it in such a position that you have to get out of bed and go round several pieces of furniture in order to silence it.

Tribune, 3 January 1947

70. As I Please

The *Daily Herald* for January 1, 1947, has a headline MEN WHO SPOKE FOR HITLER HERE, and underneath this a photograph of two Indians who are declared to be Brijlal Mukerjee and Anjit Singh, and are described as having come "from Berlin". The news column below the photograph goes on to say that "four Indians who might have been shot as traitors" are staying at a London hotel, and further describes the group of Indians who broadcast over the German radio during the war as "collaborators". It is worth looking a bit more closely at these various statements.

To begin with, there are at least two errors of fact, one of them a very serious one. Anjit Singh did not broadcast on the Nazi radio, but only from Italian stations, while the man described as "Brijlal

Mukerjee" is an Indian who has been in England throughout the war and is well known to myself and many other people in London. But these inaccuracies are really the symptom of an attitude of mind which comes out more clearly in the phraseology of the report.

What right have we to describe the Indians who broadcast on the German radio as "collaborators"? They were citizens of an occupied country, hitting back at the occupying power in the way that seemed to them best. I am not suggesting that the way they chose was the right one. Even from the narrow point of view which would assume that Indian independence is the only cause that matters, I think they were gravely wrong, because if the Axis had won the war—and their efforts must have aided the Axis to some extent—India would merely have had a new and worse master. But the line they took was one that could perfectly well be taken in good faith. and cannot with fairness or even with accuracy be termed "collaboration". The word "collaboration" is associated with people like Quisling and Laval. It implies, first of all, treachery to one's own country, secondly, full co-operation with the conqueror, and thirdly, ideological agreement, or at least partial agreement. But how does this apply to the Indians who sided with the Axis? They were not being traitors to their own country—on the contrary, they were working for its independence, as they believed—and they recognised no obligation to Britain. Nor did they co-operate in the same manner as Quisling, etc. The Germans allowed them a separate broadcasting unit on which they said what they liked and followed, in many cases, a political line quite different from the Axis one. In my opinion they were mistaken and mischievous, but in moral attitude, and probably in the effects of what they did, they were quite different from ordinary renegades.

Meanwhile one has to consider the effect of this kind of thing in India. Rightly or wrongly, these men will be welcomed as heroes when they get home, and the fact that British newspapers insult them will not go unnoticed. Nor will the slovenly handling of the photographs. The caption "Brijlal Mukerjee" appears under the face of a totally different person. No doubt the photograph was taken at the reception which the repatriated Indians were given by their fellow countrymen in London, and the photographer snapped the wrong man by mistake. But suppose the person in question had been William Joyce. In that case, don't you think the *Daily Herald* would have taken good care that it *was* photographing William Joyce and not somebody else? But since it's only an Indian, a mistake of this kind doesn't matter—so runs the unspoken thought. And this happens not in the *Daily Graphic*, but in Britain's sole Labour newspaper.

I hope everyone who can get access to a copy will take at least a glance at Victor Gollancz's recently published book, *In Darkest Germany*. It is not a literary book, but a piece of brilliant journalism intended to shock the public of this country into some kind of consciousness of the hunger, disease, chaos and lunatic mismanagement prevailing in the British Zone. This business of making people *conscious* of what is happening outside their own small circle is one of the major problems of our time, and a new literary technique will have to be evolved to meet it. Considering that the people of this country are not having a very comfortable time, you can't, perhaps, blame them for being somewhat callous about suffering elsewhere, but the remarkable thing is the extent to which they manage to remain unaware of it. Tales of starvation, ruined cities, concentration camps, mass deportations, homeless refugees, persecuted Jews—all this is received with a sort of incurious surprise, as though such things had never been heard of before but at the same time were not particularly interesting. The now-familiar photographs of skeleton-like children make very little impression. As time goes on and the horrors pile up, the mind seems to secrete a sort of self-protecting ignorance which needs a harder and harder shock to pierce it, just as the body will become immunised to a drug and require bigger and bigger doses.

Half of Victor Gollancz's book consists of photographs, and he has taken the wise precaution of including himself in a good many of them. This at least proves that the photographs are genuine and cuts out the routine charge that they have been obtained from an agency and are "all propaganda". But I think the best device in the book, after innumerable descriptions of people living on "biscuit soup", potatoes and cabbage, skim milk and ersatz coffee, was to include some menus of dinners in the messes provided for the Control Commission. Mr Gollancz says that he slipped a menu card into his pocket whenever he could do so unobserved, and he prints half a dozen of them. Here is the first on the list:

Consommé in cups

————

Fried Soles in Butter
Fresh Potatoes

————

Dutch Steak
Mashed Potatoes
Cauliflower

————

Raspberry Cream

————

Cheese

————

Coffee

These accounts of starvation in Europe seem to link up with a paragraph, headed "This Week's Hint for Dog-Lovers", which I cut out of the *Evening Standard* just before Christmas:

> Your dog may also have that "after Christmas hangover" feeling if you have been indulging him with too many titbits. Many owners like to give their pets "a taste of everything", regardless of the fact that many of the items of Christmas fare are unsuitable for dogs.
>
> No permanent harm may be done, but if the dog seems dull, the tongue loses colour and the breath becomes offensive, a dose of castor oil is indicated.
>
> Twelve hours rest from food, followed by a light diet for a few days, usually effects a speedy cure—and from eight to twelve grains of carbonate of bismuth may be given three times a day. The dog should be encouraged to drink barley water rather than plain water.

Signed by a Fellow of the Zoological Society.

Looking through what I have written above, I notice that I have used the phrase "a totally different person". For the first time it occurs to me what a stupid expression this is. As though there could be such a thing as a partially different person! I shall try to cut this phrase (and also "a very different person" and "a different person altogether") out of my vocabulary from now onwards.

Ko—iv

But there are other words and phrases which obviously deserve to go on the scrap-heap, but which continue to be used because there seems to be no convenient substitute. An example is the word "certain". We say, for instance, "After a certain age one's hair turns grey", or "There will probably be a certain amount of snow in February". In all such sentences, "certain" means *uncertain*. Why do we have to use this word in two opposite meanings? And yet, unless one pedantically says "after an uncertain age", etc, there appears to be no other word which will exactly cover the required meaning.

Tribune, 17 January 1947

71. As I Please

Recently I was listening to a conversation between two small businessmen in a Scottish hotel. One of them, an alert-looking, well-dressed man of about forty-five, was something to do with the Federation of Master Builders. The other, a good deal older, with white hair and a broad Scottish accent, was some kind of wholesale tradesman. He said grace before his meals, a thing I had not seen anyone do for many a year. They belonged, I should say, in the £2,000-a-year and the £1,000-a-year income groups respectively.

We were sitting round a rather inadequate peat fire, and the conversation started off with the coal shortage. There was no coal, it appeared, because the British miners refused to dig it out, but on the other hand it was important not to let Poles work in the pits because this would lead to unemployment. There was severe unemployment in Scotland already. The older man then remarked with quiet satisfaction that he was very glad—"varra glad indeed"—that Labour had won the General Election. Any government that had to clean up after the war was in for a bad time, and as a result of five years of rationing, housing shortage, unofficial strikes and so forth, the general public would see through the promises of the Socialists and vote Conservative next time.

They began talking about the housing problem, and almost immediately they were back to the congenial subject of the Poles. The younger man had just sold his flat in Edinburgh at a good profit and was trying to buy a house. He was willing to pay £2,700. The other was trying to sell his house for £1,500 and buy a smaller one. But it seemed that it was impossible to buy houses or flats nowadays. The Poles were buying them all up, and "where they get the money from is a mystery". The Poles were also invading the medical profession. They even had their own medical school in Edinburgh or Glasgow (I forget which) and were turning out doctors in great numbers while "our lads" found it impossible to buy practices. Didn't everyone know that Britain had more doctors than it could use? Let the Poles go back to their own country. There were too many people in this country already. What was needed was emigration.

The younger man remarked that he belonged to several business and civic associations, and that on all of them he made a point of putting forward resolutions that the Poles should be sent back to their own country. The older one added that the Poles were "very degraded in their morals." They were responsible for much of the immorality that was prevalent nowadays. "Their ways are not our ways," he concluded piously. It was not mentioned that the Poles pushed their way to the head of queues, wore bright-coloured clothes and displayed cowardice during air raids, but if I had put forward a suggestion to this effect I am sure it would have been accepted.

One cannot of course, do very much about this kind of thing. It is the contemporary equivalent of antisemitism. By 1947, people of the kind I am describing would have caught up with the fact that antisemitism is discreditable, and so the scapegoat is sought elsewhere. But the race hatred and mass delusions which are part of the pattern of our time might be somewhat less bad in their effects if they were not reinforced by ignorance. If in the years before the war, for instance, the facts about the persecution of Jews in Germany had been better known, the subjective popular feeling against Jews would probably not have been less, but the actual treatment of Jewish refugees might have been better. The refusal to allow refugees in significant numbers into this country would have been branded as disgraceful. The average man would still have felt a grudge against the refugees, but in practice more lives would have been saved.

So also with the Poles. The thing that most depressed me in the above-mentioned conversation was the recurrent phrase, "let them go back to their own country". If I had said to those two business-men, "Most of these people have no country to go back to," they would have gaped. Not one of the relevant facts would have been known to them. They would never have heard of the various things that have happened to Poland since 1939, any more than they would have known that the over-population of Britain is a fallacy or that local unemployment can coexist with a general shortage of labour. I think it is a mistake to give such people the excuse of ignorance. You can't actually change their feelings, but you can make them understand what they are saying when they demand that homeless refugees shall be driven from our shores, and the knowledge may make them a little less actively malignant.

The other week, in the *Spectator*, Mr Harold Nicolson was consoling himself as best he could for having reached the age of sixty. As he perceived, the only positive satisfaction in growing older is that after a certain point you can begin boasting of having seen things that no one will ever have the chance to see again. It set me wondering what boasts I could make myself, at forty-four, or nearly. Mr Nicolson had seen the Czar, surrounded by his bodyguard of enormous Cossacks, blessing the Neva. I never saw that, but I did see Marie Lloyd, already almost a legendary figure, and I saw Little Tich—who, I think, did not die till about 1928, but who must have retired at about the same time as Marie Lloyd—and I have seen a whole string of crowned heads and other celebrities from Edward VII onwards. But on only two occasions did I feel, at the time, that I was seeing something significant, and on one of these occasions it was the circumstances and not the person concerned that made me feel this.

One of these celebrities was Pétain. It was at Foch's funeral in 1929. Pétain's personal prestige in France was very great. He was honoured as the defender of Verdun, and the phrase "They shall not pass" was popularly supposed to have been coined by him. He was given a place to himself in the procession, with a gap of several yards in front of and behind him. As he stalked past—a tall, lean, very erect figure, though he must have been seventy years old or thereabouts, with great sweeping white moustaches like the wings of a gull—a whisper of *Voilà Pétain!* went rippling through the vast crowd. His appearance impressed me so much that I dimly felt, in spite of his considerable age, that he might still have some kind of distinguished future ahead of him.

The other celebrity was Queen Mary. One day I was walking past Windsor Castle when a sort of electric shock seemed to go through the street. People were taking their hats off, soldiers springing to attention. And then, clattering over the cobbles, there came a huge, plum-coloured open carriage drawn by four horses with postilions. I believe it was the first and last time in my life that I have seen a postilion. On the rear seat, with his back to the carriage, another groom sat stiffly upright, with his arms folded. The groom who sat at the back used to be called the tiger. I hardly noticed the Queen, my eyes were fixed on that strange, archaic figure at the back, immobile as a waxwork, with his white breeches that looked as though he had been poured into them, and the cockade on his top-hat. Even at that date (1920 or thereabouts) it gave me a wonderful feeling of looking backwards through a window into the nineteenth century.

Tribune, 24 January 1947

72. Letter to Rayner Heppenstall

27B Canonbury Square
Islington, N1
25 January 1947

Dear Rayner,

Thanks for your letter Re *Animal Farm*.[1] I had a number of people here to listen to it on the first day, and they all seemed to think it was good, and Porteous,[2] who had not read the book, grasped what was happening after a few minutes. I also had one or two fan letters and the press notices were good except on my native ground, i.e. *Tribune*. As to what I thought myself, it's hard to get a detached view, because whenever I write anything for the air I have the impression it has been spoiled, owing to its inevitably coming out different to one's conception of it. I must say I don't agree about there being too much narrator. If anything I thought there should have been more explanation. People are always yearning to get rid of the narrator, but it seems to me that until certain problems have been overcome you only get rid of the narrator at the expense of having to play a lot of stupid tricks in order to let people know what is happening. The thing is to make the narrator a good turn in himself. But that means

[1] *Animal Farm* had been adapted by Orwell for radio and produced by Rayner Heppenstall in the BBC Third Programme on 14 January 1947.
[2] Hugh Gordon Porteous, literary critic and sinologist.

writing serious prose, which people don't, and making the actors stick to it instead of gagging and trying to make everything homey and naturalistic.

I can't write or promise to write anything more at present, I am too busy. I've still got ideas about fairy stories. I wish they would dig up and re-b'cast my adaptation of "The Emperor's New Clothes". It was done on the Eastern and African services, but in those days I wasn't well-connected enough to crash the Home. I expect the discs would have been scrapped, however. I had them illicitly re-recorded at a commercial studio, but that lot of discs got lost. I've often pondered over Cinderella, which of course is the tops so far as fairy stories go but on the face of it is too visual to be suitable for the air. But don't you think one could make the godmother turn her into a wonderful singer who could sing a higher note than anyone else, or something of that kind? The best way would be if she had a wonderful voice but could not sing in tune, like Trilby, and the godmother cured this. One could make it quite comic with the wicked sisters singing in screeching voices. It might be worth talking over some time.

Give my love to Margaret.[1]

Yours
Eric

73. As I Pleased

One's relations with a newspaper or a magazine are more variable and intermittent than they can be with a human being. From time to time a human being may dye his hair or become converted to Roman Catholicism, but he cannot change himself fundamentally, whereas a periodical will go through a whole series of different existences under the same name. *Tribune* in its short life has been two distinct papers, if not three, and my own contacts with it have varied sharply, starting off, if I remember rightly, with a rap on the knuckles.

I did not learn of the existence of *Tribune* till some time in 1939. It had started early in 1937, but of the thirty months that intervened before the outbreak of war I spent five in hospital and thirteen abroad. What first drew my attention to it, I believe, was a none too

[1] Mrs Rayner Heppenstall.

friendly review of a novel of mine. During the period 1939–42 I produced three or four books and reprints, and I think it is true that I never had what is called a "good" review in *Tribune* until after I became a member of the staff. (The two events were unconnected, needless to say.) Somewhat later, in the cold winter of 1939, I started writing for *Tribune*, though at first, curiously enough, without seeing it regularly or getting a clear idea of what kind of paper it was.

Raymond Postgate, who was then editor, had asked me to do the novel reviews from time to time. I was not paid (until recently it was unusual for contributors to left-wing papers to be paid), and I only saw the paper on the somewhat rare occasions when I went up to London and visited Postgate in a bare and dusty office near London Wall. *Tribune* (until a good deal later everyone called it "the" *Tribune*) was at that time in difficulties. It was still a threepenny paper aimed primarily at the industrial workers and following more or less the Popular Front line which had been associated with the Left Book Club and the Socialist League. With the outbreak of war its circulation had taken a severe knock, because the Communists and near-Communists who had been among its warmest supporters now refused to help in distributing it. Some of them went on writing for it, however, and the futile controversy between "supporters" and "opposers" of the war continued to rumble in its columns while the German armies gathered for the spring offensives.

Early in 1940 there was a large meeting in a public hall, the purpose of which was to discuss both the future of *Tribune* and the policy of the left wing of the Labour Party. As is usual on such occasions nothing very definite was said, and what I chiefly remember is a political tip which I received from an inside source. The Norway campaign was ending in disaster, and I had walked to the hall past gloomy posters. Two MPs, whom I will not name, had just arrived from the House.

"What chance is there," I asked them, "of this business getting rid of Chamberlain?"

"Not a hope," they both said. "He's solid."

I don't remember dates, but I think it can only have been a week or two before Chamberlain was out of the Premiership.

After that *Tribune* passed out of my consciousness for nearly two years. I was very busy trying to earn a living and write a book amid the bombs and the general disorganisation, and any spare time I had was taken up by the Home Guard, which was still an amateur force and demanded an immense amount of work from its members. When I became aware of *Tribune* again I was working in the Eastern Service of the BBC. It was now an almost completely different paper. It had a different make-up, cost sixpence, was orientated chiefly towards foreign policy, and was rapidly acquiring a new public which mostly belonged, I should say, to the out-at-elbow middle class. Its prestige among the BBC personnel was very striking. In the libraries where commentators went to prime themselves it was one of the most sought-after periodicals, not only because it was largely written by people who knew something at first hand about Europe, but because it was then the only paper of any standing which criticised the Government. Perhaps "criticised" is an over-mild word. Sir Stafford Cripps had gone into the Government, and the fiery personality of Aneurin Bevan gave the paper its tone. On one occasion there were some surprisingly violent attacks on Churchill by someone who called himself Thomas Rainsboro'. This was obviously a pseudonym, and I spent a whole afternoon trying to determine the authorship by stylistic evidence, as the literary critics employed by the Gestapo were said to do with anonymous pamphlets. Finally I decided that "Thomas Rainsboro'" was a certain W———. A day or two later I met Victor Gollancz, who said to me: "Do you know who wrote those Thomas Rainsboro' articles in *Tribune*? I've just heard. It was W———." This made me feel very acute, but a day or two later I heard that we were both wrong.

During this period I occasionally wrote articles for *Tribune*, but only at long intervals, because I had little time or energy. However, towards the end of 1943 I decided to give up my job in the BBC, and I was asked to take over the literary editorship of *Tribune*, in place of John Atkins, who was expecting call-up. I went on being literary editor, as well as writing the "As I Please" column, until the beginning of 1945. It was interesting, but it is not a period that I look back on with pride. The fact is that I am no good at editing. I hate planning ahead, and I have a psychical or even physical inability to answer letters. My most essential memory of that time is of pulling out a drawer here and a drawer there, finding it in each case to be stuffed with letters and manuscripts which ought to have been dealt with weeks earlier, and hurriedly shutting it up again. Also, I have a fatal tendency to accept manuscripts which I know very well are too bad to be printed. It is questionable whether anyone who has had long experience as a free-lance journalist ought to become an editor. It is too like taking a convict out of his cell and making him governor of the prison. Still, it was "all experience", as they say, and I have friendly memories of my cramped little office looking out on a back-yard, and the three of us who shared it huddling in the corner as the doodlebugs came zooming over, and the peaceful click-click of the typewriters starting up again as soon as the bomb had crashed.

Early in 1945 I went to Paris as correspondent for the *Observer*. In Paris *Tribune* had a prestige which was somewhat astonishing and which dated from before the liberation. It was impossible to buy it, and the ten copies which the British Embassy received weekly did not, I believe, get outside the walls of the building. Yet all the French journalists I met seemed to have heard of it and to know that it was the one paper in England which had neither supported the Government uncritically, nor opposed the war, nor swallowed the Russian myth. At that time there was—I should like to be sure that it still exists—a weekly paper named *Libertés*, which was roughly speaking the opposite number of *Tribune* and which during the occupation had been clandestinely produced on the same machines as printed the *Pariser Zeitung*.

Libertés, which was opposed to the Gaullists on one side and the Communists on the other, had almost no money and was distributed by groups of volunteers on bicycles. On some weeks it was mangled out of recognition by the censorship; often nothing would be left of an article except some such title as "The Truth About Indo-China" and a completely blank column beneath it. A day or two after I reached Paris I was taken to a semi-public meeting of the supporters of *Libertés*, and was amazed to find that about half of them knew all about me and about *Tribune*. A large working man in black corduroy breeches came up to me, exclaimed "Ah, vous êtes Georges Orrvell!" and crushed the bones of my hand almost to pulp. He had heard of me because *Libertés* made a practice of translating extracts from *Tribune*. I believe one of the editors used to go to the British Embassy every week and demand to see a copy. It seemed to me somehow touching that one could have acquired, without knowing it, a public among people like this: whereas among the huge tribe of American journalists at the Hotel Scribe, with their glittering uniforms and their stupendous salaries, I never encountered one who had heard of *Tribune*.

For six months during the summer of 1946 I gave up being a writer in *Tribune* and became merely a reader, and no doubt from time to time I shall do the same again; but I hope that my association with with it may long continue, and I hope that in 1957 I shall be writing another anniversary article. I do not even hope that by that time *Tribune* will have slaughtered all its rivals. It takes all sorts to make a world, and if one could work these things out one might discover that even the————serves a useful purpose. Nor is *Tribune* itself perfect, as I should know, having seen it from the inside. But I do think that it is the only existing weekly paper that makes a genuine effort to be both progressive and humane—that is, to combine a radical Socialist policy with a respect for freedom of speech and a civilised attitude towards literature and the arts: and I think that its relative popularity, and even its survival in its present form for five years or more, is a hopeful symptom.

Tribune, 31 January 1947

74. As I Please

Recently I have been looking through Mr Peter Hunot's *Man About the House*, published a month or two back by the Pilot Press. Books telling you how to do household repairs are fairly numerous, but I think this is about the best I have seen. The author gathered his experience the hard way by taking over a nearly derelict house and making it habitable with his own hands. He thus concentrates on the sort of difficulties that do actually arise in real life, and does not, like the author of another book in my possession, tell you how to mend Venetian blinds while ignoring electrical fittings. I looked up all the domestic calamities that I have had to deal with during the past year, and found all of them mentioned, except mice, which perhaps hardly come under the heading of decorations and repairs. The book is also simply written and well illustrated, and takes account of the difficulty nowadays of getting hold of tools and materials.

But I still think that there is room for a very large, comprehensive book of this type, a sort of dictionary or encyclopaedia with every conceivable household job tabulated under alphabetical headings. You would then be able to look up *Tap, how to stop a dripping*, or *Floorboards, causes of squeaking in*, with the same certainty of getting the right answer as when you look up madeira cake or Welsh rarebit in Mrs Beeton's cookery book. The time was when the amateur handyman, with his tack hammer and his pocketful of rawl-plugs, was looked on as a mere eccentric, a joke to his friends and a nuisance to his women-folk. Nowadays, however, you either do your repairs yourself or they don't get done, and most of us are still remarkably helpless. How many people even know how to replace a broken sash-cord, for instance?

As Mr Hunot points out, much of the tinkering that now goes on would be unnecessary, or would be much easier, if our houses were sensibly built. Even so simple a precaution as putting fuse boxes in get-at-able places would save a lot of nuisance, and the miserable business of putting up shelves could be greatly simplified without any extra materials or radical change in methods. I hear rumours that the new houses now being built will have the pipes so placed that they will not freeze, but surely this cannot be true. There will be a snag somewhere, and the annual freeze-up will happen as usual. Burst water-pipes are a part of the English winter, no less than muffins or roasted chestnuts, and doubtless Shakespeare would have mentioned them in the song at the end of *Love's Labour's Lost*, if there had been water-pipes in those days.

It is too early to cheer, but I must say that up to date the phenomena of the freeze-up have been less unpleasant than those of 1940. On that occasion the village where I lived was not only so completely snowed up that for a week or more it was impossible to get out of it, or for any food vans to get in, but every tap and pump in the village froze so hard that for several days we had no water except melted snow. The disagreeable thing about this is that snow is always dirty, except just after it has fallen. I have noticed this even in the high peaks of the Atlas mountains, miles from human habitation. The everlasting snow which looks so virginal, is in fact distinctly grimy when you get close to it.

About the time when Sir Stafford Cripps came back from India, I heard it remarked that the Cripps offer had not been extended to Burma because the Burmese would have accepted it. I don't know whether any such calculation really entered into the minds of Churchill and the rest. It is perfectly possible: at any rate, I think that responsible Burmese politicians would have accepted such an offer, although at that moment Burma was in process of being overrun by the Japanese. I also believe that an offer of Dominion status would have been gladly accepted if we had made it in 1944 and had named a definite date. As it is, the suspicions of the Burmese have been well roused, and it will probably end by our simply getting out of Burma on the terms least advantageous to both countries.

If that happens, I should like to think that the position of the racial minorities could be safeguarded by something better than promises. They number ten to twenty per cent of the population, and they present several different kinds of problem. The biggest group, the Karens, are a racial enclave living largely within Burma proper. The Kachins and other frontier tribes are a good deal more backward and more different from the Burmese in customs and appearance. They have never been under Burmese rule—indeed, their territories were only very sketchily occupied even by the British. In the past they were well able to maintain their independence, but probably would not be able to do so in the face of modern weapons. The other big group, the Shans, who are racially akin to the Siamese, enjoyed some faint traces of autonomy under British rule. The minority who are in the most difficult position of all are the Indians. There were over a million of them in Burma before the war. Two hundred thousand of them fled to India at the time of the Japanese invasion— an act which demonstrated better than any words could have done their real position in the country.

I remember twenty years ago a Karen remarking to me, "I hope the British will stay in Burma for two hundred years." "Why?"— "Because we do not wish to be ruled by Burmese." Even at the time it struck me that sooner or later this would become a problem. The fact is that the question of minorities is literally insoluble so long as nationalism remains a real force. The desire of some of the peoples of Burma for autonomy is genuine, but it cannot be satisfied in any secure way unless the sovereignty of Burma as a whole is interfered with. The same problem comes up in a hundred other places. Ought the Sudan to be independent of Egypt? Ought Ulster to be independent of Eire? Ought Eire to be independent of Britain? And so on. Whenever A is oppressing B, it is clear to people of goodwill that B ought to be independent, but then it always turns out that there is another group, C, which is anxious to be independent of B. The question is always *how large* must a minority be before it deserves autonomy. At best, each case can only be treated on its merits in a rough and ready way: in practice, no one is consistent in his thinking on this subject, and the minorities which win the most sympathy are those that have the best means of publicity. Who is there who champions equally the Jews, the Balts, the Indonesians, the expelled Germans, the Sudanese, the Indian Untouchables and the South African Kaffirs? Sympathy for one group almost invariably entails callousness towards another.

When H.G. Wells's *The Island of Doctor Moreau* was reprinted in the Penguin Library, I looked to see whether the slips and misprints which I remembered in earlier editions had been repeated in it. Sure enough, they were still there. One of them is a particularly stupid misprint, of a kind to make most writers squirm. In 1941 I pointed this out to H.G. Wells, and asked him why he did not remove it. It had persisted through edition after edition ever since 1896. Rather to my surprise, he said that he remembered the misprint, but could not be bothered to do anything about it. He no longer took the faintest interest in his early books: they had been written so long ago that he no longer felt them to be part of himself. I have never been quite sure whether to admire this attitude or not. It is magnificent to be so free from literary vanity. And yet, what writer of Wells's gifts, if he had had any power of self-criticism or regard for his own reputation, would have poured out in fifty years a total of ninety-five books, quite two-thirds of which have already ceased to be readable?

Tribune, 7 February 1947

75. As I Please

Here are some excerpts from a letter from a Scottish Nationalist. I have cut out anything likely to reveal the writer's identity. The frequent references to Poland are there because the letter is primarily concerned with the presence of exiled Poles in Scotland:

> The Polish forces have now discovered how untrue it is to say "An Englishman's word is his bond". We could have told you so hundreds of years ago. The invasion of Poland was only an excuse for these brigands in bowler hats to beat up their rivals the Germans and the Japs, with the help of Americans, Poles, Scots, Frenchmen, etc etc. Surely no Pole believes any longer in

English promises. Now that the war is over you are to be cast aside and dumped in Scotland. If this leads to friction between the Poles and Scots so much the better. Let them slit each other's throats and two problems would be thereupon "solved". Dear, kind little England! It is time for all Poles to shed any ideas they may have about England as a champion of freedom. Look at her record in Scotland, for instance. And please don't refer to us as "Britons". There is *no* such race. We are Scots and that's good enough for us. The English changed their name to British; but even if a criminal changes his name he can be known by his fingerprints. . . . Please disregard any anti-Polish statement in the ——. It is a boot-licking pro-English (pro-Moscow you would call it) rag. Scotland experienced her Yalta in 1707 when English gold achieved what English guns could not do. But we will never accept defeat. After more than two hundred years we are still fighting for our country and will never acknowledge defeat whatever the odds.

There is a good deal more in the letter, but this should be enough. It will be noted that the writer is not attacking England from what is called a "left" standpoint, but on the ground that Scotland and England are enemies *as nations*. I don't know whether it would be fair to read race-theory into this letter, but certainly the writer hates us as bitterly as a devout Nazi would hate a Jew. It is not a hatred of the capitalist class, or anything like that, but of *England*. And though the fact is not sufficiently realised, there is an appreciable amount of this kind of thing knocking about. I have seen almost equally violent statements in print.

Up to date the Scottish Nationalist movement seems to have gone almost unnoticed in England. To take the nearest example to hand, I don't remember having seen it mentioned in *Tribune*, except occasionally in book reviews. It is true that it is a small movement, but it could grow, because there is a basis for it. In this country I don't think it is enough realised—I myself had no idea of it until a few years ago—that Scotland has a case against England. On economic grounds it may not be a very strong case. In the past, certainly, we have plundered Scotland shamefully, but whether it is *now* true that England as a whole exploits Scotland as a whole, and that Scotland would be better off if fully autonomous, is another question. The point is that many Scottish people, often quite moderate in outlook, are beginning to think about autonomy and to feel that they are pushed into an inferior position. They have a good deal of reason. In some areas, at any rate, Scotland is almost an occupied country. You have an English or anglicised upper class, and a Scottish working class which speaks with a markedly different accent, or even, part of the time, in a different language. This is a more dangerous kind of class division than any now existing in England. Given favourable circumstances it might develop in an ugly way, and the fact that there was a progressive Labour Government in London might not make much difference.

No doubt Scotland's major ills will have to be cured along with those of England. But meanwhile there are things that could be done to ease the cultural situation. One small but not negligible point is the language. In the Gaelic-speaking areas, Gaelic is not taught in the schools. I am speaking from limited experience, but I should say that this is beginning to cause resentment. Also, the BBC only broadcasts two or three half-hour Gaelic programmes a week, and they give the impression of being rather amateurish programmes. Even so they are eagerly listened to. How easy it would be to buy a little goodwill by putting on a Gaelic programme at least once daily.

At one time I would have said that it is absurd to keep alive an archaic language like Gaelic, spoken by only a few hundred thousand people. Now I am not so sure. To begin with, if people feel that they have a special culture which ought to be preserved, and that the language is part of it, difficulties should not be put in their way when they want their children to learn it properly. Secondly, it is probable that the effort of being bilingual is a valuable education in itself. The Scottish Gaelic-speaking peasants speak beautiful English, partly, I think, because English is an almost foreign language which they sometimes do not use for days together. Probably they benefit intellectually by having to be aware of dictionaries and grammatical rules, as their English opposite numbers would not be.

At any rate, I think we should pay more attention to the small but violent separatist movements which exist within our own island. They may look very unimportant now, but, after all, the Communist Manifesto was once a very obscure document, and the Nazi Party only had six members when Hitler joined it.

To change the subject a bit, here is an excerpt from another letter. It is from a whisky distiller:

We regret we are reluctantly compelled to return your cheque as owing to Mr Strachey's failure to fulfil his promise to release barley for distilling in Scotland we dare not take on any new business. . . . When you have difficulty in obtaining a drink it will be some consolation to you to know that Mr Strachey has sent 35,000 tons of barley to NEUTRAL Eire for brewing purposes.

People must be feeling very warmed-up when they put that kind of thing into a business letter which, by the look of it, is almost a circular letter. It doesn't matter very much, because whisky distillers and even their customers don't add up to many votes. But I wish I could feel sure that the people who make remarks like the one I overheard in the greengrocer's queue yesterday—"Government! They couldn't govern a sausage-shop, this lot couldn't!"—were equally few in numbers.

Skelton is not an easy poet to get hold of, and I have never yet possessed a complete edition of his works. Recently, in a selection I had picked up, I looked for and failed to find a poem which I remember reading years ago. It was what is called a macaronic poem —part English, part Latin—and was an elegy on the death of somebody or other. The only passage I can recall runs:

> Sepultus est among the weeds,
> God forgive him his misdeeds,
> With hey ho, rumbelo,
> Rumpopulorum,
> Per omnia saecula,
> Saecula saeculorum.

It has stuck in my mind because it expresses an outlook totally impossible in our own age. Today there is literally no one who could write of death in that light-hearted manner. Since the decay of the belief in personal immortality, death has never seemed funny, and it will be a long time before it does so again. Hence the disappearance of the facetious epitaph, once a common feature of country church-yards. I should be astonished to see a comic epitaph dated later than 1850. There is one in Kew, if I remember rightly, which might be about that date. About half the tombstone is covered with a long panegyric on his dead wife by a bereaved husband: at the bottom of the stone is a later inscription which reads, "Now he's gone, too".

One of the best epitaphs in English is Landor's epitaph on "Dirce", a pseudonym for I do not know whom. It is not exactly comic, but it is essentially profane. If I were a woman it would be my favourite epitaph—that is to say, it would be the one I should like to have for myself. It runs:

> Stand close around, ye Stygian set,
> With Dirce in one boat conveyed,
> Or Charon, seeing, may forget
> That he is old and she a shade.

It would almost be worth being dead to have that written about you.

Tribune, 14 February 1947

76. Lear, Tolstoy and the Fool

Tolstoy's pamphlets are the least-known part of his work, and his attack on Shakespeare[1] is not even an easy document to get hold of, at any rate in an English translation. Perhaps, therefore, it will be useful if I give a summary of the pamphlet before trying to discuss it.

Tolstoy begins by saying that throughout life Shakespeare has aroused in him "an irresistible repulsion and tedium". Conscious that the opinion of the civilised world is against him, he has made one attempt after another on Shakespeare's works, reading and rereading them in Russian, English and German; but "I invariably underwent the same feelings: repulsion, weariness and bewilderment". Now, at the age of seventy-five, he has once again reread the entire works of Shakespeare, including the historical plays, and

> I have felt with even greater force, the same feelings—this time, however, not of bewilderment, but of firm, indubitable conviction that the unquestionable glory of a great genius which Shakespeare enjoys, and which compels writers of our time to imitate him and readers and spectators to discover in him non-existent merits—thereby distorting their aesthetic and ethical understanding—is a great evil, as is every untruth.

[1] *Shakespeare and the Drama.* Written about 1903 as an introduction to another pamphlet, *Shakespeare and the Working Classes*, by Ernest Crosby. [Author's footnote.]

Shakespeare, Tolstoy adds, is not merely no genius, but is not even "an average author", and in order to demonstrate this fact he will examine *King Lear*, which, as he is able to show by quotations from Hazlitt, Brandes and others, has been extravagantly praised and can be taken as an example of Shakespeare's best work.

Tolstoy then makes a sort of exposition of the plot of *King Lear*, finding it at every step to be stupid, verbose, unnatural, unintelligible, bombastic, vulgar, tedious and full of incredible events, "wild ravings", "mirthless jokes", anachronisms, irrelevancies, obscenities, worn-out stage conventions and other faults both moral and aesthetic. *Lear* is, in any case, a plagiarism of an earlier and much better play, *King Leir*, by an unknown author, which Shakespeare stole and then ruined. It is worth quoting a specimen paragraph to illustrate the manner in which Tolstoy goes to work. Act III, Scene 2 (in which Lear, Kent and the Fool are together in the storm) is summarised thus:

> Lear walks about the heath and says words which are meant to express his despair: he desires that the winds should blow so hard that they (the winds) should crack their cheeks and that the rain should flood everything, that lightning should singe his white head, and the thunder flatten the world and destroy all germs "that make ungrateful man"! The fool keeps uttering still more senseless words. Enter Kent: Lear says that for some reason during this storm all criminals shall be found out and convicted. Kent, still unrecognised by Lear, endeavours to persuade him to take refuge in a hovel. At this point the fool utters a prophecy in no wise related to the situation and they all depart.

Tolstoy's final verdict on *Lear* is that no unhypnotised observer, if such an observer existed, could read it to the end with any feeling except "aversion and weariness". And exactly the same is true of "all the other extolled dramas of Shakespeare, not to mention the senseless dramatised tales, *Pericles, Twelfth Night, The Tempest, Cymbeline, Troilus and Cressida*".

Having dealt with *Lear* Tolstoy draws up a more general indictment against Shakespeare. He finds that Shakespeare has a certain technical skill which is partly traceable to his having been an actor, but otherwise no merits whatever. He has no power of delineating character or of making words and actions spring naturally out of

situations, his language is uniformly exaggerated and ridiculous, he
constantly thrusts his own random thoughts into the mouth of any
character who happens to be handy, he displays a "complete absence
of aesthetic feeling", and his words "have nothing whatever in
common with art and poetry". "Shakespeare might have been whatever you like," Tolstoy concludes, "but he was not an artist." Moreover, his opinions are not original or interesting, and his tendency is
"of the lowest and most immoral". Curiously enough, Tolstoy does
not base this last judgement on Shakespeare's own utterances, but
on the statements of two critics, Gervinus and Brandes. According
to Gervinus (or at any rate Tolstoy's reading of Gervinus) "Shakespeare taught . . . that one *may be too good*," while according to
Brandes "Shakespeare's fundamental principle . . . is that *the end
justifies the means.*" Tolstoy adds on his own account that Shakespeare was a jingo patriot of the worst type, but apart from this he
considers that Gervinus and Brandes have given a true and adequate
description of Shakespeare's view of life.

Tolstoy then recapitulates in a few paragraphs the theory of art
which he had expressed at greater length elsewhere. Put still more
shortly, it amounts to a demand for dignity of subject-matter,
sincerity, and good craftsmanship. A great work of art must deal
with some subject which is "important to the life of mankind", it must
express something which the author genuinely feels, and it must use
such technical methods as will produce the desired effect. As Shakespeare is debased in outlook, slipshod in execution and incapable of
being sincere even for a moment, he obviously stands condemned.

But here there arises a difficult question. If Shakespeare is all that
Tolstoy has shown him to be, how did he ever come to be so generally
admired ? Evidently the answer can only lie in a sort of mass hypnosis,
or "epidemic suggestion". The whole civilised world has somehow
been deluded into thinking Shakespeare a good writer, and even the
plainest demonstration to the contrary makes no impression, because
one is not dealing with a reasoned opinion but with something akin
to religious faith. Throughout history, says Tolstoy, there has been
an endless series of these "epidemic suggestions"—for example, the
Crusades, the search for the Philosopher's Stone, the craze for tulip
growing which once swept over Holland, and so on and so forth.
As a contemporary instance he cites, rather significantly, the Dreyfus
Case, over which the whole world grew violently excited for no
sufficient reason. There are also sudden short-lived crazes for new

political and philosophical theories, or for this or that writer, artist or
scientist—for example, Darwin, who (in 1903) is "beginning to be
forgotten". And in some cases a quite worthless popular idol may
remain in favour for centuries, for "it also happens that such crazes,
having arisen in consequence of special reasons accidentally favour-
ing their establishment, correspond in such a degree to the views of
life spread in society, and especially in literary circles, that they are
maintained for a long time". Shakespeare's plays have continued to
be admired over a long period because "they corresponded to the
irreligious and immoral frame of mind of the upper classes of his time
and ours".

As to the manner in which Shakespeare's fame *started*, Tolstoy
explains it as having been "got up" by German professors towards
the end of the eighteenth century. His reputation "originated in
Germany, and thence was transferred to England". The Germans
chose to elevate Shakespeare because, at a time when there was no
German drama worth speaking about and French classical literature
was beginning to seem frigid and artificial, they were captivated by
Shakespeare's "clever development of scenes" and also found in him
a good expression of their own attitude towards life. Goethe pronounced Shakespeare a great poet, whereupon all the other critics
flocked after him like a troop of parrots, and the general infatuation
has lasted ever since. The result has been a further debasement of
the drama—Tolstoy is careful to include his own plays when condemning the contemporary stage—and a further corruption of the
prevailing moral outlook. It follows that "the false glorification of
Shakespeare" is an important evil which Tolstoy feels it his duty to
combat.

This, then, is the substance of Tolstoy's pamphlet. One's first
feeling is that in describing Shakespeare as a bad writer he is saying
something demonstrably untrue. But this is not the case. In reality
there is no kind of evidence or argument by which one can show that
Shakespeare, or any other writer, is "good". Nor is there any way of
definitely proving that—for instance—Warwick Deeping is "bad".
Ultimately there is no test of literary merit except survival, which is
itself merely an index to majority opinion. Artistic theories such as
Tolstoy's are quite worthless, because they not only start out with
arbitrary assumptions, but depend on vague terms ("sincere",
"important" and so forth) which can be interpreted in any way one
chooses. Properly speaking one cannot *answer* Tolstoy's attack. The

interesting question is: why did he make it? But it should be noticed in passing that he uses many weak or dishonest arguments. Some of these are worth pointing out, not because they invalidate his main charge but because they are, so to speak, evidence of malice.

To begin with, his examination of *King Lear* is not "impartial", as he twice claims. On the contrary, it is a prolonged exercise in misrepresentation. It is obvious that when you are summarising *King Lear* for the benefit of someone who has not read it, you are not really being impartial if you introduce an important speech (Lear's speech when Cordelia is dead in his arms) in this manner: "Again begin Lear's awful ravings, at which one feels ashamed, as at unsuccessful jokes." And in a long series of instances Tolstoy slightly alters or colours the passages he is criticising, always in such a way as to make the plot appear a little more complicated and improbable, or the language a little more exaggerated. For example, we are told that Lear "has no necessity or motive for his abdication", although his reason for abdicating (that he is old and wishes to retire from the cares of state) has been clearly indicated in the first scene. It will be seen that even in the passage which I quoted earlier, Tolstoy has wilfully misunderstood one phrase and slightly changed the meaning of another, making nonsense of a remark which is reasonable enough in its context. None of these misreadings is very gross in itself, but their cumulative effect is to exaggerate the psychological incoherence of the play. Again, Tolstoy is not able to explain why Shakespeare's plays were still in print, and still on the stage, two hundred years after his death (*before* the "epidemic suggestion" started, that is); and his whole account of Shakespeare's rise to fame is guesswork punctuated by outright mis-statements. And again, various of his accusations contradict one another: for example, Shakespeare is a mere entertainer and "not in earnest", but on the other hand he is constantly putting his own thoughts into the mouths of his characters. On the whole it is difficult to feel that Tolstoy's criticisms are uttered in good faith. In any case it is impossible that he should fully have believed in his main thesis—believed, that is to say, that for a century or more the entire civilised world had been taken in by a huge and palpable lie which he alone was able to see through. Certainly his dislike of Shakespeare is real enough, but the reasons for it may be different, or partly different, from what he avows; and therein lies the interest of his pamphlet.

At this point one is obliged to start guessing. However, there is one

possible clue, or at least there is a question which may point the way
to a clue. It is: why did Tolstoy, with thirty or more plays to choose
from, pick out *King Lear* as his especial target? True, *Lear* is so well
known and has been so much praised that it could justly be taken as
representative of Shakespeare's best work: still, for the purpose of a
hostile analysis Tolstoy would probably choose the play he disliked
most. Is it not possible that he bore an especial enmity towards this
particular play because he was aware, consciously or unconsciously,
of the resemblance between Lear's story and his own? But it is better
to approach this clue from the opposite direction—that is, by examining *Lear* itself, and the qualities in it that Tolstoy fails to mention.

   One of the first things an English reader would notice in Tolstoy's
pamphlet is that it hardly deals with Shakespeare as a poet. Shakespeare is treated as a dramatist, and in so far as his popularity is not
spurious, it is held to be due to tricks of stagecraft which give good
opportunities to clever actors. Now, so far as the English-speaking
countries go, this is not true. Several of the plays which are most
valued by lovers of Shakespeare (for instance, *Timon of Athens*) are
seldom or never acted, while some of the most actable, such as *A
Midsummer Night's Dream*, are the least admired. Those who care
most for Shakespeare value him in the first place for his use of language, the "verbal music" which even Bernard Shaw, another hostile
critic, admits to be "irresistible". Tolstoy ignores this, and does not
seem to realise that a poem may have a special value for those who
speak the language in which it was written. However, even if one
puts oneself in Tolstoy's place and tries to think of Shakespeare as a
foreign poet it is still clear that there is something that Tolstoy has
left out. Poetry, it seems, is *not* solely a matter of sound and association, and valueless outside its own language-group: otherwise, how
is it that some poems, including poems written in dead languages,
succeed in crossing frontiers? Clearly a lyric like "Tomorrow is Saint
Valentine's Day" could not be satisfactorily translated, but in
Shakespeare's major work there is something describable as poetry
that can be separated from the words. Tolstoy is right in saying that
Lear is not a very good play, as a play. It is too drawn-out and has
too many characters and sub-plots. One wicked daughter would have
been quite enough, and Edgar is a superfluous character: indeed it
would probably be a better play if Gloucester and both his sons were
eliminated. Nevertheless, something, a kind of pattern, or perhaps
only an atmosphere, survives the complications and the *longueurs*.

Lear can be imagined as a puppet show, a mime, a ballet, a series of pictures. Part of its poetry, perhaps the most essential part, is inherent in the story and is dependent neither on any particular set of words, nor on flesh-and-blood presentation.

Shut your eyes and think of *King Lear*, if possible without calling to mind any of the dialogue. What do you see? Here at any rate is what I see: a majestic old man in a long black robe, with flowing white hair and beard, a figure out of Blake's drawings (but also, curiously enough, rather like Tolstoy), wandering through a storm and cursing the heavens, in company with a Fool and a lunatic. Presently the scene shifts, and the old man, still cursing, still under-standing nothing, is holding a dead girl in his arms while the Fool dangles on a gallows somewhere in the background. This is the bare skeleton of the play, and even here Tolstoy wants to cut out most of what is essential. He objects to the storm, as being unnecessary, to the Fool, who in his eyes is simply a tedious nuisance and an excuse for making bad jokes, and to the death of Cordelia, which, as he sees it, robs the play of its moral. According to Tolstoy, the earlier play, *King Leir*, which Shakespeare adapted

> terminates more naturally and more in accordance with the moral demands of the spectator than does Shakespeare's: namely, by the King of the Gauls conquering the husbands of the elder sisters, and by Cordelia, instead of being killed, restoring Leir to his former position.

In other words the tragedy ought to have been a comedy, or perhaps a melodrama. It is doubtful whether the sense of tragedy is com-patible with belief in God: at any rate, it is not compatible with disbelief in human dignity and with the kind of "moral demand" which feels cheated when virtue fails to triumph. A tragic situation exists precisely when virtue does *not* triumph but when it is still felt that man is nobler than the forces which destroy him. It is perhaps more significant that Tolstoy sees no justification for the presence of the Fool. The Fool is integral to the play. He acts not only as a sort of chorus, making the central situation clearer by commenting on it more intelligently than the other characters, but as a foil to Lear's frenzies. His jokes, riddles and scraps of rhyme, and his endless digs at Lear's high-minded folly, ranging from mere derision to a sort of melancholy poetry ("All thy other titles thou hast given away; that thou wast born with"), are like a trickle of sanity running through the play, a reminder that somewhere or other, in spite of the injustices, cruelties, intrigues, deceptions and misunderstandings that are being enacted here, life is going on much as usual. In Tolstoy's impatience with the Fool one gets a glimpse of his deeper quarrel with Shakespeare. He objects, with some justification, to the raggedness of Shakespeare's plays, the irrelevancies, the incredible plots, the exaggerated language: but what at bottom he probably most dislikes is a sort of exuberance, a tendency to take—not so much a pleasure, as simply an interest in the actual process of life. It is a mistake to write Tolstoy off as a moralist attacking an artist. He never said that art, as such, is wicked or meaningless, nor did he even say that technical virtuosity is unimportant. But his main aim, in his later years, was to narrow the range of human consciousness. One's interests, one's points of attachment to the physical world and the day-to-day struggle, must be as few and not as many as possible. Literature must consist of parables, stripped of detail and almost independent of language. The parables—this is where Tolstoy differs from the average vulgar puritan—must themselves be works of art, but pleasure and curiosity must be excluded from them. Science, also, must be divorced from curiosity. The business of science, he says, is not to discover what happens, but to teach men how they ought to live. So also with history and politics. Many problems (for example, the Dreyfus Case) are simply not worth solving, and he is willing to leave them as loose ends. Indeed his whole theory of "crazes" or "epidemic suggestions", in which he lumps together such things as the Crusades and the Dutch passion of tulip growing, shows a willingness to regard many human activities as mere ant-like rushings to and fro, inexplicable and uninteresting. Clearly he could have no patience with a chaotic, detailed, discursive writer like Shakespeare. His reaction is that of an irritable old man who is being pestered by a noisy child. "Why do you keep jumping up and down like that? Why can't you sit still like I do?" In a way the old man is in the right, but the trouble is that the child has a feeling in its limbs which the old man has lost. And if the old man knows of the existence of this feeling, the effect is merely to increase his irritation: he would make children senile, if he could. Tolstoy does not know, perhaps, just *what* he misses in Shakespeare, but he is aware that he misses something, and he is determined that others shall be deprived of it as well. By nature he was imperious as well as egotistical. Well after he was grown up he would still occasionally strike his servant in moments of anger, and somewhat later, according to his English biographer, Derrick Leon, he felt "a frequent desire upon the slenderest provocation to slap the faces of those with whom he disagreed". One does not necessarily get rid of that kind of temperament by undergoing religious conversion, and indeed it is obvious that the illusion of having been reborn may allow one's native vices to flourish more freely than ever, though perhaps in subtler forms. Tolstoy was capable of abjuring physical violence and of seeing what this implies, but he was not capable of tolerance or humility, and even if one knew nothing of his other writings, one could deduce his tendency towards spiritual bullying from this single pamphlet.

However, Tolstoy is not simply trying to rob others of a pleasure he does not share. He is doing that, but his quarrel with Shakespeare goes further. It is the quarrel between the religious and the humanist attitudes towards life. Here one comes back to the central theme of *King Lear*, which Tolstoy does not mention, although he sets forth the plot in some detail.

Lear is one of the minority of Shakespeare's plays that are unmistakably *about* something. As Tolstoy justly complains, much rubbish has been written about Shakespeare as a philosopher, as a psychologist, as a "great moral teacher", and what not. Shakespeare was not a systematic thinker, his most serious thoughts are uttered irrelevantly or indirectly, and we do not know to what extent he wrote with a "purpose" or even how much of the work attributed to him was actually written by him. In the Sonnets he never even refers to the plays as part of his achievement, though he does make what seems to be a half-ashamed allusion to his career as an actor. It is perfectly possible that he looked on at least half of his plays as mere pot-boilers and hardly bothered about purpose or probability so long as he could patch up something, usually from stolen material, which would more or less hang together on the stage. However, that is not the whole story. To begin with, as Tolstoy himself points out, Shakespeare has a habit of thrusting uncalled-for general reflections into the mouths of his characters. This is a serious fault in a dramatist but it does not fit in with Tolstoy's picture of Shakespeare as a vulgar hack who has no opinions of his own and merely wishes to produce the greatest effect with the least trouble. And more than this, about a dozen of his plays, written for the most part later than 1600, do unquestionably have a meaning and even a moral. They revolve round a central subject which in some cases can be reduced to a single word. For example, *Macbeth* is about ambition, *Othello* is about jealousy, and *Timon of Athens* is about money. The subject of *Lear* is renunciation, and it is only by being wilfully blind that one can fail to understand what Shakespeare is saying.

Lear renounces his throne but expects everyone to continue treating him as a king. He does not see that if he surrenders power, other people will take advantage of his weakness: also that those who flatter him the most grossly, i.e. Regan and Goneril, are exactly the ones who will turn against him. The moment he finds that he can no longer make people obey him as he did before, he falls into a rage which Tolstoy describes as "strange and unnatural", but which in fact is perfectly in character. In his madness and despair, he passes through two moods which again are natural enough in his circumstances, though in one of them it is probable that he is being used partly as a mouthpiece for Shakespeare's own opinions. One is the mood of disgust in which Lear repents, as it were, for having been a king, and grasps for the first time the rottenness of formal justice and vulgar morality. The other is a mood of impotent fury in which he wreaks imaginary revenges upon those who have wronged him. "To have a thousand with red burning spits Come hissing in upon 'em!", and:

> It were a delicate stratagem to shoe
> A troop of horse with felt: I'll put't in proof;
> And when I have stol'n upon these sons-in-law,
> Then kill, kill, kill, kill, kill!

Only at the end does he realise, as a sane man, that power, revenge and victory are not worth while:

> No, no, no, no! Come, let's away to prison . . .
> . . . . .and we'll wear out,
> In a wall'd prison, packs and sects of great ones
> That ebb and flow by the moon.

But by the time he makes this discovery it is too late, for his death and Cordelia's are already decided on. That is the story, and, allowing for some clumsiness in the telling, it is a very good story.

But is it not also curiously similar to the history of Tolstoy himself? There is a general resemblance which one can hardly avoid seeing, because the most impressive event in Tolstoy's life, as in Lear's, was a huge and gratuitous act of renunciation. In his old age he renounced his estate, his title and his copyrights, and made an attempt—a sincere attempt, though it was not successful—to escape from his privileged position and live the life of a peasant. But the deeper resemblance lies in the fact that Tolstoy, like Lear, acted on mistaken motives and failed to get the results he had hoped for. According to Tolstoy, the aim of every human being is happiness, and happiness can only be attained by doing the will of God. But doing the will of God means casting off all earthly pleasures and ambitions, and living only for others. Ultimately, therefore, Tolstoy renounced the world under the expectation that this would make him happier. But if there is one thing certain about his later years, it is that he was *not* happy. On the contrary, he was driven almost to the edge of madness by the behaviour of the people about him, who persecuted him precisely *because* of his renunciation. Like Lear, Tolstoy was not humble and not a good judge of character. He was inclined at moments to revert to the attitudes of an aristocrat, in spite of his peasant's blouse, and he even had two children whom he had believed in and who ultimately turned against him—though, of course, in a less sensational manner than Regan and Goneril. His exaggerated revulsion from sexuality was also distinctly similar to Lear's. Tolstoy's remark that marriage is "slavery, satiety, repulsion" and means putting up with the proximity of "ugliness, dirtiness, smell, sores", is matched by Lear's well-known outburst:

> But to the girdle do the gods inherit,
> Beneath is all the fiends;
> There's hell, there's darkness, there's the sulphurous pit,
> Burning, scalding, stench, consumption, etc etc.

And though Tolstoy could not foresee it when he wrote his essay on Shakespeare, even the ending of his life—the sudden unplanned flight across country, accompanied only by a faithful daughter, the death in a cottage in a strange village—seems to have in it a sort of phantom reminiscence of *Lear*.

Of course, one cannot assume that Tolstoy was aware of this resemblance, or would have admitted it if it had been pointed out to him. But his attitude towards the play must have been influenced by its theme. Renouncing power, giving away your lands, was a subject on which he had reason to feel deeply. Probably, therefore, he would be more angered and disturbed by the moral that Shakespeare draws than he would be in the case of some other play—*Macbeth*, for example—which did not touch so closely on his own life. But what exactly *is* the moral of *Lear*? Evidently there are two morals, one explicit, the other implied in the story.

Shakespeare starts by assuming that to make yourself powerless is to invite an attack. This does not mean that *everyone* will turn against you (Kent and the Fool stand by Lear from first to last), but in all probability *someone* will. If you throw away your weapons, some less scrupulous person will pick them up. If you turn the other cheek, you will get a harder blow on it than you got on the first one. This does not always happen, but it is to be expected, and you ought not to complain if it does happen. The second blow is, so to speak, part of the act of turning the other cheek. First of all, therefore, there is the vulgar, common-sense moral drawn by the Fool: "Don't relinquish power, don't give away your lands." But there is also another moral. Shakespeare never utters it in so many words, and it does not very much matter whether he was fully aware of it. It is contained in the story, which, after all, he made up, or altered to suit his purposes. It is: "Give away your lands if you want to, but don't expect to gain happiness by doing so. Probably you won't gain happiness. If you live for others, you must live *for others*, and not as a roundabout way of getting an advantage for yourself."

Obviously neither of these conclusions could have been pleasing to Tolstoy. The first of them expresses the ordinary, belly-to-earth selfishness from which he was genuinely trying to escape. The other conflicts with his desire to eat his cake and have it—that is, to destroy his own egoism and by so doing to gain eternal life. Of course, *Lear* is not a sermon in favour of altruism. It merely points out the results of practising self-denial for selfish reasons. Shakespeare had a considerable streak of worldliness in him, and if he had been forced to take sides in his own play, his sympathies would probably have lain with the Fool. But at least he could see the whole issue and treat it at the level of tragedy. Vice is punished, but virtue is not rewarded. The morality of Shakespeare's later tragedies is not religious in the ordinary sense, and certainly is not Christian. Only two of them, *Hamlet* and *Othello*, are supposedly occurring inside the Christian era, and even in those, apart from the antics of the ghost in *Hamlet*, there is no indication of a "next world" where everything is to be put right. All of these tragedies start out with the humanist assumption that life, although full of sorrow, is worth living, and that Man is a noble animal—a belief which Tolstoy in his old age did not share.

Tolstoy was not a saint, but he tried very hard to make himself into a saint, and the standards he applied to literature were other-worldly ones. It is important to realise that the difference between a saint and an ordinary human being is a difference of kind and not of degree. That is, the one is not to be regarded as an imperfect form of the other. The saint, at any rate Tolstoy's kind of saint, is not trying to work an improvement in earthly life: he is trying to bring it to an end and put something different in its place. One obvious expression of this is the claim that celibacy is "higher" than marriage. If only, Tolstoy says in effect, we would stop breeding, fighting, struggling and enjoying, if we could get rid not only of our sins but of everything else that binds us to the surface of the earth—including love, in the ordinary sense of caring more for one human being than another —then the whole painful process would be over and the Kingdom of Heaven would arrive. But a normal human being does not want the Kingdom of Heaven: he wants life on earth to continue. This is not solely because he is "weak", "sinful" and anxious for a "good time". Most people get a fair amount of fun out of their lives, but on balance life is suffering, and only the very young or the very foolish imagine otherwise. Ultimately it is the Christian attitude which is self-interested and hedonistic, since the aim is always to get away from the painful struggle of earthly life and find eternal peace in some kind of Heaven or Nirvana. The humanist attitude is that the struggle must continue and that death is the price of life. "Men must endure Their going hence, even as their coming hither: Ripeness is all"— which is an un-Christian sentiment. Often there is a seeming truce between the humanist and the religious believer, but in fact their attitudes cannot be reconciled: one must choose between this world and the next. And the enormous majority of human beings, if they understood the issue, would choose this world. They do make that choice when they continue working, breeding and dying instead of crippling their faculties in the hope of obtaining a new lease of existence elsewhere.

We do not know a great deal about Shakespeare's religious beliefs, and from the evidence of his writings it would be difficult to prove that he had any. But at any rate he was not a saint or a would-be saint: he was a human being, and in some ways not a very good one. It is clear, for instance, that he liked to stand well with the rich and powerful, and was capable of flattering them in the most servile way. He is also noticeably cautious, not to say cowardly, in his manner of uttering unpopular opinions. Almost never does he put a subversive or sceptical remark into the mouth of a character likely to be identified with himself. Throughout his plays the acute social critics, the people who are not taken in by accepted fallacies, are buffoons, villains, lunatics or persons who are shamming insanity or are in a state of violent hysteria. *Lear* is a play in which this tendency is particularly well marked. It contains a great deal of veiled social criticism—a point Tolstoy misses—but it is all uttered either by the Fool, by Edgar when he is pretending to be mad, or by Lear during his bouts of madness. In his sane moments Lear hardly ever makes an intelligent remark. And yet the very fact that Shakespeare had to use these subterfuges shows how widely his thoughts ranged. He could not restrain himself from commenting on almost everything, although he put on a series of masks in order to do so. If one has once read Shakespeare with attention, it is not easy to go a day without quoting him, because there are not many subjects of major importance that he does not discuss or at least mention somewhere or other, in his unsystematic but illuminating way. Even the irrelevancies that litter every one of his plays—the puns and riddles, the lists of names, the scraps of reportage like the conversation of the carriers in *Henry IV*, the bawdy jokes, the rescued fragments of forgotten ballads—are merely the products of excessive vitality. Shakespeare was not a philosopher or a scientist, but he did have curiosity: he loved the surface of the earth and the process of life— which, it should be repeated, is *not* the same thing as wanting to have a good time and stay alive as long as possible. Of course, it is not because of the quality of his thought that Shakespeare has survived, and he might not even be remembered as a dramatist if he had not also been a poet. His main hold on us is through language. How deeply Shakespeare himself was fascinated by the music of words can probably be inferred from the speeches of Pistol. What Pistol says is largely meaningless, but if one considers his lines singly they are magnificent rhetorical verse. Evidently, pieces of resounding nonsense ("Let floods o'erswell, and fiends for food howl on", etc) were constantly appearing in Shakespeare's mind of their own accord, and a half-lunatic character had to be invented to use them up. Tolstoy's native tongue was not English, and one cannot blame him for being unmoved by Shakespeare's verse, nor even, perhaps, for refusing to believe that Shakespeare's skill with words was something out of the ordinary. But he would also have rejected the whole notion of valuing poetry for its texture—valuing it, that is to say, as a kind of music. If it could somehow have been proved to him that his whole explanation of Shakespeare's rise to fame is mistaken, that inside the English-speaking world, at any rate, Shakespeare's popularity is genuine, that his mere skill in placing one syllable beside another has given acute pleasure to generation after generation of English-speaking people— all this would not have been counted as a merit to Shakespeare, but rather the contrary. It would simply have been one more proof of the irreligious, earthbound nature of Shakespeare and his admirers. Tolstoy would have said that poetry is to be judged by its meaning, and that seductive sounds merely cause false meanings to go unnoticed. At every level it is the same issue—this world against the next: and certainly the music of words is something that belongs to this world.

A sort of doubt has always hung round the character of Tolstoy, as round the character of Gandhi. He was not a vulgar hypocrite, as some people declared him to be, and he would probably have imposed even greater sacrifices on himself than he did, if he had not been interfered with at every step by the people surrounding him, especially his wife. But on the other hand it is dangerous to take such men as Tolstoy at their disciples' valuation. There is always the possibility—the probability, indeed—that they have done no more than exchange one form of egoism for another. Tolstoy renounced wealth, fame and privilege; he abjured violence in all its forms and was ready to suffer for doing so; but it is not so easy to believe that he abjured the principle of coercion, or at least the *desire* to coerce others. There are families in which the father will say to his child, "You'll get a thick ear if you do that again," while the mother, her eyes brimming over with tears, will take the child in her arms and murmur lovingly, "Now, darling, *is* it kind to Mummy to do that?" And who would maintain that the second method is less tyrannous than the first? The distinction that really matters is not between violence and non-violence, but between having and not having the appetite for power. There are people who are convinced of the wickedness both of armies and of police forces, but who are nevertheless much more intolerant and inquisitorial in outlook than the normal person who believes that it is necessary to use violence in certain circumstances. They will not say to somebody else, "Do this, that and the other or you will go to prison," but they will, if they can, get inside his brain and dictate his thoughts for him in the minutest particulars. Creeds like pacifism and anarchism, which seem on the surface to imply a complete renunciation of power, rather encourage this habit of mind. For if you have embraced a creed which appears to be free from the ordinary dirtiness of politics—a creed from which you yourself cannot expect to draw any material advantage—surely that proves that you are in the right? And the more you are in the right, the more natural that everyone else should be bullied into thinking likewise.

If we are to believe what he says in his pamphlet, Tolstoy had never been able to see any merit in Shakespeare, and was always astonished to find that his fellow writers, Turgenev, Fet and others, thought differently. We may be sure that in his unregenerate days Tolstoy's conclusion would have been: "You like Shakespeare—I don't. Let's leave it at that." Later, when his perception that it takes all sorts to make a world had deserted him, he came to think of Shakespeare's writings as something dangerous to himself. The more pleasure people took in Shakespeare, the less they would listen to Tolstoy. Therefore nobody must be *allowed* to enjoy Shakespeare, just as nobody must be allowed to drink alcohol or smoke tobacco. True, Tolstoy would not prevent them by force. He is not demanding that the police shall impound every copy of Shakespeare's works. But he will do dirt on Shakespeare, if he can. He will try to get inside the mind of every lover of Shakespeare and kill his enjoyment by every trick he can think of, including—as I have shown in my summary of his pamphlet—arguments which are self-contradictory or even doubtfully honest.

But finally the most striking thing is how little difference it all makes. As I said earlier, one cannot *answer* Tolstoy's pamphlet, at least on its main counts. There is no argument by which one can defend a poem. It defends itself by surviving, or it is indefensible. And if this test is valid, I think the verdict in Shakespeare's case must be "not guilty". Like every other writer, Shakespeare will be forgotten sooner or later, but it is unlikely that a heavier indictment will ever be brought against him. Tolstoy was perhaps the most admired literary man of his age, and he was certainly not its least able pamphleteer. He turned all his powers of denunciation against Shakespeare, like all the guns of a battleship roaring simultaneously. And with what result? Forty years later, Shakespeare is still there, completely unaffected, and of the attempt to demolish him nothing remains except the yellowing pages of a pamphlet which hardly anyone has read, and which would be forgotten altogether if Tolstoy had not also been the author of *War and Peace* and *Anna Karenina*.

Polemic, No. 7, March 1947; SE; OR; CB

77. As I Please

Some time ago a foreign visitor asked me if I could recommend a good, representative anthology of English verse. When I thought it over I found that I could not name a single one that seemed to me satisfactory. Of course there are innumerable period anthologies, but nothing, so far as I know, that attempts to cover the whole of English literature except Palgrave's *Golden Treasury* and, more comprehensive and more up-to-date, *The Oxford Book of English Verse*.

Now, I do not deny that *The Oxford Book* is useful, that there is a great deal of good stuff in it, and that every schoolchild ought to have a copy, in default of something better. Still, when you look at the last fifty pages, you think twice about recommending such a book to a foreigner who may imagine that it is really representative of English verse. Indeed, the whole of this part of the book is a lamentable illustration of what happens to professors of literature when they have to exercise independent judgement. Up to 1850, or thereabouts, one could not go very wrong in compiling an anthology, because, after all, it is on the whole the best poems that have survived. But as soon as Sir Arthur Quiller-Couch reached his contemporaries, all semblance of taste deserted him.

The Oxford Book stops at 1900, and it is true that the last decades of the nineteenth century were a poor period for verse. Still, there were poets even in the 'nineties. There was Ernest Dowson— "Cynara" is not my idea of a good poem, but I would sooner have it than Henley's "England, My England"—there was Hardy, who published his first poems in 1898, and there was Housman, who published *A Shropshire Lad* in 1896. There was also Hopkins, who was not in print or barely in print, but whom Sir Arthur Quiller-Couch must have known about. None of these appears in *The Oxford Book*. Yeats, who had already published a great deal at that date, does appear shortly, but he is not represented by his best poems: neither is Kipling, who, I think, did write one or two poems (for instance, "How far is St Helena") which deserve to be included in a serious anthology. And on the other hand, just look at the stuff that *has* been included! Sir Henry Newbolt's Old Cliftonian keeping a stiff upper lip on the North-West Frontier; other patriotic pieces by Henley and Kipling; and page after page of weak, sickly, imitative

verse by Andrew Lang, Sir William Watson, A.C. Benson, Alice
Meynell and others now forgotten. What is one to think of an
anthologist who puts Newbolt and Edmund Gosse in the same
volume with Shakespeare, Wordsworth and Blake?

Perhaps I am just being ignorant and there does already exist a
comprehensive anthology running all the way from Chaucer to
Dylan Thomas and including no tripe. But if not, I think it is time
to compile one, or at least to bring *The Oxford Book* up to date by
making a completely new selection of poets from Tennyson onwards.

Looking through what I have written above, I see that I have
spoken rather snootily of Dowson's "Cynara". I know it is a bad
poem, but it is bad in a good way, or good in a bad way, and I do
not wish to pretend that I never admired it. Indeed, it was one of the
favourites of my boyhood. I am quoting from memory:

> I have forgot much, Cynara! gone with the wind,
> Flung roses, roses, riotously with the throng,
> Dancing, to put thy pale lost lilies out of mind;
> But I was desolate and sick of an old passion,
> Yea, all the time, because the dance was long—
> I have been faithful to thee, Cynara! in my fashion.

Surely those lines possess, if not actual merit, at least the same kind
of charm as belongs to a pink geranium or a soft-centre chocolate.

Tribune, 7 March 1947

78. As I Please

I have not yet read more than a newspaper paragraph about Nu
Speling, in connection with which somebody is introducing a Bill in
Parliament, but if it is like most other schemes for rationalising our
spelling, I am against it in advance, as I imagine most people will be.

Probably the strongest reason for resisting rationalised spelling is
laziness. We have all learned to read and write already, and we don't
want to have to do it over again. But there are other more respectable
objections. To begin with, unless the scheme were rigidly enforced,
the resulting chaos, with some newspapers and publishing houses
accepting it, others refusing it, and others adopting it in patches,

would be fearful. Then again, anyone who had learned only the new system would find it very difficult to read books printed in the old one, so that the huge labour of respelling the entire literature of the past would have to be undertaken. And again, you can only fully rationalise spelling if you give a fixed value to each letter. But this means standardising pronunciation, which could not be done in this country without an unholy row. What do you do, for instance, about words like "butter" or "glass," which are pronounced in different ways in London and Newcastle? Other words, such as "were", are pronounced in two different ways according to individual inclination, or according to context.

However, I do not want to prejudge the inventors of Nu Speling. Perhaps they have already thought of a way round these difficulties. And certainly our existing spelling system is preposterous and must be a torment to foreign students. This is a pity, because English is well fitted to be the universal second language, if there ever is such a thing. It has a large start over any natural language and an enormous start over any manufactured one, and apart from the spelling it is very easy to learn. Would it not be possible to rationalise it by little and little, a few words every year? Already some of the more ridiculous spellings do tend to get killed off unofficially. For instance, how many people now spell "hiccup" as "hiccough"?

Another thing I am against in advance—for it is bound to be suggested sooner or later—is the complete scrapping of our present system of weights and measures.

Obviously you have got to have the metric system for certain purposes. For scientific work it has long been in use, and it is also needed for tools and machinery, especially if you want to export them. But there is a strong case for keeping on the old measurements for use in everyday life. One reason is that the metric system does not possess, or has not succeeded in establishing, a large number of units that can be visualised. There is, for instance, effectively no unit between the metre, which is more than a yard, and the centimetre, which is less than half an inch. In English you can describe someone as being five feet three inches high, or five feet nine inches, or six feet one inch, and your hearer will know fairly accurately what you mean. But I have never heard a Frenchman say, "He is a hundred and forty-two centimetres high"; it would not convey any visual image. So also with the various other measurements. Rods and acres, pints, quarts and gallons, pounds, stones and hundredweights, are all of them units with which we are intimately familiar, and we should be slightly poorer without them. Actually, in countries where the metric system is in force a few of the old measurements tend to linger on for everyday purposes, although officially discouraged.

There is also the literary consideration, which cannot be left quite out of account. The names of the units in the old system are short homely words which lend themselves to vigorous speech. Putting a quart into a pint pot is a good image, which could hardly be expressed in the metric system. Also, the literature of the past deals only in the old measurements, and many passages would become an irritation if one had to do a sum in arithmetic when one read them, as one does with those tiresome versts in a Russian novel.

> The emmet's inch and eagle's mile
> Make lame philosophy to smile:

fancy having to turn that into millimetres!

I have just been reading about a party of German teachers, journalists, trade union delegates and others who have been on a visit to this country. It appears that while here they were given food parcels by trade unions and other organisations, only to have them taken away again by the Customs officials at Harwich. They were not even allowed to take out of the country the 15 lb of food which is permitted to a returning prisoner of war. The newspaper reporting this adds without apparent irony that the Germans in question had been here "on a six weeks' course in democracy".

The other day I had occasion to write something about the teaching of history in private schools, and the following scene, which was only rather loosely connected with what I was writing, floated into my memory. It was less than fifteen years ago that I witnessed it.

"Jones!"

"Yessir!"

"Causes of the French Revolution."

"Please, sir, the French Revolution was due to three causes, the teachings of Voltaire and Rousseau, the oppression of the nobles by the people and—"

At this moment a faint chill, like the first premonitory symptom of an illness, falls upon Jones. Is it possible that he has gone wrong somewhere? The master's face is inscrutable. Swiftly Jones casts his mind back to the unappetising little book, with the gritty brown cover, a page of which is memorised daily. He could have sworn he had the whole thing right. But at this moment Jones discovers for the first time the deceptiveness of visual memory. The whole page is clear in his mind, the shape of every paragraph accurately recorded, but the trouble is that there is no saying which way round the words go. He had made sure it was the oppression of the nobles by the people; but then it might have been the oppression of the people by the nobles. It is a toss-up. Desperately he takes his decision—better to stick to his first version. He gabbles on:

"The oppression of the nobles by the people and—"

"JONES!"

Is that kind of thing still going on, I wonder?

Tribune, 14 March 1947

79. Letter to Victor Gollancz

27B Canonbury Square
Islington, N1
14 March 1947

Dear Gollancz,[1]

I believe Leonard Moore has already spoken to you about the contract which I still have with you and about my wish to be released from it. I believe that the contract that still subsists between us is the one made for *Keep the Aspidistra Flying* in 1937, which provided that I would give you the first refusal of my next three novels. *Coming Up for Air* worked off one of these, but you did not accept *Animal Farm*, which you saw and refused in 1944, as working off another. So that by the terms of the contract I still owe you the refusal of two other novels.

I know that I am asking you a very great favour in asking that you should cancel the contract, but various circumstances have changed in the ten years since it was made, and I believe that it might be to your advantage, as it certainly would be to mine, to bring it to an end. The position is that since then you have published three books

---

[1] Victor Gollancz (1893–1967), Kt 1965, publisher. From 1933 to 1940 he had published seven of Orwell's books, but had rejected *Homage to Catalonia* and *Animal Farm* on political grounds.

of mine but you have also refused two others on political grounds, and there was also another which you did not refuse but which it seemed natural to take to another publisher. The crucial case was *Animal Farm*. At the time when this book was finished, it was very hard indeed to get it published, and I determined then that if possible I would take all my future output to the publisher who would produce it, because I knew that anyone who would risk this book would risk anything. Secker & Warburg were not only ready to publish *Animal Farm* but are willing, when paper becomes available, to do a uniform edition of such of my books as I think worth reprinting, including some which are at present very completely out of print. They are also anxious to reprint my novel *Coming Up for Air* in an ordinary edition this year, but, not unnaturally, they are only willing to do all this if they can have a comprehensive contract giving them control of anything I write.

From my own point of view it is clearly very unsatisfactory to have to take my novels to one publisher and at the same time be obliged, at any rate in some cases, to take non-fiction books elsewhere. I recognise, of course, that your political position is not now exactly what it was when you refused *Animal Farm*, and in any case I respect your unwillingness to publish books which go directly counter to your political principles. But it seems to me that this difficulty is likely to arise again in some form or other, and that it would be better if you are willing to bring the whole thing to an end.

If you wish to see me personally about this, I am at your disposal. I shall be at this address until about April 10th.

Yours sincerely,
Geo. Orwell

80. Letter to Victor Gollancz

27B Canonbury Square
Islington
London N1
25 March 1947

Dear Gollancz,

I must thank you for your kind and considerate letter, and I have thought it over with some care. I nevertheless still think, if you are willing to agree, that it would be better to terminate our contract. It is not that anything in the book I am now writing is likely to lead to trouble, but I have to think of the overall position. Neither Warburg nor anyone else can regard me as a good proposition unless he can have an option on my whole output, which is never very large in any case. It is obviously better if I can be with one publisher altogether, and, as I don't suppose I shall cease writing about politics from time to time, I am afraid of further differences arising, as in the past. You know what the difficulty is, i.e. Russia. For quite 15 years I have regarded that régime with plain horror, and though, of course, I would change my opinion if I saw reason, I don't think my feelings are likely to change so long as the Communist Party remains in power. I know that your position in recent years has been not very far from mine, but I don't know what it would be if, for instance, there is another seeming rapprochement between Russia and the West, which is a possible development in the next few years. Or again in an actual war situation. I don't, God knows, want a war to break out, but if one were compelled to choose between Russia and America—and I suppose that is the choice one might have to make—I would always choose America. I know Warburg and his opinions well enough to know that he is very unlikely ever to refuse anything of mine on political grounds. As you say, no publisher can sign blind an undertaking to print anything a writer produces, but I think Warburg is less likely to jib than most.

I know that I am asking a great deal of you, since after all we have a contract which I signed freely and by which I am still bound. If you decide that the contract must stand, of course I shall not violate it. But so far as my own feelings go I would rather terminate it. Please forgive me for what must seem like ungraciousness, and for causing you all this trouble.

Yours sincerely,
Geo. Orwell

81. As I Please

I have been reading with interest the February–March bulletin of Mass Observation, which appears just ten years after this organisation first came into being. It is curious to remember with what hostility it was greeted at the beginning. It was violently attacked in the *New Statesman*, for instance, where Mr Stonier declared that the typical Mass Observer would have "elephant ears, a loping walk and a permanent sore eye from looking through keyholes", or words to that effect. Another attacker was Mr Stephen Spender. But on the whole the opposition to this or any other kind of social survey comes from people of conservative opinions, who often seem to be genuinely indignant at the idea of finding out what the big public is thinking.

If asked why, they generally answer that what is discovered is of no interest, and that in any case any intelligent person always knows already what are the main trends of public opinion. Another argument is that social surveys are an interference with individual liberty and a first step towards totalitarianism. The *Daily Express* ran this line for several years and tried to laugh the small social survey unit instituted by the Ministry of Information out of existence by nick-naming it Cooper's Snoopers. Of course, behind much of this opposition there lies a well-justified fear of finding that mass sentiment on many subjects is not conservative.

But some people do seem sincerely to feel that it is a bad thing for the government to know too much about what people are thinking, just as others feel that it is a kind of presumption when the government tries to educate public opinion. Actually you can't have democracy unless both processes are at work. Democracy is only possible when the law-makers and administrators know what the masses want, and what they can be counted on to understand. If the present Government paid more attention to this last point, they would word some of their publicity differently. Mass Observation issued a report last week on the White Paper on the economic situation. They found, as usual, that the abstract words and phrases which are flung to and fro in official announcements mean nothing to countless ordinary citizens. Many people are even flummoxed by the word "assets", which is thought to have something to do with "assist"!

The *Mass Observation Bulletin* gives some account of the methods its investigators use, but does not touch on a very important point, and that is the manner in which social surveys are financed. Mass Observation itself appears to keep going in a hand-to-mouth way by publishing books and by undertaking specific jobs for the Government or for commercial organisations. Some of its best surveys, such as that dealing with the birthrate, were carried out for the Advertising Service Guild. The trouble with this method is that a subject only gets investigated if some large, wealthy organisation happens to be interested in it. An obvious example is antisemitism, which I believe has never been looked into, or only in a very sketchy way. But antisemitism is only one variant of the great modern disease of nationalism. We know very little about the real causes of nationalism, and we might conceivably be on the way towards curing it if we knew more. But who is sufficiently interested to put up the thousands of pounds that an exhaustive survey would cost?

For some weeks there has been correspondence in the *Observer* about the persistence of "spit and polish" in the armed forces. The last issue had a good letter from someone who signed himself "Conscript", describing how he and his comrades were forced to waste their time in polishing brass, blacking the rubber hoses on stirrup pumps with boot polish, scraping broom handles with razor blades, and so on. But "Conscript" then goes on to say:

> When an officer (a major) carried out routine reading of King's Regulations regarding venereal disease, he did not hesitate to add: "There is nothing to be ashamed of if you have the disease —it is quite natural. But make sure that you report for treatment at once."

I must say that it seems to me strange, amid the other idiocies mentioned, to object to one of the few sensible things in the army system, i.e. its straightforward attitude towards venereal disease. We shall never be able to stamp out syphilis and gonorrhoea until the stigma of sinfulness is removed from them. When full conscription was introduced in the 1914–18 war it was discovered, if I remember rightly, that nearly half the population suffered or had suffered from some form of venereal disease, and this frightened the authorities into taking a few precautions. During the inter-war years the struggle against venereal disease languished, so far as the civilian population went. There was provision for treatment of those already infected, but the proposal to set up "early treatment centres", as in the army, was quelled by the puritans. Then came another war, with the increase in venereal disease that war necessarily causes, and another attempt to deal with the problem. The Ministry of Health posters are timid enough, but even these would have provoked an outcry from the pious ones if military necessity had not called them into being.

You can't deal with these diseases so long as they are thought of as visitations of God, in a totally different category from all other diseases. The inevitable result of that is concealment and quack remedies. And it is humbug to say that "clean living is the only real remedy". You are bound to have promiscuity and prostitution in a society like ours, where people mature sexually at about fifteen and are discouraged from marrying till they are in their twenties, where conscription and the need for mobility of labour break up family life, and where young people living in big towns have no regular way of forming acquaintanceships. It is impossible to solve the problem by making people more moral, because they won't, within any foreseeable time, become as moral as all that. Besides, many of the victims of venereal disease are husbands or wives who have not themselves committed any so-called immoral act. The only sensible course is to recognise that syphilis and gonorrhoea are merely *diseases*, more preventable if not more curable than most, and that to suffer from them is not disgraceful. No doubt the pious ones would squeal. But in doing so they might avow their real motives, and then we should be a little nearer to wiping out this evil.

For the last five minutes I have been gazing out of the window into the square, keeping a sharp look-out for signs of spring. There is a thinnish patch in the clouds with a faint hint of blue behind it, and on a sycamore tree there are some things that look as if they might be buds. Otherwise it is still winter. But don't worry! Two days ago, after a careful search in Hyde Park, I came on a hawthorn bush that was definitely in bud, and some birds, though not actually singing, were making noises like an orchestra tuning up. Spring is coming after all, and recent rumours that this was the beginning of another Ice Age were unfounded. In only three weeks' time we shall be listening to the cuckoo, which usually gives tongue about the fourteenth of April. Another three weeks after that, and we shall be basking under blue skies, eating ices off barrows and neglecting to lay up fuel for next winter.

How appropriate the ancient poems in praise of spring have seemed these last few years! They have a meaning that they did not have in the days when there was no fuel shortage and you could get almost anything at any time of year. Of all passages celebrating spring, I think I like best those two stanzas from the beginning of one of the Robin Hood ballads. I modernise the spelling:

When shaws be sheen and swards full fair,
And leaves both large and long,
It is merry walking in the fair forest
To hear the small birds' song.

The woodwele sang and would not cease,
Sitting upon the spray,
So loud he wakened Robin Hood
In the greenwood where he lay.

But what exactly was the woodwele? The Oxford Dictionary seems to suggest that it was the woodpecker, which is not a notable songster, and I should be interested to know whether it can be identified with some more probable bird.

Tribune, 28 March 1947

82. Burnham's View of the Contemporary World Struggle

One fallacy left over from the nineteenth century and still influencing our thoughts is the notion that two major wars cannot happen within a few years of one another. The American civil war and the Franco-Prussian war, it is true, occurred almost simultaneously, but they were fought in different continents and by different people. Otherwise the rule seemed to hold good that you can only get people to fight when everyone who remembers what the last war was like is beyond military age. Even the gap between the two world wars—twenty-one years—was large enough to ensure that very few men took part in both of them as common soldiers. Hence the widespread vague belief, or hope, that a third world war could not break out before about 1970, by which time, it is hopefully argued, "all sorts of things may have happened".

As James Burnham points out,[1] the atomic bomb has altered all that. His book is, in effect, a product of atomic weapons: it is a revision, almost an abandonment of his earlier world-picture, in the light of the fact that the great nations are now in a position actually to annihilate one another. When weapons have reached this level of

[1] *The Struggle for the World* by James Burnham.

deadliness, one cannot take the risk of letting the enemy get his blow
in first, so that as soon as *two* hostile nations possess atomic bombs,
the explosion will follow almost immediately. In Burnham's opinion,
we have perhaps ten years, but more probably only five, before the
third world war, which has been raging unofficially ever since 1944,
enters its open phase.

No doubt it is not necessary to say what powers this war will be
between. Burnham's main aim in writing his book is to urge the
United States to seize the initiative and establish what amounts to a
world empire now, before Communism swallows the whole of
Eurasia. The actual continuity of civilisation, he says, is threatened
by the existence of atomic weapons, and there is no safeguard except
to make sure that only one nation possesses them. Ideally, atomic
energy would be controlled by an international authority, but no such
thing exists or is likely to exist for a long time to come, and meanwhile the only serious competitors for world power are the United
States and the USSR. However, the struggle is not merely between
western democracy and Communism. Burnham's definition of
Communism is central to the book, and it is worth stopping to
examine it.

He does not accept the now widely-spread belief that Communism
is simply Russian imperialism: in its way, it is a genuinely international movement, and the USSR is merely the base, or nucleus,
from which it expands, sucking one territory after another into its
system. Even if the system covered the whole earth, the real centre
of power and government would no doubt continue to be the
Eurasian "heartland"; but world Communism does not so much
mean conquest by Russia as conquest by a special form of social
organisation. Communism is not in the ordinary sense a political
movement: it is a world-wide conspiratorial movement for the
capture of power. Its aim is to establish everywhere a system similar
to that which prevails in Soviet Russia—that is, a system which is
technically collectivist, but which concentrates all power in a very
few hands, is based on forced labour, and eliminates all real or
imaginary opponents by means of terrorism. It can expand, even
outside the striking range of the Red army, because in every country
there are a few people who are its devoted adherents, others, more
numerous, who are in some degree deceived, and yet others who will
more or less accept Communism so long as it seems to be winning
and they are offered no alternative. In every country which they are

unable to dominate, the Communists act as a Fifth Column, working through cover organisations of every kind, playing on working-class aspirations and the ignorance of well-meaning liberals, always with the object of sowing demoralisation against the day when war breaks out. All Communist activities are really directed towards this war. Unless Communism can be forced back upon the defensive, there is no chance of the war being averted, since the inevitability of a "final struggle" is part of the Leninist mythology and is believed in as an article of faith.

After discussing the nature of Communism and of Soviet foreign policy, Burnham examines the strategic situation. "Communism"—that is to say, the USSR with its satellite nations and Fifth Columns—has enormous advantages in manpower, in natural resources, in the inaccessibility of the Eurasian "heartland", in the quasi-religious appeal of the Communist myth, and above all, perhaps, in the quality of its leadership. The supreme commanders of the Communist movement are men who have no aim in life except to capture power and who are not troubled by scruples nor obliged to take much account of public opinion. They are both experts and fanatics, whereas their opponents are bungling, half-hearted amateurs. On the other hand, "Communism" is technologically backward and suffers from the disadvantage that its mythology is most easily swallowed by people who have not seen Russian rule at close quarters. The United States is relatively weak in manpower and its geographical position is none too strong, but in industrial output and technique it is far ahead of all rivals, and it has potential allies all over the world, especially in western Europe. The greatest handicap of the United States, therefore, is the lack of any definite world-view: if the American people understood their own strength, and also the danger that threatens them, the situation would be retrievable.

Burnham discusses what ought to be done, what could be done, and what probably will be done. He writes off pacifism as a practical remedy. In principle it could solve the world's ills, but since significant numbers of people cannot be induced to adopt it, it can only provide salvation for scattered individuals, not for societies. The real alternatives before the world are domination by Communism and domination by the United States. Obviously the latter is preferable, and the United States must act swiftly and make its purpose unmistakably clear. It must start off by proposing a union—not an alliance, but a complete fusion—with Britain and the British

Dominions, and strive to draw the whole of western Europe into its orbit. It must ruthlessly extirpate Communism within its own borders. It must frankly set itself up as the world's champion against Communism, and conduct unremitting propaganda to the people of the Russian-occupied countries, and still more to the Russian people themselves, making clear to them that not they but their rulers are regarded as the enemy. It must take up the firmest possible attitude towards the USSR, always understanding that a threat or gesture not backed by military force is useless. It must stick by its friends and not make gifts of food and machinery to its enemies. And above all, the United States must have a clear policy. Unless it has a definite, intelligible plan for world organisation, it cannot seize the initiative from Communism. It is on this point that Burnham is most pessimistic. At present, the American people as a whole have no grasp of the world situation, and American foreign policy is weak, unstable and contradictory. It must be so, because—quite apart from the sabotage of "fellow-travellers" and the intrusion of home politics—there is no general, overriding purpose. In outlining a policy for the United States, Burnham says, he is only pointing out what *could* be done. What probably *will* happen is yet more confusion and vacillation, leading in five or ten years to a war which the United States will enter at grave disadvantage.

That is the general outline of Burnham's argument, though I have slightly rearranged the order in which he presents it. It will be seen that he is demanding, or all but demanding, an immediate preventive war against Russia. True, he does not *want* the war to happen, and he thinks that it may possibly be prevented if sufficient firmness is shown. Still, the main point of his plan is that only one country should be allowed to possess the atomic bombs: and the Russians, unless crippled in war, are bound to get hold of them sooner or later. It will also be seen that Burnham is largely scrapping his earlier world-picture, and not merely the geographical aspect of it. In *The Managerial Revolution*, Burnham foretold the rise of three super-states which would be unable to conquer one another and would divide the world between them. Now the super-states have dwindled to two, and, thanks to atomic weapons, neither of them is invincible. But more has changed than that. In *The Managerial Revolution* it was implied that all three super-states would be very much alike. They would all be totalitarian in structure: that is, they would be collectivist but not democratic, and would be ruled over by a caste of managers, scientists and bureaucrats who would destroy old-style capitalism and keep the working class permanently in subjection. In other words, something rather like "Communism" would prevail everywhere. In *The Machiavellians*, Burnham somewhat toned down his theory, but continued to insist that politics is only the struggle for power, and that government has to be based on force and fraud. Democracy is unworkable, and in any case the masses do not want it and will not make sacrifices in defence of it. In his present book, however, Burnham is in effect the champion of old-style democracy. There is, he now decides, a great deal in western society that is worth preserving. Managerialism, with its forced labour, deportation, massacres and frame-up trials, is not really the unavoidable next stage in human development, and we must all get together and quell it before it is too late. All the available forces must rally immediately under the banner of anti-Communism. It is essentially a conservative programme, making its appeal to the love of liberty and ordinary decency, but not to international sentiment.

Before criticising Burnham's thesis, there is one thing that must be said. This is that Burnham has intellectual courage, and writes about real issues. He is certain to be denounced as a war-monger for writing this book. Yet if the danger is as acute as he believes, the course he suggests would probably be the right one: and more than this, he avoids the usual hypocritical attitude of "condemning" Russian policy while denying that it could be right in any circumstances to go to war. In international politics, as he realises, you must either be ready to practise appeasement indefinitely, or at some point you must be ready to fight. He also sees that appeasement is an unreal policy, since a great nation, conscious of its own strength, never really carries it through. All that happens is that sooner or later some demand is felt to be intolerable, and one flounders into a war that might have been avoided by taking a firm attitude earlier. It is not fashionable to say such things nowadays, and Burnham deserves credit for saying them. However, it does not follow that he is right in his main argument. The important thing is the time factor. How much time have we got before the moment of crisis? Burnham, as usual, sees everything in the darkest colours and allows us only five years, or at most ten. If that were right, an American world empire would probably be the only hope. On the other hand, if we have twenty years in which to manoeuvre, there are other and better possibilities which ought not to be abandoned.

Unless the signs are very deceiving, the USSR is preparing for war against the western democracies. Indeed, as Burnham rightly says, the war is already happening in a desultory way. How soon it could break out into full-scale conflict is a difficult question, bringing in all kinds of military, economic and scientific problems on which the ordinary journalist or political observer has no data. But there is one point, very important to Burnham's argument, which can be profitably discussed, and that is the position of the Communist parties and the "fellow-travellers" and the reliance placed on them by Russian strategy.

Burnham lays great stress on the Communist tactic of "infiltration". The Communists and their associates, open and secret, and the liberals who play their game unknowingly, are everywhere. They are in the trade unions, in the armed forces, in the State Department, in the press, in the churches, in cultural organisations, in every kind of league or union or committee with ostensibly progressive aims, seeping into everything like a filter-passing virus. For the moment they spread confusion and disaffection, and presently, when the crisis comes, they will hit out with all their strength. Moreover, a Communist is psychologically quite different from an ordinary human being. According to Burnham:

> The true Communist . . . is a "dedicated man". He has no life apart from his organisation and his rigidly systematic set of ideas. Everything that he does, everything that he has, family, job, money, belief, friends, talents, life, everything is subordinated to his Communism. He is not a Communist just on election day or at Party headquarters. He is a Communist always. He eats, reads, makes love, thinks, goes to parties, changes residence, laughs, insults, always as a Communist. For him, the world is divided into just two classes of human beings: the Communists, and all the rest.

And again:

> The Moscow Show Trials revealed what has always been true of the Communist morality: that it is not merely the material possessions or the life of the individual which must be subordinated, but his reputation, his conscience, his honour, his dignity. He must lie and grovel, cheat and inform and betray, for Communism, as well as die. There is no restraint, no limit.

There are many similar passages. They all sound true enough until one begins applying them to the Communists whom one actually knows. No doubt, Burnham's description of the "true Communist" holds good for a few hundred thousand or a few million fanatical, dehumanised people, mostly inside the USSR, who are the nucleus of the movement. It holds good for Stalin, Molotov, Zhdanov, etc and the more faithful of their agents abroad. But if there is one well-attested fact about the Communist parties of almost all countries, it is the rapid turnover in membership. People drift in, sometimes by scores of thousands at a time, and presently drift out again. In a country like the United States or Britain, a Communist Party consists essentially of an inner ring of completely subservient long-term members, some of whom have salaried jobs; a larger group of industrial workers who are faithful to the Party but do not necessarily grasp its real aims; and a shifting mass of people who are full of zeal to start with, but rapidly cool off. Certainly every effort is made to induce in Communist Party members the totalitarian mentality that Burnham describes. In a few cases this succeeds permanently, in many others temporarily: still, it is possible to meet thinking people who have remained Communists for as much as ten years before resigning or being expelled, and who have not been intellectually crippled by the experience. In principle, the Communist Parties all over the world are quisling organisations, existing for the purpose of espionage and disruption, but they are not necessarily so efficient and dangerous as Burnham makes out. One ought not to think of the Soviet Government as controlling in every country a huge secret army of fanatical warriors, completely devoid of fear or scruples and having no thought except to live and die for the Workers' Fatherland. Indeed, if Stalin really disposed of such a weapon as that, one would be wasting one's time in trying to resist him.

Also, it is not altogether an advantage to a political party to sail under false colours. There is always the danger that its followers may desert it at some moment of crisis when its actions are plainly against the general interest. Let me take an example near at hand. The British Communist Party appears to have given up, at any rate for the time being, the attempt to become a mass party, and to have concentrated instead on capturing key positions, especially in the trade unions. So long as they are not obviously acting as a sectional group, this gives the Communists an influence out of proportion to their numbers. Thus, owing to having won the leadership of several important unions, a handful of Communist delegates can swing several million votes at a Labour Party conference. But this results from the undemocratic inner working of the Labour Party, which allows a delegate to speak on behalf of millions of people who have barely heard of him and may be in complete disagreement with him. In a parliamentary election, where the individual votes on his own behalf, a Communist candidate can as a rule get almost no support. In the 1945 General Election, the Communist Party won only 100,000 votes in the country as a whole, although in theory it controls several million votes merely inside the trade unions. When public opinion is dormant, a great deal can be achieved by groups of wire-pullers, but in moments of emergency a political party must have a mass following as well. An obvious illustration of this was the failure of the British Communist Party, in spite of much trying, to disrupt the war effort during the period 1939–41. Certainly the Communists are everywhere a serious force, above all in Asia, where they have, or can plausibly present themselves as having, something to offer to the colonial populations. But one should not assume, as Burnham seems to do, that they can draw their followers after them, whatever policy they choose to adopt.

There is also the question of the "fellow-travellers", "cryptos" and sympathisers of various shades who further the aims of the Communists without having any official connection with them. Burnham does not claim that these people are all crooks or conscious traitors, but he does seem to believe that they will always continue in the same strain, even if the world situation deteriorates into open warfare. But after all, the disillusioned "fellow-traveller" is a common figure, like the disillusioned Communist. The important thing to do with these people—and it is extremely difficult, since one has only inferential evidence—is to sort them out and determine which of them is honest and which is not. There is, for instance, a whole group of MPs in the British Parliament (Pritt, Zilliacus, etc) who are commonly nicknamed "the cryptos". They have undoubtedly done a great deal of mischief, especially in confusing public opinion about the nature of the puppet régimes in eastern Europe; but one ought not hurriedly to assume that they are all equally dishonest or even that they all hold the same opinions. Probably some of them are actuated by nothing worse than stupidity. After all, such things have happened before.

There was also the pro-Fascist bias of British Tories and corresponding strata in the United States in the years before 1939. When one saw British Conservative MPs cheering the news that British ships had been bombed by Italian aeroplanes in the service of Franco, it was tempting to believe that these people were actually treacherous to their own country. But when the pinch came, it was found that they were subjectively quite as patriotic as anyone else. They had merely based their opinions on a syllogism which lacked a middle term: Fascism is opposed to Communism; therefore it is on our side. In left-wing circles there is the corresponding syllogism: Communism is opposed to capitalism; therefore it is progressive and democratic. This is stupid, but it can be accepted in good faith by people who will be capable of seeing through it sooner or later. The question is not whether the "cryptos" and "fellow-travellers" advance the interests of the USSR against those of the democracies. Obviously they do so. The real question is, how many of them would continue on the same lines if war were really imminent? For a major war—unless it is a war waged by a few specialists, a Pearl Harbor with atomic bombs—is not possible until the issues have become fairly clear.

I have dwelt on this question of the Communist fifth columns inside the democratic countries, because it is more nearly verifiable than the other questions raised by Burnham's book. About the USSR itself we are reduced to guesswork. We do not know how strong the Russians are, how badly they have been crippled by the war, to what extent their recovery will depend on American aid, how much internal disaffection they have to contend with, or how soon they will get hold of atomic weapons. All we know with certainty is that at present no great country except the United States is physically able to make war, and the United States is not psychologically prepared to do so. At the one point where some kind of evidence is available, Burnham seems to me to overstate his case. After all, that is his besetting sin. He is too fond of apocalyptic visions, too ready to believe that the muddled processes of history will happen suddenly and logically. But suppose he is wrong. Suppose the ship is not sinking, only leaking. Suppose that Communism is not yet strong enough to swallow the world and that the danger of war can be staved off for twenty years or more: then we don't have to accept Burnham's remedy—or, at least, we don't have to accept it immediately and without question.

Burnham's thesis, if accepted, demands certain immediate actions.

One thing that it *appears* to demand is a preventive war in the very near future, while the Americans have atomic bombs and the Russians have not. Even if this inference is unjustified, there can be no doubt about the reactionary nature of other points in Burnham's programme. For instance, writing in 1946, Burnham considers that, for strategic reasons, full independence ought not to be granted to India. This is the kind of decision that sometimes has to be taken under pressure of military necessity, but which is indefensible in any normal circumstances. And again, Burnham is in favour of suppressing the American Communist Party, and of doing the job thoroughly, which would probably mean using the same methods as the Communists, when in power, use against *their* opponents. Now, there are times when it is justifiable to suppress a political party. If you are fighting for your life, and if there is some organisation which is plainly acting on behalf of the enemy, and is strong enough to do harm, then you have got to crush it. But to suppress the Communist Party *now*, or at any time when it did not unmistakably endanger national survival, would be calamitous. One has only to think of the people who would approve! Burnham claims, perhaps rightly, that when once the American empire had been established, it might be possible to pass on to some more satisfactory kind of world organisation. But the first appeal of his programme must be to conservatives, and if such an empire came into being, the strongest intellectual influence in it would probably be that of the Catholic Church.

Meanwhile there is one other solution which is at any rate thinkable, and which Burnham dismisses almost unmentioned. That is, somewhere or other—not in Norway or New Zealand, but over a large area—to make democratic Socialism work. If one could somewhere present the spectacle of economic security without concentration camps, the pretext for the Russian dictatorship would disappear and Communism would lose much of its appeal. But the only feasible area is western Europe plus Africa. The idea of forming this vast territory into a Socialist United States has as yet hardly gained any ground, and the practical and psychological difficulties in the way are enormous. Still, it is a *possible* project if people really wanted it, and if there were ten or twenty years of assured peace in which to bring it about. And since the initiative would have to come in the first place from Britain, the important thing is that this idea should take root among British Socialists. At present, so far as the idea of a unified Europe has any currency at all, it is associated with Churchill. Here one comes back to one of the main points in Burnham's programme—the fusion of Britain with the United States.

Burnham assumes that the main difficulty in the way of this would be national pride, since Britain would be very much the junior partner. Actually there is not much pride of that kind left, and has not been for many years past. On the whole, anti-American feeling is strongest among those who are also anti-imperialist and anti-military. This is true not only of Communists and "fellow-travellers" who are anxious to make mischief, but of people of goodwill who see that to be tied to America probably means preserving capitalism in Britain. I have several times overheard or taken part in conversations something like this:

"How I hate the Americans! Sometimes they make me feel almost pro-Russian."

"Yes, but they're not actually our enemies. They helped us in 1940, when the Russians were selling oil to the Germans. We can't stand on our own feet much longer, and in the end we may have to choose between knuckling under to Russia or going in with America."

"I refuse to choose. They're just a pair of gangsters."

"Yes, but supposing you *had* to choose. Suppose there was no other way out, and you had to live under one system or the other. Which would you choose, Russia or America?"

"Oh, well, of course, if one *had* to choose, there's no question about it—America."

Fusion with the United States is widely realised to be one way out of our difficulties. Indeed, we have been almost a dependency of the United States ever since 1940, and our desperate economic plight drives us in this direction all the faster. The union desired by Burnham may happen almost of its own accord, without formal arrangement and with no plan or idea behind it. A noisy but, I believe, very small minority would like Britain to be integrated into the Soviet system. The mass of the British people would never accept this, but the thinking ones among them do not regard the probable alternative —absorption by America—with enthusiasm. Most English left-wingers at present favour a niggling policy of "getting along with Russia" by being strong enough to prevent an attack and weak enough to disarm suspicion. Under this lies the hope that when the Russians become more prosperous, they may become more friendly.

The other way out for Britain, the Socialist United States of Europe, has not as yet much magnetism. And the more the pessimistic world-view of Burnham and others like him prevails, the harder it is for such ideas to take hold.

Burnham offers a plan which would probably work, but which is a *pis aller* and should not be accepted willingly. In the end, the European peoples may have to accept American domination as a way of avoiding domination by Russia, but they ought to realise, while there is yet time, that there are other possibilities. In rather the same way, English Socialists of almost all colours accepted the leadership of Churchill during the war. Granted that they did not want Britain to be defeated, they could hardly help themselves, because effectively there was no one else, and Churchill was preferable to Hitler. But the situation might have been different if the European peoples could have grasped the nature of Fascism about five years earlier. In that case the war, if it happened at all, might have been a different kind of war, fought under different leaders for different ends.

The tendency of writers like Burnham, whose key concept is "realism", is to overrate the part played in human affairs by sheer force. I do not say that he is wrong all the time. He is quite right to insist that gratitude is not a factor in international politics; that even the most high-minded policy is no use unless you can show a practical way of putting it into effect, and that in the affairs of nations and societies, as opposed to individuals, one cannot hope for more than temporary and imperfect solutions. And he is probably right in arguing from this that one cannot apply to politics the same moral code that one practises or tries to practise in private life. But somehow his picture of the world is always slightly distorted. *The Managerial Revolution*, for instance, seemed to me a good description of what is actually happening in various parts of the world, i.e. the growth of societies neither capitalist nor Socialist, and organised more or less on the lines of a caste system. But Burnham went on to argue that because this *was* happening, nothing else *could* happen, and the new, tightly-knit totalitarian state *must* be stronger than the chaotic democracies. Therefore, among other things, Germany had to win the war. Yet in the event Germany collapsed at least partly because of her totalitarian structure. A more democratic, less efficient country would not have made such errors in politics and strategy, nor would it have aroused such a volume of hatred throughout the world.

Of course, there is more in Burnham's book than the mere proposal for the setting-up of an American empire, and in detail there is much with which one can agree. I think he is mainly right in his account of the way in which Communist propaganda works, and the difficulty of countering it, and he is certainly right in saying that one of the most important problems at this moment is to find a way of speaking to the Russian people over the heads of their rulers. But the central subject of this book, as of almost everything that Burnham writes, is power. Burnham is always fascinated by power, whether he is for it or against it, and he always sees it a little larger than life. First it was Germany that was to swallow the world, then Russia, now perhaps America. When *The Managerial Revolution* was published, I for one derived the impression that Burnham's sympathies were on the whole with Germany, and at any rate that he was anxious that the United States should not throw good money after bad by coming to the rescue of Britain. The much-discussed essay, "Lenin's Heir", which was a dissertation—a rhapsody, rather—on the strength, cunning and cruelty of Stalin, could be interpreted as expressing either approval or disapproval. I myself took it to be an expression of approval, though of a rather horrified kind.

It now appears that this was wrong. Burnham is not in favour of Stalin or Stalinism, and he has begun to find virtues in the capitalist democracy which he once considered moribund. But the note of fascination is still there. Communism may be wicked, but at any rate it is *big*: it is a terrible, all-devouring monster which one fights against but which one cannot help admiring. Burnham thinks always in terms of monsters and cataclysms. Hence he does not even mention, or barely mentions, two possibilities which should at least have been discussed in a book of this scope. One is that the Russian régime may become more liberal and less dangerous a generation hence, if war has not broken out in the meantime. Of course, this would not happen with the consent of the ruling clique, but it is thinkable that the mechanics of the situation may bring it about. The other possibility is that the great powers will be simply too frightened of the effects of atomic weapons ever to make use of them. But that would be much too dull for Burnham. Everything must happen suddenly and completely, and the choice must be all or nothing, glory or bust:

It may be that the darkness of great tragedy will bring to a quick end the short, bright history of the United States—for there is enough truth in the dream of the New World to make the action tragic. The United States is called before the rehearsals are completed. Its strength and promise have not been matured by the wisdom of time and suffering. And the summons is for nothing less than the leadership of the world, for that or nothing. If it is reasonable to expect failure, that is only a measure of how great the triumph could be.

It may be that modern weapons have speeded things up to the point at which Burnham would be right. But if one can judge from the past, even from such huge calamities as the fall of the Roman Empire, history never happens quite so melodramatically as that.

New Leader (New York), 29 March 1947

83. Letter[1] to Victor Gollancz

27B Canonbury Square
Islington, N1
9 April 1947

Dear Gollancz,

I should have written several days earlier, but I have been ill in bed. Very many thanks for your generous action.

Yours sincerely,
Geo. Orwell

84. Letter to Sonia Brownell

Barnhill
Isle of Jura
Argyllshire
12 April 1947

Dearest Sonia,[2]

I am handwriting this because my typewriter is downstairs. We arrived OK & without incident yesterday. Richard was as good as

---

[1] From a typed copy.
[2] Sonia Brownell (1918–), editorial secretary of *Horizon* 1945–50, who became Orwell's second wife in 1949.

gold & rather enjoyed having a sleeper to himself after he had got over the first strangeness, & as soon as we got into the plane at Glasgow he went to sleep, probably because of the noise. I hadn't been by plane before & I think it's really better. It costs £2 or £3 more, but it saves abt 5 hours & the boredom of going on boats, & even if one was sick it's only three quarters of an hour whereas if one goes by sea one is sick for five or six hours, i.e. if it is bad weather. Everything up here is just as backward as in England, hardly a bud showing & I saw quite a lot of snow yesterday. However it's beautiful spring weather now & the plants I put in at the new year seem to be mostly alive. There are daffodils all over the place, the only flower out. I'm still wrestling with more or less virgin meadow, but I think by next year I'll have quite a nice garden here. Of course we've had a nightmare all today getting things straight, with Richard only too ready to help, but it's more or less right now & the house is beginning to look quite civilised. It will be some weeks before we've got the transport problem fully solved, but otherwise we are fairly well appointed. I'm going to send for some hens as soon as we have put the hen house up, & this year I have been also able to arrange for alcohol so that one has just a little, a sort of rum ration, each day. Last year we had to be practically TT. I think in a week everything will be straight & the essential work in the garden done, & then I can get down to some work.

I wrote to Janetta[1] asking her to come whenever she liked & giving instructions abt the journey. So long as she's bringing the child, not just sending it, it shld be simple enough. I want to give you the complete details abt the journey, which isn't so formidable as it looks on paper. The facts are these:

There are boats to Jura on *Mondays, Wednesdays & Fridays.* You have to catch the boat train at Glasgow at 8 am, which means that it's safer to sleep the preceding night at Glasgow, because the all-night trains have a nasty way of coming in an hour or two hours late, & then one misses the boat train. The times & so on are as follows:

8 am leave Glasgow Central for GOUROCK.
Join boat for Tarbert (TARBERT) at Gourock.
Abt 12 noon arrive East Tarbert.

---

[1] Janetta Kee (now Jackson), a friend of Sonia Brownell and of the writers connected with *Horizon* and *Polemic*.

Travel by bus to West Tarbert (bus runs in conjunction with the boats).

Join boat for CRAIGHOUSE (Jura) at West Tarbert.

Abt 3.30 pm arrive Craighouse.

Take hired car to LEALT, where we meet you.

If you want to go by plane, the planes run daily (except Sundays I think), & they nearly always take off unless it's very misty. The itinerary then is:

10.30 arrive at Scottish Airways office at St Enoch Station, Glasgow (the air office is in the railway station).

10.40 leave by bus for RENFREW.

11.15 leave by plane for ISLAY. (Pronounced EYELY).

12 noon arrive Islay.

Hire a car (or take bus) to the ferry which leads to Jura.

Abt 1 pm cross ferry.

Hired car to LEALT.

It's important to let us know in advance when you are coming, because of the hired car. There are only 2 posts a week here, & only 2 occasions on which I can send down to Craighouse to order the car. If you come by boat, you could probably get a car all right by asking on the quay, but if you come by air there wouldn't be a car at the ferry (which is several miles from Craighouse) unless ordered before-hand. Therefore if you proposed coming on, say, June 15th, it wld be as well to write abt June 5th because, according to the day of the week, it may be 4 or 5 days before your letter reaches me, & another 3 or 4 days before I can send a message. It's no use wiring because the telegrams come by the postman.

You want a raincoat & if possible stout boots or shoes—gum boots if you have them. We may have some spare gum boots, I'm not sure. We are fairly well off for spare oilskins & things like that. It wld help if you brought that week's rations, because they're not quick at getting any newcomer's rations here, & a little flour & tea.

I am afraid I am making this all sound very intimidating, but really it's easy enough & the house is quite comfortable. The room you wld have is rather small, but it looks out on the sea. I do so want to have you here. By that time I hope we'll have got hold of an engine for the boat, & if we get decent weather we can go round to the com-pletely uninhabited bays on the west side of the island, where there is beautiful white sand & clear water with seals swimming abt in it. At one of them there is a cave where one can take shelter when it rains, & at another there is a shepherd's hut which is disused but quite livable where one could even picnic for a day or two. Anyway do come, & come whenever you like for as long as you like, only try to let me know beforehand. And meanwhile take care of yourself & be happy.

I've just remembered I never paid you for that brandy you got for me, so enclose £3. I think it was abt that wasn't it? The brandy was very nice & was much appreciated on the journey up because they can't get alcohol here at all easily. The next island, Islay, distils whisky, but it all goes to America. I gave the lorry driver a large wallop, more than a double, & it disappeared so promptly that it seemed to hit the bottom of his belly with a click.

With much love
George

85. Letter to F. J. Warburg

Barnhill
Isle of Jura
Argyllshire
31 May 1947

Dear Fred,

Many thanks for your letter. I have made a fairly good start on the book[1] and I think I must have written nearly a third of the rough draft. I have not got as far as I had hoped to do by this time, because I have really been in most wretched health this year ever since about January (my chest as usual) and can't quite shake it off. However I keep pegging away, and I hope that when I leave here in October I shall either have finished the rough draft or at any rate broken its back. Of course the rough draft is always a ghastly mess having very little relation to the finished result, but all the same it is the main part of the job. So if I do finish the rough draft by October I might get the book done fairly early in 1948, barring illnesses. I don't like talking about books before they are written, but I will tell you now that this is a novel about the future—that is, it is in a sense a fantasy,

---

[1] *Nineteen Eighty-Four.*

but in the form of a naturalistic novel. That is what makes it a difficult job—of course as a book of anticipations it would be comparatively simple to write.

I am sending you separately a long autobiographical sketch[1] which I originally undertook as a sort of pendant to Cyril Connolly's *Enemies of Promise*, he having asked me to write a reminiscence of the preparatory school we were at together. I haven't actually sent it to Connolly or *Horizon*, because apart from being too long for a periodical I think it is really too libellous to print, and I am not disposed to change it, except perhaps the names. But I think it should be printed sooner or later when the people most concerned are dead, and maybe sooner or later I might do a book of collected sketches. I must apologise for the typescript. It is not only the carbon copy, but is very bad commercial typing which I have had to correct considerably—however, I think I have got most of the actual errors out.

Richard is very well in spite of various calamities. First he fell down and cut his forehead and had to have two stitches put in, and after that he had measles. He is talking a good deal more now (he was three a week or two ago). The weather has cheered up after being absolutely stinking, and the garden we are creating out of virgin jungle is getting quite nice. Please remember me to Pamela[2] and Roger.[3]

Yours
George

86. Such, Such Were the Joys[4]

i

Soon after I arrived at St Cyprian's (not immediately, but after a week or two, just when I seemed to be settling into the routine of school life) I began wetting my bed. I was now aged eight, so that

---

[1] "Such, Such Were the Joys".   [2] Mrs F.J. Warburg.   [3] Roger Senhouse.
[4] In the version of this piece already published in the United States, St Cyprian's was called "Crossgates". Other old boys writing of the school followed Cyril Connolly and called it "St Wulfric's", the name it was first given in *Enemies of Promise*. The text printed here is of Orwell's original typescript, but the names of his school fellows and the assistant masters have been changed.

this was a reversion to a habit which I must have grown out of at least four years earlier.

Nowadays, I believe, bed-wetting in such circumstances is taken for granted. It is a normal reaction in children who have been removed from their homes to a strange place. In those days, however, it was looked on as a disgusting crime which the child committed on purpose and for which the proper cure was a beating. For my part I did not need to be told it was a crime. Night after night I prayed, with a fervour never previously attained in my prayers, "Please God, do not let me wet my bed! Oh, please God, do not let me wet my bed!", but it made remarkably little difference. Some nights the thing happened, others not. There was no volition about it, no consciousness. You did not properly speaking *do* the deed: you merely woke up in the morning and found that the sheets were wringing wet.

After the second or third offence I was warned that I should be beaten next time, but I received the warning in a curiously roundabout way. One afternoon, as we were filing out from tea, Mrs W——, the Headmaster's wife, was sitting at the head of one of the tables, chatting with a lady of whom I knew nothing, except that she was on an afternoon's visit to the school. She was an intimidating, masculine-looking person wearing a riding-habit, or something that I took to be a riding-habit. I was just leaving the room when Mrs W—— called me back, as though to introduce me to the visitor.

Mrs W—— was nicknamed Flip, and I shall call her by that name, for I seldom think of her by any other. (Officially, however, she was addressed as Mum, probably a corruption of the "Ma'am" used by public schoolboys to their housemasters' wives.) She was a stocky square-built woman with hard red cheeks, a flat top to her head, prominent brows and deep-set, suspicious eyes. Although a great deal of the time she was full of false heartiness, jollying one along with mannish slang ("*Buck* up, old chap!" and so forth), and even using one's Christian name, her eyes never lost their anxious, accusing look. It was very difficult to look her in the face without feeling guilty, even at moments when one was not guilty of anything in particular.

"Here is a little boy," said Flip, indicating me to the strange lady, "who wets his bed every night. Do you know what I am going to do if you wet your bed again?" she added, turning to me. "I am going to get the Sixth Form to beat you."

The strange lady put on an air of being inexpressibly shocked, and exclaimed "I-should-*think*-so!" And here there occurred one of those wild, almost lunatic misunderstandings which are part of the daily experience of childhood. The Sixth Form was a group of older boys who were selected as having "character" and were empowered to beat smaller boys. I had not yet learned of their existence, and I mis-heard the phrase "the Sixth Form" as "Mrs Form". I took it as referring to the strange lady—I thought, that is, that her name was Mrs Form. It was an improbable name, but a child has no judgement in such matters. I imagined, therefore, that it was *she* who was to be deputed to beat me. It did not strike me as strange that this job should be turned over to a casual visitor in no way connected with the school. I merely assumed that "Mrs Form" was a stern disciplinarian who enjoyed beating people (somehow her appearance seemed to bear this out) and I had an immediate terrifying vision of her arriving for the occasion in full riding kit and armed with a hunting-whip. To this day I can feel myself almost swooning with shame as I stood, a very small, round-faced boy in short corduroy knickers, before the two women. I could not speak. I felt that I should die if "Mrs Form" were to beat me. But my dominant feeling was not fear or even resentment: it was simply shame because one more person, and that a woman, had been told of my disgusting offence.

A little later, I forget how, I learned that it was not after all "Mrs Form" who would do the beating. I cannot remember whether it was that very night that I wetted my bed again, but at any rate I did wet it again quite soon. Oh, the despair, the feeling of cruel injustice, after all my prayers and resolutions, at once again waking between the clammy sheets! There was no chance of hiding what I had done. The grim statuesque matron, Margaret by name, arrived in the dormitory specially to inspect my bed. She pulled back the clothes, then drew herself up, and the dreaded words seemed to come rolling out of her like a peal of thunder:

"REPORT YOURSELF to the Headmaster after breakfast!"

I put REPORT YOURSELF in capitals because that was how it appeared in my mind. I do not know how many times I heard that phrase during my early years at St Cyprian's. It was only very rarely that it did not mean a beating. The words always had a portentous sound in my ears, like muffled drums or the words of the death sentence.

When I arrived to report myself, Flip was doing something or other at the long shiny table in the ante-room to the study. Her uneasy eyes searched me as I went past. In the study the Headmaster, nicknamed Sambo, was waiting. Sambo was a round-shouldered, curiously oafish-looking man, not large but shambling in gait, with a chubby face which was like that of an overgrown baby, and which was capable of good humour. He knew, of course, why I had been sent to him, and had already taken a bone-handled riding-crop out of the cupboard, but it was part of the punishment of reporting yourself that you had to proclaim your offence with your own lips. When I had said my say, he read me a short but pompous lecture, then seized me by the scruff of the neck, twisted me over and began beating me with the riding-crop. He had a habit of continuing his lecture while he flogged you, and I remember the words "you dir-ty lit-tle boy" keeping time with the blows. The beating did not hurt (perhaps, as it was the first time, he was not hitting me very hard), and I walked out feeling very much better. The fact that the beating had not hurt was a sort of victory and partially wiped out the shame of the bed-wetting. I was even incautious enough to wear a grin on my face. Some small boys were hanging about in the passage outside the door of the ante-room.

"D'you get the cane?"

"It didn't hurt," I said proudly.

Flip had heard everything. Instantly her voice came screaming after me:

"Come here! Come here this instant! What was that you said?"

"I said it didn't hurt," I faltered out.

"How dare you say a thing like that? Do you think that is a proper thing to say? Go in and REPORT YOURSELF AGAIN!"

This time Sambo laid on in real earnest. He continued for a length of time that frightened and astonished me—about five minutes, it seemed—ending up by breaking the riding-crop. The bone handle went flying across the room.

"Look what you've made me do!" he said furiously, holding up the broken crop.

I had fallen into a chair, weakly snivelling. I remember that this was the only time throughout my boyhood when a beating actually reduced me to tears, and curiously enough I was not even now crying because of the pain. The second beating had not hurt very much either. Fright and shame seemed to have anaesthetised me. I was crying partly because I felt that this was expected of me, partly from genuine repentance, but partly also because of a deeper grief which is peculiar to childhood and not easy to convey: a sense of desolate loneliness and helplessness, of being locked up not only in a hostile world but in a world of good and evil where the rules were such that it was actually not possible for me to keep them.

I knew that the bed-wetting was (a) wicked and (b) outside my control. The second fact I was personally aware of, and the first I did not question. It was possible, therefore, to commit a sin without knowing that you committed it, without wanting to commit it, and without being able to avoid it. Sin was not necessarily something that you did: it might be something that happened to you. I do not want to claim that this idea flashed into my mind as a complete novelty at this very moment, under the blows of Sambo's cane: I must have had glimpses of it even before I left home, for my early childhood had not been altogether happy. But at any rate this was the great, abiding lesson of my boyhood: that I was in a world where it was *not possible* for me to be good. And the double beating was a turning-point, for it brought home to me for the first time the harshness of the environment into which I had been flung. Life was more terrible, and I was more wicked, than I had imagined. At any rate, as I sat snivelling on the edge of a chair in Sambo's study, with not even the self-possession to stand up while he stormed at me, I had a conviction of sin and folly and weakness, such as I do not remember to have felt before.

In general, one's memories of any period must necessarily weaken as one moves away from it. One is constantly learning new facts, and old ones have to drop out to make way for them. At twenty I could have written the history of my schooldays with an accuracy which would be quite impossible now. But it can also happen that one's memories grow sharper after a long lapse of time, because one is looking at the past with fresh eyes and can isolate and, as it were, notice facts which previously existed undifferentiated among a mass of others. Here are two things which in a sense I remembered, but which did not strike me as strange or interesting until quite recently. One is that the second beating seemed to me a just and reasonable punishment. To get one beating, and then to get another and far fiercer one on top of it, for being so unwise as to show that the first had not hurt—that was quite natural. The gods are jealous, and when you have good fortune you should conceal it. The other is that

I accepted the broken riding-crop as my own crime. I can still recall my feeling as I saw the handle lying on the carpet—the feeling of having done an ill-bred clumsy thing, and ruined an expensive object. *I* had broken it: so Sambo told me, and so I believed. This acceptance of guilt lay unnoticed in my memory for twenty or thirty years.

So much for the episode of the bed-wetting. But there is one more thing to be remarked. This is that I did not wet my bed again—at least, I did wet it once again, and received another beating, after which the trouble stopped. So perhaps this barbarous remedy does work, though at a heavy price, I have no doubt.

ii

St Cyprian's was an expensive and snobbish school which was in process of becoming more snobbish, and, I imagine, more expensive. The public school with which it had special connections was Harrow, but during my time an increasing proportion of the boys went on to Eton. Most of them were the children of rich parents, but on the whole they were the un-aristocratic rich, the sort of people who live in huge shrubberied houses in Bournemouth or Richmond, and who have cars and butlers but not country estates. There were a few exotics among them—some South American boys, sons of Argentine beef barons, one or two Russians, and even a Siamese prince, or someone who was described as a prince.

Sambo had two great ambitions. One was to attract titled boys to the school, and the other was to train up pupils to win scholarships at public schools, above all at Eton. He did, towards the end of my time, succeed in getting hold of two boys with real English titles. One of them, I remember, was a wretched drivelling little creature, almost an albino, peering upwards out of weak eyes, with a long nose at the end of which a dewdrop always seemed to be trembling. Sambo always gave these boys their titles when mentioning them to a third person, and for their first few days he actually addressed them to their faces as "Lord So-and-so". Needless to say he found ways of drawing attention to them when any visitor was being shown round the school. Once, I remember, the little fair-haired boy had a choking fit at dinner, and a stream of snot ran out of his nose on to his plate in a way horrible to see. Any lesser person would have been called a dirty little beast and ordered out of the room instantly: but Sambo and Flip laughed it off in a "boys will be boys" spirit.

All the very rich boys were more or less undisguisedly favoured.

The school still had a faint suggestion of the Victorian "private academy" with its "parlour boarders", and when I later read about that kind of school in Thackeray I immediately saw the resemblance. The rich boys had milk and biscuits in the middle of the morning, they were given riding lessons once or twice a week, Flip mothered them and called them by their Christian names, and above all they were never caned. Apart from the South Americans, whose parents were safely distant, I doubt whether Sambo ever caned any boy whose father's income was much above £2,000 a year. But he was sometimes willing to sacrifice financial profit to scholastic prestige. Occasionally, by special arrangement, he would take at greatly reduced fees some boy who seemed likely to win scholarships and thus bring credit on the school. It was on these terms that I was at St Cyprian's myself: otherwise my parents could not have afforded to send me to so expensive a school.

I did not at first understand that I was being taken at reduced fees; it was only when I was about eleven that Flip and Sambo began throwing the fact in my teeth. For my first two or three years I went through the ordinary educational mill: then, soon after I had started Greek (one started Latin at eight, Greek at ten), I moved into the scholarship class, which was taught, so far as classics went, largely by Sambo himself. Over a period of two or three years the scholarship boys were crammed with learning as cynically as a goose is crammed for Christmas. And with what learning! This business of making a gifted boy's career depend on a competitive examination, taken when he is only twelve or thirteen, is an evil thing at best, but there do appear to be preparatory schools which send scholars to Eton, Winchester, etc without teaching them to see everything in terms of marks. At St Cyprian's the whole process was frankly a preparation for a sort of confidence trick. Your job was to learn exactly those things that would give an examiner the impression that you knew more than you did know, and as far as possible to avoid burdening your brain with anything else. Subjects which lacked examination-value, such as geography, were almost completely neglected, mathematics was also neglected if you were a "classical", science was not taught in any form—indeed it was so despised that even an interest in natural history was discouraged—and even the books you were encouraged to read in your spare time were chosen with one eye on the "English paper". Latin and Greek, the main scholarship subjects, were what counted, but even these were deliberately taught in a flashy, unsound way. We never, for example, read right through even a single book of a Greek or Latin author: we merely read short passages which were picked out because they were the kind of thing likely to be set as an "unseen translation". During the last year or so before we went up for our scholarships, most of our time was spent in simply working our way through the scholarship papers of previous years. Sambo had sheaves of these in his possession, from every one of the major public schools. But the greatest outrage of all was the teaching of history.

There was in those days a piece of nonsense called the Harrow History Prize, an annual competition for which many preparatory schools entered. It was a tradition for St Cyprian's to win it every year, as well we might, for we had mugged up every paper that had been set since the competition started, and the supply of possible questions was not inexhaustible. They were the kind of stupid question that is answered by rapping out a name or a quotation. Who plundered the Begams? Who was beheaded in an open boat? Who caught the Whigs bathing and ran away with their clothes? Almost all our historical teaching was on this level. History was a series of unrelated, unintelligible but—in some way that was never explained to us—important facts with resounding phrases tied to them. Disraeli brought peace with honour. Clive was astonished at his moderation. Pitt called in the New World to redress the balance of the Old. And the dates, and the mnemonic devices! (Did you know, for example, that the initial letters of "A black Negress was my aunt: there's her house behind the barn" are also the initial letters of the battles in the Wars of the Roses?) Flip, who "took" the higher forms in history, revelled in this kind of thing. I recall positive orgies of dates, with the keener boys leaping up and down in their places in their eagerness to shout out the right answers, and at the same time not feeling the faintest interest in the meaning of the mysterious events they were naming.

"1587?"

"Massacre of St Bartholomew!"

"1707?"

"Death of Aurangzeeb!"

"1713?"

"Treaty of Utrecht!"

"1773?"

"Boston Tea Party!"

"1520?"

"Oo, Mum, please, Mum—"

"Please, Mum, please, Mum! Let me tell him, Mum!"

"Well! 1520?"

"Field of the Cloth of Gold!"

And so on.

But history and such secondary subjects were not bad fun. It was in "classics" that the real strain came. Looking back, I realise that I then worked harder than I have ever done since, and yet at the time it never seemed possible to make quite the effort that was demanded of one. We would sit round the long shiny table, made of some very pale-coloured hard wood, with Sambo goading, threatening, exhorting, sometimes joking, very occasionally praising, but always prodding, prodding away at one's mind to keep it up to the right pitch of concentration, as one might keep a sleepy person awake by sticking pins into him.

"Go on, you little slacker! Go on, you idle, worthless little boy! The whole trouble with you is that you're bone and horn idle. You eat too much, that's why. You wolf down enormous meals, and then when you come here you're half asleep. Go on, now, put your back into it. You're not *thinking*. Your brain doesn't sweat."

He would tap away at one's skull with his silver pencil, which, in my memory, seems to have been about the size of a banana, and which certainly was heavy enough to raise a bump: or he would pull the short hairs round one's ears, or, occasionally, reach out under the table and kick one's shin. On some days nothing seemed to go right, and then it would be: "All right, then, I know what you want. You've been asking for it the whole morning. Come along, you useless little slacker. Come into the study." And then whack, whack, whack, whack, and back one would come, red-wealed and smarting—in later years Sambo had abandoned his riding-crop in favour of a thin rattan cane which hurt very much more—to settle down to work again. This did not happen very often, but I do remember, more than once, being led out of the room in the middle of a Latin sentence, receiving a beating and then going straight ahead with the same sentence, just like that. It is a mistake to think such methods do not work. They work very well for their special purpose. Indeed, I doubt whether classical education ever has been or can be successfully carried on without corporal punishment. The boys themselves believed in its efficacy. There was a boy named Beacham,

with no brains to speak of, but evidently in acute need of a scholarship. Sambo was flogging him towards the goal as one might do
with a foundered horse. He went up for a scholarship at Uppingham,
came back with a consciousness of having done badly, and a day or
two later received a severe beating for idleness. "I wish I'd had that
caning before I went up for the exam," he said sadly—a remark
which I felt to be contemptible, but which I perfectly well understood.

The boys of the scholarship class were not all treated alike. If a
boy were the son of rich parents to whom the saving of fees was not
all-important, Sambo would goad him along in a comparatively
fatherly way, with jokes and digs in the ribs and perhaps an occasional
tap with the pencil, but no hair-pulling and no caning. It was the
poor but "clever" boys who suffered. Our brains were a gold-mine
in which he had sunk money, and the dividends must be squeezed
out of us. Long before I had grasped the nature of my financial
relationship with Sambo, I had been made to understand that I was
not on the same footing as most of the other boys. In effect there were
three castes in the school. There was the minority with an aristocratic
or millionaire background, there were the children of the ordinary
suburban rich, who made up the bulk of the school, and there were a
few underlings like myself, the sons of clergyman, Indian civil
servants, struggling widows and the like. These poorer ones were
discouraged from going in for "extras" such as shooting and
carpentry, and were humiliated over clothes and petty possessions.
I never, for instance, succeeded in getting a cricket bat of my own,
because "Your parents wouldn't be able to afford it". This phrase
pursued me throughout my schooldays. At St Cyprian's we were not
allowed to keep the money we brought back with us, but had to "give
it in" on the first day of term, and then from time to time were
allowed to spend it under supervision. I and similarly-placed boys
were always choked off from buying expensive toys like model
aeroplanes, even if the necessary money stood to our credit. Flip, in
particular, seemed to aim consciously at inculcating a humble outlook
in the poorer boys. "Do you think that's the sort of thing a boy like
you should buy?" I remember her saying to somebody—and she
said this in front of the whole school: "You know you're not going
to grow up with money, don't you? Your people aren't rich. You
must learn to be sensible. Don't get above yourself!" There was also
the weekly pocket-money, which we took out in sweets, dispensed
by Flip from a large table. The millionaires had sixpence a week,

but the normal sum was threepence. I and one or two others were only allowed twopence. My parents had not given instructions to this effect, and the saving of a penny a week could not conceivably have made any difference to them: it was a mark of status. Worse yet was the detail of the birthday cakes. It was usual for each boy, on his birthday, to have a large iced cake with candles, which was shared out at tea between the whole school. It was provided as a matter of routine and went on his parents' bill. I never had such a cake, though my parents would have paid for it readily enough. Year after year, never daring to ask, I would miserably hope that this year a cake would appear. Once or twice I even rashly pretended to my companions that this time I *was* going to have a cake. Then came tea-time, and no cake, which did not make me more popular.

Very early it was impressed upon me that I had no chance of a decent future unless I won a scholarship at a public school. Either I won my scholarship, or I must leave school at fourteen and become, in Sambo's favourite phrase "a little office boy at forty pounds a year". In my circumstances it was natural that I should believe this. Indeed, it was universally taken for granted at St Cyprian's that unless you went to a "good" public school (and only about fifteen schools came under this heading) you were ruined for life. It is not easy to convey to a grown-up person the sense of strain, of nerving oneself for some terrible, all-deciding combat, as the date of the examination crept nearer—eleven years old, twelve years old, then thirteen, the fatal year itself! Over a period of about two years, I do not think there was ever a day when "the exam", as I called it, was quite out of my waking thoughts. In my prayers it figured invariably: and whenever I got the bigger portion of a wishbone, or picked up a horseshoe, or bowed seven times to the new moon, or succeeded in passing through a wishing-gate without touching the sides, then the wish I earned by doing so went on "the exam" as a matter of course. And yet curiously enough I was also tormented by an almost irresistible impulse *not* to work. There were days when my heart sickened at the labours ahead of me, and I stood stupid as an animal before the most elementary difficulties. In the holidays, also, I could not work. Some of the scholarship boys received extra tuition from a certain Mr Batchelor, a likeable, very hairy man who wore shaggy suits and lived in a typical bachelor's "den"—book-lined walls, overwhelming stench of tobacco—somewhere in the town. During the holidays Mr Batchelor used to send us extracts from Latin authors to translate, and we were supposed to send back a wad of work once a week. Somehow I could not do it. The empty paper and the black Latin dictionary lying on the table, the conscious-ness of a plain duty shirked, poisoned my leisure, but somehow I could not start, and by the end of the holidays I would only have sent Mr Batchelor fifty or a hundred lines. Undoubtedly part of the reason was that Sambo and his cane were far away. But in term-time, also, I would go through periods of idleness and stupidity when I would sink deeper and deeper into disgrace and even achieve a sort of feeble, snivelling defiance, fully conscious of my guilt and yet unable or unwilling—I could not be sure which—to do any better. Then Sambo or Flip would send for me, and this time it would not even be a caning.

Flip would search me with her baleful eyes. (What colour were those eyes, I wonder? I remember them as green, but actually no human being has green eyes. Perhaps they were hazel.) She would start off in her peculiar, wheedling, bullying style, which never failed to get right through one's guard and score a hit on one's better nature. "I don't think it's awfully decent of you to behave like this, is it? Do you think it's quite playing the game by your mother and father to go on idling your time away, week after week, month after month? Do you *want* to throw all your chances away? You know your people aren't rich, don't you? You know they can't afford the same things as other boys' parents. How are they to send you to a public school if you don't win a scholarship? I know how proud your mother is of you. Do you *want* to let her down?"

"I don't think he wants to go to a public school any longer," Sambo would say, addressing himself to Flip with a pretence that I was not there. "I think he's given up that idea. He wants to be a little office boy at forty pounds a year."

The horrible sensation of tears—a swelling in the breast, a tickling behind the nose—would already have assailed me. Flip would bring out her ace of trumps:

"And do you think it's quite fair to *us*, the way you're behaving? After all we've done for you? You *do* know what we've done for you, don't you?" Her eyes would pierce deep into me, and though she never said it straight out, I did know. "We've had you here all these years—we even had you here for a week in the holidays so that Mr Batchelor could coach you. We don't *want* to have to send you away, you know, but we can't keep a boy here just to eat up our food, term after term. *I* don't think it's very straight, the way you're behaving. Do you?"

I never had any answer except a miserable "No, Mum", or "Yes, Mum", as the case might be. Evidently it was *not* straight, the way I was behaving. And at some point or other the unwanted tear would always force its way out of the corner of my eye, roll down my nose, and splash.

Flip never said in plain words that I was a non-paying pupil, no doubt because vague phrases like "all we've done for you" had a deeper emotional appeal. Sambo, who did not aspire to be loved by his pupils, put it more brutally, though, as was usual with him, in pompous language. "You are living on my bounty" was his favourite phrase in this context. At least once I listened to these words between blows of the cane. I must say that these scenes were not frequent, and except on one occasion they did not take place in the presence of other boys. In public I was reminded that I was poor and that my parents "wouldn't be able to afford" this or that, but I was not actually reminded of my dependent position. It was a final unanswerable argument, to be brought forth like an instrument of torture when my work became exceptionally bad.

To grasp the effect of this kind of thing on a child of ten or twelve, one has to remember that the child has little sense of proportion or probability. A child may be a mass of egoism and rebelliousness, but it has no accumulated experience to give it confidence in its own judgements. On the whole it will accept what it is told, and it will believe in the most fantastic way in the knowledge and powers of the adults surrounding it. Here is an example.

I have said that at St Cyprian's we were not allowed to keep our own money. However, it was possible to hold back a shilling or two, and sometimes I used furtively to buy sweets which I kept hidden in the loose ivy on the playing-field wall. One day when I had been sent on an errand I went into a sweet-shop a mile or more from the school and bought some chocolates. As I came out of the shop I saw on the opposite pavement a small sharp-faced man who seemed to be staring very hard at my school cap. Instantly a horrible fear went through me. There could be no doubt as to who the man was. He was a spy placed there by Sambo! I turned away unconcernedly, and then, as though my legs were doing it of their own accord, broke into a clumsy run. But when I got round the next corner I forced myself to walk again, for to run was a sign of guilt, and obviously there would be other spies posted here and there about the town. All that day and the next I waited for the summons to the study, and was surprised when it did not come. It did not seem to me strange that the headmaster of a private school should dispose of an army of informers, and I did not even imagine that he would have to pay them. I assumed that any adult, inside the school or outside, would collaborate voluntarily in preventing us from breaking the rules. Sambo was all-powerful; it was natural that his agents should be everywhere. When this episode happened I do not think I can have been less than twelve years old.

I hated Sambo and Flip, with a sort of shamefaced, remorseful hatred, but it did not occur to me to doubt their judgement. When they told me that I must either win a public-school scholarship or become an office boy at fourteen, I believed that those were the unavoidable alternatives before me. And above all, I believed Sambo and Flip when they told me they were my benefactors. I see now, of course, that from Sambo's point of view I was a good speculation. He sank money in me, and he looked to get it back in the form of prestige. If I had "gone off", as promising boys sometimes do, I imagine that he would have got rid of me swiftly. As it was I won him two scholarships when the time came, and no doubt he made full use of them in his prospectuses. But it is difficult for a child to realise that a school is primarily a commercial venture. A child believes that the school exists to educate and that the schoolmaster disciplines him either for his own good, or from a love of bullying. Flip and Sambo had chosen to befriend me, and their friendship included canings, reproaches and humiliations, which were good for me and saved me from an office stool. That was their version, and I believed in it. It was therefore clear that I owed them a vast debt of gratitude. But I was *not* grateful, as I very well knew. On the contrary, I hated both of them. I could not control my subjective feelings, and I could not conceal them from myself. But it is wicked, is it not, to hate your benefactors? So I was taught, and so I believed. A child accepts the codes of behaviour that are presented to it, even when it breaks them. From the age of eight, or even earlier, the consciousness of sin was never far away from me. If I contrived to seem callous and defiant, it was only a thin cover over a mass of shame and dismay. All through my boyhood I had a profound conviction that I was no good, that I was wasting my time, wrecking my talents, behaving with monstrous folly and wickedness and ingratitude—and all this,

it seemed, was inescapable, because I lived among laws which were
absolute, like the law of gravity, but which it was not possible for
me to keep.

iii

No one can look back on his schooldays and say with truth that they
were altogether unhappy.

I have good memories of St Cyprian's, among a horde of bad ones.
Sometimes on summer afternoons there were wonderful expeditions
across the Downs to a village called Birling Gap, or to Beachy Head,
where one bathed dangerously among the chalk boulders and came
home covered with cuts. And there were still more wonderful midsummer evenings when, as a special treat, we were not driven off
to bed as usual but allowed to wander about the grounds in the long
twilight, ending up with a plunge into the swimming bath at about
nine o'clock. There was the joy of waking early on summer mornings
and getting in an hour's undisturbed reading (Ian Hay, Thackeray,
Kipling and H.G. Wells were the favourite authors of my boyhood)
in the sunlit, sleeping dormitory. There was also cricket, which I
was no good at but with which I conducted a sort of hopeless love
affair up to the age of about eighteen. And there was the pleasure of
keeping caterpillars—the silky green and purple puss-moth, the
ghostly green poplar-hawk, the privet-hawk, large as one's third
finger, specimens of which could be illicitly purchased for sixpence at
a shop in the town—and, when one could escape long enough from
the master who was "taking the walk", there was the excitement of
dredging the dew-ponds on the Downs for enormous newts with
orange-coloured bellies. This business of being out for a walk,
coming across something of fascinating interest and then being
dragged away from it by a yell from the master, like a dog jerked
onwards by the leash, is an important feature of school life, and helps
to build up the conviction, so strong in many children, that the things
you most want to do are always unattainable.

Very occasionally, perhaps once during each summer, it was
possible to escape altogether from the barrack-like atmosphere of
school, when Brown, the second master, was permitted to take one
or two boys for an afternoon of butterfly hunting on a common a
few miles away. Brown was a man with white hair and a red face
like a strawberry, who was good at natural history, making models
and plaster casts, operating magic lanterns, and things of that kind.

He and Mr Batchelor were the only adults in any way connected with the school whom I did not either dislike or fear. Once he took me into his room and showed me in confidence a plated, pearl-handled revolver—his "six-shooter", he called it—which he kept in a box under his bed. And oh, the joy of those occasional expeditions! The ride of two or three miles on a lonely little branch line, the afternoon of charging to and fro with large green nets, the beauty of the enormous dragonflies which hovered over the tops of the grasses, the sinister killing-bottle with its sickly smell, and then tea in the parlour of a pub with large slices of pale-coloured cake! The essence of it was in the railway journey, which seemed to put magic distances between yourself and school.

Flip, characteristically, disapproved of these expeditions, though not actually forbidding them. "And have you been catching *little butterflies*?" she would say with a vicious sneer when one got back, making her voice as babyish as possible. From her point of view, natural history ("bug-hunting" she would probably have called it) was a babyish pursuit which a boy should be laughed out of as early as possible. Moreover it was somehow faintly plebeian, it was traditionally associated with boys who wore spectacles and were no good at games, it did not help you to pass exams, and above all it smelt of science and therefore seemed to menace classical education. It needed a considerable moral effort to accept Brown's invitation. How I dreaded that sneer of *little butterflies*! Brown, however, who had been at the school since its early days, had built up a certain independence for himself: he seemed able to handle Sambo, and ignored Flip a good deal. If it ever happened that both of them were away, Brown acted as deputy headmaster, and on those occasions instead of reading the appointed lesson for the day at morning chapel, he would read us stories from the Apocrypha.

Most of the good memories of my childhood, and up to the age of about twenty, are in some way connected with animals. So far as St Cyprian's goes, it also seems, when I look back, that all my good memories are of summer. In winter your nose ran continually, your fingers were too numb to button your shirt (this was an especial misery on Sundays, when we wore Eton collars), and there was the daily nightmare of football—the cold, the mud, the hideous greasy ball that came whizzing at one's face, the gouging knees and trampling boots of the bigger boys. Part of the trouble was that in winter, after the age of about ten, I was seldom in good health, at any rate

during term-time. I had defective bronchial tubes and a lesion in one
lung which was not discovered till many years later. Hence I not
only had a chronic cough, but running was a torment to me. In those
days however, "wheeziness", or "chestiness", as it was called, was
either diagnosed as imagination or was looked on as essentially a
moral disorder, caused by overeating. "You wheeze like a concer-
tina," Sambo would say disapprovingly as he stood behind my
chair; "You're perpetually stuffing yourself with food, that's why."
My cough was referred to as a "stomach cough", which made it
sound both disgusting and reprehensible. The cure for it was hard
running, which, if you kept it up long enough, ultimately "cleared
your chest".

It is curious, the degree—I will not say of actual hardship, but of
squalor and neglect—that was taken for granted in upper-class schools
of that period. Almost as in the days of Thackeray, it seemed natural
that a little boy of eight or ten should be a miserable, snotty-nosed
creature, his face almost permanently dirty, his hands chapped, his
nails bitten, his handkerchief a sodden horror, his bottom frequently
blue with bruises. It was partly the prospect of actual physical
discomfort that made the thought of going back to school lie in one's
breast like a lump of lead during the last few days of the holidays.
A characteristic memory of St Cyprian's is the astonishing hardness
of one's bed on the first night of term. Since this was an expensive
school, I took a social step upwards by attending it, and yet the
standard of comfort was in every way far lower than in my own
home, or, indeed, than it would have been in a prosperous working-
class home. One only had a hot bath once a week, for instance. The
food was not only bad, it was also insufficient. Never before or since
have I seen butter or jam scraped on bread so thinly. I do not think
I can be imagining the fact that we were underfed, when I remember
the lengths we would go in order to steal food. On a number of
occasions I remember creeping down at two or three o'clock in the
morning through what seemed like miles of pitch-dark stairways and
passages—barefooted, stopping to listen after each step, paralysed
with about equal fear of Sambo, ghosts and burglars—to steal stale
bread from the pantry. The assistant masters had their meals with
us, but they had somewhat better food, and if one got half a chance
it was usual to steal left-over scraps of bacon rind or fried potato
when their plates were removed.

As usual, I did not see the sound commercial reason for this underfeeding. On the whole I accepted Sambo's view that a boy's appetite is a sort of morbid growth which should be kept in check as much as possible. A maxim often repeated to us at St Cyprian's was that it is healthy to get up from a meal feeling as hungry as when you sat down. Only a generation earlier than this it had been common for school dinners to start off with a slab of unsweetened suet pudding, which, it was frankly said, "broke the boys' appetites". But the underfeeding was probably less flagrant at preparatory schools, where a boy was wholly dependent on the official diet, than at public schools, where he was allowed—indeed, expected—to buy extra food for himself. At some schools, he would literally not have had enough to eat unless he had bought regular supplies of eggs, sausages, sardines, etc; and his parents had to allow him money for this purpose. At Eton, for instance, at any rate in College, a boy was given no solid meal after midday dinner. For his afternoon tea he was given only tea and bread and butter, and at eight o'clock he was given a miserable supper of soup or fried fish, or more often bread and cheese, with water to drink. Sambo went down to see his eldest son at Eton and came back in snobbish ecstasies over the luxury in which the boys lived. "They give them fried fish for supper!" he exclaimed, beaming all over his chubby face. "There's no school like it in the world." Fried fish! The habitual supper of the poorest of the working class! At very cheap boarding schools it was no doubt worse. A very early memory of mine is of seeing the boarders at a grammar school—the sons, probably, of farmers and shopkeepers—being fed on boiled lights.

Whoever writes about his childhood must beware of exaggeration and self-pity. I do not want to claim that I was a martyr or that St Cyprian's was a sort of Dotheboys Hall. But I should be falsifying my own memories if I did not record that they are largely memories of disgust. The overcrowded, underfed, underwashed life that we led *was* disgusting, as I recall it. If I shut my eyes and say "school", it is of course the physical surroundings that first come back to me: the flat playing-field with its cricket pavilion and the little shed by the rifle range, the draughty dormitories, the dusty splintery passages, the square of asphalt in front of the gymnasium, the raw-looking pinewood chapel at the back. And at almost every point some filthy detail obtrudes itself. For example, there were the pewter bowls out of which we had our porridge. They had overhanging rims, and under the rims there were accumulations of sour porridge, which could be flaked off in long strips. The porridge itself, too, contained more lumps, hairs and unexplained black things than one would have thought possible, unless someone were putting them there on purpose. It was never safe to start on that porridge without investigating it first. And there was the slimy water of the plunge bath—it was twelve or fifteen feet long, the whole school was supposed to go into it every morning, and I doubt whether the water was changed at all frequently—and the always-damp towels with their cheesy smell: and, on occasional visits in the winter, the murky sea-water of the local Baths, which came straight in from the beach and on which I once saw floating a human turd. And the sweaty smell of the changing-room with its greasy basins, and, giving on this, the row of filthy, dilapidated lavatories, which had no fastenings of any kind on the doors, so that whenever you were sitting there someone was sure to come crashing in. It is not easy for me to think of my schooldays without seeming to breathe in a whiff of something cold and evil-smelling—a sort of compound of sweaty stockings, dirty towels, faecal smells blowing along corridors, forks with old food between the prongs, neck-of-mutton stew, and the banging doors of the lavatories and the echoing chamber-pots in the dormitories.

It is true that I am by nature not gregarious, and the WC and dirty-handkerchief side of life is necessarily more obtrusive when great numbers of human beings are crushed together in a small space. It is just as bad in an army, and worse, no doubt, in a prison. Besides, boyhood is the age of disgust. After one has learned to differentiate, and before one has become hardened—between seven and eighteen, say—one seems always to be walking the tight-rope over a cesspool. Yet I do not think I exaggerate the squalor of school life, when I remember how health and cleanliness were neglected, in spite of the hoo-ha about fresh air and cold water and keeping in hard training. It was common to remain constipated for days together. Indeed, one was hardly encouraged to keep one's bowels open, since the only aperients tolerated were castor oil or another almost equally horrible drink called liquorice powder. One was supposed to go into the plunge bath every morning, but some boys shirked it for days on end, simply making themselves scarce when the bell sounded, or else slipping along the edge of the bath among the crowd, and then wetting their hair with a little dirty water off the floor. A little boy of eight or nine will not necessarily keep himself clean unless there is someone to see that he does it. There was a new boy named Hazel, a pretty, mother's darling of a boy, who came a little while before I left. The first thing I noticed about him was the beautiful pearly whiteness of his teeth. By the end of that term his teeth were an extraordinary shade of green. During all that time, apparently, no one had taken sufficient interest in him to see that he brushed them.

But of course the differences between home and school were more than physical. That bump on the hard mattress, on the first night of term, used to give me a feeling of abrupt awakening, a feeling of: "This is reality, this is what you are up against." Your home might be far from perfect, but at least it was a place ruled by love rather than by fear, where you did not have to be perpetually on your guard against the people surrounding you. At eight years old you were suddenly taken out of this warm nest and flung into a world of force and fraud and secrecy, like a gold-fish into a tank full of pike. Against no matter what degree of bullying you had no redress. You could only have defended yourself by sneaking, which, except in a few rigidly defined circumstances, was the unforgivable sin. To write home and ask your parents to take you away would have been even less thinkable, since to do so would have been to admit yourself unhappy and unpopular, which a boy will never do. Boys are Erewhonians: they think that misfortune is disgraceful and must be concealed at all costs. It might perhaps have been considered permissible to complain to your parents about bad food, or an unjustified caning, or some other ill-treatment inflicted by masters and not by boys. The fact that Sambo never beat the richer boys suggests that such complaints were made occasionally. But in my own peculiar circumstances I could never have asked my parents to intervene on my behalf. Even before I understood about the reduced fees, I grasped that they were in some way under an obligation to Sambo, and therefore could not protect me against him. I have mentioned already that throughout my time at St Cyprian's I never had a cricket bat of my own. I had been told this was because "your parents couldn't afford it". One day in the holidays, by some casual remark, it came out that they had provided ten shillings to buy me one: yet no cricket bat appeared. I did not protest to my parents, let alone raise the subject with Sambo. How could I? I was dependent on him, and the ten shillings was merely a fragment of what I owed him. I realise now, of course, that it is immensely unlikely that Sambo had simply stuck to the money. No doubt the matter had slipped his memory. But the point is that I assumed that he had stuck to it, and that he had a right to do so if he chose.

How difficult it is for a child to have any real independence of attitude could be seen in our behaviour towards Flip. I think it would be true to say that every boy in the school hated and feared her. Yet we all fawned on her in the most abject way, and the top layer of our feelings towards her was a sort of guilt-stricken loyalty. Flip, although the discipline of the school depended more on her than on Sambo, hardly pretended to dispense strict justice. She was frankly capricious. An act which might get you a caning one day might next day be laughed off as a boyish prank, or even commended because it "showed you had guts". There were days when everyone cowered before those deep-set, accusing eyes, and there were days when she was like a flirtatious queen surrounded by courtier-lovers, laughing and joking, scattering largesse, or the promise of largesse ("And if you win the Harrow History Prize I'll give you a new case for your camera!"), and occasionally even packing three or four favoured boys into her Ford car and carrying them off to a teashop in town, where they were allowed to buy coffee and cakes. Flip was inextricably mixed up in my mind with Queen Elizabeth, whose relations with Leicester and Essex and Raleigh were intelligible to me from a very early age. A word we all constantly used in speaking of Flip was "favour". "I'm in good favour," we would say, or "I'm in bad favour." Except for the handful of wealthy or titled boys, no one was permanently in good favour, but on the other hand even the outcasts had patches of it from time to time. Thus, although my memories of Flip are mostly hostile, I also remember considerable periods when I basked under her smiles, when she called me "old chap" and used my Christian name, and allowed me to frequent her private library, where I first made acquaintance with *Vanity Fair*. The high-water mark of good favour was to be invited to serve at table on Sunday nights when Flip and Sambo had guests to dinner. In clearing away, of course, one had a chance to finish off the scraps, but one also got a servile pleasure from standing behind the seated guests and darting deferentially forward when something was wanted. Whenever one had the chance to suck up, one did suck up, and at the first smile one's hatred turned into a sort of cringing love. I was always tremendously proud when I succeeded in making Flip laugh. I have even, at her command, written *vers d'occasion*, comic verses to celebrate memorable events in the life of the school.

I am anxious to make it clear that I was not a rebel, except by force of circumstances. I accepted the codes that I found in being. Once, towards the end of my time, I even sneaked to Brown about a suspected case of homosexuality. I did not know very well what homosexuality was, but I knew that it happened and was bad, and that this was one of the contexts in which it was proper to sneak. Brown told me I was "a good fellow", which made me feel horribly ashamed. Before Flip one seemed as helpless as a snake before the snake-charmer. She had a hardly-varying vocabulary of praise and abuse, a whole series of set phrases, each of which promptly called forth the appropriate response. There was "*Buck* up, old chap!", which inspired one to paroxysms of energy; there was "Don't *be* such a fool!" (or, "It's path*e*tic, isn't it?"), which made one feel a born idiot; and there was "It isn't very straight of you, is it?", which always brought one to the brink of tears. And yet all the while, at the middle of one's heart, there seemed to stand an incorruptible inner self who knew that whatever one did—whether one laughed or snivelled or went into frenzies of gratitude for small favours—one's only true feeling was hatred.

iv

I had learned early in my career that one can do wrong against one's will, and before long I also learned that one can do wrong without ever discovering what one has done or why it was wrong. There were sins that were too subtle to be explained, and there were others that were too terrible to be clearly mentioned. For example, there was sex, which was always smouldering just under the surface and which suddenly blew up into a tremendous row when I was about twelve.

At some preparatory schools homosexuality is not a problem, but I think that St Cyprian's may have acquired a "bad tone" thanks to the presence of the South American boys, who would perhaps mature a year or two earlier than an English boy. At that age I was not interested, so I do not actually know what went on, but I imagine it was group masturbation. At any rate, one day the storm suddenly burst over our heads. There were summonses, interrogations, confessions, floggings, repentances, solemn lectures of which one understood nothing except that some irredeemable sin known as "swinishness" or "beastliness" had been committed. One of the ring-leaders, a boy named Horne, was flogged, according to eye-witnesses, for a quarter of an hour continuously before being expelled. His yells rang through the house. But we were all implicated, more or less, or felt ourselves to be implicated. Guilt seemed to hang in the air like a pall of smoke. A solemn, black-haired imbecile of an assistant master, who was later to be a Member of Parliament, took the older boys to a secluded room and delivered a talk on the Temple of the Body.

"Don't you realise what a wonderful thing your body is?" he said gravely. "You talk of your motor-car engines, your Rolls-Royces and Daimlers and so on. Don't you understand that no engine ever made is fit to be compared with your body? And then you go and wreck it, ruin it—for life!"

He turned his cavernous black eyes on me and added sadly:

"And you, whom I'd always believed to be quite a decent person after your fashion—you, I hear, are one of the very worst."

A feeling of doom descended upon me. So I was guilty too. I too had done the dreadful thing, whatever it was, that wrecked you for life, body and soul, and ended in suicide or the lunatic asylum. Till then I had hoped that I was innocent, and the conviction of sin which now took possession of me was perhaps all the stronger because I did not know what I had done. I was not among those who were interrogated and flogged, and it was not until the row was well over that I even learned about the trivial accident that had connected my name with it. Even then I understood nothing. It was not till about two years later that I fully grasped what that lecture on the Temple of the Body had referred to.

At this time I was in an almost sexless state, which is normal, or at any rate common, in boys of that age; I was therefore in the position of simultaneously knowing and not knowing what used to be called the Facts of Life. At five or six, like many children, I had passed through a phase of sexuality. My friends were the plumber's children up the road, and we used sometimes to play games of a vaguely erotic kind. One was called "playing at doctors", and I remember getting a faint but definitely pleasant thrill from holding a toy trumpet, which was supposed to be a stethoscope, against a little girl's belly. About the same time I fell deeply in love, a far more worshipping kind of love than I have ever felt for anyone since, with a girl named Elsie at the convent school which I attended. She seemed to me grown up, so I suppose she must have been fifteen. After that, as so often happens, all sexual feelings seemed to go out of me for many years. At twelve I knew more than I had known as a young child, but I understood less, because I no longer knew the essential fact that there is something pleasant in sexual activity. Between roughly seven and fourteen, the whole subject seemed to me uninteresting and, when for some reason I was forced to think of it, disgusting. My knowledge of the so-called Facts of Life was derived from animals, and was therefore distorted, and in any case was only intermittent. I knew that animals copulated and that human beings had bodies resembling those of animals: but that human beings also copulated I only knew, as it were, reluctantly, when something, a phrase in the Bible, perhaps, compelled me to remember it. Not having desire, I had no curiosity, and was willing to leave many questions unanswered. Thus, I knew in principle how the baby gets into the woman, but I did not know how it gets out again, because I had never followed the subject up. I knew all the dirty words, and in my bad moments I would repeat them to myself, but I did not know what the worst of them meant, nor want to know. They were abstractly wicked, a sort of verbal charm. While I remained in this state, it was easy for me to remain ignorant of any sexual misdeeds that went on about me, and to be hardly wiser even when the row broke. At most, through the veiled and terrible warnings of Flip, Sambo and all the rest of them, I grasped that the crime of which we were all guilty was somehow connected with the sexual organs. I had noticed, without feeling much interest, that one's penis sometimes stands up of its own accord (this starts happening to a boy long before he has any conscious sexual desires), and I was inclined to believe, or half-believe, that *that* must be the crime. At any rate, it was something to do with the penis—so much I understood. Many other boys, I have no doubt, were equally in the dark.

After the talk on the Temple of the Body (days later, it seems in retrospect: the row seemed to continue for days), a dozen of us were seated at the long shiny table which Sambo used for the scholarship class, under Flip's lowering eye. A long, desolate wail rang out from a room somewhere above. A very small boy named Ronalds, aged no more than about ten, who was implicated in some way, was being flogged, or was recovering from a flogging. At the sound, Flip's eyes searched our faces, and settled upon me.

"*You see,*" she said.

I will not swear that she said "You see what you have done," but that was the sense of it. We were all bowed down with shame. It was *our* fault. Somehow or other we had led poor Ronalds astray: *we* were responsible for his agony and his ruin. Then Flip turned upon

354 *Such, Such Were the Joys*

another boy named Heath. It is thirty years ago, and I cannot remember for certain whether she merely quoted a verse from the Bible, or whether she actually brought out a Bible and made Heath read it; but at any rate the text indicated was: "Whoso shall offend one of these little ones that believe in me, it were better for him that a millstone were hanged about his neck, and that he were drowned in the depth of the sea."

That, too, was terrible. Ronalds was one of these little ones, we had offended him; it were better that a millstone were hanged about our necks and that we were drowned in the depth of the sea.

"Have you thought about that, Heath—have you thought what it means?" Flip said. And Heath broke down into snivelling tears.

Another boy, Beacham, whom I have mentioned already, was similarly overwhelmed with shame by the accusation that he "had black rings round his eyes".

"Have you looked in the glass lately, Beacham?" said Flip. "Aren't you ashamed to go about with a face like that? Do you think everyone doesn't know what it means when a boy has black rings round his eyes?"

Once again the load of guilt and fear seemed to settle down upon me. Had *I* got black rings round my eyes? A couple of years later I realised that these were supposed to be a symptom by which masturbators could be detected. But already, without knowing this, I accepted the black rings as a sure sign of depravity, *some* kind of depravity. And many times, even before I grasped the supposed meaning, I have gazed anxiously into the glass, looking for the first hint of that dreaded stigma, the confession which the secret sinner writes upon his own face.

These terrors wore off, or became merely intermittent, without affecting what one might call my official beliefs. It was still true about the madhouse and the suicide's grave, but it was no longer acutely frightening. Some months later it happened that I once again saw Horne, the ringleader who had been flogged and expelled. Horne was one of the outcasts, the son of poor middle-class parents, which was no doubt part of the reason why Sambo had handled him so roughly. The term after his expulsion he went on to Eastbourne College, the small local public school, which was hideously despised at St Cyprian's and looked on as "not really" a public school at all. Only a very few boys from St Cyprian's went there, and Sambo always spoke of them with a sort of contemptuous pity. You had no chance if you went to a school like that: at the best your destiny would be a clerkship. I thought of Horne as a person who at thirteen had already forfeited all hope of any decent future. Physically, morally and socially he was finished. Moreover I assumed that his parents had only sent him to Eastbourne College because after his disgrace no "good" school would have him.

During the following term, when we were out for a walk, we passed Horne in the street. He looked completely normal. He was a strongly-built, rather good-looking boy with black hair. I immediately noticed that he looked better than when I had last seen him—his complexion, previously rather pale, was pinker and that he did not seem embarrassed at meeting us. Apparently he was not ashamed either of having been expelled, or of being at Eastbourne College. If one could gather anything from the way he looked at us as we filed past, it was that he was glad to have escaped from St Cyprian's. But the encounter made very little impression on me. I drew no inference from the fact that Horne, ruined in body and soul, appeared to be happy and in good health. I still believed in the sexual mythology that had been taught me by Sambo and Flip. The mysterious, terrible dangers were still there. Any morning the black rings might appear round your eyes and you would know that you too were among the lost ones. Only it no longer seemed to matter very much. These contradictions can exist easily in the mind of a child, because of its own vitality. It accepts—how can it do otherwise?—the nonsense that its elders tell it, but its youthful body, and the sweetness of the physical world, tell it another story. It was the same with Hell, which up to the age of about fourteen I officially believed in. Almost certainly Hell existed, and there were occasions when a vivid sermon could scare you into fits. But somehow it never lasted. The fire that waited for you was real fire, it would hurt in the same way as when you burnt your finger, and *for ever*, but most of the time you could contemplate it without bothering.

v

The various codes which were presented to you at St Cyprian's—religious, moral, social and intellectual—contradicted one another if you worked out their implications. The essential conflict was between the tradition of nineteenth-century asceticism and the actually existing luxury and snobbery of the pre-1914 age. On the one side were low-church Bible Christianity, sex puritanism, insistence

on hard work, respect for academic distinction, disapproval
of self-indulgence: on the other, contempt for "braininess", and
worship of games, contempt for foreigners and the working class,
an almost neurotic dread of poverty, and, above all, the assumption
not only that money and privilege are the things that matter, but
that it is better to inherit them than to have to work for them.
Broadly, you were bidden to be at once a Christian and a social
success, which is impossible. At the time I did not perceive that the
various ideals which were set before us cancelled out. I merely saw
that they were all, or nearly all, unattainable, so far as I was concerned, since they all depended not only on what you did but on
what you *were*.

Very early, at the age of only ten or eleven, I reached the conclusion—no one told me this, but on the other hand I did not simply
make it up out of my own head: somehow it was in the air I breathed
—that you were no good unless you had £100,000. I had perhaps
fixed on this particular sum as a result of reading Thackeray. The
interest on £100,000 would be £4,000 a year (I was in favour of a
safe 4 per cent), and this seemed to me the minimum income that
you must possess if you were to belong to the real top crust, the
people in the country houses. But it was clear that I could never
find my way into that paradise, to which you did not really belong
unless you were born into it. You could only *make* money, if at all,
by a mysterious operation called "going into the City", and when you
came out of the City, having won your £100,000, you were fat and
old. But the truly enviable thing about the top-notchers was that
they were rich while young. For people like me, the ambitious
middle class, the examination-passers, only a bleak, laborious kind
of success was possible. You clambered upwards on a ladder of
scholarships into the Civil Service or the Indian Civil Service, or
possibly you became a barrister. And if at any point you "slacked"
or "went off" and missed one of the rungs in the ladder, you became
"a little office boy at forty pounds a year". But even if you climbed
to the highest niche that was open to you, you could still only be an
underling, a hanger-on of the people who really counted.

Even if I had not learned this from Sambo and Flip, I would have
learned it from the other boys. Looking back, it is astonishing how
intimately, intelligently snobbish we all were, how knowledgeable
about names and addresses, how swift to detect small differences in
accents and manners and the cut of clothes. There were some boys

who seemed to drip money from their pores even in the bleak misery of the middle of a winter term. At the beginning and end of the term, especially, there was naively snobbish chatter about Switzerland, and Scotland with its ghillies and grouse moors, and "my uncle's yacht", and "our place in the country", and "my pony" and "my pater's touring car". There never was, I suppose, in the history of the world a time when the sheer vulgar fatness of wealth, without any kind of aristocratic elegance to redeem it, was so obtrusive as in those years before 1914. It was the age when crazy millionaires in curly top-hats and lavender waistcoats gave champagne parties in rococo house-boats on the Thames, the age of diabolo and hobble skirts, the age of the "knut" in his grey bowler and cutaway coat, the age of *The Merry Widow*, Saki's novels, *Peter Pan* and *Where the Rainbow Ends*, the age when people talked about chocs and cigs and ripping and topping and heavenly, when they went for divvy week-ends at Brighton and had scrumptious teas at the Troc. From the whole decade before 1914 there seems to breathe forth a smell of the more vulgar, un-grown-up kinds of luxury, a smell of brilliantine and *crème-de-menthe* and soft-centred chocolates—an atmosphere, as it were, of eating everlasting strawberry ices on green lawns to the tune of the Eton Boating Song. The extraordinary thing was the way in which everyone took it for granted that this oozing, bulging wealth of the English upper and upper-middle classes would last for ever, and was part of the order of things. After 1918 it was never quite the same again. Snobbishness and expensive habits came back, certainly, but they were self-conscious and on the defensive. Before the war the worship of money was entirely unreflecting and un-troubled by any pang of conscience. The goodness of money was as unmistakable as the goodness of health or beauty, and a glittering car, a title or a horde of servants was mixed up in people's minds with the idea of actual moral virtue.

At St Cyprian's, in term-time, the general bareness of life enforced a certain democracy, but any mention of the holidays, and the con-sequent competitive swanking about cars and butlers and country houses, promptly called class distinctions into being. The school was pervaded by a curious cult of Scotland, which brought out the fundamental contradiction in our standard of values. Flip claimed Scottish ancestry, and she favoured the Scottish boys, encouraging them to wear kilts in their ancestral tartan instead of the school uniform, and even christened her youngest child by a Gaelic name.

Ostensibly we were supposed to admire the Scots because they were "grim" and "dour" ("stern" was perhaps the key word), and irresistible on the field of battle. In the big schoolroom there was a steel engraving of the charge of the Scots Greys at Waterloo, all looking as though they enjoyed every moment of it. Our picture of Scotland was made up of burns, braes, kilts, sporrans, claymores, bagpipes and the like, all somehow mixed up with the invigorating effects of porridge, Protestantism and a cold climate. But underlying this was something quite different. The real reason for the cult of Scotland was that only very rich people could spend their summers there. And the pretended belief in Scottish superiority was a cover for the bad conscience of the occupying English, who had pushed the Highland peasantry off their farms to make way for the deer forests, and then compensated them by turning them into servants. Flip's face always beamed with innocent snobbishness when she spoke of Scotland. Occasionally she even attempted a trace of Scottish accent. Scotland was a private paradise which a few initiates could talk about and make outsiders feel small.

"You going to Scotland this hols?"

"Rather! We go every year."

"My pater's got three miles of river."

"My pater's giving me a new gun for the twelfth. There's jolly good black game where we go. Get out, Smith! What are you listening for? You've never been in Scotland. I bet you don't know what a blackcock looks like."

Following on this, imitations of the cry of a blackcock, of the roaring of a stag, of the accent of "our ghillies", etc etc.

And the questionings that new boys of doubtful social origin were sometimes put through—questionings quite surprising in their mean-minded particularity, when one reflects that the inquisitors were only twelve or thirteen!

"How much a year has your pater got? What part of London do you live in? Is that Knightsbridge or Kensington? How many bathrooms has your house got? How many servants do your people keep? Have you got a butler? Well, then, have you got a cook? Where do you get your clothes made? How many shows did you go to in the hols? How much money did you bring back with you?" etc etc.

I have seen a little new boy, hardly older than eight, desperately lying his way through such a catechism:

"Have your people got a car?"

"Yes."

"What sort of car?"

"Daimler."

"How many horse-power?"

(Pause, and leap in the dark.) "Fifteen."

"What kind of lights?"

The little boy is bewildered.

"What kind of lights? Electric or acetylene?"

(A longer pause, and another leap in the dark.) "Acetylene."

"Coo! He says his pater's car's got acetylene lamps. They went out years ago. It must be as old as the hills."

"Rot! He's making it up. He hasn't got a car. He's just a navvy. Your pater's a navvy."

And so on.

By the social standards that prevailed about me, I was no good, and could not be any good. But all the different kinds of virtue seemed to be mysteriously interconnected and to belong to much the same people. It was not only money that mattered: there were also strength, beauty, charm, athleticism and something called "guts" or "character", which in reality meant the power to impose your will on others. I did not possess any of these qualities. At games, for instance, I was hopeless. I was a fairly good swimmer and not altogether contemptible at cricket, but these had no prestige value, because boys only attach importance to a game if it requires strength and courage. What counted was football, at which I was a funk. I loathed the game, and since I could see no pleasure or useful-ness in it, it was very difficult for me to show courage at it. Football, it seemed to me, is not really played for the pleasure of kicking a ball about, but is a species of fighting. The lovers of football are large, boisterous, nobbly boys who are good at knocking down and trampling on slightly smaller boys. That was the pattern of school life—a continuous triumph of the strong over the weak. Virtue consisted in winning: it consisted in being bigger, stronger, hand-somer, richer, more popular, more elegant, more unscrupulous than other people—in dominating them, bullying them, making them suffer pain, making them look foolish, getting the better of them in every way. Life was hierarchical and whatever happened was right. There were the strong, who deserved to win and always did win, and there were the weak, who deserved to lose and always did lose, everlastingly.

I did not question the prevailing standards, because so far as I could see there were no others. How could the rich, the strong, the elegant, the fashionable, the powerful, be in the wrong? It was their world, and the rules they made for it must be the right ones. And yet from a very early age I was aware of the impossibility of any *subjective* conformity. Always at the centre of my heart the inner self seemed to be awake, pointing out the difference between the moral obligation and the psychological *fact*. It was the same in all matters, worldly or other-worldly. Take religion, for instance. You were supposed to love God, and I did not question this. Till the age of about fourteen I believed in God, and believed that the accounts given of him were true. But I was well aware that I did not love him. On the contrary, I hated him, just as I hated Jesus and the Hebrew patriarchs. If I had sympathetic feelings towards any character in the Old Testament, it was towards such people as Cain, Jezebel, Haman, Agag, Sisera: in the New Testament my friends, if any, were Ananias, Caiaphas, Judas and Pontius Pilate. But the whole business of religion seemed to be strewn with psychological impossibilities. The Prayer Book told you, for example, to love God and fear him: but how could you love someone whom you feared? With your private affections it was the same. What you *ought* to feel was usually clear enough, but the appropriate emotion could not be commanded. Obviously it was my duty to feel grateful towards Flip and Sambo; but I was not grateful. It was equally clear that one ought to love one's father, but I knew very well that I merely disliked my own father, whom I had barely seen before I was eight and who appeared to me simply as a gruff-voiced elderly man forever saying "Don't". It was not that one did not want to possess the right qualities or feel the correct emotions, but that one could not. The good and the possible never seemed to coincide.

There was a line of verse that I came across not actually while I was at St Cyprian's, but a year or two later, and which seemed to strike a sort of leaden echo in my heart. It was: "The armies of unalterable law". I understood to perfection what it meant to be Lucifer, defeated and justly defeated, with no possibility of revenge. The schoolmasters with their canes, the millionaires with their Scottish castles, the athletes with their curly hair—these were the armies of unalterable law. It was not easy, at that date, to realise that in fact it *was* alterable. And according to that law I was damned. I had no money, I was weak, I was ugly, I was unpopular, I had a chronic cough, I was cowardly, I smelt. This picture, I should add, was not altogether fanciful. I was an unattractive boy. St Cyprian's soon made me so, even if I had not been so before. But a child's belief in its own shortcomings is not much influenced by facts. I believed, for example, that I "smelt", but this was based simply on general probability. It was notorious that disagreeable people smelt, and therefore presumably I did so too. Again, until after I had left school for good I continued to believe that I was preternaturally ugly. It was what my schoolfellows had told me, and I had no other authority to refer to. The conviction that it was *not possible* for me to be a success went deep enough to influence my actions till far into adult life. Until I was about thirty I always planned my life on the assumption not only that any major undertaking was bound to fail, but that I could only expect to live a few years longer.

But this sense of guilt and inevitable failure was balanced by something else: that is, the instinct to survive. Even a creature that is weak, ugly, cowardly, smelly and in no way justifiable still wants to stay alive and be happy after its own fashion. I could not invert the existing scale of values, or turn myself into a success, but I could accept my failure and make the best of it. I could resign myself to being what I was, and then endeavour to survive on those terms.

To survive, or at least to preserve any kind of independence, was essentially criminal, since it meant breaking rules which you yourself recognised. There was a boy named Johnny Hale who for some months oppressed me horribly. He was a big, powerful, coarsely handsome boy with a very red face and curly black hair, who was forever twisting somebody's arm, wringing somebody's ear, flogging somebody with a riding-crop (he was a member of the Sixth Form), or performing prodigies of activity on the football field. Flip loved him (hence the fact that he was habitually called by his Christian name) and Sambo commended him as a boy who "had character" and "could keep order". He was followed about by a group of toadies who nicknamed him Strong Man.

One day, when we were taking off our overcoats in the changing-room, Hale picked on me for some reason. I "answered him back", whereupon he gripped my wrist, twisted it round and bent my forearm back upon itself in a hideously painful way. I remember his handsome, jeering red face bearing down upon mine. He was, I think, older than I, besides being enormously stronger. As he let go of me a terrible, wicked resolve formed itself in my heart. I would get back on him by hitting him when he did not expect it. It was a strategic moment, for the master who had been "taking" the walk would be coming back almost immediately, and then there could be no fight. I let perhaps a minute go by, walked up to Hale with the most harmless air I could assume, and then, getting the weight of my body behind it, smashed my fist into his face. He was flung backwards by the blow, and some blood ran out of his mouth. His always sanguine face turned almost black with rage. Then he turned away to rinse his mouth at the washing-basins.

"All right!" he said to me between his teeth as the master led us away.

For days after this he followed me about, challenging me to fight. Although terrified out of my wits, I steadily refused to fight. I said that the blow in the face had served him right, and there was an end of it. Curiously enough he did not simply fall upon me there and then, which public opinion would probably have supported him in doing. So gradually the matter tailed off, and there was no fight.

Now, I had behaved wrongly, by my own code no less than his. To hit him unawares was wrong. But to refuse afterwards to fight knowing that if we fought he would beat me—that was far worse: it was cowardly. If I had refused because I disapproved of fighting, or because I genuinely felt the matter to be closed, it would have been all right; but I had refused merely because I was afraid. Even my revenge was made empty by that fact. I had struck the blow in a moment of mindless violence, deliberately not looking far ahead and merely determined to get my own back for once and damn the consequences. I had had time to realise that what I did was wrong, but it was the kind of crime from which you could get some satisfaction. Now all was nullified. There had been a sort of courage in the first act, but my subsequent cowardice had wiped it out.

The fact I hardly noticed was that though Hale formally challenged me to fight, he did not actually attack me. Indeed, after receiving that one blow he never oppressed me again. It was perhaps twenty years before I saw the significance of this. At the time I could not see beyond the moral dilemma that is presented to the weak in a world governed by the strong: Break the rules, or perish. I did not see that in that case the weak have the right to make a different set of rules for themselves; because, even if such an idea had occurred to me, there was no one in my environment who could have confirmed me in it. I lived in a world of boys, gregarious animals, questioning nothing, accepting the law of the stronger and avenging their own humiliations by passing them down to someone smaller. My situation was that of countless other boys, and if potentially I was more of a rebel than most, it was only because, by boyish standards, I was a poorer specimen. But I never did rebel intellectually, only emotionally. I had nothing to help me except my dumb selfishness, my inability—not, indeed, to despise myself, but to *dislike* myself— my instinct to survive.

It was about a year after I hit Johnny Hale in the face that I left St Cyprian's for ever. It was the end of a winter term. With a sense of coming out from darkness into sunlight I put on my Old Boy's tie as we dressed for the journey. I well remember the feeling of that brand-new silk tie round my neck, a feeling of emancipation, as though the tie had been at once a badge of manhood and an amulet against Flip's voice and Sambo's cane. I was escaping from bondage. It was not that I expected, or even intended, to be any more successful at a public school than I had been at St Cyprian's. But still, I was escaping. I knew that at a public school there would be more privacy, more neglect, more chance to be idle and self-indulgent and degenerate. For years past I had been resolved—unconsciously at first, but consciously later on—that when once my scholarship was won I would "slack off" and cram no longer. This resolve, by the way, was so fully carried out that between the ages of thirteen and twenty-two or three I hardly ever did a stroke of avoidable work.

Flip shook hands to say good-bye. She even gave me my Christian name for the occasion. But there was a sort of patronage, almost a sneer, in her face and in her voice. The tone in which she said good-bye was nearly the tone in which she had been used to say *little butterflies*. I had won two scholarships, but I was a failure, because success was measured not by what you did but by what you *were*. I was "not a good type of boy" and could bring no credit on the school. I did not possess character or courage or health or strength or money, or even good manners, the power to look like a gentleman.

"Good-bye," Flip's parting smile seemed to say; "it's not worth quarrelling now. You haven't made much of a success of your time at St Cyprian's, have you? And I don't suppose you'll get on awfully well at a public school either. We made a mistake, really, in wasting our time and money on you. This kind of education hasn't much to offer to a boy with your background and your outlook. Oh, don't think we don't understand you! We know all about those ideas

you have at the back of your head, we know you disbelieve in everything we've taught you, and we know you aren't in the least grateful
for all we've done for you. But there's no use in bringing it all up
now. We aren't responsible for you any longer, and we shan't be
seeing you again. Let's just admit that you're one of our failures and
part without ill-feeling. And so, good-bye."

That at least was what I read into her face. And yet how happy
I was, that winter morning, as the train bore me away with the
gleaming new silk tie (dark green, pale blue and black, if I remember
rightly) round my neck! The world was opening before me, just a
little, like a grey sky which exhibits a narrow crack of blue. A public
school would be better fun than St Cyprian's, but at bottom equally
alien. In a world where the prime necessities were money, titled
relatives, athleticism, tailor-made clothes, neatly-brushed hair, a
charming smile, I was no good. All I had gained was a breathing-
space. A little quietude, a little self-indulgence, a little respite from
cramming—and then, ruin. What kind of ruin I did not know:
perhaps the colonies or an office stool, perhaps prison or an early
death. But first a year or two in which one could "slack off" and get
the benefit of one's sins, like Doctor Faustus. I believed firmly in my
evil destiny, and yet I was acutely happy. It is the advantage of being
thirteen that you can not only live in the moment, but do so with full
consciousness, foreseeing the future and yet not caring about it.
Next term I was going to Wellington. I had also won a scholarship
at Eton, but it was uncertain whether there would be a vacancy, and
I was going to Wellington first. At Eton you had a room to yourself
—a room which might even have a fire in it. At Wellington you had
your own cubicle, and could make yourself cocoa in the evenings.
The privacy of it, the grown-upness! And there would be libraries to
hang about in, and summer afternoons when you could shirk games
and mooch about the countryside alone, with no master driving you
along. Meanwhile there were the holidays. There was the ·22 rifle
that I had bought the previous holidays (the Crackshot, it was called,
costing twenty-two and sixpence), and Christmas was coming next
week. There were also the pleasures of overeating. I thought of
some particularly voluptuous cream buns which could be bought for
twopence each at a shop in our town. (This was 1916, and food-
rationing had not yet started.) Even the detail that my journey-
money had been slightly miscalculated, leaving about a shilling over
—enough for an unforeseen cup of coffee and a cake or two some-

where on the way—was enough to fill me with bliss. There was time
for a bit of happiness before the future closed in upon me. But I did
know that the future was dark. Failure, failure, failure—failure
behind me, failure ahead of me—that was by far the deepest conviction that I carried away.

vi

All this was thirty years ago and more. The question is: Does a child
at school go through the same kind of experiences nowadays?

The only honest answer, I believe, is that we do not with certainty
know. Of course it is obvious that the present-day *attitude* towards
education is enormously more humane and sensible than that of the
past. The snobbishness that was an integral part of my own education
would be almost unthinkable today, because the society that
nourished it is dead. I recall a conversation that must have taken
place about a year before I left St Cyprian's. A Russian boy, large
and fair-haired, a year older than myself, was questioning me.

"How much a year has your father got?"

I told him what I thought it was, adding a few hundreds to make
it sound better. The Russian boy, neat in his habits, produced a
pencil and a small note-book and made a calculation.

"My father has over two hundred times as much money as yours,"
he announced with a sort of amused contempt.

That was in 1915. What happened to that money a couple of
years later, I wonder? And still more I wonder, do conversations of
that kind happen at preparatory schools now?

Clearly there has been a vast change of outlook, a general growth
of "enlightenment", even among ordinary, unthinking middle-class
people. Religious belief, for instance, has largely vanished, dragging
other kinds of nonsense after it. I imagine that very few people
nowadays would tell a child that if it masturbates it will end in the
lunatic asylum. Beating, too, has become discredited, and has even
been abandoned at many schools. Nor is the underfeeding of
children looked on as a normal, almost meritorious act. No one
now would openly set out to give his pupils as little food as they
could do with, or tell them that it is healthy to get up from a meal as
hungry as you sat down. The whole status of children has improved,
partly because they have grown relatively less numerous. And the
diffusion of even a little psychological knowledge has made it harder
for parents and schoolteachers to indulge their aberrations in the

name of discipline. Here is a case, not known to me personally, but known to someone I can vouch for, and happening within my own lifetime. A small girl, daughter of a clergyman, continued wetting her bed at an age when she should have grown out of it. In order to punish her for this dreadful deed, her father took her to a large garden party and there introduced her to the whole company as a little girl who wetted her bed: and to underline her wickedness he had previously painted her face black. I do not suggest that Flip and Sambo would actually have done a thing like this, but I doubt whether it would have much surprised them. After all, things do change. And yet—!

The question is not whether boys are still buckled into Eton collars on Sunday, or told that babies are dug up under gooseberry bushes. That kind of thing is at an end, admittedly. The real question is whether it is still normal for a schoolchild to live for years amid irrational terrors and lunatic misunderstandings. And here one is up against the very great difficulty of knowing what a child really feels and thinks. A child which appears reasonably happy may actually be suffering horrors which it cannot or will not reveal. It lives in a sort of alien under-water world which we can only penetrate by memory or divination. Our chief clue is the fact that we were once children ourselves, and many people appear to forget the atmosphere of their own childhood almost entirely. Think for instance of the unnecessary torments that people will inflict by sending a child back to school with clothes of the wrong pattern, and refusing to see that this matters! Over things of this kind a child will sometimes utter a protest, but a great deal of the time its attitude is one of simple concealment. Not to expose your true feelings to an adult seems to be instinctive from the age of seven or eight onwards. Even the affection that one feels for a child, the desire to protect and cherish it, is a cause of misunderstanding. One can love a child, perhaps, more deeply than one can love another adult, but it is rash to assume that the child feels any love in return. Looking back on my own childhood, after the infant years were over, I do not believe that I ever felt love for any mature person, except my mother, and even her I did not trust, in the sense that shyness made me conceal most of my real feelings from her. Love, the spontaneous, unqualified emotion of love, was something I could only feel for people who were young. Towards people who were old—and remember that "old" to a child means over thirty, or even over twenty-five—I could feel reverence, respect, admiration or compunction, but I seemed cut off from them by a veil of fear and shyness mixed up with physical distaste. People are too ready to forget the child's *physical* shrinking from the adult. The enormous size of grown-ups, their ungainly, rigid bodies, their coarse, wrinkled skins, their great relaxed eyelids, their yellow teeth, and the whiffs of musty clothes and beer and sweat and tobacco that disengage from them at every movement! Part of the reason for the ugliness of adults, in a child's eyes, is that the child is usually looking upwards, and few faces are at their best when seen from below. Besides, being fresh and unmarked itself, the child has impossibly high standards in the matter of skin and teeth and complexion. But the greatest barrier of all is the child's misconception about age. A child can hardly envisage life beyond thirty, and in judging people's ages it will make fantastic mistakes. It will think that a person of twenty-five is forty, that a person of forty is sixty-five, and so on. Thus, when I fell in love with Elsie I took her to be grown-up. I met her again, when I was thirteen and she, I think, must have been twenty-three; she now seemed to me a middle-aged woman, somewhat past her best. And the child thinks of growing old as an almost obscene calamity, which for some mysterious reason will never happen to itself. All who have passed the age of thirty are joyless grotesques, endlessly fussing about things of no importance and staying alive without, so far as the child can see, having anything to live for. Only child life is real life. The schoolmaster who imagines that he is loved and trusted by his boys is in fact mimicked and laughed at behind his back. An adult who does not seem dangerous nearly always seems ridiculous.

I base these generalisations on what I can recall of my own childhood outlook. Treacherous though memory is, it seems to me the chief means we have of discovering how a child's mind works. Only by resurrecting our own memories can we realise how incredibly distorted is the child's vision of the world. Consider this, for example. How would St Cyprian's appear to me now, if I could go back, at my present age, and see it as it was in 1915? What should I think of Sambo and Flip, those terrible, all-powerful monsters? I should see them as a couple of silly, shallow, ineffectual people, eagerly clambering up a social ladder which any thinking person could see to be on the point of collapse. I would no more be frightened of them than I would be frightened of a dormouse. Moreover, in those days they seemed to me fantastically old, whereas—though of this I am not certain—I imagine they must have been somewhat younger than I am now. And how would Johnny Hale appear, with his blacksmith's arms and his red, jeering face? Merely a scruffy little boy, barely distinguishable from hundreds of other scruffy little boys. The two sets of facts can lie side by side in my mind, because those happen to be my own memories. But it would be very difficult for me to see with the eyes of any other child, except by an effort of the imagination which might lead me completely astray. The child and the adult live in different worlds. If that is so, we cannot be certain that school, at any rate boarding school, is not still for many children as dreadful an experience as it used to be. Take away God, Latin, the cane, class distinctions and sexual taboos, and the fear, the hatred, the snobbery and the misunderstanding might still all be there. It will have been seen that my own main trouble was an utter lack of any sense of proportion or probability. This led me to accept outrages and believe absurdities, and to suffer torments over things which were in fact of no importance. It is not enough to say that I was "silly" and "ought to have known better". Look back into your own childhood and think of the nonsense you used to believe and the trivialities which could make you suffer. Of course my own case had its individual variations, but essentially it was that of countless other boys. The weakness of the child is that it starts with a blank sheet. It neither understands nor questions the society in which it lives, and because of its credulity other people can work upon it, infecting it with the sense of inferiority and the dread of offending against mysterious, terrible laws. It may be that everything that happened to me at St Cyprian's could happen in the most "enlightened" school, though perhaps in subtler forms. Of one thing, however, I do feel fairly sure, and that is that boarding schools are worse than day schools. A child has a better chance with the sanctuary of its home near at hand. And I think the characteristic faults of the English upper and middle classes may be partly due to the practice, general until recently, of sending children away from home as young as nine, eight or even seven.

I have never been back to St Cyprian's. Reunions, old boys' dinners and such-like leave me something more than cold, even when my memories are friendly. I have never even been down to Eton, where I was relatively happy, though I did once pass through it in 1933 and noted with interest that nothing seemed to have changed, except that the shops now sold radios. As for St Cyprian's, for years I loathed its very name so deeply that I could not view it with enough detachment to see the significance of the things that happened to me there. In a way, it is only within the last decade that I have really thought over my schooldays, vividly though their memory has always haunted me. Nowadays, I believe, it would make very little impression on me to see the place again, if it still exists. (I remember hearing a rumour some years ago that it had been burnt down.) If I had to pass through Eastbourne I would not make a detour to avoid the school: and if I happened to pass the school itself I might even stop for a moment by the low brick wall, with the steep bank running down from it, and look across the flat playing field at the ugly building with the square of asphalt in front of it. And if I went inside and smelt again the inky, dusty smell of the big schoolroom, the rosiny smell of the chapel, the stagnant smell of the swimming bath and the cold reek of the lavatories, I think I should only feel what one invariably feels in revisiting any scene of childhood: How small everything has grown, and how terrible is the deterioration in myself! But it is a fact that for many years I could hardly have borne to look at it again. Except upon dire necessity I would not have set foot in Eastbourne. I even conceived a prejudice against Sussex, as the county that contained St Cyprian's, and as an adult I have only once been in Sussex, on a short visit. Now, however, the place is out of my system for good. Its magic works no longer, and I have not even enough animosity left to make me hope that Flip and Sambo are dead or that the story of the school being burnt down was true.

Written by May 1947; *Partisan Review*, September–October 1952; SJ; OR

87. Letter to George Woodcock

Barnhill
Isle of Jura
Argyllshire
18 June 1947

Dear George,

Yes, certainly the people in Munich may reprint the piece from *Now*.[1]

I'm glad you are managing to do some work, and that you

[1] "How the Poor Die". See 58.

contemplate writing something on Wilde. I've always been very pro-Wilde. I particularly like *Dorian Grey*, absurd as it is in a way. I just recently read Hesketh Pearson's life of him—only the ordinary hack biography, but I found bits of it quite interesting, especially the part about Wilde's time in prison. I don't think I'd read a life of Wilde before, though years ago I read some reminiscences by Frank Harris, obviously untruthful, and part of a book by Sherard,[1] answering Harris's biography. I should like to read a more detailed account of the two trials. I was amused by that woman's remarks in the American magazine you sent me. What an ass! The weather here has turned filthy again after being nice for a week or two.

Yours
George

88. Toward European Unity

A Socialist today is in the position of a doctor treating an all but hopeless case. As a doctor, it is his duty to keep the patient alive, and therefore to assume that the patient has at least a chance of recovery. As a scientist, it is his duty to face the facts, and therefore to admit that the patient will probably die. Our activities as Socialists only have meaning if we assume that Socialism *can* be established, but if we stop to consider what probably *will* happen, then we must admit, I think, that the chances are against us. If I were a bookmaker, simply calculating the probabilities and leaving my own wishes out of account, I would give odds against the survival of civilisation within the next few hundred years. As far as I can see, there are three possibilities ahead of us:

1. That the Americans will decide to use the atomic bomb while they have it and the Russians haven't. This would solve nothing. It would do away with the particular danger that is now presented by the USSR, but would lead to the rise of new empires, fresh rivalries, more wars, more atomic bombs, etc. In any case this is, I think, the least likely outcome of the three, because a preventive war is a crime not easily committed by a country that retains any traces of democracy.

[1] Robert Harborough Sherard.

2. That the present "cold war" will continue until the USSR, and several other countries, have atomic bombs as well. Then there will only be a short breathing-space before whizz! go the rockets, wallop! go the bombs, and the industrial centres of the world are wiped out, probably beyond repair. Even if any one state, or group of states, emerges from such a war as technical victor, it will probably be unable to build up the machine civilisation anew. The world, therefore, will once again be inhabited by a few million, or a few hundred million human beings living by subsistence agriculture, and probably, after a couple of generations, retaining no more of the culture of the past than a knowledge of how to smelt metals. Conceivably this is a desirable outcome, but obviously it has nothing to do with Socialism.

3. That the fear inspired by the atomic bomb and other weapons yet to come will be so great that everyone will refrain from using them. This seems to me the worst possibility of all. It would mean the division of the world among two or three vast super-states, unable to conquer one another and unable to be overthrown by any internal rebellion. In all probability their structure would be hierarchic, with a semi-divine caste at the top and outright slavery at the bottom, and the crushing out of liberty would exceed anything that the world has yet seen. Within each state the necessary psychological atmosphere would be kept up by complete severance from the outer world, and by a continuous phony war against rival states. Civilisations of this type might remain static for thousands of years.

Most of the dangers that I have outlined existed and were foreseeable long before the atomic bomb was invented. The only way of avoiding them that I can imagine is to present somewhere or other, on a large scale, the spectacle of a community where people are relatively free and happy and where the main motive in life is not the pursuit of money or power. In other words, democratic Socialism must be made to work throughout some large area. But the only area in which it could conceivably be made to work, in any near future, is western Europe. Apart from Australia and New Zealand, the tradition of democratic Socialism can only be said to exist—and even there it only exists precariously—in Scandinavia, Germany, Austria, Czechoslovakia, Switzerland, the Low Countries, France, Britain, Spain, and Italy. Only in those countries are there still large numbers of people to whom the word "Socialism" has some appeal and for whom it is bound up with liberty, equality, and internationalism.

Elsewhere it either has no foothold or it means something
different. In North America the masses are contented with
capitalism, and one cannot tell what turn they will take when capitalism begins to collapse. In the USSR there prevails a sort of
oligarchical collectivism which could only develop into democratic
Socialism against the will of the ruling minority. Into Asia even the
word "Socialism" has barely penetrated. The Asiatic nationalist
movements are either Fascist in character, or look towards Moscow,
or manage to combine both attitudes: and at present all movements
among the coloured peoples are tinged by racial mysticism. In most
of South America the position is essentially similar, so is it in Africa
and the Middle East. Socialism does not exist anywhere, but even
as an idea it is at present valid only in Europe. Of course, Socialism
cannot properly be said to be established until it is world-wide, but
the process must begin somewhere, and I cannot imagine it beginning
except through the federation of the western European states,
transformed into Socialist republics without colonial dependencies.
Therefore a Socialist United States of Europe seems to me the only
worth-while political objective today. Such a federation would contain about 250 million people, including perhaps half the skilled
industrial workers of the world. I do not need to be told that the
difficulties of bringing any such thing into being are enormous and
terrifying, and I will list some of them in a moment. But we ought not
to feel that it is of its nature impossible, or that countries so different
from one another would not voluntarily unite. A western European
union is in itself a less improbable concatenation than the Soviet
Union or the British Empire.

Now as to the difficulties. The greatest difficulty of all is the apathy
and conservatism of people everywhere, their unawareness of danger,
their inability to imagine anything new—in general, as Bertrand
Russell put it recently, the unwillingness of the human race to
acquiesce in its own survival. But there are also active malignant
forces working against European unity, and there are existing
economic relationships on which the European peoples depend for
their standard of life and which are not compatible with true
Socialism. I list what seem to me to be the four main obstacles,
explaining each of them as shortly as I can manage:

1. Russian hostility. The Russians cannot but be hostile to any
European union not under their own control. The reasons, both
the pretended and the real ones, are obvious. One has to count,

therefore, with the danger of a preventive war, with the systematic terrorising of the smaller nations, and with the sabotage of the Communist Parties everywhere. Above all there is the danger that the European masses will continue to believe in the Russian myth. As long as they believe it, the idea of a Socialist Europe will not be sufficiently magnetic to call forth the necessary effort.

2. American hostility. If the United States remains capitalist, and especially if it needs markets for exports, it cannot regard a Socialist Europe with a friendly eye. No doubt it is less likely than the USSR to intervene with brute force, but American pressure is an important factor because it can be exerted most easily on Britain, the one country in Europe which is outside the Russian orbit. Since 1940 Britain has kept its feet against the European dictators at the expense of becoming almost a dependency of the USA. Indeed, Britain can only get free of America by dropping the attempt to be an extra-European power. The English-speaking Dominions, the colonial dependencies, except perhaps in Africa, and even Britain's supplies of oil, are all hostages in American hands. Therefore there is always the danger that the United States will break up any European coalition by drawing Britain out of it.

3. Imperialism. The European peoples, and especially the British, have long owed their high standard of life to direct or indirect exploitation of the coloured peoples. This relationship has never been made clear by official Socialist propaganda, and the British worker, instead of being told that, by world standards, he is living above his income, has been taught to think of himself as an overworked, downtrodden slave. To the masses everywhere "Socialism" means, or at least is associated with, higher wages, shorter hours, better houses, all-round social insurance, etc etc. But it is by no means certain that we can afford these things if we throw away the advantages we derive from colonial exploitation. However evenly the national income is divided up, if the income as a whole falls, the working-class standard of living must fall with it. At best there is liable to be a long and uncomfortable reconstruction period for which public opinion has nowhere been prepared. But at the same time the European nations *must* stop being exploiters abroad if they are to build true Socialism at home. The first step toward a European Socialist federation is for the British to get out of India. But this entails something else. If the United States of Europe is to be self-sufficient and able to hold its own against Russia and America, it must include Africa and the

Middle East. But that means that the position of the indigenous peoples in those countries must be changed out of recognition—that Morocco or Nigeria or Abyssinia must cease to be colonies or semi-colonies and become autonomous republics on a complete equality with the European peoples. This entails a vast change of outlook and a bitter, complex struggle which is not likely to be settled without bloodshed. When the pinch comes the forces of imperialism will turn out to be extremely strong, and the British worker, if he has been taught to think of Socialism in materialistic terms, may ultimately decide that it is better to remain an imperial power at the expense of playing second fiddle to America. In varying degrees all the European peoples, at any rate those who are to form part of the proposed union, will be faced with the same choice.

4. The Catholic Church. As the struggle between East and West becomes more naked, there is danger that democratic Socialists and mere reactionaries will be driven into combining in a sort of Popular Front. The Church is the likeliest bridge between them. In any case the Church will make every effort to capture and sterilise any movement aiming at European unity. The dangerous thing about the Church is that it is *not* reactionary in the ordinary sense. It is not tied to *laissez-faire* capitalism or to the existing class system, and will not necessarily perish with them. It is perfectly capable of coming to terms with Socialism, or appearing to do so, provided that its own position is safeguarded. But if it is allowed to survive as a powerful organisation, it will make the establishment of true Socialism impossible, because its influence is and always must be against freedom of thought and speech, against human equality, and against any form of society tending to promote earthly happiness.

When I think of these and other difficulties, when I think of the enormous mental readjustment that would have to be made, the appearance of a Socialist United States of Europe seems to me a very unlikely event. I don't mean that the bulk of the people are not prepared for it, in a passive way. I mean that I see no person or group of persons with the slightest chance of attaining power and at the same time with the imaginative grasp to see what is needed and to demand the necessary sacrifices from their followers. But I also can't at present see any other hopeful objective. At one time I believed that it might be possible to form the British Empire into a federation of Socialist republics, but if that chance ever existed, we lost it by failing to liberate India, and by our attitude toward the coloured peoples generally. It may be that Europe is finished and that in the long run some better form of society will arise in India or China. But I believe that it is only in Europe, if anywhere, that democratic Socialism could be made a reality in short enough time to prevent the dropping of the atom bombs.

Of course, there are reasons, if not for optimism, at least for suspending judgement on certain points. One thing in our favour is that a major war is not likely to happen immediately. We could, I suppose, have the kind of war that consists in shooting rockets, but not a war involving the mobilisation of tens of millions of men. At present any large army would simply melt away, and that may remain true for ten or even twenty years. Within that time some unexpected things might happen. For example, a powerful Socialist movement might for the first time arise in the United States. In England it is now the fashion to talk of the United States as "capitalistic", with the implication that this is something unalterable, a sort of racial characteristic like the colour of eyes or hair. But in fact it cannot be unalterable, since capitalism itself has manifestly no future, and we cannot be sure in advance that the next change in the United States will not be a change for the better.

Then, again, we do not know what changes will take place in the USSR if war can be staved off for the next generation or so. In a society of that type, a radical change of outlook always seems unlikely, not only because there can be no open opposition but because the régime, with its complete hold over education, news, etc deliberately aims at preventing the pendulum swing between generations which seems to occur naturally in liberal societies. But for all we know the tendency of one generation to reject the ideas of the last is an abiding human characteristic which even the NKVD will be unable to eradicate. In that case there may by 1960 be millions of young Russians who are bored by dictatorship and loyalty parades, eager for more freedom, and friendly in their attitude toward the West.

Or again, it is even possible that if the world falls apart into three unconquerable super-states, the liberal tradition will be strong enough within the Anglo-American section of the world to make life tolerable and even offer some hope of progress. But all this is speculation. The actual outlook, so far as I can calculate the probabilities, is very dark, and any serious thought should start out from that fact.

Partisan Review, July–August 1947

89. Letter to George Woodcock

Barnhill,
Isle of Jura
Argyllshire
9 August 1947

Dear George,

I at last get round to answering your letter of 25th July. I am, as you say, in principle prepared to do an article in the series you mention, but "in principle" is about right, because I am busy and don't want to undertake any more work in the near future. I am struggling with this novel which I hope to finish early in 1948. I don't even expect to finish the rough draft before about October, then I must come to London for about a month to see to various things and do one or two articles I have promised, then I shall get down to the rewriting of the book which will probably take me 4 or 5 months. It always takes me a hell of a time to write a book even if I am doing nothing else, and I can't help doing an occasional article, usually for some American magazine, because one must earn some money occasionally.

I think probably I shall come back in November and we shall spend the winter here. I can work here with fewer interruptions, and I think we shall be less cold here. The climate, although wet, is not quite so cold as England, and it is much easier to get fuel. We are saving our coal as much as possible and hope to start the winter with a reserve of 3 tons, and you can get oil by the 40-gallon drum here, whereas last winter in London you had to go down on your knees to get a gallon once a fortnight. There are also wood and peat, which are a fag to collect but help out the coal. Part of the winter may be pretty bleak and one is sometimes cut off from the mainland for a week or two, but it doesn't matter so long as you have flour in hand to make scones. Latterly the weather has been quite incredible, and I am afraid we shall be paying for it soon. Last week we went round in the boat and spent a couple of days on the completely uninhabited Atlantic side of the island in an empty shepherd's hut—no beds, but otherwise quite comfortable. There are beautiful white beaches round that side, and if you do about an hour's climb into the hills you come to lochs which are full of trout but never fished because too unget-atable. This last week of course we've all been breaking our backs helping to get the hay in, including Richard, who likes to roll about in the hay stark naked. If you want to come here any time, of course do, only just give me a week's notice because of meeting. After September the weather gets pretty wild, though I know there are very warm days even in mid-winter.

I got two copies of the FDC[1] bulletin. I am not too happy about following up the Nunn May case, i.e. building him up as a well-meaning man who has been victimised. I think the Home Secretary can make hay of this claim if he wants to. I signed the first petition,[2] not without misgivings, simply because I thought 10 years too stiff a sentence (assuming that *any* prison sentence is ever justified). If I had had to argue the case, I should have pointed out that if he had communicated the information to the USA he would probably have got off with 2 years at most. But the fact is that he was an ordinary spy—I don't mean that he was doing it for money—and went out to Canada as part of a spy ring. I suppose you read the Blue Book on the subject. It also seems to me a weak argument to say that he felt information was being withheld from an ally, because in his position he must have known that the Russians never communicated military information to anybody. However, in so far as the object is simply to get him out of jail somewhat earlier, I am not against it.

Yours
George

90. Letter to Anthony Powell

Barnhill,
Isle of Jura
Argyllshire
8 September 1947

Dear Tony,[3]
Thanks so much for your postcard which I think was rather lucky to get here—at any rate I think the crofter who brings the post the

[1] "The Freedom Defence Committee was founded in 1945 to deal with cases of the infringement of the civil liberties of any citizens of the British Empire, and since its foundation it has intervened successfully in a considerable number of cases, which have been duly reported in its Bulletin. . . ." Letter to *Tribune*, 7 February 1947, signed Herbert Read (Chairman), George Orwell (Vice-Chairman), George Woodcock (Secretary).

[2] Orwell signed the petition on 6 August 1946.

[3] Anthony Powell (1905–   ), the novelist, who had written Orwell a fan letter about *Keep the Aspidistra Flying*; they met in 1941 and remained friends until Orwell's death.

last seven miles might have suppressed it if he had seen it.[1] I am coming down to London about the beginning of November, but probably only for about a month. We are planning to spend the winter here, because I can get on with my work without constantly getting bogged down in journalism, and also I think it will be a bit more comfortable here in spite of the mud and isolation. One is better off for fuel here, and on the whole better off for food. The worst privation really is bread rationing, and the new petrol cut, as we unavoidably have to make a car journey once a week to fetch groceries etc. We have got the house quite comfortable now, except that of course we are still using oil lamps for lighting, and I have got a bit of garden round. We have had incredible weather, indeed a severe drought, with the result that there was no water in the taps for about a fortnight, during which time nobody had a bath. Theoretically one can bathe in the sea, but I find it much too cold at my time of life and have never been in it except once or twice involuntarily. Recently four of us including Richard were all but drowned in the famous whirlpool of Corrievrechan which came into a film called "I Know Where I'm Going". There was a very incorrect account of the disaster in the *Daily Express*. It was very unpleasant while it lasted, and it ended by our being literally wrecked on a desert island where we might have been stranded for a day or two, but very luckily some lobster fishermen saw the fire we lit for a signal and got us off. Richard loved every moment of it except when he was actually in the water. He is getting enormous and talking a good deal more. He had a bad fall earlier in the year and scarred his forehead, but I imagine the scar will disappear after a year or two. I am getting on with my novel and hope to finish it in the spring if I don't do anything else. I know that if I return to London and get caught up in weekly articles I shall never get on with anything longer. One just seems to have a limited capacity for work nowadays and one has to husband it. Mrs Christen[2] says you sent me a book[3]— I think a reprint of some Victorian novels to which you wrote an

[1] The postcard was of the Donald McGill type: "Male Customer: 'Do you keep stationery, miss?' Young Lady Assistant: 'Sometimes I wriggle a little.'" See II, 27.

[2] Mrs Christen, had worked as secretary at Duckworth & Co, the publishers, when Powell was employed there before the war; then at the Oxford University Press in India. She had recently returned to England after spending the war in Japanese-occupied territory. Orwell, while in Jura, lent her his Canonbury flat before she returned temporarily to the Far East.

[3] *Novels of High Society from the Victorian Age*, edited by Anthony Powell.

introduction—but she hasn't sent it on yet. Many thanks any way. I'll ring you up as soon as I return to London. Please give my love to Violet.[1]

Yours
George

91. Letter to Arthur Koestler

Barnhill,
Isle of Jura
Argyllshire
20 September 1947

Dear Arthur,

I think a Ukrainian refugee named Ihor Sevcenko may have written to you—he told me that he had written and that you had not yet answered.

What he wanted to know was whether they could translate some of your stuff into Ukrainian, without payment of course, for distribution among the Ukrainian DPs, who now seem to have printing outfits of their own going in the American Zone and in Belgium. I told him I thought you would be delighted to have your stuff disseminated among Soviet citizens and would not press for payment, which in any case these people could not make. They made a Ukrainian translation of *Animal Farm* which appeared recently, reasonably well printed and got up, and, so far as I could judge by my correspondence with Sevcenko, well translated. I have just heard from them that the American authorities in Munich have seized 1,500 copies of it and handed them over to the Soviet repatriation people, but it appears about 2,000 copies got distributed among the DPs first. If you decide to let them have some of your stuff, I think it is well to treat it as a matter of confidence and not tell too many people this end, as the whole thing is more or less illicit. Sevcenko asked me simultaneously whether he thought Laski[2]

[1] The Lady Violet Powell, Anthony Powell's wife.
[2] Harold J. Laski (1893–1950), political theorist, Marxist, author and journalist. Connected with the London School of Economics from 1920 and Professor of Political Science in the University of London from 1926. Member of the Fabian Executive 1922 and 1936. Member of the Executive Committee of the Labour Party 1936–49.

would agree to let them have some of his stuff (they are apparently trying to get hold of representative samples of western thought). I told him to have nothing to do with Laski and by no means let a person of that type know that illicit printing in Soviet languages is going on in the allied zones, but I told him you were a person to be trusted. I am sure we ought to help these people all we can, and I have been saying ever since 1945 that the DPs were a godsent opportunity for breaking down the wall between Russia and the West. If our government won't see this, one must do what one can privately.

I shall be in London during November but am going to spend the winter up here because I think it will be easier to keep warm (more coal etc) and because I want to get on with the novel I am doing. I hope to finish it about next spring, and I am not doing much else in the meantime. I have been in wretched health a lot of the year—my chest as usual—starting with last winter. But we are quite comfortable here and better off for food than in London. Richard is getting enormous. Love to Mamaine.

Yours
George

92. Letter to Julian Symons

Barnhill,
Isle of Jura
Argyllshire
9 October 1947

Dear Julian,[1]

I'm going to be in London for November, arriving about the 5th I think, and hope we can meet. I'll ring or write nearer the time.

You gave me much too kind a review of that silly little *English People*[2] book in the *M[anchester] E[vening] News*. The only real excuse for it was that I was almost physically bullied into writing

[1] Julian Symons (1912–), poet, novelist, biographer and crime writer; edited *Twentieth Century Verse* 1937-9. He met Orwell during the war and remained friends with him until Orwell's death.

[2] See III, 1.

it by Turner.[1] It was written about the beginning of 1944, but this didn't appear from the text, as last year the proof-reader hurriedly went through it shoving in a remark here and there to show the general election had happened in the mean time.

... We have also been able to make an arrangement by which the derelict croft on which this house stands is to be farmed after all, so I shan't have [a] bad conscience about keeping someone else off cultivable land. Richard is getting enormous and talking a lot more. He has had quite an eventful summer including having measles and cutting an enormous chunk out of his forehead on a broken jug, also being wrecked on a desert island and nearly drowned. The weather on the whole has been marvellous. We had six consecutive weeks without rain, in fact even no water in the taps for a week or two. Later it has rained a good deal, but they got the harvest in with less agony than last year.

Please remember me to your wife.

Yours
Geo. Orwell

93. Letter to Roger Senhouse

Barnhill,
Isle of Jura
Argyllshire
22 October 1947

Dear Roger,

I'm returning the proofs of *Coming Up for Air*.

There are not many corrections. In just one or two cases I've altered something that had been correctly transcribed, including one or two misprints that existed in the original text. I note that on p. 46 the compositor has twice altered "Boars" to "Boers," evidently taking it for a misprint. "Boars" was intentional, however (a lot of people used to pronounce it like that).

What about dates? On the title page it says "1947", but it isn't

[1] W.J. Turner (1889–1946), poet, novelist and music critic who did various publishing and journalistic work. When he asked Orwell to contribute to the series "Britain in Pictures" for Collins he was also literary editor of the *Spectator*.

going to be published in 1947. And should there not somewhere be a mention of the fact that the book was first published in 1939?

Did you know by the way that this book hasn't got a semicolon in it? I had decided about that time that the semicolon is an unnecessary stop and that I would write my next book without one.

I'm coming up to London on November 7th and shall be there for about a month. I have various time-wasting things to do, lectures and so on. I *hope* before I arrive to have finished the rough draft of my novel,[1] which I'm on the last lap of now. But it's a most dreadful mess and about two-thirds of it will have to be rewritten entirely besides the usual touching up. I don't know how long that will take —I hope only 4 to 5 months but it might well be longer. I've been in such wretched health all this year that I never seem to have much spare energy. I wonder if Fred will be back by November. I hope to see you both then.

Yours
George

94. Letter to Anthony Powell

Barnhill,
Isle of Jura,
Argyllshire
23 October 1947

Dear Tony,

Re the Gissing book[2]—I'd love to do it but I'm really afraid I must say no. The thing is I'm not only struggling with this book of mine but shall also be pretty busy while in London. I've got all manner of time-wasting things to do, and in addition I've been landed with another long article which I can't dodge out of. I hope to at any rate break the back of it while in London, but that means not undertaking anything else. I'm sorry—I'd much rather have done the Gissing article.

I'm coming up on the 7th and will ring you up. Winter is setting

[1] *Nineteen Eighty-Four.*

[2] Anthony Powell had asked him to review *A Life's Morning* by George Gissing for the middle page of the *Times Literary Supplement.*

in here, rather dark and gloomy. Already we light the lamps at about half past five. However we've got a lot more coal here than we should have in London, and this house is a lot more weather-proof than my flat, where the water was coming through the roof in twelve places last winter. Please give my love to Violet.

Yours
George

95. Letter to Julian Symons

Barnhill,
Isle of Jura,
Argyllshire
25 October 1947

Dear Julian,

I can't resist taking up a point of pedantry. Kid Lewis[1] *may* have been a welter-weight, but I think he was a light-weight. At any rate he wasn't a heavy or a light-heavy, and I'll tell you how I remember. He fought Carpentier, a sort of grudge battle, Lewis having challenged Carpentier, whom he declared to be overrated. At first Carpentier (a light-heavy-weight) said that he refused to fight someone who was below his own weight. In the end they fought and Lewis was knocked out, his supporters claiming that he had been fouled. This was about 1922. (Perhaps later.)

He was a supporter of Mosley in the New Party,[2] and stood for Whitechapel in the election—I suppose it was 1931—in which the New Party had its fiasco. I think he must have stuck to Mosley a bit longer and after M started calling himself a Fascist, because I remember Boothroyd ("Yaffle" of *Reynolds's*) telling me about an affray at a public meeting, about 1932, in which Lewis was involved. I believe Mosley at the beginning had a regular bodyguard of Jewish

---

[1] Orwell had referred to Kid Lewis's boxing and political career in *The English People* which Symons had reviewed for the *Manchester Evening News*.

[2] Sir Oswald Mosley, Bt (1896–), politician, successively Conservative, Independent and Labour MP. In 1931 he broke away from the Labour Party to form the "New Party". Later he became fanatically pro-Hitler and turned his party into the British Union of Fascists.

Letter to Julian Symons

prize-fighters. Fascism was not then thought of as antisemitic, and
Mosley did not take up antisemitism until about 1933 or 1934.
Look forward to seeing you.

Yours
George

96. Letter to Anthony Powell

Barnhill,
Isle of Jura
Argyllshire
29 November 1947

Dear Tony,
Thanks so much for your letter. I'm still on my back, but I think
really getting better after many relapses. I'd probably be all right by
this time if I could have got to my usual chest specialist, but I dare
not make the journey to the mainland while I have a temperature.
It's really a foul journey in winter even if one flies part of the way.
However I've now arranged for a man to come from Glasgow & give
me the once-over, & then maybe I'll get up to London later, or
perhaps only as far as Glasgow. I think I'll have to go into hospital
for a bit, because apart from treatment there's the X-raying etc, &
after that I might have a stab at going abroad for a couple of months
if I can get a newspaper assignment to somewhere warm. Of course
I've done no work for weeks—have only done the rough draft of my
novel, which I always consider as the half-way mark. I was supposed
to finish it by May—now, God knows when. I'm glad the Aubrey[1]
book is coming along at last. I think in these days besides putting the
date of publication in books one also ought to put the date of writing.
In the spring I'm reprinting a novel which came out in 1939[2] & was
rather killed by the war, so that makes up a little for being late with
my new one.
 Apparently Mrs Christen has just sailed. What I partly wrote about
was this: have you got, or do you know anyone who has got, a saddle

---

[1] *John Aubrey and His Friends* by Anthony Powell.
[2] *Coming Up for Air.*

for sale? Good condition doesn't matter very much so long as it has a sound girth & stirrups. It's for a horse only abt 14 h but on the stout side, so very likely a saddle belonging to a big horse would do. It's the sort of thing someone might have kicking round, & you can't buy them for love or money. The farm pony we have here is ridden for certain errands to save petrol, & it's so tiring riding bareback. I am ready to pay a reasonable price.

Richard is *offensively* well & full of violence. He went through whooping cough without noticing that he had it. My love to everyone. I hope to see you all some day.

Yours
George

97. Letter to Celia Kirwan

Barnhill,
Isle of Jura
Argyllshire
7 December 1947

Dearest Celia,

How nice it was to get your letter. Unfortunately I can't reply at any length, because I'm really very ill. As to your query abt Inez.[1] I haven't actually heard from her, but when I found I couldn't go up to London (because of this illness) I wrote asking her to ring up & inform various friends, which she did, so she's abt, anyway.

I've been in bed 6 weeks, & was feeling unwell some time before that. I kept trying to get just well enough to make the journey to London—finally I brought a chest specialist here. He says I have got to go into a sanatorium, probably for abt 4 months. It's an awful bore, however perhaps it's all for the best if they can cure me. I don't think living in Jura has had a bad effect on my health—in any case the sanatorium I'm going to is near Glasgow, which is the same climate. Actually we've had marvellous weather this year & very dry. Even now I'm looking out on what might be a spring day if the bracken was green.

[1] Inez Holden, author and journalist, a cousin of Celia Kirwan and a friend of Orwell.

Richard is ever so well & getting very solid & heavy. I'll let you
know the address of the sanatorium when I get there, & I'll also try
to write you a better letter, that is if they let you sit up there. I would
love to see you some time—but heaven knows when that will happen.

With much love
George

98. Letter to T.R. Fyvel

Ward 3
Hairmyres Hospital
East Kilbride
Lanarkshire
31 December 1947

Dear Tosco,[1]

Thanks so much for your letter. I'd love it if you did come & see me
some time. Don't put yourself out, of course, but if it was convenient.
They don't seem very lavish with their visiting hours, though. The
official hours are: Sundays, Weds. & Sats., 2.30–3.30 pm Tuesdays
6–7 pm. This is a long way to come. I came by car so I'm not sure
how far out of Glasgow it is, but I think abt 20 minutes drive.

I've only been in the hospital abt 10 days, but I've been deadly sick
for abt 2–3 months & not very well the whole year. Of course I've
had this disease before, but not so seriously. I was very well last year,
& I think this show really started in that beastly cold of last winter.[2]
I was conscious early this year of being seriously ill & thought I'd
probably got TB, but like a fool I decided not to go to a doctor as I
knew I'd be stuck in bed & I wanted to get on with the book I was
writing. All that happened is that I've half written the book, which
in my case is much the same as not starting it. However, they seem
pretty confident they can patch me up, so I might be able to get back
to some serious work some time in 1948. I am going shortly to start a
little book reviewing for the *Observer*. I might as well earn a bit of

[1] T.R. (Tosco) Fyvel (1907–   ), author and journalist, a friend of Orwell and
at this time literary editor of *Tribune*.
[2] The winter of 1946–7 was exceptionally cold and the country's fuel stocks
appallingly low.

money while on my back, & I've felt somewhat better the last week
or so. The treatment is to put the affected lung out of action, which is
supposed to give it a better chance to heal. It is a slow job, I suppose,
but meanwhile it does me good to have proper nursing here. It is a
nice hospital & everyone is very kind to me. The next thing is to
prevent Richard getting this disease, though I must say by his
physique he doesn't look much like it at present. He is developing
into a regular tough & loves working on the farm & messing abt
with machinery. I kept him away from me as best I could after I
knew what was wrong with me, & we are getting a TT cow so as to
feel a bit surer abt his milk. We have been boiling his milk, but of
course one can forget sometimes. Early in the year when my sister
goes up to London for shopping etc I am going to have him X-rayed
just to make sure.

I should think it would be quite nice living at Amersham. It's
beautiful country round there. I remember we went on Home Guard
manoeuvres on Berkhamsted common, & everywhere there were
wild cherry trees weighted down with fruit. That night we were
billeted in a barn, & early in the morning I woke up & was seriously
alarmed to hear a lion roaring. Of course we were near Whipsnade,
which I didn't know.

Please give my love to Mary[1] & all the others. I don't know if it's
much use now worrying abt Palestine or anything else. This stupid
war is coming off in abt 10–20 years, & this country will be blown off
the map whatever else happens. The only hope is to have a home
with a few animals in some place not worth a bomb.

Hoping to see you some time.

Yours
George

Encounter, January 1962

---

[1] Mrs T.R. Fyvel.

1948

99. Letter to Gwen O'Shaughnessy

Ward 3
Hairmyres Hospital
East Kilbride
Nr Glasgow
1 January 1948

Dear Gwen,[1]
I thought you'd like to hear how I was getting on. I believe Mr Dick[2] sent you a line abt my case. As soon as he listened to me he said I had a fairly extensive cavity in the left lung—& also a small patch at the top of the other lung—this, I think, the old one I had before. The X-ray confirms this, he says. I have now been here nearly a fortnight, & the treatment they are giving me is to put the left lung out of action, apparently for abt 6 months, which is supposed to give it a better chance to heal. They first crushed the phrenic nerve, which I gather is what makes the lung expand & contract, & then pumped air into the diaphragm, which I understand is to push the lung into a different position & get it away from some kind of movement which occurs automatically. I have to have "refills" of air in the diaphragm every few days, but I think later it gets down to once a week or less. For the rest, I am still really very ill & weak, & on getting here I found I had lost 1½ stone, but I have felt better since being here, don't sweat at night like I used & have more appetite. They make me eat a tremendous lot. At present I am not allowed out of bed because apparently one has to get adjusted to having the extra air inside. It is a nice hospital & everyone is extremely kind to me. I have also got a room to myself, but I don't know whether that will be permanent. I have of course done no work for 2–3 months, but I think I may be

[1] Dr Gwen O'Shaughnessy, widow of Eileen Blair's brother, Laurence (Eric) O'Shaughnessy.
[2] The specialist at Hairmyres Hospital.

equal to some light work soon & I am arranging to do a little book reviewing.

Richard was tremendously well when I came away. After I was certain what was wrong with me I tried to keep him out of my room, but of course couldn't do so entirely. When Avril[1] goes up to London in Jan or Feb to do some shopping I am going to take the opportunity of having Richard thoroughly examined to make sure he is OK. We boiled his milk ever since you warned us, but of course one can forget sometimes. I am trying to buy a TB-tested cow, & I think we are on the track of one now. With Bill Dunn[2] in the house it is easier abt animals, as he is going to pay part of his board by looking after our cows, which means that at need we can go away. I must say Richard doesn't look very TB, but I would like to be sure. I think they had quite a good Christmas at Barnhill. There were 4 of them including Richard, & there was a nice goose we bought off the Kopps.[3] I was glad to get away before Xmas so as not to be a death's head. I am afraid I didn't write any Xmas letters or anything & it's now a bit late even for New Year wishes. I hope by the summer I shall be well enough to go back to Barnhill for a bit & you & the kids will come again. Maybe there'll be a pony to ride this time—we have got one at present but he is only borrowed. They had a New Year party for the patients here, all the beds dragged into one ward & there were singers & a conjuror. I hope you had a good Christmas. Love to the kids.

Yours
George

[1] Avril Blair, Orwell's younger sister who was acting as his housekeeper and looking after his son.

[2] Bill Dunn, a young Scotsman, invalided out of the army, while working on Jura in 1947 had met Sir Richard Rees and entered into partnership with him to farm Barnhill for Orwell. In 1951 he married Avril Blair.

[3] Georges Kopp had been Commandant of the POUM militia in which Orwell served in the Spanish civil war. They had remained friends and Kopp had married Gwen O'Shaughnessy's sister, Doreen. At this time the Kopps were running a farm at Biggar outside Edinburgh.

100. Letter to Julian Symons

Ward 3
Hairmyres Hospital
East Kilbride
Lanarkshire
2 January 1948

Dear Julian,
Thanks ever so for sending the pen, which as you see I'm using. Of course it'll do just as well as a Biro & I prefer the colour of the ink. My other was just on its last legs & you can't use ink in bed.

I think I'm getting a bit better. I don't feel quite so deathlike & am eating a lot more. They stuff food into me all the time here. I don't know whether my weight is going up, because I'm kept strictly in bed at this stage of the treatment. . . . It's funny you always think Scotland must be cold. The west part isn't colder than England, & the islands I should think decidedly warmer on average, though probably the summer isn't so hot. When I'm well enough to leave hospital I shall have to continue with this air-pumping business, so shall stay either in Glasgow or London for some months & just dodge up to Jura when I can. I have arranged things fairly well there. We, i.e. my sister & I, have the house, & a young chap who lost a foot in the war & is taking up farming lives with us & farms the croft. Another friend of mine[1] acts as a sort of sleeping partner, financing the croft & coming to help at the busy times. So I don't have bad conscience abt living in a farmhouse & keeping someone else off the land, & at the same time can go away whenever I want to as our animals will be looked after in our absence. I'm just going to embark on cows, just one or two, because I'm in terror of Richard getting this disease & the safest thing is to have a TT cow. . . .

Abt book reviewing. I had no thoughts of going back to the M[anchester] E[vening] News. I am merely arranging to do a review once a fortnight for the Observer, & I think I shall try & fix one once a fortnight for someone else, as I'm probably up to doing one article a week now. I think that shows I'm better, as I couldn't have contemplated that a few weeks ago. I can't do any serious work—I never can do in bed, even when I feel well. I can't show you the part-finished novel. I never show them to anybody, because they are just a

[1] Sir Richard Rees, Bt.

mess & don't have much relationship to the final draft. I always say a book doesn't exist until it is finished. I am glad you finished the life of your brother.[1] It is such a ghastly effort ever to finish a book nowadays.

I agree with you abt *Tribune*, though I think it's probably Fyvel rather than Kimche[2] who is responsible for the over-emphasis on Zionism. They would have done better when Labour got in to label themselves frankly a government organ, (a) because in all major matters they *are* in agreement with the government, (b) because Labour has no weekly paper definitely faithful to it & is in fact on the defensive so far as the press goes. The evil genius of the paper has I think been Crossman,[3] who influences it through Foot[4] & Fyvel. Crossman & the rest of that gang thought they saw an opening for themselves in squealing abt foreign policy, which in the circumstances was bound to go badly, & so *Tribune* has been in the position of coming down on the side of the government whenever there is a major issue, e.g. conscription, & at the same time trying to look fearfully Left by raising an outcry about Greece etc. I really think I prefer the Zilliacus lot, since after all they do have a policy, i.e. to appease Russia. I started writing an open letter to *Tribune* abt this, but was taken ill before I finished it.[5] I particularly hate that trick of sucking up to the Left cliques by perpetually attacking America while relying on America to feed & protect us. I even get letters from American university students asking why *Tribune* is always going for the USA, & in such an ignorant way.

Well, this is quite a long letter. So many thanks again for sending the pen. I'll send my old Biro sometime when I've got a bit of paper & perhaps you'd be kind enough to get it refilled. My best respects to your wife.

Yours
George

[1] A.J.A. Symons, a well-known personality of the London literary scene, scholar, bibliophile, author of *The Quest for Corvo*.

[2] Jon Kimche (1909–), author and journalist, editor of *Tribune* 1942–46; editor of the *Jewish Observer* 1952–67.

[3] R.H.S. Crossman (1907–), scholar, intellectual, journalist and left-wing politician. Fellow and tutor of New College, Oxford 1930–7. Assistant editor of the *New Statesman* 1938–55. Labour MP since 1945. Minister of Housing and Local Government 1964–6. President of the Council and Leader of the House since 1966.

[4] Michael Foot, MP.   [5] "In Defence of Comrade Zilliacus".

101. In Defence of Comrade Zilliacus

Some weeks ago Mr K. Zilliacus addressed a long and, as usual, abusive letter to *Tribune*, in which he accused it of having no definite and viable foreign policy, but of being in effect an anti-Russian paper while keeping up a show of hostility to Ernest Bevin. Bevin, he said, was far more realistic than *Tribune*, since he grasped that to oppose Russia it was necessary to rely on America and "bolster up Fascism", while *Tribune* was merely sitting on the fence, uttering contradictory slogans and getting nowhere.

I am not often in agreement with Mr Zilliacus, and it is therefore all the more of a pleasure to record my agreement with him on this occasion. Granting him his own special terminology, I think his accusation is fully justified. One must remember, of course, that in the mouths of Mr Zilliacus and his associates, words like democracy, Fascism or totalitarianism do not bear quite their normal meanings. In general they tend to turn into their opposites, Fascism meaning unfaked elections, democracy meaning minority rule, and so on. But this does not alter the fact that he is dwelling on real issues—issues on which *Tribune* has consistently, over a period of years, failed to make its position clear. He knows that the only big political questions in the world today are: for Russia—against Russia, for America— against America, for democracy—against democracy. And though he may describe his own activities in different words from what most of us would use, at least we can see at a glance where he stands.

But where does *Tribune* stand? I know, or think I know, what foreign policy *Tribune* favours, but I know it by inference and from private contacts. Casual readers can, and to my knowledge do, draw very different impressions. If one had to sum up *Tribune's apparent* policy in a single word, the name one would have to coin for it would be anti-Bevinism. The first rule of this "ism" is that when Bevin says or does something, a way must be found of showing that it is wrong, even if it happens to be what *Tribune* was advocating in the previous week. The second rule is that though Russian policy may be criticised, extenuating circumstances must always be found. The third rule is that when the United States can be insulted, it must be insulted. The effect of framing a policy on these principles is that one cannot even find out what solution *Tribune* offers for the specific problems it most discusses. To take some examples. Is *Tribune* in favour of clearing

out of Greece unconditionally? Does *Tribune* think the USSR should
have the Dardanelles? Is *Tribune* in favour of unrestricted Jewish
immigration into Palestine? Does *Tribune* think Egypt should be
allowed to annex the Sudan? In some cases I know the answers, but
I think it would be very difficult to discover them simply by reading
the paper.

Part of the trouble, I believe, is that after building Bevin up into
Public Enemy Number One, *Tribune* has found out that it is not
genuinely in disagreement with him. Certainly there are real differences over Palestine, Spain and perhaps Greece, but broadly, I
think, he and *Tribune* stand for the same kind of policy. There are, it
is generally agreed, only three possible foreign policies for Great
Britain. One is to do as Mr Zilliacus would have us do, i.e. to become
part of the Russian system, with a government perhaps less servile
than that of Poland or Czechoslovakia, but essentially similar.
Another is to move definitely into the orbit of the United States.
And another is to become part of a federation of western European
Socialist republics, including if possible Africa, and again if possible
(though this is less likely) the British Dominions. *Tribune*, I infer—
for it has never been clearly stated—favours the third policy, and so
I believe does Bevin, that is to say, the Government. But *Tribune* is
not only involved in its personal feud with Bevin; it is also unwilling to face two facts—very unpopular facts at the moment—
which must be faced if one is to discuss a western union seriously.
One is that such a union could hardly succeed without a friendly
America behind it, and the other is that however peaceful its intentions might be, it would be bound to incur Russian hostility. It is
exactly here that *Tribune* has failed as an organ of opinion. All its
other equivocations, I believe, spring from a dread of flouting
fashionable opinion on the subject of Russia and America.

One very noticeable thing in *Tribune* is the pretence that Bevin's
policy is exclusively his own. Apparently he is a sort of runaway
horse dragging an unwilling Cabinet behind him, and our policy
would have been quite different—above all, our relations with the
USSR would have been better—if only we had had a more enlightened Foreign Secretary. Now it is obvious that this cannot be
so. A Minister who is really thwarting the will of the rest of the
government does not stay in office for two years. Why then the
attempt to put all the blame on one person? Was it not because
otherwise it would have been necessary to say a very unpopular thing:

namely, that a Labour government, as such, is almost bound to be on bad terms with the government of the USSR? With a government headed by Pritt and Zilliacus we could no doubt have excellent relations, of a kind, with Russia, and with a government headed by Churchill and Beaverbrook we could probably patch up some kind of arrangement: but any government genuinely representative of the Labour movement *must* be regarded with hostility. From the point of view of the Russians and the Communists, Social Democracy is a deadly enemy, and to do them justice they have frequently admitted it. Even such controversial questions as the formation of a western union are irrelevant here. Even if we had no influence in Europe and made no attempt to interfere there, it would still be to the interest of the Russian Government to bring about the failure of the British Labour Government, if possible. The reason is clear enough. Social Democracy, unlike capitalism, offers an alternative to Communism, and if somewhere or other it can be made to work on a big scale—if it turns out that after all it *is* possible to introduce Socialism without secret police forces, mass deportations and so forth—then the excuse for dictatorship vanishes. With a Labour Government in office, relations with Russia, bad already, were bound to deteriorate. Various observers pointed this out at the time of the General Election, but I do not remember *Tribune* doing so, then or since. Was it not because it was easier, more popular, to encourage the widespread delusion that "a government of the Left can get on better with Russia" and that Communism is much the same thing as Socialism, only more so—and then, when things didn't turn out that way, to register pained surprise and look round for a scapegoat?

And what, I wonder, is behind *Tribune*'s persistent anti-Americanism? In *Tribune* over the past year I can recall three polite references to America (one of those was a reference to Henry Wallace) and a whole string of petty insults. I have just received a letter from some students at an American university. They ask me if I can explain why *Tribune* thinks it necessary to boo at America. What am I to say to these people? I shall tell them what I believe to be the truth—namely that *Tribune*'s anti-Americanism is not sincere but is an attempt to keep in with fashionable opinion. To be anti-American nowadays is to shout with the mob. Of course it is only a minor mob, but it is a vocal one. Although there was probably some growth of ill-feeling as a result of the presence of the American troops, I do not believe the mass of the people in this country are anti-American politically, and certainly they are not so culturally. But politico-literary intellectuals are not usually frightened of mass opinion. What they are frightened of is the prevailing opinion within their own group. At any given moment there is always an orthodoxy, a parrot-cry which must be repeated, and in the more active section of the Left the orthodoxy of the moment is anti-Americanism. I believe part of the reason (I am thinking of some remarks in Mr G.D.H. Cole's last 1,143 page compilation)[1] is the idea that if we can cut our links with the United States we might succeed in staying neutral in the case of Russia and America going to war. How anyone can believe this, after looking at the map and remembering what happened to neutrals in the late war, I do not know. There is also the rather mean consideration that the Americans are *not* really our enemies, that they are unlikely to start dropping atomic bombs on us or even to let us starve to death, and therefore that we can safely take liberties with them if it pays to do so. But at any rate the orthodoxy is there. To speak favourably of America, to recall that the Americans helped us in 1940 when the Russians were supplying the Germans with oil and setting on their Communist Parties to sabotage the war effort, is to be branded as a "reactionary". And I suspect that when *Tribune* joins in the chorus it is more from fear of this label than from genuine conviction.

Surely, if one is going to write about foreign policy at all, there is one question that should be answered plainly. It is: "If you *had* to choose between Russia and America, which would you choose?" It will not do to give the usual quibbling answer, "I refuse to choose." In the end the choice may be forced upon us. We are no longer strong enough to stand alone, and if we fail to bring a western European union into being, we shall be obliged, in the long run, to subordinate our policy to that of one Great Power or the other. And in spite of all the fashionable chatter of the moment, everyone knows in his heart that we should choose America. The great mass of people in this country would, I believe, make this choice almost instinctively. Certainly there is a small minority that would choose the other way. Mr Zilliacus, for instance, is one of them. I think he is wrong, but at least he makes his position clear. I also know perfectly well what *Tribune*'s position is. But has *Tribune* ever made it clear?

How subject we are in this country to the intellectual tyranny of minorities can be seen from the composition of the press. A foreign observer who judged Britain solely by its press would assume that

[1] *The Intelligent Man's Guide to the Post-War World.*

the Conservative Party was out and away the strongest party, with the Liberals second, the Communists third and the Labour Party nowhere. The one genuine mass party has no daily paper that is undisputedly its own, and among the political weeklies it has no reliable supporter. Suppose *Tribune* came out with a plain statement of the principles that are implicit in some of its individual decisions—in its support of conscription, for instance. Would it be going against the main body of Labour Party opinion? I doubt it. But it would be going against the fashionable minority who can make things unpleasant for a political journalist. These people have a regular technique of smears and ridicule—a whole specialised vocabulary designed to show that anyone who will not repeat the accepted catchwords is a rather laughable kind of lunatic. Mr Zilliacus, for instance, accuses *Tribune* of being "rabidly anti-Russian" (or "rabidly anti-Communist"—it was one or the other). The key-word here is rabid. Other words used in this context are insensate, demented, "sick with hatred" (the *New Republic*'s phrase) and maniacal. The upshot is that if from time to time you express a mild distaste for slave-labour camps or one-candidate elections, you are either insane or actuated by the worst motives. In the same way, when Henry Wallace is asked by a newspaper interviewer why he issues falsified versions of his speeches to the press, he replies: "So you are one of these people who are clamouring for war with Russia?" It doesn't answer the question, but it would frighten most people into silence. Or there is the milder kind of ridicule that consists in pretending that a reasoned opinion is indistinguishable from an absurd out-of-date prejudice. If you do not like Communism you are a Red-baiter, a believer in Bolshevik atrocities, the nationalisation of women, Moscow Gold, and so on. Similarly, when Catholicism was almost as fashionable among the English intelligentsia as Communism is now, anyone who said that the Catholic Church was a sinister organisation and no friend to democracy was promptly accused of swallowing the worst follies of the No-Popery organisations, of looking under his bed lest Jesuits should be concealed there, of believing stories about babies' skeletons dug up from the floors of nunneries, and all the rest of it. But a few people stuck to their opinion, and I think it is safe to say that the Catholic Church is less fashionable now than it was then.

After all, what does it matter to be laughed at? The big public, in any case, usually doesn't see the joke, and if you state your principles clearly and stick to them, it is wonderful how people come round to you in the end. There is no doubt about whom *Tribune* is frightened of. It is frightened of the Communists, the fellow-travellers and the fellow-travellers of fellow-travellers. Hence its endless equivocations: a paragraph of protest when this one of our friends is shot—silence when that one is shot, denunciation of this faked election—qualified approval of that one, and so on. The result is that in American papers I have more than once seen the phrase "the Foot[1]-Zilliacus group" (or words to that effect). Of course Foot and Zilliacus are not allies, but they can appear so from the outside. Meanwhile, does this kind of thing even conciliate the people it is aimed at? Does it conciliate Mr Zilliacus, for instance? He has been treated with remarkable tenderness by *Tribune*. He has been allowed to infest its correspondence columns like a perennial weed, and when a little while ago *Tribune* reviewed a book of his, I looked in vain in that review[2] for any plain statement of what he is or whose interests he is serving. Instead there was only a mild disagreement, a suggestion that he was perhaps a little over-zealous, a little given to special pleading—all this balanced by praise wherever possible, and headed by the friendly title, "The Fighting Propagandist". But is Mr Zilliacus grateful? On the contrary, only a few weeks later he turns round and without any provocation delivers a good hard boot on the shins.

It is hard to blame him, since he knows very well that *Tribune* is not on his side and does not really like him. But whereas he is willing to make this clear, *Tribune*, in spite of occasional side-thrusts, is not. I do not claim for Mr Zilliacus that he is honest, but at least he is sincere. We know where he stands, and he prefers to hit his enemies rather than his friends. Of course it is true that he is saying what is safe and fashionable at this moment, but I imagine he would stick to his opinions if the tide turned.

Written [October 1947–January? 1948]

---

[1] Michael Foot, MP.
[2] By T.R. Fyvel of *Mirror of the Present* by Konni Zilliacus, *Tribune*, 6 June 1947.

102. Letter to George Woodcock

Ward 3
Hairmyres Hospital
East Kilbride
Lanarkshire
4 January 1948

Dear George,
I'd been meaning to write for some time to explain I wouldn't be coming down to London after all. As I feared, I am seriously ill, TB in the left lung. . . .

I hope the FDC is doing something abt these constant demands to outlaw Mosley & Co. *Tribune*'s attitude I think has been shameful, & when the other week Zilliacus wrote in demanding what amounts to Fascist legislation & creation of 2nd-class citizens, nobody seems to have replied. The whole thing is simply a thinly-disguised desire to persecute someone who can't hit back, as obviously the Mosley lot don't matter a damn & can't get a real mass following. I think it's a case for a pamphlet, & I only wish I felt well enough to write one. The central thing one has [to] come to terms with is the argument, always advanced by those advocating repressive legislation, that "you cannot allow democracy to be used to overthrow democracy— you cannot allow freedom to those who merely use it in order to destroy freedom." This of course is true, & both Fascists & Communists do aim at making use of democracy in order to destroy it. But if you carry this to its conclusion, there can be no case for allowing any political or intellectual freedom whatever. Evidently therefore it is a matter of distinguishing between a real & a merely theoretical threat to democracy, & no one should be persecuted for expressing his opinions, however antisocial, & no political organisation suppressed, unless it can be shown that there is *a substantial threat to the stability of the state*. That is the main point I should make any way. Of course there are many others.
. . . All the best to Inge.

Yours
George

103. Letter to Celia Kirwan

Ward 3
Hairmyres Hospital
East Kilbride
Lanarkshire
20 January 1948

Dearest Celia,

How delightful to get your nice long letter. I've been here abt a month after being ill for abt two months at home. I thought I'd told you what was wrong with me. It is TB, which of course was bound to get me sooner or later, in fact I've had it before, though not so badly. However I don't think it is very serious, & I seem to be getting better slowly. I don't feel so death-like as I did a month ago, & I now eat quite a lot & have started to gain weight slowly, after losing nearly 2 stone. Today when I was X-rayed the doctor said he could see definite improvement. But I'm likely to be here a long time, as it's a slow treatment, & I don't think I shall even be fit to get out of bed for about 2 months. . . . This is the second Christmas I've spent in hospital. It's always rather harrowing, with the "parties" they have—all the beds dragged into one ward, & then a concert & a Christmas tree. This is a very nice hospital & everyone is most kind to me, & I have a room to myself. I'm starting to attempt a very little work, i.e. an occasional book review, after doing nothing for 3 months.

Yes, I remember the Deux Magots. I think I saw James Joyce there in 1928, but I've never quite been able to swear to that because J was not of very distinctive appearance. I also went there to meet Camus who was supposed to have lunch with me, but he was ill & didn't come. I suppose Paris has cheered up a bit since I was there at the beginning of 1945. It was too gloomy for words then, & of course it was almost impossible to get anything to eat & drink, & everybody was so shabby & pale. But I can't believe it is what it used to be. It's lucky for you you're too young to have seen it in the 'twenties, it always seemed a bit ghostlike after that, even before the war. I don't know when I'll see France again, as at present one can't travel because of this currency business, but if one of my books *did* strike it lucky I'd get them to keep some of the francs in France so that I could go & spend them. If I'm cured & abt by then, as I assume I shall be, I am going to try & wangle a correspondent's job this winter so as to winter in a warm place. The winter of 1946–7 in

London was really a bit too thick, & I think it was probably what started me on this show. In Jura it's a bit better, because it isn't quite so cold & we get more coal, also more food, but it's a bit awkward if one needs medical attention at a time when one can't get to the mainland. Early last year my sister dislocated her arm & was nearly drowned going across to the doctor in a tiny motor boat. Inez exaggerated our later adventure a bit, but we did have a very nasty accident in the famous whirlpool of Corrievrechan (which comes into a film called "I Know Where I'm Going") & were lucky not to be drowned. The awful thing was having Richard with us, however he loved every moment of it except when we were in the water. I think Jura is doing him good except that he doesn't see enough of other children & therefore is still very backward in talking. Otherwise he is most enterprising & full of energy, & is out working on the farm all day long. It's nice to be able to let him roam abt with no traffic to be afraid of. Write again if you get time. I love getting letters.

With much love
George

104. Letter to Anthony Powell

Ward 3
Hairmyres Hosp
East Kilbride
Lanarkshire
25 January 1948

Dear Tony,
Thanks so much for your letter. It doesn't matter abt the saddle. We're supposed to have one coming, but if you do chance to run across another I'll always buy it because it wouldn't hurt to have two. The petrol situation is so calamitous that one has to use horses for certain purposes, & also the chap who lives with us & farms the croft lost a foot in Italy & it's easier for him to round up cattle etc on horseback. No, I don't think one could use a side saddle. It would be like shooting a fox sitting or something. I must say in the days when I used to ride I sometimes secretly thought I'd like to try a side saddle, because I believe it's almost impossible to fall off. . . .

All the best to Violet. I hope to see you within a few months anyway.

Yours
George

105. Letter to F. J. Warburg

Ward 3
Hairmyres Hospital
East Kilbride
Lanarkshire
4 February 1948

Dear Fred,

Thanks so much for your letter. As you inferred, my beginning to do articles in the *Observer* is a sign of partial revival, though even that is an effort, especially as I now have my right arm in plaster. I can't attempt any serious work while I am like this ($1\frac{1}{2}$ stone under weight) but I like to do a little to keep my hand in and incidentally earn some money. I've been definitely ill since abt October, and really, I think, since the beginning of 1947. I believe that frightful winter in London started it off. I didn't really feel well all last year except during that hot period in the summer. Before taking to my bed I had finished the rough draft of my novel all save the last few hundred words, and if I had been well I might have finished it by abt May. If I'm well and out of here by June, I might finish it by the end of the year—I don't know. It is just a ghastly mess as it stands, but the idea is so good that I could not possibly abandon it. If anything should happen to me I've instructed Richard Rees, my literary executor, to destroy the MS without showing it to anybody, but it's unlikely that anything like that would happen. This disease isn't dangerous at my age, and they say the cure is going on quite well, though slowly. . . . We are now sending for some new American drug called streptomycin which they say will speed up the cure.

Richard is getting enormous and is very forward in everything except talking. . . . It's sad that I can't see him again till I'm non-infectious. Please remember me to Pamela and Roger.

Yours
George

106. Letter to John Middleton Murry

Ward 3
Hairmyres Hospital
East Kilbride
Lanarkshire
5 March 1948

Dear Murry,[1]

Thanks very much for the book,[2] which I read with interest. I agree with your general thesis, but I think that in assessing the world situation it is very rash to assume that the rest of the world would combine against Russia. We have a fearful handicap in the attitude towards us of the coloured races, & the under-privileged peoples generally (e.g. in S. America), which we possibly don't deserve any longer but which we have inherited from our imperial past. I also think it is rash to assume that most orientals, or indeed any, except a few westernised ones, would prefer democracy to totalitarianism. It seems to me that the great difficulty of our position is that in the coming show-down we must have the peoples of Africa & the Middle East—if possible of Asia too, of course—on our side, & they will all look towards Russia unless there is a radical change of attitude, especially in the USA. I doubt whether we can put things right in Africa, at least in some parts of it, without quite definitely siding with the blacks against the whites. The latter will then look to the USA for support, & they will get it. It can easily turn out that we & America are alone, with all the coloured peoples siding with Russia. Perhaps even then we could win a war against Russia, but only by laying the world in ruins, especially this country.

I'm sorry to hear abt your illness. My own seems to be getting better rapidly. They can't say yet whether the streptomycin is doing its stuff, but I certainly have been a lot better the last week or so. . . .

Please remember me to your wife.

Yours sincerely
Geo. Orwell

[1] John Middleton Murry (1889–1957), prolific writer, critic and polemicist. He founded the *Adelphi* in 1923 and controlled it for the next twenty-five years, and was successively a fervent disciple of D.H. Lawrence, unorthodox Marxist, unorthodox Christian, pacifist and "back to the land" farmer. From July 1940 to April 1946 he was editor of *Peace News*.

[2] Murry's *The Free Society*.

107. Letter to Julian Symons

Ward 3
Hairmyres Hospital
East Kilbride
Lanarkshire
21 March 1948

Dear Julian,

I've at last found a box to put this pen in, so I'd be much obliged if you could get me a refill. No hurry, of course. Herewith also postal order for 3/6 which I found among my papers. I forget what the refills cost.

I thought you'd like to hear that I am getting a lot better. I have been having the streptomycin for abt a month, & evidently it is doing its stuff. I haven't gained much weight, but I am much better in every other way, & longing to get up, which of course they won't let me do for ages yet. I can really only do light work still, i.e. book reviews. I did write two longer articles, but I find my fingers are all thumbs as soon as I attempt anything serious. However, the doctor is very pleased with the way I am going on & says I should be up & abt by the summer. I may have to continue with periodical treatment for some months after that, but in that case I shall get a room in Glasgow & run up to Jura or down to London between treatments. Apparently even after they have killed off the germs they often keep the lung collapsed until they consider it is healed.

Richard is very well, &, so far as I can judge from photographs, growing rapidly. I can't see him till I am non-infectious, which is rather annoying. Various people have been to see me, including Fred Warburg who brought a blank of my uniform edition which we are starting this year. I was rather dismayed to find he had chosen a light green cover, but maybe he'll be able to get hold of some darker stuff. I think a uniform edition should always be very chaste-looking & preferably dark blue. I read your article on George Eliot in the *Windmill*[1] with interest, but I must say I've never been able to read G.E herself. No doubt I'll get round to it someday. Recently I read one or two of the minor novels of Charlotte Brontë which I hadn't read before—was astounded by how sexy they were. I've just read

[1] The *Windmill*, a literary magazine published by William Heinemann Ltd. From 1944–8 twelve issues appeared irregularly.

Mauriac's *Thérèse*, not so good as *A Woman of the Pharisees*, I thought, but it started me thinking abt Catholic novelists, & after reading Heppenstall's article in *P[artisan] R[eview]* I am trying to get hold of Léon Bloy whom I have never read. The *Politics & Letters*[1] people sent me a copy of their magazine & I wrote a piece[2] for the "Critic & Leviathan" series, though, as I say, I really can't write long articles now. I was quite well impressed by the magazine, which I hadn't seen before, & maybe it will develop into the sort of thing we need so badly. The trouble always is that you must have an angel or you can't keep the magazine alive. *Politics* is evidently already tottering—it's become a quarterly which is usually a very bad symptom. Dwight Macdonald sent me a copy of a little book on Wallace which he has just published—very good, & I am urging Gollancz to publish it over here. I am afraid W may well cause "our" man to lose the election, & then Lord knows what may happen. However, whichever way one looks the news is really too depressing to talk about.

Write, if you get time, & please remember me to your wife. I do hope I'll be abt in the summer & will be able to see everybody again.

Yours
George

108. Writers and Leviathan

The position of the writer in an age of State control is a subject that has already been fairly largely discussed, although most of the evidence that might be relevant is not yet available. In this place I do not want to express an opinion either for or against State patronage of the arts, but merely to point out that *what kind* of State rules over us must depend partly on the prevailing intellectual atmosphere: meaning, in this context, partly on the attitude of writers and artists themselves, and on their willingness or otherwise to keep the spirit of liberalism alive. If we find ourselves in ten years' time cringing before

---

[1] *Politics and Letters* was a short-lived Cambridge magazine edited by Raymond Williams, C.S. Collins and Wolf Mankowitz.
[2] "Writers and Leviathan".

somebody like Zhdanov, it will probably be because that is what we have deserved. Obviously there are strong tendencies towards totalitarianism at work within the English literary intelligentsia already. But here I am not concerned with any organised and conscious movement such as Communism, but merely with the effect, on people of goodwill, of political thinking and the need to take sides politically.

This is a political age. War, Fascism, concentration camps, rubber truncheons, atomic bombs, etc are what we daily think about, and therefore to a great extent what we write about, even when we do not name them openly. We cannot help this. When you are on a sinking ship, your thoughts will be about sinking ships. But not only is our subject-matter narrowed, but our whole attitude towards literature is coloured by loyalties which we at least intermittently realise to be non-literary. I often have the feeling that even at the best of times literary criticism is fraudulent, since in the absence of any accepted standards whatever—any *external* reference which can give meaning to the statement that such and such a book is "good" or "bad"— every literary judgement consists in trumping up a set of rules to justify an instinctive preference. One's real reaction to a book, when one has a reaction at all, is usually "I like this book" or "I don't like it", and what follows is a rationalisation. But "I like this book" is not, I think, a non-literary reaction; the non-literary reaction is "This book is on my side, and therefore I must discover merits in it". Of course, when one praises a book for political reasons one may be emotionally sincere, in the sense that one does feel strong approval of it, but also it often happens that party solidarity demands a plain lie. Anyone used to reviewing books for political periodicals is well aware of this. In general, if you are writing for a paper that you are in agreement with, you sin by commission, and if for a paper of the opposite stamp, by omission. At any rate, innumerable controversial books—books for or against Soviet Russia, for or against Zionism, for or against the Catholic Church, etc—are judged before they are read, and in effect before they are written. One knows in advance what reception they will get in what papers. And yet, with a dishonesty that sometimes is not even quarter-conscious, the pretence is kept up that genuinely literary standards are being applied.

Of course, the invasion of literature by politics was bound to happen. It must have happened, even if the special problem of totalitarianism had never arisen, because we have developed a sort of compunction which our grandparents did not have, an awareness of the enormous injustice and misery of the world, and a guilt-stricken feeling that one ought to be doing something about it, which makes a purely aesthetic attitude towards life impossible. No one, now, could devote himself to literature as single-mindedly as Joyce or Henry James. But unfortunately, to accept political responsibility now means yielding oneself over to orthodoxies and "party lines", with all the timidity and dishonesty that that implies. As against the Victorian writers, we have the disadvantage of living among clear-cut political ideologies and of usually knowing at a glance what thoughts are heretical. A modern literary intellectual lives and writes in constant dread—not, indeed, of public opinion in the wider sense, but of public opinion within his own group. As a rule, luckily, there is more than one group, but also at any given moment there is a dominant orthodoxy, to offend against which needs a thick skin and sometimes means cutting one's income in half for years on end. Obviously, for about fifteen years past, the dominant orthodoxy, especially among the young, has been "left". The key words are "progressive", "democratic" and "revolutionary", while the labels which you must at all costs avoid having gummed upon you are "bourgeois", "reactionary" and "Fascist". Almost everyone nowadays, even the majority of Catholics and Conservatives, is "progressive", or at least wishes to be thought so. No one, so far as I know, ever describes himself as a "bourgeois", just as no one literate enough to have heard the word ever admits to being guilty of antisemitism. We are all of us good democrats, anti-Fascist, anti-imperialist, contemptuous of class distinctions, impervious to colour prejudice, and so on and so forth. Nor is there much doubt that the present-day "left" orthodoxy is better than the rather snobbish, pietistic Conservative orthodoxy which prevailed twenty years ago, when the *Criterion* and (on a lower level) the *London Mercury* were the dominant literary magazines. For at the least its implied objective is a viable form of society which large numbers of people actually want. But it also has its own falsities which, because they cannot be admitted, make it impossible for certain questions to be seriously discussed.

The whole left-wing ideology, scientific and Utopian, was evolved by people who had no immediate prospect of attaining power. It was, therefore, an extremist ideology, utterly contemptuous of kings, governments, laws, prisons, police forces, armies, flags, frontiers, patriotism, religion, conventional morality, and, in fact, the whole

existing scheme of things. Until well within living memory the forces
of the Left in all countries were fighting against a tyranny which
appeared to be invincible, and it was easy to assume that if only *that*
particular tyranny—capitalism—could be overthrown, Socialism
would follow. Moreover, the Left had inherited from Liberalism
certain distinctly questionable beliefs, such as the belief that the truth
will prevail and persecution defeats itself, or that man is naturally
good and is only corrupted by his environment. This perfectionist
ideology has persisted in nearly all of us, and it is in the name of it
that we protest when (for instance) a Labour government votes huge
incomes to the King's daughters or shows hesitation about nation-
alising steel. But we have also accumulated in our minds a whole
series of unadmitted contradictions, as a result of successive bumps
against reality.

The first big bump was the Russian Revolution. For somewhat
complex reasons, nearly the whole of the English Left has been driven
to accept the Russian régime as "Socialist", while silently recognising
that its spirit and practice are quite alien to anything that is meant by
"Socialism" in this country. Hence there has arisen a sort of schizophrenic manner of thinking, in which words like "democracy" can
bear two irreconcilable meanings, and such things as concentration
camps and mass deportations can be right and wrong simultaneously.
The next blow to the left-wing ideology was the rise of Fascism,
which shook the pacifism and internationalism of the Left without
bringing about a definite restatement of doctrine. The experience of
German occupation taught the European peoples something that the
colonial peoples knew already, namely, that class antagonisms are
not all-important and that there is such a thing as national interest.
After Hitler it was difficult to maintain seriously that "the enemy is
in your own country" and that national independence is of no value.
But though we all know this and act upon it when necessary, we still
feel that to say it aloud would be a kind of treachery. And finally, the
greatest difficulty of all, there is the fact that the Left is now in power
and is obliged to take responsibility and make genuine decisions.

Left governments almost invariably disappoint their supporters
because, even when the prosperity which they have promised is
achievable, there is always need of an uncomfortable transition
period about which little has been said beforehand. At this moment
we see our own Government, in its desperate economic straits, fighting in effect against its own past propaganda. The crisis that we are

now in is not a sudden unexpected calamity, like an earthquake, and it was not caused by the war, but merely hastened by it. Decades ago it could be foreseen that something of this kind was going to happen. Ever since the nineteenth century our national income, dependent partly on interest from foreign investments, and on assured markets and cheap raw materials in colonial countries, had been extremely precarious. It was certain that, sooner or later, something would go wrong and we should be forced to make our exports balance our imports: and when that happened the British standard of living, including the working-class standard, was bound to fall, at least temporarily. Yet the left-wing parties, even when they were vociferously anti-imperialist, never made these facts clear. On occasion they were ready to admit that the British workers had benefited, to some extent, by the looting of Asia and Africa, but they always allowed it to appear that we could give up our loot and yet in some way contrive to remain prosperous. Quite largely, indeed, the workers were won over to Socialism by being told that they were exploited, whereas the brute truth was that, in world terms, they were exploiters. Now, to all appearances, the point has been reached when the working-class living-standard *cannot* be maintained, let alone raised. Even if we squeeze the rich out of existence, the mass of the people must either consume less or produce more. Or am I exaggerating the mess we are in? I may be, and I should be glad to find myself mistaken. But the point I wish to make is that this question, among people who are faithful to the Left ideology, cannot be genuinely discussed. The lowering of wages and raising of working hours are felt to be inherently anti-Socialist measures, and must therefore be dismissed in advance, whatever the economic situation may be. To suggest that they may be unavoidable is merely to risk being plastered with those labels that we are all terrified of. It is far safer to evade the issue and pretend that we can put everything right by redistributing the existing national income.

To accept an orthodoxy is always to inherit unresolved contradictions. Take for instance the fact that all sensitive people are revolted by industrialism and its products, and yet are aware that the conquest of poverty and the emancipation of the working class demand not less industrialisation, but more and more. Or take the fact that certain jobs are absolutely necessary and yet are never done except under some kind of coercion. Or take the fact that it is impossible to have a positive foreign policy without having powerful armed forces. One

could multiply examples. In every such case there is a conclusion
which is perfectly plain but which can only be drawn if one is
privately disloyal to the official ideology. The normal response is to
push the question, unanswered, into a corner of one's mind, and then
continue repeating contradictory catchwords. One does not have to
search far through the reviews and magazines to discover the effects
of this kind of thinking.

I am not, of course, suggesting that mental dishonesty is peculiar to
Socialists and left-wingers generally, or is commonest among them. It
is merely that acceptance of *any* political discipline seems to be
incompatible with literary integrity. This applies equally to movements like Pacifism and Personalism, which claim to be outside the
ordinary political struggle. Indeed, the mere sound of words ending
in -ism seems to bring with it the smell of propaganda. Group
loyalties are necessary, and yet they are poisonous to literature, so
long as literature is the product of individuals. As soon as they are
allowed to have any influence, even a negative one, on creative
writing, the result is not only falsification, but often the actual drying-
up of the inventive faculties.

Well, then what? Do we have to conclude that it is the duty of
every writer to "keep out of politics"? Certainly not! In any case, as
I have said already, no thinking person can or does genuinely keep
out of politics, in an age like the present one. I only suggest that we
should draw a sharper distinction than we do at present between our
political and our literary loyalties, and should recognise that a
willingness to *do* certain distasteful but necessary things does not
carry with it any obligation to swallow the beliefs that usually go
with them. When a writer engages in politics he should do so as a
citizen, as a human being, but not *as a writer*. I do not think that he
has the right, merely on the score of his sensibilities, to shirk the
ordinary dirty work of politics. Just as much as anyone else, he
should be prepared to deliver lectures in draughty halls, to chalk
pavements, to canvass voters, to distribute leaflets, even to fight in
civil wars if it seems necessary. But whatever else he does in the
service of his party, he should never write for it. He should make it
clear that his writing is a thing apart. And he should be able to act
co-operatively while, if he chooses, completely rejecting the official
ideology. He should never turn back from a train of thought because
it may lead to a heresy, and he should not mind very much if his
unorthodoxy is smelt out, as it probably will be. Perhaps it is even a

bad sign in a writer if he is not suspected of reactionary tendencies today, just as it was a bad sign if he was not suspected of Communist sympathies twenty years ago.

But does all this mean that a writer should not only refuse to be dictated to by political bosses, but also that he should refrain from writing *about* politics? Once again, certainly not! There is no reason why he should not write in the most crudely political way, if he wishes to. Only he should do so as an individual, an outsider, at the most an unwelcome guerrilla on the flank of a regular army. This attitude is quite compatible with ordinary political usefulness. It is reasonable, for example, to be willing to fight in a war because one thinks the war ought to be won, and at the same time to refuse to write war propaganda. Sometimes, if a writer is honest, his writings and his political activities may actually contradict one another. There are occasions when that is plainly undesirable: but then the remedy is not to falsify one's impulses, but to remain silent.

To suggest that a creative writer, in a time of conflict, must split his life into two compartments, may seem defeatist or frivolous: yet in practice I do not see what else he can do. To lock yourself up in an ivory tower is impossible and undesirable. To yield subjectively, not merely to a party machine, but even to a group ideology, is to destroy yourself as a writer. We feel this dilemma to be a painful one, because we see the need of engaging in politics while also seeing what a dirty, degrading business it is. And most of us still have a lingering belief that every choice, even every political choice, is between good and evil, and that if a thing is necessary it is also right. We should, I think, get rid of this belief, which belongs to the nursery. In politics one can never do more than decide which of two evils is the lesser, and there are some situations from which one can only escape by acting like a devil or a lunatic. War, for example, may be necessary, but it is certainly not right or sane. Even a General Election is not exactly a pleasant or edifying spectacle. If you have to take part in such things —and I think you do have to, unless you are armoured by old age or stupidity or hypocrisy—then you also have to keep part of yourself inviolate. For most people the problem does not arise in the same form, because their lives are split already. They are truly alive only in their leisure hours, and there is no emotional connection between their work and their political activities. Nor are they generally asked, in the name of political loyalty, to debase themselves as workers. The artist, and especially the writer, is asked just that—in fact, it is the only thing that politicians ever ask of him. If he refuses, that does not mean that he is condemned to inactivity. One half of him, which in a sense is the whole of him, can act as resolutely, even as violently if need be, as anyone else. But his writings, in so far as they have any value, will always be the product of the saner self that stands aside, records the things that are done and admits their necessity, but refuses to be deceived as to their true nature.

Written [March] 1948; *Politics and Letters*, Summer 1948; *New Leader* (New York), 19 June 1948; SJ; EYE; CE

109. Letter to George Woodcock

Ward 3
Hairmyres Hospital
East Kilbride
Lanarkshire
23 March 1948

Dear George,

Thanks so much for the 3 pamphlets, & for your own poems.[1] I intend to write to you at greater length abt the latter, but first, two points.

1. There's a slip in your introduction to Tolstoy's pamphlet. He didn't die in 1901. I *think* he died in 1912—any way he was over 80, & I imagine he wrote a good many pamphlets after this one.

2. Is the Freedom Defence Committee taking up any position abt this ban on Communists & Fascists? (It's only important at this moment in relation to Communists, & is aimed only at them.) It's not easy to have a clear position, because, if one admits the right of governments to govern, one must admit their right to choose suitable agents, & I think *any* organisation, e.g. a political party, has a right to protect itself against infiltration methods. But at the same time, the *way* in which the Government seems to be going to work is

---

[1] The three pamphlets were the first, and only, publications in a series "The Porcupine Pamphlets", edited by George Woodcock for the Porcupine Press: *The Soul of Man under Socialism* by Oscar Wilde, *The Slavery of Our Times* by Leo Tolstoy and *A Defence of Poetry and a Letter to Lord Ellenborough* by Percy Bysshe Shelley. Orwell reviewed *The Soul of Man under Socialism* in the *Observer*, 9 May 1948 (see 118). The poems for which Orwell also thanks Woodcock were his book of poems, *Imagine the South*, 1947.

vaguely disquieting, & the whole phenomenon seems to me part of the general breakdown of the democratic outlook. Only a week or two ago the Communists themselves were shouting for unconstitutional methods to be used against Fascists, now the same methods are to be used against themselves, & in another year or two a pro-Communist government might be using them against us. Meanwhile the general apathy abt freedom of speech etc constantly grows, & that matters much more than what may be in the statute books. It seems to me a case for a pamphlet—but, at any rate, the FDC ought to declare its attitude, I think.

More later. I hope the Canada business comes off. It would be an interesting change. I believe there's incredible fishing in Canada, if you care abt that.

Yours
George

110. Letter to Julian Symons

Ward 3
Hairmyres Hospital
East Kilbride
Lanark
20 April 1948

Dear Julian,

Thanks so much for sending the pen, & prospectively for some chocolate you mentioned. I am so glad to hear you are going to have a baby. They're awful fun in spite of the nuisance, & as they develop one has one's own childhood over again. I suppose one thing one has to guard against is imposing one's own childhood on the child, but I do think it is relatively easy to give a child a decent time nowadays & allow it to escape the quite unnecessary torments that I for instance went through. I'm not sure either that one ought to trouble too much abt bringing a child into a world of atomic bombs, because those born now will never have known anything except wars, rationing etc and can probably be quite happy against that background if they've had a good psychological start.

I am a lot better, but I had a bad fortnight with the secondary effects of the streptomycin. I suppose with all these drugs it's rather a

case of sinking the ship to get rid of the rats. However they've
stopped the strepto now & evidently it has done its stuff. I am still
fearfully weak & thin, but they seem pleased with my case & I think
I may get out some time during the summer. If I do, I imagine I shall
have to stay in Glasgow, or at any rate somewhere near, so as to
come in abt once a fortnight & be examined & "refilled" (with air).
No doubt I shall be able between times to get down to London & up
to Jura, though they tell me I shall have to travel as little as possible,
& in any case to take things easy for abt a year. It's better to keep on
with the treatment at this hospital, as it's a very good hospital &
they know my case. I am longing to get up to Jura at any rate for a
few days, to see Richard & see how the farm work is going, but I
should have to be careful not to do much. I'm afraid that even when
completely cured I shall be not much good physically for the rest of
my life—I never was strong or athletic, but I don't like an altogether
sedentary life, & I shall have to readjust my habits so that I can get
abt without making too much muscular effort, no more digging or
chopping wood, for instance.

It's funny you should have mentioned Gissing. I am a great fan of
his (though I've never read *Born in Exile*, which some say is his
masterpiece, because I can't get hold of a copy), & was just in the act
of rereading two reprints, which I promised to review for *Politics &
Letters*. I think I shall do a long article on him, for them or someone
else.[1] I think *The Odd Women* is one of the best novels in English.
You asked abt my uniform edition. They're starting with a novel
called *Coming Up for Air*, which was published in 1939 & rather
killed by the war, & doing *Burmese Days* later in the year. I just
corrected the proofs of the latter, which I wrote more than 15 years
ago & probably hadn't looked at for 10 years. It was a queer experience—almost like reading a book by somebody else. I'm also going
to try & get Harcourt Brace to reprint these two books in the USA,
but even if they do so they'll probably only take "sheets", which
never does one much good. It's funny what BFs American publishers
are abt reprints. Harcourt Brace have been nagging me for 2 years
for a manuscript, any kind of manuscript, & are now havering with
the idea of doing a series of reprints, but when I urged them to reprint
Burmese Days immediately after they had cleaned up on *Animal
Farm*, they wouldn't do so. Nor would the original publishers of
BD, though they too were trying to get something out of me.

[1] See 119.

Apparently reprints in the USA are done mostly by special firms which only take them on if they are safe for an enormous sale.

Yes, I thought the last number of *Politics* quite good, but I must say that in spite of all their elegies I retain dark suspicions about Gandhi, based only on gossip, but such a lot of gossip that I think there must be something in it.

Please remember me to your wife.

Yours
George

111. Letter to Gleb Struve

Ward 3
Hairmyres Hospital
East Kilbride
Lanarkshire (Scotland)
21 April 1948

Dear Struve,[1]

I'm awfully sorry to have to send this[2] back, after such a long delay, having finally failed to find a home for it. But as you see by the above, I am in hospital (tuberculosis), & at the time of receiving your letter I wasn't able to do very much. I am better now, & hope to get out of here some time during the summer, but of course the treatment of this disease is always a slow job.

I have arranged to review *We*[3] for the *Times Lit. Supp.*[4] when the English translation comes out. Did you tell me that Zamyatin's widow is still alive & in Paris? If so, & she can be contacted, it might be worth doing so, as there may be others of his books which some English publisher might be induced to take, if *We* is a success. You told me that his satire on England, *The Islanders*, had never been translated, & perhaps it might be suitable.

---

[1] Gleb Struve (1898–), born in St Petersburg. Taught at the School of Slavonic and East European Studies, London University 1932–47; since 1947 Professor of Slavic Languages and Literature, University of California, Berkeley. Author of *Soviet Literature 1917–1950* and *Russian Literature in Exile*.
[2] Presumably the Mandelstam sketches mentioned in this letter.
[3] See 17 for Orwell's review of the French translation.
[4] Orwell did not review it, as the plans for the English publication fell through.

I hope you will forgive me for my failure to find an editor for Mandelstam's sketches. There are so few magazines in England now. *Polemic* died of the usual disease, & the other possible one, *Politics & Letters*, was no good.

You asked abt my novel, *Burmese Days*. I think it is still in print as a Penguin, but there won't be many copies left. It is being reprinted abt the end of this year, as I am beginning a uniform edition, & that is second on the list. I *may* succeed in getting some of these books reprinted in the USA as well.

Yours sincerely
Geo. Orwell

PS. This address will find me for some months, I'm afraid.

112. Letter to George Woodcock

Ward 3
Hairmyres Hosp.
East Kilbride
Lanark
24 April 1948

Dear George,
I haven't written earlier because I've been having a bad time for a fortnight or so with the secondary effects of the streptomycin. I have read your poems with attention. I liked best the long poem at the end, "Waterloo Bridge", & after that I think "Ancestral Tablet", "The Agitator", & "The Island". I think you get your best effects with 10-syllable lines which are a bit irregular so as to give a sort of broken-backed movement, like "And again, I am thinking of the angels & William Blake" or "This is the preposterous hour when Caesars rise". But, I think you need to make up your mind a bit better on the subject of rhyme. Part of the time you use ordinary rhymes, but a good deal of the time assonances like thought-white, hours-fears, etc. I must say I am against this kind of rhyme, which seems to me only, as it were, an intellectual rhyme, existing on the paper because we can see that the final consonant is the same. The lack of rhymes in English is a very serious difficulty & gets more serious all the time, as familiar rhymes get more & more hackneyed,

but I have always felt that if one is to use imperfect rhymes, it would be better to make the vowel sound & not the consonant the same. E.g. open-broken, fate-shape, sound to me more like rhymes than eyes-voice, town-again & so forth. However, I'm no judge of such things.

I did a short article—not actually a review but one of those articles they have on the leader page—for the *Observer* on Wilde's *Soul of Man under Socialism*,[1] which may help it a little. Charles Davy, one of the sub-eds, asked me if I could do a short article, when they have a pretext for it, on the Freedom Defence Committee, its aims & scope. I will do so, of course, & no doubt it would bring in a few contributions. I suppose I should be correct in saying that there is not now any other organisation having just those aims (except of course the NCCL,[2] which I might be able to give a quiet kick at in passing)? . . .

Yours
George

PS. I've lost your new address—I'm going to send this care of the FDC.

113. Letter to Roger Senhouse

[Hairmyres Hospital]
3 May 1948

Dear Roger,

I had managed to get a copy of *L'Univers Concentrationnaire*[3] from another source and have read it in conjunction with your translation. I'm not sure whether your approach is right. I don't know French well enough to judge, but Rousset's style doesn't seem to be a particularly unusual or lyrical one—at any rate, not beyond the first chapter. In many cases I would have used a simpler phrase than you do, and often more literal. For instance I would translate the first sentence of the book as "The great lonely city of Buchenwald." A little further down, "Squalid sheds squatting in a semi-circle" etc. I don't see any alliteration in the French to correspond to squalid-squatting, and you seem to me to alter the sense of some words, e.g.

[1] See 118.   [2] National Council for Civil Liberties.
[3] By David Rousset.

420 Letter to Roger Senhouse

"haute" translated gaunt. I would have translated the first part of the sentence "Helmstedt: sheds grouped in a circle, and camouflaged by the seeping of their own filth, uncovered stacks of cases containing bombs and torpedoes, fields of wheat and mustard, and, across the plain, the tall black silhouettes of pit shafts." (I take it from you that "puits" means that. It sounds as if it ought to mean the actual hole in the ground, but it can't in the context, and I suppose it must mean the winding gear above the shaft.) I may be wrong, but my instinct is simplicity every time. The "dramatic present" is a great difficulty. Personally I am against it except when it is used for generalisation, i.e. describes something typical. I think in genuine narration one should avoid it. One great difficulty also is that there is no proper English equivalent for "concentrationnaire". Obviously one can't say "concentrationary". One can use "concentration-camp" as an adjective, but it is very cumbersome. In the extracts in an American magazine in which I first came across this book, the expression used was "KZ" which I think stands for something or other in German. In the title, if you try to translate the original, I think I'd avoid "universe" if possible and use "world".

I rather think I missed out one correction in that list I sent you with the proof of *Burmese Days*. Page 97, line 13 from top: "of blue rings of hills". Should be "by blue rings of hills". Perhaps you could add this?

I am getting up for an hour a day now and beginning to put on a few clothes. They haven't let me out yet, but I think they would if it was warmer. I'll send back the MS separately, because I must get hold of a bit of string. Please give all the best to Fred.

Yours
George

114. Letter to Roger Senhouse

[Hairmyres Hospital]
Thursday [6? May 1948]
Dear Roger,
I'm awfully sorry abt the delay in sending this back. I trust it will arrive all right.

I've already got Rousset's *Les Jours de Notre Mort*, but haven't read it yet. The trouble with this concentration-camp literature is that there is such a lot of it. I wanted to read Rousset because from extracts I had seen I thought he had more grasp than most of the people who have written on the subject. The point is that these forced-labour camps are part of the pattern of our time, & are a very interesting though horrible phenomenon. What is wanted now is for someone to write a scholarly work on concentration & forced-labour camps, drawing on Rousset & all the others.

I've started revising the novel,[1] but I do only a very little, perhaps an hour's work each day. However at that rate I should get through several chapters before leaving hospital. I am still not certain when this will happen, nor whether I shall have to continue out-patient treatment after leaving. Richard Rees is up at Jura, or has been for the week-end. I imagine they must have had lovely weather. Please remember me to Fred.

Yours
George

115. Letter to Julian Symons

Ward 3
Hairmyres Hospital
East Kilbride, Lanark
10 May 1948

Dear Julian,

Thanks ever so much to yourself and your wife for the chocolate and the tea and rice, which got here last week. I'd been meaning to write. You see I've organised a typewriter at last. It's a bit awkward to use in bed, but it saves hideous misprints in reviews etc caused by my handwriting. As you say, the ball-bearing pen is the last stage in the decay of handwriting, but I've given mine up years ago. At one time I used to spend hours with script pens and squared paper, trying to re-teach myself to write, but it was no use after being taught copperplate and on top of that encouraged to write a "scholarly" hand. The writing of children nowadays is even worse than ours used to be,

---

[1] *Nineteen Eighty-Four.*

because they will teach them this disconnected script which is very slow to write. Evidently the first thing is to get a good simple cursive script, but on top of that you have to teach hand control, in fact learning to write involves learning to draw. Evidently it can be done, as in countries like China and Japan anyone who can write at all writes more or less gracefully.

I am glad E and S[1] are pleased with the biography, but don't let them get away with "The Quest for A.J.A. Symons" as a title. It is true that if a book is going to sell no title can kill it, but I am sure that is a bad one. Of course I can't make suggestions without seeing the book, but if they insist on having the name, something like "A.J.A. Symons: a Memoir" is always inoffensive.

Coming Up for Air isn't much, but I thought it worth reprinting because it was rather killed by the outbreak of war and then blitzed out of existence, so thoroughly that in order to get a copy from which to reset it we had to steal one from a public library. Of course you are perfectly right about my own character constantly intruding on that of the narrator. I am not a real novelist anyway, and that particular vice is inherent in writing a novel in the first person, which one should never do. One difficulty I have never solved is that one has masses of experience which one passionately wants to write about, e.g. the part about fishing in that book, and no way of using them up except by disguising them as a novel. Of course the book was bound to suggest Wells watered down. I have a great admiration for Wells, i.e. as a writer, and he was a very early influence on me. I think I was ten or eleven when Cyril Connolly and I got hold of a copy of Wells's *The Country of the Blind* (short stories) and were so fascinated by it that we kept stealing it from one another. I can still remember at 4 o'clock on a midsummer morning, with the school fast asleep and the sun slanting through the window, creeping down a passage to Connolly's dormitory where I knew the book would be beside his bed. We also got into severe trouble (and I think a caning—I forget) for having a copy of Compton Mackenzie's *Sinister Street*.

They now tell me that I shall have to stay here till about August. The germs are evidently liquidated, but the actual healing of the lung and build-up of strength takes a long time. I'm still terribly short of breath and I suppose shall continue to be as long as they keep the lung collapsed, which might be a year or more. However it's worth it to get a good mend. They now let me out of doors for a little each

[1] Eyre and Spottiswoode, the publishers.

day, and I feel so much better that I think I shall be able to do a little serious work again. What chiefly worries me is Richard, whom I haven't seen for 4 or 5 months. However I may be able to arrange for him to have a short stay in Glasgow, and then he can come and visit me. I don't know who put that par in the *Standard*[1]—someone who knew me, though there were the usual mistakes. I don't think they ought to have given my real name.

Please remember me to your wife.

Yours
George

116. Letter to George Woodcock

[Hairmyres Hospital]
24 May 1948

Dear George,

I received another letter from Charles Davy, drawing my attention to the fact that E.M. Forster has resigned from the NCCL. I then sat down, or sat up rather, with the idea of writing that article on the FDC, but on second thoughts I really don't think I can do it. To begin with I have two long articles on hand and I can't do much yet, but what is more to the point, I don't know enough factually about the FDC for the purpose. Do you think you could do the article? I think you said Davy had written to you. Perhaps you could ring him up. I don't know if you know him—he is a very nice chap. I don't know exactly what they want, but I assume they would want an account of the Committee and its activities, in general terms, with some remarks on the threat to individual liberty contained in the modern centralised state. I don't like shoving this off on to you, on the other hand if they are willing for you to write the article they'll pay you quite well for it.

I hadn't yet thanked you for the copy of the book of essays.[2] Of course I was delighted to see the one on myself appearing in book

---

[1] On 5 May 1948 in the "Londoner's Diary", a gossip column in the *Evening Standard*, there was a paragraph about Orwell which referred to his wife's death.

[2] *The Writer and Politics* by George Woodcock.

424 *Letter to George Woodcock*

form. I liked the one on Bates,[1] whose book I read years ago. All nineteenth-century books about S. America have a wonderful Arcadian atmosphere, though I think I was always more attracted by the pampas than by the forest. I suppose you've read *The Purple Land.* Also the one on hymns, which I'd always been meaning to write something about myself. I think you're wrong in saying that people respond to a hymn like "Abide with me" (by the way shouldn't it be "the darkness deepens", not "gathers") chiefly because of wars, unemployment etc. There is a great deal of inherent sadness and loneliness in human life that would be the same whatever the external circumstances. You don't mention two of the best hymns, "Praise to the holiest" and "Jerusalem my happy home"—this one, I think, however, must be a great deal earlier than the other groups you were studying. In *Ancient and Modern* if I remember rightly it's heavily expurgated to get the Catholic imagery out.

I am much better and now get up for two hours a day, and even go out a little when it is warm. They haven't told me definitely when I can leave hospital, but probably about August. They now seem to think that I won't have to continue with treatment when I leave, which would be a great blessing as it would mean I could go back to Jura instead of having to hang about in Glasgow or Edinburgh. Richard is by all accounts extremely well and growing enormous. Of course I haven't seen him for months, but I am trying to arrange for him to be brought here for at any rate an afternoon, now that I can go out of doors and can see him in the grounds.

Please give all the best to Inge. I've gone and lost your new address, but I will think of someone to send this care of. I will write to Charles Davy about the article.

Yours
George

[1] Henry Walter Bates (1825–92), who visited South America in 1848; author of *The Naturalist on the River Amazons*, 1863.

117. Letter to Celia Kirwan

Ward 3
Hairmyres Hospital
East Kilbride
Lanarkshire
27 May 1948

Dearest Celia,

Thanks ever so much for your letter. I must say, anything to do with UNESCO sounds pretty discouraging. Any way, I should knock all the money you can out of them, as I don't suppose they'll last much longer.

I am ever so much better & for some time past they have not been able to find any germs in me. They are now having a last try, & if they don't find any this time we can presumably regard the germs as quelled, though of course the healing-up process takes a long time. I am still frightfully weak & thin, but I get up for 2 hours every day & go outside a little. I still can't work a great deal, but I get a little done each day. They haven't said definitely when I shall leave hospital, but probably abt August, & what is very good news, they now seem to think I shan't have to continue with out-patient treatment, which means I can go back to Jura instead of having to hang abt in Glasgow or Edinburgh. They seem to have been having marvellous weather in Jura & are very busy with the farm work, Richard included. I haven't seen him since before Christmas, for fear of infection, but I could see him now if I can fix for him to be brought here for a day or two. He is getting enormous & is evidently learning to talk more. He had his fourth birthday this month.

How I wish I were with you in Paris, now that spring is there. Do you ever go to the Jardin des Plantes? I used to love it, though there was really nothing of interest except the rats, which at one time over-ran it & were so tame that they would almost eat out of your hand. In the end they got to be such a nuisance that they introduced cats & more or less wiped them out. The plane trees are so beautiful in Paris, because the bark isn't blackened by smoke the way it is in London. I suppose the food & so on is still pretty grisly, but that will improve if the Marshall plan gets working. I see you have to put a 10 franc stamp on your letter, which gives one an idea of what meals must cost now.

I can't help feeling that it's a bit treacherous on Arthur's[1] part if he does settle down in the USA. He was talking abt doing it before. I suppose he is furious abt what is happening in Palestine, though what else was to be expected I don't know. His lecture tour seems to have been quite a success. I wonder if he has got back yet, & what he will do abt his place in Wales. It seems a pity to start sending roots down somewhere & then tear them up again, & I can imagine Mamaine not liking it.

It seems years since I have seen you, & in fact it must be 15 months. It's funny to think I haven't been out of Scotland for over a year, though I wld have been if I had stayed well. This business has put my work back frightfully. The book I am at work on was to be finished at the beginning of this year—now it can't be finished before the end of the year, which means not coming out till the end of 1949. However it's something to be capable of working again. Last year before they brought me here I really felt as though I were finished. Thank Heaven Richard looks as if he is going to have good health. We have got 2 tested cows now, so at any rate he won't get this disease through milk, which is the usual way with children. Take care of yourself & write to me again some time.

With love
George

118. Review

The Soul of Man under Socialism by Oscar Wilde

Oscar Wilde's work is being much revived now on stage and screen, and it is well to be reminded that Salome and Lady Windermere were not his only creations. Wilde's *The Soul of Man under Socialism*, for example, first published nearly sixty years ago, has worn remarkably well. Its author was not in any active sense a Socialist himself, but he was a sympathetic and intelligent observer; although his prophecies have not been fulfilled, they have not been made simply irrelevant by the passage of time.

[1] Arthur Koestler, who had been living with his wife Mamaine in Wales, decided he would like to move to the United States. The Koestlers lived there for a short time.

Wilde's vision of Socialism, which at that date was probably shared by many people less articulate than himself, is Utopian and anarchistic. The abolition of private property, he says, will make possible the full development of the individual and set us free from "the sordid necessity of living for others". In the Socialist future there will not only be no want and no insecurity, there will also be no drudgery, no disease, no ugliness, no wastage of the human spirit in futile enmities and rivalries.

Pain will cease to be important: indeed, for the first time in his history, Man will be able to realise his personality through joy instead of through suffering. Crime will disappear, since there will be no economic reason for it. The State will cease to govern and will survive merely as an agency for the distribution of necessary commodities. All the disagreeable jobs will be done by machinery, and everyone will be completely free to choose his own work and his own manner of life. In effect, the world will be populated by artists, each striving after perfection in the way that seems best to him.

Today, these optimistic forecasts make rather painful reading. Wilde realised, of course, that there were authoritarian tendencies in the Socialist movement, but he did not believe they would prevail, and with a sort of prophetic irony he wrote: "I hardly think that any Socialist, nowadays, would seriously propose that an inspector should call every morning at each house to see that each citizen rose up and did manual labour for eight hours"—which, unfortunately, is just the kind of thing that countless modern Socialists would propose. Evidently something has gone wrong. Socialism, in the sense of economic collectivism, is conquering the earth at a speed that would hardly have seemed possible sixty years ago, and yet Utopia, at any rate Wilde's Utopia, is no nearer. Where, then, does the fallacy lie?

If one looks more closely one sees that Wilde makes two common but unjustified assumptions. One is that the world is immensely rich and is suffering chiefly from maldistribution. Even things out between the millionaire and the crossing-sweeper, he seems to say, and there will be plenty of everything for everybody. Until the Russian Revolution, this belief was very widely held—"starving in the midst of plenty" was a favourite phrase—but it was quite false, and it survived only because Socialists thought always of the highly developed western countries and ignored the fearful poverty of Asia and Africa. Actually, the problem for the world as a whole is not how to distribute such wealth as exists but how to increase production, without which economic equality merely means common misery.

Secondly, Wilde assumes that it is a simple matter to arrange that all the unpleasant kinds of work shall be done by machinery. The machines, he says, are our new race of slaves: a tempting metaphor, but a misleading one, since there is a vast range of jobs—roughly speaking, any job needing great flexibility—that no machine is able to do. In practice, even in the most highly-mechanised countries, an enormous amount of dull and exhausting work has to be done by unwilling human muscles. But this at once implies direction of labour, fixed working hours, differential wage rates, and all the regimentation that Wilde abhors. Wilde's version of Socialism could only be realised in a world not only far richer but also technically far more advanced than the present one. The abolition of private property does not of itself put food into anyone's mouth. It is merely the first step in a transitional period that is bound to be laborious, uncomfortable, and long.

But that is not to say that Wilde is altogether wrong. The trouble with transitional periods is that the harsh outlook which they generate tends to become permanent. To all appearances this is what has happened in Soviet Russia. A dictatorship supposedly established for a limited purpose has dug itself in, and Socialism comes to be thought of as meaning concentration camps and secret police forces. Wilde's pamphlet and other kindred writings—*News from Nowhere*, for instance—consequently have their value. They may demand the impossible, and they may—since a Utopia necessarily reflects the aesthetic ideas of its own period—sometimes seem "dated" and ridiculous, but they do at least look beyond the era of food queues and party squabbles, and remind the Socialist movement of its original, half-forgotten objective of human brotherhood.

Observer, 9 May 1948

119. George Gissing

In the shadow of the atomic bomb it is not easy to talk confidently about progress. However, if it can be assumed that we are *not* going to be blown to pieces in about ten years' time, there are many reasons, and George Gissing's novels are among them, for thinking that the present age is a good deal better than the last one. If Gissing were still alive he would be younger than Bernard Shaw, and yet already the London of which he wrote seems almost as distant as that of Dickens. It is the fog-bound, gas-lit London of the 'eighties, a city of drunken puritans, where clothes, architecture and furniture had reached their rock-bottom of ugliness, and where it was almost normal for a working-class family of ten persons to inhabit a single room. On the whole Gissing does not write of the worst depths of poverty, but one can hardly read his descriptions of lower-middle-class life, so obviously truthful in their dreariness, without feeling that we have improved perceptibly on that black-coated, money-ruled world of only sixty years ago.

Everything of Gissing's—except perhaps one or two books written towards the end of his life—contains memorable passages, and anyone who is making his acquaintance for the first time might do worse than start with *In the Year of the Jubilee*. It was rather a pity, however, to use up paper in reprinting two of his minor works[1] when the books by which he ought to be remembered are and have been for years completely unprocurable. *The Odd Women*, for instance, is about as thoroughly out of print as a book can be. I possess a copy myself, in one of those nasty little red-covered cheap editions that flourished before the 1914 war, but that is the only copy I have ever seen or heard of. *New Grub Street*, Gissing's masterpiece, I have never succeeded in buying. When I have read it, it has been in soup-stained copies borrowed from public lending libraries: so also with *Demos*, *The Nether World* and one or two others. So far as I know only *The Private Papers of Henry Ryecroft*, the book on Dickens, and *A Life's Morning*, have been in print at all recently. However, the two now reprinted are well worth reading, especially *In the Year of the Jubilee*, which is the more sordid and therefore the more characteristic.

In his introduction Mr William Plomer remarks that "generally speaking, Gissing's novels are about money and women," and Miss Myfanwy Evans says something very similar in introducing *The Whirlpool*. One might, I think, widen the definition and say that Gissing's novels are a protest against the form of self-torture that goes by the name of respectability. Gissing was a bookish, perhaps

[1] *In the Year of the Jubilee* and *The Whirlpool* by George Gissing. [Author's footnote.]

over-civilised man, in love with classical antiquity, who found himself
trapped in a cold, smoky, Protestant country where it was impossible
to be comfortable without a thick padding of money between yourself
and the outer world. Behind his rage and querulousness there lay a
perception that the horrors of life in late-Victorian England were
largely unnecessary. The grime, the stupidity, the ugliness, the sex-
starvation, the furtive debauchery, the vulgarity, the bad manners,
the censoriousness—these things were unnecessary, since the puritanism of which they were a relic no longer upheld the structure of
society. People who might, without becoming less efficient, have
been reasonably happy chose instead to be miserable, inventing
senseless taboos with which to terrify themselves. Money was a
nuisance not merely because without it you starved; what was more
important was that unless you had quite a lot of it—£300 a year, say
—society would not allow you to live gracefully or even peacefully.
Women were a nuisance because even more than men they were the
believers in taboos, still enslaved to respectability even when they had
offended against it. Money and women were therefore the two
instruments through which society avenged itself on the courageous
and the intelligent. Gissing would have liked a little more money for
himself and some others, but he was not much interested in what we
should now call social justice. He did not admire the working class as
such, and he did not believe in democracy. He wanted to speak not
for the multitude, but for the exceptional man, the sensitive man,
isolated among barbarians.

In *The Odd Women* there is not a single major character whose life
is not ruined either by having too little money, or by getting it too
late in life, or by the pressure of social conventions which are
obviously absurd but which cannot be questioned. An elderly spinster
crowns a useless life by taking to drink; a pretty young girl marries a
man old enough to be her father; a struggling schoolmaster puts off
marrying his sweetheart until both of them are middle-aged and
withered; a good-natured man is nagged to death by his wife; an
exceptionally intelligent, spirited man misses his chance to make an
adventurous marriage and relapses into futility; in each case the
ultimate reason for the disaster lies in obeying the accepted social
code, or in not having enough money to circumvent it. In *A Life's
Morning* an honest and gifted man meets with ruin and death because
it is impossible to walk about a big town with no hat on. His hat is
blown out of the window when he is travelling in the train, and as he

has not enough money to buy another, he misappropriates some money belonging to his employer, which sets going a series of disasters. This is an interesting example of the changes in outlook that can suddenly make an all-powerful taboo seem ridiculous. Today, if you had somehow contrived to lose your trousers, you would probably embezzle money rather than walk about in your underpants. In the 'eighties the necessity would have seemed equally strong in the case of a hat. Even thirty or forty years ago, indeed, bare-headed men were booed at in the street. Then, for no very clear reason, hatlessness became respectable, and today the particular tragedy described by Gissing—entirely plausible in its context— would be quite impossible.

The most impressive of Gissing's books is *New Grub Street*. To a professional writer it is also an upsetting and demoralising book, because it deals among other things with that much-dreaded occupational disease, sterility. No doubt the number of writers who suddenly lose the power to write is not large, but it is a calamity that *might* happen to anybody at any moment, like sexual impotence. Gissing, of course, links it up with his habitual themes—money, the pressure of the social code, and the stupidity of women.

Edwin Reardon, a young novelist—he has just deserted a clerkship after having a fluky success with a single novel—marries a charming and apparently intelligent young woman, with a small income of her own. Here, and in one or two other places, Gissing makes what now seems the curious remark that it is difficult for an educated man who is not rich to get married. Reardon brings it off, but his less successful friend, who lives in an attic and supports himself by ill-paid tutoring jobs, has to accept celibacy as a matter of course. If he did succeed in finding himself a wife, we are told, it could only be an uneducated girl from the slums. Women of refinement and sensibility will not face poverty. And here one notices again the deep difference between that day and our own. Doubtless Gissing is right in implying all through his books that intelligent women are very rare animals, and if one wants to marry a women who is intelligent *and* pretty, then the choice is still further restricted, according to a well-known arithmetical rule. It is like being allowed to choose only among albinos, and left-handed albinos at that. But what comes out in Gissing's treatment of his odious heroine, and of certain others among his women, is that at that date the idea of delicacy, refinement, even intelligence, in the case of a woman, was hardly separable from the idea of superior social status and expensive physical surroundings. The sort of woman whom a writer would want to marry was also the sort of woman who would shrink from living in an attic. When Gissing wrote *New Grub Street* that was probably true, and it could, I think, be justly claimed that it is not true today.

Almost as soon as Reardon is married it becomes apparent that his wife is merely a silly snob, the kind of woman in whom "artistic tastes"are no more than a cover for social competitiveness. In marrying a novelist she has thought to marry someone who will rapidly become famous and shed reflected glory upon herself. Reardon is a studious, retiring, ineffectual man, a typical Gissing hero. He has been caught up in an expensive, pretentious world in which he knows he will never be able to maintain himself, and his nerve fails almost immediately. His wife, of course, has not the faintest understanding of what is meant by literary creation. There is a terrible passage— terrible, at least, to anyone who earns his living by writing—in which she calculates the number of pages that it would be possible to write in a day, and hence the number of novels that her husband may be expected to produce in a year—with the reflection that really it is not a very laborious profession. Meanwhile Reardon has been stricken dumb. Day after day he sits at his desk; nothing happens, nothing comes. Finally, in panic, he manufactures a piece of rubbish; his publisher, because Reardon's previous book had been successful, dubiously accepts it. Thereafter he is unable to produce anything that even looks as if it might be printable. He is finished.

The desolating thing is that if only he could get back to his clerk- ship and his bachelorhood, he would be all right. The hard-boiled journalist who finally marries Reardon's widow sums him up accurately by saying that he is the kind of man who, if left to himself, would write a fairly good book every two years. But, of course, he is not left to himself. He cannot revert to his old profession, and he cannot simply settle down to live on his wife's money: public opinion, operating through his wife, harries him into impotence and finally into the grave. Most of the other literary characters in the book are not much more fortunate, and the troubles that beset them are still very much the same today. But at least it is unlikely that the book's central disaster would now happen in quite that way or for quite those reasons. The chances are that Reardon's wife would be less of a fool, and that he would have fewer scruples about walking out on her if she made life intolerable for him. A woman of rather similar type turns up in *The Whirlpool* in the person of Alma Frothingham. By contrast there are the three Miss Frenches in *The Year of the Jubilee*, who represent the emerging lower-middle class—a class which, according to Gissing, was getting hold of money and power which it was not fitted to use—and who are quite surprisingly coarse, rowdy, shrewish and unmoral. At first sight Gissing's "ladylike" and "un-ladylike" women seem to be different and even opposite kinds of animal, and this seems to invalidate his implied condemnation of the female sex in general. The connecting link between them, however, is that all of them are miserably limited in outlook. Even the clever and spirited ones, like Rhoda in *The Odd Women* (an interesting early specimen of the New Woman), cannot think in terms of generalities, and cannot get away from ready-made standards. In his heart Gissing seems to feel that women are natural inferiors. He wants them to be better educated, but on the other hand he does not want them to have freedom, which they are certain to misuse. On the whole the best women in his books are the self-effacing, home-keeping ones.

There are several of Gissing's books that I have never read, because I have never been able to get hold of them, and these unfortunately include *Born in Exile*, which is said by some people to be his best book. But merely on the strength of *New Grub Street*, *Demos* and *The Odd Women* I am ready to maintain that England has produced very few better novelists. This perhaps sounds like a rash statement until one stops to consider what is meant by a novel. The word "novel" is commonly used to cover almost any kind of story—*The Golden Asse*, *Anna Karenina*, *Don Quixote*, *The Improvisatore*, *Madame Bovary*, *King Solomon's Mines* or anything else you like—but it also has a narrower sense in which it means something hardly existing before the nineteenth century and flourishing chiefly in Russia and France. A novel, in this sense, is a story which attempts to describe credible human beings, and—without necessarily using the technique of naturalism—to show them acting on everyday motives and not merely undergoing strings of improbable adventures. A true novel, sticking to this definition, will also contain at least two characters, probably more, who are described from the inside and on the same level of probability—which, in effect, rules out the novels written in the first person. If one accepts this definition, it becomes apparent that the novel is not an art-form in which England has excelled. The writers commonly paraded as "great English novelists" have a way of turning out either not to be true novelists, or not to be

Englishmen. Gissing was not a writer of picaresque tales, or bur-
lesques, or comedies, or political tracts: he was interested in individual human beings, and the fact that he can deal sympathetically
with several different sets of motives, and makes a credible story out
of the collision between them, makes him exceptional among English
writers.

Certainly there is not much of what is usually called beauty, not
much lyricism, in the situations and characters that he chooses to
imagine, and still less in the texture of his writing. His prose, indeed,
is often disgusting. Here are a couple of samples:

> Not with impunity could her thought accustom itself to stray in
> regions forbidden, how firm soever her resolve to hold bodily
> aloof. (*The Whirlpool.*)
>
> The ineptitude of uneducated English women in all that relates
> to their attire is a fact that it boots not to enlarge upon. (*In the
> Year of the Jubilee.*)

However, he does not commit the faults that really matter. It is
always clear what he means, he never "writes for effect", he knows
how to keep the balance between *récit* and dialogue and how to make
dialogue sound probable while not contrasting too sharply with the
prose that surrounds it. A much more serious fault than his inelegant
manner of writing is the smallness of his range of experience. He is
only acquainted with a few strata of society, and, in spite of his vivid
understanding of the pressure of circumstance on character, does not
seem to have much grasp of political or economic forces. In a mild
way his outlook is reactionary, from lack of foresight rather than
from ill-will. Having been obliged to live among them, he regarded
the working class as savages, and in saying so he was merely being
intellectually honest; he did not see that they were capable of becoming civilised if given slightly better opportunities. But, after all, what
one demands from a novelist is not prophecy, and part of the charm
of Gissing is that he belongs so unmistakably to his own time,
although his time treated him badly.

The English writer nearest to Gissing always seems to be his contemporary, or near-contemporary, Mark Rutherford. If one simply
tabulates their outstanding qualities, the two men appear to be very
different. Mark Rutherford was a less prolific writer than Gissing, he
was less definitely a novelist, he wrote much better prose, his books
belong less recognisably to any particular time, and he was in out-

look a social reformer and, above all, a puritan. Yet there is a sort of haunting resemblance, probably explained by the fact that both men lack that curse of English writers, a "sense of humour". A certain low-spiritedness, and air of loneliness, is common to both of them. There are, of course, funny passages in Gissing's books, but he is not chiefly concerned with getting a laugh—above all, he has no impulse towards burlesque. He treats all his major characters more or less seriously, and with at least an attempt at sympathy. Any novel will inevitably contain minor characters who are mere grotesques or who are observed in a purely hostile spirit, but there is such a thing as impartiality, and Gissing is more capable of it than the great majority of English writers. It is a point in his favour that he had no very strong moral purpose. He had, of course, a deep loathing of the ugliness, emptiness and cruelty of the society he lived in, but he was concerned to describe it rather than to change it. There is usually no one in his books who can be pointed to as the villain, and even when there is a villain he is not punished. In his treatment of sexual matters Gissing is surprisingly frank, considering the time at which he was writing. It is not that he writes pornography or expresses approval of sexual promiscuity, but simply that he is willing to face the facts. The unwritten law of English fiction, the law that the hero as well as the heroine of a novel should be virgin when married, is disregarded in his books, almost for the first time since Fielding.

Like most English writers subsequent to the mid-nineteenth century, Gissing could not imagine any desirable destiny other than being a writer or a gentleman of leisure. The dichotomy between the intellectual and the lowbrow already existed, and a person capable of writing a serious novel could no longer picture himself as fully satisfied with the life of a businessman, or a soldier, or a politician, or what not. Gissing did not, at least consciously, even want to be the kind of writer that he was. His ideal, a rather melancholy one, was to have a moderate private income and live in a small comfortable house in the country, preferably unmarried, where he could wallow in books, especially the Greek and Latin classics. He might perhaps have realised this ideal if he had not managed to get himself into prison immediately after winning an Oxford scholarship: as it was he spent his life in what appeared to him to be hack work, and when he had at last reached the point where he could stop writing against the clock, he died almost immediately, aged only about forty-five. His death, described by H.G. Wells in his *Experiment in*

Autobiography, was of a piece with his life. The twenty novels, or thereabouts, that he produced between 1880 and 1900 were, so to speak, sweated out of him during his struggle towards a leisure which he never enjoyed and which he might not have used to good advantage if he had had it: for it is difficult to believe that his temperament really fitted him for a life of scholarly research. Perhaps the natural pull of his gifts would in any case have drawn him towards novel writing sooner or later. If not, we must be thankful for the piece of youthful folly which turned him aside from a comfortable middle-class career and forced him to become the chronicler of vulgarity, squalor and failure.

Written [May–June] 1948 for *Politics and Letters* which ended before this essay could be published; *London Magazine*, June 1960.

120. Letter to Anthony Powell

Ward 3
Hairmyres Hospital
East Kilbride
Lanarkshire
25 June 1948

Dear Tony,
I received a letter from your friend Cecil Roberts[1] asking me if he could have my flat. I had to write and tell him it was impossible. I am awfully sorry about this, but they have already been riding me like the nightmare for lending it to Mrs Christen, and threatening to let the Borough take it away from me. I don't want this to happen because I must have *a* pied à terre in London, and also I have a little furniture still there and a lot of papers which it's awkward to store elsewhere. Even if I gave up the flat they won't let you transfer the lease, and of course they have their own candidates ready many deep, with bribes in their hands.

If you happen to see Graham Greene, could you break the news to him that I have written a very bad review of his novel[2] for the *New Yorker*. I couldn't do otherwise—I thought the book awful, though of course don't put it as crudely as that. I am going to review Kings-

[1] Cecil A. ("Bobby") Roberts, sometime manager of Sadler's Wells Theatre, who had been recently demobilised from the Royal Air Force.
[2] *The Heart of the Matter*. See 122.

mill's book for the *Obs.*[1] as soon as possible, but I still have another book to get out of the way first. I seem to be getting quite back into the journalistic mill, however I do tinker a little at my novel and no doubt shall get it done by the end of the year.

I am a lot better and now get up for three hours a day. I have been playing a lot of croquet, which seems quite a tough game when you've been on your back for 6 months. In the ward below me the editor of the *Hotspur*[2] is a patient. He tells me their circulation is 300,000. He says they don't pay very good rates per thou, but they can give people regular work and also give them the plots so that they only have to do the actual writing. In this way a man can turn out 40,000 words a week. They had one man who used to do 70,000, but his stuff was "rather stereotyped". I hope to get out in August, but the date isn't fixed because it depends on when my lung resumes its normal shape after the collapse therapy has worn off. Richard is coming to see me early in July. He couldn't before because of infection. I suppose I shall hardly know him after six months.

It's my birthday today—45, isn't it awful. I've also got some more false teeth, and, since being here, a lot more grey in my hair. Please remember me to Violet.

Yours
George

121. Letter to Julian Symons

Ward 3
Hairmyres Hospital
East Kilbride
Lanarkshire
10 July 1948

Dear Julian,
I must thank you for a very kind review in the *M.E. News*[3] which I have just had a cutting of. I hope your wife is well and that everything is going all right. I thought you would like to hear that I am

---

[1] *The Dawn's Delay* by Hugh Kingsmill, *Observer*, 18 July 1948.
[2] A weekly paper for boys.
[3] Julian Symons had reviewed the reprint of *Coming Up for Air* in the *Manchester Evening News*, 19 May 1948.

leaving here on the 25th. They seem to think I am pretty well all
right now, though I shall have to take things very quietly for a long
time, perhaps a year or so. I am only to get up for six hours a day,
but I don't know that it makes much difference as I have got quite
used to working in bed. My sister brought Richard over to see me this
week, the first time I had seen him since Christmas. He is tremendously well and almost frighteningly energetic. His talking still
seems backward, but in other ways I should say he was forward.
Farm life seems to suit him, though I am pretty sure he is one for
machines rather than animals. I get up for three hours a day at
present, and go for short walks and play croquet, but I'm getting
rather bored here and looking forward to getting home. I don't
think I shall be in London until the winter, by which time I hope I'll
have finished this blasted novel which should have been finished this
spring. Also I'm afraid that if I go up to London I shan't stay in
bed etc. There is no one much to talk to here. In the ward below this
the editor of the *Hotspur* is a patient, but he's rather dull. He tells me
their circulation is 300,000. I recently wrote a long essay on Gissing
for *Politics and Letters*, but I had to do it almost without books as
you simply can't get Gissing's books now. As far as I can discover
there is no biography of Gissing, except that silly one in the form of a
novel by Morley Roberts. It is a job that is crying out to be done. A
year or two back Home and Van Thal[1] asked me if I would do one,
but of course I couldn't do all the research that would be needed. I
recently read Graham Greene's new novel and thought it was just
awful. I also wasn't so up in the air as most people about Evelyn
Waugh's *The Loved One*, though of course it was amusing. Unlike a
lot of people I thought *Brideshead Revisited* was very good, in spite
of hideous faults on the surface. I have been trying to read a book
of extracts from Léon Bloy, whose novels I have never succeeded in
getting hold of. He irritates me rather, and Péguy, whom I also tried
recently, made me feel unwell. I think it's about time to do a new
counter-attack against these Catholic writers. I also read Farrell's
Studs Lonigan for the first time, and was very disappointed by it. I
don't know that I've read much else.

The weather here was filthy all June but now it's turning at last
and they are getting the hay in with great speed. I am longing to go
fishing, but I suppose I shan't be able to this year, not because fishing

[1] The publishers.

in itself is much of an exertion, but because you always have to walk five or ten miles and end up by getting soaked to the skin. Please remember me to your wife. After the 25th my address will be as before, i.e. Barnhill, Isle of Jura, Argyllshire.

Yours
George

122. Review
The Heart of the Matter by Graham Greene

A fairly large proportion of the distinguished novels of the last few decades have been written by Catholics and have even been describable as Catholic novels. One reason for this is that the conflict not only between this world and the next world but between sanctity and goodness is a fruitful theme of which the ordinary, unbelieving writer cannot make use. Graham Greene used it once successfully, in *The Power and the Glory*, and once, with very much more doubtful success, in *Brighton Rock*. His latest book, *The Heart of the Matter*, is, to put it as politely as possible, not one of his best, and gives the impression of having been mechanically constructed, the familiar conflict being set out like an algebraic equation, with no attempt at psychological probability.

Here is the outline of the story: The time is 1942 and the place is a West African British colony, unnamed but probably the Gold Coast. A certain Major Scobie, Deputy Commissioner of Police and a Catholic convert, finds a letter bearing a German address hidden in the cabin of the captain of a Portuguese ship. The letter turns out to be a private one and completely harmless, but it is, of course, Scobie's duty to hand it over to higher authority. However, the pity he feels for the Portuguese captain is too much for him, and he destroys the letter and says nothing about it. Scobie, it is explained to us, is a man of almost excessive conscientiousness. He does not drink, take bribes, keep Negro mistresses, or indulge in bureaucratic intrigue, and he is, in fact, disliked on all sides because of his uprightness, like Aristides the Just. His leniency toward the Portuguese captain is his first lapse. After it, his life becomes a sort of fable on the theme of "Oh, what a tangled web we weave", and in every single instance it is the goodness of his heart that leads him astray. Actuated at the start by pity, he has a love affair with a girl who has been rescued from a torpedoed ship. He continues with the affair largely out of a sense of duty, since the girl will go to pieces morally if abandoned; he also lies about her to his wife, so as to spare her the pangs of jealousy. Since he intends to persist in his adultery, he does not go to confession, and in order to lull his wife's suspicions he tells her that he has gone. This involves him in the truly fearful act of taking the Sacrament while in a state of mortal sin. By this time, there are other complications, all caused in the same manner, and Scobie finally decides that the only way out is through the unforgivable sin of suicide. Nobody else must be allowed to suffer through his death; it will be so arranged as to look like an accident. As it happens, he bungles one detail, and the fact that he has committed suicide becomes known. The book ends with a Catholic priest's hinting, with doubtful orthodoxy, that Scobie is perhaps not damned. Scobie, however, had not entertained any such hope. White all through, with a stiff upper lip, he had gone to what he believed to be certain damnation out of pure gentlemanliness.

I have not parodied the plot of the book. Even when dressed up in realistic details, it is just as ridiculous as I have indicated. The thing most obviously wrong with it is that Scobie's motives, assuming one could believe in them, do not adequately explain his actions. Another question that comes up is: Why should this novel have its setting in West Africa? Except that one of the characters is a Syrian trader, the whole thing might as well be happening in a London suburb. The Africans exist only as an occasionally mentioned background, and the thing that would actually be in Scobie's mind the whole time—the hostility between black and white, and the struggle against the local nationalist movement—is not mentioned at all. Indeed, although we are shown his thoughts in considerable detail, he seldom appears to think about his work, and then only of trivial aspects of it, and never about the war, although the date is 1942. All he is interested in is his own progress toward damnation. The improbability of this shows up against the colonial setting, but it is an improbability that is present in *Brighton Rock* as well, and that is bound to result from foisting theological preoccupations upon simple people anywhere.

The central idea of the book is that it is better, spiritually higher, to be an erring Catholic than a virtuous pagan. Graham Greene would probably subscribe to the statement of Maritain, made apropos of Léon Bloy, that "there is but one sadness—not to be a saint." A saying of Péguy's is quoted on the title page of the book to the effect that the sinner is "at the very heart of Christianity" and knows more of Christianity than anyone else does, except the saint. All such sayings contain, or can be made to contain, the fairly sinister suggestion that ordinary human decency is of no value and that any one sin is no worse than any other sin. In addition, it is impossible not to feel a sort of snobbishness in Mr Greene's attitude, both here and in his other books written from an explicitly Catholic standpoint. He appears to share the idea, which has been floating around ever since Baudelaire, that there is something rather *distingué* in being damned; Hell is a sort of high-class night club, entry to which is reserved for Catholics only, since the others, the non-Catholics, are too ignorant to be held guilty, like the beasts that perish. We are carefully informed that Catholics are no better than anybody else; they even, perhaps, have a tendency to be worse, since their temptations are greater. In modern Catholic novels, in both France and England, it is, indeed, the fashion to include bad priests, or at least inadequate priests, as a change from Father Brown. (I imagine that one major objective of young English Catholic writers is not to resemble Chesterton.) But all the while—drunken, lecherous, criminal, or damned outright—the Catholics retain their superiority since they alone know the meaning of good and evil. Incidentally, it is assumed in *The Heart of the Matter*, and in most of Mr Greene's other books, that no one outside the Catholic Church has the most elementary knowledge of Christian doctrine.

This cult of the sanctified sinner seems to me to be frivolous, and underneath it there probably lies a weakening of belief, for when people really believed in Hell, they were not so fond of striking graceful attitudes on its brink. More to the point, by trying to clothe theological speculations in flesh and blood, it produces psychological absurdities. In *The Power and the Glory*, the struggle between this-worldly and other-worldly values is convincing because it is not occurring inside one person. On the one side, there is the priest, a poor creature in some ways but made heroic by his belief in his own thaumaturgic powers; on the other side, there is the lieutenant, representing human justice and material progress, and also a heroic figure after his fashion. They can respect each other, perhaps, but not understand each other. The priest, at any rate, is not credited with any very complex thoughts. In *Brighton Rock*, on the other hand, the central situation is incredible, since it presupposes that the most brutishly stupid person can, merely by having been brought up a Catholic, be capable of great intellectual subtlety. Pinkie, the race-course gangster, is a species of satanist, while his still more limited girl friend understands and even states the difference between the categories "right and wrong" and "good and evil". In, for example, Mauriac's *Thérèse* sequence, the spiritual conflict does not outrage probability, because it is not pretended that Thérèse is a normal person. She is a chosen spirit, pursuing her salvation over a long period and by a difficult route, like a patient stretched out on the psychiatrist's sofa. To take an opposite instance, Evelyn Waugh's *Brideshead Revisited*, in spite of improbabilities, which are traceable partly to the book's being written in the first person, succeeds because the situation is itself a normal one. The Catholic characters bump up against problems they would meet with in real life; they do not suddenly move on to a different intellectual plane as soon as their religious beliefs are involved. Scobie is incredible because the two halves of him do not fit together. If he were capable of getting into the kind of mess that is described, he would have got into it years earlier. If he really felt that adultery was mortal sin, he would stop committing it; if he persisted in it, his sense of sin would weaken. If he believed in Hell, he would not risk going there merely to spare the feelings of a couple of neurotic women. And one might add that if he were the kind of man we are told he is—that is, a man whose chief characteristic is a horror of causing pain—he would not be an officer in a colonial police force.

There are other improbabilities, some of which arise out of Mr Greene's method of handling a love affair. Every novelist has his own conventions, and, just as in an E.M. Forster novel there is a strong tendency for the characters to die suddenly without sufficient cause, so in a Graham Greene novel there is a tendency for people to go to bed together almost at sight and with no apparent pleasure to either party. Often this is credible enough, but in *The Heart of the Matter* its effect is to weaken a motive that, for the purposes of the story, ought to be a very strong one. Again, there is the usual, perhaps unavoidable, mistake of making everyone too highbrow. It is not only that Major Scobie is a theologian. His wife, who is represented as an almost complete fool, reads poetry, while the detective who is sent by the Field Security Corps to spy on Scobie even writes poetry. Here one is up against the fact that it is not easy for most modern writers to imagine the mental processes of anyone who is not a writer.

It seems a pity, when one remembers how admirably he has written of Africa elsewhere, that Mr Greene should have made just this book out of his war-time African experiences. The fact that the book is set in Africa while the action takes place almost entirely inside a tiny white community gives it an air of triviality. However, one must not carp too much. It is pleasant to see Mr Greene starting up again after so long a silence, and in post-war England it is a remarkable feat for a novelist to write a novel at all. At any rate, Mr Greene has not been permanently demoralised by the habits acquired during the war, like so many others. But one may hope that his next book will have a different theme, or, if not, that he will at least remember that a perception of the vanity of earthly things, though it may be enough to get one into Heaven, is not sufficient equipment for the writing of a novel.

New Yorker, 17 July 1948

123. Review

Great Morning by Osbert Sitwell

As the successive wars, like ranges of hills, rear their bulk between ourselves and the past, autobiography becomes a sort of antiquarianism. One need only be a little over forty to remember things that are as remote from the present age as chain armour or girdles of chastity. Many people have remarked nostalgically on the fact that before 1914 you could travel to any country in the world, except perhaps Russia, without a passport. But what strikes me in retrospect as even more startling is that in those days you could walk into a bicycle shop—an ordinary bicycle shop, not even a gunsmith's—and buy a revolver and cartridges, with no questions asked. Clearly, that is not the kind of social atmosphere that we shall ever see again, and when Sir Osbert Sitwell writes of "before 1914" with open regret, his emotion can hardly be called reactionary. Reaction implies an effort to restore the past, and though the world might conceivably be pushed back to the pattern of 1938, there can be no more question of restoring the Edwardian age than of reviving Albigensianism.

Not that Sir Osbert's early years were altogether carefree, as readers of the first two volumes of his autobiography will have noticed. His father, Sir George Sitwell, was a trying man to have any dealings with: an architectural genius gone astray, who squandered fantastic sums in megalomaniac building schemes, which extended even to altering the landscape and constructing artificial lakes whose water seeped into the coal mines below and caused endless lawsuits—all this while considering a shilling a week sufficient pocket-money for a boy of nineteen, and even refusing to rescue his wife from the clutches of a money-lender. Architecture apart, his main purpose in life—not, perhaps, from downright malice but as a sort of prolonged practical joke—was to force everyone connected with him into doing whatever he or she most disliked. Osbert, whose antipathy to horses was well known, was driven into a cavalry regiment, then escaped into the Grenadier Guards, then, when he seemed too happy in the Guards, was found a job in the Town Clerk's office in Scarborough, after receiving lessons in pot-hooks (to improve his handwriting) at the age of twenty. The war rescued him from this, but his brother and sister were similarly treated. Nevertheless the last few years before the war were happy ones, and, making all allowance for his abnormal position as a rich man's son, he is probably right in feeling that English life then had a gaiety that has never been recovered.

Life in the Guards was pleasant because it meant being stationed in London, which in its turn meant theatres, music and picture galleries. Osbert's brother officers were civilised and tolerant, and his colonel even excused him for sitting in a café with Jacob Epstein, who was in private's uniform. It was the age of Chaliapin and the Russian Ballet, and of the revival in England of a serious interest in music and painting. It was also the age of rag-time and the tango, of the "knuts" in their grey top-hats, of house-boats and hobble skirts, and of a splashing to and fro of wealth such as the world had not seen since the early Roman empire. The Victorian puritanism had at last broken down, money was pouring in from all directions, and the sense of guilt which is now inseparable from a privileged position had not yet developed. Barney Barnato and Sir William Whiteley were held up as models to emulate, and it was meritorious not merely to be rich, but to look rich. Life in London was a ceaseless round of entertainment, on a scale unheard-of before and barely imaginable now:

> One band in a house was no longer enough, there must be two,
> even three. Electric fans whirled on the top of enormous blocks
> of ice, buried in banks of hydrangeas, like the shores from which

the barque departs for Cythera. Never had there been such
displays of flowers. . . . Never had Europe seen such mounds of
peaches, figs, nectarines and strawberries at all seasons, brought
from their steamy tents of glass. Champagne bottles stood
stacked on the sideboards. . . . As guests, only the poor of every
race were barred. Even foreigners could enter, if they were rich.

There was also the life of the country houses, with their platoons of
servants. Osbert, inimical to horses, was no hunting man, but he
enjoyed his shooting expeditions in spite of, or perhaps because of,
the fact that he never succeeded in killing anything, and his talks
with the crabbed old gamekeeper, a type of man now extinct—the
type that accepts a position of vassalage, and within that framework
is able to enjoy a considerable independence.

Of course, if you happened not to belong to the world of champagne and hot-house strawberries, life before 1914 had serious disadvantages. Even today, after two murderous wars, the manual
workers throughout most of the world are probably better off, in a
physical sense, than they were then. In Britain they are unquestionably better off. But will this still be true after a third world war, this
time conducted with atom bombs? Or even after another fifty years of
soil erosion and squandering of the world's fuel resources? Before
1914, moreover, people had the inestimable advantage of not knowing that war was coming, or, if they did know it, of not foreseeing
what it would be like. Sir Osbert does not claim much more than that
life in those days was fun for a privileged minority, and, as anyone
who has read *Before the Bombardment* will know, he is perfectly alive
to the vulgarity and grotesqueness of the whole epoch. His political
outlook, in so far as this book implies one at all, seems to be a mild
liberalism. "In those days," he says, "the rich were as much and
unjustly revered as they are now reviled." But in the golden summer
of 1914 he greatly enjoyed being rich, and he is honest enough to say so.

There is now a widespread idea that nostalgic feelings about the
past are inherently vicious. One ought, apparently, to live in a continuous present, a minute-to-minute cancellation of memory, and if
one thinks of the past at all it should merely be in order to thank God
that we are so much better than we used to be. This seems to me a
sort of intellectual face-lifting, the motive behind which is a snobbish
terror of growing old. One ought to realise that a human being cannot continue developing indefinitely, and that a writer, in particular,

is throwing away his heritage if he repudiates the experience of his early life. In many ways it is a grave handicap to remember that lost paradise "before the war"—that is, before the other war. In other ways it is an advantage. Each generation has its own experience and its own wisdom, and though there is such a thing as intellectual progress, so that the ideas of one age are sometimes demonstrably less silly than those of the last—still, one is likelier to make a good book by sticking to one's early-acquired vision than by a futile effort to "keep up". The great thing is to be your age, which includes being honest about your social origins. In the nineteen-thirties we saw a whole literary generation, or at least the most prominent members of a generation, either pretending to be proletarians or indulging in public orgies of self-hatred because they were not proletarians. Even if they could have kept up this attitude (today, a surprising number of them have either fled to America or found themselves jobs in the BBC or the British Council), it was a stupid one, because their bourgeois origin was not a thing that could be altered. It is to Sir Osbert Sitwell's credit that he has never pretended to be other than he is: a member of the upper classes, with an amused and leisurely attitude which comes out in his manner of writing, and which could only be the product of an expensive upbringing. Probably, so far as his memory serves him, he records his likes and dislikes accurately, which always needs moral courage. How easy it would have been to write of Eton or the Grenadier Guards in a spirit of sneering superiority, with the implication that from earliest youth he was the holder of enlightened sentiments which, in fact, no comfortably-placed person did hold a generation ago. Or how easy, on the other hand, to stand on the defensive and try to argue away the injustice and inequality of the world in which he grew up. He has done neither, with the result that these three volumes (*Left Hand, Right Hand, The Scarlet Tree* and *Great Morning*), although the range they cover is narrow, must be among the best autobiographies of our time.

Adelphi, July–September 1948

124. The Freedom Defence Committee

The British people accept freedom as a matter of course and tend to forget that its price is "eternal vigilance".

Even if they remember that famous saying, they do not seem to realise that vigilance is an activity involving time, energy and money.

The Freedom Defence Committee was set up in 1945 "to uphold the essential liberty of individuals and organisations, and to defend those who are persecuted for exercising their rights to freedom of speech, writing and action".

Our Bulletin, which is available to anyone who applies to the Secretary, shows to what an extent our existence has been justified. Cases of unjust imprisonment, excessive sentences and racial discrimination are frequent.

Threats to freedom of speech, writing and action, though often trivial in isolation, are cumulative in their effect and, unless checked, lead to a general disrespect for the rights of the citizen.

The Committee gives aid to individuals or organisations irrespective of their political views, the nature of the attack on their freedom being the sole criterion on which it is determined whether or not action should be taken.

The Committee is opposed in principle to all forms of military and industrial conscription, and works for the abolition of the Emergency Powers Act, Defence Regulations and all existing statutes restricting the freedom of political action.

We need a regular income of at least £1,000 if we are to carry on efficiently. This has not been forthcoming in the past year and our accounts now show a deficit of over £145. To enable our work to go forward, therefore, we need an immediate sum of at least £500.

Our basic requirements are modest enough—a thousand regular subscribers at a guinea a year; but we are also in desperate need of lump-sum donations to enable us to pay our debts and keep our office open.

Subscriptions and donations should be sent to Herbert Read, Chairman, Freedom Defence Committee, 8 Endsleigh Gardens, London, WC1

(Signed) Benjamin Britten,
E.M. Forster,
Augustus John,
George Orwell,
Herbert Read,
Osbert Sitwell.

Socialist Leader, 18 September 1948

125. Letter to F. J. Warburg

Barnhill
Isle of Jura
Argyllshire
22 October 1948

Dear Fred,

You will have had my wire by now, and if anything crossed your mind I dare say I shall have had a return wire from you by the time this goes off. I shall finish the book, DV, early in November, and I am rather flinching from the job of typing it, because it is a very awkward thing to do in bed, where I still have to spend half the time. Also there will have to be carbon copies, a thing which always fidgets me, and the book is fearfully long, I should think well over 100,000 words, possibly 125,000. I can't send it away because it is an unbelievably bad MS and no one could make head or tail of it without explanation. On the other hand a skilled typist under my eye could do it easily enough. If you can think of anybody who would be willing to come, I will send money for the journey and full instructions. I think we could make her quite comfortable. There is always plenty to eat and I will see that she has a comfortable warm place to work in.

I am not pleased with the book but I am not absolutely dissatisfied. I first thought of it in 1943. I think it is a good idea but the execution would have been better if I had not written it under the influence of TB. I haven't definitely fixed on the title but I am hesitating between "Nineteen Eighty-Four" and "The Last Man in Europe".

I have just had Sartre's book on antisemitism, which you published, to review.[1] I think Sartre is a bag of wind and I am going to give him a good boot.

Please give everyone my love.

Yours
George

[1] *Portrait of the Antisemite.* See 127.

126. Letter to Julian Symons

Barnhill
Isle of Jura
Argyllshire
29 October 1948

Dear Julian,

I can't thank you enough for the tea, which I do hope you could spare. My sister, who keeps house for me, was enchanted to see it and asked me to say she will pack up a little butter for you next churning day. I am so glad to hear that all is well with your wife and daughter and that you enjoy having a baby. They're really great fun, so much so that I find myself wishing at each stage that they could stay like that. I suppose you are on the steady grind of 5 bottles and 15 nappies a day. It's funny that they are so insatiably greedy when they are small babies and then between about 2 and 6 it is such a fight to get them to eat, except between meals. I wonder which milk you are using. We brought up Richard on Ostermilk, which seemed to be better than National Dried. . . . You've got a big battle ahead when it comes to weaning time.

I was very well for some time after leaving hospital but have been very poorly again for the last month. Ironically it started with my going back to the hospital to be re-examined and being upset by the journey. We had a filthy summer, which doesn't help one to recover. Latterly the weather has been quite nice but I have been too sick and sorry to go out of the house much. I can work, but that is about all I can do. Even to walk half a mile upsets me. I was going to come down to London in January, but I am consulting with my doctor and if he thinks it best I shall go into a private sanatorium, if I can find one, for the worst of the winter, i.e. Jan–Feb. I could go abroad perhaps, but the journey might be the death of me, so perhaps a sanatorium would be best. I think I am going to give up my London flat, as I never use it at present and it costs me about £100 a year and a lot of nuisance. Of course I shall have to get another London place later. I shall finish my book, DV, in a week or ten days, but I am rather flinching from typing it, which is a tiring job and in any case can't be done in bed where I have to be half the day. So I am trying to get a good stenog to come here for a fortnight. I can't send the MS away because it is in too much of a mess to be intelligible unless I am there to explain. The trouble is it's not easy to get typists for short periods nowadays, at least good ones, and some might funk the journey. It's only a two-hour crossing, but one can be very sick in two hours, as I well know.

I am rather surprised to hear of John Davenport[1] associating himself with a CP or near CP paper.[2] He used not to be that way inclined, that I knew of. *Politics & Letters* I am sorry to say has disappeared and is supposed to be reappearing next year as a monthly, rather to my annoyance as they had an article of mine. It is nonsense what Fyvel said about Eliot being antisemitic. Of course you can find what would now be called antisemitic remarks in his early work, but who didn't say such things at that time? One has to draw a distinction between what was said before and what after 1934. Of course all these nationalistic prejudices are ridiculous, but disliking Jews isn't intrinsically worse than disliking Negroes or Americans or any other block of people. In the early 'twenties, Eliot's antisemitic remarks were about on a par with the automatic sneer one casts at Anglo-Indian colonels in boarding houses. On the other hand if they had been written after the persecutions began they would have meant something quite different. Look for instance at the Anglophobia in the USA, which is shared even by people like Edmund Wilson. It doesn't matter, because we are not being persecuted. But if 6 million Englishmen had recently been killed in gas vans, I imagine I should feel insecure if I even saw a joke in a French comic paper about Englishwomen's teeth sticking out. Some people go round smelling after antisemitism all the time. I have no doubt Fyvel thinks I am antisemitic. More rubbish is written about this subject than any other I can think of. I have just had Sartre's book on the subject for review, and I doubt whether it would be possible to pack more nonsense into so short a space. I have maintained from the start that Sartre is a bag of wind, though possibly when it comes to Existentialism, which I don't profess to understand, it may not be so.

Richard is blooming. He is still I think backward about talking, but lively enough in other ways and really almost helpful about the farm and garden. Something tells me he won't be one for book-

[1] John Davenport (1906–1966), critic and man of letters, a friend of many writers and painters.

[2] Probably *Our Time*, to which John Davenport was a contributor. In the autumn of 1948 it was edited by Frank Jellinek and in 1949 by Randall Swingler.

learning and that his bent is for mechanics. I shan't try to influence him, but if he grew up with the ambition of being a farmer I should be pleased. Of course that may be the only job left after the atom bombs. If the show does start and is as bad as one fears, it would be fairly easy to be self-supporting on these islands provided one wasn't looted. The winters are a good deal milder than in England, which means that at a pinch one can keep animals through the winter without fodder, and in fact the sheep are very rarely fed in a normal winter. For the first time in my life I have tried the experiment of keeping a pig. They really are disgusting brutes and we are all longing for the day when he goes to the butcher, but I am glad to see they do well here. He has grown to a stupendous size purely on milk and potatoes, without our buying any food for him from outside. In another year or so I shall have to be thinking about Richard's schooling, but I am not making any plans because one can't see far ahead now. I am not going to let him go to a boarding school before he is ten, and I would like him to start off at the elementary school. If one could find a good one. It's a difficult question. Obviously it is democratic for everyone to go to the same schools, or at least start off there but when you see what the elementary schools are like, and the results, you feel that any child that has the chance should be rescued from them. It is quite easy, for instance, to leave those schools at 14 without having learned to read. I heard on the wireless lately that 10 per cent of army recruits, aged 19, have to be taught to read after they join the army. I remember in 1936 meeting John Strachey[1] in the street—then a CP member or at least on the staff of the [*Daily*] *Worker*—and him telling me he had just had a son and was putting him down for Eton. I said "How can you do that?" and he said that given our existing society it was the best education. Actually I doubt whether it is the best, but in principle I don't feel sure that he was wrong. However I am taking no decisions about Richard one way or the other. Of course we may all have been blown to hell before it becomes urgent, but personally I don't expect a major shooting war for 5 or 10 years. After the Russians have fully recovered and have atomic bombs, I suppose it isn't avoidable. And even if it is avoided, there are a lot of other unpleasantnesses blowing up.

[1] John Strachey (1901–63), politician and political theorist; Labour MP 1929–31, 1945–63; his book *The Coming Struggle for Power*, 1932, was the most influential exercise in Marxism produced by the English Left. In 1946 he bcame a prominent member of the Labour Government.

Please remember me to your wife and give my best regards to your daughter.

Yours
George

127. Review

Portrait of the Antisemite by Jean-Paul Sartre, translated from the French by Erik de Mauny

Antisemitism is obviously a subject that needs serious study, but it seems unlikely that it will get it in the near future. The trouble is that so long as antisemitism is regarded simply as a disgraceful aberration, almost a crime, anyone literate enough to have heard the word will naturally claim to be immune from it; with the result that books on antisemitism tend to be mere exercises in casting motes out of other people's eyes. M. Sartre's book is no exception, and it is probably no better for having been written in 1944, in the uneasy, self-justifying, quisling-hunting period that followed on the Liberation.

At the beginning, M. Sartre informs us that antisemitism has no rational basis: at the end, that it will not exist in a classless society, and that in the meantime it can perhaps be combated to some extent by education and propaganda. These conclusions would hardly be worth stating for their own sake, and in between them there is, in spite of much cerebration, little real discussion of the subject, and no factual evidence worth mentioning.

We are solemnly informed that antisemitism is almost unknown among the working class. It is a malady of the bourgeoisie, and, above all, of that goat upon whom all our sins are laid, the "petty bourgeois". Within the bourgeoisie it is seldom found among scientists and engineers. It is a peculiarity of people who think of nationality in terms of inherited culture and of property in terms of land.

Why these people should pick on Jews rather than some other victim M. Sartre does not discuss, except, in one place, by putting forward the ancient and very dubious theory that the Jews are hated because they are supposed to have been responsible for the Crucifixion. He makes no attempt to relate antisemitism to such obviously allied phenomena as for instance, colour prejudice.

Part of what is wrong with M. Sartre's approach is indicated by his title. "The" antisemite, he seems to imply all through the book, is always the same kind of person, recognisable at a glance and, so to speak, in action the whole time. Actually one has only to use a little observation to see that antisemitism is extremely widespread, is not confined to any one class, and, above all, in any but the worst cases, is intermittent.

But these facts would not square with M. Sartre's atomised vision of society. There is, he comes near to saying, no such thing as a human being, there are only different categories of men, such as "the" worker and "the" bourgeois, all classifiable in much the same way as insects. Another of these insect-like creatures is "the" Jew, who, it seems, can usually be distinguished by his physical appearance. It is true that there are two kinds of Jew, the "Authentic Jew", who wants to remain Jewish, and the "Inauthentic Jew", who would like to be assimilated; but a Jew, of whichever variety, is not just another human being. He is wrong, at this stage of history, if he tries to assimilate himself, and we are wrong if we try to ignore his racial origin. He should be accepted into the national community, not as an ordinary Englishman, Frenchman, or whatever it may be, but as a Jew.

It will be seen that this position is itself dangerously close to antisemitism. Race prejudice of any kind is a neurosis, and it is doubtful whether argument can either increase or diminish it, but the net effect of books of this kind, if they have an effect, is probably to make antisemitism slightly more prevalent than it was before. The first step towards serious study of antisemitism is to stop regarding it as a crime. Meanwhile, the less talk there is about "the" Jew or "the" antisemite, as a species of animal different from ourselves, the better.

Observer, 7 November 1948

454

128. Letter to Anthony Powell

Barnhill
Isle of Jura
Argyllshire
15 November 1948

Dear Tony,
Please excuse bad typing, but I am in bed and this is a very decrepit typewriter. Thanks so much for your letter. Yes, *do* send the Barry Pain[1] etc books. I love anything like that. Maybe some of them would be worth binding. There are people in Edinburgh who bind books. I came out of hospital in July very much better, but have been in lousy health for the last month or more and am trying to arrange to spend the worst of the winter in a sanatorium. I suppose it's a step up over last winter, i.e. a sanatorium not a hospital—perhaps in 1949 I might manage to spend the winter at home. I could go abroad perhaps, but I am afraid the journey would literally be the death of me. I can work, but that is about all I can do. To walk even a few hundred yards promptly upsets me. It's annoying that after a filthy summer we've been having nice autumn weather but I can't so much as pull a weed up in the garden. I am just on the grisly job of typing out my novel. I can't type much because it tires me too much to sit up at table, and I asked Roger Senhouse to try and send me a stenog for a fortnight, but of course it's not so easy to get people for short periods like that. It's awful to think I've been mucking about with this book since June of 1947, and it's a ghastly mess now, a good idea ruined, but of course I was seriously ill for 7 or 8 months of the time. Richard is blooming and getting enormous. I don't think somehow he'll be much of a one for booklearning. He is rather backward in talking and shows no interest in learning his letters (age $4\frac{1}{2}$), but on the other hand is good with machinery and likes working on the farm, fishing and things like that. I'm not going to influence him, but would like it if he went in for farming, perhaps the only job there will be left after the atom bombs. Another year and I suppose he will be going to school. I just reread *From a View to a Death*[2] and enjoyed it immensely. I put in for the Aubrey[3] book with the *Observer* but I

[1] Barry Pain (1864–1928), humorous novelist, author of the *Eliza* books, etc, very popular in the Edwardian era.
[2] A novel by Anthony Powell, 1933.
[3] *John Aubrey and his Friends* by Anthony Powell.

don't know whether I shall get it. If you see Malcolm[1] tell him from me that I recently read his book on Samuel Butler[2] and that though I enjoyed it I consider it quite shameful. Please remember me to Violet. I hope the family are well.

Yours
George

129. Review

Notes towards the Definition of Culture by T.S. Eliot

In his new book, *Notes towards the Definition of Culture*, Mr T.S. Eliot argues that a truly civilised society needs a class system as part of its basis. He is, of course, only speaking negatively. He does not claim that there is any method by which a high civilisation can be created. He maintains merely that such a civilisation is not likely to flourish in the absence of certain conditions, of which class distinctions are one.

This opens up a gloomy prospect, for on the one hand it is almost certain that class distinctions of the old kind are moribund, and on the other hand Mr Eliot has at the least a strong *prima facie* case.

The essence of his argument is that the highest levels of culture have been attained only by small groups of people—either social groups or regional groups—who have been able to perfect their traditions over long periods of time. The most important of all cultural influences is the family, and family loyalty is strongest when the majority of people take it for granted to go through life at the social level at which they were born. Moreover, not having any precedents to go upon, we do not know what a classless society would be like. We know only that, since functions would still have to be diversified, classes would have to be replaced by "élites", a term Mr Eliot borrows with evident distaste from the late Karl Mannheim. The élites will plan, organise and administer: whether they can become the guardians and transmitters of culture, as certain social classes have been in the past, Mr Eliot doubts, perhaps justifiably.

[1] Malcolm Muggeridge (1903–), novelist, critic, journalist and television personality. In the late 'thirties he had corresponded with Orwell about the Spanish civil war. During the war Anthony Powell introduced them and they remained friends until Orwell's death.

[2] *Samuel Butler* by Malcolm Muggeridge.

As always, Mr Eliot insists that tradition does not mean worship of the past; on the contrary, a tradition is alive only while it is growing. A class can preserve a culture because it is itself an organic and changing thing. But here, curiously enough, Mr Eliot misses what might have been the strongest argument in his case. This is, that a classless society directed by élites may ossify very rapidly, simply because its rulers are able to choose their successors, and will always tend to choose people resembling themselves.

Hereditary institutions—as Mr Eliot might have argued—have the virtue of being unstable. They must be so, because power is constantly devolving on people who are either incapable of holding it, or use it for purposes not intended by their forefathers. It is impossible to imagine any hereditary body lasting so long, and with so little change, as an adoptive organisation like the Catholic Church. And it is at least thinkable that another adoptive and authoritarian organisation, the Russian Communist Party, will have a similar history. If it hardens into a class, as some observers believe it is already doing, then it will change and develop as classes always do. But if it continues to co-opt its members from all strata of society, and then train them into the desired mentality, it might keep its shape almost unaltered from generation to generation. In aristocratic societies the eccentric aristocrat is a familiar figure, but the eccentric commissar is almost a contradiction in terms.

Although Mr Eliot does not make use of this argument, he does argue that even the antagonism between classes can have fruitful results for society as a whole. This again is probably true. Yet one continues to have, throughout his book, the feeling that there is something wrong, and that he himself is aware of it. The fact is that class privilege, like slavery, has somehow ceased to be defensible. It conflicts with certain moral assumptions which Mr Eliot appears to share, although intellectually he may be in disagreement with them.

All through the book his attitude is noticeably defensive. When class distinctions were vigorously believed in, it was not thought necessary to reconcile them either with social justice or with efficiency. The superiority of the ruling classes was held to be self-evident, and in any case the existing order was what God had ordained. The mute inglorious Milton was a sad case, but not remediable on this side of the grave.

This, however, is by no means what Mr Eliot is saying. He would like, he says, to see in existence both classes *and* élites. It should be normal for the average human being to go through life at his predestined social level, but on the other hand the right man must be able to find his way into the right job. In saying this he seems almost to give away his whole case. For if class distinctions are desirable in themselves, then wastage of talent, or inefficiency in high places, are comparatively unimportant. The social misfit, instead of being directed upwards or downwards, should learn to be contented in his own station.

Mr Eliot does not say this: indeed, very few people in our time would say it. It would seem morally offensive. Probably, therefore, Mr Eliot does not believe in class distinctions as our grandfathers believed in them. His approval of them is only negative. That is to say, he cannot see how any civilisation worth having can survive in a society where the differences arising from social background or geographical origin have been ironed out.

It is difficult to make any positive answer to this. To all appearances the old social distinctions are everywhere disappearing, because their economic basis is being destroyed. Possibly new classes are appearing, or possibly we are within sight of a genuinely classless society, which Mr Eliot assumes would be a cultureless society. He may be right, but at some points his pessimism seems to be exaggerated. "We can assert with some confidence," he says, "that our own period is one of decline; that the standards of culture are lower than they were fifty years ago; and that the evidence of this decline is visible in every department of human activity."

This seems true when one thinks of Hollywood films or the atomic bomb, but less true if one thinks of the clothes and architecture of 1898, or what life was like at that date for an unemployed labourer in the East End of London. In any case, as Mr Eliot himself admits at the start, we cannot reverse the present trend by conscious action. Cultures are not manufactured, they grow of their own accord. Is it too much to hope that the classless society will secrete a culture of its own? And before writing off our own age as irrevocably damned, is it not worth remembering that Matthew Arnold and Swift and Shakespeare—to carry the story back only three centuries—were all equally certain that they lived in a period of decline?

Observer, 28 November 1948

130. Letter to Gwen O'Shaughnessy

Barnhill
Isle of Jura
Argyllshire
28 November 1948

Dear Gwen,

I wonder whether you know of a private sanatorium where they would be likely to have room for me. I have not felt really well since September, and sometimes felt very bad, and I thought it would be a good idea to go into a sanatorium for the worst of the winter, i.e. January and February and perhaps part of March. Dr Dick agreed with me and recommended me to a place called the Grampian Sanatorium at Kingussie, which is the only private sanatorium in Scotland. However, they are full up. I have no doubt there are many more in England, however. It must be a private place, because the public ones will all have waiting lists, and also I must have a room to myself, otherwise I can't work. I can't of course pay things like 30 guineas a week, but can pay anything reasonable. Do you know of anywhere?

I hope the kids are well. All is well here and Richard is bursting with energy. He goes out fishing with the others now, and sometimes catches quite a lot of fish. The weather just lately has been very nice, beautiful still sunny days and not at all cold, but I hardly ever go out of doors because the smallest exertion upsets me. The pig has grown to a stupendous size and goes to the butcher next week. We are all longing to get rid of him, as he is so destructive and greedy, even gets into the kitchen sometimes. Bill has got a young bull which seems a nice quiet beast and I trust will remain so. Avril is going up to London for a week or so in December to do some shopping and to see about giving up the Islington flat, which I don't want to keep on as it is simply an expense. I have finished my book, which I had been messing about with since some time in 1947. I am busy typing it out now, a ghastly job as it tires me to sit up much and I have to do most of it in a sofa. I tried to get a stenog to come here for a fortnight and do it for me, but the arrangements went wrong. Avril sends love.

Yours
George

131. Letter to F. J. Warburg

Barnhill
21 December 1948

Dear Fred,

Thanks for two letters. I am really very unwell indeed & am arranging to go into a sanatorium early in January. I suppose there *may* be some slip-up, but if not my address as from 7.1.49 will be The Cotswold Sanatorium, Cranham, Glos. But better consider Barnhill my address till I confirm the other. I ought to have done this 2 months ago but I wanted to get that bloody book finished.

Abt photos. I have none here, but I'm pretty certain I had a number at my flat, which my sister has just been closing up & dismantling. The photos will have been in a file which will be coming up here, but I suppose not for ages, as anything sent by rail takes months. I'll send you any photos I can when they arrive, but meanwhile could you try first Moore, who I *think* has one or two, & then Vernon & Marie-Louise Richards,[1] who took a lot 3 years ago & should have a lot of prints if they haven't chucked them away. You could get their address from that little Anarchist bookshop near you, or from Herbert Read or others. They'd want copyright of course, but not much. They took a number, some very good, some bad— don't pick out the awful ones, will you. At need we could bring a photographer to the sanatorium, but I am really a deaths-head at present, & I imagine shall be in bed for a month or so.

I'm glad you liked the book. It isn't a book I would gamble on for a big sale, but I suppose one could be sure of 10,000 anyway. It's still beautiful weather here, but I never stir out of doors & seldom off the sofa. Richard is offensively well, & everything else flourishing except me. I am trying to finish off my scraps of book reviewing etc & must then just strike work for a month or so. I can't go on as at present. I have a stunning idea for a very short novel which has been in my head for years, but I can't start anything until I am free from high temperatures etc.

Love to all
George

[1] They both took photographs for newspapers and magazines and in 1946, at Orwell's request, they took several photographs of him and his adopted son, Richard.

132. Letter to Roger Senhouse

Barnhill
Isle of Jura
Argyll.
26 December 1948

Dear Roger,

Thanks so much for your letter. As to the blurb,[1] I really don't think the approach in the draft you sent me is the right one. It makes the book sound as though it were a thriller mixed up with a love story, & I didn't intend it to be primarily that. What it is really meant to do is to discuss the implications of dividing the world up into "Zones of influence" (I thought of it in 1944 as a result of the Teheran Conference), & in addition to indicate by parodying them the intellectual implications of totalitarianism. It has always seemed to me that people have not faced up to these & that, e.g. the persecution of scientists in Russia, is simply part of a logical process which should have been foreseeable 10–20 years ago. When you get to the proof stage, how would it be to get some eminent person who might be interested, e.g. Bertrand Russell or Lancelot Hogben, to give his opinions abt the book, & (if he consented) use a piece of that as the blurb? There are a number of people one might choose from.

I am going into a sanatorium as from 6th Jan & unless there is some last-minute slip-up my address will be, The Cotswold Sanatorium, Cranham, Glos.

Love to all
George

---

[1] For *Nineteen Eighty-Four*

1949

133. Reflections on Gandhi

Saints should always be judged guilty until they are proved innocent, but the tests that have to be applied to them are not, of course, the same in all cases. In Gandhi's case the questions one feels inclined to ask are: to what extent was Gandhi moved by vanity—by the consciousness of himself as a humble, naked old man, sitting on a praying-mat and shaking empires by sheer spiritual power—and to what extent did he compromise his own principles by entering into politics, which of their nature are inseparable from coercion and fraud? To give a definite answer one would have to study Gandhi's acts and writings in immense detail, for his whole life was a sort of pilgrimage in which every act was significant. But this partial autobiography, which ends in the nineteen-twenties, is strong evidence in his favour, all the more because it covers what he would have called the unregenerate part of his life and reminds one that inside the saint, or near-saint, there was a very shrewd, able person who could, if he had chosen, have been a brilliant success as a lawyer, an administrator or perhaps even a businessman.

At about the time when the autobiography[1] first appeared I remember reading its opening chapters in the ill-printed pages of some Indian newspaper. They made a good impression on me, which Gandhi himself, at that time, did not. The things that one associated with him—homespun cloth, "soul forces" and vegetarianism—were unappealing, and his medievalist programme was obviously not viable in a backward, starving, overpopulated country. It was also apparent that the British were making use of him, or thought they were making use of him. Strictly speaking, as a Nationalist, he was an enemy, but since in every crisis he would exert himself to prevent violence—which, from the British point of view, meant preventing any effective action whatever—he could be regarded as "our man".

[1] *The Story of my Experiments with Truth* by M.K. Gandhi, translated from the Gujarati by Mahadev Desai.

In private this was sometimes cynically admitted. The attitude of the
Indian millionaires was similar. Gandhi called upon them to repent,
and naturally they preferred him to the Socialists and Communists
who, given the chance, would actually have taken their money away.
How reliable such calculations are in the long run is doubtful; as
Gandhi himself says, "in the end deceivers deceive only themselves";
but at any rate the gentleness with which he was nearly always
handled was due partly to the feeling that he was useful. The British
Conservatives only became really angry with him when, as in 1942,
he was in effect turning his non-violence against a different conqueror.

But I could see even then that the British officials who spoke of
him with a mixture of amusement and disapproval also genuinely
liked and admired him, after a fashion. Nobody ever suggested that
he was corrupt, or ambitious in any vulgar way, or that anything he
did was actuated by fear or malice. In judging a man like Gandhi one
seems instinctively to apply high standards, so that some of his virtues
have passed almost unnoticed. For instance, it is clear even from the
autobiography that his natural physical courage was quite outstanding: the manner of his death was a later illustration of this, for a
public man who attached any value to his own skin would have been
more adequately guarded. Again, he seems to have been quite free
from that maniacal suspiciousness which, as E.M. Forster rightly
says in *A Passage to India*, is the besetting Indian vice, as hypocrisy
is the British vice. Although no doubt he was shrewd enough in
detecting dishonesty, he seems wherever possible to have believed
that other people were acting in good faith and had a better nature
through which they could be approached. And though he came of a
poor middle-class family, started life rather unfavourably, and was
probably of unimpressive physical appearance, he was not afflicted
by envy or by the feeling of inferiority. Colour feeling, when he first
met it in its worst form in South Africa, seems rather to have astonished him. Even when he was fighting what was in effect a colour war
he did not think of people in terms of race or status. The governor of
a province, a cotton millionaire, a half-starved Dravidian coolie, a
British private soldier, were all equally human beings, to be approached in much the same way. It is noticeable that even in the worst
possible circumstances, as in South Africa, when he was making
himself unpopular as the champion of the Indian community, he did
not lack European friends.

Written in short lengths for newspaper serialisation, the autobiography is not a literary masterpiece, but it is the more impressive because of the commonplaceness of much of its material. It is well to be reminded that Gandhi started out with the normal ambitions of a young Indian student and only adopted his extremist opinions by degrees and, in some cases, rather unwillingly. There was a time, it is interesting to learn, when he wore a top-hat, took dancing lessons, studied French and Latin, went up the Eiffel Tower, and even tried to learn the violin—all this with the idea of assimilating European civilisation as thoroughly as possible. He was not one of those saints who are marked out by their phenomenal piety from childhood onwards, nor one of the other kind who forsake the world after sensational debaucheries. He makes full confession of the misdeeds of his youth, but in fact there is not much to confess. As a frontispiece to the book there is a photograph of Gandhi's possessions at the time of his death. The whole outfit could be purchased for about £5, and Gandhi's sins, at least his fleshly sins, would make the same sort of appearance if placed all in one heap. A few cigarettes, a few mouthfuls of meat, a few annas pilfered in childhood from the maidservant, two visits to a brothel (on each occasion he got away without "doing anything"), one narrowly escaped lapse with his landlady in Plymouth, one outburst of temper—that is about the whole collection. Almost from childhood onwards he had a deep earnestness, an attitude ethical rather than religious, but, until he was about thirty, no very definite sense of direction. His first entry into anything describable as public life was made by way of vegetarianism. Underneath his less ordinary qualities one feels all the time the solid middle-class businessmen who were his ancestors. One feels that even after he had abandoned personal ambition he must have been a resourceful, energetic lawyer and a hard-headed political organiser, careful in keeping down expenses, an adroit handler of committees and an indefatigable chaser of subscriptions. His character was an extraordinarily mixed one, but there was almost nothing in it that you can put your finger on and call bad, and I believe that even Gandhi's worst enemies would admit that he was an interesting and unusual man who enriched the world simply by being alive. Whether he was also a lovable man, and whether his teachings can have much value for those who do not accept the religious beliefs on which they are founded, I have never felt fully certain.

Of late years it has been the fashion to talk about Gandhi as

though he were not only sympathetic to the western left-wing movement, but were even integrally part of it. Anarchists and pacifists, in
particular, have claimed him for their own, noticing only that he was
opposed to centralism and State violence and ignoring the other-
worldly, anti-humanist tendency of his doctrines. But one should, I
think, realise that Gandhi's teachings cannot be squared with the
belief that Man is the measure of all things, and that our job is to
make life worth living on this earth, which is the only earth we have.
They make sense only on the assumption that God exists and that the
world of solid objects is an illusion to be escaped from. It is worth
considering the disciplines which Gandhi imposed on himself and
which—though he might not insist on every one of his followers
observing every detail—he considered indispensable if one wanted to
serve either God or humanity. First of all, no meat eating, and if
possible no animal food in any form. (Gandhi himself, for the sake
of his health, had to compromise on milk, but seems to have felt this
to be a backsliding.) No alcohol or tobacco, and no spices or condi-
ments, even of a vegetable kind, since food should be taken not for its
own sake, but solely in order to preserve one's strength. Secondly, if
possible, no sexual intercourse. If sexual intercourse must happen,
then it should be for the sole purpose of begetting children and
presumably at long intervals. Gandhi himself, in his middle thirties,
took the vow of *bramahcharya*, which means not only complete
chastity but the elimination of sexual desire. This condition, it seems,
is difficult to attain without a special diet and frequent fasting. One
of the dangers of milk drinking is that it is apt to arouse sexual desire.
And finally—this is the cardinal point—for the seeker after goodness
there must be no close friendships and no exclusive loves whatever.

Close friendships, Gandhi says, are dangerous, because "friends
react on one another" and through loyalty to a friend one can be led
into wrong-doing. This is unquestionably true. Moreover, if one is to
love God, or to love humanity as a whole, one cannot give one's
preference to any individual person. This again is true, and it marks
the point at which the humanistic and the religious attitudes cease to
be reconcilable. To an ordinary human being, love means nothing if
it does not mean loving some people more than others. The autobiography leaves it uncertain whether Gandhi behaved in an incon-
siderate way to his wife and children, but at any rate it makes clear
that on three occasions he was willing to let his wife or a child die
rather than administer the animal food prescribed by the doctor. It is

true that the threatened death never actually occurred, and also that
Gandhi—with, one gathers, a good deal of moral pressure in the
opposite direction—always gave the patient the choice of staying
alive at the price of committing a sin: still, if the decision had been
solely his own, he would have forbidden the animal food, whatever
the risks might be. There must, he says, be some limit to what we will
do in order to remain alive, and the limit is well on this side of chicken
broth. This attitude is perhaps a noble one, but, in the sense which—
I think—most people would give to the word, it is inhuman. The
essence of being human is that one does not seek perfection, that one
is sometimes willing to commit sins for the sake of loyalty, that one
does not push asceticism to the point where it makes friendly intercourse impossible, and that one is prepared in the end to be defeated
and broken up by life, which is the inevitable price of fastening one's
love upon other human individuals. No doubt alcohol, tobacco and
so forth are things that a saint must avoid, but sainthood is also a
thing that human beings must avoid. There is an obvious retort to
this, but one should be wary about making it. In this yogi-ridden age,
it is too readily assumed that "non-attachment" is not only better
than a full acceptance of earthly life, but that the ordinary man only
rejects it because it is too difficult: in other words, that the average
human being is a failed saint. It is doubtful whether this is true. Many
people genuinely do not wish to be saints, and it is probable that
some who achieve or aspire to sainthood have never felt much
temptation to be human beings. If one could follow it to its psychological roots, one would, I believe, find that the main motive for
"non-attachment" is a desire to escape from the pain of living, and
above all from love, which, sexual or non-sexual, is hard work. But
it is not necessary here to argue whether the other-worldly or the
humanistic ideal is "higher". The point is that they are incompatible.
One must choose between God and Man, and all "radicals" and
"progressives", from the mildest Liberal to the most extreme
Anarchist, have in effect chosen Man.

However, Gandhi's pacifism can be separated to some extent from
his other teachings. Its motive was religious, but he claimed also for
it that it was a definite technique, a method, capable of producing
desired political results. Gandhi's attitude was not that of most
western pacifists. *Satyagraha*, first evolved in South Africa, was a
sort of non-violent warfare, a way of defeating the enemy without
hurting him and without feeling or arousing hatred. It entailed such

things as civil disobedience, strikes, lying down in front of railway
trains, enduring police charges without running away and without
hitting back, and the like. Gandhi objected to "passive resistance" as
a translation of *Satyagraha*: in Gujarati, it seems, the word means
"firmness in the truth". In his early days Gandhi served as a stretcher-
bearer on the British side in the Boer war, and he was prepared to do
the same again in the war of 1914–18. Even after he had completely
abjured violence he was honest enough to see that in war it is usually
necessary to take sides. He did not—indeed, since his whole political
life centred round a struggle for national independence, he could not
—take the sterile and dishonest line of pretending that in every war
both sides are exactly the same and it makes no difference who wins.
Nor did he, like most western pacifists, specialise in avoiding awkward questions. In relation to the late war, one question that every
pacifist had a clear obligation to answer was: "What about the Jews?
Are you prepared to see them exterminated? If not, how do you propose to save them without resorting to war?" I must say that I have
never heard, from any western pacifist, an honest answer to this
question, though I have heard plenty of evasions, usually of the
"you're another" type. But it so happens that Gandhi was asked a
somewhat similar question in 1938 and that his answer is on record
in Mr Louis Fischer's *Gandhi and Stalin*. According to Mr Fischer
Gandhi's view was that the German Jews ought to commit collective
suicide, which "would have aroused the world and the people of
Germany to Hitler's violence". After the war he justified himself: the
Jews had been killed anyway, and might as well have died significantly. One has the impression that this attitude staggered even so
warm an admirer as Mr Fischer, but Gandhi was merely being
honest. If you are not prepared to take life, you must often be prepared for lives to be lost in some other way. When, in 1942, he urged
non-violent resistance against a Japanese invasion, he was ready to
admit that it might cost several million deaths.

At the same time there is reason to think that Gandhi, who after
all was born in 1869, did not understand the nature of totalitarianism
and saw everything in terms of his own struggle against the British
Government. The important point here is not so much that the British
treated him forbearingly as that he was always able to command
publicity. As can be seen from the phrase quoted above, he believed
in "arousing the world", which is only possible if the world gets a
chance to hear what you are doing. It is difficult to see how Gandhi's

methods could be applied in a country where opponents of the régime disappear in the middle of the night and are never heard of again. Without a free press and the right of assembly, it is impossible not merely to appeal to outside opinion, but to bring a mass movement into being, or even to make your intentions known to your adversary. Is there a Gandhi in Russia at this moment? And if there is, what is he accomplishing? The Russian masses could only practise civil disobedience if the same idea happened to occur to all of them simultaneously, and even then, to judge by the history of the Ukraine famine, it would make no difference. But let it be granted that non-violent resistance can be effective against one's own government, or against an occupying power: even so, how does one put it into practice internationally? Gandhi's various conflicting statements on the late war seems to show that he felt the difficulty of this. Applied to foreign politics, pacifism either stops being pacifist or becomes appeasement. Moreover the assumption, which served Gandhi so well in dealing with individuals, that all human beings are more or less approachable and will respond to a generous gesture, needs to be seriously questioned. It is not necessarily true, for example, when you are dealing with lunatics. Then the question becomes: Who is sane? Was Hitler sane? And is it not possible for one whole culture to be insane by the standards of another? And, so far as one can gauge the feelings of whole nations, is there any apparent connection between a generous deed and a friendly response? Is gratitude a factor in international politics?

These and kindred questions need discussion, and need it urgently, in the few years left to us before somebody presses the button and the rockets begin to fly. It seems doubtful whether civilisation can stand another major war, and it is at least thinkable that the way out lies through non-violence. It is Gandhi's virtue that he would have been ready to give honest consideration to the kind of question that I have raised above; and, indeed, he probably did discuss most of these questions somewhere or other in his innumerable newspaper articles. One feels of him that there was much that he did not understand, but not that there was anything that he was frightened of saying or thinking. I have never been able to feel much liking for Gandhi, but I do not feel sure that as a political thinker he was wrong in the main, nor do I believe that his life was a failure. It is curious that when he was assassinated, many of his warmest admirers exclaimed sorrowfully that he had lived just long enough to see his life work in ruins, because India was engaged in a civil war which had always been fore-seen as one of the by-products of the transfer of power. But it was not in trying to smooth down Hindu-Moslem rivalry that Gandhi had spent his life. His main political objective, the peaceful ending of British rule, had after all been attained. As usual, the relevant facts cut across one another. On the one hand, the British did get out of India without fighting, an event which very few observers indeed would have predicted until about a year before it happened. On the other hand, this was done by a Labour Government, and it is certain that a Conservative Government, especially a government headed by Churchill, would have acted differently. But if, by 1945, there had grown up in Britain a large body of opinion sympathetic to Indian independence, how far was this due to Gandhi's personal influence? And if, as may happen, India and Britain finally settle down into a decent and friendly relationship, will this be partly because Gandhi, by keeping up his struggle obstinately and without hatred, dis-infected the political air? That one even thinks of asking such ques-tions indicates his stature. One may feel, as I do, a sort of aesthetic distaste for Gandhi, one may reject the claims of sainthood made on his behalf (he never made any such claim himself, by the way), one may also reject sainthood as an ideal and therefore feel that Gandhi's basic aims were anti-human and reactionary: but regarded simply as a politician, and compared with the other leading political figures of our time, how clean a smell he has managed to leave behind!

Partisan Review, January 1949; SE; OR; CE

134. Letter to Reginald Reynolds

The Cotswold Sanatorium
Cranham
Glos.
17 January 1949

Dear Reg,[1]
Re pamphlets. I've just been reading the Hammonds' book *The English Labourer*. Don't you think there's sure to be some good inflammatory pamphlet, round abt 1800, abt either the enclosure of the commons, or the workhouses, or the game laws? I'd never realised before that the game laws by which poachers were transported to Australia etc were new abt that date, or at least were tightened up then. I thought they were a Norman survival. The innumerable footnotes etc in the Hammonds' book might put you on to something.

As to modern ones. One I imagine we might include is Keynes's *Economic Consequences of the Peace*? In a way it's well-known, but I've never seen a copy of it myself. Lawrence's *Pornography & Obscenity* I have already suggested. There's also an attack on Lawrence by Norman Douglas (re their mutual friend Magnus) that might be worth looking at.[2]

Don't worry abt Laski. In the second introduction I'll pick out one of his choicer bits of writing & use it as an example of what political writing in our time has sunk to.

The above address will find me for some months, I fear.

Yours
George

[1] Reginald Reynolds (1905–1958), journalist and author. A Quaker, he was early on greatly influenced by Gandhi and became a passionate supporter of the cause of freedom for India. In 1937 he supported the non-Communist Republicans in Spain and became a brilliant speaker for the Independent Labour Party. He was a pacifist in the second world war. Joint editor of the two volume collection *British Pamphleteers*, volume one of which appeared in 1948 with an introduction by Orwell.

[2] *D. H. Lawrence and Maurice Magnus: A Plea for Better Manners* by Norman Douglas.

135. Letter to Sir Richard Rees, Bt

Cranham
28 January 1949

Dear Richard,

I thought over what you said, & it seems to me that unless Bill definitely wants to, it would be a great pity to sever his connection with Barnhill, into which he has put so much work. To move the stock would also cost a great deal, or on the other hand to sell it & start again would presumably involve a loss. I should have thought the Fletchers,[1] who are interested in keeping the North End under cultivation, might be able to arrange for someone to keep house for Bill during the winter. I suggested to Avril that if she *wants* to, she could stay on there & I would make arrangements for R & myself during the winter months. So far as I am concerned I should be very sorry not to be able to have Barnhill as a place during the summer. Most of my furniture & books are now there, & the garden is more or less under control & could be reorganised so as not to need much doing to it. On the other hand I have no doubt I shall have to live an invalid life in the winters from now on. In the beginning, of course, we took the place as a summer place, & my idea had been to spend the winters in London. It is very unfortunate that the continued working of the farm more or less depends on our presence, although we are not the farmers, & I feel unhappy that my health should interfere with this. I should think it a possible arrangement that Bill should live in winter with the Rosgas,[2] if he & they agreed & if he took his milch cows over there. It occurs to me that as the Rosgas would have to be paid for his keep, it might sweeten them to the arrangement if they made a bit of profit on the transaction, & I wouldn't mind contributing something a week to this. I am in favour of keeping the establishment going & the North End inhabited. You might tell me what you think of all this.

Don't forget that I owe you various sums of money. For a consignment of drink, for a rug & two cushions, & no doubt for other things I've forgotten. We'd better settle this before it gets too muddled up. I was also to contribute £25 towards the lorry.

The American publishers seem quite excited abt my book, so they

[1] The Fletchers owned the north end of the isle of Jura and rented Barnhill to Orwell.
[2] The Rosgas farmed the croft a little to the north of Barnhill.

are going to go ahead without waiting for proofs from Warburg. This will mean 2 sets of proofs to correct. I don't suppose it will arise, but *if* I should feel very poorly & unequal to correcting proofs, do you think you could do them for me? As there are a lot of neologisms there are bound to be many printers' errors of a stupid kind, & American compositors are very tiresome to deal with as they always think they know better than the author. I wouldn't trust publishers or agents to do the job. On the other hand you could trust the MS, in which I don't expect there are more than a very few slips. It is most important that there shouldn't be misprints in a book of this kind. However, as I say, I don't imagine this will arise. I have been feeling better & don't have temperatures now, though I don't exactly know how much progress I am making as I haven't been weighed or X-rayed since the first time. This PAS stuff makes me feel sick but otherwise doesn't seem to have secondary effects. One is very well looked after here but the doctors pay very little attention. The chief doctor, Dr Hoffmann, I have never seen, & the other, a woman, simply looks in every morning & asks how I feel, and never even uses her stethoscope. However, I suppose they know best. When I am abt again, I suppose in the summer, I shall see a London specialist, if possible the man I saw just before the war. They can't do anything for you, but I want an expert opinion on how long I am likely to live, because I must make my plans accordingly.

I enclose the remarks from the Russian magazine which Struve translated. Don't lose them, will you, because I haven't a copy. Even allowing for possible unfairness in translation, doesn't it strike you that there is something queer abt the *language* of totalitarian literature—a curious mouthing sort of quality, as of someone who is choking with rage & can never quite hit on the words he wants?

I hope you have been able to read this. The bad handwriting is due to my hands being cold. It's turned colder after being incredibly mild for some days. I'm quite warm in bed, however, as I now have an electric blanket, much better than a hot water bottle.

Yours
Eric

136. Letter to Julian Symons

The Cotswold Sanatorium
Cranham
Glos.
2 February 1949

Dear Julian,

I wonder how you & family are getting on. I have been in this place abt a month. I think I told you last time I wrote that I had been feeling very bad again. . . .

Your baby must be getting quite a size & must be cutting teeth & eating solid food. I wonder if you had the battle over weaning that we had with Richard. It's like Machiavelli says abt government, you can't do it except by force or fraud. Richard is getting [on] for 5 now & is enormous & very healthy, though still not interested in learning his letters. He likes to be read to, but doesn't see that as a reason for learning to read himself. I suppose this coming winter he will have to start going to school, which he is certain to enjoy as he is very gregarious.

My new book is supposed to come out in July (Warburg said May or June, which means July in publisher's language) but maybe the American edition will be out first. Anyway I'll see you get a copy. I must thank you for some friendly references in the *M.E. News* including one to that ghastly book of pamphlets in which I reluctantly collaborated. I am having another try to get Warburg to reprint some of Gissing's books, to which I would write introductions. They reprinted (I forget which publishers) those 3 last year, but of course the wrong ones. Meanwhile I am still trying to get hold of a copy of *New Grub Street*, & am now trying in New York. Somewhat to my annoyance that paper *Politics & Letters* got me to write an essay on Gissing & then died, & have never sent my article back or answered my queries abt it, though it appears distinctly unlikely that the magazine will reappear. What a calamity that we can't find a way of financing *one* decent magazine in this country. I suppose it's only a question of losing abt £2,000 a year. The *Partisan Review* have either increased their sales or got hold of some money from somewhere, as I notice they now pay one quite decently. For all those articles I did during the war for them I got only 10 dollars a time.

I don't know this part of the country but it's supposed to be a beauty spot. Professor Tawney[1] lives nearby, but unfortunately he's had to go back to London as the LSE[2] term had started. The weather is quite incredible, bright sunshine & birds singing as though it were April. Please remember me to your wife & excuse this bad handwriting.

Yours
George

137. Letter to Julian Symons

The Cotswold Sanatorium
Cranham
Glos.
4 February 1949

Dear Julian,

Thanks so much for your letter. Do send me a copy of your thriller.[3] I'm sure I should enjoy it. I do nothing now except read anyway, and I'm rather an amateur of detective stories, although, as you know, I have old-fashioned tastes in them. I recently by the way read for the first time *The Postman Always Rings Twice*—what an awful book.

I'd love it if you could come and see me any time, though of course don't put yourself out. I think someone else is coming on either Feb 12th or Feb 26th; but any other date. Tony Powell said he might be able to come and see me—if so perhaps you could come the same day. You get here by coming to Stroud on the GWR.[4]...

My new book is a Utopia in the form of a novel. I ballsed it up rather, partly owing to being so ill while I was writing it, but I think some of the ideas in it might interest you. We haven't definitely fixed the title, but I think it will be called "Nineteen Eighty-Four". Tony

---

[1] Professor R.H. Tawney (1888–1962), the historian, author of *Religion and the Rise of Capitalism*, *Equality*, etc and his wife, were very old friends of Sir Richard Rees who had asked them to visit Orwell as they were on holiday near Cranham, at their country home.

[2] London School of Economics.

[3] *Bland Beginning*.   [4] Great Western Railway.

says Malcolm Muggeridge has a novel coming out about the same time.[1]

Please remember me to the family.

Yours
George

138. Letter to Sir Richard Rees, Bt

The Cotswold Sanatorium
Cranham
Glos.
4 February 1949

Dear Richard,

I enclose cheque for what I owed you. You will notice I have added £3. Do you think you could be kind enough to get your wine merchant to send me 2 bottles of rum, which I suppose will come to about that. I assume he will know how to pack them so as not to get them broken.

I have heard from Avril who says she and Bill both think it would be better to move to a farm on the mainland. I think they are right, but can't help feeling bad about it as I feel my health is the precipitating factor, though the state of the road is a good second. I think you would be rash to sink more money in any non-removable improvements etc, because such a place might of its nature become untenable at some time. I trust it will be possible to move without selling off the stock and losing on the transaction. I am afraid the actual move will be a godawful business from which I shall probably absent myself whenever it happens. I have asked Avril to tell Robin[2] that unless he happens on a tenant who would actually farm the place, I would like to keep on the lease of the house. I don't see why we shouldn't have it as a summer holiday place, and one could leave camp beds etc there. Of course I may never be strong enough for that kind of thing again even in the summer, but others may be and the rent is next to nothing.

I am reading B. Russell's latest book,[3] about human knowledge.

---

[1] *Affairs of the Heart*, 1949.　　[2] Robin Fletcher.
[3] *Human Knowledge: Its Scope and Limits.*

He quotes Shakespeare, "Doubt that the stars are fire, Doubt that the earth doth move" (it goes on I think, "Doubt truth to be a liar, But never doubt I love.") But he makes it "Doubt that the *sun* doth move", and uses this as an instance of S's ignorance. Is that right? I had an idea it was "the earth". But I haven't got Shakespeare here and I can't even remember where the lines come (must be one of the comedies I think). I wish you'd verify this for me if you can remember where it comes.[1] I see by the way that the Russian press has just described B.R as a wolf in a dinner-jacket and a wild beast in philosopher's robes.

I don't know really that I'd be very interested in that book about the cards etc. I had heard of that chap before,[2] but I can't get very interested in telepathy unless it could be developed into a reliable method.

I've been reading *The First Europe*[3] (history of the Dark Ages), very interesting though written in a rather tiresome way. For the first week or two here I hadn't got my book supply going and had to rely on the library, which meant reading some fearful trash. Among other things I read a Deeping for the first time—actually not so bad as I expected, a sort of natural novelist like A.S.M. Hutchinson. Also a Peter Cheyney. He evidently does well out of his books as I used often to get invites from him for slap-up parties at the Dorchester. I have sent for several of Hardy's novels and am looking at them rather unenthusiastically.

Yours
Eric

139. Letter to the Editor of the *News Chronicle*

Cranham
Gloucestershire

I appeal on behalf of Enrique Marco Nadal, a Spanish Republican now under sentence of death in Spain.

[1] Russell was right. The quotation is from *Hamlet*, II, ii, 116–19.
[2] Professor J.B. Rhine, Director of the Parapsychology Laboratory, Duke University, N. Carolina.
[3] By Cecil Delisle Burns.

He was taken prisoner by the Italians when the Spanish Government collapsed in 1939; then by the Germans in 1944–5 after fighting for the French.

He re-entered Spain clandestinely after the war, and was sentenced to death without trial. He has probably not done anything that would constitute a legal offence in any democratic country.[1]

George Orwell

News Chronicle, 3 March 1949

140. Letter to Sir Richard Rees, Bt

Cranham
3 March 1949

Dear Richard,

Thanks so much for your letter, with the cuttings, which I thought gave quite a good exposition of CP policy. I always disagree, however, when people end by saying that we can only combat Communism, Fascism or what not if we develop an equal fanaticism. It appears to me that one defeats the fanatic precisely by *not* being a fanatic oneself, but on the contrary by using one's intelligence. In the same way, a man can kill a tiger because he is *not* like a tiger & uses his brain to invent the rifle, which no tiger could ever do.

I looked up the passage in Russell's book.[2] If the antithesis to a "some" statement is always an "all" statement, then it seems to me that the antithesis of "some men are tailless" is not "all men have tails," but "all men are tailless". Russell seems, in that paragraph, to be citing only pairs of statements of which one is untrue, but clearly there must be many cases when both "some" & "all" are true, except that "some" is an understatement. Thus "some men are tailless" is true, unless you are implying by it that some men have tails. But I never can follow that kind of thing. It is the sort of thing that makes me feel that philosophy should be forbidden by law.

I have arranged to write an essay on Evelyn Waugh & have just read his early book on Rossetti & also *Robbery under Law* (abt

[1] Nadal was released from Burgos prison at the end of 1964.
[2] *Human Knowledge: Its Scope and Limits* by Bertrand Russell.

Mexico). I am now reading a new life of Dickens by Hesketh Pearson, which I have to review.[1] It isn't awfully good. There doesn't seem to be a perfect life of Dickens—perverse & unfair though it is, I really think Kingsmill's book[2] is the best. You were right abt Huxley's book[3]—it is awful. And do you notice that the more holy he gets, the more his books stink with sex. He cannot get off the subject of flagellating women. Possibly, if he had the courage to come out & say so, that is the solution to the problem of war. If we took it out in a little private sadism, which after all doesn't do much harm, perhaps we wouldn't want to drop bombs etc. I also reread, after very many years, *Tess of the D'Urbervilles*, & *Jude the Obscure* (for the first time). *Tess* is really better than I had remembered, & incidentally is quite funny in places, which I didn't think Hardy was capable of.

The doctor says I shall have to stay *in bed* for another 2 months, i.e. till abt May, so I suppose I shan't actually get out till abt July. However I don't know that it matters except for being expensive & not seeing little R. I am so afraid of his growing away from me, or getting to think of me as just a person who is always lying down & can't play. Of course children can't understand illness. He used to come to me & say "Where have you hurt yourself?"—I suppose the only reason he could see for always being in bed. But otherwise I don't mind being here & I am comfortable & well cared-for. I feel much better & my appetite is a lot better. (By the way I never thanked you for sending that rum. Did I pay you enough for it?) I hope to start some serious work in April, & I think I could work fairly well here, as it is quiet & there are not many interruptions. Various people have been to see me, & I manage to keep pretty well supplied with books. Contrary to what people say, time seems to go very fast when you are in bed, & months can whizz by with nothing to show for it.

Yours
Eric

---

[1] Orwell's review of *Dickens: His Character, Comedy and Career* by Hesketh Pearson appeared in the *New York Times Book Review*, 15 May 1949.
[2] *The Sentimental Journey: A Life of Charles Dickens* by Hugh Kingsmill.
[3] *Ape and Essence* by Aldous Huxley.

141. Letter to Michael Meyer [in Sweden]

The Cotswold Sanatorium
Cranham
Glos.
12 March 1949

Dear Michael,

Thanks ever so much for sending all that food, which arrived a day or two ago, and for your letter. You really shouldn't have sent the food, but I take your word that you could spare it, and of course I am delighted to receive it. As a matter of fact I'm sending most of it on to Jura, where food is always welcome as there's usually someone staying. . . .

I always thought Sweden sounded a dull country, much more so than Norway or Finland. I should think there would probably be very good fishing, if you can whack up any interest in that. But I have never been able to like these model countries with everything up to date and hygienic and an enormous suicide rate. I also have a vague feeling that in our century there is some sort of interconnection between the quality of thought and culture in a country, and the *size* of the country. Small countries don't seem to produce interesting writers any longer, though possibly it is merely that one doesn't hear about them. I have ideas about the reason for this, if it is true, but of course only guesswork. I hope your novel[1] gets on. Even if one makes a mess of it the first time, one learns a great deal in making the attempt, also if you once have a draft finished, however discouraging it is, you can generally pull it into shape. I simply destroyed my first novel after unsuccessfully submitting it to one publisher, for which I'm rather sorry now. I think Thomas Hood is a very good subject. He is incidentally no longer as well known as he should be, and very thoroughly out of print. I have only a selection of his poems, and have for a long time been trying in vain to get the rest. I want particularly the one where he is writing a poem on the beauties of childhood but can't get on with it because the children are making such a noise (I remember it has the beautiful line, "Go to your mother, child, and blow your nose.") I don't know whether one could call him a serious poet—he is what I call a good bad poet. I am glad you like Surtees. I think after being so long abandoned to the hunting people, who I

---

[1] *The End of the Corridor.*

don't suppose read him, he is beginning to be appreciated again. I
haven't however read much of his works, and am trying to get hold of
several now. At present I do nothing except read—I'm not going to
try and start any work till some time next month. I have been rereading some of Hardy's novels, after very many years, and was
agreeably surprised. There is a new life of Dickens coming out, which
I had to review, by Hesketh Pearson. It's a bit more readable than
old Pope-Hennessy's[1] book but not any good really. Huxley's new
book[2], which I expect you have seen, is awful. Koestler's new book[3]
I haven't seen yet. I am going to do an essay on Evelyn Waugh for
the *Partisan Review*, and have been reading his early works, including
a quite good life of Rossetti. My novel is supposed to come out in
June. I don't know whether the American edition may come out
before the English, but I should think not. I hope to hear from you
again some time. This place will be my address till about July, I'm
afraid.

Yours
George

142. Letter to Julian Symons

Cranham
15 March 1949

Dear Julian,
As you are doing that life of Dickens I thought you might care to
glance at this[4] (I don't want it back). It hasn't been published in this
country yet so far as I know. I don't think there's anything in [it] you
wouldn't get out of old Pope-Hennessy, but he raises one or two
minor points of interest. He makes out for instance that D's acceptance of a baronetcy just before his death was merely a sort of practical joke. P-H in her book seems to suggest that this is not so. I have
never followed this up, and I must say I don't regard it as important,
since by that time D's mind was probably giving way anyway. He

---

[1] *Charles Dickens* by Dame Una Pope-Hennessy, 1945.
[2] *Ape & Essence.*   [3] *Insight and Outlook.*
[4] *Dickens: His Character, Comedy and Career* by Hesketh Pearson, published
in New York.

also says, what I didn't know before, that D was impressed by
Edgar Allen Poe, who must then (1842) have been very obscure, and
tried unsuccessfully to get his *Tales* published for him in book form.
I have often wondered whether Poe was influenced by the madman's
tale in Pickwick.

Yours
George

143. Letter to Sir Richard Rees, Bt

Cranham
16 March 1949

Dear Richard,
I hope all is going well with you. I have heard once or twice from
Barnhill and things seem to be fairly prosperous. Avril says Bill is
going to plant about an acre of kale. Ian McKechnie[1] is there at
present, working on the road, and Francis Boyle[1] has done some
work in the garden. Bill suggested we should sell off the milch cows,
as some of his own cows will be calving and will have surplus milk,
and of course it would make more room in the byre. On the other
hand there is the question of overlapping, so I suggested keeping one
Ayrshire. The boat is apparently in good order and they have been
over to Crinan in her. Avril says Richard has found out about
money, i.e. has grasped that you can buy sweets with it, so I expect I
had better start giving him pocket money, though at present he
hasn't any opportunity to spend it. Incidentally, getting pocket
money would probably teach him the days of the week.
I have been feeling fairly good, though of course they won't
dream of letting me up. Most of the time it has been beautiful
spring-like weather. I have been reading Evelyn Waugh's very early
books (on Rossetti, and one or two others) as I undertook to write an
essay on him for the *Partisan Review*. Also a not very good life of
Dickens by Hesketh Pearson which I had to review. Also rereading
Israel Zangwill's *Children of the Ghetto*, a book I hadn't set eyes on
for very many years. I am trying to get hold of the sequel to it,
Grandchildren of the Ghetto, which I remember as being better than
the other. I don't know what else he wrote, but I believe a whole lot.

[1] Neighbours on Jura.

I think he is a very good novelist who hasn't had his due, though I notice now that he has a very strong tinge of Jewish nationalism, of a rather tiresome kind. I sent for Marie Bashkirtseff's diary, which I had never read, and it is now staring me in the face, an enormous and rather intimidating volume. I haven't seen Koestler's new book, which I think has only been published in the USA, but I think I shall send for it. My book is billed to come out on June 15th. It is going to be the *Evening Standard* book of the month, which I believe doesn't mean anything in particular.

Have you torn up your clothing book?[1] The reaction of everybody here was the same—"it must be a trap". Of course clothes are now sufficiently rationed by price. I think I shall order myself a new jacket all the same.

Yours
Eric

144. Letter to Leonard Moore

The Cotswold Sanatorium
Cranham
Glos.
17 March 1949

Dear Moore,
You will have had Robert Giroux's[2] letter, of which he sent me a duplicate.

I can't possibly agree to the kind of alteration and abbreviation suggested. It would alter the whole colour of the book and leave out a good deal that is essential. I think it would also—though the judges, having read the parts that it is proposed to cut out, may not appreciate this—make the story unintelligible. There would also be something visibly wrong with the structure of the book if about a fifth or a quarter were cut out and the last chapter then tacked on to the abbreviated trunk. A book is built up as a balanced structure and one cannot simply remove large chunks here and there unless one is ready to recast the whole thing. In any case, merely to cut out the suggested chapters and abridge the passages from the "book within

[1] Clothes rationing ended on 1 February 1949.
[2] An editor at Harcourt, Brace and Company.

the book" would mean a lot of rewriting which I simply do not feel equal to at present.

The only terms on which I could agree to any such arrangement would be if the book were published definitely as an abridged version and if it were clearly stated that the English edition contained several chapters which had been omitted. But obviously the Book of the Month people couldn't be expected to agree to any such thing. As Robert Giroux says in his letter, they have not promised to select the book in any case, but he evidently hopes they might, and I suppose it will be disappointing to Harcourt Brace if I reject the suggestion. I suppose you, too, stand to lose a good deal of commission. But I really cannot allow my work to be mucked about beyond a certain point, and I doubt whether it even pays in the long run. I should be much obliged if you would make my point of view clear to them.

Yours sincerely
Eric Blair

145. Letter to Sir Richard Rees, Bt

Cranham
18 March 1949

Dear Richard,

I'm sorry I didn't answer directly your previous letter. It was very kind of you to offer to lend me money, but really I don't need it. I am quite comfortable for some time to come. The only thing that worries me about my financial position is the possibility that I might become like some of the people here, i.e. able to stay alive but unable to work. However it's not very likely. Re your other query, I didn't think a great deal of Slater's book.[1] It seemed to me perfunctory, and I thought, as you did yourself, that the sex stuff was out of place and in poor taste. I really think that this modern habit of describing love-making in detail is something that future generations will look back on as we do on things like the death of Little Nell.

I haven't any reason to think my letters are tampered with. On one occasion ten years ago a letter of mine actually was opened by the police, but that was because it was addressed to a Paris publisher

[1] *The Conspirator* by Humphrey Slater.

whose books were banned en bloc. Other people have sometimes told me they thought theirs were opened, and at one time I tried to devise an envelope which couldn't be opened without the fact becoming apparent. But I don't think there's any reason to think the CP have any hand in that kind of thing or any power of getting at people's letters.

Thanks for sending the *Highway*.[1] I thought the article quite good, but I didn't think a great deal of Weidlé's book when I tried to read it some time back—actually it seemed to me that he had got himself into rather a muddle.

Robert Wheeler[2] looked in this afternoon. He has just been to Switzerland.

Yours
Eric

PS. Did you read my article on Gandhi in the *PR*?[3] If so, did you agree with what I said?

146. Letter to F. J. Warburg

Cranham
30 March 1949

Dear Fred,

Thanks for your letter. I read *We* abt a couple of years ago & don't think I particularly want the galleys. I didn't wish to force it on you, & I merely thought it might be worth your while & at any rate ought to be re-issued by somebody. Certainly it has faults, but it seems to me to form an interesting link in the chain of Utopia books. On the one hand it debunks the super-rational, hedonistic type of Utopia (I think Aldous Huxley's *Brave New World* must be plagiarised from it to some extent), but on the other hand it takes account of the diabolism & the tendency to return to an earlier form of

---

[1] *Highway*, organ of the WEA (Workers' Educational Association). In its February number, 1949, there was a review by J.M. Cameron of *The Dilemma of the Arts* by Vladimir Weidlé.
[2] Robert Wheeler, a Gloucestershire farmer living near Cranham, had been asked by his friend, Sir Richard Rees, to visit Orwell.
[3] See 133.

civilisation which seem to be part of totalitarianism. It seems to me a good book in the same way as *The Iron Heel*, but better written. But of course there's no knowing whether it wld sell & I have no wish to land you with a white elephant. I just think *somebody* ought to print it & that it is disgraceful that a book of this kind, with its curious history as well as its intrinsic interest, should stay out of print when so much rubbish is published every day.

I have been rather poorly & have been having "haemoptyses". That is why I have written this by hand. They have forbidden me to use my typewriter for a week, as it is supposed to tire me. Please give everyone my love.

Yours
George

147. Letter to Sir Richard Rees, Bt

Cranham
31 March 1949

Dear Richard,

Thanks so much for your letter. I send herewith a copy of *PR* with the article I spoke of. I'd have sent it before, as I thought it would interest you, but I was under the impression that you took in *PR*. Celia Kirwan was here the other day & she will send me a copy of that number of *Polemic* which I lost & which has the essay on Tolstoy in it.[1] It really connects up with the Gandhi article.

Yes, I must get this will business sewn up. I had my will properly drawn up by a solicitor, then, as I wanted to make some alterations, rewrote it myself, & I dare say this second draft, though duly witnessed etc is not legal. Have you got a solicitor in Edinburgh? I am out of touch with my London ones. It is important to get the literary executorship sewn up properly, & also to be quite sure abt Richard's position, because there is some legal difference, I forget what, in the case of an adopted child. In addition I must bring up to date the notes I left for you abt my books, which editions to follow, etc. When Avril came back from town she brought some box files marked "Personal" which I *think* have all the relevant stuff in them. Do you

[1] See 76.

think when you are at Barnhill you could go through these files & send the relevant papers to me. I want my will, i.e. the second will, dated abt the beginning of 1947 I think, the notes I left for you, & a notebook marked "Reprintable Essays" which wants bringing up to date. It's important that your powers should be made clear, i.e. that you should have the final say when any definitely literary question is involved. For example. The American Book of the Month people, though they didn't actually promise, half promised to select my present book if I could cut out abt a quarter of it. Of course I'm not going to do this, but if I had died the week before, Moore & the American publishers wld have jumped at the offer, ruining the book & not even benefiting my estate much, because whenever you make a large sum you are in the surtax class & it is all taken away again.

I have been very poorly, spitting up quantities of blood. This doesn't necessarily do any harm, indeed Morlock,[1] the specialist I went to before the war, said it might even do good, but it always depresses & disgusts me, & I have been feeling rather down. There is evidently nothing very definite they can do for me. They talked of doing the "thora" operation, but the surgeon wouldn't undertake it because you have to have one sound lung which I haven't. Evidently the only thing to do is to keep quiet. It worries me not to see little R, but perhaps later I can arrange somehow for him to visit me. If I do get up this year I want to take him for a trip to London.

Yours
Eric

Excuse this writing. They've forbidden me to use a typewriter at present because it is tiring!

148. Letter to Sir Richard Rees, Bt

Cranham
8 April 1949

Dear Richard,
I thought you'd all like to know that I have just had a cable saying that the Book of the Month Club have selected my novel after all, in

[1] Dr H.V. Morlock.

spite of my refusing to make the changes they demanded. So that
shows that virtue is its own reward, or honesty is the best policy, I
forget which. I don't know whether I shall ultimately end up with a
net profit, but at any rate this should pay off my arrears of income
tax.

I've had the sanatorium cable the magazines to which I had
promised articles saying I am unfit to do any work, which is the truth.
Don't depress the others too much with this, but the fact is I am in a
bad way at present. They are going to try streptomycin again, which
I had previously urged them to do & which Mr Dick thought might
be a good idea. They had been afraid of it because of the secondary
effects, but they now say they can offset these to some extent with
nicotine, or something, & in any case they can always stop if the
results are too bad. *If* things go badly—of course we'll hope they
won't, but one must be prepared for the worst—I'll ask you to bring
little Richard to see me before I get too frightening in appearance. I
think it wld upset you less than it wld Avril, & there may be business
deals to talk over as well. If the stuff works, as it seemed to do last
time, I shall take care this time to keep the improvement by leading
an invalid life for the rest of the year.

I forgot to say, I wish some time you'd have a look at my books &
see they're not getting too mildewy (I asked Avril to light a fire from
time to time for that reason) & that the magazines in the bottom
shelf are in some sort of order. I want to keep all the magazines that
are there, as some of them have articles of mine that I might want to
reprint. The books are piling up here & I'm going to start sending
them home some time, but I can't do up parcels at present.

Love to all
Eric

149. Conrad's Place and Rank in English Letters

[*Wiadomości*, the Polish émigré literary weekly published in London, sent
a questionnaire on Joseph Conrad to several English writers asking them
the following two questions:

First, what do you believe to be his permanent place and rank in
English letters? When Conrad died, some critics were uncertain of his

final position, and Virginia Woolf, in particular, doubted whether any of his later novels would survive. Today, on the occasion of a new edition of his collected writings, Mr Richard Curle wrote in *Time and Tide* that Conrad's works now rank among the great classics of the English novel. Which of these views, in your opinion, is correct?

The other question to which we would like to have your answer, is whether you detect in Conrad's work any oddity, exoticism and strangeness (of course, against the background of the English literary tradition), and if so, do you attribute it to his Polish origin?

Orwell sent the following reply:]

I cannot answer at great length, as I am ill in bed, but I am happy to give you my opinions for what they are worth.

1. I regard Conrad as one of the best writers of this century, and—supposing that one can count him as an English writer—one of the very few true novelists that England possesses. His reputation, which was somewhat eclipsed after his death, has risen again during the past ten years, and I have no doubt that the bulk of his work will survive. During his lifetime he suffered by being stamped as a writer of "sea stories", and books like *The Secret Agent* and *Under Western Eyes* went almost unnoticed. Actually Conrad only spent about a third of his life at sea and he had only a sketchy knowledge of the Asiatic countries of which he wrote in *Lord Jim*, *Almayer's Folly*, etc. What he did have, however, was a sort of grown-upness and political understanding which would have been almost impossible to a native English writer at that time. I consider that his best work belongs to what might be called his middle period, roughly between 1900 and 1914. This period includes *Nostromo*, *Chance*, *Victory*, the two mentioned above, and several outstanding short stories.

2. Yes, Conrad has definitely a slight exotic flavour to me. That is part of his attraction. In the earlier books, such as *Almayer's Folly*, his English is sometimes definitely incorrect, though not in a way that matters. He used I believe to think in Polish and then translate his thoughts into French and finally into English, and one can sometimes follow the process back at least as far as French, for instance in his tendency to put the adjective after the noun. Conrad was one of those writers who in the present century civilised English literature and brought it back into contact with Europe, from which it had been almost severed for a hundred years. Most of the writers who did this were foreigners, or at any rate not quite English—Eliot and

James (Americans), Joyce and Yeats (Irish), and Conrad himself, a transplanted Pole.

Wiadomości, 10 April 1949

150. The Question of the Pound Award

[When Ezra Pound was awarded the Bollingen Foundation Prize for *The Pisan Cantos* as the best book of poetry for 1948, the editors of *Partisan Review* in April 1949 asked several writers to discuss the issues connected with the award. Orwell sent the following piece]

I think the Bollingen Foundation were quite right to award Pound the prize, if they believed his poems to be the best of the year, but I think also that one ought to keep Pound's career in memory and not feel that his ideas are made respectable by the mere fact of winning a literary prize.

Because of the general revulsion against Allied war propaganda, there has been—indeed, there was, even before the war was over—a tendency to claim that Pound was "not really" a Fascist and an anti-semite, that he opposed the war on pacifist grounds, and that in any case his political activities only belonged to the war years. Some time ago I saw it stated in an American periodical that Pound only broadcast on the Rome radio when "the balance of his mind was upset", and later (I think in the same periodical) that the Italian Government had blackmailed him into broadcasting by threats to relatives. All this is plain falsehood. Pound was an ardent follower of Mussolini as far back as the nineteen-twenties, and never concealed it. He was a contributor to Mosley's review, the *British Union Quarterly*, and accepted a professorship from the Rome Government before the war started. I should say that his enthusiasm was essentially for the Italian form of Fascism. He did not seem to be very strongly pro-Nazi or anti-Russian, his real underlying motive being hatred of Britain, America and "the Jews". His broadcasts were disgusting. I remember at least one in which he approved the massacre of the East European Jews and "warned" the American Jews that their turn was coming presently. These broadcasts—I did not hear them, but only read them in the BBC monitoring report—did not

Review   491

give me the impression of being the work of a lunatic. Incidentally I
am told that in delivering them Pound used to put on a pronounced
American accent which he did not normally have, no doubt with the
idea of appealing to the isolationists and playing on anti-British
sentiment.

   None of this is a reason against giving Pound the Bollingen Prize.
There are times when such a thing might be undesirable—it would
have been undesirable when the Jews were actually being killed in the
gas vans, for instance—but I do not think this is one of them. But
since the judges have taken what amounts to the "art for art's sake"
position, that is, the position that aesthetic integrity and common
decency are two separate things, then at least let us keep them separate and not excuse Pound's political career on the ground that he is a
good writer. He *may* be a good writer (I must admit that I personally
have always regarded him as an entirely spurious writer), but the
opinions that he has tried to disseminate by means of his works are
evil ones, and I think that the judges should have said so more firmly
when awarding him the prize.

Partisan Review, May 1949

151. Review[1]

Their Finest Hour by Winston S. Churchill

It is difficult for a statesman who still has a political future to reveal
everything that he knows: and in a profession in which one is a baby
at fifty and middle-aged at seventy-five, it is natural that anyone who
has not actually been disgraced should feel that he still has a future.
A book like Ciano's diaries, for instance, would not have been published if its author had remained in good standing. But it is fair to
Winston Churchill to say that the political reminiscences which he
has published from time to time have always been a great deal above
the average, in frankness as well as in literary quality. Churchill is
among other things a journalist, with a real if not very discriminating
feeling for literature, and he also has a restless, enquiring mind,

---

[1] This review is included as it is the last piece of writing Orwell completed
and deals with events he recorded in his first war-time diary. See II, 57.

interested both in concrete facts and in the analysis of motives, sometimes including his own motives. In general, Churchill's writings are more like those of a human being than of a public figure. His present book does, of course, contain passages which give the appearance of having escaped from an election address, but it also shows a considerable willingness to admit mistakes.

This volume, the second in the series, covers the period between the opening of the German attack on France and the end of 1940. Its main events, therefore, are the collapse of France, the German air attacks on Britain, the increasing involvement of the United States in the war, the stepping-up of the U-boat warfare, and the beginning of the long struggle in North Africa. The book is heavily documented, with excerpts from speeches or despatches at each step, and though it leads to a great deal of reduplication, it makes it possible to compare what was said and thought at the time with what actually happened.

As he himself admits, Churchill had underestimated the effect of recent changes in the technique of war, but he reacted quickly when the storm broke in 1940. His great achievement was to grasp even at the time of Dunkirk that France was beaten and that Britain, in spite of appearances, was not beaten; and this last judgement was not based simply on pugnacity but on a reasonable survey of the situation.

The only way in which the Germans could win the war quickly was to conquer the British Isles, and to conquer the British Isles they had to get there, which meant having command of the sea over the Channel. Churchill, therefore, steadily refused to throw the whole of the British metropolitan air force into the Battle of France. It was a harsh decision, which naturally caused bitterness at the time and probably weakened Reynaud's position against the defeatists in the French Government, but it was strategically correct. The twenty-five fighter squadrons held to be indispensable were kept in Britain, and the threatened invasion was beaten off. Long before the year was over the danger had receded sufficiently for guns, tanks and men to be transferred from Britain to the Egyptian front. The Germans could still defeat Britain by the U-boat, or conceivably by bombing, but it would take several years, and in the meantime the war could be relied upon to spread.

Churchill knew, of course, that the United States would enter the war sooner or later; but at this stage he does not seem to have expected that an American army of millions of men would ultimately arrive in Europe. He foresaw even in 1940 that the Germans would probably attack Russia, and he rightly calculated that Franco, whatever promises he might make, would not come into the war on the Axis side. He also saw the importance of arming the Palestine Jews and of fomenting rebellion in Abyssinia. Where his judgement went astray, it was chiefly because of his undiscriminating hatred of "Bolshevism" and consequent tendency to ignore political distinctions. He says revealingly that when he sent Sir Stafford Cripps as Ambassador to Moscow, he did not realise that Communists hate Socialists more than they hate Conservatives. No British Tory, indeed, seems to have grasped this simple fact until the advent of the Labour Government in 1945; failure to do so was partly responsible for the mistaken British policy during the Spanish civil war. Churchill's attitude towards Mussolini, although it probably did not affect the course of events in 1940, was also based on a miscalculation. In the past he had admired Mussolini as a "bulwark against Bolshevism" and had belonged to the school that believed it possible to draw Italy out of the Axis by means of bribes. He would never, he says frankly, have quarrelled with Mussolini over such an issue as Abyssinia. When Italy entered the war, Churchill did not, of course, pull his punches, but the over-all situation would have been better if the British Tories could have grasped ten years earlier that Italian Fascism was not just another version of Conservatism but must of its nature be hostile to Britain.

One of the most interesting chapters in *Their Finest Hour* deals with the exchange of American destroyers for bases in the British West Indies. The letters that passed between Churchill and Roosevelt form a sort of commentary on democratic politics. Roosevelt knew that it was in the American interest that Britain should have the destroyers, and Churchill knew that it was not to the disadvantage of Britain—rather the contrary—that the United States should have the bases. Nevertheless, apart from the legal and constitutional difficulties, it was impossible for the ships to be simply handed over without haggling. With the election ahead of him, and with one eye on the Isolationists, Roosevelt had to give the appearance of driving a hard bargain. He also had to demand an assurance that even if Britain lost the war, the British fleet would in no circumstances be handed over to the Germans. This, of course, was a senseless condition to impose. It could be taken as certain that Churchill would not hand over the fleet: but, on the other hand, if the Germans succeeded in overrunning Britain, they would set up some kind of puppet government, for whose actions Churchill could not answer. He was unable, therefore, to give as firm an assurance as was demanded, and the bargaining was prolonged accordingly. The one quick solution would have been to secure a pledge from the whole British people, including the crews of the ships. But Churchill, curiously enough, seems to have shrunk from publicising the facts. It would have been dangerous, he says, to let it be known how near Britain was to defeat—perhaps the only occasion throughout this period when he underrated public morale.

The book ends in the dark winter of 1940, when unexpected victories in the desert, with vast hauls of Italian prisoners, were offset by the bombing of London and the increased sinkings at sea. Unavoidably, as one reads, the thought moves to and fro in one's mind: "How freely is Churchill capable of speaking?" For the main interest of these memoirs is bound to come later, when Churchill tells us (if he does decide to tell us) what really happened at Teheran and Yalta, and whether the policies there adopted were ones that he himself approved of, or whether they were forced upon him by Roosevelt. But at any rate, the tone of this and the preceding volume suggests that when the time comes, he will tell us more of the truth than has been revealed hitherto.

Whether or not 1940 was anyone else's finest hour, it was certainly Churchill's. However much one may disagree with him, however thankful one may be that he and his party did not win the 1945 election, one has to admire in him not only his courage but also a certain largeness and geniality which comes out even in formal memoirs of this type, much less personal than a book like *My Early Life*. The British people have generally rejected his policies, but they have always had a liking for him, as one can see from the tone of the stories about him that have been told throughout most of his life. Often, no doubt, these stories were apocryphal, and sometimes they were also unprintable, but the fact of their circulating is significant. At the time of the Dunkirk evacuation, for instance, when Churchill made his often-quoted fighting speech, it was rumoured that what he actually said, when recording the speech for broadcasting, was: "We will fight on the beaches, we will fight in the streets. . . . We'll throw bottles at the b–s, it's about all we've got left"—but, of course the BBC's switch-censor pressed his thumb on the key at the right moment. One may assume that this story is untrue, but at the time it was felt that it ought to be true. It was a fitting tribute from ordinary

people to the tough and humorous old man whom they would not
accept as a peace-time leader but whom in the moment of disaster
they felt to be representative of themselves.

Written by 9 April 1949; *New Leader* (New York), 14 May 1949

152. Letter to Robert Giroux

> The Cotswold Sanatorium
> Cranham
> Glos.
> 14 April 1949

Dear Mr Giroux,
Many thanks for your letter of the 11th. Naturally I am delighted
that the Book of the Month Club selected *1984* after all. A little
before publication date I am going to ask you to be kind enough to
send complimentary copies to about a dozen people in the USA. I
will send you the names through Leonard Moore. Actually I dare say
some of them are on your list already.

The essay on *Lear* that you asked after (actually it's on Tolstoy's
essay on Shakespeare)[1] appeared about two years ago in a short-lived
magazine called *Polemic*. Unfortunately I haven't a copy myself, and
have been trying to get hold of one, as I might want to reprint it some
time. I would be interested to know where Empson's[2] essay appeared,
as I'd like to know what he has to say about *Lear*. He has disappeared
into China the way people do, and I did not even know he was writing
anything at present.

I have been very ill the last few weeks, but am now somewhat
better. I trust that I am now on the way to recovery and shall be out
of here before the summer is over, but it is certain to be a slow job
at best. I have my next novel mapped out, but I am not going to
touch it until I feel stronger. It is not only that it tires me to work, but
also that I am afraid of making a false start and getting discouraged.

> Yours sincerely
> Geo. Orwell

[1] See 76.   [2] William Empson (1906–), the poet and critic.

Ro—IV

153. Letter[1] to T. R. Fyvel

Cranham
15 April 1949

Dear Tosco,

Thanks so much for sending Ruth Fischer's book.[2] I had intended buying it, but perhaps after reading a borrowed copy I shan't need to. I'll see you get it back. I read Margarete Neumann's book[3] with some interest. It wasn't a particularly good book but she struck me as a sincere person. Gollancz also has a quite remarkable novel about the forced-labour camps coming along, by someone calling himself pseudonymously "Richard Cargoe"—a Pole I should say—how authentic I couldn't be sure, but quite a striking book, in the Slav manner.[4]

There were several points in your articles that I had been meaning to take up with you. One is about Graham Greene. You keep referring to him as an extreme Conservative, the usual Catholic reactionary type. This isn't so at all, either in his books or privately. Of course he is a Catholic and in some issues has to take sides politically with the church, but in outlook he is just a mild Left with faint CP leanings. I have even thought that he might become our first Catholic fellow-traveller, a thing that doesn't exist in England but does in France, etc. If you look at books like *A Gun for Sale, England Made Me, The Confidential Agent* and others, you will see that there is the usual left-wing scenery. The bad men are millionaires, armaments manufacturers etc and the good man is sometimes a Communist. In his last book there is also the usual inverted colour-feeling. According to Rayner Heppenstall, Greene somewhat reluctantly supported Franco during the Spanish civil war, but *The Confidential Agent* is written from the other point of view.

The other thing is that you are always attacking novelists for not writing about the contemporary scene. But can you think of a novel that ever was written about the strictly contemporary scene? It is very unlikely that any novel, i.e. worth reading, would ever be set

---

[1] As the original of this letter has been lost, the text has been taken from *Encounter*, January 1962, where it was first printed.
[2] *Stalin and German Communism* by Ruth Fischer.
[3] *Under Two Dictators* by Margarete Buber-Neumann.
[4] *The Tormentors* by Richard Cargoe, one of the pseudonyms of Robert Payne.

back less than three years at least. If you tried, *in* 1949, to write a novel about 1949 it would simply be "reportage" and probably would seem out of date and silly before you could get it into print. I have a novel dealing with 1945 in my head now, but even if I survive to write it I shouldn't touch it before 1950. The reason is not only that one can't see the events of the moment in perspective, but also that a novel has to be lived with for years before it can be written down, otherwise the working-out of detail, which takes an immense time and can only be done at odd moments, can't happen. This is my experience and I think it is also other people's. I have sometimes written a so-called novel within about two years of the original conception, but then they were always weak, silly books which I afterwards suppressed. You may remember that nearly all the worthwhile books about the 1914 war appeared five, ten or even more years after it was over, which was when one might have expected them. I think books about the late war are about due to appear now, and books about the immediate post-war at some time in the 'fifties.

I've been horribly ill the last few weeks. I had a bit of a relapse, then they decided to have another go with streptomycin, which previously did me a lot of good, at least temporarily. This time only one dose of it had ghastly results, as I suppose I had built up an allergy or something. I'm a bit better now, however, but I can't work and don't know when I shall be able to. I've no hope of getting out of here before the late summer. If the weather is good I might then get up to Scotland for a few weeks, but not more, and then I shall have to spend the autumn and winter somewhere near a doctor, perhaps even in some kind of residential sanatorium. I can't make plans till my health takes a more definite turn one way or the other. Richard is blooming, or was when I last saw him. He will be five in May. I think he will go to the village school this winter, but next year I shall have to remove him to the mainland so that he can go to a proper day school. . . . If he grew to be a farmer I should be pleased, though I shan't try to influence him . . .[1]

Yours
George

---

[1] Richard Blair did take up farming as his career. In 1964 he married Eleanor Moir, and they have two sons.

154. Letter to Sir Richard Rees, Bt

Cranham
25 April 1949

Dear Richard,
Thanks for your letter. I have been sort of up & down in health but on the whole am a little better, I think. I still can't make any plans, but if I am up & abt for the winter, I thought it might not be a bad idea to go abroad somewhere, & Orlando[1] (I don't know if you know him, he writes for the *Observer* sometimes) suggested Capri as a good place to stay. It sounds as if it wld have good food & wine, & Silone,[2] who is a friend of mine & lives there, wld no doubt be able to arrange somewhere for me to stay. Any way it's worth thinking over. The Tawneys came in the other day. I think they're going back to London almost immediately, so I'm afraid I may not see them again. For little Richard's birthday, Inez[3] is going to try & get me one of those children's typewriters you see advertised now, if not too impossibly expensive. I thought if he could be kept from smashing it, it wld come in useful when he begins to learn his letters in earnest, & it wld also keep him off my typewriter. The Tawneys took that book of yours I had & are going to send it to you. When Brenda[4] comes I am going to get her to make up some parcels for me & send home some of the books, which are piling up fearfully. I still can't do any work. Some days I take pen & paper & try to write a few lines, but it's impossible. When you are in this state you have the impression that your brain is working normally until you try to put words together, & then you find that you have acquired a sort of awful heaviness & clumsiness, as well as inability to concentrate for more than a few seconds. I am reading *Mr Sponge's Sporting Tour*, which I had never read before. I don't think it's as good as *Handley Cross*. I also recently reread *Little Dorrit* for the first time in a good many years. It's a dull book in a way, but it contains a really subtle character, William Dorrit, quite unlike most of Dickens's people. Someone in the USA has managed to get me a copy of Gissing's *New Grub Street* at last. Don't lose *The Odd Women*, will you.

Yours
Eric

[1] Ruggero Orlando, a journalist.   [2] Ignazio Silone.
[3] Inez Holden.   [4] Brenda Salkeld, who had known Orwell since 1928.

155. Letter to Anthony Powell

Cranham
11 May 1949

Dear Tony,

Thanks so much for your letter. I at last (only yesterday as a matter of fact) got hold of a copy of John Aubrey & am reading it with interest. I had not realised he was such an all-round chap—had simply thought of him in connection with scandalous anecdotes. I look forward to seeing your selections. Yes, I read Margarete Neumann's book. I thought it was quite good, obviously written by a sincere person. Tell Malcolm[1] if he hasn't seen it that he ought to read Ruth Fischer's book (*Stalin & German Communism*)—at any rate it is a useful book to have by one as a reference. I am so sorry abt poor old Hugh Kingsmill.[2] I don't know if you see him, but if you do, tell him I just reread his book on Dickens, which I got hold of with some difficulty, & that I think the same as before—it's a brilliant book, but it's the case for the prosecution. I wonder why somebody doesn't reprint *After Puritanism*. I put in a mention of it when I reviewed that other book of his that they reprinted, but it got cut out the way things do in reviews. I have by the way at last got hold of a copy of *New Grub Street* & am having another try at getting someone to reprint it. One would think the Everyman Library would have at least one book of Gissing's, but I don't know how one approaches them—at least I have no wire I can pull there.

I have been beastly ill, on & off. I can't make any firm plans. If I'm reasonably well this winter I shall go abroad for some months. If I'm able to walk but can't face a journey I shall stay in somewhere like Brighton. If I have to continue in bed I shall try to move to some sanatorium near London where people can come & see me more easily. It looks as if I may have to spend the rest of my life, if not actually in bed, at any rate at the bath-chair level. I could stand that for say 5 years if only I could work. At present I can do nothing, not even a book review.

Please give everyone my love. Yours
George

[1] Malcolm Muggeridge.
[2] Hugh Kingsmill, writer and critic, had been present at least once at the weekly luncheons held in 1945 by Orwell, Powell and Muggeridge. His book that Orwell reviewed was *The Dawn's Delay* (*Observer*, 18 July 1948). Kingsmill went into hospital on 14 April 1949 and died on 15 May.

156. Letter to F.J. Warburg

Cranham
16 May 1949

Dear Fred,

Thanks so much for your letter. As she may have told you, I had to put Sonia Brownell off. I am in most ghastly health, & have been for some weeks. I am due for another X-ray picture, but for some days I have been too feverish to go over to the X-ray room & stand up against the screen. When the picture is taken I am afraid there is not much doubt it will show that both lungs have deteriorated badly. I asked the doctor recently whether she thought I would survive, & she wouldn't go further than saying she didn't know. If the "prognosis" after this photo is bad, I shall get a second opinion. Can you give me the name of that specialist you mentioned? Then I will suggest either him or Dr Morlock, another specialist whom I consulted before the war. They can't *do* anything, as I am not a case for operation, but I would like an expert opinion on how long I am likely to stay alive. I do hope people won't now start chasing me to make me go to Switzerland, which is supposed to have magical qualities. I don't believe it makes any difference where you are, & a journey would be the death of me. The one chance of surviving, I imagine, is to keep quiet. Don't think I am making up my mind to peg out. On the contrary, I have the strongest reasons for wanting to stay alive. But I want to get a clear idea of *how long* I am likely to last, & not just be jollied along the way doctors usually do.

Yes, do come & see me. I hope & trust that by the beginning of June I may be a bit better, at any rate less feverish. I am glad *1984* has done so well before publication. The *World Review* published a most stupid extract, abridged in such a way as to make nonsense of it.[1] I wouldn't have let Moore arrange this if I'd known they meant to hack it abt. However, I suppose it's advertisement. That *Evening Standard* man, Mr Curran, came to interview me, & had arranged to come again, but I'm thinking of putting him off, because he tired me so last time, arguing abt politics. Please give everyone my love.

Yours
George

[1] "1984 and Newspeak", *World Review*, May 1949.

157. Letter to Anthony Powell

Cranham Lodge
Cranham
Gloucester
6 June 1949

Dear Tony,

Thanks ever so for sending me the Aubrey book.[1] I'm so glad you *did* put in my favourite Mrs Overall after all, also the story abt Sir W. Raleigh & his son. I was so sorry about Hugh Kingsmill. If they are trying to get a pension for his widow, if my signature would be useful in any way, of course include me. I'm a good deal better, & trust this will continue. I had a specialist from London, who said much the same as the people here, i.e. that if I get round *this* corner I could be good for quite a few years, but that I have got to keep quiet & not try to work for a long time, possibly as long as a year or two years—I trust it won't be as long as that. It's a great bore, but worth while if it means I can work again later. Richard[2] is staying nearby for the summer, & comes over & sees me once or twice a week. Please remember me to everybody. I hope you & Malcolm[3] will come & see me some time—but of course don't put yourselves out. I know what a tiresome journey it must be.

Yours
George

PS. I'm reading Dante! (With a crib of course.)

---

[1] *Brief Lives: and Other Selected Writings of John Aubrey* edited by Anthony Powell.
[2] His adopted son.   [3] Malcolm Muggeridge.

502

*Nineteen Eighty-Four was published in London by Secker & Warburg
on 8 June 1949 and in New York by Harcourt, Brace on 13 June 1949*

158. Letter to Francis A. Henson (extract)

[Part of a letter, since lost, written on 16 June 1949 by Orwell to Francis
A. Henson of the United Automobile Workers answering questions about
Nineteen Eighty-Four. Excerpts from the letter were published in *Life*, 25
July 1949, and the *New York Times Book Review*, 31 July 1949; the
following is an amalgam of these.]

My recent novel is NOT intended as an attack on Socialism or on the
British Labour Party (of which I am a supporter) but as a show-up of
the perversions to which a centralised economy is liable and which
have already been partly realised in Communism and Fascism. I do
not believe that the kind of society I describe necessarily *will* arrive,
but I believe (allowing of course for the fact that the book is a satire)
that something resembling it *could* arrive. I believe also that totalitarian ideas have taken root in the minds of intellectuals everywhere,
and I have tried to draw these ideas out to their logical consequences.
The scene of the book is laid in Britain in order to emphasise that the
English-speaking races are not innately better than anyone else and
that totalitarianism, *if not fought against*, could triumph anywhere.

159. Letter to Julian Symons

Cranham Lodge
Cranham
Gloucester
16 June 1949

Dear Julian,
I think it was you who reviewed *1984* in the *TLS*.[1] I must thank you
for such a brilliant as well as generous review. I don't think you
could have brought out the sense of the book better in so short a
space. You are of course right abt the vulgarity of the "Room 101"

[1] *Times Literary Supplement*, 10 June 1949.

business. I was aware of this while writing it, but I didn't know
another way of getting somewhere near the effect I wanted.

I have been horribly ill since last seeing you, but a lot better in the
last few weeks, & I hope perhaps now I have turned the corner. The
various doctors I have seen are all quite encouraging but say I must
remain quiet & not work for a long time, possibly as much as a year
—I hope it won't be so long, of course. It's a bore, but worth while if
it means recovering. Richard is staying nearby for the summer &
comes & sees me every week. He has started kindergarten school &
this winter is going to the village school in Jura, I don't know for how
long. I have been thinking about Westminster for him when he is
older. They have abandoned their top-hats, I learn. It is a day school,
which I prefer, & I think has other good points. Anyway I'm going to
make enquiries & put his name down if it seems suitable. Of course
god knows what will have happened by then, say 1956, but one has to
plan as though nothing would change drastically.

Have you any news of the Empsons, who were in Pekin? I don't
know whether you knew them. There have been various rumours, & I
am trying to get some news from Empson's American publishers.

Did you read Ruth Fischer's book *Stalin & German Communism*?
She's coming to see me tomorrow, I think.

Hope all is well & baby flourishing. Please remember me to your
wife.

Yours
George

160. Letter to Vernon Richards

Cranham Lodge
Cranham
Gloucester
22 June 1949

Dear Vernon,
Thanks so much for your letter, & the press-cuttings. Yes, I got the
copy of the memorial number[1] all right.

Sell as many photos as you can. It doesn't cost *me* anything, & is
all advertisement. I had a lot of fuss with *Life*, who wanted to send

---

[1] *Freedom*, 28 May 1949, which was devoted to the memory of Vernon
Richards's wife, Marie Louise, who had died of pneumonia on 13 April 1949.

interviewers here etc, but I put them off because that kind of thing tires me too much. I am afraid some of the US Republican papers have tried to use *1984* as propaganda against the Labour Party, but I have issued a sort of démenti which I hope will be printed.

Yes, send me the list of questions & I'll do my best. You will understand that I cannot answer at great length. The more this issue is cleared up, the better.

I'd love to see you some time. But let me know when you're coming. (I think there are people coming the next 3 week-ends) so as not to clash with anyone else, & so that I can arrange abt a car.

Yours
George

161. Letter to Sir Richard Rees, Bt

Cranham Lodge
Cranham
Gloucester
28 July 1949

Dear Richard,

Thanks so much for your letter, with cutting. Do you think you could get your Mr Roberts to make me a bookcase, same dimensions as yours but 5 feet wide, if he can manage it. If, as I assume, it will be of white wood, I suppose it should be stained or painted, I don't much mind which, except that if painted I think off-white is the best colour. I'd be much obliged if you could get him to do this & send it up to Barnhill.

I think you'll find at Barnhill one novel by Charles Williams, called *The Place of the Lion* or something like that (published by Gollancz). He's quite unreadable, one of those writers who just go on and on & have no idea of selecting. I think Eliot's approval of him must be purely sectarian (Anglo-Catholic). It wouldn't surprise me to learn that Eliot approves of C.S. Lewis as well. The more I see the more I doubt whether people ever really make aesthetic judgements at all. Everything is judged on political grounds which are then given an aesthetic disguise. When, for instance, Eliot can't see anything good in Shelley or anything bad in Kipling, the real underlying reason must be that the one is a radical and the other a conservative, of sorts. Yet evidently one does have aesthetic reactions, especially as a lot of art and even literature is politically neutral, and also certain unmistakable standards do exist, e.g. Homer is better than Edgar Wallace. Perhaps the way we should put it is: the more one is aware of political bias the more one can be independent of it, & the more one claims to be impartial the more one is biassed.

1984 has had good reviews in the USA, such as I have seen of them, but of course also some very shame-making publicity. You'll be glad to hear *Animal Farm* has been translated into Russian at last, in a DP paper in Frankfurt. I'm trying to arrange for it to be done in book form.

Yours
Eric

Encounter, January 1962

162. Letter to F. J. Warburg

Cranham Lodge
Cranham
Gloucester
22 August 1949

Dear Fred,
Could you please send one copy each of *Burmese Days* & *Coming Up for Air* to Sonia Brownell, care of *Horizon*.

I have Morland[1] coming to see me again this evening. On & off I have been feeling absolutely ghastly. It comes & goes, but I have periodical bouts of high temperatures etc. I will tell you what Morland says. Richard has just gone back to Jura & is going to the village school for the winter term. Beyond that I can't make plans for the moment. I have put him down for Westminster, but he wouldn't be going there till 1957, & heavens knows what may have happened by then. As I warned you I might do, I intend getting married again (to Sonia) when I am once again in the land of the living, if I ever am.

---

[1] Dr Andrew Morland, a specialist in TB, who had been called in by F.J. Warburg. Morland recommended that Orwell be moved to University College Hospital, London.

I suppose everyone will be horrified, but apart from other considerations I really think I should stay alive longer if I were married.

I have sketched out the book of essays I wld like to publish next year, but I want it to include two long new essays on Joseph Conrad & George Gissing, & of course I can't touch those till I am definitively better.

Love to all
George

163. Letter to Philip Rahv

Room 65
Private Wing
University College Hospital
Gower Street
London WC1
17 September 1949

Dear Philip Rahv,

About two weeks ago Alan Dowling[1] wrote to me from France, informing me that I had been selected for *PR's* literary award & forwarding a cheque for 1000 dollars, signed by you. I wrote to him then, & would have written to you earlier if it were not that I have been so beastly ill that writing letters is still something of an effort. I really do feel very deeply honoured, & only wish I could repay you a little by sometimes writing for *PR* again. As it is I am quite incapable of doing any work, even if the doctors would allow me to, & in fact I have hardly set pen to paper since last December. This beastly disease (TB) works very slowly, & though I am supposed to be getting on fairly well it is possible that I shall be incapacitated for the better part of another year.

I must also thank you for your very long & kind review of *1984* in *PR*. I expect you will forgive me for not writing a better letter. At any rate, very many thanks again.

Yours sincerely
Geo. Orwell

[1] Alan Dowling had helped to finance *Partisan Review* and was on the editorial board.

164. Letter to Julian Symons

Room 65
Private Wing
UC Hospital
Gower St. WC.1
[17? September 1949]

Dear Julian,
Thanks so much for your letter. I've been here a fortnight & was meaning to write or ring up, but till a day or two ago I was not supposed to have visitors. I was really ghastly ill for some months. Now I'm slightly better, but it's a very slow business & lord knows when I shall be able to get up or work again. As you saw from those nasty pars in the newspapers, Sonia & I contemplate getting married while I am still an invalid, among other things because it would make it easier for her to come & look after me wherever I go after leaving here.

Do come & see me some time. I'm supposed to have only 1 visitor a day for 20 minutes (of course it stretches itself out a bit) so it's not worth making a special expedition. Perhaps you could ring up & arrange a day that suited you. If you ring up the hospital they'll put you through to my room. In the evening, any time after 5, is the best time to come. I'd like very much to see the biography of your brother[1] if you'll bring it along.

I can sympathise with you trying to write in a flat with a small child. If you don't find a suitable place in Essex you might try Hertfordshire. It's a very attractive county in places, very agricultural. I should say Gollancz is talking rot about having to produce your novel under another name. I suppose it might be true if you were Peter Cheyney or James Hadley Chase.

Richard was staying near me for the summer (at the anarchist colony at Whiteway) & has now gone back to Jura. He is attending the village school, which I think he will enjoy. He is getting enormous & is extremely active, though still a bit backward in talking. He loves farming & boats, & even last year he helped with the farm work to the extent of being quite useful. I shan't influence him if I can help it, but if he does grow up to be a farmer, a sailor, a civil engineer or something useful of that description I should be very pleased.

[1] *A.J.A. Symons* by Julian Symons, 1950.

What do you think of devaluation? I imagine they had to do it
sooner or later, but I wasn't expecting it till after the election.
Please remember me to your wife.

Yours
George

165. Letter to Leonard Moore

Room 65
Private Wing
UC Hospital
11 October 1949

Dear Moore,
I wonder if you could deal with the enclosed letters.

I am still very weak & ill, but I think better on the whole. I am
getting married very unobtrusively this week. It will probably be a
long time before I can get out of bed, but if I am equal to travelling
by the end of the year the doctor suggests that I should spend the
worst of the winter abroad, probably in France. They will no doubt
allow me some currency, but probably not enough & I want to
wangle some more francs if possible. If I have any francs due to me
(e.g. from the French translation of *1984*), do you think you could
arrange for them to remain in France, after deducting your commission.

Yours sincerely
Eric Blair

166. Letter to T. R. Fyvel

Room 65
Private Wing
UC Hospital
25 October 1949

Dear Tosco,
I have to write to you instead of Mary, because I can't remember or
find your Amersham address, so have to send this to *Tribune*. It was

so awfully kind of you both to send me that beautiful box of crystal-
lised fruits, & then on top of that for Mary to send me those packets
of tea. Sonia asks me to thank you from her too.

I am getting on pretty well, but they evidently won't let me out
of bed for a long time to come. However, I enjoy my food very much
more than I did, which makes a great difference. I hope you will come
& see me again some time, & please convey my thanks to Mary. I
tried to ring up Evelyn[1] the other day to ask her to come & see me,
but she was out.

Yours
George

167. Extracts from a Manuscript Note-book

[During the last year of his life Orwell kept a manuscript note-book in
which he made notes for a long short story, "A Smoking Room Story",
and for essays on Joseph Conrad and Evelyn Waugh. He also used it for
occasional jottings from which the following selection is taken. Before 21
March 1949 none of the entries is dated.]

Probably there was some truth in Pétain's remark, at the time when
he became ruler of France, that the French defeat was due partly to
the low birthrate. Where families are small, the civilian population
cannot regard the killing of their sons with indifference, & the
soldier's own attitude is probably affected by his having learned to
think of himself as more of an individual, & more important, than if
he had had to scramble for survival in a hungry peasant family of
five or ten children.

One great difference between the Victorians & ourselves was that
they looked on the adult as more important than the child. In a
family of ten or twelve it was almost inevitable that one or two should
die in infancy, & though these deaths were sad, of course, they were
soon forgotten, as there were always more children coming along. In
St John's Church, near Lord's, there are many memorial tablets of
East India nabobs, etc with the usual column of lies in praise of the

---

[1] Evelyn Anderson, who had worked on *Tribune* at the same time as Orwell.

dead man, then a line or two abt "Sarah, relict of the above", and then perhaps another line saying that one male & two female children, or words to that effect, are buried in the same vault. No names given, & in one case the inscription reads *two or three children*. By the time the stone was put up, it had been forgotten how many had died.

Nowadays the death of a child is the worst thing that most people are able to imagine. If one has only *one* child, to recover from losing it would be almost impossible. It would darken the universe, permanently. Even two generations ago I doubt whether people had this feeling. Cf in *Jude the Obscure*, in the preposterous incident where the eldest child hangs the two younger ones & then hangs itself. Jude & Sue are, of course, distressed, but they do not seem to feel that after such an event their own lives must cease. Sue (I think Hardy realises that she is an intolerable character, but I don't think he is being ironical in this place) says after a while that she sees why the children had to die: it was to make her a better woman & help her to begin her life anew. It does not occur to her that the children were more important creatures than herself & that in comparison with their death, nothing that can now happen to her is of much significance.

I read recently in the newspaper that in Shanghai (now full of refugees) abandoned children are becoming so common on the pavement that one no longer notices them. In the end, I suppose, the body of a dying child becomes simply a piece of refuse to be stepped over. Yet all these children started out with the expectation of being loved & protected & with the conviction which one can see even in a very young child that the world is a splendid place & there are plenty of good times ahead.

Qy. are you the same again if you have walked home stepping over the bodies of abandoned children, & not succouring even one of them? (Even to take care not to tread on them is a sort of hypocrisy.) M.M[1] says that anyone who has lived in Asia has in effect done this kind of thing already. Perhaps not quite true, insomuch that when he & I lived in Asia we were young men who wd hardly notice babies.

It is now (1949) 16 years since my first book was published, & abt 21 years since I started publishing articles in the magazines. Throughout that time there has literally been not one day in which I did not feel that I was idling, that I was behind with the current job, & that

[1] Malcolm Muggeridge.

my total output was miserably small. Even at the periods when I was working 10 hours a day on a book, or turning out 4 or 5 articles a week, I have never been able to get away from this neurotic feeling, that I was wasting time. I can never get any sense of achievement out of the work that is actually in progress, because it always goes slower than I intend, & in any case I feel that a book or even an article does not exist until it is finished. But as soon as a book is finished, I begin, actually from the next day, worrying because the next one is not begun, & am haunted with the fear that there never will be a next one —that my impulse is exhausted for good & all. If I look back & count up the actual amount that I have written, then I see that my output has been respectable: but this does not reassure me, because it simply gives me the feeling that I once had an industriousness & a fertility which I have now lost.

Recently I was reading somewhere or other abt an Italian curio-dealer who attempted to sell a 17th-century crucifix to J.P. Morgan. It was not at first sight a particularly interesting work of art. But it turned out that the real point was that the crucifix took to pieces & inside it was concealed a stiletto. What a perfect symbol of the Christian religion.

For & against novels in the first person.

Actually, to write a novel in the first person is like dosing yourself with some stimulating but very deleterious & very habit-forming drug. The temptation to do it is very great, but at every stage of the proceedings you know perfectly well that you are doing something wrong & foolish. However, there are two great advantages:

i. In the first person, one can always get the book actually written, & fairly quickly, as the use of the "I" seems to do away with the shyness & feeling of helplessness which often prevent one from getting well started. In the first person, one can always get somewhere near the conception with which one starts out.

ii. In the first person *anything* can be made to sound credible. This is so in the first place because whatever he writes seems credible to the author, for you can daydream abt *yourself* doing no matter what, whereas third-person adventures have to be comparatively probable. The reader, again, finds anything told in the first person credible, because he either identifies himself with the "I" of the story, or, because an "I" is talking to him, accepts it as a real person.

Disadvantages:

i. The narrator is never really separable from the author. It is impossible to avoid crediting him with one's own thoughts occasionally, &, since even in a novel the author must occasionally comment, one's own comments unavoidably become those of the narrator (which would not be so in a third-person novel). At the least, the narrator must have the author's prose style (example, *Great Expectations*, which is otherwise not a very autobiographical book).

ii. If the arrangement is strictly kept to, the events of the story are seen only through the consciousness of one person. Merely in order to find out what is happening, this involves the narrator in eavesdropping & amateur detective work, or makes it necessary for people to do things in company which in real life they would only do alone. If the thoughts of the other characters are to be revealed, then they have to be made to talk more freely than any real person would do, or else the narrator has to say something which amounts to, "I could see what he was thinking, namely," etc etc. (Cf fearful scene in E. Waugh's *Brideshead Revisited*.) But in general an "I" novel is simply the story of one person—a three-dimensional figure among caricatures—& therefore cannot be a true novel.

iii. Range of feeling much narrowed, as there are many kinds of appeal that you can make on behalf of others but not for yourself.

For article on E. Waugh.
The advantages of not being part of the movement, irrespective of whether the movement is in the right direction or not.

But disadvantage in holding false (indefensible) opinions.

The movement (Auden etc).

W's driving forces. Snobbery. Catholicism.

Note even the early books not anti-religious or demonstrably anti-moral. But note the persistent snobbishness, rising in the social scale but always centring round the idea of continuity/aristocracy/a country house. Note that everyone is snobbish, but that Waugh's loyalty is to a form of society no longer viable, of which he must be aware.

Untenable opinions *cf* Poe.

Catholicism. Note that a Catholic writer does not have to be Conservative in a political sense. Differentiate G. Greene. Advantage to a novelist of being a Catholic—theme of collision between two kinds of good.

Analyse *Brideshead Revisited*. (Note faults due to being written in first person.) Studiously detached attitude. Not puritanical. Priests not superhuman. Real theme—Sebastian's drunkenness, & family's unwillingness to cure this at the expense of committing a sin. Note that this is a real departure from the humanist attitude, with which no compromise possible.

But. Last scene, where the unconscious man makes the sign of the Cross. Note that after all the veneer is bound to crack sooner or later. One cannot really be Catholic & grown-up.

Conclude. Waugh is abt as good a novelist as one can be (i.e. as novelists go today) while holding untenable opinions.

21 March 1949

The routine here (Cranham Sanatorium) is quite different from that of Hairmyres Hospital. Although everyone at Hairmyres was most kind & considerate to me—quite astonishingly so, indeed—one cannot help feeling at every moment the difference in the *texture* of life when one is paying one's own keep.

The most noticeable difference here is that it is much quieter than the hospital, & that everything is done in a more leisurely way. I live in a so-called chalet, one of a row of continuous wooden huts, with glass doors, each chalet measuring abt 15′ by 12′. There are hot water pipes, a washing basin, a chest of drawers & wardrobe, besides the usual bed-tables etc. Outside is a glass-roofed verandah. Everything is brought by hand—none of those abominable rattling trolleys which one is never out of the sound of in a hospital. Not much noise of radios either—all the patients have headphones. (Here these are permanently tuned in to the Home Service. At Hairmyres, usually to the Light.) The most persistent sound is the song of birds.

In 1943, when I was working for the BBC, one of the weekly "newsletters" that I was responsible for was the Marathi one. These newsletters—actually news commentaries issued once or twice a week in minor languages in which it was impossible to broadcast daily—were composed by someone in the BBC, then translated by a speaker of that language & broadcast by him, under the supervision of a censor who as a rule was also an employee of the BBC.

We always had difficulty with the Marathi newsletter, because, apparently, Indians of that race when living in England soon lose their command of their native tongue. So though there were a number of Marathi students in England, there were not many who were suitable as broadcasters. In 1943 the job was being done by a little man named Kothari, who was almost completely spherical. He had I think been a Communist & certainly been an extreme Nationalist, but was quite reliable because he was genuinely anti-Nazi & pro-Allied. Suddenly the so-called "College", the mysterious body (actually I think MI.5) which had to OK all broadcasters, got onto the fact that Kothari had been in prison—for some political offence while a student, I think. At once Kothari was banned from the air on the ground that no-one who had been in prison could be allowed to broadcast. With some difficulty we got hold of another youth named Jatha, & all went well for some time. Then, after this had been going on for some months, my Marathi assistant, Miss Chitale, came to me & suddenly revealed with great secretiveness that Jatha was not actually writing the broadcasts. He had partly forgotten his own language, & though he could broadcast the newsletter when once written, he could not translate it. Kothari was actually doing the translations & he & Jatha were splitting the fee. I felt it my duty to tell my superior, Dr Rushbrook-Williams, abt this. As it would be very difficult, if possible at all, to find another Marathi broadcaster, he decided that we must wink our eye at what was happening. So the arrangement continued, & we did not officially know anything abt it.

It seemed to me that this was a little bit of India transplanted to Britain. But the *perfectly* Indian touch was Miss Chitale holding up her information for several months before disclosing it.

Gross unfairness & misleadingness of much criticism of both USA & USSR, because of failure to allow for the *size* of those countries. Obvious absurdity of comparing a small homogenous population, e.g. of Britain, packed together in a small area, with a multi-racial state sprawling across a continent. Clearly one cannot reasonably compare conditions in Britain with those in, say, Siberia. One might compare Siberia with Canada, or Turkestan with Northern India, or Leningrad with Edinburgh. Ditto with USA. People in Britain very high-minded abt American treatment of Negroes, but cf conditions in South Africa. Certainly we, in Britain, have no control over S. Africa, but neither have the people in the Northern States much control over what happens in Alabama. Meanwhile we profit indirectly from what happens in S. Africa, in Jamaica, in Malaya etc.

But these places are separated from us *by water*. On this last fact the essential hypocrisy of the British labour movement is based.

17 April 1949
Curious effect, here in the sanatorium, on Easter Sunday, when the people in this (the most expensive) block of "chalets" mostly have visitors, of hearing large numbers of upper-class English voices. I have been almost out of the sound of them for two years, hearing them at most one or two at a time, my ears growing more & more used to working-class or lower-middle-class Scottish voices. In the hospital at Hairmyres, for instance, I literally never heard a "cultivated" accent except when I had a visitor. It is as though I were hearing these voices for the first time. And what voices! A sort of over-fedness, a fatuous self-confidence, a constant bah-bahing of laughter abt nothing, above all a sort of heaviness & richness combined with a fundamental ill-will—people who, one instinctively feels, without even being able to see them, are the enemies of anything intelligent or sensitive or beautiful. No wonder everyone hates us so.

The big cannibal critics that lurk in the deeper waters of American quarterly reviews.

The greatest of all the disadvantages under which the left-wing movement suffers: that being a newcomer to the political scene, & having to build itself up out of nothing, it had to create a following by telling lies. For a left-wing party in power, its most serious antagonist is always its own past propaganda.

Greater and ever-increasing softness & luxuriousness of modern life. Rise in the standard of physical courage, improvement in health & physique, continuous supersession of athletic records. Qy. how to reconcile?

At 50, everyone has the face he deserves.

Appendix I

BOOKS BY OR CONTAINING CONTRIBUTIONS BY GEORGE ORWELL

Down and Out in Paris and London, London, 1933; New York, 1933.
Burmese Days, New York, 1934; London, 1935.
A Clergyman's Daughter, London, 1935; New York, 1936.
Keep the Aspidistra Flying, London, 1936; New York, 1956.
The Road to Wigan Pier, London, 1937; New York, 1958.
Homage to Catalonia, London, 1938; New York, 1952.
Coming Up for Air, London, 1939; New York, 1950.
Inside the Whale, London, 1940.
The Lion and the Unicorn, London, 1941.
The Betrayal of the Left, by Victor Gollancz, George Orwell, John Strachey and others, London, 1941.
Victory or Vested Interest? by G.D.H. Cole, George Orwell and others, London, 1942.
Talking to India, edited with an introduction by George Orwell, London, 1943.
Animal Farm, London, 1945; New York, 1946.
Critical Essays, London, 1946; (American title) *Dickens, Dali and Others*, New York, 1946.
James Burnham and the Managerial Revolution, London, 1946. (Pamphlet.)
Love of Life and Other Stories, by Jack London. Introduction by George Orwell, London, 1946.
The English People, London, 1947.
British Pamphleteers, Vol. 1, edited by George Orwell and Reginald Reynolds. Introduction by George Orwell, London, 1948.
Nineteen Eighty-Four, London, 1949; New York, 1949.

POSTHUMOUS COLLECTIONS

Shooting an Elephant, London, 1950; New York, 1950
Such, Such Were the Joys, New York, 1953.
England Your England, London, 1953.
The Orwell Reader, edited by Richard H. Rovere, New York, 1956.
Collected Essays, London, 1961.

Appendix II

Chronology

1945

After eighteen months of rejections and setbacks *Animal Farm* was published on 17 August by Secker & Warburg.

From 10 to 22 September Orwell paid his first visit to Jura in the Hebrides and stayed in a crofter's cottage in a remote part of the island. On his return to his flat, 27B Canonbury Square, Islington, he resumed writing regularly again for *Tribune*, the *Observer*, and the *Manchester Evening News*.

Although his friends had expected Orwell to give up his adopted son after the death of his wife, Eileen Blair, in March, Orwell refused to part with the child and had young Richard Blair looked after by Gwen O'Shaughnessy's children's nurse, Joyce Pritchard, then by Doreen Kopp until the summer, when for the next twelve months Susan Watson, who had a young child of her own, became Orwell's housekeeper. Orwell and Richard Blair spent Christmas with Arthur Koestler and his wife, Mamaine, at their home in North Wales.

1946

Critical Essays was published on 14 February by Secker & Warburg and with the title *Dickens, Dali and Others* on 29 April by Reynal & Hitchcock in New York. From mid-April Orwell gave up all journalism for six months and until the end of July took a complete rest from writing.

On 3 May his elder sister, Marjorie Dakin, died of a kidney disease at the age of 48. A few days after attending her funeral in Nottingham Orwell set off north from London and stayed for a week with George Kopp and his wife, Doreen, at their home at Biggar, not far from Edinburgh. He arrived on 23 May at Barnhill, a house he had rented on Jura to find some peace away from journalism, the telephone, etc, and start writing books again, and began putting it in order. His sister, Avril Blair, came on 31 May to help and in early July he went down to London and fetched young Richard and Susan Watson, who, however, did not stay long. From then on his sister Avril became Orwell's housekeeper and looked after young Richard.

On 26 August *Animal Farm* was published in New York by Harcourt, Brace. It was also published as the American Book of the Month Club choice in an edition which sold over half a million copies and freed him from financial worries for the first time in his life. In early August he began work on *Nineteen Eighty-Four*. He returned to Canonbury Square on 13 October. In November he gave up his book review column in the *Manchester Evening News* and made his last contribution for the next fifteen months to the *Observer*. He started writing weekly again for *Tribune* until the "As I Please" of 4 April 1947, which was the last piece he wrote for it. In November Paul Elek published Jack London's *Love of Life and Other Stories* for which Orwell had written the Introduction in November 1945.

On 29 December Orwell went up to Jura to plant fruit trees and rose bushes and was back in Canonbury Square by 8 January.

1947
On 11 April he arrived on Jura with young Richard and Avril Blair. For the week before leaving London Orwell had been ill in bed and until after the middle of May he was not well enough to do much out of doors.

From April onwards, apart from fifteen reviews for the *Observer* between February 1948 and February 1949, Orwell did no more regular journalism, but wrote individual articles and reviews for either American magazines which paid well, like the *New Yorker* or the *New York Times Book Review*, or minority magazines, such as *Politics and Letters*, which he felt needed encouragement and support. By 31 May he had written "Such, Such Were the Joys".

Sir Richard Rees, Orwell's close friend, arrived at Barnhill in early July and stayed until the end of September. In the same month Orwell gave up The Stores, the cottage he had rented at Wallington, Hertfordshire, since 1936, as he now intended to make Jura his summer home and keep 27B Canonbury Square as a *pied à terre* in London.

In October Orwell prepared *Coming Up for Air* to appear as the first volume in the uniform edition of his works which Secker & Warburg were undertaking. In November Bill Dunn, a young Scotsman recently demobilised from the army, came to live at Barnhill, having entered into partnership with Sir Richard Rees to farm it for Orwell.

Orwell had become increasingly unwell with inflammation of the

lungs throughout September and October, but by the time he was
forced to take to his bed in late October he had finished the first
draft of *Nineteen Eighty-Four*. A chest specialist diagnosed tuberculosis of the left lung and five days before Christmas Orwell entered
Hairmyres Hospital, East Kilbride, near Glasgow.

1948
In the second half of January Orwell felt well enough to do a little
book reviewing. In March he wrote "Writers and Leviathan" for
Politics and Letters and in April corrected the proofs for a reprint of
Burmese Days. On 13 May *Coming Up for Air* was published in the
uniform edition. Orwell responded sufficiently well to the two-month
course of streptomycin he had started in February for him to begin
in May the second draft of *Nineteen Eighty-Four* and write an article
"Britain's Left Wing Press" for the June issue of the *Progressive*
(Madison, Wisconsin). About this time he wrote "George Gissing"
for *Politics and Letters*.

On 28 July he returned to Barnhill, but in September his health
began to relapse. He put off going for treatment in order to finish
Nineteen Eighty-Four, which he did by early November, then typed
it himself and sent the copies off on 4 December. During the autumn
he wrote "Reflections on Gandhi" for *Partisan Review*. On 15
November Allan Wingate published *British Pamphleteers*, Vol. I,
for which Orwell had written the introduction in spring 1947. In
December he gave up his flat in Canonbury Square.

Throughout November and December Orwell was too unwell to go
out of doors and on 6 January, seriously ill with tuberculosis, he went
into the Cotswold Sanatorium, Cranham, Gloucestershire.

1949
In January *Burmese Days* appeared as the second volume in the
uniform edition. By mid-February Orwell felt well enough to agree to
do for *Partisan Review* a 5,000 word article on Evelyn Waugh, which
he began but never completed. In March he corrected the proofs of
Nineteen Eighty-Four. He had a relapse, yet managed to finish the
review he had promised of Winston Churchill's *Their Finest Hour*,
sending it off on 9 April to the *New Leader* (New York), in which it
appeared on 14 May 1949. This was the last completed review or
article he wrote. In April he had plans for writing a novel set in 1945,

but never felt well enough to write it. In the course of the year he did a synopsis and wrote four pages of a 30–40,000 word long short story called "A Smoking Room Story" and began making notes for a long essay on Joseph Conrad.

In June *Nineteen Eighty-Four* was published by Secker & Warburg and in New York by Harcourt, Brace. In July it was chosen by the American Book of the Month Club. In August Orwell began planning a book of reprinted essays.

On 3 September, seriously ill again, Orwell was transferred to University College Hospital, London. On 13 October he married Sonia Brownell, editorial assistant on *Horizon*, whom he had met in 1945.

1950
On 21 January, a few days before he was to travel to a Swiss sanatorium, Orwell died of pulmonary tuberculosis. He was 46. He was buried in the churchyard of All Saints, Sutton Courtenay, Berkshire.

Ian Angus

INDEX

Compiled by Oliver Stallybrass

For reasons of space it was not possible to include a consolidated index to the four volumes of *The Collected Essays, Journalism and Letters of George Orwell*. Instead, all index entries in volumes I, II and III, with the exceptions noted below, are here indicated, in parentheses, by roman figures immediately following the *main* headings (as opposed to subheadings). Thus, "(Bayswater, I, III)" means that there are one or more entries in volumes I and III but none in this volume (or, obviously, in volume II); while "Zamyatin (III): *We*, 72–5, 163, 417(n), 485–6" means that there are one or more entries on Zamyatin (not necessarily on his novel *We*) in volume III as well as on the pages shown for this volume. If, therefore, a heading is not found here it is unnecessary to search for it elsewhere, with the following exceptions:

1. Titles of books (other than anonymous ones) found only in volumes I–III are repeated here *only under their authors*; a reader who does not know the author of a book will therefore need to look for it under its title in the earlier indexes.

2. Orwell's own books, essays etc are listed, *in this volume*, only under Orwell, G., subheading *writings*.

3. References from the second half of a hyphenated name to the first (e.g. "Cooke, Rupert Croft-, *see* Croft-Cooke") have been omitted from this volume; all hyphenated names being given under the first element. Other forms of "*see*" reference have been repeated (in parentheses where they apply only to earlier volumes).

To save space, headings have here been shortened as much as possible (unadorned surnames refer to the obvious holder), and blocks of headings referring only to earlier volumes have been "set solid". This means that some of these headings occur in the middle of lines, and it is not, therefore, sufficient, in searching for references to earlier volumes, to run the eye down the left edge of the column.

All arabic numbers refer to pages, not to items. Footnotes are indicated by "n" or "(n)" after the page number: "n" refers *only* to the footnote, "(n)" to text *and* footnote. The *first* footnote on any individual person usually includes a brief biographical outline.

Subheadings are arranged in order of first page reference, except where chronological order (e.g. Orwell: *chronology*) or alphabetical order (e.g. Orwell: *writings:* individual titles) is clearly more appropriate.

George Orwell is abbreviated to GO throughout.

So—IV

536

Index

Intelligentsia—*cont.*
and the war, 67, 173; and Communist Party, 68; and power worship, 173–4; and totalitarianism, 502
Interglossa, see Hogben, L.
(International, the, II)
— affairs, 254–5, 370–5, 395–400; and atom bomb, 8–10; Burnham's view, 160–81, 313–26; a day's news, 247–8
— Brigade, *see* Spanish civil war
(— law, II)
— Rescue and Relief Committee, 120–1, 126
(Invasion, II, III; Inventions, III)
Iran (II, III), 187
(Iraq, II; Ireland, II, III; Irish in America, III; — labourers, II, III)
Irish nationalism (III), 13–15, 39
Iron Heel (London; II, III), 24, 26, 29, 163, 486
(Ironside, II; Irujo, I; Isherwood, I; Islam, III)
Island of Doctor Moreau (Wells), 283
Islanders, The (Zamyatin), 417
(Italians, II)
Italy (I, II, III), 371, 490
Izvestia, 267

(Jack the Giant-Killer, I, III)
— the Ripper, 98, 99
Jacket, The (London), 29
Jackson, Barbara, Lady, *see* Ward
—, Janetta, 327(n)
(—, L., III; —, T.A., I)
Jacobs, W.W. (I, II, III), 20
(James, A., III; —, C.L.R., I)
—, Henry (II, III), 409, 490
Japan and Japanese (II, III), 8, 35; and Burma, 112, 114; reason for losing war, 125; Burnham's view, 167, 172
(Jaques, E., *see* Collings)
Jargon, *see* English language
Jarrolds, Messrs, 99
(Jefferies, R., I)
Jellinek, Frank (I), 450n
(Jerome, J.K., III; Jerrold, D., I, III)
Jerusalem, 248
(—, Mufti of, II)
Jesse, F.T.: *Story of Burma*, 111–13; letters from GO, 113(n)–14
(Jesuits, I; Jesus Christ, III)
Jews (I, II, III): an Austrian, 3–4; refugees, 238; and Palestine, 250–1,

396; prizefighters, as Mosley's bodyguard, 383–4. *See also* Antisemitism
Joad, C.E.M. (II, III), 116
(Joan, Saint, III)
John, Augustus, 447
— *Aubrey and His Friends* (Powell), 384(n), 454(n)–5
(— *Bull*, I)
Johnson, Hewlett (II), 97
(—, Samuel, III)
Jolis, Bert, 121
Jones, Elizabeth, 100–1
(—, I., II; —, Tom, II; Jordan, P., III; Joseph, Saint, III)
Joubert, Sir Philip, 82–5
(Journalism, III)
Jours de Notre Mort (Rousset), 421
(Joyce, A.H., I)
—, James (I, II, III), 402, 409, 490; *Finnegans Wake*, 14; *Ulysses*, 257
—, William (II), 269–70
Jude the Obscure (Hardy), 479, 510
Jugoslavia (II, III), 30, 266
Jura, Hebrides (III): GO's rented house on, 87(n), 105, 126, 149, 392, 393, 403, 416, 421, 425, 426, 472, 476, 480, 482, 487, 504, 505, 518–20; GO's letters from, 196–200, 203–5, 326–30, 369–70, 376–86, 448–52, 454–5, 458–60; crofters' lives, 203–4; falling population, 204

(Kahane, J., I; Kaiser, the, III)
Kamenev, 63
(Kaye, Len, I; Kaye-Smith, S., I; Keats, III)
Kee, Janetta, *see* Jackson
(Kemal, M., II, III; Kennan, J., I; Kennedy, Joseph, II; —, Margaret, I; Kensington, III; Kerensky, I)
Kew, 286–7
Keynes, J.M.: *Economic Consequences of the Peace*, 471
(Kharkov trials, III)
Kimche, Jon (III), 394(n)
King Lear (Shakespeare; II, III), 44, 184, 220–1; and Tolstoy, 287–302
— *Solomon's Mines* (Haggard), 22
(King-Farlow, D., I)
King-Hall, S., 145(n)
Kingsley, C. (I), 12, 501
Kingsmill, Hugh (III), 499(n); *After Puritanism*, 499; *Dawn's Delay*,

Moral Re-Armament, *see* Oxford Group
(Morale, II, III)
Morality: and politics, 153–60
Morgan, J.P., 511
Morland, Dr A., 505n
(Morley, F.V., I; — College, II)
Morlock, Dr H.V., 487(n), 500
Mormons, 39
Morning Star, *see Daily Worker*
(Morocco, I, II, III; Morris, Stuart, II)
Morris, W., 164; *News from Nowhere*, 428
(Morrison, F., III; —, H., II, III; Mortimer, R., I, III; Morton, J.B., *see* Beachcomber)
Moscow Dynamos, 40(n)–1, 43
Mosley (I, II, III), 38, 383(n)–4, 401, 490
(Mottistone, II; Mountbatten, II)
Mr Sponge's Sporting Tour (Surtees), 498
(Mudlarks, III)
Muggeridge, M. (I, II, III), 499(n), 501, 510(n); *Affairs of the Heart*, 476(n); *Samuel Butler*, 455(n)
Mukerjee, Brijlal, 268–9
(Mumford, L., I)
Munich crisis, *see* Czechoslovakia
(Munitions, II)
Munro, H.H., *see* Saki
(Munson, G., II)
Munthe: *Story of San Michele*, 232
Murder: in England, 98–101; political, how to blur edges of, 136–7
(Muriel, goat, I; Murray, G., II)
Murry, J.M. (I, II, III): letter from GO, 405(n); *Free Society*, 405(n)
Music-halls (III), 22
Mussolini, Benito (I, II, III), 5, 102, 490, 493
(—, Bruno, III)
My Early Life (Churchill), 494
Myers, L.H. (I, II), 104n
(Mynors, R., I)

Nadal, E. M., 477–8
(Names, II)
Napoleon I (II, III), 168n
(Napoleonic war, III; *Nation*, II, III; National anthems, II, III)
National Council for Civil Liberties, 419(n), 423

(National Theatre, III; — Trust, III; — Unemployed Workers' Movement, I)
Nationalisation (II, III), 186, 188
Nationalism (I, II, III): and science, 11; Irish, 13–15; and sport, 40–4; need for research on, 311; in Asia, 372; antisemitism as a form of, 450
Nature: not wicked to enjoy, 142–5
(Navy, II)
Nazis and Nazism, *see* Fascism; Germany; Hitler
Negrin (I), 77(n)
(Negroes, I, II, III; Nehru, II; Nelson, Lord, III; —, T., I)
Nesbit, E.: *Treasure Seekers*, 20
Nether World (Gissing), 429
Netherlands, *see* Holland
(Nettleton, *see* King-Farlow)
Neumann, Margarete, *see* Buber-Neumann
(Neutrals, II; Never Again Society, III; *New Adelphi*, *see Adelphi*; — *Apocalypse*, II; — British Broadcasting Station, II; — *English Review*, III; — — *Weekly*, I, II)
New Grub Street (Gissing), 55, 429, 431–2, 433, 498, 499
(— *Leader*, London, I, II, III)
— —, N.Y.: GO's contributions, 313–26, 407–14, 491–5, 520
(— *Masses*, II)
— *Republic*, N.Y., 399; GO's contributions, 141–5, 181–4
— —, *The* (Mallock; III), 102
(— *Road*, II, III; — *Saxon Pamphlets*, II; — *Signatures*, I)
— *Statesman* (I, II, III), 189, 310. *See also* Martin, K.
(— *Writing*, I, II)
— *York Times* (III) *Book Review*: GO's contributions, 479(n), 519; letter of GO published in, 502
— *Yorker* (II, III): GO's contributions 233–4, 436(n), 439–43, 519
— *Zealand*, 371
Newark Advertiser, 261n
Newbolt, Sir H. (I, III), 303–4
(Newcastle, II)
Newhaven, 107
News Chronicle (I, II, III), 41, 185–6, 241; letter from GO, 477–8
— *from Nowhere* (Morris), 428

Orwell, George: *health—cont.*
458–60; *1949*, 473–88 *passim*, 495–
509 *passim*
—, *miscellaneous observations:* on a
dog that praises its fleas, 13; "but
where is the omelette?", 16; on
adding to a vast fund of ill-will, 43;
on political writing and Meccano,
66; on human needs, 81; on hobby-
horses and unicorns, 88; on God as
author, 109; on the non-Euclidean
world of politics, 125; on not unblack dogs, 138n; on the earth and
the sun, 145; on the Latin for a
whopping, 156; on a major mental
disease, 173; on being filthier than
oneself, 218; on compensations of
death, 287; on irritable old men and
noisy children, 294; on two forms of
tyranny, 301; on reviving Albigensianism, 443; on 1898 and 1948, 457;
on judging saints, 463; on one's face
at fifty, 515
—, *predictions and forebodings:* on the
future of literature, 69; on Anglo-
American alliance against Russia,
175; war in 10-20 years, and England
blown off the map, 387; similar
prediction, 451
—, *recreations and outdoor activities:*
croquet, 437, 438; fishing, 199, 438;
gardening, 199, 327, 330, 378;
harvesting, 203, 376; natural history,
141–5, 312–13, 344–5; poultry, 327;
riding, 403; shooting, 199; swimming, 344, 359
—, *writing and writings (italic figures
indicate texts):* books listed, 517;
writing weekly articles for *Evening
Standard*, 87; plans to drop journalism and write another novel, 87,
105, 111, 140, 146, 149; doing four
articles a week, 105; in excessively
heavy demand, 146; problems as
writer, 146–7; confessions of a book
reviewer, *181–5*; attitude to being
"edited", 233–4; agrees to write for
New Yorker, 233–4; views and ideas
on radio programmes, 275–6; adaptation of "The Emperor's New
Clothes", 276; writing for *Tribune*,
277–9; intends reviewing for *Observer* while in hospital, 386, 392, 393;

able to do one article a week, but on
serious work, 393; uniform edition
of books, 406, 416; attitude to
writing on politics, 412–14; possible
American reprints, 416–17, 418;
tries to clear up reviewing etc
commitments, 459; has stunning
idea for short novel, 459; destroyed
first novel after rejection by one
publisher, 480; attempts to write
essay on Evelyn Waugh for *Partisan
Review*, 482; notes for this essay,
512–13; instructions to Sir Richard
Rees as literary executor, 486–7, 488;
unable to do any work, 488, 499;
next novel mapped out, 495; set in
1945, 497; plans book of essays,
including two unwritten essays on
Conrad and Gissing, 506; extracts
from a notebook, *509–15*; constant
sense of idling, 510–11. **Animal
Farm** (I, II, III), 148; French
publisher gets cold feet, 77, 88, 140;
American edition (Harcourt, Brace),
77, 87–8, 110–11, 416, 518–19;
many translations, 88, 110, 140;
Eileen had helped in planning of,
104; has sold well, 104; possibility of
illustrated edition, 104–5; write-up
in *Time*, 110, 140; rejected by Dial
Press because of impossibility of
selling animal stories in US, 110;
French publisher found in Monte
Carlo, 140; broadcast as radio
play, 275(n)–6; Gollancz's refusal,
307(n)–8; 1,500 copies of Ukrainian
edition seized by Americans and
handed over to Russians, 379;
Russian translation published in
Frankfurt DP newspaper, 505;
"Arthur Koestler" (III), 77(n); "As I
Please" (16 items), *234–42, 247–75,
280–7, 303–7, 309–13*; "As I
Pleased", *276–80*; "Books v. Cigarettes", *92–6*; "Boys' Weeklies" (I),
146(n); "Britain's Left Wing Press",
520; *British Pamphleteers*, 471(n),
474; *Burmese Days* (I, II, III), 114,
505; reprinted in uniform edition,
416, 418, 520; difficulties over
American reprint, 416–17; in
print as a Penguin, 418; a last-
minute correction to reprint, 420;

552

Index

Times, The (I, II, III), 241
— *Literary Supplement*, 417(n)
(Timmermans, R., I)
Timon of Athens (II, III), 292, 296
(Timoshenko, II; *Tit-Bits*, I; *Titanic*, I; Titles, III; Tito, III)
Toads, 141–5
(Tobruk, II; Tolstoy, A., II)
Tolstoy, L. (I, II, III), 253; and Swift, 211, 217; *Shakespeare and the Drama*, 287–302; *Slavery of Our Times*, 414(n)
Tom Sawyer (Twain; II), 243
(Top-hats, III; Topis, III)
Tormentors, The (Cargoe), 496(n)
Tory Party, *see* Conservative Party
— Reform Committee (III), 209
Toryism, *see* Conservatism
Totalitarianism (I, II, III), 30, 59–72 *passim;* how to blur outlines of, 136–7; and corruption of language, 156–7, 473; *1984* and, 460, 502; Gandhi and, 468–9
(Tourism, III; *Towards a Free Revolutionary Art*, I; Town-planning, III; Trachtenberg, J., III; Trade, III)
Trade unions (I, II, III), 237–8, 319–20
Traitors, *see* Quislings
(Tramps, I)
"Transfer of population", 136
Translation: GO's views on, 419–20
(Transport, II; Travel, I, III)
Travels in Tartary (Huc), 20
Traven, W.B., 29
Treasure Seekers (Nesbit), 20
(Treece, H., II)
Trees: on planting, 150–3
(Treitschke, III)
Tressell, R. (II), 29
Trevelyan, G.M. (II): *England under Queen Anne*, 207
Tribune (I, II, III), 10, 34, 35, 37, 129, 135, 145n, 189, 191, 253, 275, 284, 386n, 401, 508, 509n; GO's contributions (40), 3–13, 19–22, 30–48, 72–5, 78–85, 88–96, 98–101, 106–9, 116–20, 122–5, 141–5, 149–53, 181–4, 192–4, 234–75, 276–87, 303–7, 309–13, 519; summary of his relations with and view of, 276–80; policy of under Labour Government, 394(n); an open letter to, on this, 395–400
Trieste, 43, 188

Trilby (du Maurier), 53, 251–3
(Trinder, T., III; *Triumph*, I)
Trollope (I, II, III), 21
Tropic of Cancer (Miller; I), 106–9
Trotsky (I, II, III), 18, 63, 121n, 168; alleged association with Germany, 115–16, 157; *Life of Stalin*, 194–6
Trotskyism and Trotskyists (I, II, III), 39, 77, 120, 195; in France, 141
Truman, Harry S., 7
(Trusts, I)
Truth (II, III), 38, 153
(— *about Russia*, II; Tunes, I, II; Turkey, II, III)
Turner, W.J. (III), 381(n)
Twain, Mark (I, II, III), 246; *Life on the Mississippi*, 246; *Tom Sawyer*, 243
(Twentieth century, II)
Twenty-Five Years of Soviet Russian Literature (Struve; III), 72

Ukraine and Ukrainians (II, III), 379–80
Ulysses (Joyce; I, II, III), 257
Uncle Tom's Cabin (Stowe; III), 21–2, 243
Under Two Dictators (Buber-Neumann), 496(n), 499
(Undset, S., I)
Unemployment (I, II, III), 185. *See also* (National Unemployed Workers' Movement); Poverty; Working class
Union for Democratic Action, 121(n)
United Nations, 124, 247, 254–5
— States (I, II, III), 165; and Russia, 7, 188, 255, 370, 395, 398; and famine in Europe, 83, 85; and England, 86, 88, 188, 397–8, 450; managerialism in, 163; Burnham's views, 175–6, 314–26 *passim*; a symbol of American civilisation, 235; and Jewish refugees, 238; in 19th century, 243; GO prefers to Russia, 309; as do many others, 323; and European unity, 373; not unalterably capitalist, 375; *Tribune* and, 394, 395–400; and coloured races, 405; size of, an important factor, 514–15. *See also headings beginning* American
(Unity Theatre, II)